BLUENOSE

MONICA GRAHAM

BLUENOSE

MONICA GRAHAM

NIMBUS
PUBLISHING

INTRODUCTION

BLUENOSE has sailed across the flip side of our dime for as long as most Canadians can remember.

The image looks like the *Bluenose II*, seen around Nova Scotia harbours and across the world, but the schooner commemorated on the ten-cent piece is an earlier template for *Bluenose II*, one known in its time as the Queen of the North Atlantic.

The Nova Scotia schooner's position on our money places it in the company of other national icons like the beaver and the maple leaf. We rarely question these national symbols, or wonder why they represent Canada. Why *Bluenose*? Why not another historically important ship, like explorer John Cabot's *Matthew* or Jacques Cartier's *La Grande Hermine*?

Maybe *Bluenose* is on our money because Canadians could put their money on *Bluenose*.

Back in 1937, when the Royal Canadian Mint designed the new dime to honour the coronation of King George VI, *Bluenose* had held the *Halifax Herald*'s International Fishermen's Trophy—also known as the Herald Trophy—for sixteen years. A year later the aging, creaking schooner would win the race series again, against all the gamblers' odds. Each victory represented not just one race,

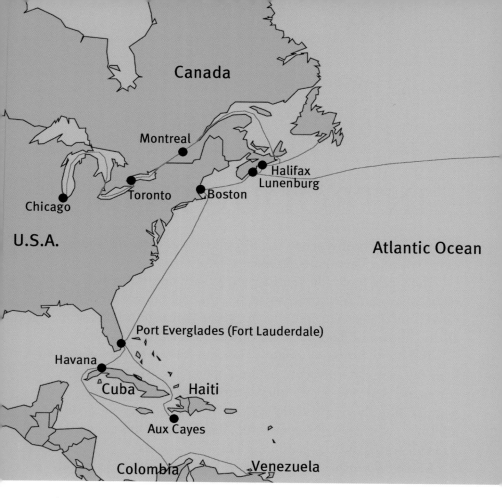

but a series. First, ships raced in Nova Scotia waters to determine the Canadian champion, which would then compete against the American contender in a second series at home or off Massachusetts.

Bluenose could boast of other victories besides the Herald Trophy. In 1926 it beat *Haligonian*, a Nova Scotia ship designed specifically to outrun the schooner. While representing Canada at the 1933 World's Fair, *Bluenose* won a 136-kilogram cheese in a sailing race on Lake Michigan. And while

As well as fishing the banks, *Bluenose* sailed across the Atlantic, and into the Great Lakes and the Caribbean. It was finally wrecked on the south coast of Haiti.

visiting England during the 1935 Silver Jubilee celebration for King George V, *Bluenose* won twenty-five pounds sterling in a race around the Isle of Wight. Not only was *Bluenose* recognized as the fastest fishing schooner in North America and an international sailing ambassador for Canada, but the captain and crew bore a reputation for daring seamanship.

If ever a ship could be a superstar, it was *Bluenose*. Indeed, it could be said that the Royal Canadian Mint suffered from "*Bluenose*-mania" just like everyone else in the country.

But the schooner was also a fishing vessel, representing the hardiness and the work ethic of people who earned their living from a dangerous sea. When the dime was minted, *Bluenose* had already survived eleven gruelling fishing seasons in the wild North Atlantic, a winter freighting salt fish to the Caribbean, and uncounted deadly storms. *Bluenose* was nearly wrecked on Sable Island in April 1926, and again that August. And in the fall of 1935, *Bluenose* keeled over in a vicious storm while returning from England; thankfully it righted itself and was able to limp into port.

The famed Canadian schooner also survived numerous attempts to sell it, until two Americans finally purchased the vessel in 1942 to freight wartime supplies around the Caribbean. When the people at the mint put *Bluenose* on the dime, they had no idea

A Genuine Silver Sailboat

When the *Bluenose* was first featured on the reverse of the Canadian ten-cent piece in 1937, the federal government didn't say it was *Bluenose*, but everyone knew the familiar silhouette. In 1938, an enterprising *Bluenose* crew member took a bag of newly-minted Canadian dimes to the United States for the ship's last race. He sold them to Americans unfamiliar with Canadian coins, charging $2 each for "genuine silver engravings" of *Bluenose*. The schooner still appears on the dime, except for special editions of the coin for the 1967 Canadian Centennial and the 2001 Year of the Volunteer. At first, dimes were 80 percent silver and 20 percent copper. Since 2000, the dime has been made of 92 percent steel and a blend of copper and nickel.

A boy plays with *Bluenose* model, with the ferry MV *Bluenose* in the background

that the ship's international fame would survive until January 1946, when it ran onto a Haitian reef.

The *Bluenose* drama might have ended on that coral reef, twenty-five years and one month after Lunenburg's Smith and Rhuland Shipyard started building the schooner.

But the legend lives on, and the story is worth telling again.

Important *Bluenose* Dates

March 6, 1921: Launched at Smith and Rhuland Shipyard in Lunenburg

April 15, 1921: Started fishing career under Capt. Angus J. Walters

October 1921: Won the *Halifax Herald*'s International Fishermen's Trophy at Halifax, NS

October 1922: Won the trophy again, at Gloucester, MA

October 1923: Retained the trophy by default after withdrawing from race finals

1929: Featured on Canadian fifty-cent postage stamp.

October 1930: Lost Lipton Cup race to US schooner *Gertrude L. Thebaud*

October 1931: Defeated *Thebaud* for the Herald Trophy

1933: Represented Canada at Chicago World's Fair and toured Great Lakes

1935: Attended King George V's silver jubilee celebrations in England

1937: First appeared on Canadian ten-cent piece

The Halifax Herald

HALIFAX, WEDNESDAY, MAY 26, 1937

New Series Of Coins For Canada Is Issued

OTTAWA, May 14.—Reproduction of a Nova Scotian schooner, obviously designed from a photo of the Bluenose, Queen of the North Atlantic, appears on one of the new coins issued today by the Canadian Government. The new series, bearing the effigy of King George VI, range in denomination from one cent to one dollar and the Bluenose is on the reverse side of the 10-cent piece. The new coins represent the collaboration of Canadian, British and French mints. Due to the pressure of work on the royal mint in London, it was found necessary for the Canadian authorities to enlist the co-operation of the Paris mint in preparation of some of the dies. The obverse of all the coins bears King George's effigy, but the reverse varies. A list of reverse designs follows:

One Dollar—A canoe manned by an Indian and a voyageur, an islet in the background, above, the word "Canada" with the northern lights; below, the word "dollar" and the date of the year, with a graining upon the edge.

Fifty Cents—Between supporters the ensigns armorial of Canada in a shield surmounted by the royal crown, "50 cents" above and "Canada" below, with the date of the year and a graining upon the edge.

Twenty-five Cents—A caribou head, "25 cents" between the antlers, and surrounded by the word "Canada" and the date of the year, with a graining upon the edge.

Ten Cents—A fishing schooner under sail, "Canada" above and "10 cents" below, with the date of the year, and a graining upon the edge.

Five Cents—A beaver; above "5 cents" between two maple leaves, and below "Canada" and the date of the year, with a plain edge.

One Cent—A two-leaved twig of maple, "1 cent" above, and "Canada" below, with the date of the year, and a plain edge.

An article from the May 26, 1937 edition of *The Halifax Herald* announcing the issuing of a new coin series, including the dime featuring a fishing schooner later officially confirmed to be *Bluenose*

October 1938:	Defeated *Thebaud* in the last race for the *Halifax Herald*'s International Fishermen's Trophy
1942:	Sold to the West Indies Trading Company
January 1946:	Foundered on a coral reef at Haiti
1955:	*Bluenose* and Captain Angus Walters inducted into the Canadian Sports Hall of Fame
1960:	CNR ferry from Yarmouth, NS, to Bar Harbor, ME, named MV *Bluenose*
July 24, 1963:	Replica *Bluenose II* launched at Smith and Rhuland Shipyard, Lunenburg
1982:	*Bluenose* appeared on 60-cent Canadian postage stamp
1988:	Nova Scotia issued the province's first *Bluenose* licence plate
November 1988:	Captain Angus Walters featured on 37-cent postage stamp
July 1998:	45-cent postage stamp issued featuring *Bluenose* and designer William J. Roué
1999:	Canada Post issued a redesign of the original 1929 postage stamp
2002:	Canadian government officially announced that the ship on the dime is *Bluenose*

Bluenose in Halifax Harbour

CHAPTER 1:
BIRTHING A LEGEND

FISHERMEN in the Maritimes and New England snickered into their morning tea in July 1920 when newspapers reported that the final race in the America's Cup was cancelled because of a high wind.

"Twenty-three knots!" they scoffed. "Just a breeze!"

Indeed, the 23-knot (39 kilometre per hour) wind that cancelled the race is enough to shake large branches and turn an umbrella inside-out, not to mention whipping up foamy whitecaps on the sea. A breeze of that strength could knock over racing yachts, which were top-heavy because they had so many sails on their masts. But the hardy banks fishermen who sailed to work every season on the North Atlantic regularly faced high winds, as well as fog, rain, snow, and sometimes a mixture of all four. They routinely left the relative safety of the schooner to fish from small dories bobbing on waves that hid the larger vessel from view. No wonder they snorted in derision at a race that had to be called off because of a bit of wind. They figured there should be a race for real boats and real sailors: in other words, for the schooners and their crews that worked in extreme weather.

Contenders and Captains in the 1920 Race

Alcala – Roly Knickle
Bernice Zinck – Danny Zinck
Delawana – Tommy Himmelman
Democracy – Bill Deal
Freda Himmelman – Alvin Himmelman
Gilbert B. Walters – Angus Walters
Independence – Albert Himmelman
Mona Marie – Lemuel Ritchie
Ruby L. Pentz – Calvin Lohnes

Already, schooners from Lunenburg, Nova Scotia, and Gloucester, Massachusetts, tried to beat each other to the fishing banks every spring. Ships that could move their fish to market more quickly earned more money, so owners knew the advantages of having a fast vessel.

Captains and their crews talked more and more about a race for fishing schooners, and the idea spread quickly until it reached the ears of prominent Halifax yachtsmen and their business friends. They figured a race for bona fide, or genuine, fishermen would be fun to watch, and would boost morale following the devastation of the city's north end in the Halifax Explosion, which had taken place less than three years earlier.

So Senator William Dennis, owner and publisher of two Halifax newspapers, offered the *Halifax Herald* and *Evening Mail* Nova Scotia Fishing Vessel Championship Trophy and a cash prize to the fastest banks schooner. He promoted the event in his newspapers, urging businesses to decorate their storefronts, factories and ships to blow their whistles, fire stations to ring their bells, and the militia to fire the Citadel Hill cannons when the winner crossed the finish line.

Four demanding courses were planned, all beginning in Halifax Harbour and extending 35–40 miles (56–64 kilometres) into the Atlantic Ocean past Chebucto Head. Nine enthusiastic South Shore captains, just back from their fishing trips, registered their schooners for the October 11 competition. Halifax money was on the skill and experience of Captain Angus J. Walters, the thirty-seven-year-old skipper of the *Gilbert B. Walters*.

The schooners provided an exciting contest as *Walters* sailed side by side with Captain Thomas Himmelman's *Delawana*. Then *Walters*'s foretopmast cracked off and *Delawana* took the lead, to cross the finish line five minutes ahead of *Walters*. Halifax erupted in a party, oblivious to the sad fact that Captain Calvin Lohnes had drowned when seventh-place *Ruby L. Pentz*'s main boom knocked him overboard.

Surrounded by the celebrations, Senator Dennis decided there was no need to wait another year to challenge the Gloucester fleet. He put up the *Halifax Herald*'s International Fishermen's Trophy, an ornate silver urn, for the fastest ship in the North Atlantic fishery. The competition capitalized on long-standing rivalries between Lunenburg and Gloucester fishermen over who had the fastest vessels. The race would sell newspapers, too, but its stated purpose was to improve fishing schooners and sailing methods. Enthusiasts hoped it would prolong the Age of Sail, a time when wind-powered ships dominated the seas. By 1920 steam power and other new technologies were proving faster than sail, and less dependent on weather.

The formal rules of the race were simple: To prevent America's Cup yachts from entering, the contest was open only to vessels that had fished commercially on the banks for at least one season, with waterlines of 112 feet (34 metres) or less. They had to operate completely under sail, with no engines allowed. The course was 35–40 nautical miles (about 65–74 kilometres) and had to be completed within nine hours. The trophy and $4,000 purse would go to the ship that won two out of three races, with a $1,000 consolation prize to the second-place ship.

Alcala, a participant in the 1920 race

Banks fishermen from seaports in Cape Breton, New York, Newfoundland, Quebec, and Portugal were not invited; only ships from Gloucester. Fishermen there received the telegram outlining the Nova Scotia challenge a week before the race, giving them little time to find an entry among the few available vessels that met the rules. About a third of the American schooner fleet had disappeared during World War One because of German U-boat action or because the crewmen had gone to fight. Many of those that remained had diesel engines installed to assist the sails, and they normally fished all year, so they were still at sea when the race challenge arrived.

As the Gloucester men wondered what to do, *Esperanto* sailed into the harbour loaded with 275,000 pounds (125,000 kilograms) of fish and battered by a season's fishing. The fourteen-year-old schooner was named a worthy competitor, so it was scraped, painted, and polished, and sent to Halifax. The skipper was Marty Welch, born a Walsh in Digby, Nova Scotia. His origins didn't matter, as many of the Gloucester fishermen were from Nova Scotia.

In the first race, on October 30, *Delawana* led at the 9:00 AM start, but *Esperanto* overtook the Nova Scotia vessel and finished eighteen minutes ahead. The next day was Sunday, when fishermen usually took a day off. Ignoring tradition, Captain Himmelman took *Delawana* out of the harbour past Georges Island to unload some of its ballast.

The ships raced again on November 1 with light winds. With the ballast removed, *Delawana* sailed faster. It was in the lead until it went around the course's final turn to face into the wind. *Esperanto* caught up but couldn't pass because Captain Himmelman moved his vessel to block the American ship. So Captain Welch decided to pass *Delawana* on its leeward side. That meant *Esperanto* had to sail between *Delawana* and Devil's Island, dangerously close to the island's rocks. Captain Welch eventually called to the other skipper to give way, which *Delawana* had to do under the rules of the sea, losing precious minutes as it swung away. *Esperanto* passed *Delawana*, to cross the finish line seven minutes ahead of the Nova Scotia vessel, and to win the *Halifax Herald* International Fishermen's Trophy and $4,000.

Captain Welch sailed *Esperanto* home to Gloucester with the cup in the hold and a broom on the mast, signifying a sweep of the opposition. The Nova Scotia sailors went back to their ports, glum at the loss and vowing it wouldn't happen again.

Captain Walters had already contacted Smith and Rhuland Shipyard in his home port of Lunenburg about building a new fishing schooner to replace *Gilbert B. Walters*. He wanted to race it, too, so he ordered the new vessel to conform to the international race specifications. Meanwhile, Senator

William J. (Bill) Roué, 1879–1970

Born in south end Halifax, Bill Roué began making toy ships as a child. Naval architecture and sailing were his passions and hobbies, but he was working as a clerk in the family soft drink business when a schooner consortium asked him to submit a design for a fast fishing vessel. The design he named "number seventeen," *Bluenose*, won him international recognition. Roué didn't get paid right away for the commission because the board of the Bluenose Schooner Company determined that he had volunteered his services and was not owed a wage. He hired a law firm to settle the $884.20 bill. In November 1922, the company finally agreed to pay the designer $600. Over Bill Roué's long career he designed more than 250 yachts, motor vessels, ferries, and a competitor for the *Bluenose* named *Haligonian*. He invented a sectional barge used in World War Two to take troops and supplies ashore. In 1998 a postage stamp commemorated his contribution to *Bluenose*, and in 2004, he was inducted into the builder category in the Nova Scotia Sports Hall of Fame.

Dennis and his friends at the Royal Nova Scotia Yacht Squadron in Halifax talked about building a schooner that would bring the Herald Trophy back to Canada. Before long they invited self-taught naval architect William J. (Bill) Roué, a club member, to create a design.

They turned down Roué's first design because it was 8 feet (2.4 metres) longer at the waterline than the International Fishermen's Trophy race requirement of 112 feet (34.2 metres). So Roué produced a second

This cartoon from the December 20, 1920 edition of *The Halifax Herald* shows Governor General Cavendish at the keel-laying for *Bluenose*

set of drawings, which introduced some yachting concepts but met race requirements. To make the ship faster, Roué placed the ballast low on the keel. He designed the ship with the best features of both Gloucester and Lunenburg vessels, with the depth of the first and the fish-carrying capacity of the second. The vessel was, after all, supposed to earn its keep by fishing.

Nova Scotia's coastline was ringed with shipbuilding communities, but Senator Dennis and the other Halifax backers took the design to Smith and Rhuland Shipyard for construction. The publisher wanted to promote his newspaper in Lunenburg, which was also the home port of most of the skippers interested in the international race, and a community with strong business ties to Gloucester and to the banks

Construction of *Bluenose II*, a replica of the original *Bluenose*

fishery. The Halifax men met Captain Walters at the shipyard, coming to an agreement that he would command the new schooner and be its main owner.

Construction started in December 1920, in order to finish the schooner in time to qualify for the 1921 International Fishermen's Trophy race. To show their high hopes for the

Possible Origins of the Nickname Bluenose

- In 1785 an Annapolis Royal clergyman recorded the use of the term to describe older inhabitants of the area.

- In the War of 1812, a Nova Scotia privateer carried a bright blue cannon on its bow.

- In 1838 writer Thomas Chandler Haliburton referred to Nova Scotians as bluenoses in his book *The Clockmaker*.

- The term may refer to the colour of cold noses in winter.

- It may refer to noses turned blue when the dye from blue woolen mittens was transferred during nose-wiping.

- It might have to do with the blue potatoes popular in early Nova Scotia.

- Order of the Blue Nose is a navy club for those who cross the Arctic Circle in a ship.

- Schooners travelling in northern ice-filled seas once had the tips of the bowsprits (their noses) painted blue.

- Bluenose is also a little-used term for a prudish or puritanical person.

new vessel, local politicians arranged for Victor Cavendish, who was the Governor General of Canada and the Ninth Duke of Devonshire, to drive the first spike during a keel-laying ceremony on December 18. Along with other dignitaries, the Governor General was treated to Caribbean rum before the ceremony, so his aim was off when he hammered the spike. He missed three times before someone else took the big mallet from him to complete the job. It wasn't a great beginning for the ship, but history would prove that it didn't harm the results.

The builders framed *Bluenose* with local spruce and oak, and planked the hull below the waterline in birch. Oak was used for the rails and top of the hull, and local pine was sawed for the deck planking. The masts were shaped from tall pine logs imported from Oregon. Shipwrights—craftsmen who had learned their trade over long practice—cut and shaped the wood using hand tools like adzes, spoke shaves, and augers.

During construction, Captain Walters asked Roué to change the design of the fo'c'sle (forecastle) by raising its height about half a metre. The change would keep the foredeck drier in heavy seas, and would also add headroom for the crew who would sleep and eat in the fo'c'sle for weeks. The result was a unique lift in the ship's bow, giving it a recognizable profile. For years, sailors and designers debated whether the change slowed the vessel or improved its speed. Roué himself suggested it would slow the ship except in rough seas, when the bow lift would let it ride up over large waves instead of ploughing through them.

As construction began, the ship didn't have a name, although some suggested Cavendish after the Governor General. The sponsors wanted a name that would truly represent Nova Scotia in the International Fishermen's Trophy race, so they finally chose *Bluenose*, a traditional nickname for Nova Scotians. Several earlier ships had borne the name, along with a Digby newspaper, a Halifax magazine, a Windsor train, and a New Glasgow mining company. Once the ship was named, the sponsors wasted no time in setting up the Bluenose Schooner Company Limited to pay for the construction.

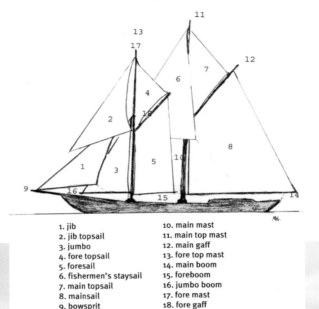

1. jib
2. jib topsail
3. jumbo
4. fore topsail
5. foresail
6. fishermen's staysail
7. main topsail
8. mainsail
9. bowsprit
10. main mast
11. main top mast
12. main gaff
13. fore top mast
14. main boom
15. foreboom
16. jumbo boom
17. fore mast
18. fore gaff

Schooners

A schooner is a ship with two or more masts, upon which the sails run lengthwise with the ship. The sails are rigged in front and behind each mast, instead of cross-ways. Banks schooners, or salt bankers, typically have about eight sails, including the mainsail, foresail, jumbo, jib, topsails, and staysail. The word schooner is likely derived from a Scottish word meaning to skim over the water. Because they stayed at sea for long periods, Nova Scotia schooners of the early 1900s developed a design with less depth and more breadth, which gave them more cargo space. They needed less ballast to remain stable in the water. They sailed fast off the wind, that is, with the wind from behind. By comparison, New England schooners' fishing grounds were close to port, so they could make quick trips back and forth between the fishing grounds and their ports, and therefore needed less cargo area. That allowed them to be narrower with a lot of ballast to give them speed, but their decks were wetter in rough weather because they rode lower in the water. They typically sailed faster than Nova Scotia vessels when heading into the wind.

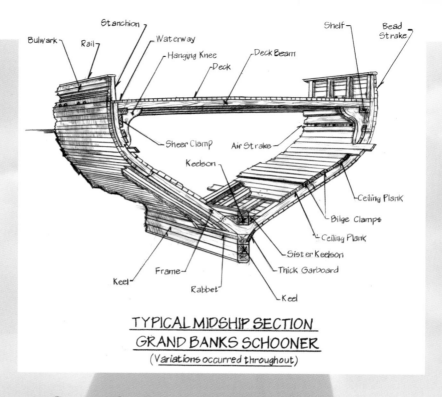

TYPICAL MIDSHIP SECTION
GRAND BANKS SCHOONER
(Variations occurred throughout)

Labels on diagram: Stanchion, Bulwark, Rail, Waterway, Hanging Knee, Deck, Deck Beam, Shelf, Bead Strake, Sheer Clamp, Air Strake, Keelson, Ceiling Plank, Bilge Clamps, Ceiling Plank, Sister Keelson, Thick Garboard, Keel, Frame, Rabbet, Keel

Some *Bluenose* Construction Expenses

Wood: $1,800
Labour: $26,584
Dories and gear: $815
Ballast: $352

Sails: $1,003
Foundry work: $760
Anchor and chain: $660
Rope: $662

One dollar in 1921 had the same buying power as $11.13 in 2010. Thus, the sails would be valued at $11,163.39 in 2010. In 1921 the average Canadian wage was $16.56 per week. *(Source: Study by Alan G. Green, Queens University, and David A. Green, University of British Columbia.)*

Lunenburg shipbuilders usually followed a traditional British practice of selling sixty-four shares in each ship to pay for building it. Each shareholder was a part owner of the vessel, and would receive a percentage of the money that the ship earned. The amount that shareholders received was based on how many shares they owned.

But the *Bluenose* cost $35,580 to build, about double the price of most schooners of the day, so the company decided to increase the number of available $100 shares to 350. Some Halifax businessmen advanced money to Captain Walters to get construction started, and he invested in ninety shares in the vessel, including twenty-one he signed over to his wife, Maggie. Some Lunenburg families who wouldn't normally buy shares in a schooner had such high hopes that they scraped money together to invest in *Bluenose*. The Halifax businessmen were quickly repaid their seed money, and shipyard owners Richard Smith and George Rhuland received their payment in both cash and in *Bluenose* shares.

Besides Captain Walters, the other company directors were Captain Adam Knickle, and Halifax businessman Hugh R. Silver. E. Fenwick Zwicker and Arthur H. Zwicker of the well-established Lunenburg fishing business Zwicker and Company, which had also invested heavily in the *Bluenose* project, were given five shares each to serve on the board. The directors named Captain Walters as managing owner, and appointed Zwicker and Company to outfit the ship and serve as agent. This meant the company would sell the schooner's catch and take the money from the sale to pay the shareholders and the crew's wages.

By March, Smith and Rhuland workers completed the vessel's housing and hull and inserted the bottom sections of the two masts through blocks placed at the keel and deck. They applied black paint to the part of the hull that would be

Masts

A 90-foot (27-metre) log is shaped into a six-sided pole with an adze, spoke shave, and plane. The edges are pared off to make an octagon, again to make a 16-sided pole, and then to create 32 sides. Then it's smoothed into the final cylindrical shape. The mast is inserted though the hole in the deck, to fit into its spot in a block above the ship's keel. The base of the mast is kept octagonal, so it locks into place. Masts are removable in case they break and need to be replaced. At launch, only the bottom portions of the masts are installed, or stepped. The top masts, foremast, booms, gaffs, and bowsprit are added after launch, along with the sails and the system of ropes, wires, and pulleys that make up the rigging.

visible above the water, and a red, copper-based wood preservative to coat the underwater part. A white stripe indicated the 34-metre waterline, so important for qualifying the schooner for the international races. The cabins, moldings, and rails were white, grey, and yellow; and the deck and masts remained as natural wood. *Bluenose* was Smith and Rhuland's 121st ship, registered at the Port of Lunenburg as vessel number 150,404. It was constructed in ninety-seven days, Lunenburg's eighth ship that year.

It was a pretty ship but, as pleased as they were, investors didn't want to jinx the schooner by bragging about how good *Bluenose* would be. Even Captain Walters, who owned more shares than any other single shareholder, wouldn't go out on a limb. He told reporters he'd make a better assessment after he'd sailed in the ship.

The ship was decorated for the March 26, 1921 launch with brightly coloured pennants and a large banner emblazoned with its name. People arrived by train, ox cart, automobile, and on foot to watch the launch. Local industries gave their employees a half-day holiday, and it was a Saturday morning, so schoolchildren swarmed the site as well.

Bluenose's launch, March 26, 1921

The official guests climbed aboard *Bluenose* where it sat high over the ways, cradled by a system of wooden blocks and wedges. At the launch master's command, workers used big sledgehammers to knock away the supporting wedges. As the wooden blocks toppled away, the ship began to slide stern first down the greased ways. Aboard *Bluenose*, Audrey Smith, the nineteen-year-old daughter of one of the shipyard owners and also Captain Walters's niece, smashed a bottle of champagne on the bow to christen the schooner. The crowd cheered, and the water lifted *Bluenose* and floated it toward the sea, which was considered a good omen.

The successful launch didn't mean construction was finished. *Bluenose* still didn't have sails, topmasts, spars, anchors, winches, and a host of other necessary equipment. So Captain Walters guided the vessel to the Zwicker and Company wharf to get *Bluenose* outfitted in time for the 1921 fishing season. Ballast was placed to weight the bottom of the ship.

Shipyard Jobs

Shipyard workers included carpenters, caulkers, painters, riggers, framers, trunnelers, and joiners. Most of the shipwrights, or ship-building craftsmen, learned their skills on the job, starting when they were twelve or thirteen years old. In the 1920s they earned about two dollars a day for a ten-hour day, six days a week, and it was considered good pay. Other industries were established in communities that had shipyards: blacksmiths to make anchors and other iron items; sail lofts; rope-makers; and merchants to stock the ships with food for long fishing trips.

Beige-painted dories were stacked on each side of the deck. Workers at Hebb's sail loft cut and sewed cotton canvas to make 10,000 square feet (930 square metres) of sails. Zwicker and Company ordered the anchors, windlass, pulleys, deck and cabin furniture, galley equipment, and all other items from local manufacturers like Lunenburg Foundry or Dauphinee's block and tackle shop. Except for the Oregon pine for the masts, *Bluenose* was entirely Nova Scotian.

Within five days the rigging team installed the system of masts, spars, ropes, chains, wires, and pulleys that held the sails and allowed them to be raised or furled. Captain Walters put the schooner through sea trials, and declared the ship worthy. On April 15, three weeks after the launch, Captain Walters took down the tall top masts, stowed the racing sails ashore, and took *Bluenose* fishing.

Bluenose in the waves—what the dorymen could see.

CHAPTER 2:
BLUENOSE, THE FISHING SCHOONER

IT WAS still dark when *Bluenose*'s dorymen climbed out of their bunks in the early morning of their first fishing trip that April, following a pattern laid down by generations of Lunenburg captains and crews.

After a hearty 4:00 AM breakfast, they baited hundreds of hooks with the frozen capelin, herring, and other fish that wasn't usually served on their dinner tables. Spending too much money on bait meant less pay for the fishermen at the end of the season, so they were careful to use enough to attract the fish without wasting it.

Each hook was attached to a metre-long tarred cotton rope called a ganging. The gangings were then attached about every two metres along a two-kilometre-long line called a trawl. As the hooks were baited, fishermen carefully coiled the trawl into a wooden tub. A couple of trawls per fisherman were placed in the dories, along with two long oars, a short mast and sail, a bin for the fish they would catch, a bailer, drinking water, a snack, a knife, a compass, a fish gaff, a winch called a hurdy-gurdy for hauling in big fish like halibut, and floats or buoys.

Fishermen baiting trawls

Bluenose carried between eight and twelve four-metre, flat-bottomed dories, their seats removed and stacked like paper cups on each side of the schooner's deck. Any water that collected in them ran out through holes that had been drilled in the bottom, so plugs were put in those holes and the seats replaced before lowering the dories into the waves. Once the boat was in the water, one fisherman would jump in, while the second man passed him the gear before he jumped into the small boat himself. It was a dangerous feat if the waves were high. Most fishermen never learned to swim, reasoning that they didn't stand a chance in the cold, wild ocean. The air inside their oilskins would keep them afloat long enough for someone to reach out and hook them aboard the dory, but survival was unlikely if they were in the sea longer than that.

Depending on the weather and the skipper's preference, the dories were either strung out behind the schooner like ducklings following their mother, or spread out from the ship like spokes from a wheel, in a pattern called a flying net. One man rowed the dory, watching for big waves that could swamp the small boat. His mate uncoiled the trawl and lowered it into the water to lie along the ocean floor, being careful not to tangle the hooks and lines. They anchored both ends of the trawl and marked them with a buoy or floating keg so they could find it again. Then they headed back to the schooner for a mug-up (tea or coffee, and snacks). An hour later, they hopped back into the dories and rowed back to the trawl. One man hauled up the line, twisted the fish off the hooks, and passed the line to the second man, who re-baited the hooks and dropped the line back into the water.

Codfish and haddock just flopped into the boat and stayed there, but halibut, which could be bigger than a large man, tended to thrash around. Fishermen carried a stick like a base-ball bat to knock halibut unconscious so they wouldn't beat up

Banks

Grand Banks is the name often given to all the underwater plateaus lying off the northeast coast of North America, but Grand Bank is the proper name for the largest, located southeast of the island of New-foundland. The others are scattered along the coast from George's Bank, east of Nantucket Island, to Banque St. Pierre and Green's Bank, south of Newfoundland and the French islands of St. Pierre and Miquelon. Whittle Bank, Milne Bank, Orphan Bank, and some others lie within the Gulf of St. Lawrence. Some are called after nearby landmarks, like Canso, Sable, or Burgeo banks. *Bluenose* and other Lunenburg schooners fished Sable, Middle, Western, and Banquero banks. Away from the banks, the sea bottom drops off to about 1,800 metres. The fishermen also gave names to the uncharted depths between the banks, such as Whale Hole, Gully, Barrel, or Hogshead.

the dory and sink it. They also carried a notched stick to reach into the halibut's throat and pull out the hook.

Sometimes sharks or whales swam through the trawls and ripped them apart, which meant the fishermen had to stay out in the dories to haul in the gear and repair it. As well as freezing their fingers and getting hungry, the fishermen wouldn't catch many fish on a day like that.

When the boat was full of a tonne or two of fish and the trawl set again, the men either rowed their cargo back to the schooner or signalled by waving an oar or a lantern flare for the skipper to pick them up. While the dories were out, the ship could stay stable and more or less in one place by setting the sails or ship's wheel a certain way, or by using the anchor and the staysail. Sometimes the dories travelled several kilometres from the schooner in the open sea, so in heavy fog or snow, or in big waves, the small boats and the schooner could easily lose sight of each other. They yelled, used a horn, or beat the halibut stick on the side of the boat to signal their location, but dories still got lost.

Fishermen knew that starting early in the morning gave more daylight at the end of the day to search for lost dories, but sometimes the men were never seen again. Other times they rowed for days before they were rescued. If a captain noticed his ship's barometer dropping, signifying a coming storm, he would ring the ship's bell or blow a whistle or horn to call the dories back to the ship. *Bluenose* didn't lose any dorymen, likely because of Captain Walters's renowned weather sense.

Once alongside the schooner, the men stood in the dories and pitch-forked the fish into a wooden pen on the deck. Then they rowed back to the trawl to haul it in again. If the weather was good and the fish were plenty, they repeated the process several times at that spot, sometimes until after dark. If they caught no fish, the schooner and all the dories moved to a new

Cod

(sketch by L. B. Jenson)

Atlantic cod (*gadus morhua*) is found mainly in cool northern seas. It has three fins on its back and two under its whitish belly, a whisker-like barbell on the chin, a large mouth, small scales, and an almost square tail. Cod may be grey-green or brown-red, depending on the habitat. A full-grown cod is usually less than 1 metre long and weighs 2 or 3 kilograms, but there are records of cod almost 2 metres long and weighing almost 100 kilograms. Cod live on the bottom of the ocean, coming near the surface only to chase prey, including schools of small capelin. Cod are found both in tight schools and in loose groups, moving to deep water to feed in winter, and closer to shore in spring. They spawn in shallow water.

location, sometimes with the schooner towing the dories behind it instead of loading them back onto the deck and sailing away. When fishing was over for the day, the fishermen hauled all the trawls into the dories and took them back to the ship. But the workday wasn't over. The fish had to be cleaned and salted before the men could turn into their bunks for a few hours' sleep. Then they started all over again the next morning. Sometimes they fished and cleaned fish for days in a row with no sleep, in order to keep up with an abundant catch.

It was exhausting, difficult, cold, wet, and dangerous work.

To keep their energy levels high, fishermen ate well and often. The cook was as important to the schooner's operation as the captain, and his abilities and personality could make or break the fishing season. He had to rise before the fishermen,

Recipe for Scouse

- 3 lbs. salt meat
- 3 onions
- 3 lbs potatoes
- 2 parsnips
- 2 lbs carrots
- 1 large turnip
- 1 small head of cabbage

Cut the meat into chunks. Soak the meat in fresh water overnight. Drain, cover with cold fresh water. Bring to a boil, then simmer for 1 hour.

Peel and slice half the potatoes and add them to the pot with the meat. Keep it simmering. Peel and slice carrots and turnip and add. After 30 minutes give the pot a good stir. Peel and slice the remaining potatoes small, chop the onions and cabbage, and add it all to the pot. Simmer until all is tender—a couple of hours.

(If using fresh meat instead of salt, cube it and brown it in hot fat first).

which could be anytime after midnight, and begin preparing a big breakfast. This often consisted of scouse—a kind of potato stew—or hash, along with sausages and hot biscuits, all gobbled down with huge amounts of tea or coffee. When the men came in for their mug-up, the cook had to have more tea and coffee ready, as well as fresh doughnuts or gingerbread or both. Dinner was shortly after noon, followed by a large snack a few hours later, and then a hearty evening meal after the last dory trip. *Bluenose*'s cook served up pies, baked beans, Jiggs' dinner, tapioca, sauerkraut, ham, fish cooked with soaked hard tack biscuit, stews and soup filled with meat and vegetables and massive dumplings, and piles of fresh bread, rolls, and biscuits. All of it was prepared on the galley stove, a cast-iron monster bolted to the floor, with a railing around the surface to stop pots from sliding off during a big sea. The galley and food lockers were situated below deck, forward of the fish holds and just behind, or aft, of the crew's quarters in the fo'c'sle.

The cook had to do more than prepare food. He was also responsible for keeping a constant fire in the galley stove to warm the fo'c'sle and to dry out the fishermen's wet clothing. He had to be a skilled sailor, strong enough to manhandle

Sketch showing the inside of a fishing schooner (L. B. Jenson)

the mountains of food supplies, and able to go long periods without sleep. A cheerful disposition was also an asset, as a cranky cook foretold an unhappy crew. Because the cook was so valuable, *Bluenose* paid him a wage instead of a share in the ship's catch, so he got paid even if the ship caught no fish. In the 1921 season, the cook on the *Bluenose* received more than $700, excellent pay for the time.

After all the work was done, everyone could sleep except the man on watch, who had to keep an eye out for ice, other ships, and sudden bad weather. Each *Bluenose* fisherman had his own bunk in the fo'c's'le, stacked two high on either side of the hull as it narrowed towards the bow. The most junior sailors slept closest to the bow, where they could hear the roar of the sea passing by their heads. The more experienced crew members' bunks were closer to the galley, and some slept in the captain's quarters at the stern of the vessel. Charts, the ship's compass and log, and other equipment were kept in the captain's cabin, but the captain ate in the fo'c'sle. A triangular table fit in the space between the two rows of bunks, where the men ate, played cards, wrote letters, or gathered to tell stories or sing. There was little space, and even less privacy. While the captain had a proper toilet, or head, in his cabin aft, the crew used a bucket that was emptied overboard.

The base of the mainmast sat in the fo'c'sle, and every available nook was filled with wet clothing steaming in the heat from the stove. The fo'c'sle smelled of damp wool, oakum, salt fish, the stove, tobacco smoke, unwashed men, and cooking; and the ship creaked and groaned as it moved through the waves. The fishermen soon learned to sleep through the reek and the noise, aided by their utter exhaustion.

Sometimes the wind rose sharply after just an hour or so of sleep. The watchman would then call everyone out of bed to help sail the ship. Bleary with sleep, the fishermen would stumble up the companionway to the deck. As the captain barked out orders, they'd begin heaving on the ropes that moved the sails, or climbing up the ladder-like ratlines on the masts to fold up the big canvas sails billowing in the wind. Sometimes the watch raised the fishermen for other dangers, as with *Bluenose*'s first fishing trip.

Captain and crew had turned in after the ship's first full day of fishing, with *Bluenose* anchored for the night. All was quiet until the watch called Captain Walters around 2:00 AM, to tell him there was another vessel approaching. The skipper peered through the gloom with his binoculars to see a fully-rigged ship bearing down on *Bluenose*. No one on the other ship seemed to notice the smaller fishing schooner directly in its path. Captain Walters ordered the watch to blow the foghorn, but the other ship paid no attention. The other vessel was getting so close it appeared it would cut the schooner in half, so Captain Walters

Fishermen's Clothing

Fishermen wore long waterproof boots, oilskins, and a waterproof sou'wester or a wool cap when they were in their dories, in the rain, or when there was spray. Depending on the weather, underneath the oilskins they wore flannel shirts, wool sweaters, the same pants for weeks, wool socks, wool mitts, and wool caps. Wool insulates even when it's wet. Fishermen didn't change out of their clothes when they slept, because they never knew when they'd be awakened to go on deck for an emergency or to help sail the boat. They just took off their oilskins and lay down.

During Angus Walters's first season as a flunky, the ship's cook fell overboard. Dorymen found his bowler-style hat floating on the water. When they picked up the hat, they discovered the cook was still wearing it. The cook survived, and wore the hat to sea for the rest of his career.

called to the crew to get the dories overboard, and gave the order to abandon ship. He got into one of the dories with two of the crew and rowed to the bigger ship, hoping he would be able to climb aboard and alert the watch.

But the ship was too high out of the water. Captain Walters yelled from the dory, and finally someone answered.

Was the ship planning to run over *Bluenose*? Captain Walters demanded. Could they not see the schooner's running lights?

The other replied he could do nothing about it.

Take in some sail, hollered Walters. At least that way the ship would drift away from the schooner.

The big ship missed *Bluenose* by an arm's length and carried on with its journey, its identity never discovered. Captain Walters and the crew climbed back aboard *Bluenose* to continue fishing, undeterred by the close call. The schooner had to fish that season if it was to enter the 1921 International Fishermen's Trophy race. Also, *Bluenose's* investors needed to be repaid, and the way to do that was to catch and sell fish. And after all, Captain Walters and his crew earned their living by fishing, just like their fathers and grandfathers had before them.

Starboard watch

Very few girls or women went to sea, but sons of fishermen grew up expecting to be fishermen. They played with boats and hung around the wharves and shipyards until they were about thirteen, old enough to go to sea with their fathers or older brothers, though some were as young as ten or eleven. They sailed first as flunkies, scaring away seagulls, helping the cook, and doing whatever jobs the crew could find aboard the ship while the dorymen set off in their little boats. After a couple of seasons, the boys graduated to the dories.

Young fishermen-in-training were paid less than experienced men. The flunky on *Bluenose*'s maiden voyage was paid $30 for a spring and summer of work, while the seasoned fishermen each received a $431 share in the first summer's profit. Boys helped clean the fish when they came aboard, often beginning their careers as throaters, headers, or gutters. These jobs involved cutting off the fish's heads, slitting the fish's bellies, and removing their guts. They tossed the organs overboard if the ship was at sea, or into a bin called a gurry kid if they were in port. Cod fish and some other species get their food from the bottom of the ocean, so the gutters occasionally found odd objects like coins in the fish's stomachs.

After it was gutted, each fish was passed along the work table, called the keeler, to the next person to split it open until it lay flat. The fish were then rinsed in buckets of sea water, sorted by species, drained, and tossed through a hatch into the hold. There, the salter's job involved carefully layering the fish in just the right amount of salt to keep them from spoiling. Salted fish could keep for months at sea, so the schooner could keep fishing until the holds were filled.

Little of the fish was wasted. Cod livers were saved in a huge barrel and cooked later to extract cod liver oil, used for medicine or for tanning leather. The headers cut out the tongues and cheeks of cod to be eaten as a delicacy. Roe, another delicacy, was collected for the European market. Swim bladders were saved to make isinglass, a substance used in cooking, to clarify wine, and to make carpenter's glue.

Cutting, gutting, splitting, sorting, and salting started as soon as the fish came aboard the schooner, and it sometimes took until midnight to finish. The boys and men worked with sharp knives by kerosene lamplight in the cold and wet, while the schooner danced up and down on the waves. Their fingers got sliced and salt water stung their raw wounds, sometimes leading to sores and infections that took a long time to heal. It was dirty, exhausting work, but it paid better than any shore job that a boy or young man could find. They considered themselves lucky if they could sail with an experienced and capable captain like Angus Walters.

Captain Walters was known as an expert sailor as well as a fish killer, that is, a captain with an uncanny sense for finding fish to catch and bring home to Lunenburg. In the 1919

Angus Walters

Young Angus shovelled salt on the wharf while attending Lunenburg Academy. When he was thirteen, he went to sea as a deckhand, or flunky, aboard the *Nyanza*, a ship owned and skippered by his father, Elias Walters. At fifteen, Angus was a doryman, partnered with an experienced member of his father's crew. He liked being at the ship's wheel, and often volunteered for the later afternoon or early evening watch. At age twenty-four, he was master of his own vessel, the *Minnie M. Cook*. His success with that ship led to the construction at Smith and Rhuland Shipyard of the *Muriel B. Walters* about a year later. He sold the *Muriel B. Walters* in 1916 and bought the *Donald Silver*, which he sailed until late 1918. Then he ordered the 170-tonne *Gilbert B. Walters* from Smith and Rhuland. His next ship was *Bluenose*, which he owned until 1942.

When young Angus Walters went to sea in 1895, his father brought in a record 100-tonne catch. In 1919, Captain Angus Walters brought in almost 400 tonnes.

Captain Angus Walters at the wheel, 1930s

season he landed 360,000 kilograms of fish, paying the *Gilbert B. Walters* shareholders more than twice their investment in a single season. The next season he again won the title of high liner by bringing home Lunenburg's largest catch, and everyone expected him to be successful with *Bluenose* in 1921. His crew earned well and were as safe under his command as banks fishermen could be.

There were hundreds of ships fishing the banks at the same time as *Bluenose*, harvesting the world's richest fishing grounds to fill a huge international demand for salt fish. In the days before refrigerators and freezers, fish were an important source of protein because once they were split, salted, and dried they would keep for months in even the warmest weather. Red meat and poultry were not as easy to preserve. Salt fish was valuable for long voyages, and it was a staple in countries that had used up their local supplies of fresh fish, or that had little farmland for producing other animal protein.

Once ashore, the fish were spread over flakes—raised platforms of mesh or lattice through which air could circulate. The fish had to be covered if it rained, and were turned often until they dried. Cod were especially prized because they were easy to catch and to preserve. They were found in abundance on the banks. The water is only 36 to 185 metres deep there, so sunlight can penetrate to promote the growth of nutrients for fish to eat. The warm Gulf Stream, flowing from the south, also nourishes marine growth, while the icy Labrador Current flows across the banks from the north, keeping the water from getting too warm for cod, halibut, and other cold-ocean fish.

Although fishermen from England, Spain, France, Portugal, and Italy began fishing the banks in the 1400s, Lunenburg ships didn't arrive on the scene until the mid-1800s, but they soon outnumbered the others on Sable, Middle, Western, and Banquero banks. In the twenty years just before *Bluenose*, the

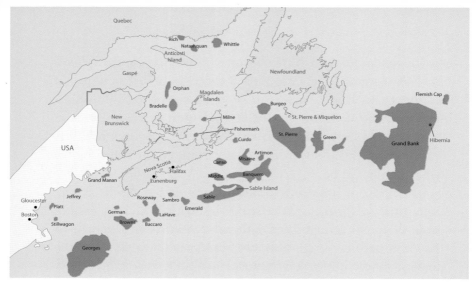

Map of fishing banks

banks yielded more than 45 million kilograms of cod, not to mention the halibut, haddock, hake, pollock, and perch that were hauled aboard (and often thrown back as shack, or useless). *Bluenose*'s crew hoped for a lucky trip, when they would fill the hold with nothing but valuable cod.

The crew depended on the skipper to get them to the banks, find the fish, and get them back to port. Salt banker captains rarely used charts, as most had a map of the ocean in their heads. Radar and radio were still in the future when *Bluenose* first went to sea, so Captain Walters and other skippers navigated by dead reckoning using a compass, the sun and stars, sniffing the wind, landmarks like lighthouses, and sometimes by noises from ashore, like barking dogs or crashing surf. On the open ocean, with no landmark in sight, they could discover their whereabouts by taking soundings. This involved dropping a long line overboard with a lead cup-like device on the end, weighing 3–8 kilograms and covered in grease. The length of line it took to reach bottom indicated the depth, and whatever stuck to the grease indicated the kind of sea bed. A sandy bottom meant codfish, mud meant hake, and gravel meant halibut. After years of fishing the banks, a fisherman became familiar with the different kinds of bottoms and could pinpoint his location by the type of sand or gravel or mud or shells that came up with the lead. If the skipper found an especially good fishing spot he guarded the secret as long as he could, but less able captains often watched where the high liners fished and followed them.

Besides keeping maps in their heads, captains also watched the wind, the clouds, the tides, the currents, and the behaviour of fish and birds. Their business considerations included the catch size, how much bait was onboard, the current price for fish, the crew's skills and experience, and the seaworthiness of the vessel. They decided where and when to fish, how to face a storm, when to adjust the sails or the ballast, how to place the cargo so it wouldn't unbalance the ship, and when to head for port. Most skippers left school when they went to sea, and learned their skills through experience. Although he was the boss, the captain had to win his crew's respect; he couldn't simply order them around. Unlike military ships, where the captain's word is law, a fishing crew listened to their skipper because they trusted him to treat them fairly, lead by brave example, help them earn a living, and get them home safely. Skippers who had good reputations as navigators, fish killers, sailors, and natural leaders had no trouble finding good crews. Captain Walters had a good reputation, so he had a good crew.

After three horrific storms plus two ice storms, losing two dories (but not the men), narrowly missing ice floes, and catching 4,200 quintals of fish, *Bluenose* arrived in port from its first fishing trip in September 1921. The schooner was early enough to get high prices for the fish. There was also plenty of time to prepare for the Trophy race.

Canadia

CHAPTER 3:
BLUENOSE'S FIRST RACE

Aғтеr unloading the season's catch, *Bluenose* was hauled ashore to scrape off five months' worth of barnacles and seaweed, and to give the hull a fresh coat of paint. The sails were examined, the rigging was overhauled, and the ballast was adjusted to ready the vessel for racing.

At the same time, seven other South Shore schooners prepared for the 1921 elimination races, hoping to challenge Gloucester for the International Fishermen's Trophy. Their skippers had seen how well *Bluenose* had performed on the banks, and some had lost to the schooner in impromptu races. But they all remained undaunted in their quest to have their ships named the fastest fishing boat in the world, or at least in their part of the world.

Canadia, a Shelburne ship that, like *Bluenose*, was built for speed, was disqualified because it was too long. New rules drafted in 1921 shortened the maximum length for ships, from 45.6 metres to 44 metres from bow to stern. When *Canadia*'s owner and captain protested that they'd followed the rules in effect when the ship was built, the race committee allowed it to

Bluenose approaches the Inner Automatic Buoy, first Halifax race, 1921

participate in the elimination race. But if it won, it had to give up its spot in the international races to the next fastest vessel. *Independence*, which had raced in the 1920 elimination series and was now ruled too big, was also allowed to enter the elimination series, but not the international race. The new rules restricted sail size and changes in ballast during the race, and allowed for changes to the course length. It wasn't the last time the race rules would be changed, nor the last time owners and skippers would protest.

In the end, it didn't matter if *Canadia* and *Independence* entered the 1921 elimination races, because *Bluenose* won. With Angus Walters at the helm and a hand-picked crew that included captains of other vessels, the schooner simply out-sailed the competition.

Old girl

Ships, even those with masculine names, have traditionally been called by feminine pronouns (she and her) in English, although not in all other languages. The origin of this very old figure of speech is uncertain. The most common practice today is to refer to a ship as "it," but many seafaring people still use the feminine.

On race day, October 15, spectators lined the shore of Halifax Harbour to watch the eight schooners, sails set, jockey for position behind the start line. When the cannon fired to start the race, *Bluenose* leaped to the front with *Alcala* and *Canadia*. Ten kilometres on to the south, at the harbour mouth, the light breeze quickened to 12 knots, allowing *Bluenose* to make the first marker four minutes ahead of *Canadia* and nine minutes ahead of *Alcala*.

Fog closed in, making it impossible to see the second leg of the race from land. When the ships came back into view around the second marker, the spectators could see that *Bluenose* had lengthened the lead. With the wind rising to 15 knots, the course took the schooners south toward Sambro light. *Bluenose* still held the lead. The course turned northward, the wind picked up to 20 knots, and *Bluenose* sped toward Halifax Harbour. *Bluenose*'s foremast passed the finish line four minutes ahead of *Canadia* and seven ahead of *Alcala*, an easy win and no great surprise.

The race's triangular course meant ships had to be able to

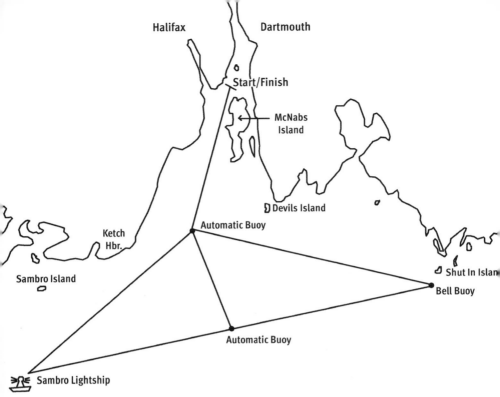

The 1922 race course involved a series of triangular routes outside Halifax Harbour, designed to prove the schooners' abilities in various wind directions and currents.

sail in different directions, regardless which way the wind blew. *Bluenose* had proven to be fast sailing against the wind, with the wind coming from behind, and in a cross wind.

The second elimination race took place two days later. This time the schooners started with a chill, 25-knot wind out of the northeast. *Delawana*, with new sails and a repaired keel, led at the halfway mark. Then *Bluenose* tore into the lead when the course turned into the wind. The timbers creaked, the sails strained, and the bow pounded the waves as *Bluenose* beat home to cross the finish line a full sixteen minutes ahead of *Delawana*. Now *Bluenose* would meet the American contender, to be chosen by a similar process in the waters off the port of Gloucester.

But the American committee was having trouble selecting a schooner to represent the United States in the race. To the supreme annoyance of the Gloucester fishermen, non-fishing business interests in Boston had become involved. A group of wealthy Boston yachtsmen had built a sleek racing schooner, the $52,000 *Mayflower*, in order to eliminate the Gloucester entry and proceed to the international series in Halifax. The schooner could carry two hundred tonnes of fish (it went on to fish successfully for seventeen years), but the Gloucester men thought the boat was a freak. It didn't even look like a fishing schooner, they said, although there was no rule governing the look of a vessel. Besides, they argued, the competition was meant for Gloucester and Lunenburg fishermen, not a bunch of fair-weather city sailors. The Gloucester men complained that *Mayflower* took too long to get the banks for the 1921 fishing season. They threatened to boycott the races, and started a rumour that Canada would too.

It could be argued that since *Bluenose* was designed and built with city money to win the International Fishermen's Trophy, it was okay for the Americans to do the same. The difference was that *Bluenose* was built in the fishing port of Lunenburg, so fishermen adopted it as theirs, whereas *Mayflower* was conceived and built in Boston instead of in the fishing port of Gloucester. It could also be argued that the race was intended to improve fishing schooners, and *Mayflower* was an improvement. But as far as the Gloucester men were concerned, the race was for fishermen, and they didn't like big Boston money trying to steal their fun and their glory.

The Canadian race committee left the decision to their American counterparts, and the fuss continued. Finally, the Canadian officials agreed with the Americans, and the

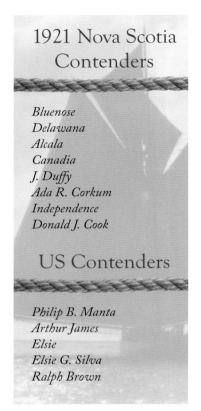

1921 Nova Scotia Contenders

Bluenose
Delawana
Alcala
Canadia
J. Duffy
Ada R. Corkum
Independence
Donald J. Cook

US Contenders

Philip B. Manta
Arthur James
Elsie
Elsie G. Silva
Ralph Brown

international committee banned *Mayflower* from the races. The committee gave no reason for its decision, but there were no rules saying it had to.

Gloucester wanted the 1920 champion *Esperanto* to enter. That hope was dashed when the schooner struck a submerged shipwreck at Sable Island on May 30. The captain and crew escaped in their dories to the rescue station on Sable Island, but *Esperanto* sank. Efforts to raise the boat failed, so the committee searched for another fast schooner. Eventually, five vessels entered the Gloucester elimination races, with *Elsie* declared the winner. The skipper was Marty Welch, who had captained the *Esperanto* for the 1920 series. The eleven-year-old *Elsie* was 26 metres shorter than *Bluenose*, and was built for fishing rather than for speed. The sweet little schooner had just returned to Gloucester after fishing from Lunenburg for two seasons and, earlier in 1921, had collected *Esperanto*'s shipwrecked crew from Sable Island.

Back in Lunenburg after the elimination races, Captain Walters had the jitters. He employed a naval captain to drill his crew in handling *Bluenose*'s sails until they could do it in their sleep. Rigging is a complicated system of wires, ropes, spars, and pulleys in which every piece has a particular function. Experienced sailors like those who crewed for *Bluenose*'s races knew a schooner's rigging like the backs of their hands.

But everyone makes mistakes, and Captain Walters wanted to make sure they didn't make them on *Bluenose* during a race.

On the way to Halifax for the October 22 race, *Bluenose* raced *Mayflower* informally. *Bluenose* won, but *Mayflower* was headed for the winter fishing grounds with the top masts removed so Captain Walters figured the race didn't prove anything. It was just a good workout. *Elsie* practised on the way to Halifax too, reaching a speed of 13 knots.

The day of the race there was a chilly 23-knot northwest breeze, the same wind that had cancelled the America's Cup race the previous year and prompted the first International Fishermen's Trophy race. *Elsie* and *Bluenose* jogged around behind the start line in Halifax Harbour, waiting for the gun. *Elsie* crossed the start before *Bluenose*, and held the lead for 10

Bluenose on the slip before the first race

Bluenose at the start

kilometres. The second leg headed into the wind, which had risen to 35 knots to create 6-metre waves, giving the men in the swaying top masts a wild ride. *Bluenose* gained quickly until the schooners were side by side. First one would pull ahead,

50   BLUENOSE

then the other, their skippers' tactics delighting spectators on shore and in boats along the course.

This was a race worth watching. It was a bit like being in a National Hockey League city during a Stanley Cup final.

Everybody talked about the race. Reporters were there from all over Canada and the United States, wiring exciting stories to their newsrooms. For the people who couldn't watch from the shore or a spectator boat, the race was repeated in Lunenburg and in downtown Halifax. Two parallel ropes were stretched across streets in both places and tiny *Bluenose* and *Elsie* models were tugged along according to reports coming in from the race by telegraph.

Up to the second marker *Bluenose* sailed fast with the four lower sails—the foresail, mainsail, jumbo, and jib—plus the staysail and the main topsail. The vessel heeled over so far that

Elsie

Bluenose Stats

- Overall length: 143 feet (43.6 metres)
- Beam: 27 feet (8.2 metres)
- Waterline length: 112 feet (34.1 metres)
- Depth (main hatch): 11 feet, 6 inches (3.5 metres)
- Draught: 15 feet, 10 inches (4.8 metres)
- Displacement: 285 tons (258.5 tonnes)
- Mainmast, above deck: 81 feet (24.6 metres)
- Foremast, above deck: 73 feet (22.2 metres)
- Main topmast: 53 feet, 6 inches (16.26 metres)
- Fore topmast: 48 feet, 6 inches (14.8 metres)
- Main boom: 81 feet (24.6 metres)
- Main gaff: 51 feet (15.5 metres)
- Fore boom: 32 feet, 6 inches (10 metres)
- Fore gaff: 32 feet, 6 inches (10 metres)
- Sail area: 10,000 square feet (930 square metres)

at times the rail and main boom were under water and spectators could see the keel. The crew on the weather, or windward, side was under strict orders to keep their heads down and out of the way of the boom when it swung across the deck, or be chastised by Captain Walters, a dreaded event given the skipper's fiery tongue and eloquence in scolding.

The captain gave the order to raise the ballooner, a smaller sail on the foremast. Wind filled the additional canvas and *Bluenose* leaped toward the finish, leaving *Elsie* farther and farther behind. To catch *Bluenose*, Captain Welch hoisted some extra sail as well, but the strain was too much for *Elsie*'s fore topmast. It cracked off and collapsed the staysail and jib topsail over *Elsie*'s bow. As *Elsie* began to dig into the water, the crew scrambled to the bowsprit to cut free the fallen rigging, getting dunked with the boat's every plunge through the waves. Captain Walters noticed the predicament and reduced *Bluenose*'s sail to match *Elsie*'s. It didn't help his opponent. *Bluenose* crossed the finish line more than twelve minutes ahead, reaching a record speed of 11 knots on the 64-kilometre course.

Two days later, the second race started with a light, 12-knot breeze. The sun shone, the sky was blue, and the schooners filled their cloud-white sails with wind: a picture-perfect day. *Elsie*, fitted with new topmasts, led *Bluenose* off the start by ninety seconds. The Gloucester vessel held the lead until the second course marker, and people

An advertisement for the Bluenose ski from the Canada Ski Company Ltd, of Annapolis Royal, Nova Scotia

began to think it might beat *Bluenose*. When the pair rounded Sambro buoy, *Bluenose* was still in *Elsie*'s wake, but just seconds behind. As the wind increased to 20 knots, *Bluenose* sailed close to *Elsie*'s windward side up to the final course marker. Now 43 kilometres into the course, *Bluenose* squeezed between *Elsie*'s leeward side and the buoy. *Bluenose* missed the marker by an arm's length, and gained the lead over *Elsie*. Heading into the wind was *Bluenose*'s specialty, and the Lunenburg vessel crossed the line first. *Elsie* trailed 5 kilometres back.

Halifax went wild. Captain Walters congratulated Captain Welch and his crew on their skill and the good race, and *Elsie*'s skipper sent a case of congratulatory champagne to *Bluenose*'s crew. The hardy crew tasted the bubbly, and then switched to a more familiar drink: Jamaican rum.

Two Champions—

Bluenose Ginger Ale established in 1831 has, like another famous beverage, "been going strong" for over a century. Mr. W. J. Roue, the founder of the Bluenose Beverage Co., designed the Bluenose, Champion of the North Atlantic fleet. We invite your inspection. We request your fair criticism of

BLUENOSE GINGER ALE

Made by

Bluenose Beverage Co.

HALIFAX, · · · · · NOVA SCOTIA

An advertisement for Bluenose Ginger Ale from the ship's designer W. J. Roué's Bluenose Beverage Co., Halifax, Nova Scotia

Elsie may have lost, but the schooner had performed well. And at least it didn't lose to that blankety-blank yacht disguised as a fishing boat, the *Mayflower*. (While the race was underway, *Delawana* beat *Mayflower* in an unofficial challenge, but, like the earlier brush with *Bluenose*, it didn't mean much. *Mayflower* kept most of its sails furled.)

Captain Walters sailed home to Lunenburg with the trophy and $1,000, his share of the prize money plus expenses. But work didn't stop for the skipper of the fastest fishing schooner in the North Atlantic. *Bluenose* exchanged racing gear for working sails, freighted two loads of salt fish to Puerto Rico, and returned with a cargo of salt for the next fishing season. It was business as usual for the fishermen, but the rest of the world was *Bluenose*-crazy. Companies leaped at the schooner as a marketing tool, naming skis, milk, and soft drinks after the vessel, and used the schooner as an endorsement for everything from underwear to photographs. The International Fishermen's Trophy race attracted tremendous world-wide attention, with sail racing enthusiasts commenting that it was as good as the America's Cup. It brought tourism, attention, and money to the hosting city of Halifax, and expanded on the popular notion of the romance of the sea.

An advertisement for B. H. marine paints, highlighting *Bluenose*'s defeat of *Elsie*

The race also gave the banks fishermen an outlet for their fiercely competitive spirits. Every trip, they competed to see which dory had the most fish, and who could dress their catch the fastest, bait their hooks the fastest, or tell the best tall tale. They raced to see which vessel would fill the hold first, get to port first, or get the best prices. They bragged about their skippers and their cooks and even their troubles, and they refused to admit defeat. It was part of the camaraderie and rivalry among the fleet of two hundred or more ships in their work-place, the fishing banks.

It's doubtful the race achieved its other goal of improving and promoting the schooner fishery. Despite the fact that 114 schooners were built in Nova Scotia after the end of World War One, sail was becoming obsolete as a means of transportation. Steel ships and steam power were taking over, and the schooner fishery was viewed as a quaint occupation of a somewhat backward part of the world. The race didn't change the danger that fishermen faced to earn a living. It proved which boat was faster, but it didn't help them catch more fish.

Regardless, 1921 was good for *Bluenose*. The vessel's profit for the year was almost $7,700, including almost $2,500 from fishing, more than $2,500 from the race, and a few dollars short of $2,700 from two freighting trips. The amount was shared among the shareholders in the Bluenose Schooner Company. On the expense side of the accounts, the company paid out $6,500 to the crew, $4,400 for supplies and outfitting, and $433 in income tax on the prize money. However, the company didn't pay *Bluenose* designer William Roué his $1,052 fee, saying it hadn't hired him in the first place. Finally, Roué hired a lawyer and, in November 1922, the board of directors paid the designer $600.

Bluenose off McNabs Island, 1922

CHAPTER 4:
BATTLING *BLUENOSE*

WHILE *Bluenose* was filling the holds with salt for the return trip to Lunenburg, the talk in Gloucester was all about how to beat the Nova Scotia schooner.

As soon as *Elsie* docked after the 1921 series, ex-Newfoundlander Ben Pine and some other Gloucester businessmen and skippers asked *Mayflower* designer Starling Burgess to design a fast schooner. They wanted the new ship to look more like a salt banker so it wouldn't be disqualified for its yacht-ish looks, as *Mayflower* had been. However, the new vessel, *Puritan*, never made it to the elimination round. With all sails set in a soupy fog, *Puritan* ran full speed into Sable Island on June 3, 1922. It was apparently going so fast that skipper Jeff Thomas didn't realize how close the shoals were. One man drowned and the schooner was destroyed.

Pine, who had developed his marine salvage business into a large fishing fleet, then leased and refitted the New York schooner *Elizabeth Howard* to enter the race. To qualify, he took it fishing on the banks. Meanwhile, a group of Boston sailors built *Yankee*, and Gloucester's Captain Clayton Morrissey ordered a schooner which he named *Henry Ford*.

Margaret K. Smith, 1922, Halifax

When *Henry Ford* launched that spring, it plunged across the estuary of the Essex River and into the muck on the opposite shore. Later the same day, it went aground on a sand bar at the river's mouth, floating dangerously close to a reef before being rescued. The vessel's fishing season was delayed while the damage was repaired, but the race officials allowed it to enter the elimination rounds anyway. That, and more changes in the race rules, prompted *Mayflower*'s owners to apply. Despite Captain Walters's willingness to race against the vessel and the fact that *Mayflower* had fished two seasons, the Canadian committee refused the schooner. Rather than see the series cancelled, the American committee also agreed to ban *Mayflower*.

In all, four American schooners officially entered the elimination race off Gloucester: *Henry Ford*, *Elizabeth Howard*, *L. A. Dunton*, and *Yankee*. (*Mayflower* joined the course and passed the others, but it didn't count. Even though *Mayflower*

Mahaska, 1922, Halifax

fished for eighteen seasons, the schooner was continually disqualified from the International Fishermen's Trophy race.)
Henry Ford won by eighteen minutes after *Elizabeth Howard*
lost its topmast. The new schooner *Yankee*, designed for speed,
never raced again. *L. A. Dunton*, built in 1921 and retired from
fishing in the 1950s, is displayed at Connecticut's Mystic Sea-
port museum.

The Halifax elimination race was a bit more exciting. Four
vessels entered there, too: *Bluenose, Mahaska, Canadia*, and the
Margaret K. Smith. Bluenose had been the third ship to leave
the banks, but the first to arrive in port, so laden with fish that
the crew announced they'd had to nail cod to the masts. *Mahaska* had won a few informal races on the banks, and skipper
Paddy Mack figured it was a contender for the international
series. *Canadia* handled better in 1922 than in the previous
year. *Margaret K. Smith* was so new it hadn't fished that season
and wouldn't qualify for the international series even if it won

Captain Morrissey

Captain Clayton "Clayte" Morrissey, like Captain Marty Welch, was a displaced Nova Scotian, originally from Lower East Pubnico on the province's western tip. To build *Henry Ford*, he sold his beloved *Arethusa*, allegedly to a rum-runner, and agreed to race the new vessel in exchange for financing from wealthy Bostonians. A quiet but experienced skipper who preferred to fish rather than race, Captain Morrissey was the model for a statue of a fisherman in Gloucester.

the elimination round, but entered for the fun of it. All except *Canadia* had been built at Smith and Rhuland in Lunenburg.

At the start of the October 7 race Captain Walters had his vessel pointed so directly into the light wind that *Bluenose* was stuck, absolutely unable to move from its position. Finally the sails caught a puff of air, and the vessel crossed the start line five minutes behind the others. As the wind picked up to 18 knots, *Bluenose* charged ahead and gained on the leader, *Margaret K. Smith*, within just twenty minutes. Then the captains of both *Bluenose* and *Smith* mistook the course and passed the marker buoy in the wrong direction. They had to change course and circle back, allowing *Canadia* to take the lead by about 2 kilometres. *Mahaska* was a close second.

Recognizing his mistake, Captain Walters yelled to his crew that the vessel would get them out of the hole he'd created. It took some fierce sailing, but *Bluenose* caught up to *Mahaska* and then to *Canadia*, sprayed past them, and crossed the finish line seven minutes ahead of the rest. The single race decided the Canadian contender, because the wind died and didn't rise again for days.

Escorted by the naval ship *Patriot*, *Bluenose* arrived in Gloucester on October 14. Huge crowds turned out to watch the races, including politicians from both sides of the border and a delegation from *Mayflower*'s owners who begged Captain Walters for an informal match to take place two days after the final race, if *Bluenose* won. Walters and the race committee agreed, as long as the offer was made to *Henry Ford*'s Captain Morrissey as well.

Long before the starting gun, the race began to go sour. When the hulls and sails were measured to make sure both schooners fit the regulations, it was discovered that *Henry Ford* carried 46 square metres of extra canvas. The sails had to be snipped down to size, a job that went through the night until 8:00 AM, just two hours before the first race was scheduled to start. Captain Morrissey, already a reluctant racer, was even more dismayed when the race was postponed because there wasn't enough wind.

So the two skippers ignored the postponement, which they considered an example of the yachting crowd trying to impose fancy racing rules on fishing schooners. They raced anyway, and *Ford* won. Race officials declared the race illegal, because it took longer than the allotted six hours and both vessels had made false starts. To add further insult, the official measurer (another introduction from the yacht-racing crowd) announced that *Ford*'s sails were still too big. Fed up, Captain Morrissey said he'd quit the race and go fishing. His crew agreed, complaining that rich yachtsmen were taking over the fishermen's series. Captain Walters declared *Ford* had won the race. *Ford*'s owners begged Captain Morrissey to stay, finally appealing to his Nova Scotia roots as well as his American pride. So Captain Morrissey had the sails cut to race again.

Unfortunately, the next race, on October 23, was as plagued as the first. *Bluenose* raised a signal flag to indicate it had a problem—a damaged keel—which the race committee ignored. Light puffs of air wafted the vessels around the course, with *Ford* finishing in front by two minutes. The committee ignored that, too, and declared the race void. The frustrated skippers argued successfully with the decision, and the committee awarded the race to *Ford*. Even though the first heat hadn't counted, Captain Morrissey now figured he'd won two races, he'd earned the trophy despite the rules, and it was time to go fishing. But *Ford*'s sponsors had gambled heavily on the vessel and told him to race again. Mrs. Morrissey, also a shareholder, told him to quit and stay home with his critically ill son. Captain Walters, busy trying to get *Bluenose*'s keel checked, told his rival that their friendship would survive whatever decision Captain Morrissey made. Amid the tension and turmoil, Captain Morrissey decided to race.

The schooners started in 20- to 25-knot gusts, crossing the start line within seconds of each other. *Bluenose* led by a minute at the first marker, but the two sailed so closely down the second leg they could call insults at each other across the swells. By the second turn, *Ford* struggled through waves washing over the deck as *Bluenose*'s unique bow kept the schooner relatively dry. Despite a sailor breaking his leg in the rigging, the Lunenburg ship took a strong lead and sailed past the finish line seven minutes before *Ford*. The next race would decide the series.

Because of rumours about sabotage to the *Ford* and Captain Walters's concerns about *Bluenose*'s damaged keel, divers examined the hulls before the last race. *Ford* was all right, but the race was briefly delayed while a large wood splinter was shaved from *Bluenose*. By the late morning start, a 30-knot northwest gale blew up big swells. *Bluenose* took the lead, with *Ford* close behind throughout most of the course. As the wind rose on the final leg, *Ford*'s staysail split. As it was hauled in, the top of the foretopmast snapped and carried away two more sails. By the time the crew cleared the tangle, *Ford* was behind *Bluenose* by seven minutes at the finish line. Then the complaints from *Ford*'s supporters began. *Bluenose* had no American observer aboard, as he'd quit and no replacement had shown up. *Bluenose*'s replacement staysail hadn't been measured before the final race, although it was well within the regulation size. *Bluenose* used special canvas in its sails, which was untrue. *Bluenose* had shifted ballast between races, for which there was no evidence. The committee had rigged the race in favour of *Bluenose*, they said.

The *Bluenose* skipper and crew viewed the American fans, media, and millionaire yachting types as sore losers. They were more concerned

A News Publishing Co. advertisement featuring *Bluenose*

about the Nova Scotia vessel's injured crew member. Worse by far was that the body of Captain Walters's nephew, Bert "Boodle" Demone, was discovered in the low water beside the wharf. Amid suspicions of foul play in the young man's death and anger over the accusations against *Bluenose*, the schooner sailed back to Lunenburg with the trophy and with the flag at half mast. Captain Walters vowed that he'd not race in the United States again that year, putting an end to the proposed race against *Mayflower* and Captain Morrissey's suggestion of a rematch.

The bitterness didn't stop anyone from anticipating the 1923 series.

In Lunenburg, Captain Albert Himmelman sold his schooner *Independence*, which had lost to *Bluenose* in the 1921 elimination round, and ordered *Keno*. Captain Himmelman

Columbia in 1923

had crewed for *Bluenose* in the 1921 and 1922 international series, an experience that might have helped him except *Keno* wasn't ready in time to fish that season. The ship was lost without a trace on New Year's Eve, so it never did race. Contenders from previous years decided against racing, so *Bluenose* proceeded unchallenged to the 1923 international series. Captain Walters arrived in port with a record catch of 213 tonnes, and proceeded to have the schooner hauled up on the ways for a good scrubbing, painting, and ballast adjustment. In the United States, *Mayflower*'s owners had given up, cutting down the masts and installing a diesel engine. Ben Pine satisfied his schooner racing obsession when he launched *Columbia* on March 17. A beautifully designed schooner, it was fitted with dories and crewmen from Shelburne, where dories were cheaper and schooner fishermen hadn't yet converted to diesel like they had in Gloucester. *Columbia* was late getting outfitted, and thus late going to the banks, but Pine persuaded the racing committee not to disqualify the vessel.

The crews of *Bluenose* and *Columbia*, 1923

Columbia almost didn't get to the races after it was damaged in a collision with a French trawler at Sable Island. The crew abandoned ship, but the captain ordered them at gunpoint to get back on board to pump out the water. *Columbia* got a tow to St. Pierre for repairs and kept fishing. Filled with salt cod, *Columbia* arrived in Gloucester that fall for an elimination race against *Henry Ford*, which was still fishing. Morrissey arrived a day later with 90 tonnes of fish and no interest in racing, but Pine was persuasive. *Columbia* easily beat *Ford*, and proceeded to Halifax for the October 27 start of the 1923 series. On the way, the schooner ran aground and had to be repaired, which delayed the series two days. Then *Columbia*'s eligibility for the race was questioned because of more new rules. The ship was found to be too short, and Captain Ben Pine had never fished the banks, but those rules were waived. Finally, the first race started on a dark, windy, rainy day.

Bluenose winning the 1923 race, with *Columbia* behind

Right away, *Bluenose* took a five-length lead on *Columbia*. It was still ahead at the first marker, and almost doubled its lead by the second while *Columbia* struggled in the swells. Once the ships headed into the wind, *Columbia* caught up with *Bluenose* and gained the lead. As *Bluenose* tried to pass, Captain Pine forced the other ship toward the rocks near Chebucto Head, so that Captain Walters had to choose whether to drop back, hit the rocks, or hit *Columbia*. He called the *Columbia* for sea room, ordered the staysail in, and yelled a warning that he was swinging hard toward his rival. The foresail swung sideways so that *Bluenose*'s boom extended over *Columbia*'s aft deck, a tactic that blocked the wind from *Columbia*'s sails. Captain Pine didn't change course. Then, as *Bluenose* passed *Columbia*, the boom hooked *Columbia*'s rigging. For a couple of brief minutes *Bluenose* towed *Columbia*. The weight pried the foot of *Bluenose*'s mast from its jaws. As seven crew members muscled the heavy timber back into place, and the mainsail stopped flapping, *Bluenose* pulled ahead. *Columbia* recovered, but it was too late. *Bluenose* won by a minute and twenty seconds.

Neither skipper lodged a complaint, but everyone else argued about the legality of both schooners' actions. To make sure a similar situation didn't happen in the second race, the committee ruled that contenders had to pass buoys on the seaward side. They didn't consult the captains.

Finding *Columbia*

On New Year's Day, 1929, a trawler fishing 37 kilometres northwest of Sable Island hooked its gear on a submerged shipwreck. Parts of the wreck were salvaged and taken to Boston, where they were identified as spars from *Columbia*.

The next race was called off for two days because there wasn't enough wind. That Thursday, November 1, 1923, was another wet day with a 20-knot wind. *Columbia* started first, but *Bluenose* soon took the lead, paced only by the destroyer *Patriot* that carried the race officials. *Bluenose* passed a customs buoy to starboard instead of to port, which violated the new rule, but the schooners were nowhere near each other, the buoy was not a course marker, and the move didn't shorten the course for *Bluenose*.

Columbia's sails dragged in the water, and a wave washed a crewman overboard; he was saved when a sailor grabbed the cuff of his trousers. Aboard *Bluenose*, the wind snapped the main topmast backstay, whipping the thick wire cable across the deck and around Captain Walters's forearm where he stood at the helm. He didn't budge.

After taking more than five hours to cover 80 kilometres of Atlantic Ocean, *Bluenose* crossed the finish line two minutes ahead of *Columbia*. As the captains and crews gathered to celebrate that evening, the committee announced that Captain Pine had lodged a protest against *Bluenose* for passing on the wrong side of the customs buoy. The committee disqualified *Bluenose*, and gave the race to *Columbia*. The committee explained to the stunned crowd that the series would now have to go to a third race.

Captain Walters and his crew were furious, as they figured they'd won fair and square. They agreed to compete again if the protested race was declared no contest. The committee said no, so Captain Walters announced he was taking *Bluenose* home. Nova Scotia Premier E. H. Armstrong begged him to reconsider, to avoid an international incident. A Bluenose Schooner Company board member tried to persuade other sailors to race *Bluenose* in the absence of its usual skipper and crew. Both men forgot that Captain Walters owned controlling interest in *Bluenose*, and was accustomed to making decisions on his own. Getting a coal scow to tow *Bluenose* out of Halifax Harbour, he sailed the schooner back to Lunenburg. Captain Pine refused to sail the course alone and take the trophy.

Accusations flew, saying that Captain Walters was a poor sportsman who was scared to race against *Columbia*, and that the race was getting too bogged down in rules to be simply a fisherman's competition. When *Columbia* supporters said *Bluenose* ran away, *Bluenose* supporters retorted that Ben Pine, who was not technically a fishing captain, knew he'd been out-sailed and needed to resort to technicalities if he wanted to win. Captain Walters agreed that it was true, he wasn't a sportsman. He was a fisherman, and the captain of his own fishing schooner at that. The Bluenose Company's board of directors backed his decision to withdraw. The disagreement halted the International Fishermen's Trophy race for seven years. The prize money was divided between the two vessels, and the cup stayed in Nova Scotia. There was talk about selling *Bluenose*, but it didn't happen. So *Bluenose* kept fishing. With no international races to worry about in 1924, the schooner worked the banks all summer to catch a record 294,000 kilograms of fish, making it high liner that year. In one trip alone, each crew member earned $336.

Regardless of *Bluenose*'s fishing ability, it still had to defend its reputation for speed. The newest contenders were a group of Halifax businessmen who persuaded Bill Roué to design a schooner to beat *Bluenose*. Likely still upset that he hadn't been paid properly for *Bluenose*, he designed *Haligonian*. The new vessel, a little smaller than *Bluenose*, was launched from Shelburne Shipbuilders Limited in March 1925. It went aground at Canso towards the end of its first season and the repairs took all winter, so there was no race with *Bluenose* that fall. Afterwards, *Haligonian* was said to be hogged, meaning the stern and bow sagged a bit, and it didn't sail straight. But the owners and Captain Moyle Crouse, who had crewed for *Bluenose* in the 1921 series, believed *Haligonian* could beat the older vessel and scheduled a race for the fall of 1926.

Bluenose almost didn't make it. During the spring fishing trip in April 1926, *Bluenose* and several other vessels were catching lots of fish in less than fifteen fathoms of water off Sable Island when a blinding snowstorm struck. Captain Walters called in the dories just in time. By suppertime there were hurricane-force winds. The mountainous waves broke into white combers in the shallow water, washing over *Bluenose* instead

1926 Storm

In the summer of 1926, both *Bluenose* and *Haligonian* missed an August gale, a seasonal storm caused by warm fronts from Bermuda meeting colder weather systems from the Gulf of St. Lawrence to stir up nasty wind and rain right over the fishing banks. The schooners had no radios to warn each other of the storm, so it was days before families back in Lunenburg discovered that two local schooners, *Sylvia Mosher* and *Sadie A. Knickle*, disappeared on August 24 and took their crews with them. Two men were lost from the *Mary Pauline*, and three other ships had injured crew and damaged gear. Weather on shore was clear and sunny, with no hint of the tragedy at sea.

of rolling under. *Bluenose*'s anchor cable broke and the vessel drifted dangerously close to Sable Island. Captain Walters sent most of his men below, and tied himself to the wheel while he tacked the schooner around the end of Sable Island, the Graveyard of the Atlantic. It took six hours, with nothing visible except the crashing white surf that drenched the skipper in icy cold water every couple of minutes. The schooner barely missed getting beaten to pieces on the sandbar, but by daylight it finally arrived at the relative safety of deeper water. One big sea smashed off the ship's rail, and swept all the fishing gear from the deck, but the men on deck hung on to the rigging for safety. When the storm ended, Sable Island sand covered the deck and the fishing gear floated around like some kind of marine yard sale. The crew salvaged what they could, and sailed back to Lunenburg for more than $2,500 worth of repairs. *Bluenose* was lucky—two other Lunenburg ships sank that night.

Bluenose returned to port to race *Haligonian* that October, beating the new boat by thirty minutes in the first race. The next two races took too long and didn't count, but then *Bluenose* beat *Haligonian* by seven minutes to win the best two out of three races. Captain Walters sarcastically suggested the ship might move faster backwards, but Ben Pine and other Gloucester skippers watched with interest. They decided to hold their own races to provide a competitor in case the International Fishermen's Trophy race was revived. Captain Pine's *Columbia* won, and he asked the Canadian committee about a race. Captain Walters was still bitter about the 1923 series and wouldn't be persuaded, but the Halifax committee suggested *Haligonian* might participate. Ben Pine looked forward to a series against a Canadian ship in the fall of 1927, but Mother Nature had other ideas.

The 1927 August gale was the worst ever. A category two hurricane, it struck without notice a few days after the anniversary of the 1926 gale, while the entire Canadian and American fleets were fishing on the banks. Eighty-five Lunenburg-area men were lost in that single storm, six from one family. In two years, the community had lost 138 men, someone from almost every family, leaving many women and children with no income. The provincial government paid a pension to the surviving widows and orphans, but the loss was felt for years.

Bluenose rode out the storm in deep water, but the wind and waves sank the Lunenburg ships *Mahala*, *Clayton Walters*, *Uda R. Corkum*, and *Joyce M. Smith* with all hands. It swept other men off their ships to their deaths, and damaged still other vessels. The sea also claimed four Newfoundland vessels and their crews, and *Bluenose*'s rival, *Columbia*, with its Liverpool skipper and twenty-two Nova Scotian crew members. Just a few weeks earlier *Columbia* had landed 160,000 kilograms of cod in Gloucester, the last salt fish ever landed there by a vessel from that port. There were huge funerals, and 120 wreaths launched into the sea. The sadness ran deeply in the fishing communities, and forced many surviving skippers to quit altogether.

Whatever the emotional reason, quitting was a good move economically, because steel trawlers had made the sail fishing fleet almost completely obsolete. The diesel-operated boats could scoop as many fish in one gulp as dories could in a whole season, while the crew never left the safety of the ship's deck. Because the trawlers made fresh fish more available, the demand for it increased, which lowered both the demand and the price for salt cod. Duty taxes kept Nova Scotia fishermen from the American markets, and Scandinavian fishermen were undercutting the salt cod prices elsewhere. Fishermen didn't know it, but the stock market was about to crash, triggering the Great Depression and making everything a lot worse.

Thebaud beating *Bluenose* to win the Lipton Cup, 1930

CHAPTER 5:
BLUENOSE, THE GRAND OLD GIRL

WITH THE stock market crash in the fall of 1929, people who already had very little were suddenly a lot poorer. That was particularly true in one-industry communities like Lunenburg, where everything revolved around fishing. Already, Captain Walters received less pay for his catch because the price of salt cod took a nosedive. That meant his crew and the *Bluenose* shareholders also got less, so they couldn't spend as much money in the community as they once had. As a result, shops and other businesses struggled to pay their employees and their debts.

Bluenose was just one of more than seventy vessels that called Lunenburg home, and Lunenburg was just one of hundreds of North Atlantic fishing ports that faced financial disaster. The situation later gave rise to a unionization movement among Nova Scotia fishermen, complaints against big trawlers plundering the once-rich fishing grounds, and the view that smuggling liquor was a reasonable employment alternative for formerly law-abiding fishermen.

But hard times didn't stop racing enthusiasts. Ben Pine teamed up with retired Montreal insurance company chairman

Louis Thebaud, who had a summer home near Gloucester, and Joe Mellow, a retired taxi company owner from Gloucester. They ordered another schooner to beat *Bluenose*. On March 17, 1930, the schooner *Gertrude L. Thebaud* (pronounced tee-bo) slid down the ways at Essex shipyard in Massachusetts. Named after Mr. Thebaud's wife, the $73,000 *Thebaud* was smaller than *Bluenose* and could carry only 79,500 kilograms of fish, but it was fast.

Fifty-cent stamp featuring *Bluenose*, issued in 1929

Captain Pine persuaded sail-racing enthusiast Sir Thomas Lipton to donate a cup for a fishermen's race to coincide with Gloucester's three hundredth anniversary and the annual America's Cup challenge. The contest was open to Canadian ships, and especially to Captain Pine's long-time rival, *Bluenose*.

Neither *Bluenose* nor *Haligonian* had wealthy businessmen paying their way; they had to earn their keep by fishing. *Bluenose* followed *Haligonian* into Lunenburg at the end of that season, battered and beaten by severe Atlantic weather. It was also a bit soggy from going aground at Placentia Bay in Newfoundland during the spring baiting trip, while under the command of Captain Walters's brother. The schooner lay on its side filling with sand and water before tugs hauled it off to a Burin shipyard for repairs. That fall, the schooner remained sluggish.

Captain Walters said he'd race *Thebaud* if it came to Halifax, but Captain Pine persisted. (After all, his rival was rubbed

Lunenburg

British army Colonel Charles Lawrence established Lunenburg in 1753 as a settlement for European Protestants of mostly German descent, to balance the province's French (Acadian) presence. Each settler received land within the town, and a farm in the forest. The first settlers were mostly farmers and craftsmen rather than fishermen, but they soon began fishing. A century later, most of the ships on the banks were from Lunenburg. The town became a noted fishing port with strong connections to Halifax and Massachusetts, and a thriving centre for fishery-related businesses like shipbuilding and outfitting. Lunenburg was also a market centre for the outlying farms, which were operated by the women of the community while their husbands and sons were at sea. Just as Lunenburg ships relied on the traditional wind energy well into the twentieth century, the farms depended on the traditional power of horses and oxen.

in his face every time he received Canadian mail bearing the new *Bluenose* postage stamp!) He promised to pay *Bluenose*'s expenses, which amounted to a $10,000 refit for the ailing schooner. The temptation lured the directors of Bluenose Schooner Company to accept, on condition that they receive the money up front and that the race was not considered to be a revived International Fishermen's Trophy race. In other words, the title of fastest fishing schooner was not at stake.

Meanwhile, *Bluenose* raced *Haligonian, Margaret K. Smith,* and *Alsatian* during the Lunenburg Fishermen's Picnic. *Haligonian* won—the first time *Bluenose* was beaten at home. But it was *Bluenose* that sailed for the Gloucester races, dressed up for the party with baggy new sails. No amount of make-up could hide the aging queen's battered hull, but no one in Gloucester sympathized. They were confident the beautiful young *Thebaud* would trounce the battle-scarred old *Bluenose*.

Gloucester's 29-kilometre triangular racecourse was easily visible from shore, because the Lipton Cup was, first and foremost, a social spectacle. Winds were light for the first race, and *Thebaud* finished an easy fifteen minutes ahead of *Bluenose*. When the races were called off for a few days because the winds were just too light, Captain Walters used the time wisely. He trimmed canvas from the sails, lightened the ballast, and repaired the keel. When the next race took place on October 15, there was a 30-knot southwest gale and choppy waves, the kind of weather that suited *Bluenose*.

The Nova Scotia ship led for the first two legs, even though it was hard to see the tiny buoys marking the course—markers that Captain Walters nicknamed "baby

Bluenose leading *Thebaud*, 1931

buoys." When rain reduced the visibility so much that spectators couldn't see the competitors, the judges called off the race. Captain Walters scorned organizers for quitting in such a light wind, but no one listened. The race was postponed three days, to October 18. The wind was light again, and *Bluenose* was out in front. Then, unluckily, Captain Walters followed the advice of the Gloucester pilot aboard *Bluenose*, who said there were

better winds closer to shore. It wasn't true. *Thebaud*, skippered by Captain Charles Johnson because Captain Pine was sick, passed *Bluenose* and crossed the finish line eight minutes ahead of its rival. The citizens of Gloucester were delighted.

Bluenose was beaten fair and square, Captain Walters agreed. But he blamed himself, not his vessel, saying he shouldn't have listened to a pilot from the opposing team. He announced that *Thebaud* hadn't beaten *Bluenose*.

The Montreal Daily Star.
Canada's Greatest Newspaper
Founded in 1869

WEDNESDAY, OCTOBER 21, 1931

BRAVO, BLUENOSE!

BY defeating the U. S. challenger, Gertrude L. Thebaud, in two straight races off Halifax, the Lunenburg fishing schooner, Bluenose, sailed by her skipper, Captain Angus Walters, retains for another year the international trophy symbolic of supremacy on the Atlantic fishing banks. The Bluenose has only been defeated once since she was built in 1921, and then the trophy was not at stake. The unpleasant memories of a former race have been completely wiped out. The best of good feeling has prevailed throughout the contest. Destroyers of the American and Canadian navies were present to witness the racing, as well as a host of smaller vessels.

A very pleasant feature of the event was the recognition by the Canadians of the fine sportsmanship of Captain Ben Pine, who, though ill, stood gallantly by his challenge and skippered the Thebaud on the first race. He was presented by Premier Harrington with a special silver cup yesterday in recognition of his pluck.

This international contest has more significance than the supremacy of the schooner. It serves to draw public attention to a body of men who are engaged every year in an extremely hazardous occupation,—deep sea fishing. They are a fine type, and they hold fast by fine traditions. The evolution of machinery has affected them more than most classes of labour, but they go their way and sail their ships and bring home their catches in a spirit of sportsmanship that has no superior anywhere in the world. Canada is proud of her fishermen, and so is the United States of hers. International amity is served by the race, and this year that fact has been emphasized in a vivid manner. Captain Pine failed in his effort to lift the cup, but he won the admiration of his opponents and he will be welcome any time he comes sailing his trim little schooner into Canadian waters again.

An article and cartoon from the October 21, 1931 edition of the *Montreal Daily Star*, following *Bluenose*'s defeat of *Thebaud* off Halifax

"She beat me," he said.

Now recovered from his illness, Captain Pine couldn't wait to challenge Captain Walters to a rematch. This time it would be in Halifax, and it would be for the Herald Trophy. Captain Walters agreed, but he knew *Bluenose* needed repairs to make it in perfect trim for the 1931 race. There was time to complete the work, because the low price of cod meant *Bluenose* fished only a few weeks that year. Captain Crouse had tied up *Haligonian* for the same reason, and everyone else had switched to diesel, so there was no Canadian competition for *Bluenose*. In Gloucester, *Elsie*'s engines were removed and her sails re-

CAPT ANGUS WALTERS

THE MOST FAMOUS SKIPPER OF THE EASTERN ATLANTIC SEABOARD.

CAPT. WALTERS WAS AT THE HELM OF THE BLUENOSE IN THE INTERNATIONAL FISHERMEN'S CUP WHICH THE CANADIAN BOAT HAS HELD FOR TEN YEARS—

THE QUEEN OF THE FLEET AND HER SKIPPER

The Bluenose is still queen of the Atlantic fishing fleet. For ten years she has turned back invaders for the right to the famed Fisherman's cup, but this year it was expected that her day was done. Opposed by a brand new, trimly designed schooner, the Gertrude L. Thebaud, the Bluenose was thought to be too old and waterlogged to stand much of a chance. But she came through with flying colors—or rather sails. In the first race, in decidedly Thebaud weather, she led the American boat to the finish line by a good two miles. In the second race, which was closer, she again emerged victorious. And so Bluenose is still the queen of the fishing fleet, and Angus Walters is still the master skipper. He has piloted his boat in these races for ten years, and his reputation is known up and down the coast as the most famous skipper on the North Atlantic seaboard. Under his skilful guiding hand, the Bluenose has answered every call, and has yet to be defeated in a Fisherman's cup series.

An article and illustration from the October 21, 1931 edition of the *Toronto Daily Star* following *Bluenose*'s defeat of *Thebaud*

placed to give *Thebaud* a run in elimination races. *Thebaud* won, and sailed for Halifax. Even Halifax gamblers put their money on the pretty new American ship, figuring *Bluenose* was past its prime. They were in for a surprise.

Expecting big winds and waves, Captain Pine had loaded extra ballast on *Thebaud*. But the first race started in a light wind on a pleasant October Saturday. *Bluenose* had a 6-kilometre lead when race officials called off the contest because it was taking too long. Two days later the wind wasn't much higher. *Bluenose* hung out every piece of canvas to pull ahead of *Thebaud*, and to stay there. The Nova Scotia vessel crossed the finish line thirty-two minutes ahead of *Thebaud*, and just six minutes short of the six-hour time limit.

The next day brought a breeze gusting to 20 knots. *Bluenose* whipped around the course again, but *Thebaud* kept pace. On the last leg, into the wind, *Bluenose* left the American schooner

Captain Angus Walters in uniform

behind to sail across the finish line with twelve minutes to spare. The trophy stayed in Nova Scotia, a decisive victory for *Bluenose*. It was also a shock to *Thebaud*'s owners, who suggested another match. Captain Walters ignored the plea, sailed his schooner home to Lunenburg, and tied it at the wharf, just in time for the town's victory parade.

The prize money helped pay the bills, because *Bluenose* lost money fishing in 1931, and again in 1932. The future of the fishermen's race looked bleak, with only *Bluenose* and *Thebaud* left as the last all-sail schooners. Newly-constructed ships came fitted with steel hulls and diesel engines, not sails. Any old wooden ships that hadn't sunk or fallen apart from age had

Passengers on *Bluenose*, 1930s

their topmasts removed and engines installed, becoming what were known as auxiliary schooners. In 1929, Lunenburg had been home to more than seventy tall ships, but two years later there were just twenty-six in the port.

Then, like a ray of sunshine in the midst of the dark Depression, tourism appeared on the horizon as a new Nova Scotia industry. Thanks to the *Bluenose* stamp and the publicity surrounding the 1931 races, everyone wanted a romantic ride on a schooner under full sail, especially if it was the Queen of the North Atlantic. So in early 1933, the Bluenose Schooner Company formed a subsidiary business called Lunenburg Exhibitors Ltd. They replaced *Bluenose*'s fish pens with cabins and offered cruises to paying customers. Captain Walters got a uniform with brass buttons and a peaked cap, and made friends with his passengers and visitors. The new company marketed playing cards and other *Bluenose* souvenirs, which was a legal enterprise unlike the alternative of smuggling booze to the

Thank You, Montreal!

On Board the Bluenose,
May 17th, 1933

Thank You, Montreal

In the name of the officers and crew of the "Bluenose," I want to extend to the Mayor and the people of Montreal our heartiest thanks for the royal reception you have given us. We are overwhelmed by your enthusiastic welcome and your generous hospitality. We have thoroughly enjoyed every minute of our stay in your beautiful city, and will never forget your kindness. It is a splendid send-off on our journey to Chicago.

ANGUS WALTERS,
Captain of the Bluenose

An advertisement from the May 18, 1933 edition of the *Montreal Gazette*

States. *Bluenose*'s more steadfast customers included Nova Scotia travel writer and photographer Clara Dennis, and marine photographer Wallace MacAskill and his wife, Elva, who travelled aboard the schooner on summer weekends.

In *Bluenose*'s first year as a tourist attraction, the organizers of the Chicago Century of Progress world's fair invited the schooner to represent Canada, all expenses paid. To prepare for the trip, the schooner's keel was altered to navigate the St. Lawrence River and the Great Lakes lock system. A freighter went with *Bluenose*, to carry the schooner's ballast through the locks and then replace it once the ship was in deep water again. The task took at least two hours each time.

Lunenburg Exhibitors Ltd. ordered postcards of the ship, *Bluenose* picture puzzles, and more playing cards to sell as souvenirs to help pay for the voyage. The crew loaded a couple of kegs of rum aboard, but the RCMP raided the vessel the night before it sailed from Halifax and seized the liquor. It didn't matter, because the captain, crew, and company officials were well wined and dined in the cities they passed on the way to Chicago. *Bluenose*'s progress was followed closely, so that at each port thousands of people greeted "The Queen of the Banks," as one newspaper called the ship.

THE EVENING TELEGRAM

EVENING TELEGRAM, TORONTO, TUESDAY, MAY 23, 1933

Thousands Hail Bluenose And Stout Racer's Crew

Hope Bluenose Will Pay Visit To 1934 C.N.E.

A headline from the May 23, 1933 edition of the *Evening Telegram*, reporting *Bluenose*'s visit to Toronto

Montreal Daily Herald

MONTREAL, MONDAY, MAY 15, 1933.   C   C

"Queen of the Bankers" in Montreal

A headline from the front page of the May 15, 1933 edition of the *Montreal Daily Herald* announcing *Bluenose*'s visit to the city

❖   ❖   ❖

The vessel had to turn visitors away in Montreal and Toronto, where crew members, including Captain Walters's son Stewart, had their photos taken with local celebrities. Stories of the ship's races filled every newspaper, and Captain Walters was guest speaker at numerous public events. Reporters professed their surprise at his eloquence, noting in Montreal that he was as comfortable behind the radio microphone as behind the mast. The *Toronto Evening Telegram* described him as "an intelligent man of the world, a graduate with honours from the school of experience...with a ready wit and a merry answer."

"No breezes in these parts," Captain Walters commented after a calm day meant *Bluenose* had to be towed from the lake off Toronto Island into the city's harbour, where it docked at Terminal Warehouse. The ship stayed in the city for the May 24th celebration of Queen Victoria's birthday before heading on to Chicago under sail. There, *Bluenose* drew big crowds who toured the ship's on-board fishing museum, bought souvenirs, and marvelled at Lunenburg artist Earle Bailey, who had no arms or legs but painted with a brush held in his mouth.

Bluenose docked at Toronto Terminal Warehouse

On July 18, *Bluenose* entered and won the twenty-sixth annual sail race between Chicago and Mackinac Island, a 530-kilometre course. The schooner finished in 54 hours, 35 minutes, and 45 seconds—almost 90 minutes ahead of the next contender. The prize was a useful 136-kilogram wheel of cheese.

Bluenose offered tours and charters for much of the summer, until a body was discovered one morning near the ship, which was docked in an area frequented by criminals; and a charter customer sued the skipper because he was dissatisfied with a tour. It was time to leave. The schooner sailed to Toronto for the winter, where Captain Walters almost sold it. The deal fell through and *Bluenose* returned to Lunenburg in the spring of 1934, having made a $1,800 net profit from the entire journey. The cruise also brought national attention to the future of the aging Canadian icon, as editors wrote pleas for

Crew members who sailed to Chicago

Mate Harris Himmelman, second mate Perry Walters (Captain Walters's brother), cook William Dauphinee, George Rose, Philip Poole, John Pardy, Stewart Walters (Captain Walters's son), George Whynacht, Sea Scouts Wallace Knock and Fred Rhuland, manager Captain Roland Knickle, treasurer Captain Carl Kohler, secretary Aubrey Walters (Captain Walters's brother).

government to preserve the ship as a historic artifact. Nothing came of the campaign, then or later.

That November, the Bluenose Schooner Company accepted an invitation to join the 1935 celebrations marking the twenty-fifth anniversary of King George V's coronation. No yacht clubs or government agencies would sponsor the schooner so the directors financed the trip to England themselves. Carrying souvenirs to sell to help pay expenses, *Bluenose* sailed for England in early May. When the ship arrived, the British government unexpectedly placed taxes on the souvenir sales and demanded a cut from admission fees to the ship.

Bluenose was the only fishing boat taking part in the royal review of the fleet, and the only one that took part in a yacht race around the Isle of Wight. The aging schooner came in third, impressive considering the competition included speedy racing yachts. The King also presented the schooner with a new mainsail from his yacht *Britannia* and invited Captain Walters aboard the royal vessel for a chat and a photo with him.

While in England, *Bluenose* welcomed thousands of sightseers, took passengers for cruises, and played a role in a movie about smuggling. But the trip made no money for the financially-strapped Bluenose Schooner Company. Then, just after

A page from *Bluenose*'s guest book, showing the ship's 1935 visit to England

the vessel left England for Nova Scotia in September, a massive storm swept the northeast Atlantic. Likely the remnants of the Labour Day hurricane that killed more than four hundred people in the Florida Keys, the storm combined with another system as it spun eastward across the North Atlantic, to catch *Bluenose* in its path about 320 kilometres from England.

In the screaming wind, Captain Walters ordered the sails reefed and oil poured on the water to calm the waves. But the sea pounded *Bluenose* all day, and the crew feared for their lives. Some of the passengers didn't understand the danger, and sat in their cabin playing music on the gramophone. Afterwards, they described how, right in the middle of Cole Porter's song "Anything Goes," a huge wave struck *Bluenose* and knocked the ship over sideways, onto its beam ends. The force broke the spars, smashed the dories, and tossed the cast-iron stove around the galley like a dollhouse toy. The ocean poured through the hatches into the holds and cabins below. Two sailors washed overboard, saved only because lifelines tethered them to the ship, and a woman passenger struck her head when she was tossed across her cabin.

As Captain Walters prepared to cut away the submerged rigging and masts so they wouldn't drag the ship under any further, *Bluenose* slowly pulled itself upright. In the following days, the crew and able-bodied passengers continuously pumped water from the now-leaking ship. As the storm subsided, the remaining tattered sails were raised so *Bluenose* could hobble to the English port of Plymouth for repairs.

Fishing superstitions

It's unlucky to:
- Fish on Sunday
- Sail on the thirteenth of the month
- Sail on a Friday
- Wear coloured mittens aboard ship
- Have a woman on board
- Say certain words, like "drowned" or "good luck"
- Hear three knocks
- Carry bananas
- Leave a hatch cover upside-down
- Whistle
- Meet the minister on the way to the wharf

It's lucky:
- To place coins under the ship's masts during construction
- When a ship swings toward the open sea during its launch
- To wear a tattoo or an earring
- To touch cold iron
- To have a ship's name include three A's

Some would say that surviving that storm with no lives lost was *Bluenose*'s greatest victory.

"I have never encountered anything like it," Captain Walters told reporters, referring to the storm.

He wired the board of directors back in Lunenburg to suggest that the ship should remain in England until the following summer and be sold there if possible. The directors agreed that Captain Walters should accept a good offer, but otherwise *Bluenose* should return to Nova Scotia as soon as the repairs were finished. They wanted *Bluenose* in Canadian waters because they predicted, correctly, that German dictator Adolf Hitler's military aggression would start a war in Europe. *Bluenose* arrived in Lunenburg on November 4, 1935, after a twenty-three-day voyage. The Queen of the North Atlantic was still for sale, but meanwhile Captain Walters, his crew, and his shareholders had to earn a living. In June 1936, they fitted *Bluenose* with two 90-horsepower diesel engines, propellers, and an exhaust stack on the deck. It was an expensive job because the ship was not designed to use propellers, and because Captain Walters made sure the $11,500 engines could be removed in case *Bluenose* ever raced again. He stored the top masts and sails for the same purpose.

After the crew was paid and a down payment was made on the engine installation, *Bluenose* had a $6,500 bank loan and a $280 profit from charter cruises and insurance claims. The still-famous vessel caught fresh fish all fall and winter, but it was hard to sell the catch for a decent price, which meant there was less pay for everyone. The few skilled sailors that remained following the switch from sail to diesel weren't eager to work if they might not get paid at the end of the season. The appearance of *Bluenose* on the dime in 1937 was a nice honour, but it didn't pay the bills.

Wallace MacAskill (1890–1956)

Born in Cape Breton and trained in New York, Wallace MacAskill's *Bluenose* portraits made his name synonymous with marine photography. A daring sailor himself, he tied himself to *Bluenose*'s mast to capture images of sailors working while big waves pounded over the deck. His photographs, often hand-tinted by his wife, Elva, can be found all over the world. MacAskill's *Bluenose* photos include racing shots and a set taken toward the end of the vessel's career that catalogues the ship's gear, possibly to help sell it.

As a result of the depressed market for fish, Captain Walters got involved in the new union, the Fishermen's Federation of Nova Scotia. He became president of the Lunenburg local, leading a campaign to get processors to raise fish prices by a quarter of a cent. He argued that the companies were getting wealthy on the backs of impoverished dory fishermen. The processors pushed back, so the fishermen went on strike for three weeks. Finally, the government arranged a compromise to end the strike, but fishermen in both Nova Scotia and Gloucester were still poor.

South of the border, the black-and-white film *Captains Courageous*—about a spoiled rich boy rescued from the Atlantic by a banks schooner crew who teach the brat to be a man over a season at sea—revived public interest in fishing schooners and in fishermen's races. People fell in love with the idea of the heroic fisherman and, once again, racing enthusiasts began talking about another International Fishermen's Trophy race between the two famous contenders: *Thebaud* and *Bluenose*.

Bluenose's stern, marine survey 1940s

CHAPTER 6:
FADED GLORY

CAPTAIN Ben Pine was one of North America's most eager schooner racers and a man who was able to get things done. He travelled to Halifax in the spring of 1938 to persuade the trustees of the Herald Trophy to offer the cup one more time, to the winner of a race at Boston and Gloucester. He promised a first prize of $3,000 and a second prize of $2,000, sponsored by an American organizing committee.

The prize money would help the now-shabby *Bluenose* pay the bill for the engine installation, but neither Captain Walters nor the directors had enough money to fix up the vessel to go to the race in the first place. They would have to remove the diesel engines, replace the masts and sails, and buy new rigging.

Captain Walters's wife, Maggie, had died in 1937, and the skipper himself was now fifty-six and thinking about retiring from the sea. He was also reluctant to race again in the States. *Bluenose* was seventeen, well past its prime. The vessel sagged where it should have been strong, and cracked where it should have flexed. As well, the American committee wanted the prize to go to the winner of three out of five races, instead of two out of three. Was the prize worth the headache and the expense?

Fearing a 1938 race wouldn't happen, Captain Pine and his backers offered to pay $8,000 towards *Bluenose*'s refit, half of it in

Fitting a jib in preparation for the 1938 race

advance of the race. Captain Walters accepted the offer because he saw an opportunity to repair his beloved ship. The refit would cost more than the offer, so he had to raise money, but where? Wealthy Lunenburg businessmen were upset with him because he'd led fishermen in a strike against them. Other townspeople still suffered from the Depression and even though *Bluenose* had paid its shareholders well over the years, they didn't have extra money to help pay for a race. Finally, with $3,500 from the Canadian and Nova Scotia governments, the captain had the ship repaired, outfitted, scraped, and painted. He left the engines in place until he got to Gloucester, rather than pay to have them taken out for nothing if the race was cancelled.

Captain Walters and *Bluenose* arrived in Gloucester that fall to find that Ben Pine's backers had withdrawn their offer to pay an advance sum towards *Bluenose*'s race preparations.

Photographer Wallace MacAskill titled this photo "All hands and the cook." It shows *Bluenose* during the 1938 race.

Captain Walters's legendary anger prompted a partial payment of $2,000, but it didn't improve the race's atmosphere. As days went by, the event was marked by suspicion, deceit, and outright hostility from both sides.

The series opened on October 9, with a northwest wind blowing when the contestants crossed the start line at Cape Ann. *Bluenose* led for a bit, but *Thebaud* soon passed the Lunenburg vessel. Then *Bluenose*'s bowsprit cracked and the foretopmast came away, which meant the ship couldn't fly as much canvas as the skipper wanted. It didn't make much difference, as *Thebaud* was already in the lead. The ship won the first race by almost three minutes, to the utter joy of the Americans.

Captain Walters spent the next day replacing the spars and adjusting the rigging, in time for the next race day. It dawned with a tiny breeze that didn't get any stronger. The committee watched the schooners float for three hours, and then called off the race because there was no way the competitors would finish in the allotted time. It was rescheduled for October 13, when an 18-knot breeze allowed *Bluenose* to take an early lead and win by eleven minutes, despite ripping a sail almost in half.

The series stood at a race each. It was too foggy and calm for racing, but there was plenty of drama behind the scenes. The Americans complained to the race committee that *Bluenose* was longer in the waterline than the required 112 feet (34 metres). They said it was because the captain was adjusting the schooner's ballast during the series, which was against the rules. Officials measured and found that the vessel was indeed too long at the waterline, and ordered Captain Walters to fix the problem one way or another. He dumped some ballast to raise the ship, which shortened the waterline. He kept adding and removing ballast during the night to get the boat in trim, but

Captain Ben Pine of *Gertrude L. Thebaud* during the 1938 race

Thebaud rounding the buoy

Thebaud fans and even the police watched *Bluenose* closely and declared it was illegal. The race committee chairman ignored their complaints, telling them *Bluenose*'s skipper was acting on his orders to shorten the waterline.

Captain Walters sent a telegram to *Bluenose* designer Bill Roué asking him to come to Gloucester to help adjust the schooner's trim and ballast. The publicity about the races and the mission's importance prompted the Yarmouth ferry operators to hold the boat to Maine until Roué could board. He rushed on to Gloucester, where he decided to lighten *Bluenose*'s load by removing five oil tanks, three air tanks, a generating plant, and five tonnes of equipment. The actual ballast stayed put.

By the time the third race started on October 20, Captain Pine was sick and was replaced by *Thebaud*'s fishing skipper, Cecil Moulton. The committee called off that race partway through because there wasn't much wind, which angered Captain Moulton because *Thebaud* was leading.

Two days later, there was no fog and an 18-knot wind: perfect racing conditions. As the schooners jogged about waiting for the starting gun, *Bluenose*'s original eighteen-year-old wheel fell off in the captain's hands. The crew did some fancy sail handling to avoid running onto a nearby reef, and ran up a flag to signal the problem. A diesel-operated fishing boat pushed the disabled schooner back to the wharf, and the race was postponed again until repairs were completed. Two frustrated cap-

Bluenose at the
finish line, 1938

tains and their edgy crews finally lined up on October 23 for
the series' third race at Gloucester. Both vessels sailed fast, but
Bluenose won, even though the wind's strain on the sails and
masts pulled up the deck planks by several centimetres.

The fourth race, on October 24 at Boston, took place in
rain and wind that gusted from 8 to 25 knots. In the first leg
of the course, *Bluenose* set a sailing speed record of 14.15 knots,
with *Thebaud* close behind. But with less than 5 kilometres left

Bluenose's deck, marine survey 1940s

in the 560-kilometre course, the stays on *Bluenose*'s foretop-mast snapped. While the crew worked on getting the flapping topsail under control, *Thebaud* passed its rival and sailed to the finish line with five minutes to spare. The series was now two wins each, with the deciding fifth race to take place on October 26.

When the starting gun went at noon that day for the world's last race between two fishing schooners, *Bluenose* leaped over the line first with every sail filled by the southwest breeze. *Thebaud* trailed, but by the second leg of the 58-ki-lometre triangular course the American ship was just three minutes behind the defending champion. *Bluenose*'s crew of experienced and aging seafarers hunched motionless by the leeward rail waiting for the skipper's instructions. As *Bluenose* rounded the final marker the wind picked up to 20 knots. Captain Walters barked commands, and the crew jumped to their stations as the ship tacked and tacked again to use every bit of wind in a display of superb seamanship. A few minutes short of the finish line, the block carrying the halyard for the main foretopmast staysail broke. The halyard stuck and the sail flapped wildly, but *Bluenose* was now too far ahead for *Thebaud* to catch up. *Bluenose* whisked across the finish almost three minutes ahead of *Thebaud*. It was official. *Bluenose* was still Queen of the North Atlantic, a title that has remained uncontested to this day.

The 1938 series was the last race between two working schooners, but crossing the finish line didn't mean it was over. To start with, Captain Walters had received only $4,000 of the $13,000 in expense and prize money he'd been promised. In addition to that insult, the Herald Trophy was missing from the Boston store window where it had been displayed. The people of Gloucester thought it was a funny prank, but offered a $5,000 reward for its return, the insured amount of the big silver mug. Captain Walters was not amused, and ordered his crew to take *Bluenose* back to Lunenburg before someone stole the schooner, too.

Captain Moulton felt he'd been robbed of the race by a pro-*Bluenose* race committee, and wanted a rematch, but the Nova Scotia skipper refused. Captain Walters said he was going home as soon as he collected the trophy. It turned up a few days later on the doorstep of a Boston orphanage, wrapped in newspapers. It took longer than that, and a lawyer's help, to get the money owed to Captain Walters. He received $3,000 on November 17, and some more in early 1939, but he never received the full amount.

In 1938 *Bluenose* earned $6,900 for its shareholders, including $5,400 from racing. The Bluenose Schooner Company needed more than that to keep the old girl afloat, because it still owed $7,000 for the diesel engines. Fairbanks-Morse, the company that had supplied the engines, planned to take *Bluenose*'s owners to court to force them to sell the ship so they

A headline from the November 15, 1939 edition of the *Halifax Herald*, announcing Captain Walters's efforts to pay off *Bluenose*'s debts

could collect. Some people in Lunenburg tried to raise money to bail out *Bluenose* in order to keep the ship as a museum piece or a sailors' memorial. But pleas to the wealthy citizens of Nova Scotia and to the provincial and federal governments went unheard. Captain Walters, still the biggest shareholder in the Bluenose Schooner Company along with Zwicker and Company, scraped up $7,000 to pay off Fairbanks-Morse. *Bluenose* was then advertised for sale, but none of the immediate offers, including one from a well-known rum-runner, was good enough for the board of directors. The company sent *Bluenose* fishing again.

Then, in August, 1941, Captain Walters raised the money to buy out his partners and become the vessel's sole owner. Still listed for sale, *Bluenose* fished, took charters, and carried freight under a series of captains, but none of the enterprises earned much money. Captain Walters was bitter that no one else seemed to care about the world's fastest fishing schooner, but everyone else was focused on the war in Europe. Potential crew members were signing up to fight, so *Bluenose* was mostly tied to the Lunenburg wharf. It was there that a pair of young, wealthy, and well-connected Americans found the vessel on January 3, 1942, after braving a snowstorm to drive from Halifax.

Jesse Spalding III and Sandy Johnson acted on advice from a mutual friend, Tom Higgins, who first saw *Bluenose* during a 1934 stop at Lunenburg while on his way to Labrador to volunteer with the Grenfell medical mission. The men had not gone to war because their families arranged for them to be declared unfit for military duty, but with others

Restoration

The schooner *Bluenose II*, like the original, has grown old. At the time of writing in 2010, the Nova Scotia Department of Tourism, Culture and Heritage, with funding assistance from the federal government, was planning to restore the ship. Completion is expected in the spring of 2011. The project aims to secure the ship's future and preserve a link with Nova Scotia's seafaring heritage.

off fighting, they were bored. In 1942, while Higgins was sailing around the Caribbean in his yacht, a businessman offered him a huge amount of money to freight some merchandise to the Bahamas from New Orleans. Higgins realized that German submarines had cut off supply routes by sinking hundreds of civilian freighters, leading to shortages of food and other goods all around the Caribbean. Only small, fast ships could avoid the German U-boats, and Higgins immediately thought of *Bluenose*. He had no money, but his buddy Spalding did, and Johnson was a good negotiator. While Higgins made arrangements in Florida and New York, the other two men made their way to Nova Scotia to meet Captain Walters.

The negotiations, involving a long charter and a complicated mortgage plan, took place at an office at the Lunenburg wharf. Captain Walters sold the Queen of the North Atlantic for $20,000, which the men carried with them in a suitcase. Right there on the spot, Captain Walters called in the people who had helped him buy out *Bluenose* the previous August, and he paid them. Captain Walters also arranged for the Americans to meet the owners of the former Coast Guard cutter *Kayemarie*, and they bought that too. Then Captain Walters found local crews to sail both boats to Cuba.

Before leaving Nova Scotia, Spalding and Johnson paid $35,000 for two ships, ordered their repairs, and accepted

Kayemarie

The other Lunenburg ship bought in 1942, *Kayemarie*, sank during a wartime storm, 160 kilometres south of Havana, while loaded with drums of aviation fuel. Captain Wilson Berringer and his crew escaped in dories. Captain Berringer went on to skipper *Bluenose*, and was in command of the schooner when it sank in January 1946.

a load of salt cod aboard *Bluenose*. They established the Halifax-based West Indies Trading Company, registered the boats under a British flag, and bought insurance from Lloyds of London. They thought they had a steal, and so did Captain Walters.

The two men went back to the United States to join Higgins in opening a shipping base in Port Everglades, Florida, and a second company in Havana, Cuba. The Cuban corporation, Compania Inter Americano de Transporte, leased *Bluenose* and *Kayemarie* from the West Indies Trading Company, a system which avoided American taxes. The first money-making sale was *Bluenose*'s load of salt cod, which the men sold for $7,000 before it arrived. The sale more than covered the crew's wages and other expenses for the voyage to Cuba.

Bluenose left Lunenburg in the spring of 1942 under the command of Edward "Crazy Capitan" Whynacht, the first of four Lunenburg skippers to handle the ship in its Caribbean career. Despite wartime censorship, word of *Bluenose*'s arrival spread through Cuba, and spectators lined the harbour to watch the famous ship arrive. The cod was unloaded and the holds and deck were filled with fruit headed for Port Everglades. Once in the United States, the West Indies Trading Company's government contacts helped secure contracts to carry dangerous cargoes of construction explosives and military ammunition to the Caribbean islands and the northern

Bluenose Skippers:

- Angus Walters: 1921–1939
- John Walters: 1930–31, 1940
- Samuel Shaw: 1938
- Lawrence Allen: 1938
- Lavinus Wentzell: date unknown
- Abraham S. "Eddie" Miles: date unknown
- Roger Conrad: date unknown
- Harry DeMone: 1941
- Edward "Crazy Capitan" Whynacht: 1942
- Amplias Berringer: 1942
- James Meisner: 1942–43
- Wilson Berringer: 1943–46

shore of South America. In one such trip, the owners paid a total of $8,000 in danger pay to the captain and crew, which the company easily recovered by selling the return cargo of Jamaican rum.

Over the next four years, *Bluenose* also carried cigars, live animals, farm machinery, canned food, fruit, fish, nylon stockings, and rum. Among the strange cargoes proposed for *Bluenose*'s new owners was a request from an exiled Bulgarian nobleman who offered a fortune if the ship sailed to Europe to retrieve a treasure he'd left there. While Spalding said he turned down the offer, there's some evidence Higgins may have taken him up on it. In another case, a rather shady adventurer offered the company $1,000 for every person they could smuggle from Cuba to Mexico. He promised to deposit the money in advance in the Havana branch of the Bank of Nova Scotia, but the men refused the tempting offer. American war shipping rules forbade human trafficking.

Bluenose's speed, wood construction, and relatively small size allowed it to slip between the islands and dodge the

U-boats and their radar, which managed to find and sink tankers and large supply ships. The owners tried to keep their blockade-running work secret, but people tended to notice *Bluenose*. In one case a movie star, who had once crewed aboard *Bluenose*'s old rival *Columbia*, came looking for a job aboard the vessel, and Spalding was certain the Germans knew all about the schooner's activities. In his 1998 memoirs, he recalled meeting a German submarine near the Florida Keys. The captain climbed from the sub's tower and asked *Bluenose* its business.

"Fishing," came the reply.

But the German captain knew his schooners. He knew it was *Bluenose*, he retorted, and he knew it was travelling from Havana to Florida. And if it wasn't for the fact that he loved the old schooner so much, he'd blow it out of the water, he told them. Next time he would, the captain warned. But *Bluenose* came under fire only once, from an American patrol boat that mistook the black-hulled schooner, riding low in the water, for a German submarine.

Toward the end of the war, Spalding, Higgins, and Johnson got involved in other business ventures. Higgins sold his *Bluenose* share to his partners, who later sold both the Nova Scotia and Cuba companies to Farr & Company of New York, owned by men who were also enthralled with *Bluenose*'s history. By that point, the schooner's planks were spreading apart, causing it to leak. It had to be pumped constantly throughout every trip.

A year after it was sold, on January 28, 1946, *Bluenose* sank while making a night run, empty, to Aux Cayes, Haiti. Captain Wilson Berringer didn't want to make the voyage at night, all for a load of bananas, but he knew how to follow orders. The coast had no lights, so when a squall struck that evening Captain Berringer couldn't see La Folle reef near the harbour entrance.

Captain Angus Walters, 1961

Captain Walters
(1882–1968)

Captain Angus J. Walters returned from *Bluenose*'s last race to marry Mildred Butler. They lived in Halifax for a while and then returned to Lunenburg. Captain Walters retired from the sea in 1939 to operate a dairy farm, Lunenburg Dairy, which he continued until he was in his eighties. His barn stood next to the sea. The second Mrs. Walters died in 1957. When Captain Walters died in August 1968, at the age of eighty-seven, Lunenburg flags flew at half-mast. Reporter Barbara Hinds of the *Halifax Mail Star* wrote that Walters's August 14 funeral took place at Zion Lutheran Church during the "kind of day a sailor likes…a fresh offshore breeze, good visibility, and warm sun." Crowded into the trim white church were *Bluenose II* designer Bill Roué, Nova Scotia Lieutenant-Governor Victor Oland, officers and crew of the *Bluenose II*, members of the Lunenburg Master Mariners Association, town officials, seaman Jack Pardy who had weathered the 1926 Sable Island storm aboard *Bluenose*, and friends from all over.

Capt. Angus Walters, First
Bluenose Skipper Dies

Crazy Capitan

Captain Eddie Whynacht served as cook aboard *Bluenose* in 1938, and was the first skipper of the vessel when it was sold to the Americans. He won the nickname Crazy Capitan (Crazee Capeetan) after ramming a Spanish ship that refused to give way. The 1942 collision caused thousands of dollars in damage to *Bluenose*, and sank the Spanish vessel.

Bluenose washed against the reef. Its starboard side lifted onto the rocks, which tipped the port rail into the sea. The crew escaped in the dories to watch the grand old ship break up on the rocks. In 1947, *Bluenose*'s masts could still be seen sticking out of the water at La Folle. The owners tried to save some of the vessel's parts, and people who lived near the reef salvaged the toilet from the captain's cabin. It is still in their home.

A few tears were shed over *Bluenose*'s sinking, which many considered an ignominious end for such a famous ship. But, as Captain Walters said, "You couldn't expect her to last forever."

Some people did think the ship would last forever, if they thought about it at all. A generation of babies had grown up in the shadow of *Bluenose*'s tall masts. For them, the ship had always been there, part of the furniture of the North Atlantic. They may have felt pride or amazement at the ship's accomplishments, but they also took its existence for granted. Their parents and grandparents had also become accustomed to *Bluenose*'s far-reaching fame. Because of *Bluenose*, Nova Scotia had developed a cultural identity based on the romance of the high sea, tall ships, daring sailors, and a hardy lifestyle. It wasn't an accurate portrayal, but it promoted the province to the world like nothing else had done to that point.

There were others, diehard *Bluenose* fans, who just didn't want to believe the ship was gone. They had cheered it on at each challenge, and exulted in its victories. When it met

The Fates of the Contenders

- *Esperanto*, 1921: sank off Sable Island
- *Columbia*, 1927: lost with all hands off Sable Island
- *Henry Ford*, 1928: went aground on Whales Back Reef, Martin's Point, NL
- *Elsie*, 1935: sank near St. Pierre and Miquelon; the crew survived by rowing 77 kilometres to shore
- *Thebaud*, 1948: broke up on a reef off the north coast of Venezuela

hard times, they assumed that someone, somewhere, would love it and have the resources to rescue it. When it retreated from public life during World War Two, they still had the vague sense that the ship was out there, somewhere, beating the pants off its rivals.

Still, no one really expected *Bluenose* to return to Nova Scotia. But on July 24, 1963, *Bluenose II* slid down the ways at the Smith and Rhuland yard in Lunenburg, with both Bill Roué and Angus Walters on hand for the occasion. The schooner was built from the same plans as the original, modified to include modern navigational and comfort features as well as two engines. The second ship was built as a provincial tourist attraction and as a marketing tool for Oland's Schooner beer. It cost about $300,000, almost nine times the price of the original.

"A very good vessel," Captain Walters declared.

Bluenose II doesn't race, but it has reached 18 knots under full sail. Nor does the schooner fish, but it has made long voyages through all kinds of weather, proving its seaworthiness. The ship takes charters and serves as a sailing ambassador for Canada and Nova Scotia in almost every port on the Atlantic coast, and more besides. It has participated in tall ship parades, visited world fairs, and welcomed thousands of visitors aboard.

Bluenose II . . . in all her Glory

July 24, 1963 — Lunenburg, Nova Scotia

Oland's advertisement featuring the launch of *Bluenose II*, July 24, 1963

And just maybe, if you step aboard and close your eyes, you might hear the men yelling from the top masts, the wind thrumming in the sails and rigging, the creak and groan of the spars, and the sea-green water hissing toward the stern. You might smell the tar and fish, taste the salt on your lips, and feel the spray sting your cheeks. Just for a moment, you might imagine yourself aboard the grand old *Bluenose*, with the hold full of cod, beating windward for Lunenburg.

GLOSSARY OF SAILING & SHIPBUILDING TERMS

Adze: a hand tool, used for shaping timbers, that looks like an axe, but with a curved blade at right angles to the handle

Aft: toward the back, or stern, of the ship

Auger: a hand-operated drill

Ballast: stones, sand, or other weight placed in the bottom of a ship to counteract the top-heaviness of sails or superstructure

Bank: an underwater shelf along the Atlantic coast of North America where the sea is shallow enough for a ship to anchor. Until the late twentieth century, fish were more plentiful on the banks than anywhere else.

Beam ends: the sides of a boat, at the ends of the beams, or timbers, which run crossways on the ship

Beating it, or beating windward: sailing into the wind

Boom: the spar or pole attached to the foot of a sail, to extend it horizontally

Bow (rhymes with how): the front of a ship

Bowsprit: the angled pole protruding forward from a ship's prow, designed to support one of the stays and to stow foresails. It's also called the widow-maker because sailors climbing out on the bowsprit to reef sails during rough seas could fall off and drown.

Ceiling: the planks lining the inside of the hull, or body, of the ship

Chart: a map of the sea, showing water depth, shorelines, lighthouses, buoys, navigational hazards, tidal information, currents, and details of bridges or harbours

Companionway: the ladder leading from the deck to the quarters below

Dead reckoning: a process of plotting a course based on a previous location or position

Dory: a flat-bottomed rowboat carried onboard a schooner and placed in the water once the ship reached the fishing grounds. Men fished from the dories and returned to the schooner when the little boats were full of fish.

Fish gaff: a pole with a sharp hook on the end for hauling large fish into the boat

Fore: toward the bow, or front, of the ship

Forecastle (also fo'c'sle): the area inside the bow of a ship where crew members live. The bunks are usually closest to the bow, while the galley is in the aft part of the fo'c'sle.

Galley: a ship's kitchen

Hard tack: bread made of flour, water, and salt, also called sea biscuits, ship's biscuits, or pilot bread. It keeps for years without spoiling, so is used as survival food. Ships' cooks soak it overnight, cook it with fish, and serve it with fried pork scraps and onions.

Heel: when the ship leans over at a sharp angle

Hull: the main part of the ship, not counting the masts and rigging and other structures above deck

Jiggs' dinner: also known as boiled dinner, typically made of pickled salt meat, potatoes, carrots, turnip, and cabbage boiled together; often accompanied by pease pudding, made of split peas cooked in a cotton bag in the pot with the meat and vegetables

Jonahs and jinkers: sailors were considered bad luck and had a hard time finding work if they survived one shipwreck then sailed on another vessel that was also wrecked or had a poor season. They were called jonahs, after the biblical story of Jonah going overboard to be swallowed by a whale, and jinkers, from the word jinx.

Keel: a timber piece along the bottom of a ship to which the stem, sternpost, and ribs are attached

Keelson: a second timber to provide additional strength, bolted on top of the keel

Knot: equal to one nautical mile per hour, or 1.852 kilometres per hour, per international agreement. Until the mid-twentieth century, a nautical mile equalled 6,080 feet (1,848 metres) compared to a land mile of 5,280 feet (1,605 metres),

and was equivalent to a minute of latitude (or one-sixtieth of a degree) on the earth's surface. Early sailors measured speed at sea by spacing apart knots in a rope, and then tying the rope to a piece of wood that they dragged behind the ship. The number of knots that fed into the water in a given time indicated the ship's speed.

Leeward: the direction toward which the wind is blowing

Oakum: tarred hemp fibres from old ropes, used for caulking the seams on the decks and sides of wooden ships

Oilskins: rain or sailing gear of overalls and jacket, originally made of canvas coated in oil. Later the fabric was coated in rubber, and is now made of synthetic petroleum products.

Privateer: a privately-owned ship authorized by the government during wartime to stop and seize other ships

Quintal: a measure of fish equal to 112 pounds (about 51 kilograms), also called a hundredweight. A metric quintal is 100 kilograms, but *Bluenose* fishermen used the imperial measure.

Rigging:

　Standing rigging consists of fixed wires, ropes, and rods that hold the masts, booms, and gaffs in place on the ship. It is not moved while the vessel is sailing, and allows the wind filling the sails to move the boat forward instead of just knocking down the masts and spars. Standard rigging includes stays, which connect masts to the front and back of the ship or to another mast; and shrouds, which are connected to the sides of the ship. Ratlines (pronounced RAT-luns) are lines set crossways in the shrouds as ladders for the sailors climbing the rigging.

Running rigging is the system of ropes and blocks (pulleys) that allow sailors to adjust the sails. Sailors pull on halyards (haul-yards) to raise and lower a yard—the spar that supports a sail. A sheet is a rope attached to a sail's lower corners, used to change the tension and direction of the canvas. Crew climbing aloft don't stand on or grab hold of the running rigging, because it moves. *Bluenose* had eight sails, and about thirty halyards running to the deck. The crew had to know what each one was for.

Scow: a flat-bottom boat with a square or blunt bow and stern, used for carrying freight

Sea room: enough space at sea for a ship to move. A skipper calls to another vessel for sea room when there is a danger of collision as they approach an obstacle.

Sharemen: fishermen who earned a share of the ship's profit, instead of a salary or wage

Skipper: from the Dutch word schipper, meaning the person in charge of the schip, or ship

Sou'wester (abbreviated from southwester): a round waterproof, felt-lined hat, tied under the chin, with a broad brim to let the water run away from the neck of the fisherman's jacket

Spar: a pole, such as a bowsprit or boom, that supports sails and rigging

Spoke shave: a blade with handles at each end, which the user grasps to draw the blade across wood thereby shaving the wood into the desired shape. A spoke shave is usually used to make wooden spokes for wheels.

Stem: the vertical post at the bow of a ship

Stern: the back of a ship

Trunnels: tree nails, or wooden dowels, which are driven through holes in wood to fasten two pieces together. They are driven through past the other side, then cut flush; the cut end is then split. A hardwood wedge is driven into the split to ensure the trunnel can't come out.

Ways: a pair of timber ramps upon which a ship is constructed. The ways are greased to help the ship slide into the harbour at launch time.

Windlass: a device used to raise weights with a rope or chain by winding the rope or chain around a drum or post

Yacht: the term originally referred to a small, fast boat used to chase criminals in the waters around the Netherlands, but later came to mean an expensive pleasure boat, whether sail or motor operated

ACKNOWLEDGEMENTS

Thanks to Captain Wayne Walters of *Bluenose II*, grandson of Captain Angus Walters; to Canadian Coast Guard Captain (retired) Eric Hann; to Philip Hartling of Nova Scotia Archives and Records Management; to Heather-Anne Getson of the Fisheries Museum of the Atlantic; to Ruth Fahie of the Canadian Coast Guard; to Vern Shea of Shea Marine Services, Pictou; and to the staff at the Pictou branch of Pictou-Antigonish Regional Library.

BIBLIOGRAPHY

Backman, Brian and Phil. *Bluenose*. Toronto: McClelland & Stewart Ltd., 1965.

"Bluenose: A Canadian Icon" digital database, Nova Scotia Archives and Records Management website: *www.nsarm.ca* (accessed 2009—2010)

De Villiers, Marq. *Witch in the Wind: The True Story of the Legendary Bluenose*. Toronto: Thomas Allen Publishers, 2007.

Getson, Heather-Anne. *Bluenose: The Ocean Knows Her Name*. Halifax: Nimbus Publishing Ltd., 2006.

Higgins, Andrew, and Jesse Spalding III. *World War II Adventures of Canada's Bluenose*. Newport Beach, CA: West Indies Trading Company, 1998.

MacLaren, R. Keith. *Bluenose & Bluenose II*. Willowdale, ON: Hounslow Press, 1981.

———. *A Race for Real Sailors*. Vancouver: Douglas and MacIntyre, 2006.

Pullen, Rear Admiral H. F., OBE, CD. *Atlantic Schooners*. Fredericton: Brunswick Press, 1967.

Robinson, Ernest Fraser. *The Saga of the Bluenose*, 3rd ed. Lunenburg: Bluenose Preservation Trust Society, 1989, 1998, 2008.

Roué, Joan E. *A Spirit Deep Within: Naval Architect W. J. Roué and the Bluenose Story*. Hantsport, NS: Lancelot Press, 1994.

Ziner, Feenie. *Bluenose, Queen of the Grand Banks*. Halifax: Nimbus Publishing Ltd., 1970.

IMAGE SOURCES

INDEX

(Page numbers in italics refer to images)

MOLECULAR
BIOPHYSICS

This book is in

THE ADDISON-WESLEY SERIES

IN THE LIFE SCIENCES

MOLECULAR
BIOPHYSICS

---

by

RICHARD B. SETLOW

Oak Ridge National Laboratory

and

ERNEST C. POLLARD

The Pennsylvania State University

ADDISON-WESLEY PUBLISHING COMPANY, INC.

READING, MASSACHUSETTS, U.S.A.

LONDON, ENGLAND

PREFACE

The subject matter of biophysics is not new. Scientists have always been interested in applying physical ideas and techniques to biological problems. Only recently, however, has biophysics emerged as a formal field of study. The rapid advances of physical science have led many more people than in the past to attempt to explain biological phenomena in terms of physical principles. A Biophysical Society has been organized, and the number of university biophysics departments and of courses in biophysics is increasing at a rapid rate.

Just as the field of physics is so large that all its material cannot possibly be incorporated into one advanced-level textbook, so is biophysics too large for such a comprehensive treatment. Since we cannot cover the entire field, we have focused our attention on the molecular aspects of biophysics. Molecular biophysics attempts to explain the properties of biological systems and biological phenomena in terms of the properties of molecules, both small and large. We have slighted, therefore, those parts of the formal field of biophysics which are closer to physiology. (Previous texts on biophysics, such as that written by Stacy, published by McGraw-Hill, stress the physiological aspects of biophysics.)

The level of the text is suitable for seniors or first-year graduate students. It presupposes some knowledge of mathematics, physics, and chemistry and biology beyond the elementary level. Since most students will not fit into this category, the text, and the course taught from it, has been designed so that students who are strong in at least two of these fields will have no difficulty in getting through the material. Numerical problems have been included at the end of each chapter, and their answers appear at the end of the book.

The book comprises fifteen chapters. The first three chapters, "Physics and Biology," "The Biophysicist's View of the Living Cell," and "Energetic and Statistical Relations in the Lving Cell," provide a general introduction to the characteristics of cells and a description of their constituents, and discuss how the laws of thermodynamics (such as the laws of conservation of energy and the flow of entropy) may be applied to living cells. They include a brief description of information theory and how it is used in describing properties of biological systems. These three chapters introduce the problems which hopefully will be solved by molecular biophysics.

The next four chapters, "Physical Methods of Determining the Sizes and Shapes of Molecules," "X-ray Analysis and Molecular Structures," "Intramolecular and Intermolecular Forces," and "Absorption Spectroscopy and Molecular Structure," describe the various techniques that have been used to analyze molecules. The techniques indicated by the titles cover many experimental fields because the macromolecules making up living systems are so complicated that one method of analysis does not give sufficient information for any clear-cut decisions about structure and function to be made. These four chapters attempt to describe what is known concerning the physics and chemistry of macromolecules associated with biological systems.

The following three chapters, "Enzymes," "Action Spectra and Quantum Yields," and "The Action of Ionizing Radiation on Cellular Constituents," are concerned with the relations between molecular structure and function covered earlier, and discuss how structure and function are influenced by various physical agents such as heat, light, and ionizing radiation, and how the effect of such perturbation may be used to infer something about the nature of the structures involved. To present a well-rounded picture of these subjects, we have found it useful to include descriptions of the various ways of studying enzyme reactions, structures, and the effects of light not only on molecules but on viruses and micro-organisms. These chapters represent the beginnings of the synthesis of biological properties in terms of the properties of individual molecules.

The theme is extended throughout the next three chapters, "The Use of Ionizing Radiation to Study Cell Structure," "Microscopes," and "Isotopic Traces in Molecular Biophysics." These chapters are concerned with the various physical techniques which may be used to find relations among the structural and functional elements of cells by use of the classical microscopic techniques as well as by such recent ones as interference microscopy and thin-section electron microscopy, and a description of the use of tracers to determine metabolic rates as well as to determine the distribution of labeled molecules from one generation to another.

The last two chapters, "Molecular Biophysics and Muscle, Nerve, and Eye Studies" and "The Physics of Cellular Processes," represent an attempt to synthesize the information from the previous chapters so as to describe on a molecular basis the properties of muscle, nerve, and eye, and the processes involved in the duplication and transmission of genetic information in cells.

The emphasis throughout the text is twofold: it is both theoretical and experimental. It attempts to describe physical ways of thinking and analyzing biological processes, as well as describing the many and powerful physical techniques which may be used to determine the relations among structures and functions of biological systems.

We are conscious of considerable debt to others. First, we should thank our students in the Biophysics Department, Yale University, who have watched us develop the material, and who have criticized and helped in improving it without, so far, rising up and smiting us. Secondly, our colleagues in the Yale Biophysics Department, notably Professor Harold J. Morowitz, have continuously helped us, by counsel and correction, over the years. One of the authors is indebted to Dr. L. H. Gray for the invigorating hospitality of the Research Unit in Radiobiology at the Mount Vernon Hospital, where several chapters were written. Mere thanks does not seem to be enough to express to the publishers who brought forth the manuscript into readable letters, but to them we do indeed express gratitude.

New Haven, Conn.   R. B. S.

E. C. P.

CONTENTS

CHAPTER 1

PHYSICS AND BIOLOGY

A biophysicist is a person who, for professional reasons, needs both physical and biological insight.

1–1 Introduction. The twofold problem of mankind in which Science has predominantly helped is that of gaining control over Nature, and of understanding Nature. Control is usually achieved first, often with a very limited understanding; as yet probably no part of Nature is completely understood. The problem of gaining control over living processes and of understanding them is the problem of biology, a problem which has proved to be the hardest yet posed by any of the accessible divisions of Nature. The problems of cosmology, and of the atomic nucleus are not solved, of course, but the difficulty there lies in gaining access to the material to be studied rather than in the inherent difficulty of the tasks themselves.

The wonderfully patient and skillful studies of biologists, involving classification, microscopical observation, comparative studies of vision, respiration, nervous and muscular action, plus biochemical discoveries linking many organisms, and above all, the pervading doctrine of organic evolution have brought a systematization to biology that gives modern Science a heritage of inestimable value. The unity of living processes is certainly as simple and single as the unity of geology, and many first-rate biologists believe that it is even more so. For this reason the geneticist works deeply with *Drosophila* or *neurospora* and is impatient of skeptics who doubt the generality of his findings. For this reason the sciatic nerve of the frog serves as a model for neurophysiology, and sea urchin eggs are used for studies of embryology. No biologist hears of a new enzyme system without thought for its generality, and indeed, specialized enzymes, operative only in a limited group of organisms, are remarkable for just that reason.

So it is that today the words "living processes" conjure up no weird range of infinite possibility, but certain broad, clear ideas. One thinks of chromosome division, of enzymatic action, of the travel of electrochemical energy in a nerve, of hormonal growth regulation, and of the physico-chemical energy transfer that underlies metabolism. At present, every one of these processes lacks complete description. In some way the chromosomes grow, divide, and separate, but by what means do they grow? Why do they divide when they do? Why only in pairs? In some way an enzyme combines with its substrate and a reaction proceeds, but how is the reaction effected? Why is it specific? And so on.

1

Much more complete descriptions of these processes are very nearly on hand, which makes this modern biology almost breathlessly exciting. Nevertheless, "complete" descriptions are more exacting today than they were a century ago. The description of a process must somehow fit with the ideas of atomic physics and chemistry, which means that it may well have to be right, all the way down to atomic detail. When this goal is realized the understanding and control of living processes will be vastly increased.

A tremendous part of the detailed description of biological processes is clearly going to be in terms of chemistry, and with this clear fact in view the biochemists have made one of the most sensational scientific advances of all time. Nevertheless, a moment's thought shows that not *all* the processes will be found to be chemical. For example, it seems certain that the cell has a vital structure and does not simply serve as a reaction vessel, like a beaker. An understanding of the relative positions of the components will be found to be important, and here is where physics takes its place in the study of biology. It is in terms of physics that we are able to describe the physical character of cellular components, how they may interact with one another, how growth and change must alter them, and how these processes play their part in the whole living process. To begin this attack, physics brings to bear one weapon of great power, and an attendant strategic disadvantage that goes with unfamiliarity with the weapon.

The weapon is the newly won knowledge of the laws of Nature: the laws of motion, of electric and magnetic actions, of quantum mechanics, and of molecular statistical behavior. In principle the physicist and physical chemist intuitively feel that these laws should be all that is necessary. They should encompass and interpret biology as they have encompassed and interpreted chemistry and spectroscopy. In practice, however, the laws can be applied only to clearly defined systems, apt for human thought and calculation. The laws *work*, says the physicist, but to figure out how they work, and how to make them work to our will, is something else. And so, the first clear problem of the biophysicist appears: the problem of describing a few important biological systems clearly and simply enough so that the physical laws can be applied.

From time to time elements of biology have become suitable for such physical thought. Our knowledge of the lens of the eye and the way in which an image is formed and with it the elementary facts of optical defects and their remedy by external lenses is a nearly complete branch of biophysics in which the laws applied, those of refraction and of light propagation, are the laws of physical optics. This application is so straightforward and clear that few physicists stop to consider that when they work problems on the eye in elementary physics they are for the moment biophysicists. Physics is so important in this application that a complete course in physical optics, more thorough than that usually given in a general physics course, is necessary before a proper understanding of the behavior of this aspect of the eye can be attained.

This aptness for physical explanation is far from the rule, even though many valuable uses of physics, as in hydrodynamic flow or total energy relations, have been made. The physicist alone will not make the attempt to sort out the proper phases of biology to attack, and the biologist is often all too busy with his own rewarding studies. It thus becomes the task of the biophysicist to study, listen, think, and experiment, with the aim of finding new areas of biology to which physics can be applied. A short account of the history of biophysics, leading up to the present, will help to show that these new areas are being discovered.

1–2 History of biophysics. History is made by people, but it is formulated by historians. Up to the present no adequate historical consideration of biophysics has been written, partly because biophysics itself is not yet organized. A brief glance shows that biophysics has a rich and exciting history.

We can begin by mentioning Galvani, though in the modern sense he was hardly a biophysicist. It is often claimed that Galvani's discovery that the muscles of frogs suspended on copper hooks from a steel wire twitched when chance contact completed the circuit was pure accident. Apparently this is not so; it seems that Galvani had been studying the effect of static electricity on muscle for some time. He correctly interpreted this "galvanic" form of electricity as being due to the dissimilar metals, and he then sought a purely physical interpretation for the flow of electricity out of the muscle through the pair of metals. His discovery, made in 1786, opened two tremendous fields, both still under vigorous research.

It is hardly fair to include Thomas Young in the narrow class of biophysicists, since, among other attainments, he knew seven languages at age 14. He obtained his M.D. at Göttingen in 1796, and in 1801 he was appointed professor of *physics* at the Royal Institution. He seems to have combined almost all possible talents and can be credited with having first proposed the wave theory of light, the theory of color vision, the hydrodynamic nature of heart action, as well as having been among the first to interpret the ancient Egyptian language! His outstanding characteristic was an incisive interest in any form of problem, and he had considerable experimental skill. The explanation of the process of accommodation of the eye and a great deal of the elementary geometrical optics of the eye were discovered by Young.

Perhaps the first real biophysicist was Julius Robert Mayer (1814–1878), who received his training in medicine. While serving as surgeon on a

Dutch ship in the tropics, he noticed that venous blood was of a brighter red color than he had expected from his experience in cooler climates, and he began to speculate whether this might be due in some way to the relationships between heat, work, and the intermediate physiological processes. It seems reasonable to assume he understood that the biological process of metabolism involves a considerable turnover in material from one chemical state to another and that in the process some mechanical work is involved. He seems to have been the first to perceive that the only alternative to a very general validity of the conservation of energy for all forms of energy, including heat, light, chemical energy, and mechanical work, was the operation of a vital force. From this he recoiled. He was astute enough to see that in Regnault's experiments on the specific heats of gases at constant pressure and volume there existed a means of estimating the mechanical equivalent of heat. In 1842 he gave this estimate (4.2 joules per calorie) with devastating accuracy. He went on to state the conservation of energy *as a general principle*, and applied his ideas to a theory of solar heat which invokes as a source of energy a ceaseless shower of meteors entering the sun's gravitational field. This theory was later propounded by Lord Kelvin.

Although Mayer anticipated Joule's careful experimental work on the mechanical equivalent of heat by two years, his claims to the enunciation of the principle of conservation of energy were attacked by physicists, notably Thompson and Tait, and Mayer suffered a great deal as a result. His case was later taken up by two able biophysicists, Tyndall and Helmholtz, and some of the harm was rectified. Even today, a biophysicist must be prepared to defend his discoveries against the skepticism of the more thoroughly entrenched branches of science.

That biology should imperatively demand the conservation of energy undoubtedly occurred first to Mayer. The energy turnover in biological systems still probably exceeds that of any other system on earth, and so only to a mechanical scientist is it remarkable that a biologist should first perceive the convertible nature of energy.

The years following Mayer's discovery were biophysically rich. The greatest biophysicist to date, Hermann Ludwig Ferdinand von Helmholtz (1821–1894), was beginning his work when Mayer made his estimate of the mechanical equivalent of heat in 1842. Helmholtz carried depth of understanding into both biology and physics equally. A list of his contributions alone would fill this chapter. He studied muscular contraction, measured the velocity of nervous impulses, did his share to confirm the law of conservation of energy, invented the ophthalmoscope (which permits observations on the retina), gave a quite reasonable theory of color vision, and aided in the understanding of hearing. The work of Helmholtz will be found to be the starting point of several complete topics considered in more detail later in this book. Some of the credit for the discovery of electromagnetic radiation should go to Helmholtz, for the experiments of Hertz were made in his laboratory and had the benefit of some of his inspiration. Helmholtz was an intellectual giant who purposefully followed scientific aims all his life.

Perhaps the greatest assets of Tyndall, a contemporary of Helmholtz, were his training by Faraday and his ability to give interesting and interpretative lectures. His lectures on "Heat, a mode of motion" are still fascinating to read, and he was clearly a master of experimental exposition. These qualities are essential in any field in which wide and clear understanding is more important than deep dedication to one subject, and they are most helpful in biophysics. Tyndall's curiosity was widespread; for example, his discovery of the scattering of light by submicroscopic objects enabled him to check on Pasteur's ideas of bacterial action. It is interesting to read of the Royal Institution being taken aback by the disastrous invasion of a durable organism, *Bacillus subtilis*, which resisted sterilization by boiling. Tyndall overcame the problem by using a method of alternate heating and cooling that preserved the food and destroyed *B. subtilis*. Tyndall believed that biology was a suitable field for physical study, and he was the first physicist to make a serious contribution to microbiology.

From the time of Tyndall's and Helmholtz' work until about 1930 there seems to have been a lull in contributions to the field of biophysics. This was probably due to the very rapid advances in fundamental physics, which took two first-rate biophysicists, Helmholtz and Gullstrand (who made basic contributions to ophthalmology), into pure physics in the latter years of the 19th century. The tremendous surge forward in atomic physics, which carried on until 1930, provided ample opportunity for the talents of physicists in that field alone. Paralleling this advance was that in the field of biochemistry, a science which proved itself capable of great value in examining some of the most fundamental problems of biology. And so, while atomic physics and quantum mechanics emerged on the one hand and enzymatic, vitaminic, and hormonal biochemistry developed on the other, biophysics was neglected.

By 1930 a change had already begun. A. V. Hill had started his study of thermal and energy effects in muscle, and his series of researches still continues. Astbury had used simple x-ray diffraction apparatus for the study of hair, silk, and wool fibers, and so discovered the three forms of fibrous proteins. Biomolecular x-ray work along these lines is still proceeding rapidly, and our knowledge of insulin, hemoglobin, myoglobin, and thymus nucleic acid is already reasonably precise. About 1930, Gates began a series of studies of biological action spectra, Hecht was involved in the biophysics of the sensitivity of the eye, and Loofbourow and Holiday began work on the absorption spectra of newly purified biological molecules. At the same time, Caspersson used the differential absorption of protein and nucleic acid to show the relation of these in the living cell.

The whole field of electrophysiology took a tremendous step forward with the work of K. S. Cole, Adrian, and Bronk, and the relation of electrical response to vision was actively studied by Hartline. Still more recently, Lea has examined the possibility of using ionizing radiation, with its unique penetrating capability, to study the size and nature of enzymes, viruses, genes, and chromosomes. The method shows promise, and will be increasingly exploited.

This renaissance of biophysics has already proved to be a strong movement, and exciting future contributions from it can be expected.

1–3 Life–order or chaos? One of the first reactions of a student of physics, particularly of experimental physics, is that of surprise at the number of precautions and preliminaries he must observe before the primary rules of Nature seem to apply to the system he is studying. The student of biology instinctively feels that it may prove impossible to reduce biological processes to order and understanding because of their inherent complexity and because they are not controlled systems. It is worth while to consider why this feeling should exist, and whether it is rationally sustained by what we know of living systems.

In the first place, consider the nature of truly chaotic forms of matter. The molecules of a gas are essentially the extreme in chaotic behavior. A statistical analysis of the behavior of a gas based solely on the conservation of energy and of number of molecules, and on the idea that the state of a gas can be described on the basis of probability alone, is quite successful. In such a system there is no continuous energy turnover, nor any ordered growth, nor any reproduction. None of the attributes of life seem to be part of such random, ceaseless, meaningless motion, and it requires a tremendous reach of intuition to explain living processes in terms of so over-randomized a world.

If we go a little further and suppose that a gas has superposed upon it an external field that is directed rather than random, the resulting distribution of gas molecules (as in an exponential atmosphere) is not that which seems to be found in living matter. Concentration gradients and the resulting diffusion processes undoubtedly play a role in the workings of a living cell, but they are not the *only* dominant factors. The gradients in a cell are multiple and changing, and can hardly be both effect and cause at the same time in so active a way. Therefore the extreme idea that primarily randomized processes underlie life is not very plausible.

Let us take exactly the opposite view and suppose that living processes are highly ordered and that they obey the known laws of Nature and perhaps conform to one or two additional general principles; i.e., they are ordered but complicated. The question then arises as to the degree of complication we must expect to find in order to explain what is seen in leaves, plants, bacteria, and human beings.

To attempt an answer, we look first at the diversity of possible kinds of atoms and molecules. The structure of atoms is based on the following three principles:

(1) The laws of electrodynamics and of quantum mechanics apply.
(2) The Pauli exclusion principle operates.
(3) A minimum total energy is sought.

The diversity of form and type among atoms is such that perhaps eight or ten species exist, with variations among them. This number is small, too small for an analogy to life.

If we now turn to molecules, we find that the same three principles are applicable, but the components of the system include not only electrons in force fields, as for the atom, but combinations of the atoms as well. Thus the diversity vastly increases, and a wide variety of kinds of matter results. Such matter, except in rather special cases, does not experience a continuous turnover of energy, does not grow and divide, and does not differentiate with functional advantage. If so large a degree of diversity results from three principles, possibly no more than two other principles are needed.

Biology is ready with one more, which works empirically from the established character of life. This is the doctrine of organic evolution, along with the modern theory of the genetic mechanism of mutation, which states that the environment forces a selection of form on systems that already grow and divide and differentiate. Clearly, this mechanism operates in cellular environments as well as macroscopically. It is possible that this one further principle may be enough, but it is also possible, and statistically likely, that at least one more great principle remains undiscovered.

1–4 Summary. To summarize, let us consider the accompanying charts. The first is a chart of the development of chemistry which, although complete, is somewhat oversimplified. The second is an incomplete chart of the development of biology.

The development of chemistry and atomic physics are portrayed, very broadly, side by side. While pure chemists such as Lavoisier and Berzelius were beginning and developing the characterization of the elements, the laws of combination, and the validity of the atomic theory, physicists such as Newton, Cavendish, and Fraunhofer were developing the laws of mechanics, light, and electricity, and discovering the spectra of elements. With the availability of the atomic theory and the ability to observe atomic spectra, physics and chemistry began to overlap. Chemists discovered the periodic systematics of valence, clearly an atomic property, and physicists discovered the Rutherford-Bohr atom, which began the explanation of spectra. This atom held no hope for the periodic systematics of valence, and in the period 1912 to 1924, we find the "physicists' atom" of Rutherford and Bohr and the "chemists' atom" of Lewis and Langmuir competing in separate worlds of thought. Both worlds of thought were separately shaken, more particularly that of the physicist, by the failure of classical quantum theory to explain the helium atom, molecular structure, and radioactivity (to mention but three examples), and the recognition by the chemist that a simple doctrine of valence could not be substantiated. Both worlds of thought were ready for new ideas, and the development of quantum mechanics and the Pauli principle gave power of interpretation in the separate worlds *and* achieved the essential unification of physics and chemistry.

In the same spirit we can attempt a developmental chart for physical science and biology. Of necessity the description is even broader, as the chart (p. 9) shows. With the arrival of a close analysis of Mendelian genetics, and the discovery, in part, of the nature of the macromolecules which we now believe to carry the stuff of heredity, a conflict may begin to develop. Or, in turn, the molecules may prove to be quite adequate to the genetic task. Possibly the conflict may arise at levels of higher complexity. Quite possibly no conflict at all may occur. In any event there is intense scientific activity in the field of molecular biology, and the approach there of the physical sciences and the biological sciences reaches a high point in what is really a new area.

One thing is evident: we live in an age when the incomplete region at the foot of the chart is ripe for challenging and exciting study. It appears as though the odds are against our finding a series of multiple complexities, and are in favor either of a deeper understanding of what we now know, or of the discovery that the formulation of one or two more principles will suffice. Even when we look only at the very fundamental and almost philosophical side of biology, we see that the unification of biology with physics poses some of the finest intellectual problems of the present age. Although we feel a real sense of inadequacy in developing the presentation of these problems, they are, nevertheless the problems of the biophysicist, challenging in nature and deeply rewarding in their solution.

In this book we have chosen to study only one branch of biophysics, molecular biophysics. We shall start with two chapters containing a general survey of the field, then proceed to develop individual topics, and finally return to a more general approach.

CHEMISTRY

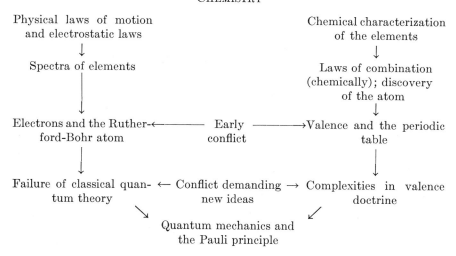

Physical laws of motion and electrostatic laws → Spectra of elements → Electrons and the Rutherford-Bohr atom ← Early conflict → Valence and the periodic table; Chemical characterization of the elements → Laws of combination (chemically); discovery of the atom → Valence and the periodic table → Complexities in valence doctrine; Failure of classical quantum theory ← Conflict demanding new ideas → Complexities in valence doctrine → Quantum mechanics and the Pauli principle

BIOLOGY

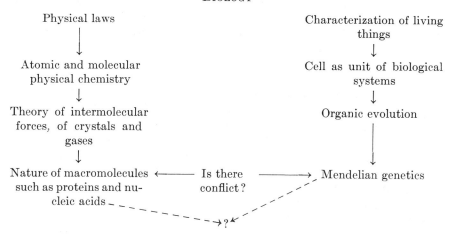

Physical laws → Atomic and molecular physical chemistry → Theory of intermolecular forces, of crystals and gases → Nature of macromolecules such as proteins and nucleic acids ← Is there conflict? → Mendelian genetics; Characterization of living things → Cell as unit of biological systems → Organic evolution → Mendelian genetics; ?

REFERENCES

1. E. SCHRÖDINGER, *What is Life?* Cambridge University Press, 1944. A very interesting and thought-provoking book.

2. A. V. HILL, "Why Biophysics," *Science* **124,** 1233 (1956).

3. W. M. ELSASSER *The Physical Foundations of Biology.* Pergamon Press, New York, 1958.

CHAPTER 2

THE BIOPHYSICIST'S VIEW OF THE LIVING CELL

Just as physicists and chemists have reduced the study of the structure of matter to relative simplicity by the discovery and description of atoms, the basic units of all matter, so the biologist has greatly simplified the study of living things by the discovery and description of cells. Muscle, nerve, brain, leaves, grass, yeast, and bacteria are all compounded of cells. The cell as the unitary living system is one of the great generalizations revealed by biology.

The cell has varied importance, and various features are emphasized, depending on how life is being studied. The geneticist continually returns in his interest to the nucleus and to chromosomes, the embryologist to the interaction between parts of cells and cells with one another, and the biochemist to the chemical content of cells. The biophysicist, too, has his special view of the living cell, and it is this which we describe in this chapter. To do so we draw boldly and in outline many properties of the cell that are known in delicate pattern to cytologists, and we also need to use terms and ideas that will be more fully described in later chapters. This account is, therefore, to be read more as a stage setting than as the drama itself.

2–1 The broad characteristics of a typical cell. In Fig. 2–1 we show the outline of three types of cell: plant, animal, and bacterial. The plant cell is characterized by a sturdy cellulose wall having structural integrity. A large part of the cell is vacuole, which means a region containing liquid, within which crystals can be seen. A nucleus is present. A dominant characteristic of plant cells is the system of choloroplasts which are concerned with the photosynthesis of sugars. Mitochondria are also visible. The parts played by all these will be described later.

The animal cell, Fig. 2–1(b), has a membrane generally lacking in structural rigidity and usually rather close to the next cell. There is not the large vacuole seen in the plant cell. The nucleus contains heterochromatin, presumably related to hereditary processes and containing DNA, and a nucleolus, which contains RNA. The nuclear membrane is seen in the electron microscope to be considerably structured, with pores, and also possibly interconnected to cytoplasmic units. In the cytoplasm great importance attaches to the *microsomes*, which in live cells are definitely implicated with protein synthesis. Their ultrastructure seems to consist of double lamellae associated with granules. Of similar importance are the

10

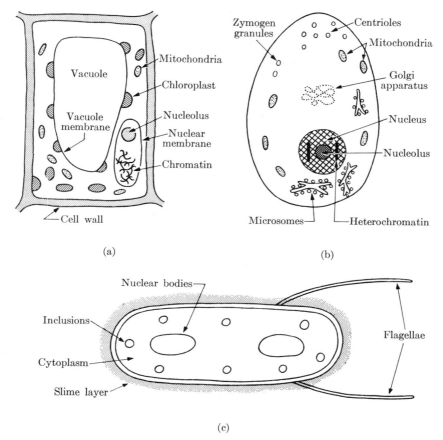

FIG. 2–1. Schematic representations of the appearance of cells under a light microscope. (a) Plant cell. (b) Animal cell. (c) Bacterial cell.

mitochondria, which contain the respiratory enzyme system, and which have a rather firm structure (as seen electron microscopically) containing what may be deep inducts. In an animal the cell is usually functional, and the elements of its functioning may be seen in enzyme-containing zymogen granules and in the Golgi apparatus which serves as a transfer system.

The bacterial cell, Fig. 2–1(c), is characterized by a cell wall containing varied amounts of polysaccharide. It has some rigidity. On the outside it merges into a slime layer containing polysaccharide and protein, and on the inside it holds in place the protoplast membrane. Many of the functions of the cell can be carried on simply as a *"protoplast,"* without the entire cell wall being present. Attached to the cell are *flagellae,* somehow

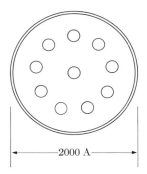

FIG. 2–2. A schematic representation of the cross section of a cilium, showing the organized sets of tubules. This type of structure is not uncommon and is shown as one illustration of the order to be found in living systems at the macromolecular level.

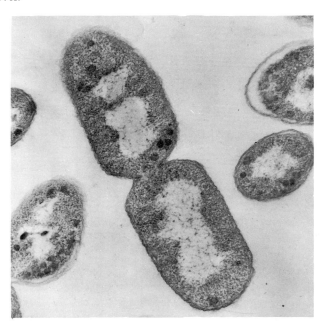

FIG. 2–3. A dividing cell of *E. coli* 15 T⁻U⁻, fixed with formalin, followed by osmium tetroxide, embedded in methacrylate, stained with lead hydroxide. The cytoplasm contains large numbers of small granules, presumably ribosomes. Also present are some larger (500 to 600 A) granules which appear after staining with lead or lanthanum. The nuclear region contains a finely fibrillar material, which shows close contact with the cytoplasmic material in many regions. There is no sign of the existence of a nuclear membrane. The cell wall shows as a double structure. The cell membrane is visible in a few places. [Photograph and preparation by L. Caro. Magnification 80,000 ×, reduced to 50%.]

concerned with motility. Inside the cell can be seen nuclear bodies, which probably contain the majority, if not all, the DNA in the cell.

Each feature of the cell has an interesting and complex microhistology. The recent development of thin-section electron microscopy has made it possible to visualize some of the detailed structure of various components. This new, greatly magnified observation is furnishing one of the liveliest advances in knowledge of the cell which has yet taken place. Thus the nuclear membrane is seen to be made up of a series of threads running crisscross, about 10,000 A long by 500 wide. In the membrane are pores, openings about 1000 A in diameter, which have dense material threading through them. Whether these pores act to permit selected diffusion is not certain. Motile structures such as *cilia* or *flagellae* show a well-defined sectional structure, as indicated in Fig. 2–2. In *cilia* there are always nine peripheral pairs of myosin fibrils and two central pairs, while in flagellae the fibrils are three-stranded.

Both nuclear and cell membranes show the presence of double fibers, or *lamellae*, which have a total thickness of about 100 A. Evidence is beginning to accumulate which shows that such lamellae are a general feature in cell substructure. They are found in mitochondria, plant plastids, and Golgi apparatus, and they appear in the grana that form part of the chloroplasts of plant cells.

The cytoplasm of a cell is a viscous fluid of unusual viscosity characteristics. It can on occasion be a relatively thick *gel* and on other occasions be far more nearly a liquid. It undoubtedly has an interlaced pattern of thin lamellae running through it. A section electron micrograph of a bacterial cell is shown in Fig. 2–3. The cell wall and the protoplast membrane can be seen. A granular structure throughout the cytoplasm is also clearly visible. The granules are probably the ribosomes, which are revealed by ultracentrifugation of the contents of the bacterium. In addition, a set of larger particles can be seen. The nuclear bodies are visible, with a dense part which is probably the result of the disruption, in preparation, of the organization of the nucleus.

Nearly every cell has a nucleus. With the possible, but doubtful, exception of the bacterial cell, the nucleus has as an important part of its structure a set of chromosomes—long, threadlike objects that are almost certainly closely concerned with the whole hereditary behavior of the cell.

2–2 Cell organelles. In a certain sense the component parts of cells have more unity and simplicity than the cells themselves. The realization that this is so had to await the development of thin-section electron microscopy. With electron microscopy we can now identify two major components of cells in many different kinds of tissue. They are the *mitochondria* and the *microsomes*. *Mitochondria*, which are the regions in the

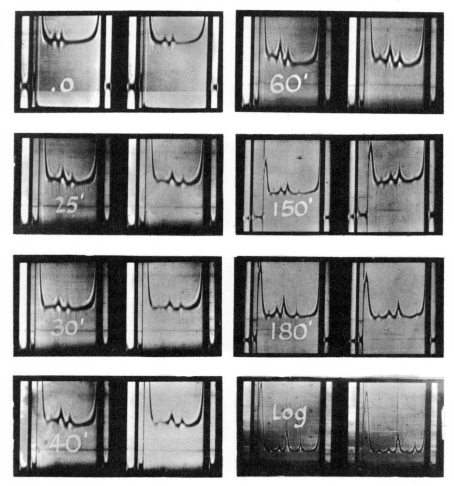

FIG. 2–4. The centrifugal pattern of disrupted cells of *Bacillus subtilis*, which is going from the spore form to the actively dividing form (due to Woese, Langridge, and Morowitz). The times of germination, in minutes, are indicated. The fully growing culture shown at the lower right is designated as in "log phase." The increased complexity of the pattern of ribosomes is clearly seen.

cell containing the array of enzymes involved in respiration, are really remarkably recognizable in many cells. The exact detail of their structure is still (and will continue to be) under some debate, but they appear to be roughly cylindrical in shape, of diameter about one-half micron or 5000 A, and of variable length, up to ten microns or so. Across the cylinder is a set of double layers, probably connecting to the outside, sometimes called *cristae*. The organization of the mitochondria contains a subarchitecture of organized enzyme systems. The revelation of this order, which is rapidly developing, is one of the tasks of molecular biophysics.

The *microsomes* are not quite so uniformly structured in all cells. They are a composite of a quite elaborately developed double layer, with particles of diameter about 300 A attached to them. It is likely that the microsomes are the region of protein synthesis.

Mention should be made of cellular *membranes*, for here too there begins to appear a unity of design that covers many cells. They appear to be made of double molecular layers of protein and lipid and seem to have a remarkable uniformity of thickness. They have very interesting functions, notably that of controlling permeability. To learn how they perform that function is another major problem of molecular biophysics.

One important avenue of study of the cell is by means of disruption and fractionation. By various means, ranging from treatment with specific enzymes to ultrasonic disintegration, the cell can be broken up and then examined. The component parts can be isolated and examined in several ways. One very good method of fractionation is centrifugation, which rapidly resolves the cell into cell-wall and cell-membrane fractions, mitochondria, microsomes, microsomal particles, and other smaller molecular fractions. By using care in choosing the proper method of fractionation, specific parts of a cell can be isolated for study. Thus mitochondria can be relatively easily separated out by centrifugation. Fractionation on an ion-exchange column, on the other hand, is more useful for macromolecular components than for the larger organelles.

An example of centrifugal fractionation is shown in Fig. 2–4. The centrifugal pattern is of germinating spores of *Bacillus subtilis* as the germination progresses. The centrifuge separates out components of microsomal particles, or "ribosomes." It can be seen that the inert, nonmetabolizing spore form has only two such components, while as the germination progresses to the actively dividing, fully "alive" form, a fresh component enters in increasing amount. Thus the molecular architecture of growing cells is itself also changing.

A great advantage of centrifugal fractionation is that it permits the use of physicochemical analysis on the various fractions. Thus the chemical composition, whether protein, lipid, polysaccharide, or nucleic acid, can be determined, and in addition the physical characteristics of sedimentation rate, light scattering, absorption spectrum, and so on, can be measured. In this way a much finer analysis of the components of the cell can be made.

On occasion, when the right auxiliary factors have been found, the individual components of the cell continue to fulfill all or part of their functions. Thus plant chloroplasts will continue to operate photosynthetically after isolation from the plant, and liver microsomes will incorporate amino acids into a proteinlike form after isolation. Such studies, with *cell-free extracts*, are tremendously informative, and form an important part of the recent advances in the detailed description of cellular mechanisms.

2–3 The molecular composition of a cell. The title of this section shows very clearly the broadness of the approach in this chapter. Since cells differ from species to species, and also change in their own life history, the variations in molecular content are highly significant. From another viewpoint, however, the molecules discussed by bacteriologists, plant physiologists, enzymologists, and even clinical pathologists, are remarkably uniform and few in number. A low-temperature physicist will have far less in common with a nuclear physicist, even though both are members of the same professional society, than a bacteriologist will have with a mammalian physiologist, even though their professional worlds are separate. Because of this amazing broad unity in living systems, we can dare to attempt a description of cells in this broad sense.

If we choose a bacterial cell suitable for chemical analysis, the following values develop:

Typical cell. Length: 3 microns (3×10^{-6} m). Diameter: 1 micron (10^{-6} m). Volume: 2.25 cubic microns (2.25×10^{-18} m^3).

Water, around 70%.
Dry weight, 6.7×10^{-13} gm.
Deoxyribonucleic acid (DNA), 3.5×10^{-14} gm, or 5% of dry weight.
Ribonucleic acid (RNA), 7×10^{-14} gm, or 10% by weight.
Lipid, 4.2×10^{-14} gm, or 6%.
Phospholipid, 2.6×10^{-14} gm, or 4%.
Polysaccharide, variable with kind of cell, to be reckoned around 5%.
Protein, around 4.7×10^{-13} gm.

To express these values in numbers of molecules per cell we must make some assumptions about the molecular weight of each kind of molecule. The two nucleic acid molecules can be considered as being of molecular weight one million, meaning that the mass of 6×10^{23} molecules is one million grams, or the mass of each molecule is 1.66×10^{-18} gm. For lipid and phospholipid no definite figure is available, but we can arbitrarily suppose molecular weights of 1000 for each of these, or *particle* weights of 1.6×10^{-21} gm. For polysaccharide about 20,000 is a good estimate, or a particle weight of 3.3×10^{-20} gm. For protein an average molecular weight of 60,000 can be taken, or a particle weight of 10^{-19} gm. The numbers of molecules per cell are then as shown in Table 2–1.

Note that the numbers in Table 2–1 are so small that the statistical regularity of ordinary matter would not be expected to hold. For instance,

TABLE 2–1

NUMBERS OF MOLECULES OF
VARIOUS KINDS IN BACTERIAL CELLS

DNA	2.1×10^4
RNA	4.2×10^4
Lipid	2.5×10^7
Phospholipid	1.6×10^7
Polysaccharide	1.0×10^6
Protein	4.7×10^6

if all motion were randomized in character in the cell, then upon division we would expect that fluctuations of as high as the square root of any number would be commonplace. Thus a 1% regularity in the DNA and RNA is all that could be expected, and much higher fluctuations should occur quite often. This is at variance with the fact that bacteria retain an accurate character over many generations, and it is this which led Schrödinger to point out that biological regularity cannot be molecular-statistical in its nature but must in some important respects be a property of individual molecular structures. The study of such structures is thus clearly of great importance, even when a most elementary numerical study of the cell is made. One very vital part of biophysics is, therefore, the study of the molecular structure of DNA, RNA, lipid, phospholipid, polysaccharide, and protein, and of the relationships among them.

The choice of a bacterial cell is in actual fact quite limiting. In a plant cell, for example, a large fraction is cellulose, a complex polymer founded on sugars for elementary units. Thus in treating the bacterial cell we have bypassed a tremendous branch of plant physiology. We do not intend to ignore this, but it will develop that the six classes of molecules described above are sufficient for an illustration of the molecular problems of biology.

In the following section, we give a short account of the six classes of molecules discussed above.

2–4 Biological molecules and their general character. In a descriptive subject such as biology in the early stages of its development, names are assigned to substances that are not known in detail but are known in broad function to be important. "Protoplasm" is such a term, and even though the detailed structure of protoplasm is still unknown, this designation has fulfilled a very valuable purpose. One reason is that the components of protoplasm are not infinitely diverse but are remarkably unified in charac-ter, as will be seen in the description below.

Proteins. Proteins are made up of twenty amino acids which are arranged in linear sequence along a polypeptide chain. An amino acid has the following typical character:

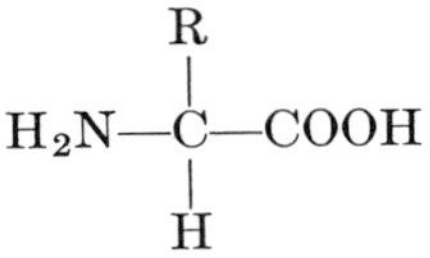

$$\begin{array}{c} R \\ | \\ H_2N-C-COOH \\ | \\ H \end{array}$$

Under varied conditions, an amino acid may behave as

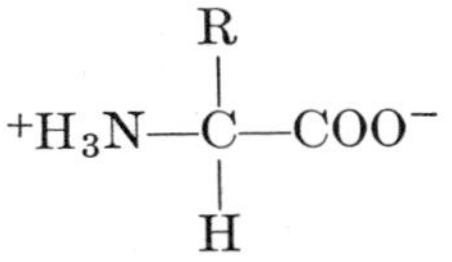

$$\begin{array}{c} R \\ | \\ {}^+H_3N-C-COO^- \\ | \\ H \end{array}$$

which is a polar combination of two ions. This ionizable behavior is a most important characteristic of proteins.

The polypeptide chain is as follows:

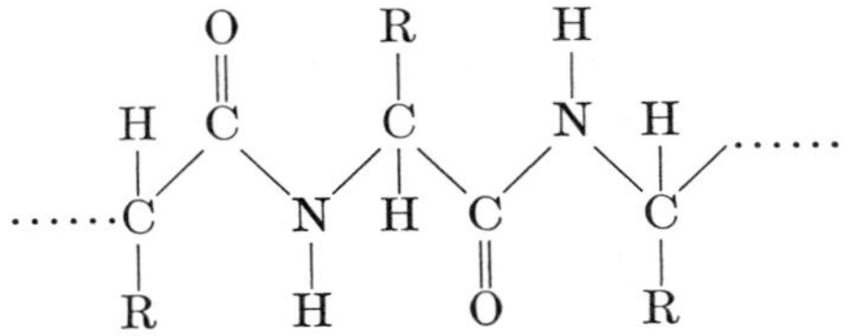

where R is one of the amino acid residues. The chain can be thought of as made by the coalescing of a multiplicity of amino acids, with loss of water as each amino acid is linked in place. Thus we must think of a number of amino acids held on a frame in some way, and of a process of *biosynthesis* by which these amino acids become linked together. This is illustrated in Fig. 2–5, which shows a *tripeptide*. Obviously the character of the framework shaded in the figure is of great interest. So also are the agency and method by which the removal of the HOH and the linking of the bonds are carried out. We shall return to this process, called *protein synthesis*, later.

The twenty amino acids, with their chemical formulas, are listed in Table 2–2. They are derived from a common group, seen most simply in glycine to be $H_2NCHCOOH$, with the addition of a side chain on the first carbon. After alanine, only the side chains are listed in Table 2–2, with the exception of cystine, proline, and hydroxyproline, which are fully given. Although detailed discussion of them is not in place here, the biophysicist must have considerable familiarity with these substances, for they are in a certain sense the alphabet of biology. The chemical and polar properties of these substances are of great importance, but the

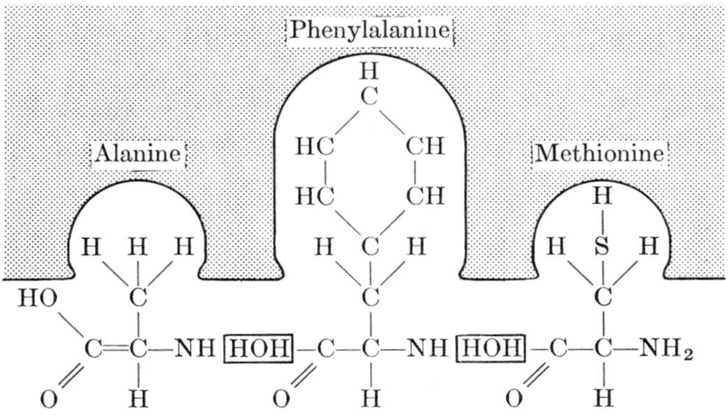

forming

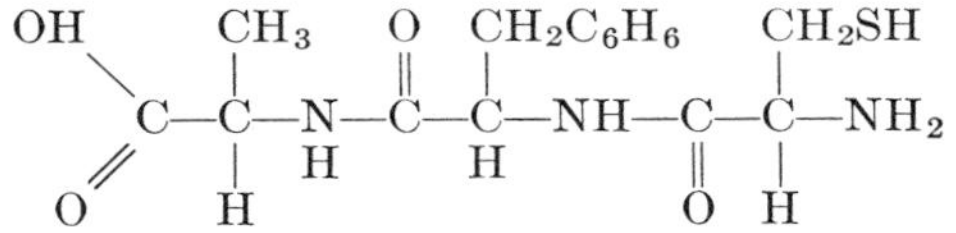

FIG. 2–5. Representation of the end result of coalescing three amino acids, *alanine*, *phenylalanine*, and *methionine*, to form a *tripeptide*: alanylphenyla-lanylmethionine.

physicist should also note their absorption spectra, length, width, and thickness. These features will be discussed in detail later.

Proteins range in molecular weight from about 3000 (gramicidin) to hundreds of thousands (myosin). They take several general physical forms. Among their outstanding characteristics is that of specific cataly-sis. In this function they are known as *enzymes*, and they undergo a most remarkable set of chemical processes. Enzyme action is undoubtedly one of the key processes of biology.

Nucleic acids, DNA and RNA. The physicist who turns from heavy contemplation of basic principles to the diversified, changing world of life will be surprised to observe that the nature of protein is so simple. Twenty amino acids comprise, after all, only a little more than two octaves of the periodic table. His surprise will be even greater when he studies nucleic acids. The intrinsic parts of these are more complex, being three-fold aggregates of purine or pyrimidine bases, sugar, and phosphoric acid. The number of "building blocks," however, is much smaller, being six altogether, and in the great majority of cases only *four*. Depending on the character of the sugar and on the presence of uracil in place of thymine, two kinds of nucleic acid—ribonucleic (RNA) and deoxyribonucleic (DNA)—are separated.

TABLE 2–2

THE AMINO ACIDS FOUND IN PROTEINS

Glycine	$H_2N-CH-H$ $\quad\quad\;\; |$ $\quad\;\; HOOC$
Alanine	$H_2N-CH-CH_3$ $\quad\quad\;\; |$ $\quad\;\; HOOC$
Valine	$-CH\big\langle{}^{CH_3}_{CH_3}$
Leucine	$-CH_2CH\big\langle{}^{CH_3}_{CH_3}$
Isoleucine	$-CH\big\langle{}^{CH_2-CH_3}_{CH_3}$
Serine	$-CH_2OH$
Threonine	$-CHOH-CH_3$
Cysteine	$-CH_2SH$
Methionine	$-CH_2CH_2SCH_3$
Glutamic acid	$-CH_2-CH_2-COOH$
Aspartic acid	$-CH_2-COOH$
Lysine	$-(CH_2)_3-CH_2NH_2$
Arginine	$-(CH_2)_3-NH-C\big\langle{}^{NH}_{NH_2}$
Phenylalanine	$-CH_2-\bigcirc$
Tyrosine	$-CH_2-\bigcirc-OH$

TABLE 2–2(*continued*)

Tryptophan	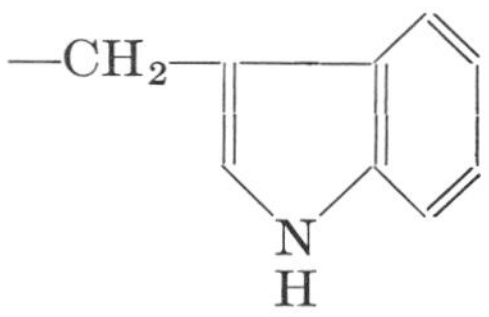 $-CH_2$ ... indole ring with $\underset{H}{N}$
Histidine	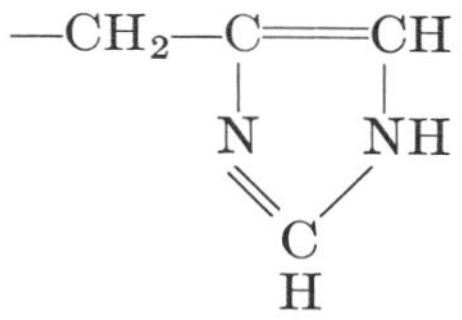 $-CH_2-C=CH$, with N, NH, and $\underset{H}{C}$
Cystine	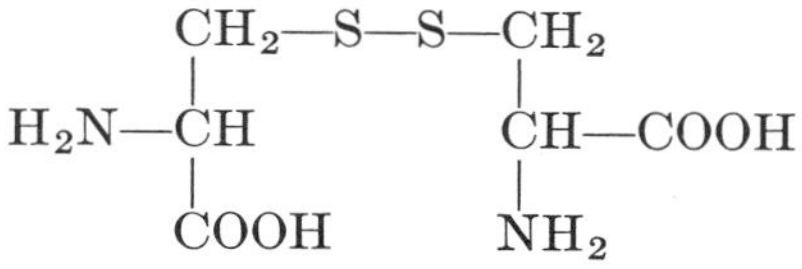 $CH_2-S-S-CH_2$ H_2N-CH $\quad$ $CH-COOH$ $COOH$ $\quad$ NH_2
Proline	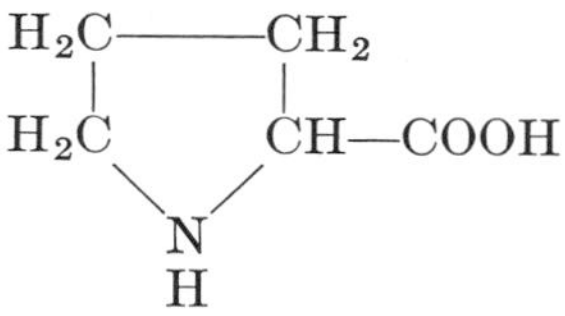 $H_2C\!-\!\!-\!\!-CH_2$ H_2C $\quad$ $CH-COOH$ $\underset{H}{N}$
Hydroxyproline	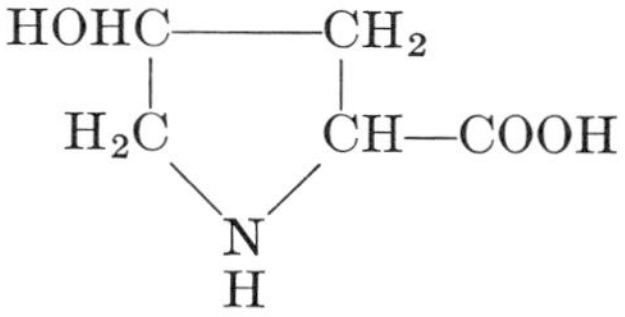 $HOHC\!-\!\!-\!\!-CH_2$ H_2C $\quad$ $CH-COOH$ $\underset{H}{N}$

The component unit, which can be thought of as analogous to an amino acid in a peptide chain, is

Base—sugar—phosphate

and the linkage is by the phosphate to two sugars in a stepwise pattern, as follows:

Base—sugar
|
phosphate
|
Base—sugar
|
phosphate
|

The component parts are often referred to separately. A combination between a base and a sugar (ribose or deoxyribose) is called, logically enough, a "nucleoside." When this is combined with phosphate, it becomes a "nucleotide."

TABLE 2–3

BASES INVOLVED IN NUCLEIC ACID

Pyrimidines
  Cytosine

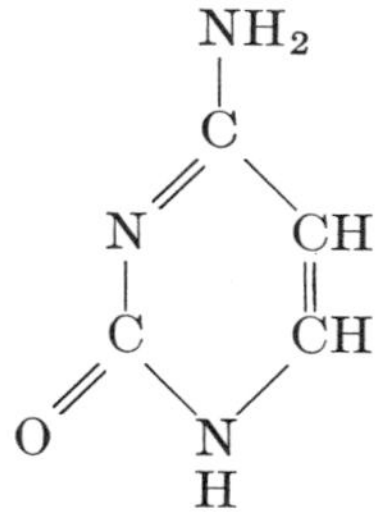

  Alpha hydroxymethyl cytosine
  (found in virus DNA in some cases)

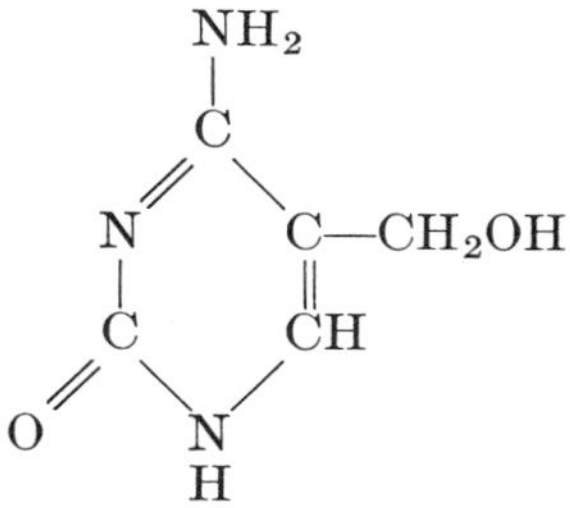

  Uracil (in RNA only)

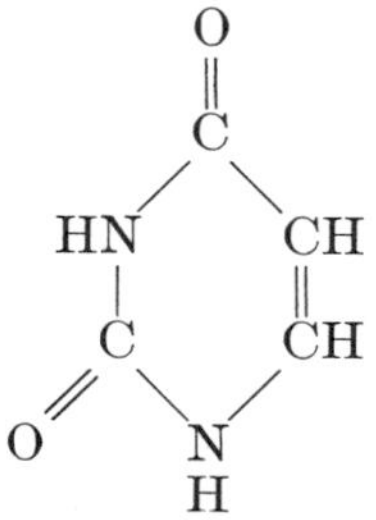

  Thymine
  (in DNA)

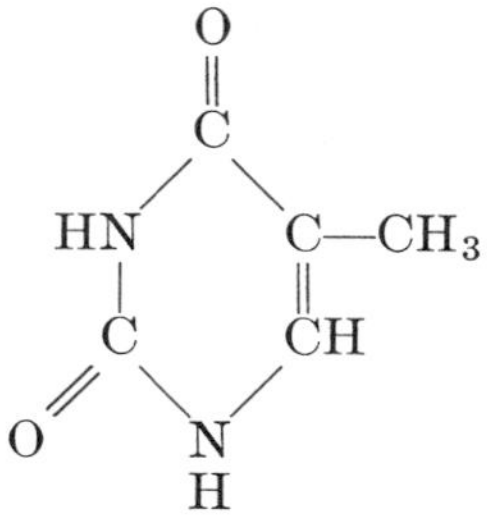

The important separate bases, six in number, are listed in Table 2–3, along with their structural formulas. These, together with their sugar and phosphate complements, are linked into enormous molecules having molecular weights in the millions. The structure of nucleic acids is gradu-

TABLE 2-3(*continued*)

Purines
   Adenine

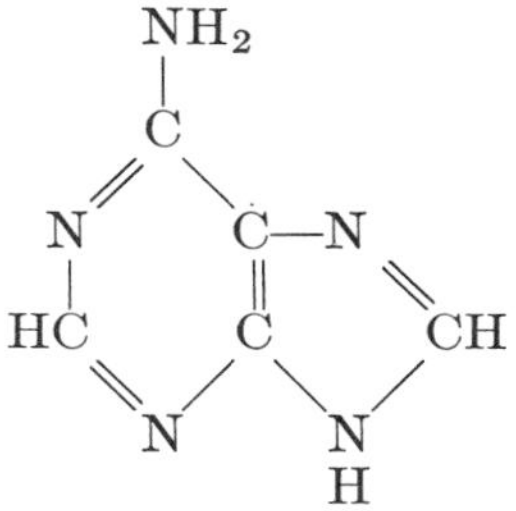

   Guanine

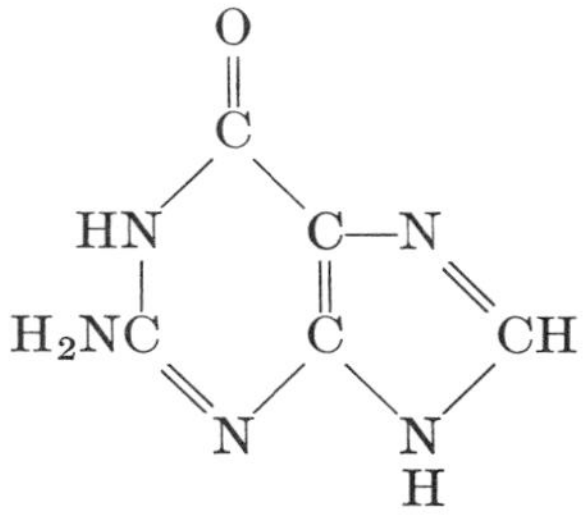

Sugars
   Ribose

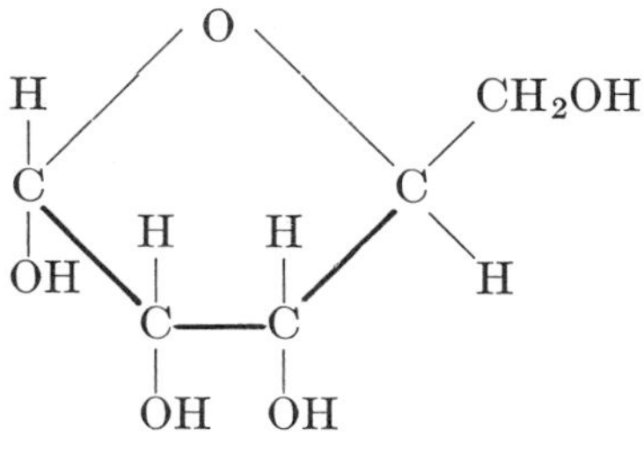

   Deoxyribose

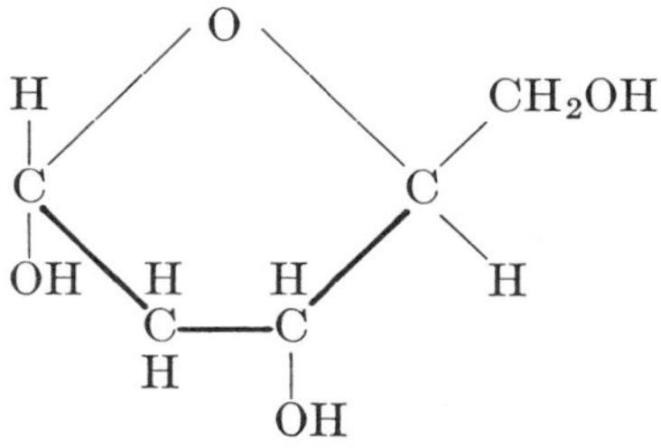

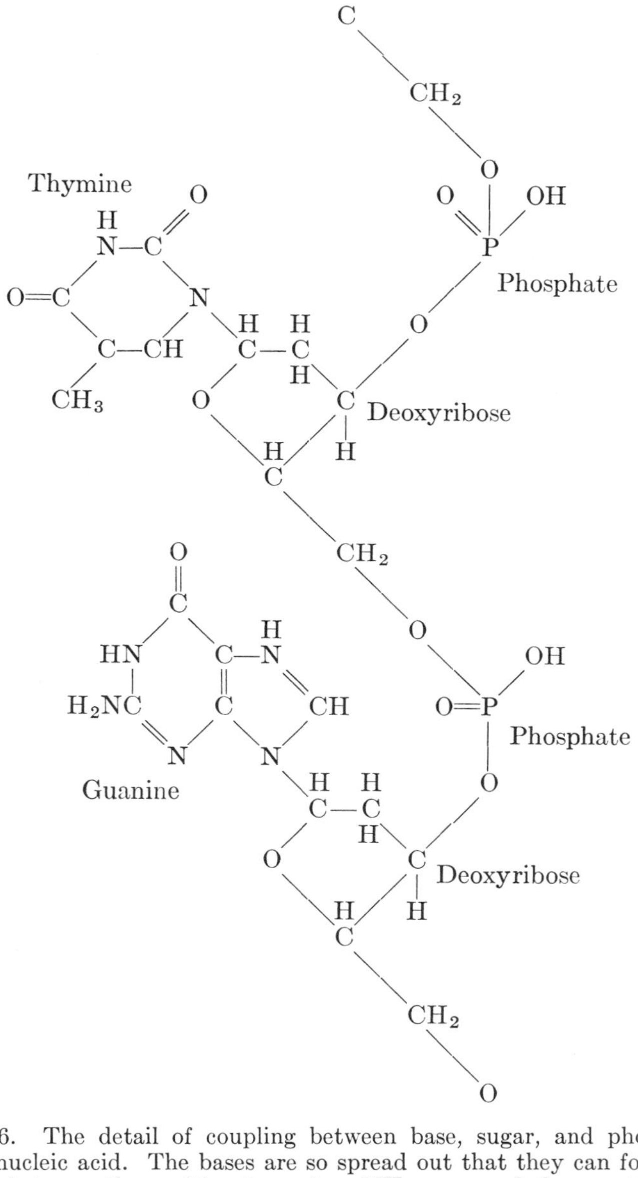

FIG. 2–6. The detail of coupling between base, sugar, and phosphate in deoxyribonucleic acid. The bases are so spread out that they can form hydrogen bonds between the positive face of an NH group and the negative face of a C=O group, at three points for guanine and cytosine or two points for adenine and thymine. This bonding between bases occurs between two intertwined chains of DNA, and gives some stability to enormous linear molecules, which seemingly carry the factors required to give hereditary control to the cell. [According to Langridge, Seeds, Wilson, Hooper, Wilkins, and Hamilton.]

ally becoming understood and is bringing with it a sensational advance in molecular biology. In some way, only partly clear, nucleic acid is related to protein and also to itself. It is almost certain that nucleic acid forms the framework that holds together the separate amino acids in their correct order. How it does this will be speculated on later.

The actual coupling between base, sugar, and phosphate is shown in terms of a structural formula in Fig. 2–6. This coupling permits the formation of a simplified double helix, as described in Chapter 5.

Again, with these six bases, which with the twenty amino acids make up the biophysicist's alphabet, it is not only their chemical properties that are important, but also their physical properties—ultraviolet absorption, size and shape, and deformability. These will all be discussed in detail later.

Lipids. Lipids are compounds of fatty acids of considerable chain length, with glycerol. A possible lipid is indicated below:

$$
\begin{array}{l}
\quad\quad\quad\quad\; O \\
\quad\quad\quad\quad\; \| \\
H_2C\!-\!O\!-\!C\!-\!(CH_2)_{16}\!-\!CH_3 \\
\;| \\
\quad\quad\quad\quad\; O \\
\quad\quad\quad\quad\; \| \\
HC\!-\!O\!-\!C\!-\!(CH_2)_{16}\!-\!CH_3 \\
\;| \\
H_2C\!-\!O\!-\!C\!-\!(CH_2)_{16}\!-\!CH_3 \\
\quad\quad\quad\;\| \\
\quad\quad\quad\; O
\end{array}
$$

Thus lipids have molecular weights of the order of 1000. They are used for food storage and in structural parts.

Phospholipids. These are also compounds of long-chain fatty acids with glycerol, but the third chain of fatty acid is replaced by phosphoric acid, which in turn can be combined with a variety of bases. The formula for lecithin follows:

$$
\begin{array}{l}
\quad\quad\quad\; O \\
\quad\quad\quad\; \| \\
CH_2O\!-\!C\!-\!(CH_2)_{16}\!-\!CH_3 \\
\;| \\
\quad\quad\quad\; O \\
\quad\quad\quad\; \| \\
CHO\!-\!C\!-\!(CH_2)_{14}\!-\!CH_3 \\
\;| \\
\quad\quad\quad\; O \\
\quad\quad\quad\; \| \\
CH_2O\!-\!P\!-\!O\!-\!CH_2\!-\!CH_2\!-\!N(CH_3)_3 \\
\quad\quad\quad\; | \\
\quad\quad\quad\; OH
\end{array}
$$

The base $HO\!-\!CH_2\!-\!CH_2\!-\!N(CH_3)_3$ is choline.

Polysaccharides. It has been observed that small sugar molecules combine to form various extremely large molecular aggregates, and the polysaccharides that result are found to play a very important role. They can combine in a specific way with some proteins, and are observed to elicit antibodies, often very efficiently. Among such polysaccharides are: *glycogen*, a branched homopolysaccharide, which can grow to have a molecular weight in the millions; *heparin*, a sulfated polysaccharide with powerful anticoagulant activity; and *hyaluronic* acid, the repeat unit of which is given below. The latter is a compound of acetylglucosamine and glucuronic acid.

Polysaccharides seem to play an important part in surface action. They form part of the slime layer of bacteria and part of the capsule of certain strains of pneumococci.

With this account of the general character of biological molecules, the reader, and particularly the biochemical reader, is bound to be dissatisfied. Where are the small molecules—the ions, the salts, the vitamins and hormones? The answer is that they are present, but in surprisingly small amounts. In yeast, which is mostly protein, only 5% of the amino acid nitrogen is present as free amino acid. The smallness of the number of small molecules in molecular aggregates is related to two things: (1) Obviously they are part of the structure of the larger molecules, and so they are *made to order* to a great extent. (2) Less obviously, the small molecules, such as vitamins and hormones, play a role that is often related to some biochemical function, and therefore their concentration need not be high. In a similar way, certain metals may play a key part in completing a structure even though they are not present in large amounts. The study of small molecules is thus of great importance to biochemistry, but in this biophysical "stage setting" we can defer their consideration until later.

2–5 Cell behavior. No verbal account of cell growth and division can equal the vividness of microscopic observation. Every biophysicist should avail himself of motion pictures, taken in phase-contrast microscopy, of all cellular processes. No attempt to describe the various forms of cell division will be made here. All that we can do is call attention to some important features now, and return to them later.

Among the many aspects of cell behavior, *growth* and *division* are two outstanding features. While the cell is functioning in its proper environment, in the correct temperature range, it is steadily growing; i.e., substances taken in through its membrane are being converted into the specific proteins, nucleic acids, lipids, vitamins, and so on, and other substances not needed in its economy are being expelled. This process of conversion is of great interest and has been a field of rapid biochemical advance. The use of isotopically labeled sugars, amino acids, purines, and pyrimidines to study this process of synthesis is producing revolutionary ideas about the nature of biological process. The techniques and early results are discussed in a later chapter.

To study cells in as simple a form as possible, it has in the past been necessary to turn to the microorganisms: bacteria, yeasts, and molds. These have the tremendous advantage that they can be grown in media which are chemically defined, or nearly so. A defined medium makes it possible, for example, to study mutants that are unable to perform some particular synthetic operation, a technique that has made microbial genetics a highly developed field. A relatively recent development has been the discovery that single cells derived from mammalian tissue, and thus having the complete complement of cytoplasm, nucleus, and chromosomes, can be grown on a medium that is very nearly fully defined. This discovery, made by Puck and Marcus, has been used to make a measurement of the radiation sensitivity of such cells. It has also been possible to show that in these fully evolved cells the synthesis of DNA does not continue throughout the cycle of division, but follows a cyclic process, as shown in Fig. 2–7. The synthesis of DNA occurs during only one-third of the cycle and neither immediately precedes, nor immediately follows cell

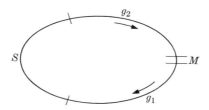

Fig. 2–7. Schematic representation of the fraction of the time S in which a cell synthesizes DNA. The synthesis occurs during only about a third of the cycle, neither just before (g_2) nor just after (g_1) cell division (M). The division process itself takes only a brief time and has two stages—the chromosome separation and the actual cell division.

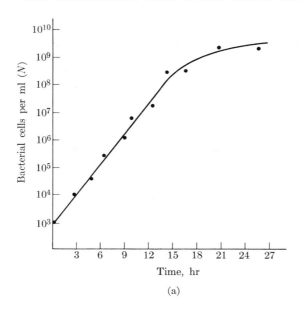

(a)

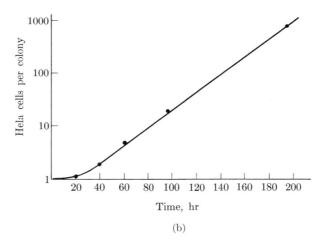

(b)

FIG. 2–8. (a) The growth of *Escherichia coli* in minimal medium as a function of the time. It can be seen that most of the increase is logarithmic, only failing as the culture becomes very dense and its relationship to the medium is altered accordingly. If I is the initial number of cells per ml and t_0 is the generation time, the relation holding is $N = I \cdot 2^{t/t_0}$. (b) The growth of Hela cells in tissue culture (after Puck).

division, a process that is remarkably short in time and occupies relatively little (5% or so) of the cycle. In one bacterium, *Escherichia coli*, this cycle cannot be observed, and DNA synthesis is continuous though not at a constant rate throughout more than 85% of the division time.

Most of the cell division we are concerned with is either the simple division of microorganisms or is *mitotic*. The process of *meiosis*, by which a germ cell deliberately reduces its complement of chromosomal material so as to require completion from an outside cell, does not often concern us. Meiosis is important in cytogenetics, and will be found so in biophysics, but since no process of division, whether of cell or organelle, has as yet been physically described, the simpler, culturable systems are still those of primary concern to us.

Cell growth. A cell grows by taking material from outside itself and converting it to make more of its own constituent material. The rate of chemical turnover and synthesis is very rapid. A fully growing bacterial cell will synthesize 40,000 amino acids of one kind *per second*, will form 150,000 peptide bonds *per second*, and if it is working against a limited metabolite, will utilize the content of 50 times its own volume of material before division. It is apparent that one problem the biophysicist has to face is whether randomly occurring processes like diffusion can possibly achieve this extremely rapid rate of specific growth and synthesis.

A bacterial cell, in the proper environment, follows a relation of the form shown graphically in Fig. 2–8(a). The mathematical form of this relation is most simply seen in terms of division:

$$N = I2^n,$$

where N is the total number of cells present (the total population), I is the initial number of cells, and n is the number of generations. This can be rewritten as

$$N = I \cdot 2^{t/t_0},$$

where the time of one generation is t_0 and the elapsed time is t, so that we have $n = t/t_0$. The behavior of an actual population of bacterial cells is somewhat more complex, because the environment is normally not ideal, and the bacterial population has to adjust to it to some degree. Also, of course, the population increase is bound to be limited at the upper end by the bacterial equivalent of overpopulation. This does not alter the essential simplicity of the major process of growth.

In Fig. 2–8(b), which shows the growth of Hela cells in a nearly defined medium (as observed by Puck), we observe the same type of adaptation and exponential increase as seen in Fig. 2–8(a). The generation time is longer in the case of these cells.

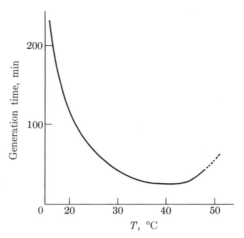

FIG. 2–9. The variation of the generation time of a bacterial culture as the temperature is changed. The rate of growth changes markedly in a way which is not characteristic of physical processes like diffusion, but is typical of processes having activation energy, as found in many enzymatic reactions.

The variation of the generation time of a bacterial cell with temperature, shown in Fig. 2–9, is highly significant. Over a temperature range of a few degrees, the rate of synthesis changes by a factor of the order of 10. This is not characteristic of any ordinary physical process, but is typical of a chemical reaction in which there is an energy threshold, or activation energy, to surmount. The study of enzymatic processes reveals temperature-dependence of this general character. Thus we see that the over-all relationship of temperature to growth is linked to the enzymatic character of the protein inside the cell.

One powerful method of studying bacterial synthesis is to supply a single limiting nutrient to the medium in amounts known to be too small. Synthesis is then held up and proceeds at a rate that depends on the rate of supply of the one nutrient. When this is done, it is found that about one-quarter of the limiting substance can be incorporated into bacteria. Also, after a time, the cells may suddenly gain the ability to bypass the bottleneck and use a different synthetic mechanism, with a consequent rapid increase in rate of growth. This process is that of adaptive enzyme formation, or "induction," and its study has provided remarkable insight into cellular processes.

Cell division. As an integral part of cell behavior, the process of cell division must be considered. Cell growth usually does not continue steadily in any one way, but after a certain stage (controlled by a variety of factors and not an immutable event) the cell divides, by a cutting-in of the cell wall, to form two cells. The process of division is most complex, and the physical viewpoint that it is simply related to surface and volume energy requirements is far from adequate.   These factors undoubtedly enter, but they do so as part of a beautifully timed series of events that seem to have little to do with surface and volume energetics.

Cell division is not of a single type.   However, there is a general pattern of requirements for cell division.   The nuclear components, the chromosomes and the adjuncts of chromosomes, need to be equally divided between parent and daughter cell.   Cytoplasmic units need to be approximately equally divided.   This means that before the observable division takes place, a whole series of submicroscopic duplications of genetically vital structures, and of synthesizing subunits, must take place.   The process is remarkably ordered.   For example, the threads of nucleoprotein that make up the individual parts of the chromosome carry small separate regions (in some way related to genes) which play an important part in controlling various cellular properties.   Prior to division these are found lined up in pairs, with the great majority of related genes precisely opposite each other.   While parts of the chromosome may break off and rejoin in other locations, the pairing of genes still takes place to the greatest possible extent in a way which seems to demand some specific interaction. The nature of this interaction is of great interest, and speculation as to its physical character is lively.

The fact that broken chromosome threads are "sticky," to quote the cytogeneticist, poses another physical problem.   What is the nature of the force that binds together broken strands of chromosome material?   Is it similar to the binding of broken parts of a long, thin virus?   Or is it a property of the whole cell in addition to being part of the rodlike structure of the chromosome, and if so, what is the precise property?

2–6 Viruses. The study of viruses has almost become a branch of molecular biophysics.   Starting from the discovery that symptoms of disease could be produced by particles which would pass through filters that stopped bacteria (giving rise to the term "filterable virus"), the study of viruses has progressed to the point where the individual particles can be described in remarkable detail and their functioning units cataloged.   To achieve this state, many physical techniques have been used, notably centrifugation, electron microscopy, light and x-ray scattering, ionizing radiation inactivation, and x-ray diffraction of crystals.   In what follows in later chapters, viruses will receive mention many times.   It is therefore in order to look at viruses themselves, for although they are not normally part of the living cell, they have a close relationship to cells and they offer a means of studying a part of the functioning of the cell.

Viruses may be categorized into four, three, or two types.   The four are *bacterial* (often called bacteriophage), *animal, plant,* and *insect* viruses.

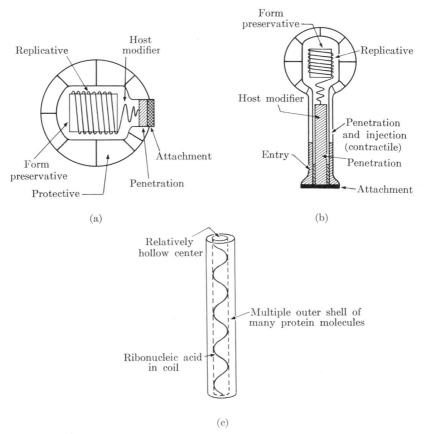

Fɪɢ. 2–10. Schematic representations of the parts and functions of viruses. (a) An animal virus, such as influenza virus. (b) A bacterial virus, T2 phage. (c) A plant virus, tobacco mosaic virus.

Since some plant viruses will grow in insects, one may question the separation of these into two categories, and perhaps, to take a large jump, we can say that there are simply viruses with single-strand or double-strand nucleic acid, making only two classes. But for now, we shall consider all four.

The best way to think about a virus is in terms of a representation of it. In Fig. 2–10 we show schematic representations of animal, bacterial, and plant viruses in varying amounts of detail. All the details will need modifying as research progresses, but nevertheless by means of the diagrams we can see what processes occur.

Consider first the animal virus. Somewhere on its outer structure is a molecular pattern that enables it to attach to a *host cell*. This attachment may be simply by electrostatic forces between $-COO^-$ and $-NH_3^+$ charges in a pattern which differs from cell to cell and virus to virus. Next, after attachment, there is an "enzyme" that acts on the cell wall so as to secure the entry of the vital part of the virus, namely the chain of nucleic acid plus one or two other not yet clearly characterized features. In the figure we have shown, first, the "host modifier," which serves to cause the host to begin to make materials needed for the virus to grow. Then there follows the nucleic acid chain, which must be coiled up in some way on what we here call the "form preservative." Once the replicative part and the host modifier have entered the cell, the external part, usually protein and lipid, becomes useless, and in the case of bacterial viruses has been shown to remain outside the host.

The processes which go on next, in terms of biochemistry, are beginning to be understood. The first event is the forced production of some needed enzymes. This can, perhaps, be dispensed with for many viruses. Then the nucleic acid multiplies rapidly at very impressive speed; for example, for bacterial viruses, 1000 or so fresh nucleic acid complements are formed in about eight minutes. If this is a process of doubling by division, then 10 divisions must occur, or one molecular chain must be made in 50 seconds. Some quite interesting physical problems are clearly associated with such a process, not the least being that of keeping things untangled!

After the nucleic acid is made, the external components—the form preservative, the penetrative, entry, and protective parts—are produced and successively assembled. In bacteria the whole process can take less than 15 minutes. The external components, although they have not been present in the cell for copies to be made, nevertheless are faithfully reproduced in response to the effect elicited by the entry of the virus nucleic acid. Thus in viruses we have quite clear proof of the process often called "information transfer," by which we mean that the molecular structure of nucleic acid, in combination with the metabolic factory of the cell, can cause the creation of very precise protein molecular structures. The process of information transfer is another of the major intellectual problems posed by molecular biophysics.

What we have said about animal viruses holds reasonably well for bacterial viruses. In the case of one such virus, T2, acting on the bacterium *Escherichia coli*, a great deal more can be said. Like many bacterial viruses, T2 has a head and a tail, as can be seen in Fig. 2–10(b). The head contains a rather large amount of a very special form of DNA that contains hydroxymethyl cytosine in place of cytosine and that also has an abonormal sugar content. The tail is made up of two parts, each of which is complex. When the first attachment process takes place, the lower outer region unwinds into four flagellalike objects that randomly move until they attach to the bacterium. Then the upper part contracts and pushes an inner plug into the host cell, a process which is followed by the entry of the nucleic acid contents of the virus. In the case of this bacteriophage, the nucleic acid is not at all related to that of the host, and accordingly at least two enzymes have to be synthesized before the components of the virus can be made.

Bacterial viruses exist in two very different forms. One, the virulent type, we have just described. The other, the type found in the phenomenon of lysogenesis, exists in a bacterial cell as part of the organized DNA structure in the cell. There it is known as *prophage*. Under such various influences as ultraviolet light, ionizing radiation, or reducing agents, or even spontaneously, the prophage can become detached and work its way out of the bacterium. If now a sensitive host cell is near, it will invade that cell and act as a virulent bacteriophage. Knowledge of this process stresses the intimate relation between virus nucleic acid and cell nucleic acid, and it is not surprising that molecular biologists have found it an interesting system to study.

The phenomenon of *transduction* is associated with bacterial viruses. A bacterium with a certain genetic lack can have the deficiency made up by infection by virus from a bacterium possessing the lacking genes. Such a bacterium must not be a host to the virulent aspect of the virus, but at the same time must be susceptible to the mechanisms of penetration.

A short but interesting digression on the process of mating of strains of bacteria which undergo conjugation is appropriate here. Conjugation between two bacteria occurs relatively infrequently. When it does take place, the DNA thread from one, the donor, passes through the short tube which occurs at conjugation and conveys its genetic markers to the recipient. This phenomenon was discovered by Lederberg (Zinder and Lederberg discovered transduction). Jacob and Wollman have further studied the process by the very simple expedient of subjecting conjugating bacteria to the high-shear gradients of a Waring blender. With this technique they have been able to break apart the bacteria after different times of mating and also to break the DNA thread that is passing through the opening. In this way the relative order of the genetic markers has been established. The process is shown, very diagrammatically, in Fig. 2–11. Of some incidental interest is the physics of shear and the possibility of studying the tensile strength of the genetic thread that passes through. Attention is beginning to be paid to this biophysical problem.

Bacterial and some animal viruses contain DNA and plant viruses contain RNA. In tobacco mosaic virus the RNA is almost certainly single-stranded, and in one case of a bacterial virus the DNA is single-stranded. The proportion of nucleic acid varies from 5% in large animal viruses to 45% in the case of T2 bacteriophage. Virus sizes vary from 200 A in diameter for foot and mouth disease and small phages to 1800 A

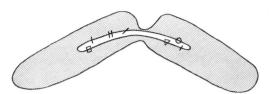

FIG. 2–11. Schematic diagram of the conjugation of two strains of *E. coli*, based on electron micrographs by Anderson, Wollman, and Jacob. The bacterial "chromosome," which analyzes genetically as if it were a closed loop, passes from one to the other. The thread can be broken by hydrodynamic shear, which separates the two bacteria.

FIG. 2–12. The double shadow of *Tipula iridescent virus,* as observed in the electron microscope by Williams and Smith, is shown on the left. On the right is the equivalent light shadow of a model of an *icosahedron.* [R. C. Williams and K. M. Smith, *B. B. Acta* **28,** 464 (1958).]

for rabies and 2600 A for vaccinia virus. Animal viruses are roughly spherical; bacterial viruses often have quite long tails; plant viruses are either rod-shaped or spherical; and insect viruses are nearly cylindrical, with not a great ratio of length to diameter.

We conclude this section with some remarks about the shape of some of the more carefully studied viruses. Kaesberg has compared the shape of shadow cast by some plant viruses in electron microscopy with models of regular solids. The insect virus of *Tipula paludosa,* studied by Williams and Smith, is an accurate icosahedron, as can be seen from the remarkable comparison in Fig. 2–12 between an electron micrograph of the virus shadowed by metal deposition at two angles 60° apart, and the light shadow of an icosahedral model. Clearly, the formation of such precision structures is an interesting crystallographic problem, and because the formation is a living process, its study will help in the understanding of other living processes.

2–7 Genetics and biophysics. The above brief discussions of cellular processes and viruses lead naturally to the subject of genetics, the precision science of biology. In many ways genetics has an intense appeal to the modern physicist and physical chemist. The whole concept of linear arrangement of genes, of linkage groups, and of all the structural interrelationships of heredity is inferential. From the statistics of various deliberately chosen crosses, the geneticist deduces the existence of linear arrays of specific determining agents. That these postulated linear arrays have a physical reality in the chromosomes has been one of the major satisfactions experienced by the scientist since scientific observation began. A moment's thought about the strength and precision of genetic analysis and its relation to the problems of the biophysicist is well repaid.

Quite independently of the discovery of the role of chromosomes in heredity and the consequent localization of a large part of the process of heredity, the geneticist has two potent means of study. The first is the study of *aberrations from linkage* (the name of the process has been paraphrased to fit the usage of physical scientists). The second is *mutation*.

As in many other phases of science, progress is made by generalization and by studied exception. One major generalization of Mendelian genetics is the process of segregation and independent assortment, a process most easily understood by imagining the random separation and re-pairing of the physical units of chromosomes. This generalization often fails, and the failure can be described in terms of the breaking and rejoining of the chromosomes in different ways, giving rise to the process of crossing over. This process means that genes become established on different linkage groups or in different orders, and the results are expressed in the nature of the whole organism, the phenotype. The study of the probability of crossing over has made possible the description of the order of the genes and also of their distance apart in admittedly strange, but nevertheless definite, units.

The unit of gene separation, the "Morgan," is the distance corresponding to unit probability of separation of two genes. Genetic analysis of bacteria will allow discrimination to 10^{-5} Morgan. Comparison with the physical dimensions of chromosome material leads to the conclusion that 10^{-5} Morgan is about 30 A. Therefore genetic analysis, from purely macroscopic observation plus the power of inference from tested theory, enables us to probe within molecular structure with the same resolving power as the electron microscope. Moreover, not only does the subject of genetics exhibit a remarkable precision, but the 30 A region of space is related to a biological functional expression. It is causative—how we do not yet know —in some chain of events whose origin lies in this small, almost submolecular region. The physical nature of that small region is obviously of paramount interest.

The study of mutation gives us the same sense of the importance of small, precisely constructed regions of the cell. Gene mutations occur spontaneously or can be induced by chemical mutagens, by ultraviolet light, and by ionizing radiation. Although the mode of action of this last method is not yet clear, it is evident that small total amounts of energy will cause mutation. Moreover, in ionizing radiation the energy is very largely distributed randomly, and this enables us to make some estimate of the region within which energy must be released to cause a mutation. The region is small, again rather less than 30 A in extent.

Modern studies of mutations have led to the observation of a beautiful and simple relationship between gene action and enzyme formation and action. The mechanism of this relation is not yet clear, but it seems certain that somehow the gene conditions the formation of a protein structure, or of an adjunct to protein structure, which is highly specific in forwarding cellular development. Thus we are led to realize not only that the gene has a part of its character which is highly localized, but also that in this region a specific framework is also localized. The nature of sensitive specific synthesis of proteins is one of the great challenges to the biophysicist as well as to all other biologists.

Gene mutation occurs in viruses, the smallest biological units that involve themselves in self-duplication and hence growth. Such systems develop their phenotypic expression very rapidly and can accordingly be studied efficiently. Here, too, small molecular units are responsible for definite functional expression. The study of the genetics of viruses has recently been advanced to a very high degree of precision by Benzer. Benzer considers three units: (1) the *recon* is the smallest interchangeable unit in a lined-up array (i.e., the length of line required to take part in recombination); (2) the *muton* is the smallest element which, when changed, causes a mutant form (i.e., the length of line within which a change will elicit a mutation); (3) the *cistron* is more subtle to define, but very interesting in its qualities. Consider a linear array represented by a line, as in Fig. 2–13, where the small blocks represent mutons. If we can devise a way to insert any two of the mutants *a*, *b*, *c*, and *d*, called a *trans* combina-

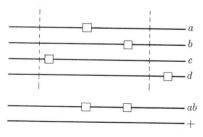

Fig. 2–13. A representation of mutants on a linear array.

tion, into an organism and see whether the two conspire to retain the mutant effect or to defeat each other, we can determine whether or not the genetic material is equivalent. Specifically, if we combine a and b or a and c or b and c, the mutant form is found, but it will not be found if d is one of the pairs, i.e., if we combine a and d, b and d, or c and d. To guard against the possibility that a double insertion, simply by having more material, overcomes a mutational appearance, a check insertion of a pair such as ab and $+$ in Fig. 2–13 can be made. This second kind of insertion, called the *cis* combination, should remove the mutant expression. By genetic analysis, limits can be set on the region within which two mutons operate to produce the same genetic effect and outside which the non-mutant material alters the effect of the mutant material. The two limits are the boundary of a *cistron*, indicated by the dashed lines in Fig. 2–13.

Benzer finds, by an elegant analysis of virus mutation, that the lowest rate of recombination is either zero or 0.02%. The total map length is estimated at 800% recombination units. When we compare this figure with the estimate of 80,000 nucleotide pairs in the genetic part of the bacterial virus studied, the correspondence indicates 0.01% recombination for one nucleotide pair, or an estimate of the *recon* as two nucleotide pairs. The same sort of reasoning gives five nucleotide pairs for the *muton*, and in one *cistron* there are over 100 locations at which a mutation can occur, or about 500 nucleotide pairs. Benzer makes the intriguing suggestion that a cistron corresponds to the whole set of nucleotides necessary to specify a single enzyme molecule. This type of study is very difficult, and it should be remembered that additional experiments are still needed to show that the conclusions are general.

In that it directly concerns enzyme formation, the phenomenon of induction of enzymes is related to genetics. Small molecules, which may or may not be substrates, can elicit the ability to synthesize new enzymes. Molecules that are very similar chemically can drastically inhibit this occurrence. The work of Pollock has shown that 100 penicillin molecules per cell will elicit the formation of penicillinase. When one considers the probable fate of many of these molecules, it seems likely that something in the order of 10 penicillin molecules, fixed in the right synthetic location, can give rise to the new enzyme synthesis. Thus the phenomenon of induction points again to the significant fact that small localized regions, of molecular or submolecular size, are basically responsible for living processes.

2–8 Molecular biophysics. The biophysicist's view of the living cell leads him to the study of the molecular processes of biology. By reviewing the content of this chapter, we can see that the chemical constitution, and the size, shape, and physicochemical behavior of biological molecules are of considerable interest. This is, however, only the beginning of molecular biophysics, for although thus far we know that the separate units involved in synthesis somehow reach their destination, we must learn *where* this is and *how* they reach it. To do so, the organization of molecular structure—the nature of the double lamellae seen in membranes, in retinal structure, and in organelles—has to be described and understood. The whole detailed character of chromosomal organization and structure must be studied, so that the effects of form and locale in the cell is known. And even when this huge task has been accomplished, the way in which molecules reach their destination—whether by diffusion, electrophoretic motion, or even by chemical destruction and resynthesis—must be described. This is a process involving almost all the kinetic knowledge of modern physics.

Even the answer to *where* and *how* is not enough, for there is then the question of the *ordered molecular development* that leads to accurate pairing of chromosomes for example, or to spindle formation in mitosis, or to sharp cleavage boundary as the cell divides. And superposed on all this is the tremendous significance of energy transfer, one of the very basic signs of life.

The topics covered in later chapters are all related to the study of molecular biophysics. Unlike the subjects of genetics or quantum mechanics, here the amount of knowledge that is solidly established is only a fraction of that needed to explain what we seek to describe. The critically minded reader must remember that without the discovery of chemical elements, e.g., of hydrogen and of discharge spectra, a finished subject like quantum mechanics could not have started. So we describe in future chapters the beginnings of cellular biophysics without apology. The finished subject, still hidden from man's imagination, will have all the beauty and precision of quantum mechanics. It is the aim of subsequent chapters to prod the imagination of research workers, and to collect in one place the modern knowledge that will lead to the finished material of the textbook of the 21st century.

PROBLEMS

1. Calculate the mass of the cell membrane of the bacterial cell described in this chapter, assuming it to consist of a layer of phospholipid-protein combination in the proportion of one molecule of phospholipid (1000 molecular weight) to one of protein (30,000 molecular weight) arranged in a double monomolecular layer. How does this compare with the total mass of phospholipid and of protein?

2. A bacterial cell divides in about 20 minutes. Assuming that every protein molecule is an enzyme and that all new protein has to be made from new amino acids, calculate the number of amino acids made per second per protein molecule. Compare this with the typical enzymatic rate given in Section 8–3.

3. Assume that a bacterium has no motility. Assume further, as found by Monod, that one-quarter of a particular small metabolite is incorporated into the bacterium. Suppose that one amino acid of limiting nature is present in the medium in a concentration of 1 mg/liter. What volume of medium must have made contact with the cell in 20 minutes? What is the radius of this volume, assumed to be spherical?

4. A single cell of *E. coli* is started on a suitable medium at (a) 15°C, (b) 35°C. How many cells will have developed in 24 hours in each case?

5. Hershey and Rotman were able to observe 0.15% separation and recombination of two genes in a bacteriophage. (a) Assuming that 10^{-5} Morgan is 30 A, calculate the separation between these genes. (b) Another pair showed a 15% figure. Assuming these to lie at opposite ends of the linkage group, calculate the length of the genetic line required. (c) The phage has a head of diameter 750 A and a tail of the same length. Comment on the molecular nature of the "gene string."

6. Novick and Szilard found that at 37°C a culture of *E. coli* gave 0.67 mutation per 10^8 bacteria per hour. Assuming there is only one gene to mutate per bacterium, calculate the half-life of the gene in years.

REFERENCES

1. A. W. POLLISTER, "Cytochemical Aspects of Protein Synthesis," in *Dynamics of Growth Processes*, ed. by E. Boell. Princeton University Press, Princeton, N. J., 1954, p. 33.

2. G. KNAYSI, "The Structure of the Bacterial Cell," in *Bacterial Physiology*, ed. by C. W. Werkman and P. W. Wilson. Academic Press, N. Y., 1951, p. 29.

3. H. QUASTLER, *Information Theory in Biology*. University of Illinois Press, Urbana, Ill., 1953.

4. *The Fine Structure of Cells*. Symposium at 8th Congress of Cell Biology, Leiden, 1954. P. Noordhof, Groningen, Netherlands.

5. G. PONTECORVO, in *Structural Aspects of Cell Physiology*. Academic Press, N. Y., 1954, and in *The Biological Replication of Macromolecules*, Academic Press, N. Y., 1958. Both are publications of the Society of Experimental Bioligists.

6. E. POLLARD, *The Physics of Viruses*. Academic Press, N. Y., 1953.

7. M. H. ADAMS, *Bacteriophages*. Interscience Publishers, N. Y., 1959.

8. S. BENZER, "The Elementary Units of Heredity," in *The Chemical Basis of Heredity*, ed. by McElroy and Glass. Johns Hopkins Press, Baltimore, Md., 1957.

9. E. BURNET and W. H. STANLEY, *The Viruses*. Academic Press, N. Y., 1959.

10. F. HERčIK, *Biophysik der Bakteriophagen*, VEB Deutscher, Verlag der Wissenschaften, Berlin, 1959.

11. F. JACOB and E. L. WOLLMAN, "The Relationship Between the Prophage and the Bacterial Chromosome in Lysogenic Bacteria," in *Recent Progress in Microbiology*, ed. by G. Tunevall. C. C. Thomas, Springfield, Ill., 1959.

12. T. F. ANDERSON, E. L. WOLLMAN, and F. JACOB, "Bacterial Conjugation." *Ann. Inst. Pasteur* **93,** 450 (1957).

CHAPTER 3

ENERGETIC AND STATISTICAL RELATIONS
IN THE LIVING CELL

3–1 Introduction. One of the basic attributes of life is its ability to utilize and convert energy. One gram of *Escherichia coli* bacteria develops energy at the rate of 0.6 watt, which is not unusual for bacteria. It is important for us to know the way in which this energy is transferred from one form to another and from one place to another. We might expect that the principles of a major branch of physics, *thermodynamics*, would be valuable in considering the biological process of energy transfer. It turns out that the contribution of thermodynamics to biology has in fact been rather unsensational, except as a form of bookkeeping. In this chapter we intend to explore the uses and the limitations of thermodynamics, treating the subject in its broad and modern sense.

Classical thermodynamics contributes two major principles to our study. The first is the generalized idea of the conservation of energy, according to which the total energy content of an isolated system remains constant, although it may change in form. When a source of energy is present, as in the case of illumination by light or consumption of food, the increase in energy of the system is exactly equal to the energy taken in by the system. This readily acceptable law, known as the *first law of thermodynamics*, is used by many sciences in different ways. In mechanical engineering it is used as a means of estimating the amount of mechanical energy available in some known transfer process. In electricity it is used to estimate the amount of chemical energy convertible into electrical energy, as in a battery, or of mechanical energy convertible to electrical energy, as in a generator. In chemistry it is used to estimate the amount of configurational energy of chemical combination that may appear or be lost in a chemical reaction. This last use is closer than any other to the one made in biology. We will discuss it at more length a little later. The other principle of classical thermodynamics we are concerned with is the *second law of thermodynamics*. This law is a statement of the impossibility of perpetual motion. In this doctrine, incorporated into the study of theoretical heat engines by Clausius and Kelvin, the term *entropy* first appeared, defined by Clausius in terms of an ideal process of heat transfer. In the hands of Gibbs and Boltzmann, entropy became a measure of the statistical probability of a system, and Gibbs was able to enlarge greatly on the laws of chemical equilibrium by using the idea that in any material change the entropy tends to increase, never to diminish. In this classical

42

form, thermodynamics has begun to be of some interest in studies of muscle action.

The 20th century has seen a new formulation of the second law of thermodynamics in terms of the statistics of molecular motion. Even more recently, an extension of thermodynamic formalism has been made by what is called *information theory*. The application of this science to biology has resulted in our acquiring some ability to classify cells and cellular units in terms of their information content and to inquire as to what changes of information take place during various cellular processes.

We must remember that thermodynamics and, indeed, information theory are not sciences which develop precise models. Thermodynamics, in its original form, was based on an entire absence of detailed description: it simply afforded a quantitative check on the possibility of some otherwise proposed set of events. So we must not expect to be led in this chapter to unravel molecular complexities or to see new simplicities in functions. We can, however, test the whole concept of molecular biophysics against these fundamental principles and attempt to gauge the plausibility of some hypotheses.

3–2 The conservation of energy in biological processes. It is now fully accepted that conservation of energy, in its general form, applies to biological systems. The experimental foundation for this belief began with Lavoisier and Laplace in 1777, was studied by Rubner in a series of experiments begun in 1885, and has been studied further by Benedict, Atwater, and Rosa.

Lavoisier and Laplace placed an animal and a block of ice in an insulated enclosure and by observing the rate at which the ice melted were able to estimate the total energy given up as heat by the animal. The amount of food that the animal used up in the process was roughly correlated with the energy released. Rubner later extended the experiment by measuring calorimetrically the total heat given off by a dog, at the same time measuring the oxygen intake and the release of carbon dioxide and water. These two end products of what could be described as combustion products that maintain the energy turnover of a living organism can be used to measure the chemical energy consumed. How this is done is now described.

Each type of science has its own convenient method of energy measurement. In electricity it is in terms of the product of voltage × current × time. In nuclear physics the velocity of single particles emitted in reactions is measured. In biology the amount of oxygen used up and CO_2 released forms the basis for the measurement of biochemical energy.

Because living tissue contains such a high proportion of carbon and hydrogen, the type of chemical-energy release in conversion of these two elements to CO_2 and water falls into a relatively narrow category. The only variable lies in the proportion of carbon to hydrogen, and this can be rather conveniently estimated from the ratio of CO_2 produced to oxygen taken in, a ratio known as the *respiratory quotient* (or RQ). Thus the oxidation of a mole of carbohydrate follows the equation

$$C_6H_{12}O_6 + 6O_2 \rightarrow 6CO_2 + 6H_2O + 678 \text{ kcal}$$

180	134.4	134.4	108
grams	liters	liters	grams

The ratio (volume CO_2)/(volume oxygen) is thus unity, and one liter of CO_2 produced yields 5.05 kcal.

The oxidation of fats, on the other hand, is not quite so simple to describe. The very simple lipid described by

$$H_2C\text{---}O\text{---}\overset{\overset{\displaystyle O}{\|}}{C}\text{---}CH_2\text{---}CH_3$$

$$HC\text{---}O\text{---}\overset{\overset{\displaystyle O}{\|}}{C}\text{---}CH_2\text{---}CH_3$$

$$H_2C\text{---}O\text{---}\underset{\underset{\displaystyle O}{\|}}{C}\text{---}CH_2\text{---}CH_3$$

would combine with $37O_2$ molecules to form $30CO_2$ and $26H_2O$, or there would be an RQ of 30/37, or 0.81 kcal. The average for lipids is 0.71 kcal, and for such oxidation each liter of oxygen used up corresponds to 4.69 kcal or 6.6 kcal for each liter of CO_2 produced.

Protein is a special case. Since protein contains a large amount of nitrogen, the amount of protein consumed can be estimated by observing the amount of nitrogen excreted. A separate calculation then determines the amount of energy turnover involved. For a typical experiment with a 12.75-kgm dog, we then obtain values like those in Table 3–1. The difference of 2.3% is reasonably expected, due to experimental errors. The aggregate of such experiments indicates the validity of the law of conservation of energy within 0.2%.

Measurements on smaller systems are complicated by the difficulty of measuring small quantities of heat. Thus, suppose we plan to work with one gram of bacteria. There is no problem at all in measuring roughly the evolution of heat by one gram, but since the check between chemical processes and heat evolution must be correct to one part in a thousand to have any particular significance, we are faced with the problem of measuring

TABLE 3-1

Total CO_2 exhaled per hour	3.44	liters
Total O_2 consumed per hour	4.35	liters
Amount of CO_2 associated with protein	0.647	liters
Amount of O_2 associated with protein	0.805	liters
Nonprotein RQ	0.79	
Caloric value per liter of O_2 at RQ 0.79	4.789	kcal
Nonprotein	16.86	kcal
Protein	3.60	kcal
Total calories by chemical reactions	20.46	
Total calories by thermal measurement	20.92	

accurately the respiration and chemical metabolism (requiring an open system with access to gas supplies) and the thermal rise (requiring a closed system). Undoubtedly modern microcalorimetry could achieve the necessary accuracy, but it has so far not been applied. In large measure this is because reasons to doubt the validity of the law of conservation of energy as applied to biology have not yet arisen.

3-3 Metabolism, or chemical and energy turnover. While a study of the applicability of the conservation of energy to biology may not be deemed rewarding, the study of respiration and of all forms of chemical turnover is important to all kinds of physiologists. Some of the results of such study are mentioned here, but the use of isotopic labeling to study molecular processes is deferred until Chapter 13.

In mammalian physiology the constancy of the total heat production per unit surface area, found among mammals, was remarkable. Over a wide range, from mouse to elephant, it was found that heat developed at the rate of about 1700 kcal/24 hr/m^2. Studies of mammalian tissue slices show that the rate of metabolism of various organs is not the same, being highest in brain and kidney cortex and relatively low in lung tissue. A part of the thermal development, especially in small animals, is muscular. For example, shivering plays a part in balancing energy produced and energy lost to environment.

Energy transfer in cells. A feature of cellular action that was pointed out by McIlwain is essential in any attempt to describe the processes of energy transfer in cells. He called attention to the rate of production of vitamin-like molecules in bacteria, which is very slow, as shown in Table 3-2. As McIlwain points out, these molecules are presumably made enzymatically, and the rate of action of almost any enzyme is of the order of 100 molecules turned out per enzyme molecule per second or *higher*. Thus in bacteria

TABLE 3–2

Compound	Organism	Molecules per cell	Average rate of production per cell per sec
Riboflavin	*Aerobacter aerogenes*	7–11,000	1.4–2
Biotin	*Aerobacter aerogenes*	400–1800	0.08–0.34
p-aminobenzoic acid	*E. coli*	17,000	3.3

there is no necessity for more than one or two enzyme molecules related to these vitamins to be present. This in turn opens the possibility that only one such enzyme molecule exists per cell.

The same sort of conclusion can be reached from a study of enzyme induction, already mentioned in Chapter 2. The enzyme beta galactosidase is present in *E. coli* cells grown on glucose in the ordinary way. If the cells are grown on lactose, which requires the adaptive formation of the same enzyme, the amount of enzyme can increase 1000 times. This amount is of the order of 1% of the protein in the cell. Since the enzyme has an unusually high molecular weight (400,000), we can conclude that before adaption, it formed one part in 100,000 of the protein in the cell, or about 5×10^{-18} gm. Converting from molecular weight to actual weight, we find that the weight of one enzyme molecule is $400,000 \times 1.67 \times 10^{-24}$, or roughly 7×10^{-19} gm. Thus there are not more than nine enzyme molecules per cell.

This leads us to the remarkable idea that for some factors (admittedly limiting) in cellular action, the whole process must take place *in the vicinity of one molecule*. Where this molecule is in the cell, how its substrate can reach it, and the considerable consequences of the formation of a second molecule are excellent subjects for thought. It is also clear that any process that occurs at a single molecule is not one to which the statistics of large numbers can be applied. So when we study the chemical and energy turnover of a living cell, the kinds of transfer mechanisms we encounter will hardly be those of a normal heat engine. Therefore we must consider the nature of chemical or configurational energy and its transfer.

Energy transfer in molecular systems. To understand energy transfer, we must discuss for a moment the nature of the forces between atoms. These are taken up in some detail in Chapter 6, but here we will need a few quite general ideas.

The forces between atoms are largely electrical in character. Superposed on the very ordinary electrical behavior, however, is the governing action of the laws of atomic physics. Thus if an electron can be shared between two atoms, a great modification occurs in the distribution of electric charge. Sometimes this modification results in a strong net attraction between the two atoms, sometimes in a repulsion. If for some reason (for example, the limitations imposed by the permissible number of electrons in an orbit) the electrons cannot be shared, only a very weak attractive force exists between the atoms. Indeed, at close separations there is a vigorous repulsion. Forces of intermediate magnitude are possible for various intermediate electronic configurations.

Suppose that two atoms which are part of a large molecular structure attract each other weakly. They will vibrate loosely about a mean position, and not a great deal of energy will be needed to separate them. But if a second large molecule approaches and by its influence so distorts the first molecule that the bonding electrons rearrange themselves so that the atoms are strongly attracted to each other, then the two atoms will now vibrate tightly in rapid oscillations and a great deal of energy will be needed to separate them. In a simple diatomic molecule, the process we have described could not happen unless some means were provided for the energy difference between the weak and strong attractive forces to leave, possibly by radiation or by transfer to some colliding molecule. In a big molecular system, the pair of atoms is surrounded by many other pairs of atoms, and what may well happen is that the energy freed by a first pair entering a more attractive state results in making another pair (or two or three other pairs) assume a less attractive state. Thus energy moves efficiently, and in big units, from one place to another. This is the standard method of energy transfer used in biological processes, and it is infinitely neater, faster, and more efficient than the statistical transfer of speed from one swarm of molecules moving at random to another swarm doing the same.

An excellent illustration of this type of configurational energy is the familiar "energy-rich phosphate bond." Such a bond is in reality itself rather weak. The attraction between oxygen and phosphorus is complicated by the fact that a second oxygen atom lies near the phosphorus. This prevents the realignment of an electron in configurations that cause attraction of phosphorus and other oxygen atoms. However, such a configuration is *stable* in the sense that there is a mean position to which the phosphorus and oxygen tend to return. Now suppose that a triphosphate, combined to some unit such as adenine and ribose, designated by A in Fig. 3–1, encounters a large molecule carrying a strategically placed and oriented water molecule. The collision results in the combination of water with the triphosphate, forming a more stable system, the diphosphate and orthophosphoric acid. Energy is released and passes directly to some point of excitation in the large molecule, where it is available, still as con-

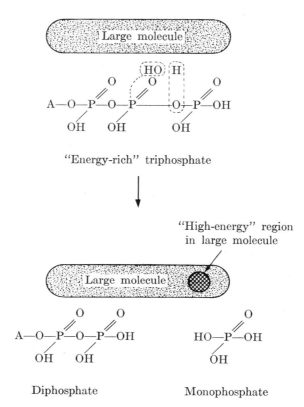

FIG. 3–1. A schematic representation of the process of transfer of the energy of chemical combination or, alternatively, of atomic configurational rearrangement.

figurational energy, for further transfer. The transfer is highly efficient. The result is the formation of a molecule of orthophosphoric acid with very stable bonding, and somewhere in the large molecule a new high-energy bond is formed. It may happen that instead of one new bond, several are formed, and this may, in turn, have an effect on the whole physical shape of the large molecule. Thus we can see how energy can in principle go directly from the original condition of latent chemical energy (or better, latent atomic configurational energy) to a molecule which can contract and actually perform work on an external system.

A great deal of biochemical literature concerns specific "high-energy" bonds. We should point out that wherever alternative atomic configurations exist in molecules and there is coupling between these different configurations, rapid and effective energy transfer can take place. It is for this reason that the subject of intermolecular forces is treated rather fully later on.

We digress for a moment to make a point about the interpretation of living synthesis and breakdown in terms of physical chemistry. In ordinary chemical processes there are two reasons for collisions between molecules. The first is the obvious one that contact must be made between the molecules that are to react, and the second is to provide a flexible means of transferring energy after the configurational alteration has happened. In biology, the nature of the cellular structure tells us that large molecular catalysts (proteins) are arrayed in their lamellae. Such proteins can easily offer a means for energy transfer, so that one of the two reasons for molecular collisions is now absent. A new question arises as to whether the cell actually gets a metabolite to the right place by waiting for it to diffuse there or whether, with the huge enzymatic surface the cell possesses and the broad similarity of chemical structure of its constituents, the cell finds it faster to *synthesize a metabolite in situ*. One task of molecular biophysics, then, is to examine the rapidity and effectiveness both of diffusion methods in transferring material from point to point in the cell and of any biosynthesis that can be conceived and described.

3–4 Statistical thermodynamics and biology. In the conventional way that the second law of thermodynamics is introduced in physics, it is clearly not applicable in biology. In physics the second law is used to discuss heat engines, where useful work is developed by means of large differences of temperature. Such temperature differences do not exist in biology; indeed, if a difference of even 10 degrees existed within a cell, the change in reaction rates would be so drastic as to render the working of the cell highly specialized, to use a great understatement. This fact has sometimes led physicists to wonder whether, in view of their rapid energy turnover, with no thermal differences, living systems operate contrary to the second law of thermodynamics. The chemist has no such worries because he is so accustomed to rapid energy transfers in chemical reactions with no thermal gradient that he is unable to see why biological systems offer any problem.

In reality, neither the old-fashioned heat-engine ideas of thermodynamics nor the Gibbsian version used in chemistry can be applied to living systems. Perhaps the most striking feature of a living system is its irreversibility or, in other terms, its lack of equilibrium. Because of this feature, all that can be done is to examine living systems in statistical terms, as is done in modern thermodynamics, and to consider the results as indicative of the way the cell operates. This use of statistics is valuable not only because it helps in cataloging and comparing cells, but also because it concentrates our attention on some of the ways in which the cell is dependent on its environment. When we use molecular statistics in this way, where rigorous application is not expected, it is worth while to go even beyond molecular statistics of the usual kind and to approach the subject

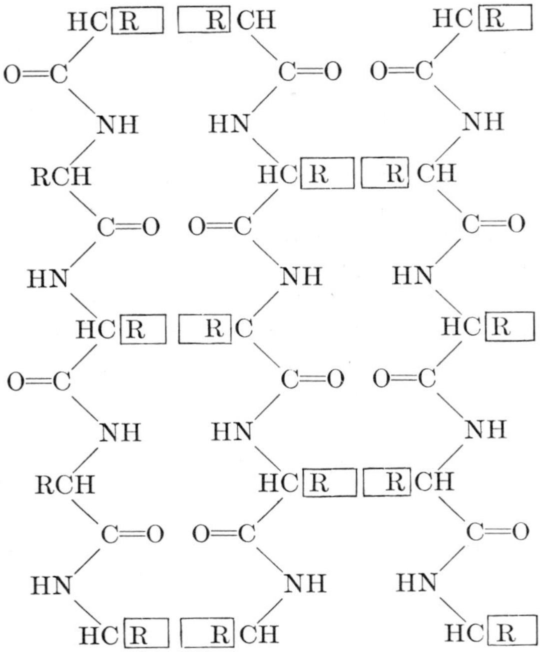

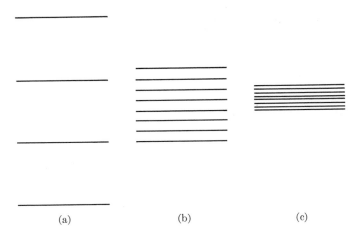

FIG. 3–2. A representation of part of a protein macromolecule. R represents an amino acid residue.

FIG. 3–3. A crude picture of the separation of the energy levels for vibration of (a) covalently bonded atoms, (b) hydrogen bonded atoms, and (c) van der Waals bonded atoms.

from the attitude of information theory, as we do the last part of this chapter. Use can also be made of the thermodynamics of irreversible systems which operate in a steady state.

The subject of thermodynamics is dominated by the use of terminology describing *quantitative* functions, such as energy and entropy, and *qualitative* functions, such as temperature and pressure. These functions were originally defined essentially experimentally. A very important feature of thermodynamics has been the absence of any model of the system, which in the past has meant an absence of error because knowledge of the actual processes is only speculative. It is possible to make the ideas expressed by these functions much clearer if a kind of schematic model is used in their definition. This use of a schematic model has been justified in atomic and molecular physics, which certainly cannot be classed as speculative subjects. Therefore, we now give a brief description of some thermodynamic functions according to a model based on the existence of energy levels.

To do this, let us take a particular substance, a protein molecule. Regardless of the actual structure proposed for it, a protein molecule possesses polypeptide chains linked to other chains in various ways to form the whole protein. The protein is represented schematically in Fig. 3–2. It can be seen in the figure that three classes of bond are present: covalent bonds in the chain itself; hydrogen bonds operating between members of the chain (if it is supposed to be a helix, as Pauling, Corey, and Branson have suggested); and van der Waals bonds between the residues of different chains. The problem of statistical description of such a molecule is to make an accounting of the degrees of vibrational excitation in the various bonds. The unfolded form was chosen for the figure because it is easy to draw, but it must be remembered that in any helical or folded form, the $C{=}O$ and NH groups take part in hydrogen bonding. For the purposes of this chapter, it is sufficient to suppose that the three general kinds of bond shown in the figure exist. These are all described in Chapter 6.

Each bond means that the atoms so attached have attained a position of equilibrium with respect to each other. If they are pushed together, they repel; if pulled apart, they attract. Each pair of atoms vibrates and, according to quantum mechanics, carries discrete amounts of vibrational energy known as *energy levels*. The stronger the bond, the farther apart and deeper are these levels. For the protein molecule, we can describe three broad classes of energy levels, as shown in Fig. 3–3.

In the process of statistical analysis we represent the number of pairs of atoms in any one of the energy levels by an occupation number, say N for the rth energy level, as pictured in Fig. 3–4, where only one set of energy levels is shown. Thus, for example, if we were treating the $-$NH groups only, the number of hydrogens attached to nitrogens and oscillating in the ground state ($r = 0$) would be counted and called N_0, the number in the

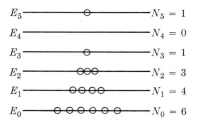

FIG. 3–4. Representation of occupation numbers for a single "ladder" of energy levels. The total energy in this form will be the sum of the occupation number times the appropriate energy of the level.

next energy level ($r = 1$) would be called N_1, and so on. If the energy value of any level is called E_r, we can see that the total energy in the macromolecule will be

$$N_0E_0 + N_1E_1 + N_2E_2 + N_3E_3 \ldots N_rE_r \qquad \text{or} \qquad \sum N_rE_r.$$

In making this kind of accounting, we need to remember that in a protein molecule there are many types of bonds, and thus many kinds of energy levels, and that they may also influence one another. So our description is intended to convey a concept rather than to be used in practice. Nevertheless, the idea is quite valid. If all types of energy levels are included and the counting is complete, we then have a definition for the most basic function in thermodynamics, the *internal energy*, defined as

$$U = \sum N_rE_r.$$

The definition is quite elementary and simple, and the usefulness of the model is at once apparent.

It is obviously very important to determine what values of N_r we may expect to encounter. In fact, one can almost say that as the energy levels and atomic configurations are settled by the rules of valence and interatomic attraction, the only factor left to thermodynamics is the determination of the values of N_r. There is one way to make a theoretical determination of the relative values of N_r, and that is to suppose that for a given form and total energy, a macromolecule will be found in the condition of maximum probability. This leads to the requirement that

$$N_r = \frac{Ne^{-E_r/kT}}{\sum e^{-E_r/kT}}, \qquad (3-1)$$

where N is the total number of vibrators, k is Boltzmann's constant, T is the absolute temperature, and the summation is over all permissible values of r. The major variable factor among the N_r is thus the Boltzmann factor, $e^{-E_r/kT}$, which is of primary importance in molecular statistics and will play a large part in any interpretations we employ in biophysics.

If we assume that equilibrium exists, i.e., that the values of N_r will not change with time, the ratio of the number of vibrators in two energy levels is given by the *Boltzmann distribution*. For example, the ratio of the number in level r to the number in level zero is given by

$$\frac{N_r}{N_0} = e^{-(E_r - E_0)/kT},$$

and if we take the lowest energy level as our zero of energy, then

$$\frac{N_r}{N_0} = e^{-E_r/kT}, \qquad E_0 = 0. \tag{3-2}$$

The total number of vibrators, N, is given by

$$N = \sum N_r = N_0 \sum e^{-E_r/kT} \tag{3-3}$$

If we solve Eq. (3–3) for N_0 and substitute it into Eq. (3–2), we obtain the result given by Eq. (3–1).

In using the above formula, we must remember that two limitations were applied in its derivation. The first was that the macromolecule actually is in the condition of maximum probability, and the second was that the values of N are large enough for approximations to factorials to apply. Both these are doubtful for a protein molecule, but they do apply to an assembly of protein molecules. Nevertheless, to see where statistical analysis leads, and not in the spirit of expecting incontrovertible predictions, we can try to apply results deduced under the assumption that these two limitations are valid. The reader should realize that in discussing single macromolecules, as we are doing here, we employ some vigorous approximations.

We can now define two more important quantities. The first is the *partition function*, Z, which is simply the sum of the Boltzmann factor for all the available energy levels:

$$Z = \sum e^{-E_r/kT}.$$

The partition function is also called the "Zustandsumme," or "sum over states." Quite apart from the fact that it is a useful function, as shown in Eq. (3–1), it has an intuitive meaning. The average energy of a vibration is given by kT, and at a given temperature this is the value we normally expect. Now, $e^{-E_r/kT}$ will only have reasonable magnitudes when E_r is not much larger than kT. Thus, even e^{-4} is 0.03 and e^{-10} is 4.5×10^{-5}. So in summing over this exponential, we are summing up the *accessible states*, the states for which any reasonable chance of becoming populated

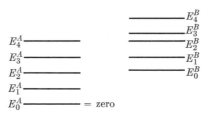

Configuration A Configuration B

FIG. 3–5. The possible energy levels of two configurations of a large protein or other macromolecule, illustrating the energy-level nomenclature used in discussing the equilibrium distribution between two possible conditions of the molecule.

exists. It is these states that will divide the occupancy. Hence the name "partition function."

The partition function is important because the *total number of molecules* in a given configuration is proportional to the partition function for that system. Suppose, when equilibrium is established, we wish to compare the number of protein molecules in the configuration shown in Fig. 3–2 with the number in a configuration in which the chains have to be split apart. Let us call the first type of protein type A, designating its energy levels by E_r^A and the number of molecules in each level by N_r^A. The broken-chain protein will be given the superscript B. A schematic representation of the energy levels is shown in Fig. 3–5. Of course, the analysis we shall go through is general and applies to all systems, not just to proteins.

In each configuration, the Boltzmann distribution holds, so we can write

$$N_r^A = N_0^A\, e^{-E_r/kT}.$$

As before, the total number N^A of type A is given by

$$N^A = \sum N_r^A$$
$$= N_0^A \sum e^{-E_r/kT},$$

which by definition of Z^A reduces to

$$N^A = N_0^A Z^A. \tag{3–4}$$

We see immediately that the total number of molecules is proportional to the partition function.

We must be slightly more careful in applying these ideas to configuration B because its lowest energy level, as shown in Fig. 3–5, is not zero energy but E_0^B. Now we have

$$N_r^B = N_0^B e^{-(E_r^B - E_0^B)/kT}$$

and

$$N^B = \sum N_r^B = N_0^B \sum e^{-(E_r^B - E_0^B)/kT}$$

$$= N_0^B e^{E_0^B/kT} \sum e^{-E_r^B/kT}$$

$$= N_0^B e^{E_0^B/kT} Z^B. \tag{3-5}$$

But the Boltzmann distribution also gives the ratio of the number of molecules in the zero levels as

$$\frac{N_0^B}{N_0^A} = e^{-E_0^B/kT},$$

and if this relation is substituted into Eq. (3–5), we see that

$$N^B = N_0^A Z^B. \tag{3-6}$$

Therefore the ratio of *total numbers of molecules* in the two configurations, which is the equilibrium constant K, is given by

$$K \equiv \frac{N^B}{N^A} = \frac{Z^B}{Z^A} = \frac{\sum e^{-E_r^B/kT}}{\sum e^{-E_r^A/kT}}. \tag{3-7}$$

As we implied before, the ratio of the total numbers of molecules depends on *all* the energy levels, not just on the energy difference between E_0^A and E_0^B. Therefore, measurements of equilibrium distributions give information about the partitition functions *only*, *not* about the energy levels. So it is fruitful to define other quantities derived from the partition function, which are also measurable. One of these is the *Helmholtz free energy per mole*, A, which is useful in discussing reactions or equilibria at constant volume. It is defined (if we use Avogadro's number, N_0, and remember that the gas constant $R = N_0 k$) as

$$A \equiv -N_0 kT \ln Z = -RT \ln Z.$$

While the partition function is simply a number, A is an *energy*. Since it contains the partition function as part of its definition, it can be looked upon as a dual quantity composed of the total average energy $N_0 kT$ times a factor that depends on how many states are available among which to divide the energy. If this definition is used in Eq. (3–7), we obtain (using ΔA to denote $A^B - A^A$)

at constant volume:

$$K = \frac{e^{-A^B/RT}}{e^{-A^A/RT}} = e^{-(A^B - A^A)} = e^{-\Delta A/RT}$$

or

$$\Delta A = -RT \ln K. \tag{3–8}$$

The measurement of the equilibrium constant at constant volume gives the change in the Helmholtz free energy.

Most biological systems are investigated under conditions of *constant pressure*; in this case, a molecular system such as a protein can change its energy not only by a change in the energy-level distribution but also by a change in its volume. A change in volume, ΔV, at constant pressure p requires an extra amount of energy, $p \Delta V$. In our previous formulation we neglected this term. If a molecular system has a volume per mole V, then we can associate an additional energy pV/N_0 with *each* molecular energy level, which means that each term in the partition function is multiplied by $e^{-pV/N_0 kT} = e^{-pV/RT}$. Thus the expression for the equilibrium constant must be written

at constant pressure:

$$K = \frac{e^{-pV^B/RT} Z^B}{e^{-pV^A/RT} Z^A} = e^{-p\Delta V/RT} \frac{Z^B}{Z^A}, \tag{3–9}$$

where ΔV represents $V^B - V^A$. If we ask that this expression have the same form as Eq. (3–8), we are led to the definition of the *Gibbs free energy* per mole, F:

$$F = pV - RT \ln Z. \tag{3–10}$$

At constant pressure $\Delta F = F^B - F^A = p \Delta V - RT \ln Z^B/Z^A$, so at constant pressure

$$e^{-\Delta F/RT} = K = N^B/N^A$$

or

$$\Delta F = -RT \ln K. \tag{3–11}$$

This is the expression we have labored so long and hard to obtain. It is important only because the value of ΔF in a reaction determines the equilibrium constant. We shall meet ΔF time and time again in our analysis of biological systems. It should go without saying that the units to be used for ΔF are those of RT. They could be ergs/mole, calories/mole, ergs/molecule, or electron volts/molecule.

In classical thermodynamics, the entropy, S, is usually defined first, and then the free energy is given as a derived function by the relation

$$F = U + pV - TS.$$

In our statistical approach, we first define the free energy, which is by far the more important quantity for us, and the entropy then appears as a secondary definition. Obviously there are no alterations in the basic thermodynamic formulas.

Although we have introduced the ideas of internal energy and of free energy, and thus can formally claim to have also introduced entropy, we have hidden one valuable intuitive aspect of entropy. It is possible to set up some simple basis for calculating the probability of some molecular condition. For example, we could say that the greater the number of ways in which the condition can be achieved, the greater the probability of that condition. When this is done, with W representing the number of ways, we can put

$$S = k \ln W.$$

Viewed in this way, entropy and order can be linked. The more ordered a system is, the fewer the number of ways in which its condition can be achieved, which means its entropy is less. By interpretation, we can therefore think of entropy as related to lack of order. A tidy room has low "entropy"; three children can rapidly increase the entropy.

The quantity W is not strictly a probability, but is a number related to it. We shall not need to calculate entropy in this way, and so for our purposes all we need is the rather simple concept expressed in the definition.

3–5 The theory of absolute reaction rates. A large range of biological and biochemical reaction rates can be understood by means of the theory of absolute reaction rates, due first to an idea put forth by Wigner and Polanyi and developed with great skill and insight by Eyring and his associates. It is interesting that the application of this theory to macromolecules is easier to discuss than the application to "simpler" chemical reactions, largely because the macromolecule forms a natural frame of reference.

In discussing this theory, let us take a very artificial process. Suppose we have a protein molecule of the form shown in Fig. 3–2, and we imagine that the whole right-hand chain becomes detached by some means. The question is, can we find some means to describe the probability per second that this may happen? Incidentally, if we have n protein molecules and the probability of transition per second is k_1, we know that in a short interval dt the probability is $k_1 \, dt$. If we retain n for the undamaged protein molecules, there results the relation

$$\frac{-dn}{n} = k_1\, dt,$$

which integrates very simply to yield

$$\ln \frac{n}{n_0} = -k_1 t,$$

where n_0 is the initial number of protein molecules for $t = 0$ and t is the total elapsed time. Since n/n_0 is a *ratio*, the above equation holds for any measurable quantity proportional to n, for example, enzyme activity or antibody precipitation. For this very simple case, n does not have to be known explicitly.

The point of view taken by Eyring is simply this. The act of moving away is always essentially *translation*, i.e., linear, one-way motion. So we surmise that the separation of the right-hand chain involves bringing it to a condition such that a translational motion will separate it, and then we see how fast such motion will make the break final. The *coup-de-grace* of translational motion turns out to be capable of very general description: if a small region of space supposedly has to be traversed to cause breaking, then the probability of traversal per unit time is independent of the size of the small region and is given (for this part only) by the expression

$$\frac{kT}{h},$$

where h is Planck's constant. Planck's constant enters because even translational motion in a small region of space is quantized, and this in turn determines the velocity of motion. So the inevitable constant of quantization shows up.

In our discussion of the act of breaking apart, we have *presupposed* that the right-hand chain has reached the condition where pure translation can remove it. To have this condition reached by the random action of thermal agitation, we have to reckon on the relative probability of reaching this unstable condition. This will depend not only on the relative probability of a certain amount of energy being available in the bonds near the right-hand chain, but also on *the number of forms over which this energy fluctuation can be distributed*. It can be seen that it is reasonable to use the free energy, which is a composite function including an energy term and a term related to the number of available energy states, to describe this requirement for starting the separation of the chain. In Eyring's formulation, the condition in which translation alone can cause separation is called the *activated state*, and it is the difference in free energy between the initial and the activated state (usually denoted as $\Delta F^{\ddagger}$) that determines the relative probability of reaching this condition. By means of our straightforward statistical analysis, we find that the probability term is the relative number of molecules in the activated state, given by Eq. (3–11), or

$$e^{-\Delta F^{\ddagger}/RT}.$$

The over-all value for k_1, the rate at which the right-hand chain splits away, is then

$$k_1 = \frac{kT}{h}\,e^{-\Delta F^{\ddagger}/RT}. \tag{3–12}$$

The value of $\Delta F^{\ddagger}$ in Eq. (3–12) is usually given in calories/mole to correspond to a value of 1.98 cal/mole/°K for R. This usage develops some rather strange listings in tables, as for example a "mole" of bacteria or even of grasshoppers. It does give the value of $\Delta F^{\ddagger}$ in units normally encountered in chemistry, which are quite as sensible as "electron volts."

If it should happen that the detached right-hand chain can return to the original configuration, then a reversible process exists. The return reaction is of course conditioned by the same relation, and if k_2 is the reaction constant and $\Delta F_1^{\ddagger}$ is the free-energy change necessary for the chain to reach the activated state, we have

$$k_2 = \frac{kT}{h}\,e^{-\Delta F_1^{\ddagger}/RT}.$$

Equilibrium is reached when as many chains break away as return per unit time, and this means that $k_1 n_1 = k_2 n_2$, where n_1 and n_2 denote the numbers of protein molecules of each kind at the equilibrium condition. Therefore

$$\frac{n_2}{n_1} = \frac{k_1}{k_2} = e^{-(\Delta F^{\ddagger} - \Delta F_1^{\ddagger})RT} = e^{-\Delta F/RT},$$

where ΔF is the difference in free energy between the original and detached forms. This illustrates that the equilibrium distribution does not depend on the speed with which equilibrium is reached.

These relations are, with certain limitations, rather easy to measure. Thus one of the conveniently numerical branches of biology is that concerned with thermal changes, whether of inactivation, or of denaturation, or of equilibrium. It is important to see what these studies can tell us. In the first place, we can *represent* the above process rather simply by a free-energy diagram as shown in Fig. 3–6. This type of representation is helpful in that it brings to mind the very simple process of crossing a hump and is helpful in forming a first concept. After this moment of insight, the reader must remind himself that it is free energy which is being plotted,

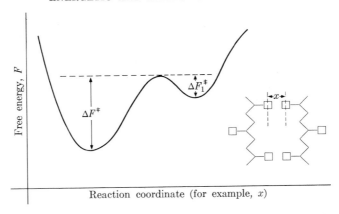

FIG. 3–6. Plot of free energy *versus* a reaction coordinate. The reaction coordinate can be quite general in nature, but a particular instance is shown in the inset. The "activated state" is shown as ‡, and the various values of free-energy changes are designated.

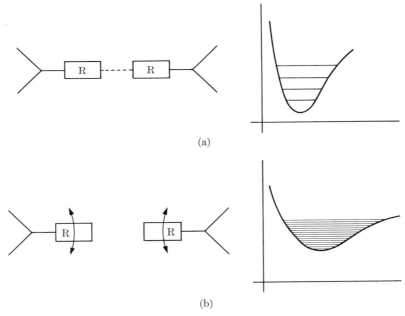

FIG. 3–7. Illustration of one way in which free energy can increase when a separation of grouping within a macromolecule occurs. In (b) a set of loose back-and-forth oscillations are possible, producing many closely spaced energy levels. In (a) the binding of the residues stiffens the oscillation, forcing the energy levels farther apart. These more widely separated levels are not as readily available for partition as the set in case (b). Thus the term $\ln Z$ is greater in case (b) than in case (a).

and that free energy contains *both* the idea of energy *and* of the ways it is shared among energy levels.

If we return to the schematic formula for the protein molecule, we can see that in the case where the chain on the right is attached, the atoms near the end of the residues are bound. Thus a whole class of pendulumlike oscillations are stiffened, with a consequent reduction of the free energy. If we consider the one such pair shown in Fig. 3–7, the bound condition shows stiff oscillations with widely separated levels, so that only one value of E_r may contribute to $\sum e^{-E_r/kT}$. When separation occurs, the levels will be much closer together and several terms may be present, making the partition function greater and accordingly making F greater.

The reader will see that groups of closely spaced levels are a big factor in changing F. Unfolding chains will increase these, but the most spectacular increase occurs when a free rotation of a small molecule is permitted. A notable small molecule is water, which can rotate in three quantized ways, with closely spaced energy levels. Therefore any water, either freed or bound, causes an appreciable change in $\sum e^{-E_r/kT}$ and so in F. Thus, when unusual values of ΔF are observed, the first cause to suspect is freed or bound water.

When measurements of enzyme inactivation (to pick one example) are made, the values of F found by applying the equation

$$k_1 = \frac{kT}{h} e^{-\Delta F^{\ddagger}/RT}$$

are not usually found to be constant. A fairly large range of results can be expressed in terms of a variation of F linearly with T. These results are usually described by invoking the thermodynamic relations

$$F = U + pV - TS \qquad \text{or} \qquad F = H - TS,$$

where the free energy F referred to is the Gibbs free energy, and H is the enthalpy. Ordinarily experiments are carried out at fixed temperatures and pressures, so that we obtain

$$\Delta F^{\ddagger} = \Delta U + p\,\Delta V^{\ddagger} - T\,\Delta S^{\ddagger} = \Delta H^{\ddagger} - T\,\Delta S^{\ddagger}.$$

When the pressures applied are high, the term in $p\,\Delta V^{\ddagger}$ can assume great importance. Ordinarily it is customary to describe $\Delta F^{\ddagger}$ simply as above, in terms of $\Delta H^{\ddagger}$ and $\Delta S^{\ddagger}$. Now we can note a very simple particular case for F, where only one additional level is introduced. Then we have

$$Z = e^{-E/kT}, \qquad \ln Z = -E/kT,$$
$$F = -N_0 kT \ln Z = +EN_0.$$

The free energy is thus the number of bonds times this energy value. *Only* in such a case can the free energy be expressed directly as an energy, regardless of the sharing among levels.

When we write $\Delta F^{\pm} = \Delta H^{\pm} - T\,\Delta S^{\pm}$, we are looking at the free energy as made up of two terms, one of which has the dimensions of a pure energy jump and the other of a more distributional character. Unfortunately the insight given by this view is largely illusory, because the value of $\Delta H^{\pm}$, being in fact *not* due to a single physical energy level but to a kind of weighted average of many, does not correlate with single processes, and the entropy term itself includes both energy changes and distribution changes. However, from the point of view of cataloging and comparing, values of $\Delta H^{\pm}$ and $\Delta S^{\pm}$ are useful. Note that the analysis of thermal inactivation of enzymes, for example, will often yield values of $\Delta H^{\pm}$ of about 60,000 calories per mole and values of $\Delta S^{\pm}$ of 30 calories per mole per degree. Identification of $\Delta H^{\pm}$ with a *single* energy transition is not experimentally justified. The theory does not suggest that it can be; it is only numerological temptation that makes us attempt the correlation.

3–6 Thermal inactivation. The behavior of enzymes at different temperatures is discussed in Chapter 8. However, a few paragraphs will be devoted here to the topic of thermal inactivations. A whole class of biological systems (viruses, bacteria, enzymes, antibodies) lose their biological function according to the simple relation,

$$\ln \frac{\text{function surviving after time } t}{\text{function orginally present at initial time}} = -k_1 t. \qquad (3\text{–}13)$$

Measurements of k_1 have been made for a great number of cases. These can be analyzed by the theory just outlined, and values of $\Delta F^{\pm}$ can be found. When this is done, one simple generalization can be made. Substances inactivated when dry yield values of $\Delta F^{\pm}$ that vary extremely slowly with temperature: often not at all, and sometimes increasing very gradually. Substances inactivated when wet show a considerable variety in the way in which $\Delta F^{\pm}$ depends on temperature, the most characteristic being a rather rapid rate of *decrease*.

These two results are of some interest both theoretically and practically. From the practical viewpoint, the decrease of $\Delta F^{\pm}$ results in a very sharp thermal instability above a certain temperature. For example, when wet, influenza virus will pass from being very nearly stable to inactivation within minutes in a range of 10 degrees. In the dry state, a much wider range of temperature can be tolerated. Indeed, tobacco mosaic virus in the dry state resists inactivation for several minutes at

TABLE 3–3

VALUES OF $\Delta H^{\neq}$ AND $\Delta S^{\neq}$ FOR SOME BIOLOGICAL
SYSTEMS WHERE FUNCTION DEPENDS ON TEMPERATURE

System	$\Delta H^{\neq}$, cal/mole	$\Delta S^{\neq}$, cal/mole/°K
Inactivation of tobacco mosaic virus (TMV)		
Dry	27,000	0
Wet	40,000	18
Denaturing TMV	195,000	410
Inactivation of bacteriophage T1		
Dry	27,500	0
Wet	95,000	207
Feeding rate of grasshoppers	20,300	—

150°C. From the theoretical point of view, the fact that a dry substance has a constant $\Delta F^{\neq}$ means that the molecule does not change its condition appreciably as temperature is increased, the only apparent effect being the release of a few vibrational energy levels due to thermal expansion. In the wet state, it is clear that the amount of hydration is exerting a big effect on the value of $\Delta F^{\neq}$. Since this is *less* as the temperature increases, we can suppose that the free energy of the activated state remains about the same but that the free energy of the normal state increases. This could possibly be due to swelling of the hydrated molecule, resulting in an increase in freedom for water molecules to vibrate or rotate. In Table 3–3 a few values for thermal inactivation constants are given.

3–7 The entropy transfer of living organisms. In the last few sections we digressed to consider rates of reactions and their relation to free-energy values. We now return to the subject of how free energy and entropy enter into the transfer processes of living systems.

Let us consider a bacterium at its maximum rate of growth. We can think of this in terms of Fig. 3–8. The bacterium is an organized structure, growing steadily and presumably developing specific protein and nucleic acid polymers, and assembling these into organelles and chromatin strings. This is an ordered structure and so will have low entropy. The first conclusion is thus that living cells diminish entropy. Since the second law of thermodynamics requires that the entropy of the inside and the outside either be unchanged or increase, there has to be a great enough increase in the entropy outside to more than match the entropy decrease

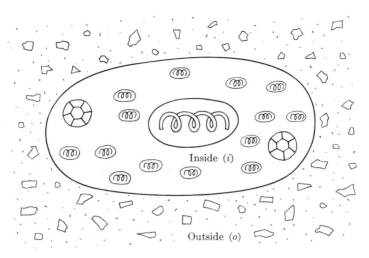

FIG. 3–8. A schematic diagram of a bacterium in its metabolic environment. The bacterium is metabolizing and growing, using small molecules in rather large amounts and incorporating them into structured organelles. Thus both free energy and entropy are being changed. Thermodynamics requires that $\Delta S_i + \Delta S_o \geq 0$ and $\Delta F_i + \Delta F_o \leq 0$.

inside, as Schrödinger pointed out very clearly in 1944. Therefore, the material on which the cell lives and grows is itself not in a high entropy state but in a low one which can, by metabolic processes, be made higher. Schrödinger describes this as "living on negative entropy."

Linschitz has made a very useful calculation of the entropy content of a bacterial cell. To do this calculation, we employ the two requirements of thermodynamics that (1) there must be either a zero change or an increase in the entropy of the entire system of Fig. 3–8 so that

$$\Delta S_i + \Delta S_o \geq 0,$$

where S_i and S_o refer to entropy inside and outside, respectively, and (2) the total free energy must either remain the same or diminish, so that, with the same kind of notation,

$$\Delta F_i + \Delta F_o \leq 0.$$

Now, in order to calculate, we need to use equalities. In reality we can expect some free-energy loss, but even so the efficiency is really quite high and our result is not much in error if we make the assumption that, in the limiting case, the above relation is an equality. So

$$\Delta F_i = -\Delta F_o.$$

Ordinarily we do not measure free energy directly, but measure heats of re-action or values of changes in H. Then, by using the relation $F = H - TS$, we have

$$\Delta H_i - T\,\Delta S_i = -\Delta F_o$$

or

$$\Delta S_i = \frac{\Delta H_i + \Delta F_o}{T}.$$

For autotrophic bacteria, growth can take place on amazingly simple media. Linschitz picked *B. pycnoticus*, which uses H_2 for energy supply, enabling us to calculate ΔF_o, and uses CO_2 (as bicarbonate) for carbon supply, enabling us to calculate ΔH_i. By using the thermal values

$$2H_2 + O_2 \rightarrow 2H_2O; \qquad \Delta H = -56 \text{ kcal per } H_2$$

and

$$6CO_2 + 6H_2O \rightarrow C_6H_{12}O_6 + 6O_2; \qquad \Delta H = +675 \text{ kcal}$$

and the fact that eight moles of H_2 are used per mole of CO_2, we find that, the figures per gram of carbon (1/12 mole),

$$\Delta F_o = \frac{8}{12}(-56) = -37.4 \text{ kcal/gm,}$$

$$\Delta H = \frac{1}{72}(675) = 9.4 \text{ kcal/gm.}$$

Note that 72 is the molecular weight of the carbon incorporated into glucose, so that for one gram, 1/72 of the thermal value for H must be taken.

When we use a value of 300°K for T, the value of ΔS_i then becomes

$$\Delta S_i = \frac{9.4 - 37.4}{300} = \frac{-28 \text{ kcal}}{300} = -93 \text{ cal/deg/gm of cellular carbon.}$$

Using the approximation that 10% of the bacterial cell is carbon and one cell has a mass of 10^{-12} gram, we find that the mass of carbon per cell is 10^{-13} gm. Therefore the *entropy per cell is* -9.3×10^{-12} cal/deg.

Morowitz has pointed out that direct measurements of the value of ΔQ, the heat associated with the production of one microorganism of *E. coli*, have been made by Bayne-Jones and Rhees, who give the figure for exponential growth as 4×10^{-10} cal per organism at 37.5°C. If we take S as $-Q/T$ and T as 310.5°K, we have $S = -1.3 \times 10^{-12}$ cal/deg, which is really rather close to Linschitz' figure, especially since it concerns a different bacterium.

These values are, in themselves, interesting data for a cell. In what follows, we show how information theory, by making use of these values, can give some idea of the inherent complexity of the cell.

3–8 Information theory. Relation between information and entropy.
Recent developments in electronics and communications have led to the
realization that general properties related to what might be called the
"assembly of a pattern" exist. The pattern may consist of the display on a
cathode-ray tube, which has to be assembled from currents developed in
a series of vacuum tubes by the received signal, or of a set of sound vibrations of variable frequency and amplitude impressed on an ear. Problems
such as these seem to have a common general feature, and this observation
has been formulated by Shannon as a new theory called "information
theory."

Information theory is recognized as having application far beyond the
telegraph wire. A collection of essays on the topic of information theory
and biology has been made by Quastler, and before we proceed to the
usual definitions and formalism, it is worth while to see what new approaches are made available by information theory. Perhaps one of the
most interesting of these is the use of known *diversity* to give a numerical
description. The mere fact that there are, say, 600 *kinds* of enzyme, enables us to make a numerical estimate of the specificity of an enzyme.
This can then be compared with, say, antigen-antibody specificity on the
same numerical basis. When we are faced with extremely complex systems, information theory can also be used to gain some idea of *how complex*
the system really is. In this sense information theory is salutory, for it
can be a starting point for a numerical analysis that may well be picked
up and finished in a quite different fashion. Quastler points out that in
biology information theory, which uses only one dimension, can be applied
to a model in which steric restraints are three dimensional and hard to
visualize. In this way it is a convenient tool for excluding hypotheses.
It does not tell how to do something, but rather *how difficult it is to do.*

With this brief introduction we can give a skeleton account of information theory and show a few applications to biology.

Definition of information. If an event has a probability p of occurring
before a "message" is received and a probability p' of occurring after the
message is received, the information in the message is **H**, where

$$\mathbf{H} = \log_2 \frac{p'}{p}.$$

To see how this operates, suppose that we have to pick out one letter from
a total of 16 letters. Then, before picking, $p = 1/16$, while after the
selection is made, $p' = 1$, so $p'/p = 16$. Now $2^4 = 16$, and $\log_2 16 = 4$,
or there are 4 *bits* of information. Thus **H** as defined above is in what we
call "bits," an attractive name and one made respectable by being the
contraction of "binary units."

This definition of information bears an obvious similarity in concept to
the definition of entropy as $k \log W$, for W is a measure of probability.

One very interesting aspect of information theory becomes evident when this similarity is examined further. The first case in which such an examination was made concerns "Maxwell's demon." This perceptive and intelligent creation of Maxwell's mind was supposed to be able to let fast molecules through and shut out slow molecules, thus raising the temperature in one place and lowering it elsewhere, without doing any work. Such a process contradicts the second law of thermodynamics. Szilard, in 1929, pointed out that the process of reducing the entropy required the use of information, and in 1951 Brillouin made the definite suggestion that the amount of negative entropy supplied had a numerical correspondence to the amount of information used to produce the entropy diminution. Brillouin, incidentally, also pointed out that if the information is obtained physically (e.g., from a flashlight illuminating the molecules), then no entropy decrease occurs.

The correspondence between entropy and information can be obtained in several ways. Perhaps the simplest, due to Linschitz, is as follows. If the total number of possible configurations available to a molecule is P, then this is a measure of the probability, and hence of the entropy, by the relation $S = k \ln P$. But to determine which configuration exists, we have to make $\mathbf{H}$ binary choices, where

$$2^{\mathbf{H}} = P \qquad \text{or} \qquad \mathbf{H} \ln 2 = \ln P.$$

Therefore

$$S = k\mathbf{H} \ln 2 \qquad \text{or} \qquad \mathbf{H} = \frac{S}{k \ln 2}.$$

The values of $\mathbf{H}$ and S refer to one molecule. Normally k is in ergs. If calories per mole per degree is used for S, we have

$$\mathbf{H} = \frac{S}{R \ln 2},$$

where $R = 1.98$ cal/mole/deg.

So far we have used the simplest kind of definition of information. If all the possible states are not equally probable, but the expected value of the ith state is p_i, then the definition of information becomes*

$$\mathbf{H} = -\Sigma p_i \log_2 p_i.$$

---

* Note that for the previously considered case, where equal expectation existed, $p_i = 1/p$ in all cases and

$$\mathbf{H} = -\sum \frac{1}{p} \log \frac{1}{p} = -\sum \frac{1}{p} (\log 1 - \log p)$$

$$= \sum \frac{1}{p} \log p = p \cdot \frac{1}{p} \log p = \log p.$$

We can show directly that the change in entropy occasioned by the selection and removal of one particular state is the negative of the information contained in that state.

Thus we have two ways of determining information: (1) directly in terms of binary choices or the more elaborate relation $\mathbf{H} = -p \log_2 p$, and (2) in terms of physical entropy changes.

3–9 Information content of some biological systems. We first employ the method of binary choices. As an example, consider a protein molecule, which by its very nature has one or more polypeptide chains. The forms of these chains are not very diverse, numbering perhaps eight. To select one kind of chain out of eight requires three binary choices, or three bits. Suppose there are 1000 residues selected from among 20 amino acids. Each selection involves very nearly four bits. (Actually one out of 16 is four bits, but the frequency of amino acids is not uniform, so that by asking for the more likely ones first, the actual amino acid can be specified in less than four bits, but not much less.) Each choice has to be made 1000 times, so there are 4×10^3 bits in a particular protein of a particular form. To choose the form requires three bits, so the total information content of a protein is still effectively 4×10^3 bits, although admittedly the computation is rough.

In a nucleic acid molecule, the four bases require that any one base can be specified by two bits. Thus, apart from any differences in type of molecule, a nucleic acid molecule contains twice the number of nucleotides. Since a nucleotide has a molecular weight of about 250, a nucleic acid molecule of molecular weight 10^6 has 4000 nucleotides, making 8000 bits altogether. It is interesting that such a nucleic acid molecule has about the same information content as a protein molecule of less than a fifth its molecular weight. Quastler has pointed out that if a correspondence between nucleic acid and protein exists, as is essential if nucleic acid is involved in protein synthesis, then to get an equivalent amount of information the nucleic acid molecule has to be bigger than a protein molecule. If there is a purine-pyrimidine correlation, as proposed in some DNA models, then there is only one bit per nucleotide, and it would be expected that for equal information content a DNA molecule would have to be 10 times as large as a protein molecule. This is, roughly speaking, what is observed.

We can now turn to a very different approach to the information content of a protein and ask about the number of bits of information involved in, say, enzyme-substrate combination or in an antigen-antibody combination. This can be answered *directly* in one or two individual cases. If we take the action of urease on urea, and assume that the urea molecule must lie in a definite orientation and have the correct molecular dimensions, we can argue thus. To specify any substrate, say urea, involves the specification that it contains 10 atoms (about three bits) and that each atom be specifically identified (about one bit per atom), making 13 bits. About four more bits may be needed, because the 10 atoms can combine in more than one way, and the right way (urea) must be chosen. Therefore the selection of the substrate involves, roughly, 17 bits.

This amount of information is more than is needed for the enzyme-substrate combination and subsequent reaction. Thus we have excluded all sorts of 10-atom combinations, and indeed configurations of more than 10 atoms, and in so doing have required information. However, the enzyme may actually react with many more combinations of atoms that are chemically much too hard to test. For example, thiourea has been totally excluded as a substrate, whereas, in fact, it is not excluded.

The problem, then, is to see how many of these 17 bits are needed if it is supposed that the important point in the interaction between urea and urease is the existence of complementary structures corresponding to the oxygen, carbon, and nitrogen atoms, as indicated in Fig. 3–9.

If we consider the pattern *alone*, without regard to any chemical similarity or attraction possibilities, then we can treat the carbon as the origin of a grid of squares, say $\frac{1}{5}$ A in size. If the requirement is that three particular squares be occupied by an atom and there are about 25 squares to choose from, then, since $25 = 2^{4.6}$, 4.6 bits are required for each square, or 13.8 bits altogether. If in place of a requirement of $\frac{1}{5}$ A and precision arrangement of all four major atoms we substitute $\frac{1}{3}$ A and only *three* major atoms (only two if the carbon is chosen as a starting point), then the number of bits shrinks to 6.5. The reader can clearly see that in this direct approach the actual process critically determines the amount of information deduced.

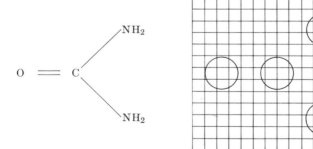

F ɪɢ. 3–9. Representation of one way to estimate the information necessary in an enzyme-substrate combination. The substrate is urea, and the specific surface of urease is divided into a grid. The fineness of division of the grid needed to specify the exact way in which the urea molecule must be placed will affect the number of bits of information required.

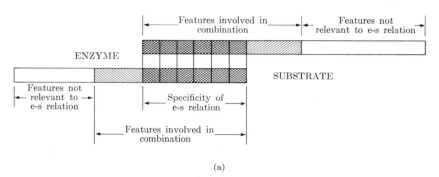

(a)

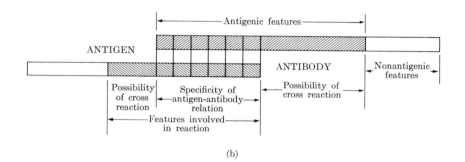

(b)

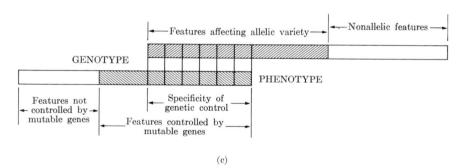

(c)

FIG. 3–10. Diagrammatic representations of the features which enter into (a) enzyme-substrate, (b) antigen-antibody, and (c) genotype-phenotype relations, due to Quastler. In each case the actual specific relation requires the common possession of a fraction of the total information present in the two related molecules.

A totally different viewpoint is possible. This is again due to Quastler. While the above treatment gives a figure for the information needed for some one method of operation, it is possible to ask how much information is biologically required regardless of any operational method. One way to answer this question is to ask how many enzymes there are, and then to say that any particular enzyme has to be chosen from among this number. Another method is to determine the number of possible substrates, and then to say that an enzyme must have the information necessary to pick out one of these. Taking the first approach, there are about 600 enzymes that can readily be conceived. To pick one out of these takes nine bits. The second approach requires some estimate of relative concentration. Quastler points out that 90% of the dry weight includes only 61 classes of substrate, and that 99% includes 300 classes of substrate. The selection of one substrate thus corresponds to seven bits, so that from the point of view of biological *necessity*, only seven to nine bits are involved in the enzyme-substrate process.

Of course, we cannot say that this last figure tells us the form of enzyme action. But we can say that if the evolutionary process has led to the simplest method that meets necessity, then highly elaborate and precision configurational matching is *not* necessary, and so may not be found. This is taken up again from a different point of view in Chapter 8.

A somewhat similar approach leads Quastler to the same kind of figure for antigen-antibody relationship and for genic control of a phenotype. The three diagrams in Fig. 3–10 illustrate how the information may be conceived as being operative for the enzyme-substrate, antigen-antibody, and gene-phenotype relationships. It will be seen that in each case there are both irrelevant features and features that might be concerned with specificity, plus the seven to nine bits concerned with specific relations.

3–10 Information content of a bacterial cell. Since a bacterial cell is actually the smallest object in which all the major functions of life are found (viruses being essentially parasites so far as this line of thought is concerned), an estimate of the information content of such a cell is of interest. Two such estimates have been made, one by Morowitz in terms of the direct approach of information theory and one by Linschitz based on physical entropy and its relation to information.

The direct approach has been likened to preparing the instructions for constructing a building from its component parts. If the building is to be made of bricks, then a three-dimensional grid can be imagined, forming a three-dimensional honeycomb of cells. To decide whether a brick is or is not in a cell is, then, the way in which the amount of information is reduced to a number. Obviously it makes a big difference whether the cellular framework set up in one's imagination is coarse or fine, and one decision that has to be made is whether the framework is too coarsely designed to describe the building, or whether it is so fine as to include slight cracks in the bricks, which are not relevant. This is one of the weaknesses of an estimate of information, but in spite of it, quite interesting figures can be developed.

A bacterial cell is made of water and solid material. A bacterial spore has nearly all its water content missing, and yet it can become vegetative and develop into a bacterium. So it is reasonable, as Morowitz points out, to consider the information content in the dry part. The problem then is to choose the right atoms and put them in the right places. The instructions for doing so, in binary form, are the information content. We give below a modification of Morowitz' method, which is very direct but not as rigorous as his.

To determine which atom of the 60 kinds present (all atoms are not found in living cells) should be chosen would appear to take nearly six bits. In fact, however, the elements are far from evenly distributed, so that the average number of binary choices to identify an atom is 1.5. We next need to know the number of atoms. If the average atomic weight is taken as six, the average atomic mass is $6 \times 1.67 \times 10^{-24}$ gm, and for a dry weight of 6×10^{-13} gm this means there are 6×10^{10} atoms to locate. Now the question of the fineness of the cellular structure has to be decided. If it is set at 2×10^{-10} cm, the vibrational amplitude of a nucleus, and we remember that the average spacing of atoms is about 2 A and we choose a cube of 8 A^3 as the region of uncertainty for an atom, the result would seem to fit with knowledge of the nature of atomic and molecular formations. This volume, in cm^3, is 8×10^{-24}, while that of vibrational amplitudes is 8×10^{-30}. The number of cells in our mental honeycomb is then $8 \times 10^{-24}/8 \times 10^{-30}$, or 10^6, an uncertainty which takes 20 binary choices. The total per atom is then 21.5, and since the total number of atoms is 6×10^{10}, the total information content is then 1.3×10^{12} or, in round numbers, 10^{12} bits.

Linschitz gave the figure 9.3×10^{-12} cal/deg or $9.3 \times 10^{-12} \times 4.2$ joules/deg for the entropy of a bacterial cell. Using the relation $\mathbf{H} = S/(k \ln 2)$, we find that the information content is

$$\frac{9.3 \times 10^{-12} \times 4.2}{1.4 \times 10^{-23} \times 0.69} = 4 \times 10^{12} \text{ bits.}$$

Morowitz' deduction from the work of Bayne-Jones and Rhees gives the lower value of 5.6×10^{11} bits, which is still in the neighborhood of 10^{12} bits. Thus two quite different approaches give rather concordant figures.

It must be pointed out that both methods tend to give high values. If the entropy calculated from the caloric values of the nutrient process is actually very wasteful, then the amount of entropy used to estimate information is lower. In the second approach, it is quite possible that many of the actual locations of atoms are not critical to life. Indeed, Holter has shown that a centrifuged amoeba that has actually developed stratification of its components can still live.

Even with these reservations, the value of 10^{12} bits is very high. Morowitz has pointed out that the random concatenation of a bacterium from its component atoms is very unlikely indeed. Those who wish to speculate on the origin of life can speculate about these values and see what impact they have on their prejudices.

We return to the method of estimating information. It is clear that the process chosen for assembly is most important. Referring again to the analogy of constructing a building, we can say that if walls are built by a process of pouring concrete into molds instead of the brick-by-brick method, the amount of information needed decreases. In the cell there is the possibility that certain growth patterns are *required* to develop from others. Thus if a string of nucleoprotein is placed in a mixture of a few enzyme molecules, salts, and amino acids and then a cell *has* to result, the information content is far less. For a bacterium, an estimate based on reasoning due to Dancoff and Quastler gives 10^4 bits. If such relative simplicity is at the base of living systems, then by all means the inevitable synthetic processes should be searched for vigorously.

Even if such processes are found, it is likely that they conform to a general principle first stated by Dancoff. Every sequential process is subject to error. We can either imagine such sequential processes as highly precise, so that no error at all can be tolerated, or we can say that the over-all demands on the sequential processes are such that the maximum possible error is allowed. Put in more specific terms, if a certain protein has to be synthesized up to 100 in number for the cell to work, then we can imagine either a process by which a precision template produces all 100, exposing the system to errors 100 times, or a process by which each protein divides, with a specific inhibitor being present to prevent the division of any incorrectly formed protein. Then any failure is stopped and the other proteins take over. This second process has a form of checking included. Dancoff suggested that a guide to setting up hypotheses about cellular action could be made in terms of choosing that hypothesis which, while still fitting the facts, allowed for the greatest error that could possibly result from its application.

One can apply this principle qualitatively to the question of whether protein or other large molecules undergo the rapid turnover of the smaller amino acids. If it is conceded that the process of exchange of one amino acid for another can involve error, then each protein must be exposed to malformation many times per second. Either this is unreasonable or the cell has a checking process of tremendous scope and efficiency. So potent would this checking process be that it should readily be observed in biochemical experiments. Until it *is* observed, it is more plausible to cast doubt on rapid amino-acid turnover. The work of Monod and Spiegelman on adaptive enzyme formation would seem to strengthen this viewpoint.

We conclude this chapter with a few information figures of interest, pointed out to us by Quastler.

Let us assume that analytical chemistry can distinguish one substance from 10^7 others, which involves 23 bits of information. Since the biological information in a DNA molecule is of the order of 10^4 bits, the biological operation of DNA is not likely to be seen in terms of analytical chemistry. On the other hand, x-ray structural analysis can readily extract 10^4 bits of information from a crystal 1 mm across. Consequently, the entry of structural analysis into biophysics is very rational.

If the figure of 10^{12} bits per bacterium is used, then 10^9 bits per second are produced as the bacterium grows and develops. This figure is so high that it makes plausible some kind of analysis in terms of a controlling set of nucleoprotein molecules. Under no circumstances can the growth of a bacterium be looked on as producing less than 1000 bits per second. It is interesting to compare this with the conscious handling of information by a human being, which Quastler sets at 25 bits per second. A printed page is about 10^4 bits, although often it contains much redundancy—a small comfort to authors.

Problems

1. Calculate (a) the internal energy, (b) the partition function, and (c) the Helmholtz free energy, for the diagram of Fig. 3–4, assuming that the levels are 1/30 ev apart and the temperature is 300°K.

2. The rate of diffusion of para-aminobenzoic acid across an area A is given by the relation

$$\frac{dn}{dt} = -DA\frac{\partial c}{\partial x},$$

where $D = 10^{-5}\text{ cm}^2/\text{sec}$. Assuming that the concentration in *E. coli* varies linearly from a value of twice the average at one end of a bacterial cell to zero at the other end, determine whether the rate of production of para-aminobenzoic acid bears any relation to its rate of diffusion.

*3. Given the relations

$$Z = \frac{\pi^{1/2}}{2}\frac{(8\pi^2 KT)^{3/2}}{h^3}(I_A I_B I_C)^{1/2},$$

----

* E. A. Moelwyn-Hughes, *Physical Chemistry*. Cambridge University Press, 1951, pp. 451–460.

where Z is the partition function for rotation, $I_A I_B I_C$ are the three moments of inertia for the rotation of water, and

$$\frac{S}{R} = \ln Z + T \frac{d}{dT} \ln Z,$$

show that the rotational entropy of water is approximately 10 cal/mole/deg. The moments of inertia are

$$I_A = 0.996 \times 10^{-40} \text{ gm/cm}^2,$$
$$I_B = 1.908 \times 10^{-40} \text{ gm/cm}^2,$$
$$I_C = 2.981 \times 10^{-40} \text{ gm/cm}^2.$$

*4. The inactivation of T1 bacteriophage gave the following data:

Temp., °C	Time, min	% Survival
90	60	85
105	60	40
125	20	2
145	5	1

Assuming that the relation $\ln n/n_0 = -k_1 t$ holds, calculate k_1 in inverse seconds and apply the theory of absolute reaction rates to calculate $\Delta F^{\ddagger}$, $\Delta H^{\ddagger}$, and $\Delta S^{\ddagger}$. Was the bacteriophage wet or dry during inactivation?

5. Estimate the information content of a brick house with five rooms.

6. Assuming that the information overlap between genotype and phenotype is seven bits, estimate the molecular weight of the gene, assuming it to be (a) nucleic-acid coded in terms of purine-pyrimidine pairs, and (b) protein coded in 20 amino acids.

7. Show that the *average energy* per molecule is related to the partition function by

$$\bar{E} = \frac{kT^2}{Z} \frac{\partial Z}{\partial t} = kT^2 \frac{\partial}{\partial T} (\ln Z).$$

8. Show that

$$T \frac{\partial A}{\partial T} = A - \bar{E} N_0 = A - U,$$

and that hence

$$\frac{S}{R} = \ln Z + T \frac{\partial}{\partial T} (\ln Z).$$

---

* Pollard and Reaume, *Arch. Bioch. Biophys.* **32**, 281 (1951).

REFERENCES

1. E. SCHRÖDINGER, *What is Life?* Cambridge University Press, 1944.
—*Statistical Thermodynamics.* Cambridge University Press, 1951.
2. R. GURNEY, *An Introduction to Statistical Mechanics.* McGraw-Hill Book Co., N. Y., 1949.
3. F. H. JOHNSON, H. EYRING, and M. J. POLLISAR, *Kinetics of Molecular Biology.* John Wiley, N. Y., 1955.
4. H. McILWAIN, "The Magnitude of Microbial Reactions Involving Vitamin-like Compounds." *Nature* **158,** 898 (1946).
5. H. QUASTLER, *Information Theory in Biology.* University of Illinois Press, Urbana, Ill., 1953.
6. H. MOROWITZ, "Some Order-Disorder Considerations in Living Systems." *Bull. Math. Biophys.* **17,** 81 (1955).

CHAPTER 4

PHYSICAL METHODS OF DETERMINING THE SIZES AND SHAPES OF MOLECULES

4-1 Introduction. The fundamental processes in metabolism, reproduction, differentiation, and irritability (four attributes of living things) involve interactions among the many and varied molecules that make up an organism. Many of these interactions or reactions are concerned with large molecules whose molecular weights are greater than 10,000. Moreover, the structural elements of living matter consist of aggregates of large molecules. Thus it is interesting and important to determine the physical characteristics of these large structures. As a first step toward knowing the mode of action of enzymes, for example, information about the sizes, shapes, and structures of protein molecules will be useful.

At present many experimental techniques are being used for the investigation of large molecules. While one technique alone may give rather scanty information and does not enable us to predict the behavior of a molecular species, the combination of two techniques may give much more than twice the information of a single one.

The most powerful technique of all is x-ray diffraction. It is also the most laborious, and hence to date only a reasonable amount of precise information has been obtained. The structures of hemoglobin, myoglobin, insulin, chymotrypsin, and ribonuclease have been investigated rather thoroughly, but only the first two have been studied more or less completely. Since the coming years will be the age of mechanical brains, the analyses of x-ray patterns of crystalline proteins should be accelerated.

Some of the techniques used and the molecular information they yield are given in Table 4–1. The many techniques not only give different types of information, but also have widely varying requirements of sample size and purity. For example, light scattering needs solutions of approximate concentration 1 mgm/ml, and x-ray diffraction needs a crystalline sample of about 1 mgm mass.

The techniques listed in Table 4–1 may be divided into two categories, the passive and the active. When using the methods of the passive group, we observe either the motion or orientation of the particles as a group or the effects of the particles on some incident form of energy. With the active methods, as exemplified by the irradiation techniques of items 17 and 18, we examine changes produced in the particle by the incident radiation, which is essentially the method of modern physics. In this method, known amounts and forms of energy are introduced into an atomic or molecular system, and the response of the system is observed.

TABLE 4–1

PHYSICAL TECHNIQUES USED FOR STUDYING LARGE MOLECULES

Technique	Information obtained	Purity needed
1. Osmotic pressure	Molecular weight	Very high
2. Diffusion	Molecular volume if shape and bound water are known	High or low
3. Sedimentation velocity	Molecular volume if shape and bound water are known	Intermediate
4. Sedimentation equilibrium	Molecular weight	High
5. Viscosity	Shape if bound water is known	High
6. Flow birefringence	Shape if bound water is known	High
7. Electric birefringence	Shape if bound water is known	High
8. Dielectric dispersion	Shape if bound water is known	High
9. Rotational dispersion	Helical fraction of molecule	High
10. Light scattering	Molecular weight, anisotropy	Very high
11. X-ray scattering	Size and shape	Very high
12. Electrophoresis	Relates charge to size and shape	Intermediate
13. Electron microscopy	Size and shape	High
14. Electron scattering	Intermolecular spacings	High
15. X-ray crystal analysis	Atomic positions	Very high
16. Electromagnetic absorption	Intramolecular forces and orientation	High
17. Charged particle irradiation	"Sensitive volume" and its location	Low
18. Photon irradiation	Structural coherence	Low

It is impossible here to analyze all the passive techniques. We will choose as examples diffusion, sedimentation, flow birefringence, x-ray diffraction, and light absorption. The first three techniques are not necessarily the easiest to use, but they do deal with a basic understanding of the properties of molecules in regard to their motions in the cell, a point to which we shall return in Chapter 15. They are sufficient to bring out most of the molecular properties we shall worry about. The last two techniques are dealt with in Chapters 10 and 9. The references there should be consulted for detailed information.

4–2 Random motion. The behavior of a molecule in a cell, i.e., the places it goes and how long it spends in various locales, is influenced by electrical forces and the short-range attractive forces that we shall consider in Chapter 6. But the major factor in molecular movement is the *random motion* of molecules, which arises from their collisions with surrounding molecules. The treatment of this random-motion problem is more complicated for the liquid phase than for gases because the motion of a large molecule through a liquid is retarded by a frictional force. It may be shown, theoretically and experimentally, that for the small velocities of molecules in solution, the frictional force is proportional to the velocity. If we designate this constant, which is the frictional coefficient per unit velocity, by f, we have for a velocity v

$$\text{Frictional force} = \mathbf{F} = -f\mathbf{v}. \tag{4–1}$$

The minus sign indicates that $\mathbf{F}$ and $\mathbf{v}$ are in opposite directions. The frictional coefficient f is intimately related to the molecular size and shape and to the viscosity of the medium. For example, if the molecule in whose motion we are interested were a sphere of radius a moving in a medium of viscosity η, we would have $f = 6\pi\eta a$. Before we worry about the details of determining f, let us take up the random-motion problem in more detail. We must do this because of the difficulties in using Eq. (4–1) directly to find the frictional coefficient.

We wish to determine something about the motion of a molecule, or particle, subject to a frictional force fv if its average kinetic energy is the same as that of the surrounding medium. We know from kinetic theory that the average kinetic energy of a molecule of mass m, $\frac{1}{2}mv^2$, is related to the absolute temperature T by

$$\overline{E_k} = \tfrac{1}{2}\overline{mv^2} = \tfrac{3}{2}kT,$$

where k is Boltzmann's constant, 1.38×10^{-23} joule/°K. The average kinetic energy associated with one degree of freedom, say in the x-direction, is

$$\overline{E_k} = \tfrac{1}{2}\overline{mv_x^2} = \tfrac{1}{2}kT. \tag{4–2}$$

Because it is difficult to determine average velocities, Eq. (4–2) cannot be used to find the mass of the particle but, as Einstein and Sutherland showed, there is a partial way out of the difficulty. The average displacement $\bar{x}$ in one direction is, of course, zero. If it were not, the motion could not be random. But the average squared displacement $\overline{x^2}$ is not zero, and the value of this quantity is related to molecular *shape* but not to mass, as we shall now show.

Suppose that at time $t = 0$ a large molecule, because of unequal bombardment by the medium, starts out with a velocity v_0 in the x-direction. Because of the frictional force $-fv$, the velocity will decrease according to Newton's second law of motion:

$$m \frac{dv}{dt} = -fv.$$

If we separate variables and integrate, we obtain for the velocity at a time t

$$v = v_0 e^{(-f/m)t}.$$

We have assumed, of course, that in the time t there have been no more unequal bombardments by the medium. This restriction does not hold for our final answer because it disappears in our averaging procedures. The kinetic energy is given by

$$E_k = \tfrac{1}{2}mv^2 = \tfrac{1}{2}mv_0^2 e^{(-2f/m)t} = E_{k,0} e^{(-2f/m)t}.$$

The average kinetic energy for a time τ is given by

$$\overline{E_k} = \frac{1}{\tau} \int_0^\tau E_k \, dt = \frac{1}{\tau} E_{k,0} \int_0^\tau e^{(-2f/m)t} \, dt,$$

$$\overline{E_k} = \frac{E_{k,0}}{\tau} \frac{m}{2f} (1 - e^{(-2f/m)\tau}). \qquad (4\text{–}3)$$

For long times τ the exponential term is negligible. If we confine our attention to times greater than 10^{-6} sec (see Problem 1), we may write

$$\overline{E_k} = \frac{E_{k,0}}{\tau} \frac{m}{2f}. \qquad (4\text{–}3')$$

We may relate $\overline{x^2}$ to $\overline{E_k}$ in the following way. The displacement of the molecule in a time τ is

$$x = \int_0^\tau v \, dt = v_0 \int_0^\tau e^{(-f/m)t} \, dt = v_0 \frac{m}{f} (1 - e^{(-f/m)\tau}),$$

and for $\tau > 10^{-6}$ sec,

$$x = v_0 \frac{m}{f}. \qquad (4\text{–}4)$$

The molecule makes a large number of these random elementary displace-ments, and because they may move either to the right or to the left, $\bar{v}_0 = 0$ and $\bar{x} = 0$. But

$$x^2 = \frac{m^2 v_0^2}{f^2} = \frac{2m}{f^2} \tfrac{1}{2} m v_0^2 = \frac{2m}{f^2} E_{k,0}. \qquad (4\text{--}5)$$

We eliminate $E_{k,0}$ from this expression by using Eq. (4–3′):

$$x^2 = \frac{4\overline{E_k}}{f} \tau. \qquad (4\text{--}5')$$

If we average over many molecules (or one molecule many times), as shown in Eq. (4–2), then

$$\overline{x^2} = 2\frac{kT}{f} \tau. \qquad (4\text{--}6)$$

This is the result we were after. It is the solution to the "random walk" with a given root-mean-square velocity. If we measure $\overline{x^2}$, we can find f. Actually, the result was first used by Perrin to determine Avogadro's number from the observed displacement of colloid particles of known size. Similar equations hold for the y- and z-directions, and so the average squared displacement moved in three dimensions in a time τ is

$$\overline{r^2} = \overline{x^2} + \overline{y^2} + \overline{z^2} = 6\frac{kT}{f} \tau. \qquad (4\text{--}6')$$

The actual distance a molecule may travel is much greater than is given by the square root of Eq. (4–6) because most of the displacements are in arbitrary directions. The implications of this fact are considered in Chapter 15.

We have calculated the *average* squared displacement. Not all molecules will have this displacement. They will be distributed about the average according to a gaussian distribution. Let us call $P(x)\,dx$ the probability of finding a displacement between x and $x + dx$. If the mean-squared displacement is $\overline{x^2}$, then

$$P(x)\,dx = \frac{1}{\sqrt{2\pi x^2}} e^{-(x^2/2\overline{x^2})}\,dx. \qquad (4\text{--}7)$$

The factor in front of the exponential has been chosen so that

$$\int_{-\infty}^{\infty} P(x)\,dx = 1.$$

Note that positive and negative displacements are equally probable, that is, $P(x) = P(-x)$.

4–3 Diffusion. The previous analysis is all very well, but it cannot be used directly because we cannot see the molecules we are interested in and so cannot measure $\overline{x^2}$ directly. Proteins and nucleic acids, for example, have dimensions ranging from 10 to 1000 A. We must adopt an indirect way of determining $\overline{x^2}$ by measurements of diffusion. Diffusion is the net flow of molecules from a region of high concentration to a region of low concentration. It is a manifestation of the random displacements of molecules that we discussed above. Since particles are just as likely to move in one direction as another, more particles will move out of a high-concentration region than move into it, simply because of the greater number of particles in such a region.

The classical way to approach the problem of diffusion is to use Fick's law (1855), which relates the rate of transport of material to the concentration gradient, i.e., the change in concentration with position. Let us consider the diffusion of molecules in a pipe parallel to the x-axis, as shown in Fig. 4–1(a). If the concentration increases to the right, there will be a net flow of molecules to the left. If we let dn/dt be the *number* of molecules that pass through the cross section A per second and call the concentration gradient $\partial c/\partial x$, Fick's law takes the form

$$\frac{dn}{dt} = -DA\,\frac{\partial c}{\partial x}.\qquad(4\text{–}8)$$

The proportionality constant D is known as the diffusion constant. Its units are

$$D = \frac{1}{Ac/x}\frac{dn}{dt} = \frac{1}{m^2\,[(\text{number/m})/m^3]}\cdot\frac{\text{number}}{\text{sec}} = \frac{m^2}{\text{sec}^{-1}}.$$

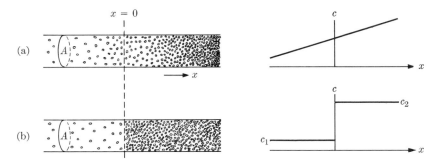

F<small>IG</small>. 4–1. The coordinate system for the one-dimensional diffusion process. (a) A uniform concentration gradient, $\partial c/\partial x$, to the right produces a net flow to the left. (b) A discontinuity at $x = 0$, $c_2 > c_1$, produces a net flow to the left, which may be computed from Eq. (4–6).

Before we worry about the relationship between the diffusion constant and molecular parameters, let us look at some of the typical numerical values shown in Table 4–2. The outstanding feature of these diffusion constants is that they are small numbers. Even though the molecular weight may range over a factor of 10^4, the diffusion constant changes only by 30 times. Before we concern ourselves with the experimental techniques that lead to these values, let us make an explicit connection between random motion and diffusion. The following derivation is crude but gives the same result as more elegant ones.

Imagine, as in Fig. 4–1(b), a long tube parallel to the x-axis. At zero time, the concentration to the right of the origin is c_2 particles/m^3, and that to the left is c_1. Let us assume $c_1 < c_2$. In a small time τ the particles will have a mean-square displacement given by Eq. (4–6), and in this time one-half of the particles within a distance $\overline{x^2}$ of the origin will pass the origin. (The factor of one-half must be used because the particles can go in either direction.) The displacements to the right and left are

$$\frac{c_1}{2} A \sqrt{\overline{x^2}} \quad \text{and} \quad \frac{c_2}{2} A \sqrt{\overline{x^2}},$$

and the *net flow* of particles per second in the $+x$-direction is

$$\frac{dn}{dt} = \frac{n}{\tau} = \frac{c_1 - c_2}{2} \frac{A}{\tau} \sqrt{\overline{x^2}}.$$

During the time τ while the molecules are executing their random walks, the concentration gradient is changing. At the end of this time, the concentration changes from c_1 to c_2 in a distance of $2\sqrt{\overline{x^2}}$, for a final gradient

TABLE 4–2

TYPICAL DIFFUSION CONSTANTS FOR
MOLECULES DIFFUSING THROUGH WATER AT 20°C

Molecule	Accepted mol. wt.	D, m^2/sec $\times 10^{11}$
Glycine	75	95
Arginine	174	58
Cytochrome C	13,000	10.1
Pepsin	35,000	9.0
CO-hemoglobin	68,000	6.2
Urease	480,000	3.5
TMV	40,000,000	0.53

of $(c_2 - c_1)/2\sqrt{\overline{x^2}}$. But clearly this value is too small. The average value during the time τ turns out to be

$$\frac{\partial c}{\partial x} = \frac{c_2 - c_1}{\sqrt{\overline{x^2}}},$$

and if we substitute this into the previous equation, we get

$$\frac{dn}{dt} = -\frac{A}{2\tau}\overline{x^2}\frac{\partial c}{\partial x}.$$

This equation has the same form as Fick's law, given in Eq. (4–8), and comparison of Eqs. (4–6) and (4–8) shows that

$$D = \frac{kT}{f} \qquad \text{and} \qquad \overline{x^2} = 2\,Dt. \qquad (4\text{–}9)$$

These equations hold the answers to our questions, for if we can measure D, we can calculate f, the frictional coefficient, and the frictional coefficient gives us information about the shape of the molecule. A knowledge of the diffusion constant is sufficient to determine $\overline{x^2}$, as indicated by the second of Eqs. (4–9), which represents the formal connection between random motion and diffusion. A more elegant way of deriving the relation between random walks and the diffusion constant is given in Section 4–4.

Assume for the moment that the diffusing molecules are *spherical*. Stoke's law gives for the frictional coefficient of a sphere of radius a moving in a fluid of viscosity η

$$f = 6\pi\eta a. \qquad (4\text{–}10)$$

For water at 20°C, the viscosity is 10^{-2} cgs units, or poise. One poise is 0.1 mks unit of viscosity. Thus from D we can calculate a, and if the density is ρ and N is Avogadro's number, the mass is given by

$$m = \tfrac{4}{3}\pi a^3 \rho, \qquad (4\text{–}11)$$

and the molecular weight M is given by

$$M = \tfrac{4}{3}\pi a^3 \rho N.$$

The important point brought out by this simple case is that the diffusion constant is *inversely proportional to the cube root of the mass*, which is the explanation for the small range of values of D given in Table 4–2. (For diffusion in gases, where the frictional coefficient is negligible, the diffusion constant is inversely proportional to the square root of the mass.)

The first application of this way of determining molecular sizes was made by W. Sutherland in 1905. He showed, experimentally, that if the diffusion data for small molecules were extrapolated to large molecules such as proteins, the product of the diffusion constant and the cube root of the gram-molecular volume was a constant. Sutherland then took Graham's data on the diffusion of egg albumin, obtained about 1860, and calculated a gram-molecular volume of 27,000 cm^3. From a knowledge of the molar volumes of the constituents of egg albumin and its percent composition, he finally derived a molecular weight of 33,000. The agreement between this value and the presently accepted one of 50,000 is somewhat fortuitous. But Sutherland was on the right track. The combination of Eqs. (4–9), (4–10), and (4–11) does yield the result that $V^{1/3}D =$ constant. It is surprising that 20 years later von Euler should have assumed that the product of the diffusion constant and the square root of the molecular weight is a constant. Thus he computed the molecular weight of invertase as 20,000, as compared with the value of 120,000 found from Eqs. (4–9), (4–10), and (4–11).

The values of molecular weights calculated in this fashion are uniformly *higher* than the accepted molecular weights, which we may take as determined by osmotic pressure, sedimentation equilibrium, or light scattering. There are two reasons for the difference. The first is that Eqs. (4–9) and (4–10) assume that the particles are spherical. If, instead, they are ellipsoidal (the only other shape that can easily be treated mathematically), then it is simple to show that for particles of the *same volume* the frictional constant for ellipsoids exceeds that for spheres. If the small value of the diffusion constant is interpreted in terms of a large radius rather than in terms of a nonspherical shape, the computed molecular volume will be too large. Of course, if the molecular shape is known, the diffusion data may be used to obtain correct molecular volumes. The reader is referred to Cohn and Edsall's book (Ref. 2) for more details.

The second reason for the incorrect values calculated from Eq. (4–11) lies in the hydration of protein molecules, spherical or otherwise. Because of the many charged side-groups on the molecules, the high local electric fields exert attractive forces on the water dipoles. These give rise to a layer of water that is firmly attached to the diffusing molecules. As a result, the frictional resistance of the medium is increased, and we are calculating a molecular volume corresponding to the hydrated molecule rather than to the unhydrated one. The quantitative correction for the bound water can be made easily if the amount of hydration is known. Values of the water of hydration run between limits of 0.20 to 0.50 gm of H_2O per gram of protein. These values can be found from measurements of the amount of water adsorbed to initially dry proteins, or by determining, in a protein solution, the fraction of the solvent which is available for dissolving salts.

The densities of dry proteins are about 1.27 gm/cm^3, but when 1 gm of protein is dissolved in water the increase in volume of the solution is not

$1/1.27 = 0.78 \text{ cm}^3$, but nearer 0.75 cm^3. The latter value is called the "apparent specific volume" of the protein. It is smaller than the reciprocal of the dry density because the attractive forces between water and protein reduce the freedom of motion of the water molecules. Alternatively, we can think of a protein molecule as having depressions in its surface into which water molecules can fit. Although these surface irregularities displace no water, they may be included in the measurement of "dry volume."

If we take 0.35 gm of H_2O per gram of protein as an average figure for hydration, then the ratio of the diffusion constant, for a hydrated sphere, D_{hyd}, to that of an unhydrated sphere, D_0, is given by the following relation:

$$\frac{D_0}{D_{hyd}} = \sqrt[3]{V_{hyd}/V_0} = \sqrt[3]{(0.75 + 0.35)/0.75} = \sqrt[3]{1.46}.$$

Hence if we compare the molecular weights, which are proportional to the volumes and thus to the cube of the ratio of the diffusion constants, we obtain

$$\frac{M_0}{M_{hyd}} = \left(\frac{D_{hyd}}{D_0}\right)^3 = \frac{1}{1.46} \qquad \text{or} \qquad M_0 = \frac{M_{hyd}}{1.46},$$

where M_{hyd} and M_0 are the molecular weights of the hydrated and unhydrated spheres, repectively. This correction factor of 1.46 for bound water holds also for nonspherical molecules. If we apply this correction to the data given in Table 4–2, we obtain the values shown in Table 4–3. If the molecules are not spherical or if the bound-water correction is incorrect, the agreement will be poor. This is obvious for tobacco mosaic virus, which is known to be a long, thin rod of length 2800 A and diameter 150 A. The factor 1.46 is just a correction term. Our knowledge of the interactions between water and proteins is nowhere near complete, so for theo-

TABLE 4–3

MOLECULAR WEIGHTS COMPUTED FROM DIFFUSION CONSTANTS

Molecule	Accepted mol. wt.	Mol. wt. from Eq. (4–1)	Corrected by division by 1.46
Hemoglobin	68,000	130,000	89,000
Cytochrome C	13,000	32,000	20,000
Pepsin	35,000	43,000	29,000
Urease	480,000	770,000	530,000
TMV	40×10^6	230×10^6	160×10^6

retical as well as experimental reasons the correction factor may have a 20% error.

Diffusion measurements clearly indicate that proteins in their native state are *not* in the form of an extended polypeptide chain. Thus serum albumin denatured by urea has a much smaller diffusion coefficient than in the native form. Since osmotic pressure measurements indicate that the molecules have not been split, it may be assumed that the dimensions of protein molecules in solution range between 20 and 100 A. If the molecules were extended polypeptide chains their length would be greater than 500 A for even the smaller proteins.

It may seem that too much time has been spent on a technique which has yielded very meager knowledge. In justification, we point out that a knowledge of diffusion constants is important in an analysis of cell metabolism and, in addition, when combined with ultracentrifuge data it can yield accurate values for molecular weights. Also, we are faced with the situation that we shall only seldom find any *one* precision method of study; most of the time we have to use all the knowledge we can get and attempt our best synthesis from the varied data.

4–4 Measurement of diffusion constants. We have talked about using the diffusion constant to obtain knowledge about molecular sizes, but we have not yet indicated how to measure it. The direct use of the defining equation, Eq. (4–8), is difficult because during diffusion the concentration gradient changes. But if we agree to *conserve the number of diffusing molecules*, we can derive, for our purposes, a more useful diffusion equation.

Let us consider diffusion taking place along the x-direction. We shall evaluate the net increase in the number of molecules within the volume $A \Delta x$ shown in Fig. 4–2. If we designate the concentration gradients at $x = 0$ and $x = \Delta x$ by $(\partial c/\partial x)_0$ and $(\partial c/\partial x)_{\Delta x}$ respectively, for the net increase in the number in $A \Delta x$ we have, from Eq. (4–8),

$$\frac{dn}{dt} = -AD\left[\left(\frac{\partial c}{\partial x}\right)_0 - \left(\frac{\partial c}{\partial x}\right)_{\Delta x}\right].$$

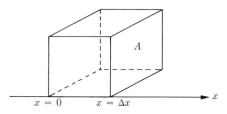

FIG. 4–2. Diffusion into and out of the volume $A \Delta x$. The concentration gradient at the origin is $(\partial c/\partial x)_0$, and at $x = \Delta x$ it is $(\partial c/\partial x)_{\Delta x}$.

(We are using partial derivatives because the concentration varies with time as well as with position.) If the concentration gradient increases linearly with x, and it does in the limit as Δx approaches zero, then

$$\left(\frac{\partial c}{\partial x}\right)_{\Delta x} = \left(\frac{\partial c}{\partial x}\right)_0 + \frac{\partial}{\partial x}\left(\frac{\partial c}{\partial x}\right)_0 \Delta x.$$

If this is substituted into the previous equation, then

$$\frac{dn}{dt} = AD\frac{\partial}{\partial x}\left(\frac{\partial c}{\partial x}\right)_0 \Delta x.$$

But $dn/(A\,dx)$ is the *concentration increase*, measured in particles/m^3; therefore as Δx approaches zero,

$$\frac{\partial c}{\partial t} = D\frac{\partial^2 c}{\partial x^2}. \tag{4-12}$$

This partial differential equation has built into itself the fact that the concentration, and hence the concentration gradient, changes during diffusion. The analytical form of the solutions of this equation depends on the boundary conditions. A solution that satisfies the boundary conditions is the general solution of the problem under investigation.

A convenient boundary condition to consider, but one not realizable in practice, is one in which *all* the molecules are at the origin at time $t = 0$ and, as time goes on, they diffuse away by a set of random walks until as $t \to \infty$, $c \to 0$ for all x. A solution for intermediate times which satisfies Eq. (4-12) and these conditions is

$$c = \frac{1}{\sqrt{4\pi\,Dt}}\,e^{-x^2/4Dt}.$$

The numerical factor of $1/\sqrt{4\pi}$ was chosen so that $\int_{-\infty}^{\infty} c\,dx = 1$. Therefore the value of c at any point and time represents the probability that a molecule will diffuse to that point in the given time, and this equation should be identical with the random-walk solution given in Eq. (4-7). The two equations are identical if we set $\overline{x^2} = 2\,Dt$. This result is the sophisticated way of deriving Eq. (4-9).

A more practical boundary condition to use is one in which at $t = 0$ there is a discontinuity at the origin, so that for all $x < 0$ the concentration is zero and for $x > 0$, $c = c_0$. As diffusion takes place the boundary becomes fuzzy and as $t \to \infty$, $c \to c_0/2$ everywhere. Figure 4-3 shows these conditions graphically. The sharpness of the boundary is indicated by the concentration gradient, $\partial c/\partial x$. At $t = 0$, $\partial c/\partial x \to \infty$, and as $t \to \infty$, $\partial c/\partial x \to 0$.

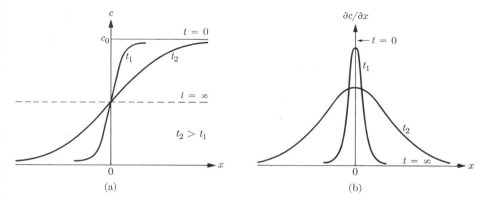

(a)   (b)

FIG. 4–3. (a) The concentration *versus* position, and (b) the concentration gradient *versus* position, for several times of diffusion if initially all the solute was to the right of the origin.

The equations for the curves in Fig. 4–3 which, of course, satisfy Eq. (4–12), are

$$c = \frac{c_0}{2}\left(1 + \frac{2}{\sqrt{\pi}}\int_0^{x/\sqrt{4Dt}} e^{-\xi^2}\,d\xi\right) \tag{4–13}$$

and

$$\frac{\partial c}{\partial x} = \frac{c_0}{\sqrt{4\pi\,Dt}}\,e^{-x^2/4Dt}.$$

The integral in Eq. (4–13) is a function of the upper limit of integration and is obviously closely related to the probability function of Eq. (4–7). It is known as the *probability integral*. For convenience in working problems, it is presented graphically in Fig. 4–4.

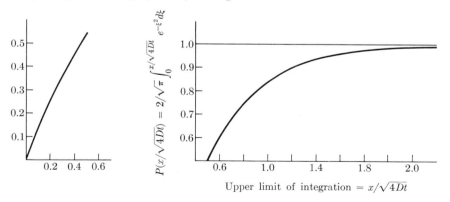

Upper limit of integration $= x/\sqrt{4Dt}$

FIG. 4–4. The value of the probability integral as a function of the numerical value of the upper limit of integration. The probability integral is an odd function.

We have written the explicit expression for the concentration gradient because in many experimental setups it is possible to measure $\partial c/\partial x$ directly by elaborate optical methods. Some of these methods will be taken up in Section 4–8. The diffusion constant can be found either by determining the shapes of the curves shown in Fig. 4–3 or by measuring the total amount of material (determined by analytical techniques) that has passed the origin in a known time and equating this quantity to the integral $\int_0^{-\infty} c\ dx$.

The necessary experimental conditions that must hold if the measured diffusion constants are to mean anything are that the diffusion be random and the initial boundary be sharp. A sharp boundary can be achieved by placing the solvent and solution in separate cells that may be moved so as to bring the two solutions into contact at $t = 0$, as shown in Fig. 4–5(a). Alternatively, the boundary problem can be evaded and a porous glass disk used to separate the two media, as shown in Fig. 4–5(b). In this case the diffusion constant cannot be found directly, because the frictional resistance of the glass pores is not known. Accordingly, the porous diaphragm must be calibrated with substances whose diffusion constants are well known.

Great care must be taken to reduce mechanical disturbances and thermal gradients to a minimum. Since free diffusion takes a time of the order of a day, it can easily be outshadowed by these extraneous effects. For example, a protein molecule with a net charge may seem to diffuse much more rapidly than a similar neutral molecule. The explanation is that if the molecule has a net plus charge, the extra $(OH)^-$ ions in solution, which can diffuse rapidly, will give rise to an electric field urging the positively charged large molecules toward the region of low concentration.

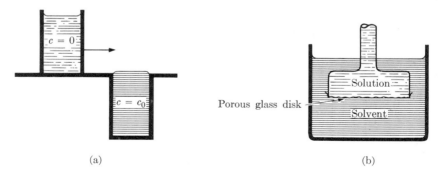

(a)   (b)

FIG. 4–5. Schematic experimental diffusion cells. (a) The two containers may be moved so as to bring the two solutions into contact at $t = 0$, thus forming a sharp initial boundary. (b) The two solutions are separated by a porous disk.

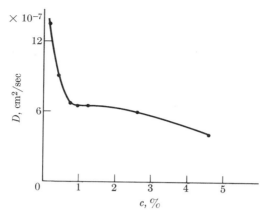

FIG. 4–6. The diffusion constant of CO-hemoglobin at pH 6.8 at different concentrations.

For this reason diffusion experiments should be run at the isoelectric point of the protein, and as a further safeguard enough electrolyte ($\sim$0.1%) should be added so that these small ions can quickly neutralize any electric field that may arise.

If the motion of dissolved molecules is to be random, the molecules must be independent of one another, which means that we should attempt to extrapolate the diffusion constants to infinite dilution. This procedure is straightforward unless the solute tends to dissociate at low concentrations. Such a case is illustrated in Fig. 4–6. At low concentration, CO-hemoglobin dissociates into subunits of the molecule of molecular weight 68,000.

4–5 Sedimentation. The usual way of determining masses is to observe the motion of particles under the action of known forces, since the operational definition of mass depends on the relative accelerations of an unknown and of a standard mass. The most convenient force to use is the force of gravity, but for small particles this force is so minute that the random bombardment of the molecules of the surrounding medium far outweighs the directing force of gravity. We can illustrate this point very simply by calculating the difference in gravitational potential energy between two points separated by a vertical distance of 1 cm, for a molecule of 10^5 molecular weight. Such a molecule has a mass of 10^5 divided by the number of molecules in a kgm-mole, or

$$\frac{10^5}{6.03 \times 10^{26}} = 0.16 \times 10^{-21} \text{ kgm.}$$

If we round off the value for the acceleration of gravity to 10 m per sec per sec, the potential energy difference, E_p, is

$$E_p = \text{mgh} = 0.16 \times 10^{-21} \times 10 \times 10^{-2} = 1.6 \times 10^{-23} \text{ joule.}$$

But 1 electron volt $= 1.6 \times 10^{-19}$ joule, so

$$E_p = \frac{1.6 \times 10^{-23} \text{ joule}}{1.6 \times 10^{-19} \text{ joule/ev}} = 10^{-4} \text{ ev.}$$

But we note that the thermal agitation energy is just kT, where k is Boltzmann's constant and T is the absolute temperature, and that at room temperature

$$kT = 1.38 \times 10^{-23} \text{ joule/}°\text{K} \cdot 2.93 \times 10^{2°}\text{K} = 4 \times 10^{-21} \text{ joule} = 1/40 \text{ ev.}$$

Since the gravitational potential energy is smaller than the average thermal energy by a factor of about 200, experimental detection of the slight additional energy due to gravity is impossible. Actually we have *overestimated* the gravitational potential energy because we have neglected the buoyant force of the surrounding medium, which effectively decreases the mass acted on by gravity.

A straightforward solution to this difficulty is to increase the gravitational potential energy to the point where it is somewhat greater than kT. This may be done by enclosing the particles in a vessel rotating at high speed. From the point of view of reference axes attached to this rotating system, the particle moves through the surrounding medium away from the axis of rotation. There is a slight complication in working problems of particles sedimenting in centrifugal fields: the acceleration varies with distance from the axis. If the angular speed is ω rad/sec and the distance from the axis is r, the linear acceleration is $a = \omega^2 r$.

Suppose that a particle of mass m and density ρ moves through a solvent of density ρ_0 under the action of a "gravitational" force $m\omega^2 r$ (the centrifugal force seen from the rotating axes). There will also be frictional and buoyant forces, caused by the action of the medium on the particle. The direction of these forces is indicated in Fig. 4–7. For example, the

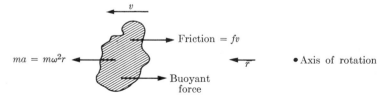

FIG. 4–7. The direction of the forces acting on a sedimenting particle in a centrifugal field.

buoyant force, in dynes or newtons, is the weight of the displaced fluid:

$$\text{Buoyant force} = \frac{m}{\rho}\rho_0 \cdot \omega^2 r,$$

and therefore the net "gravitational" force is

$$m\omega^2 r \left(1 - \frac{\rho_0}{\rho}\right).$$

Thus in a medium of density ρ_0, the particle acts as if it had an effective mass m' given by

$$m' = m \left(1 - \frac{\rho_0}{\rho}\right). \qquad (4\text{–}14)$$

The difficulty in using Eq. (4–14) is to find the proper value to use for the density ρ of the particle. Suppose, to take an extreme example, that the sedimenting particles are in the form of hollow porous spheres. We could measure the density of a number of these spheres by dividing their total mass by their total volume, but obviously this would not be the proper value to use in the sedimentation expression because the term that appears there is just the weight of the displaced fluid. Since the spheres have holes through their surfaces, the volume of the displaced fluid is the volume of the spherical shell, not the volume of the sphere. Thus the density we really should use is the density of the spherical shell. The only way we can determine this is by finding out how much water is displaced by the sphere. In place of the density, we should use the reciprocal of a quantity known as the *partial specific volume*, which is the change in volume per unit mass for an infinitesimal mass. This measurement, too, presents difficulties, as we outlined in our discussion of bound water.

4–6 Sedimentation-equilibrium method. There are two general ways in which sedimentation experiments are performed. With the method of *sedimentation equilibrium*, one waits until the average motion of the molecules has stopped. With the method of *sedimentation velocity* (Section 4–7), the average drift velocity of the molecules away from the rotation axis is measured. Let us analyze the conditions which hold in the equilibrium method.

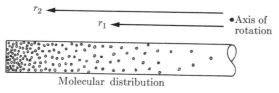

Fig. 4–8. The coordinates and the schematic distribution of particles in sedimentation equilibrium.

The molecules are subject to a net gravitational force, and they would all lie on the bottom of the sedimentation vessel if they were not also executing random walks, or diffusing. If the molecules sediment long enough (about a day) so that their average velocity is zero, the spatial distribution, indicated schematically in Fig. 4–8, is governed by the Boltzmann distribution. If we call n_1 and n_2 the number of solute molecules per unit volume at distances r_1 and r_2 from the rotation axis, at which positions the molecules have energies E_1 and E_2, then

$$\frac{n_1}{n_2} = e^{-(E_1 - E_2)/kT}$$

This equation merely expresses the balance of power between gravitational and thermal energies. The kinetic energies are the same at the two positions, so $(E_1 - E_2)$ is only the difference in potential energy. The potential energy difference is the work necessary to carry a molecule from r_2 to r_1 against the *net* force of gravity, $m'\omega^2 r$. Thus, because we are going in a direction opposite to that of the element of distance dr,

$$E_1 - E_2 = -\int_{r_2}^{r_1} m'\omega^2 r\, dr = \frac{m'\omega^2}{2}(r_2^2 - r_1^2).$$

If this expression is substituted into the Boltzmann distribution, we get

$$\frac{n_1}{n_2} = \exp\left[-\frac{m'\omega^2}{2kT}(r_2^2 - r_1^2)\right],$$

or

$$\ln\frac{n_2}{n_1} = \frac{m'\omega^2}{2kT}(r_2^2 - r_1^2). \tag{4–15}$$

If Eq. (4–15) is found to hold experimentally, then we may be fairly sure that equilibrium has been reached, and we can solve for m' and hence obtain m from Eq. (4–14). Since the derivation of Eq. (4–15) had nothing to say about the shape of the molecule or the presence of bound water, the molecular weights obtained in this fashion are independent of these parameters. This is the power of the method. With it we can ignore all factors except the effective mass, because the shape and bound water affect only the *rate* at which equilibrium is reached, not the final molecular distribution.

It is worth while at this point to get a feeling for the magnitudes of the quantities involved. Suppose that a centrifuge rotor is spinning at an angular velocity of 1000 rad/sec (about 10,000 rev/min) and that the average radius r is 10 cm. The average centrifugal acceleration, $\omega^2 r$, is 10^5 m/sec. This value, which is about 10^4 times the normal acceleration due to gravity, is called $10^4\,g$. If the molecules being spun are of molecular weight 10^5 and if $(1 - \rho_0/\rho) = 0.25$, then, as calculated in Section 4–5,

$m' = 0.4 \times 10^{-22}$ kgm and the ratio of the number of particles at 10.0 cm and 9.8 cm from the axis is given, by Eq. (4–15), as

$$\ln \left(\frac{n_{10.0}}{n_{9.8}}\right)$$
$$= \frac{0.4 \times 10^{-22} \text{ kgm} \times 10^6 \text{ sec}^{-2}}{2 \times 1.38 \times 10^{-23} \text{ joule/}^\circ\text{K} \times 3 \times 10^2 \text{ }^\circ\text{K}} (1.00 - 0.96) \text{ m}^2 = 1.9$$

or

$$\frac{n_{10.0}}{n_{9.8}} = 6.6.$$

For the system we have calculated, the change in concentration with position is too rapid for accurate measurement. For higher angular velocities, practically all the molecules would be at the bottom of the sedimentation cell.

The large centrifugal forces that can be brought to act on big molecules have been used to great advantage in a sedimentation-equilibrium method in which the molecules are spun in a *density gradient*. Such a gradient may be obtained by spinning a solution of a heavy salt, such as CsCl, until equilibrium is reached, as indicated by Eq. (4–15). Because of the concentration difference between the top and the bottom of the cell, there is also a density gradient. If a molecule whose density ρ falls between the two extreme densities of the solution is also centrifuged in the solution, it will tend to accumulate at the lowest energy position. The lowest energy corresponds to the position where the effective mass m', given by Eq. (4–14), is zero. At this point $\rho_0 = \rho$. The distribution about this point is very narrow because of the high speeds used, and the resolution is good enough so that DNA containing N^{15} is clearly separated from the normal N^{14} variety. Meselson, Stahl, and Vinograd* grew *E. coli* in an N^{15}-containing medium so that all the DNA had a higher density than normal. They found that when the bacteria were transferred to and then grown in a N^{14} medium, the extracted DNA had only *three* observed densities: that of N^{15}-DNA, N^{14}-DNA, and one halfway between. The amount of N^{14}-DNA increases with time, and the amount of the intermediate remains constant. The fact that, in addition, there is only *one intermediate density* is evidence for the intact nature of the macromolecular DNA, its manufacture in large pieces, and a pairing between new and old pieces.

4–7 Sedimentation-velocity method. The second way of obtaining sedimentation data is by use of *sedimentation-velocity* techniques. Here, instead of waiting the long time necessary for an equilibrium distribution to be established, we make use of the fact that the sedimenting particles

---

* *Proc. Nat. Acad. Sci.* **43,** 581 (1957).

have a constant drift velocity away from the rotation axis. Since the forces of friction, fv, increase with velocity, the particle will quickly reach equilibrium under the action of the three forces shown in Fig. 4–7. We then have

$$ma \left(1 - \frac{\rho_0}{\rho} \right) = fv.$$

This yields for the average velocity $\bar{v}$,

$$\bar{v} = \frac{ma}{f} \left(1 - \frac{\rho_0}{\rho} \right). \tag{4–16}$$

In an actual experiment, both velocity and acceleration are known. We define their ratio as the *sedimentation constant*

$$s \equiv \frac{\bar{v}}{a}.$$

The sedimentation constant has the units of $(\text{m/sec})/(\text{m/sec}^2)$. A value of $s = 10^{-13}$ sec is called 1 svedberg, in honor of the centrifugation pioneer. If the definition of sedimentation constant is substituted into Eq. (4–16) and we solve for m, we find

$$m = \frac{sf}{1 - (\rho_0/\rho)}. \tag{4–17}$$

The analysis presented here applies only if sedimentation rather than diffusion predominates, so that the dense sedimenting particles move from the axis of rotation and a sharp boundary is formed between solvent and solution. During the course of a run, diffusion causes this initial sharp boundary to become fuzzy, but the average velocity (which in diffusion is zero) is still given by Eq. (4–16).

Equation (4–17) is just as powerless as the expression derived for molecular weight on the basis of diffusion measurements, because the shape of the molecule and the amount of hydrated water will influence the frictional force. In the absence of other information, we could use a spherical model with about 0.35 gm of water per gram of protein. Since the mass given by Eq. (4–17) depends directly on f, then as before we obtain

$$\frac{f_\text{hyd}}{f_0} = \sqrt[3]{1.46} = 1.13,$$

where $f_0 = 6\pi\eta a$ is the frictional coefficient for a sphere, and we must reduce the molecular weights obtained by the sedimentation-velocity method by a factor of 1.13. The effect of bound water is obviously less than in the case of diffusion measurements.

There is a simple way out of this dilemma of unknown shape and associated water. We use the results of diffusion to obtain f and then substitute this value into the sedimentation equation. From Eq. (4–9),

$$f = kT/D.$$

Substituted into Eq. (4–17), this gives

$$m = \frac{kTs}{D[1 - (\rho_0/\rho)]}. \tag{4–18}$$

Or, if we multiply both sides of the equation by Avogadro's number, then the particle weight m becomes the molecular weight M and Boltzmann's constant k becomes R, the gas constant, 8.3×10^3 joules/kgm·mole·°K. Therefore we get

$$M = \frac{RTs}{D[1 - (\rho_0/\rho)]},$$

where ρ is still the reciprocal of the partial specific volume.

The combined application of two techniques is more than twice as powerful as one method alone. From a single technique we can get only a relation between three unknowns: size, shape, and the amount of water. From the combination we can get a definite value for size and a relation between the other two. Table 4–4 shows some typical data.

TABLE 4–4

SEDIMENTATION AND DIFFUSION DATA OF
SOME MOLECULES AND VIRUSES IN MKS UNITS*

Molecule	$\dfrac{1}{\rho}$	$S \times 10^{13}$ ($\pm 2\%$)	$D \times 10^{11}$ ($\pm 5\%$)	M (± 5–10%)	$\dfrac{f}{f_0}$
Cytochrome C	0.707	1.9	10.1	15,600	1.29
Myoglobin	0.741	2.04	11.3	17,200	1.11
Ribonuclease	0.709	1.85	13.6	12,900	1.04
Pepsin	0.750	3.3	9.0	37,000	1.08
Hemoglobin	0.749	4.41	6.3	68,000	1.24
Urease	0.73	18.6	3.46	480,000	1.19
Hemocyanin	0.738	98.9	1.38	6,600,000	1.24
Bushy stunt virus	0.739	132	1.15	10,600,000	1.27
Tobacco mosaic virus	0.73	193	0.53	32,000,000	3.1
Nucleohistone	0.658	31	0.93	2,100,000	2.5

* The molecular weights found by a combination of sedimentation and diffusion methods are in good agreement with values found by osmotic-pressure, sedimentation-equilibrium, and light-scattering methods.

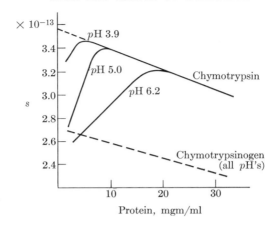

FIG. 4–9. Sedimentation data for chymotrypsinogen and chymotrypsin at different concentrations. [From Swert, *J. Biol. Chem.* **179**, 655 (1949).]

The relation between the possible shape of a molecule and the amount of bound water associated with it is usually expressed in terms of the frictional ratio of the measured frictional coefficient f to the value f_0 calculated for a sphere of equal mass. A value of $f/f_0 > 1$ arises from a combination of bound water and nonspherical shape. Values of f/f_0 up to about 1.1 can be ascribed to bound water. Higher values may be interpreted as due to the ellipsoidal shape of a molecule. Calf nucleohistone, for example, would have an axial ratio of about 40:1. There is no reason to suppose, of course, that actual molecules are ellipsoidal. TMV, for example, is known to be much closer to a cylindrical shape.

Sedimentation measurements, like those for diffusion, should be taken over a range of concentrations. An extrapolation of s to infinite dilution will yield the appropriate value to use in Eqs. (4–17) or (4–18). Figure 4–9 shows such data for the enzymatically inactive protein chymotrypsinogen and for the active enzyme derived from it, chymotrypsin. The data for chymotrypsinogen extrapolate to a unique value of s which corresponds to a molecular weight of 25,000. The value obtained for chymotrypsin, however, depends on whether the extrapolation is made from high concentrations or low concentrations. The molecular weight obtained by extrapolating to zero concentration from values of less than 10 mgm/ml is 22,000. That obtained from the high concentration data is about double this value. Chymotrypsin obviously forms dimers at high concentration.

4–8 Analytical centrifuges and optical detection methods. Centrifuges may be driven by air, oil, electric motors, or rotating magnetic fields. At the high speeds necessary in the sedimentation-velocity method, the rotor must spin in an evacuated chamber, so as to minimize heating ef-

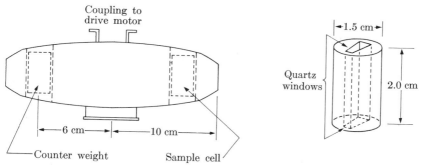

Fig. 4–10. A typical analytical centrifugal rotor and sample cell. [Courtesy of Beckman Instruments, Inc.]

fects. A view of a typical rotor and a schematic diagram of a sedimentation cell are shown in Fig. 4–10. Because the centrifugal force is radial, the cell has a sector shape, so that the sedimenting particles travel along the radii and there is no other component of force on the particles other than those of gravity and friction. The windows in the cell permit the sample to be observed during sedimentation. Rotors of the type indicated in Fig. 4–10 can spin at speeds up to 60,000 rev/min, which corresponds to 300,000 g. Such an instrument can resolve molecular weights of 20,000 and 40,000. The position of the sedimenting boundary may be followed by one of a number of optical techniques. These techniques may also, of course, be used in diffusion measurements, where there is not the added complication of a rotating sample. In a centrifuge the sample is observed for only the short period of time it passes by an observation window in the chamber surrounding the rotor. The optical techniques use either the fact that a solution *absorbs* more light than the solvent or that a solution has a *refractive index* different from that of the solvent. The general principles and techniques are very similar to those used in light microscopy for producing contrast between an image and its surroundings.

Light absorption. Suppose that molecules are sedimenting in a centrifuge and, at a particular time, the distribution of molecules is as shown in Fig. 4–11(a). If the cell is illuminated by light absorbed by the molecules, the intensity of the light might be as shown in Fig. 4–11(b). And if the complete optical setup of Fig. 4–11(c) is used, so that the lens forms an image of the cell on the photographic plate, we can use our knowledge of light absorption (see Chapter 6) to measure concentration *versus* position.

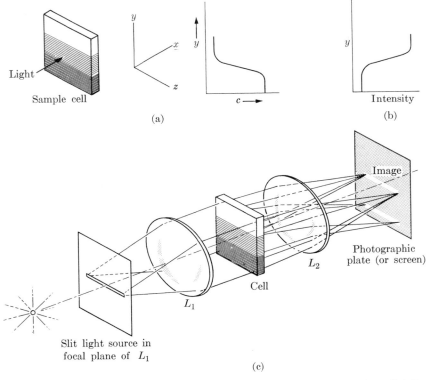

Fig. 4–11. The use of absorption optics to measure concentration distributions. (a) A possible concentration curve. (b) The wavefront emerging from the cell. (c) A schematic diagram of the complete optical system. The lens L_2 focuses the cell on the photographic plate.

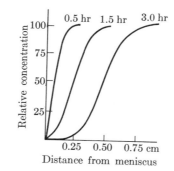

FIG. 4–12. Concentration *versus* position curves for CO-hemoglobin spun several times at 115,000 *g*. Note how the boundary becomes more diffuse as time goes on. [From Svedberg and Nichols, *J. Am. Chem. Soc.* **49**, 2920 (1927).]

By taking pictures at several different times, we can obtain the sedimentation or diffusion constants. Because proteins (those without porphyrin rings or other conjugated groups) and nucleic acids absorb light only in the ultraviolet region, i.e., at wavelengths below 3000 A, quartz optical elements must be used. If the cell has a light path 1 cm wide, concentrations of nucleic acids of 20 μgm/ml and protein concentrations of 200 μgm/ml may be used. Some data obtained by this method are shown in Fig. 4–12.

Schlieren optics. A large class of optical techniques makes use of the fact that the index of refraction of a solution is larger than that of the solvent. As a result, a plane wavefront passing through a medium that has a concentration gradient is no longer a plane wavefront. The high concentration regions have a high refractive index, or a low light velocity, and the wavefront is retarded more than in the low refractive index regions. Suppose that sedimentation or diffusion is taking place in the y-direction and, as in Fig. 4–11(a), that the concentration changes with position. If the refractive index n is proportional to the solute concentration c and the constant of proportionality is called $\partial n/\partial c$, and n_0 is the refractive index of the solvent, then the refractive index *versus* y-curve is parallel to the concentration curve, because

$$n = n_0 + \frac{\partial n}{\partial c} \cdot c.$$

A plane wave incident on the sedimentation cell will emerge as shown in Fig. 4–13. For a protein in water solution, $n_0 = 1.33$ and $\partial n/\partial c = 0.18$ per gm/ml. Clearly, the plot of n versus y in the figure and the shape of the emergent wavefront are grossly exaggerated. The emergent wavefront is just the reflection of the concentration gradient and, as the follow-

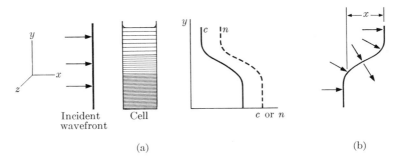

(a)   (b)

FIG. 4–13. If a plane wave is incident on a cell whose concentration and refractive index vary as shown in (a), the emergent wavefront will have the form shown in (b). The arrows show the directions of the normals to the wavefront.

ing simple analysis shows, the *slope* of the normal to the wavefront is proportional to the *concentration gradient*.

The horizontal displacement x of the wavefront, in a cell of thickness t, is equal to $\Delta n t$ or, in general, to $[(\partial n/\partial y) \, dy]t$. Thus,

$$\text{Slope of normal} = \frac{\partial x}{\partial y} = t \frac{\partial n}{\partial y} = t \frac{\partial n}{\partial c} \cdot \frac{\partial c}{\partial y} \propto \frac{\partial c}{\partial y}.$$

An easy way to detect the regions of high concentration gradient is to use a system such as the one shown in Fig. 4–14. Light from the slit is made parallel by the lens L_1. The plane wavefronts entering the cell are converted to emergent wavefronts of the form shown in Fig. 4–13(b). Those parts of the wavefront, such as a and c, whose normals have not been deviated, pass through the *focal point* of L_2 and go on to form on the screen inverted images of the regions a and c of the cell. Light from the region b,

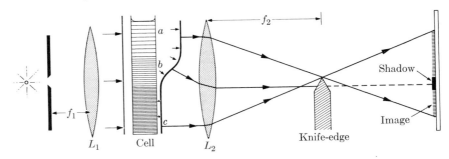

FIG. 4–14. A schlieren optical system to detect the regions of high concentration gradient. The lens L_2 is so placed that it focuses the cell on the screen (or photographic plate). The knife-edge in the focal plane of L_2 produces a shadow on the screen in the region b.

or maximum concentration gradient, would pass *below* the focal point and continue in a straight line to form an image on the screen at region *b*. If, however, an opaque knife-edge is placed just below the focal point of L_2, all the deviated rays are cut out and no light from the concentration gradient region appears on the screen. With this optical system, regions of rapid changes in refractive index appear as shadows on the screen, hence the name *schlieren* (German, "streaked") optics. As sedimentation continues, the boundary moves down and the shadow up. In a diffusion cell the region of the concentration gradient gets larger and the shadow grows.

By use of an appropriate optical system devised by Philpot,* it is possible to translate the deviations of the wavefront normals (which appeared as shadows in the above analysis) into *horizontal* deflections. The optical system is the same as that shown in Fig. 4–14, except for the addition of an inclined slit in the focal plane of L_2 and a cylindrical lens L_3 which is positioned to focus the focal plane of L_2 on the screen. These optical components are shown in Fig. 4–15. If the inclined slit and cylindrical lens

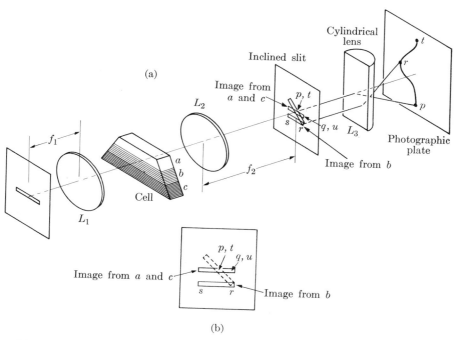

FIG. 4–15. An optical system designed to present the concentration gradient *versus* position. (a) The location of the optical components and the final image on the photographic plate. (b) The inclined slit in the focal plane of L_2.

* *Nature* **141,** 283 (1938).

were not used, the final image would be inverted, and no effect of the wavefront deviation by the refractive index gradient would be noticed. This is the case because, since the slit is an extended source and the light leaving levels a, b, and c of the cell is not confined to particular directions, the final image of the cell is formed by rays leaving all parts of the slit. The refractive index gradient at level b splits the images of the source slit in the focal plane of L_2 but does not affect the image of the cell formed on the photographic plate. The cylindrical lens which focuses the slit images on the photographic plate has *no* focusing properties in the vertical direction, and the position of the images of the cell at a, b, and c are unchanged except for an interchange of the side (p, q), (r, s), and (t, u), as shown in Fig. 4–15. If we now put an inclined slit in the focal plane of the L_2, then the line images of a, b, and c can appear on the screen only as points, such as p, r, and t. This fancy optical setup has converted a vertical change in wavefront direction into a horizontal deflection.

If we now fill in the intermediate points between a, b, and c, a curve is obtained whose deflection in the z-direction is proportional to the original wavefront deflection from the horizontal, which in turn is proportional to the refractive index gradient, as is indicated in Fig. 4–15. The area under this curve is proportional to the concentration. Usually the inclined slit is replaced by an opaque bar 1.5 mm in width, whose inclination from the vertical may be changed. The image on the screen is then just the negative of what we have described. This modification, besides being mechanically simpler, has the advantage that interference fringes due to diffraction from the bar can easily be observed, provided the light used is monochromatic. Since the interference fringes are sharp, they are much easier to measure than the broad central maximum, and they allow the measurement of sedimentation constants to be made to within less than 1%. The lowest concentration limit that can be used in this method is about 0.1%, or 1 mgm of protein per milliliter.

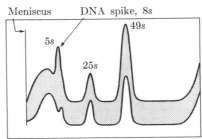

FIG. 4–16. The ultracentrifuge pattern of an extract of *E. coli*. The 49s and 25s peaks represent RNA-protein particles. The 8s peak is DNA and the 5s peak is the soluble protein. [After H. K. Schachman, A. B. Pardee, and R. Y. Stanier, *Arch. Biochem. Biophys.* **38**, 245 (1952).]

Figure 4–16 shows the sedimentation pattern of an extract of *E. coli* obtained with this type of optical system. The several peaks, whose sedimentation rates can be measured, have been identified, as indicated, with the DNA, RNA particles, and protein components of the bacterium. The DNA peak is sharp because of its low diffusion constant.

4–9 Rotational diffusion and birefringence. The diffusion and sedimentation constants of molecules depend on the molecular size and shape, and the amount of bound water. As we saw in Tables 4–2 and 4–4, neither of these constants is a very sensitive function of the molecular parameters. Therefore it is difficult to obtain accurate shape data about long, thin structures such as myosin and DNA. The *rotational diffusion constant*, on the other hand, does depend strongly on the length of long, thin structures. This constant, Θ, is defined in a manner similar to the linear diffusion constant defined in Eq. (4–8). Consider a cone, as shown in Fig. 4–17(a), whose surface makes an angle ϕ with the x-axis. If the number of molecules whose axes lie between ϕ and $(\phi + d\phi)$ is dn, the density in ϕ-space is $\rho(\phi) = \partial n/\partial \phi$, and the rate at which molecules rotate out of the cone is given by

$$\frac{dn}{dt} = -\Theta \frac{\partial \rho}{\partial \phi}.$$ (4–19)

The negative sign, as before, implies a net flow to the low concentration region. The rotational diffusion constant Θ has the units of $\sec^{-1}$.

Just as the linear diffusion constant depends on molecular form and dimensions, so does the rotational diffusion constant. For a long, thin molecule, which may be thought of as a prolate ellipsoid [Fig. 4–17(b)], it may be shown that the rotational diffusion constant Θ_b for rotation about the b-axis is given by the approximate expression

$$\Theta_b = \frac{3kT}{16\pi\eta a^3}\left(2 \ln \frac{2a}{b} - 1\right),$$

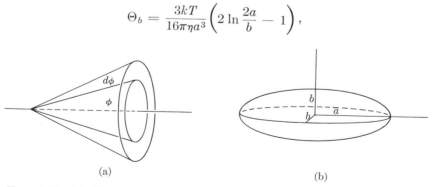

(a)   (b)

Fig. 4–17. (a) The coordinates used for defining the rotational diffusion constant. (b) A prolate ellipsoid of revolution.

TABLE 4–5

SOME VALUES OF ROTATIONAL DIFFUSION CONSTANTS

Molecule	Θ
Hemoglobin	$6 \times 10^6 \text{ sec}^{-1}$
TMV	5.5×10^2
DNA	37
Myosin	7

where the symbols have their usual meanings. The small dimension b appears only in the logarithm, and so a large change in it produces only a small change in Θ_b. Some typical values of Θ are given in Table 4–5. The range of values, a factor of 10^6, is really impressive compared with the range of values shown for the linear diffusion constant. The reason is that the value of Θ is approximately inversely proportional to the cube of the dimension of a molecule, but the value of D depends, as we saw, on the dimension to the first power. Thus the rotational diffusion constant may be used to measure the *length* of a molecule. As in the previous techniques we have discussed, we must start with known boundary conditions, or impress an orienting force on the molecules, and we must be able to detect the orientation. The preferred orientation of a set of long, thin molecules may be detected by shining polarized light on them and observing the absorption of the light or the refractive index for different polarization directions. Although the two techniques will be taken up in greater detail in Chapters 7 and 12, here we shall give a brief description of the latter technique.

Suppose, as in Fig. 4–18, we have a number of molecules oriented so that their axes make an angle θ with the y-axis. If polarized light, with

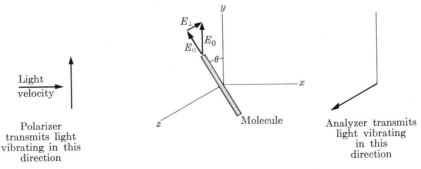

FIG. 4–18. The relative orientations of polarizer, molecular axes, and analyzer. The molecules split the electric field of incident light into components $E_{||}$ and $E_{\perp}$.

the electric field vibrating in the y-direction, is incident on the molecules, it will be split into components $E_{||}$ and $E_\perp$ because the refractive index is different for vibrations in these two directions. We say that the oriented structure is *birefringent*. If the incident electric field is E_0, then $E_{||} = E_0 \cos \theta$ and $E_\perp = E_0 \sin \theta$. The light that passes through the oriented molecules now must pass the analyzer, which is set to transmit vibrations parallel to the z-axis. If θ is zero or $\pi/2$, the incident polarized light will *not* be split into components, the field incident on the analyzer will be parallel to y, and *no* light will be transmitted. For all other orientation angles, some light will be transmitted. If the orientation is not perfect, $\theta = 0$, and $\pi/2$ will still represent *minimum* transmitted intensity.

Two convenient ways of orienting molecules are by electric fields and flowing fluids. The orientation produced by electric fields, so-called *electric birefringence*, is not as great as in *flow birefringence*. A long, thin molecule in a fluid whose layers are moving with different speeds will tend to be aligned with the streamlines because of the torque exerted by the moving fluid. From the point of view of the center of mass of the molecules shown in Fig. 4–19, the fluid moves in opposite directions at the two ends of the molecule. The torque clearly depends on the velocity gradient, $\partial v/\partial y$, and on the molecular length. We do not have to go into the detailed mathematics of the situation to see that the way the molecules are distributed around the direction of the streamlines will depend on both the velocity gradient and the rotational diffusion constant. As the velocity gradient increases, the most probable position for a long, thin molecule will be more closely parallel to a streamline. The actual form of the distribution can be found only by the solution of the rotational analog of the continuity expression, Eq. (4–12). It would take us too far afield to go into these explicit mathematical solutions.

There are two standard ways of producing a velocity gradient. The first is by flowing a solution through a capillary tube. The fluid has zero velocity at the walls and a maximum velocity at the center of the tube,

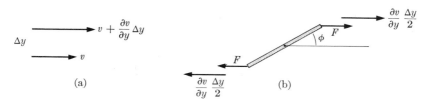

FIG. 4–19. The direction of the forces on a long molecule in a fluid with velocity gradient $\partial v/\partial y$. (a) The fluid velocity relative to a stationary observer. (b) The relative fluid velocity observed from the center of a molecule moving with the average fluid velocity. The two descriptions are equivalent so far as rotation about the center of mass is concerned.

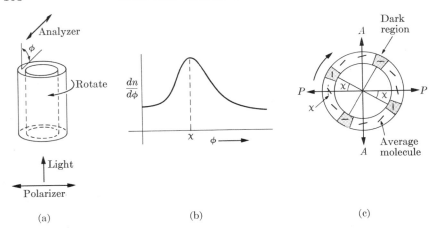

FIG. 4–20. A flow birefringence arrangement. (a) The various components. (b) The average orientation of molecules. (c) The observation in crossed polarizer and analyzer.

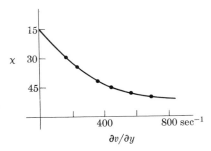

FIG. 4–21. The average orientation direction of DNA for different velocity gradients. [After H. Schwander and R. Cerf, *Helv. Chim. Acta.* **34**, 436 (1951).]

but because the velocity gradient varies from zero at the center to a maximum at the walls, this is not a useful way of producing a gradient for analytical work. A better way is to use coaxial cylinders, one of which rotates relative to the other. If the difference in the diameters is small, the velocity gradient is close to constant. A typical setup is shown in Fig. 4–20(a). A rotational speed of 100 rev/min will give a velocity gradient of about 20 sec^{-1}. As a result of the velocity gradient and rotational diffusion, the molecules make a most probable angle χ with the streamlines, as in Fig. 4–20(b).

If the solution is viewed between a crossed polarizer and analyzer, as described above, the minimum intensity will occur when the most probable position is parallel to either the polarizer or the analyzer. As is shown in Fig. 4–20(c), the most probable angle between the molecules and the streamlines is the same as the angular displacement between the polarizer and the position of minimum intensity. As the velocity gradient increases, the angle χ gets smaller. Figure 4–21 shows the effect of increasing velocity gradient on the orientation of DNA in salt solution. Because of inhomogeneity in the sample of DNA and the temperature rise at high velocity gradients, the angle χ does not approach zero. Since the distribution of molecules depends on $\partial v/\partial y$ and Θ (even though we have not given the explicit expression) and we know $\partial v/\partial y$, these measurements permit us to calculate the rotational diffusion constant.

By taking measurements at different temperatures and viscosities, it is possible to determine whether the particle is rigid. If, for example, the particle were not rigid, but a random coil, we would expect that its length would increase with increasing velocity gradient and hence that the rotational diffusion constant would decrease with increasing gradient. Tobacco mosaic virus acts like a rigid rod, and the behavior of two-stranded DNA seems to be close to that of a rigid rod.

4–10 Conclusion. We have examined in some detail three techniques by which we can learn something about the gross physical appearance of large molecules. Other experimental methods, such as light-scattering, viscosity, and dielectric-constant measurements, give similar information. The use of many lines of evidence can give an excellent picture of a molecule as a whole. We know, for example, that many protein molecules are approximately spherical, with radii that may range from 15 A (with a corresponding molecular weight of 11,000) to 70 A (for molecular weight about 10^6). Other molecules must be hydrodynamically treated as though they were long, thin ellipsoids. Such knowledge is essential to an understanding of the role of large molecules in living systems, but it is far from being sufficient. We must know the internal structure of these spherical and elliptical aggregates before we can make a guess as to how they operate. To illustrate the kind of complexity that may be faced, consider a molecule of glycogen. It is made up of chains of sugar molecules joined either end-to-end or in such a way that they start a branch. A molecule of glycogen is thus structurally like a tree, and a small molecule of glycogen can hardly be called spherical. On the other hand, as the branches increase, the chains become more tightly packed and the molecule becomes more nearly spherical, so that for large glycogen molecules the physical approximations we have just used are probably quite valid. Thus, as we have stressed before, it is the total evidence we seek.

Problems

1. Given a spherical molecule of molecular weight 100,000 and density 1.33 gm/cm^3. If the molecule is in water (but binds no water) of viscosity 10^{-2} poise, calculate: (a) its radius, (b) the frictional coefficient, and (c) the time it would take for the velocity to decay to 1/e of its initial value.

2. Use the known molecular weights and densities to calculate: (a) the radii of pepsin and urease. Neglect hydration. Use the results of Problem 2(a) to calculate: (b) the diffusion, and (c) the sedimentation constants of the two molecules.

3. Use the diffusion constant of pepsin in water to calculate the time for a molecule to go a root-mean-square distance equal to the approximate diameter of an *E. coli*. (Assume, incorrectly, that the viscosity of the inside of the bacterium is the same as that of water.)

4. (a) What is the probability of a pepsin molecule diffusing a distance between $x = 10\mu$ and $x = 11\mu$ in 0.10 sec? (b) What is the probability of finding a displacement in greater than 10μ? in 0.10 sec? (c) What are the probabilities in (a) and (b) if the time is 1 sec or 10^{-3} sec?

5. What are the concentrations of urease at $x = 0.10$ cm and $x = -0.10$ cm one hour after diffusion has started if at $t = 0$ and $x < 0$, $c = 1.00\%$, and for $x > 0$, $c = 0.000$?

6. The first reliable determination of the diffusion constant of a protein (invertase) was made by von Euler, *et al.* [*Hoppeseylers Zeit.* **130**, 87 (1923)]. He obtained $D = 0.05$ cm^2/day at 20°C. Assume that invertase is spherical and has an average amount of bound water. Calculate its molecular weight (von Euler obtained 20,000).

7. Sutherland found experimentally that for large molecules $V^{1/3}D$ is constant, where D is the diffusion constant and V is the gram-molecular volume. Use our present knowledge of physical constants to calculate the value of $V^{1/3}D$ for spherical proteins (Sutherland found 2.1 × 10^{-5} cgs units).

8. Show that in a diffusion cell in which at $t = 0$, $c = c_0$ for $x < 0$ and $c = 0$ for $x > 0$, the positions at which the concentration gradient is half maximum are given by $x = \pm1.64\sqrt{Dt}$.

9. (a) A molecule of what molecular weight will have a potential energy change in 1.00 cm equal to kT in the earth's gravitational field if its density in water is 1.33 gm/cm^3? (b) How long would it take for such a molecule to sediment 1.0 cm, neglecting diffusion? (c) What root-mean-square distance would it diffuse through in this time?

10. (a) How long would it take an *E. coli* ($\rho = 1.10$ gm/cm^3) to sediment 1.0 cm in water in the earth's field? (b) How long would it take to obtain an rms diffusion distance equal to 1.0 cm? (c) At equilibrium, what is the ratio of number of bacteria at a height h to the number at $h + 1$?

11. For an unhydrated molecule of $M = 10^5$ and density 1.33 gm/cm^3, calculate the ratio of the number of molecules at the top to the number at the bottom of a cell 1.00 cm deep if the sedimenting field is constant and equal to (a) 100,000 g, and (b) 1000 g.

12. Calculate the time for the molecule of Problem 11 to sediment 1.0 cm in fields of (a) 100,000 g, and (b) 1000 g.

13. If molecules with sedimentation constant s move in a centrifugal field $\omega^2 r$, show that at times t_2 and t_1 the distances from the axis, r_2 and r_1 respectively, are related by $\ln r_2/r_1 = \omega^2 s(t_2 - t_1)$.

14. From the following data obtained on the sedimentation of ribonuclease, calculate the average value of the sedimentation constant. The angular velocity of the rotor was 52,400 rev/min.

Time, min	Distance of boundary from axis, cm
0	5.908
32.0	5.980
64.0	6.045
96.0	6.112
128.0	6.176

15. (a) Light of wavelength 5000 A is split into two beams and passes through a 1.0% protein solution and a cell containing only solvent. If both solutions are 1.20 cm thick, by how many wavelengths does the light passing through the protein lag the reference solution? (b) What concentration would give a retardation of $\lambda/2$?

16. At 3°C, the rotational diffusion constant of myosin is 7 sec^{-1}. Take the viscosity of water as 0.016 cgs units, and assume that the molecule is long and thin and that its length is (a) 100 times its width, (b) 10 times its width. Compute the length of myosin under these two assumptions.

REFERENCES

1. H. B. BULL, *Physical Biochemistry*, 2nd ed. Wiley, N. Y., 1951.

2. E. J. COHN and J. T. EDSALL, *Proteins, Amino Acids, and Peptides*. Reinhold, N. Y., 1943.

3. O. GLASSER, Ed., *Medical Physics*. Year Book Publishers, Inc., Chicago, Ill. Vol. 1 (1944); Vol. 2 (1950).

4. F. M. UBER, Ed., *Biophysical Research Methods*. Interscience, N. Y., 1950.

5. F. HAUROWITZ, *Chemistry and Biology of Proteins*. Academic Press, N. Y., 1950.

6. T. SVEDBERG and K. O. PEDERSEN, *The Ultracentrifuge*. Oxford University Press, 1940.

7. H. GUTFREUND, "Properties of Solutions of Large Molecules," *Prog. Biophys.* **1**, 1 (1950).

8. C. SADRON, "Methods of Determining the Form and Dimensions of Particles in Solution, A Critical Survey," *Prog. Biophys.* **3**, 237 (1953).

9. G. WEBER, "Rotational Brownian Motion and Polarization of the Fluorescence of Solutions," *Adv. Protein Chem.* **8**, 416 (1953).

10. L. J. GROSTING, "Measurement and Interpretation of Diffusion Coefficients of Proteins," *Adv. Protein Chem.* **11,** 430 (1956).

11. E. C. POLLARD, *The Physics of Viruses.* Academic Press, N. Y., 1953.

12. H. D. SPRINGALL, *The Structural Chemistry of Proteins.* Academic Press, N. Y., 1954.

13. A. NORMAN and J. A. FELD, "Electric Birefringence Studies of Irradiated Deoxyribonucleic Acid," *Arch. Biochem. Biophys.* **71,** 170 (1957).

14. W. MOFFITT, D. FITTS, and J. KIRKWOOD, "Critique of the Theory of Optical Activity of Helical Polymers," *Proc. Nat. Aca. Sci.* **43,** 723 (1957).

15. K. A. STACEY, *Light Scattering in Physical Chemistry.* Academic Press, N. Y., 1956.

16. J. EDSALL and J. WYMAN, *Biophysical Chemistry.* Academic Press, N. Y., 1958.

CHAPTER 5

X-RAY ANALYSIS AND MOLECULAR STRUCTURES

5–1 Introduction. We saw in the previous chapter that sedimentation and diffusion experiments indicate that protein molecules have approximately spherical or ellipsoidal shapes, with dimensions varying from 30 to 200 A, and that birefringence studies show that DNA is a long, thin structure. Experiments of this type, however, tell us nothing about the internal structure of large molecules, what holds them together, and how the various components are arranged. The arrangement of individual atoms may be studied in two ways. One is a purely chemical analysis, which tells us that proteins, for example, are made up of amino acids that are joined by polypeptide bonds and that DNA is a polynucleotide, as was outlined in Chapter 2. Thus a typical protein would have a generalized structure like that shown below, where the R groups represent the various side chains of amino acids. These side chains are shown in Table 2–2.

$$
\begin{array}{c}
\mathrm{R_1} \qquad \mathrm{H} \qquad \overset{\displaystyle \mathrm{O}}{\underset{\displaystyle \parallel}{\mathrm{C}}} \qquad \mathrm{R_3} \\
\mathrm{C} \qquad \mathrm{N} \quad \mathrm{H} \qquad \mathrm{C} \\
{}^{+}\mathrm{H_3N} \quad \mathrm{H} \quad \mathrm{C} \qquad \mathrm{C} \qquad \mathrm{N} \quad \mathrm{H} \quad \mathrm{COO^-} \\
\underset{\displaystyle \mathrm{O}}{\overset{\displaystyle \parallel}{}} \qquad \mathrm{R_2} \qquad \mathrm{H}
\end{array}
$$

In a few proteins, such as insulin and ribonuclease, it has been possible to determine the order of the amino acids in the polypeptide chains. The method used, pioneered by Sanger, consists of splitting the protein into fragments in many different ways, analyzing these fragments by chromatography, and then fitting them back together conceptually to form the insulin molecule. The order of linkages in insulin is shown in Fig. 5–1, and the structure of ribonuclease is shown in Fig. 8–9.

The functions of large molecules depend on more than the order of their subunits. The spatial arrangement may be just as important, as will be seen in Chapters 6 and 8, where the subjects of antibody-antigen reactions and enzyme specificity are taken up. Even though we know the order of the amino acids along the polypeptide chain, or of nucleotides along a DNA chain, we do not necessarily have any knowledge about the configuration of the chain. It is with the second method of studying the arrangement of individual atoms, x-ray diffraction, that the relative positions of atoms in a molecule may be found.

One can imagine three structural levels for large molecules such as proteins. The *primary* structure is the order of the amino acids or subunits.

113

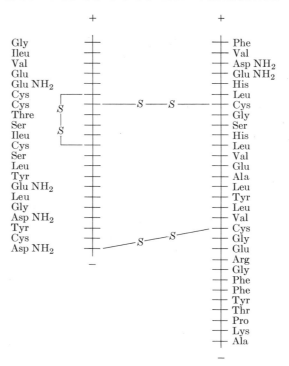

FIG. 5–1. The order and linkages of amino acids in insulin.

The *secondary* structure is the orientation of neighboring subunits, such as the coiling of a polypeptide chain to make an α-helix. The *tertiary* structure is the orientation of one chain with respect to another and gives the molecule its external form. The secondary and tertiary structures are best found by x-ray diffraction techniques.

In favorable cases, such as that of sodium chloride, the positions of the atoms in a crystal lattice may be found with little difficulty. For more complex crystals, such as protein crystals, an x-ray analysis may yield only partial information about structure, but even this is more than is given by other methods.

There are four techniques that make use of the properties of x-rays to investigate biological structures. They are: (1) x-ray absorption, (2) x-ray scattering, (3) x-ray diffraction, and (4) inactivation by x-rays. The fourth technique, the destruction of a biological function by x-rays, is fully discussed in Chapter 11. The first technique is useful because the absorption coefficient of x-rays may change rapidly with atomic number for constant wavelength (or with wavelength for constant atomic number, as indicated below). Thus, as in the case of visible and ultraviolet light taken up in Chapter 7, a measurement of the absorption of x-rays leads to a knowledge of the *atomic* composition of the absorbing material. The fact that long wavelength x-rays are strongly absorbed means that x-ray microscopes show good contrast of the image. An analysis of these techniques here would take us too far afield; the interested reader should consult the review article by Engstrom (Ref. 3).

Both x-ray scattering and x-ray diffraction techniques make use of the wave properties of x-rays. The wavelengths of x-rays are of the order of atomic dimensions, i.e., 1 A, which is small compared with the sizes of the molecules we are interested in. The x-rays that are scattered by the atoms making up an aggregate of molecules interfere and give rise to an interference pattern whose intensities and positions depend on the arrangement of atoms in each molecule and upon the position of the molecules relative to one another. If the molecules occupy random positions, as in a dilute solution, the observed scattered x-rays depend mostly on the size and shape of the scattering molecules. The dependence on internal structure almost vanishes because of the random orientation of the molecules. We shall not be concerned with this type of x-ray analysis, but shall devote our attention to x-ray diffraction—the case in which the molecules have a regular orientation and position relative to one another. The types of structures we shall look at are fibers, molecular crystals, and virus crystals.

X-ray diffraction is now used extensively for the analysis of biological systems because techniques of growing good crystals have improved, new experimental tricks that help determine structures have been developed, and high-speed computers simplify the analysis of data. Under ideal circumstances, x-ray diffraction techniques may be used to locate the positions of all atoms except hydrogen, whose scattering power is too small to be detected by this means. However, the orientation of H atoms may be found by infrared absorption techniques (see Chapter 7).

5–2 Production of x-rays. X-rays are produced when fast electrons are stopped by a target, usually a metal. The resulting x-ray spectrum is composed of two parts, a continuous background, due to (classical) electron deceleration, and a characteristic part which depends on the energy levels of the target atoms. The manner of production of the characteristic lines of copper is represented schematically in Fig. 5–2. As shown in the figure, an incoming electron makes an inelastic collision with a copper atom and ejects an electron from the inner or K-shell of the atom. Electrons from outer levels that may fall into the vacancy lose energy in the amount ΔE, and photons of frequency ν are emitted, such that $\Delta E = h\nu$. If c is the velocity of light, the wavelength is given by

$$\lambda = \frac{c}{\nu} = \frac{hc}{\Delta E}.$$

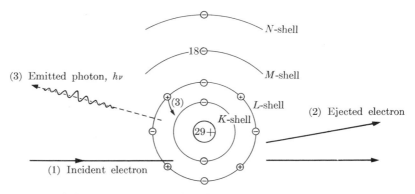

FIG. 5–2. Schematic representation of x-ray production in copper. The events take place in the order 1, 2, 3.

The wavelength emitted when an electron jumps from the L-shell to the vacant K-shell is known as the K_α-line. The K_β line is identified with a transition from M- to K-shells. The L-series of lines represent transitions from higher energy levels to an L-shell with a vacancy. The L-series represents smaller energy changes and hence longer wavelengths than the K-series. The wavelengths of lines in the L-series are about 13 A, and those of the K-series are 1.4 A.

The K_α-lines of copper will not be strongly absorbed by copper, since it is not possible to promote a K-electron to an already filled L-shell. However, absorption may take place by the ejection of electrons from the L- or higher shells. X-ray photons will not be absorbed unless their energies are greater than the binding energy of one of the atomic electrons. The processes involved in the disposition of absorbed x-ray energy will be taken up in detail in Chapter 10. At the moment all we have to know is that when x-rays pass through matter, they are attenuated according to the relation

$$\frac{I}{I_0} = e^{-\mu x},$$

where I_0 represents the x-ray intensity incident on a sample of thickness x, and I is the intensity emerging from the sample. The quantity μ, called the absorption coefficient of the material, depends on the wavelength and the atomic constitution of the material. The behavior of the absorption coefficient for different incident wavelengths is shown in Fig. 5–3, where it can be seen that the absorption spectrum is clearly different from the emission spectrum. The sharp breaks in the absorption coefficient are known as absorption edges. To the left of the K-edge, the incident x-ray photons have enough energy to eject K-electrons; to the right of the peak, their energy is too small to ionize the atoms in the K-

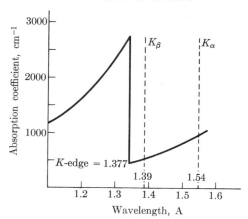

FIG. 5–3. The absorption spectrum in the x-ray region of copper. The positions of some of the emission lines are indicated.

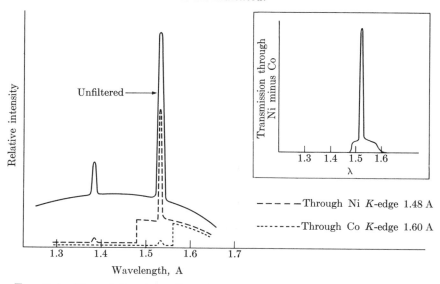

FIG. 5–4. The relative intensity of x-rays emitted from copper by electrons of 30,000 volt energy. The intensity distribution through filters that transmit 50% of 1.57 A radiation is indicated, and the insert shows the difference in intensity transmitted through nickel and cobalt.

shell. Similar statements hold for the other absorption edges. The existence of absorption edges makes it possible to produce nearly monochromatic radiation by appropriate filter choices.

The K-edge of nickel is at 1.48 A, and therefore it will transmit the K_α-line of copper but will strongly absorb the K_β-line. The next higher ele-

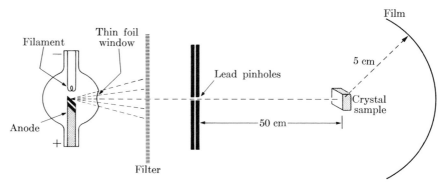

Fig. 5–5. Schematic diagram (not to scale) of apparatus for producing collimated x-rays for crystal analysis.

ment in the periodic table is cobalt. Its K-edge is at 1.60 A, and so it absorbs both the K-lines of copper. It is possible to adjust, or balance, thin films of these two metals so that the *difference* between their transmissions represents monochromatic x-rays, the K_α-line of copper. Figure 5–4 shows the emission spectrum of copper before and after filtration. Apparatus for producing collimated, monochromatic x-rays for crystal analysis would look something like that illustrated in Fig. 5–5.

5–3 Diffraction of x-rays. Shortly after the discovery of x-rays it was found by Laue, Friedrich, and Knipping (1912) that the diffraction of x-rays could be analyzed from the point of view of the summation of disturbances from individual atoms or scattering centers. Thus an incident electromagnetic wave of x-rays falling on two scattering centers A and B will give an intensity at the observer that depends on the resultant electric field at the observer. The intensity I is proportional to $(\mathbf{E}_A + \mathbf{E}_B)^2$. When the differences in path between the scattering centers and observer are integral multiples of the wavelength, constructive interference will occur. In general, the resultant intensity scattered from many scattering centers will be of the form $I = (\sum_i \mathbf{E}_i)^2$ where $\mathbf{E}_i$ is the field scattered by the ith scatterer. As a simple example, consider the scattering from a single row of atoms that is parallel to the wavefront of the incident x-ray beam, as shown in Fig. 5–6. Each atom may be thought of as scattering light in all directions, but the resultant wave will exist only for those directions for which the wave from one atom is an integral number of wavelengths out of step with the others. Such a constructive interference condition will hold if the path difference between adjacent atoms can be expressed as

$$b \sin \phi = k\lambda, \qquad k = 0, 1, 2, \ldots, \tag{5–1}$$

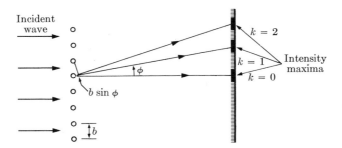

FIG. 5–6. The diffraction of x-rays by a row of atoms.

where k is an integer. There exist only particular angles ϕ which satisfy this relation.

The analysis of a three-dimensional array of scattering centers by the summation of individual scattered waves is a very difficult procedure. A great simplification was introduced by Bragg, who proposed that the ob-served interference pattern be analyzed in terms of reflections from planes of atoms rather than from individual atoms. The three-dimensional property of a crystal can be examined from a two-dimensional viewpoint, as shown in Fig. 5–7. As before, we obtain constructive interference when the path differences between adjacent rays is an integral multiple of the wavelength. The path difference between adjacent rays is $2d \sin \theta$, and the same condition will hold for all other pairs of rays. If the crystal is thick, then the constructive superposition of waves scattered from the

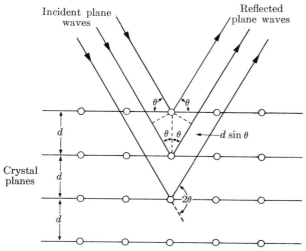

FIG. 5–7. A cross section of a crystal, showing some crystal planes and the reflection of x-rays from them.

lower planes will give rise to a very high scattered intensity only when

$$n\lambda = 2d \sin \theta, \qquad n = 0, 1, 2, \ldots . \tag{5-2}$$

Equation (5–2) is very different from Eq. (5–1), even though they show a formal similarity. The difference is that the angle θ (see Fig. 5–7) is a reflection angle, not a scattering angle. This angle is fixed once the crystal planes are oriented relative to the incident x-ray beam. The interplanar spacing d in Eq. (5–2) is not a variable, and for monochromatic x-rays, λ is constant. We see that the three quantities λ, d, and θ are not variables but are fixed independently of one another by the experimenter. Therefore it is not reasonable to suppose that the value of d will be such as to satisfy Eq. (5–2), and in general *no* intensity maxima will appear. There are two general ways to satisfy Eq. (5–2). The first method is to use non-monochromatic radiation, so that there will be some wavelength that satisfies the equation for fixed θ and d. The analysis of the resulting diffraction pattern, known as a Laue pattern, is impossible for complicated systems. The second method is to use monochromatic x-rays and rotate the crystal shown in Fig. 5–7 about an axis perpendicular to the page. The grazing angle, θ, will vary over a range of angles, and it will pass through angles θ_1, θ_2, . . . , known as Bragg angles, for which Eq. (5–2) will be satisfied for $n = 1, 2, \ldots .$ The reflections shown in Fig. 5–8 might occur. In the figure we have greatly simplified the diffraction pattern, since there obviously exist many other sets of crystal planes that, during the rotation of the crystal, will give rise to diffraction maxima. Before discussing these other planes, we must investigate some of the elements of crystal structure.

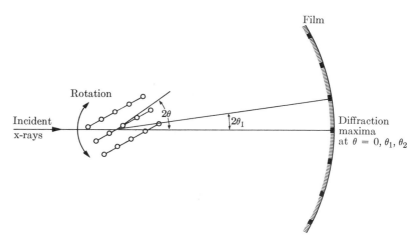

FIG. 5–8. The diffraction pattern obtained from one set of planes in the rotating crystal method. The rotation axis is perpendicular to the page.

If we think of a crystal as made up of many sets of planes all with different interplanar distances d, we see from Eq. (5–2) that small values of d correspond to large angles θ. The largest value of sin θ, namely unity, gives the minimum spacing, d_{min}, that will give constructive interference.

$$d_{min} = \lambda/2 .$$

If copper K_α radiation is used, $d_{min} = 0.7$ A.

5–4 Crystal structure and the unit cell. A crystal is an orderly three-dimensional array of subunits. The subunits may be atoms, molecules, or groups of particles. It is useful to consider the smallest subdivision of the crystal that has the properties of the crystal. The *unit cell* is the smallest possible subdivision which has the properties of the macrocrystal and which, by repetition or translation of itself in all directions, builds the crystal. Figure 5–9 shows the unit cells of some two-dimensional arrays and of a rectangular three-dimensional array. The unit cell is important because of its following properties.

1. The *positions* of intensity maxima are determined by the unit cell dimensions.

2. The magnitudes of the *intensity* of the maxima depend on the *distribution* of electrons.

3. The angular *length* of the intensity maxima depends on the degree of *orientation* of the unit cells relative to one another.

4. The angular *width* of the intensity maxima depends on the *number* of unit cells in the crystal.

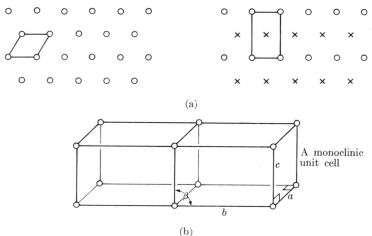

(a)

(b)

FIG. 5–9. The unit cell of (a) some two-dimensional arrays, and (b) of a three-dimensional array whose unit cell lengths are a, b, and c.

TABLE 5–1

UNIT CELL DIMENSIONS*

Material	a	b	c	β	Number of molecules per cell	Mol. wt. per molecule
Insulin						
Wet	49.2 A	57.6 A	39.5 A		4	——
Dry	44 A	51.4 A	30.4 A		——	——
Chymotrypsin						
Wet	49.6 A	67.8 A	66.5 A	102°	4	——
Dry	45 A	62.5 A	57.5 A	112°	——	21,500
Hemoglobin						
Wet	109 A	63.2 A	54.2 A	111°	2	——
Dry	102 A	56 A	49 A	134°	——	66,700
Ribonuclease						
Wet	30.9 A	38.8 A	54.1 A	106°	2	13,000
Dry	29.1 A	30.1 A	51.0 A	114°	——	——

* From J. C. Kendrew, *Prog. Biophys.* **4**, 244 (1954).

Table 5–1 gives some unit cell dimensions of protein crystals. The dimensions of the unit cell, which can be found by the techniques described in Section 5–5, may be used to obtain accurate values of molecular weights. The mass of the unit cell may be obtained from the dimensions and the density. If the approximate molecular weight is known by other means, such as sedimentation and diffusion techniques, the number of molecules per unit cell may be found, and thus the precise molecular mass obtained. Multiplication by Avogadro's number, 6.02×10^{26} molecules/kgm mole, gives the molecular weight. Since wet crystals include water bound to and between the molecules, it is necessary to know what fraction of the crystal mass is solvent. Dry crystals may be used to obtain molecular weights, but they are not usually as perfect as wet ones.

We have seen that the diffraction of x-rays by crystals is best analyzed in terms of the reflection of x-rays from the planes making up a crystal. There are, of course, many more sets of planes than those shown in Fig. 5–7. The orientation of a set of planes may be found from the fact that if the reflected x-rays make an angle 2θ with the incident beam, the planes are oriented so that they make an angle θ with the incident beam, as shown in Fig. 5–7. If such a set of planes contains a large number of atoms, the reflected intensity is high, but if the plane contains only a few atoms, the intensity maximum is practically nonobservable. A crystallographic plane

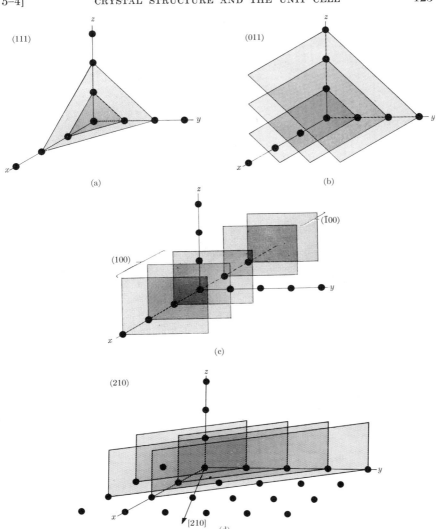

FIG. 5–10. The orientation of some crystal planes with indices (hkl). Note that planes with high values of (hkl) have fewer atoms per plane.

may be represented in terms of its intercepts on the axes a, b, and c of the unit cell of Fig. 5–9. These intercepts are a/h, b/k, and c/l, where h, k, and l are integers. The triplet (hkl) is known as the *Miller indices* of a given plane, and each set of crystallographic planes, represented by integral multiples of the above intercepts, may be designated by a set of indices. Planes parallel to a given axis, the c-axis for example, intercept that axis at ∞, and hence its intercept is represented by $l = 0$. The orientation of some crystallographic planes is shown in Fig. 5–10. It is left as an exercise to show that reflections from sets of planes $(2h2k2l)$ are the same as the $n = 2$ reflections from planes (hkl). Planes with given indices not only have their direction specified but also have d given. For example, for a cubic crystal,

$$\frac{1}{d^2} = \frac{h^2}{a^2} + \frac{k^2}{b^2} + \frac{l^2}{c^2}. \tag{5–3}$$

Because the Bragg angles are determined by the orientation of the planes and the distance between them, the dimensions of the unit cell determine the positions of intensity maxima in the diffraction pattern.

5–5 Layer lines and crystal arrays. We have derived two expressions relating crystal dimensions to the directions in which constructive interference, or intensity maxima, take place. The first expression, Eq. (5–1), gives the vertical deflection, ϕ, by a row of repeating units with spacing b. The second, Eq. (5–2), gives the total angular deviation of the incident beam, 2θ, in terms of $\sin\theta$ and the interplanar spacing d. For any given wavelength and repeat distance b, *all* the intensity maxima given by Bragg's law, $n\lambda = 2d\sin\theta$, must lie on the cones, $\sin\phi = $ constant, shown in Fig. 5–6. Thus the individual diffraction maxima obtained by rotating the crystal about a direction parallel to the side of a unit cell all lie on parallel lines, called *layer lines*, as is shown in Fig. 5–11. The vertical

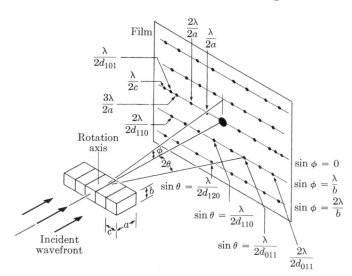

FIG. 5–11. The diffraction of x-rays by a crystal rotated about an axis parallel to the side of a unit cell. The vertical deflection of the layer lines is given by ϕ, and the various diffraction maxima have deflections 2θ.

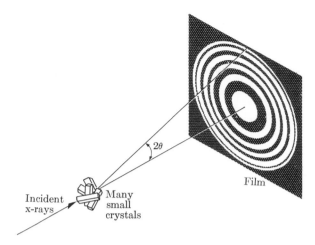

FIG. 5–12. The reflection pattern from an array of small crystals.

deflection of the layer lines is given by $\sin \phi_k = k\lambda/b$. A measurement of the vertical separation of the layer lines yields the unit cell length b. Measurements made when the crystal is rotated about axes parallel to **a** and to **c** yield the other dimensions of the unit cell. If the crystal is not rotated about an axis parallel to unit cell edges, the layer lines are not perpendicular to the rotation axis.

Instead of rotating a crystal about axes parallel to the unit cell sides so as to satisfy the Bragg relation, we may use an aggregate of many randomly oriented crystals, i.e., a powder. Each small crystal will give rise to reflections if the equation $n\lambda = 2d \sin \theta$ is satisfied. As we pointed out before, the great majority of these crystals will give no reflections. Provided there are enough small crystals, however, some will be set at the correct angles and give rise to intensity maxima. Since the reflecting crystals are *randomly* oriented, the diffraction pattern will be similar to a layer-line pattern which has been rotated about the x-ray beam. It will consist of concentric circles, as shown in Fig. 5–12. Note that the inner circles represent large d and that many orders and interplanar spacings appear intermingled. The analysis of such a pattern usually yields only spacings $d_i = n\lambda/(2 \sin \theta_i)$, but sometimes may yield unit cell size and shape.

If all the small crystals are aligned parallel to an axis perpendicular to the incident beam (but with random orientation about this axis), we get a layer-line pattern, as we did from a single crystal rotated about an axis perpendicular to the beam (Fig. 5–11). If the orientation of the small crystals is not perfect, but is given by a distribution like that of b in Fig. 5–13, then the points of the layer lines broaden out and become arcs of circles. The length of the arcs is a measure of the degree of orientation of the reflecting planes.

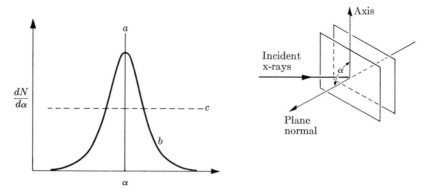

Fig. 5–13. Possible distributions of the orientation of crystal planes, showing the number of planes $dN/d\alpha$ whose normals make angles between α and $\alpha + d\alpha$ with a given direction. The distributions give rise to patterns which are a layer lines, b arcs of circles, c circles.

5–6 Vector representation of amplitudes and the width of diffraction maxima. Much information about crystal structure may be found, as we have seen, from measurements of the positions of the diffraction maxima. Even more useful information comes from knowing the magnitude of the intensity maxima. The intensity of electromagnetic waves, such as x-rays, is proportional to the square of the amplitude of the electric field. Therefore it is necessary to investigate how the resultant electric field may be obtained from the sum of the electric fields scattered by the individual atoms. The electric fields we are speaking of are alternating fields. The electric field, E, is given by an expression of the form

$$E = F \cos \omega t, \qquad \omega = 2\pi\nu, \tag{5–4}$$

where ω is related to the frequency ν of the wave whose amplitude is F. A simple way to represent Eq. (5–4) is to consider a *vector* of length F rotating with an angular velocity ω about an axis perpendicular to the page. The projection of F on the horizontal axis represents E. The utility of this representation becomes apparent when we try to determine the sum of two or more simple harmonic waves of the form of Eq. (5–4) when the waves have similar frequencies but are out of phase by an angle δ and have different amplitudes. Suppose, for example, that we want the sum of $E = E_1 + E_2$, where

$$E_1 = F_1 \cos \omega t, \qquad E_2 = F_2 \cos(\omega t + \delta).$$

The vector way of solving the problem is to add $\mathbf{F}_1$ and $\mathbf{F}_2$ vectorially to give a resultant $\mathbf{F}$, as shown in Fig. 5–14. Since the vectors $\mathbf{F}_1$ and $\mathbf{F}_2$ are

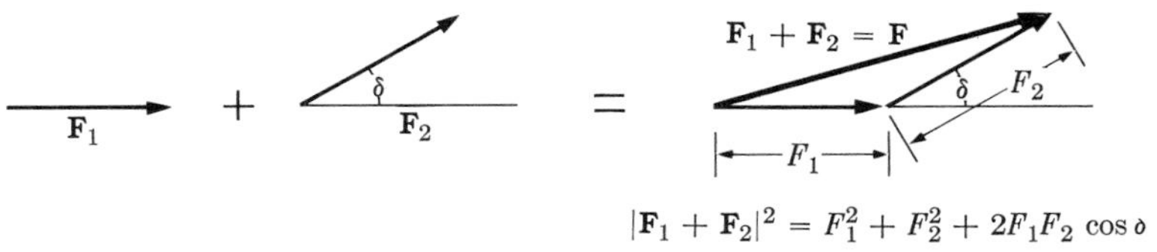

$$\mathbf{F}_1 + \mathbf{F}_2 = \mathbf{F}$$

$$|\mathbf{F}_1 + \mathbf{F}_2|^2 = F_1^2 + F_2^2 + 2F_1F_2 \cos \delta$$

FIG. 5–14. Vector addition of the amplitudes of two simple harmonic waves which differ by a phase angle δ.

rotating with the same frequency, the resultant rotates with frequency ω and the projection of $\mathbf{F}$ on the horizontal axis represents E at any time. The average intensity is proportional to the time average of E^2, which is given by

$$I\alpha(E^2)_{\mathrm{av}} = \tfrac{1}{2}F^2.$$

A knowledge of the *amplitude* of the resultant wave suffices to specify the intensity.

As an example of the utility of the vector representation of amplitudes, we shall calculate the dependence of the angular width of the diffraction pattern on the number, N, of reflecting planes in the crystal. At angles θ_B which satisfy the Bragg relation $n\lambda = 2d \sin \theta_B$, the relation among the amplitudes $F_1, F_2, \ldots, F_N$ of the waves reflected from the planes is as shown in Fig. 5–15(a). If the angle of reflection is slightly greater than the Bragg angle, the amplitudes of the waves reflected from successive planes are no longer in phase (or out of phase by 360°), but are out of phase by a small angle δ. It should be clear from Fig. 5–15(b) that the *resultant* intensity will be zero when the path difference between adjacent planes is λ/N, corresponding to $\delta = (2\pi/\lambda) \cdot (\lambda/N)$. For smaller path differences, the intensity is intermediate between these extremes, and a plot of intensity *versus* angle will be similar to those shown in Chapter 12 for the diffraction

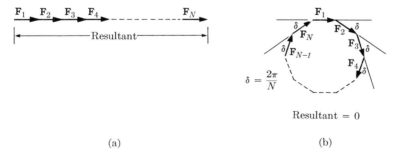

$$\delta = \frac{2\pi}{N}$$

Resultant = 0

(a)   (b)

FIG. 5–15. The addition of the vector amplitudes of waves reflected from crystal planes. (a) Crystal set at the Bragg angle θ_B. (b) Crystal set at an angle $\theta_B + \Delta\theta$, so that the *resultant* amplitude is zero.

patterns of slits. When the intensity falls to zero, the path differences become

$$n\lambda + \frac{\lambda}{N} = 2d \sin(\theta_B + \Delta\theta)$$

$$= 2d(\sin\theta_B \cos\Delta\theta + \cos\theta_B \sin\Delta\theta).$$

Because $\Delta\theta$ is small,

$$n\lambda + \frac{\lambda}{N} = 2d \sin\theta_B + 2d\,\Delta\theta \cos\theta_B.$$

But since $n\lambda = 2d \sin\theta_B$, we have

$$\Delta\theta = \pm\,\frac{\lambda}{2Nd \cos\theta_B}\,, \tag{5-5}$$

and a similar expression holds for $-\Delta\theta$. Since the incident beam makes an angle θ_B, *not* $\theta_B + \Delta\theta$ with the planes, the reflected rays are deviated through twice $2\,\Delta\theta$ on each side of the center of the line, and we have

$$\text{Total angular width} = \frac{2\lambda}{Nd \cos\theta} = \frac{2\lambda}{t \cos\theta}\,, \tag{5-6}$$

where $t = Nd$ is the thickness of the crystal. We now must add the minimum obtainable line width to this angular width. Since crystals with dimensions greater than 10^{-4} cm give line widths equal to the minimum, in practice crystals of microscopic sizes may be analyzed. Thus it is possible to make determinations on crystals of viruses or proteins when only small samples are available.

5–7 Density distribution within a unit cell. X-ray diffraction results are important because they open up the possibility of calculating the density of electrons as a function of position in the unit cell. If this density function were known with a resolution of about 1 A, we could infer the positions of all the atoms except hydrogen, and the structure of the molecules making up the unit cell would be known. The determination of the density distribution is a difficult job. There is, as yet, no complete determination for proteins. We can, however, indicate the magnitude of the three-dimensional problem by taking up some simple one-dimensional cases.

The basic ideas in structure analysis are simple enough. Remember that intensity maxima are obtained only when the Bragg relation is satisfied. This means that we look only in directions specified by the indices (hkl) of the planes. Let us take the (100) planes as an example. These planes intersect the a-axis at 0, a, $2a$, ... and are parallel to the b- and c-axes. When we speak of the reflection from these adjacent planes, we say that the waves are λ out of step or an angle $(2\pi/\lambda) \lambda$ out of phase. But the fact that a is the repeat distance does not imply that there are no atoms at positions other than 0 and a. The region between 0 and a may have a very complicated atomic density distribution. The general expression for the amplitude, $F(100)$, of the x-rays scattered in the [100] direction [that is, from (100) planes] is

$$\mathbf{F}(100) = \sum_i \mathbf{f}_i(100),$$

where $\mathbf{f}_i$ are the vector amplitudes of the radiation scattered by the individual atoms in the [100] direction. In general, for directions [hkl],

$$\mathbf{F}(hkl) = \sum_i \mathbf{f}_i(hkl). \tag{5-7}$$

Figure 5–16 indicates that if the path difference between planes 0 and a is λ, the path difference between 0 and i is $\lambda(x_i/a)$ and the corresponding phase difference is $(2\pi/\lambda)\lambda(x_i/a) = 2\pi(x_i/a)$. If we were to look in the [h00] direction, the phase difference would be $2\pi h(x_i/a)$. If we set $|\mathbf{f}_i(h00)| = f_i(h00) = f_i$, we see from Eq. (5–7) and Fig. 5–16 that the two components of F, F_X, and F_Y, are given by

$$F_X(h00) = \sum_i f_i \cos 2\pi h \frac{x_i}{a}, \qquad F_Y(h00) = \sum_i f_i \sin 2\pi h \frac{x_i}{a}. \tag{5-8}$$

Needless to say, the X- and Y-axes represent the coordinates of the electric field, and x, y, and z represent coordinates in the unit cell. If the resultant amplitude makes an angle α with the X-axis, we may write the above equations as

$$F_X(h00) = |\mathbf{F}| \cos \alpha, \qquad F_Y(h00) = |\mathbf{F}| \sin \alpha, \tag{5-9}$$

where

$$|\mathbf{F}|^2 = F_X^2 + F_Y^2, \qquad \tan \alpha = \frac{F_Y}{F_X}.$$

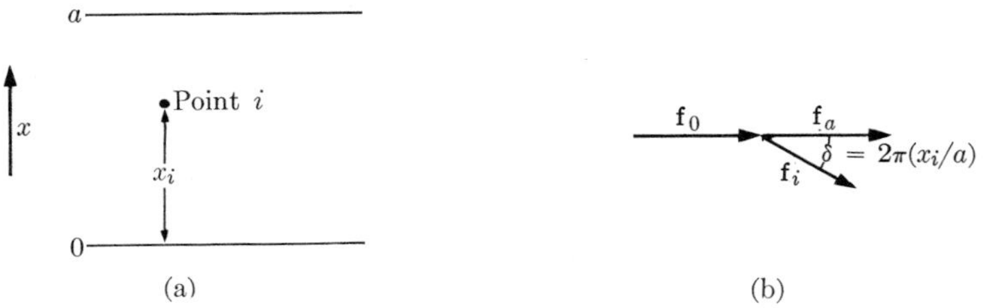

(a) (b)

FIG. 5–16. The (100) planes, showing an arbitrary point i and the relative phases of 0, a, and i.

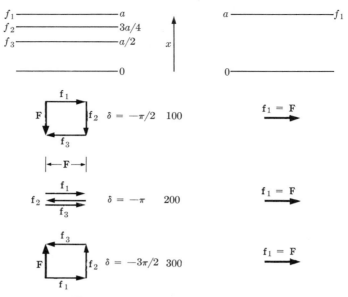

FIG. 5–17. Two different density distributions and the resulting reflected amplitudes in the [h00] direction, $f_1 = f_2 = f_3$.

The quantity **F**, called the *structure factor*, is a function of the density distribution and the direction [hkl]. It is clear from the above argument that, given the density distribution, the structure factor may be calculated for any direction. Likewise, a knowledge of the structure factor in all directions permits calculation of the density distribution.

It is *impossible*, without additional information, to determine the structure factor from an x-ray diffraction photograph. The reason is simple. The intensity of a given spot (hkl) in the diffraction diagram is proportional to the square of the absolute value of the amplitude of the electric field, which is proportional to the structure factor. That is,

$$I(hkl) \alpha |\mathbf{F}(hkl)|^2.$$

But, as is shown by Eqs. (5–8) and (5–9), the density distribution is related to the vector structure factor. Both amplitude, $|\mathbf{F}|$, and phase, α, must be found. *The intensity measures only the amplitude.*

To understand the necessity for knowing the phase of the resultant amplitude, consider the case of two unit cells with the same dimension a but with different density distributions, shown in Fig. 5–17. If the dimension a is small enough, the only observable reflections are 100, 200, and 300. In this case the magnitudes of the diffracted amplitudes are the same for the two density distributions. Since the phase cannot be found from

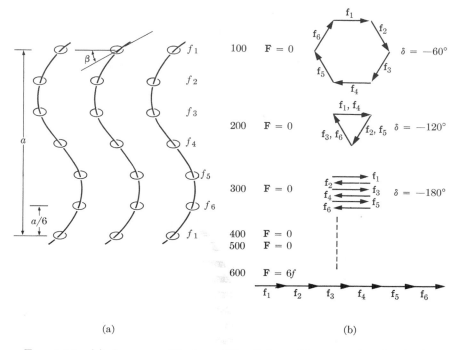

(a)   (b)

FIG. 5–18. (a) An array of helices with pitch **a**. There are six subunits in a pitch distance. (b) Vector addition of amplitudes to yield the structure factors $F(h00)$.

the intensity alone, the diffraction patterns of the two distributions are the same in the [h00] direction. There are experimental tricks, which we shall not go into, that help to determine the phases of the diffracted waves. Needless to say, all evidence, not just x-ray diffraction, is useful in determining structures.

An important application of vector amplitudes is to the analysis of the diffraction pattern obtained from an array of helical structures. Suppose that the pitch of the helix is a and that there are an integral number of similar (but not necessarily identical) subunits, such as nucleotides, spaced along the helix, as shown in Fig. 5–18. In the [100] direction, where the phase difference between the extremes of the pitch is 2π, the phase difference between adjacent units is $2\pi \, \Delta x/a = 2\pi/6$. As the vector sum shows, $\sum_{i=1}^{6} \mathbf{f}_i = 0$. For the second-order reflection, (200), the phase differences are $2\pi/3$ and the structure factor is still zero. Likewise, $F(300)$, $F(400)$, and $F(500)$ are zero. The first nonzero amplitude in the [h00] direction occurs for the sixth-order reflection, (600), of planes separated a distance a.

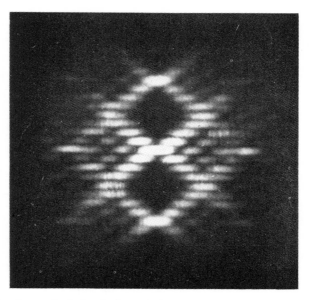

FIG. 5–19. An optical simulation of the x-ray diffraction pattern of a helix with six subunits per pitch. [After A. R. Stokes, "The Theory of X-ray Fibre Diagrams," *Prog. Biophys.* **5,** 140 (1955).]

Calculation of the magnitudes of the structure factors for directions other than [$h00$] is more involved. The intensity does not vanish for the reflections ($1kl$) and ($7kl$) as it does when both k and l are zero, but it may be shown that the intensity of the diffraction pattern vanishes in regions that are at an angle β (the helix angle) with the vertical (or meridional) direction. The layer lines 1 through 7 have zero intensity along the meridian, as indicated in Fig. 5–19. For a helix with N subunits per pitch, the first ($N - 1$) layer lines will show no spots on the meridian. This type of diffraction pattern is very easy to recognize.

5–8 The diffraction patterns of some protein fibers. The work of Astbury has shown that, on the basis of x-ray diffraction patterns, fibrous proteins may be divided into two groups. One group consists of fibrinogen, keratin, and myosin—blood-clotting proteins and proteins found in epidermal tissue and in muscle. The other group is comprised of proteins of the connective tissue—the collagen group.

Figure 5–20 shows the major features of the x-ray patterns of unstretched and stretched hair, which are characteristic of structures known as α-keratin and β-keratin. Part (a) of the figure shows that in α-keratin the 9.7 A spacing is strong compared with the 5.2 A spacing. When the hair

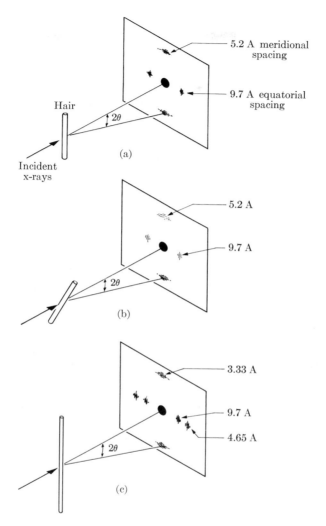

Fig. 5–20. The x-ray diffraction patterns from (a) unstretched hair (α-keratin), (b) unstretched hair tilted relative to the incident beam, and (c) stretched hair (β-keratin).

is tilted as shown in part (b), the 5.2 A spacing is greatly intensified. This result is to be expected if the 5.2 A spacing represents the distance between planes which are mostly perpendicular to the length of the hair and have a distribution about this average position like that given by b in Fig. 5–13. When the hair is tilted, many more planes will be oriented such that the Bragg relation is obeyed for $d = 5$ A. We shall see shortly that the

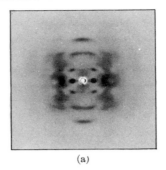

(a)

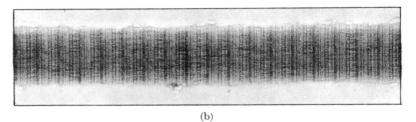

(b)

Fig. 5–21. (a) The diffraction pattern of slightly stretched collagen obtained from rat-tail tendon. Note the fine structure in the low-angle part of the pattern. [Courtesy A. C. T. North.] (b) An electron micrograph of collagen stained with phosphotungstic acid. The repeat distance is 640 A. [Courtesy A. J. Hodge.] × 125,000.

meridional spacing is associated with a repeat distance along the poly-peptide chain. The 9.8 A spacing represents distances between the poly-peptide chains that run parallel to the hair axis. The width and arc length of the diffraction patterns of Fig. 5–20 indicate that the orientation of the polypeptide chains is nowhere near perfect. The x-ray pattern of β-keratin (Fig. 5–20b), which is typical of stretched hair, natural silk fibroin, and of the grosser features of natural feather keratin, shows a spacing of 3.3 A parallel to the fiber and spacings of 9.8 A and 4.6 A perpendicular to the hair. These latter spacings are actually perpendicular to each other, as can be shown by compressing the hair during stretching. The actual configuration of amino acids responsible for the α- and β-keratin patterns will be described in Section 5–12, after we have examined another powerful analytical method, that of building a model (Section 5–10).

The x-ray pattern of collagen exhibits a wealth of detail compared with diagrams of hair. There are reflections of very small angle corresponding to spacings of ∼100 A and angular deviations corresponding to spacings of ∼10 A. The large spacings show up beautifully in electron micro-graphs of stained preparations. Figure 5–21 shows both an x-ray pattern and an electron micrograph of collagen. The long repeat distance of 640 A shows many subunits in Fig. 5–21(b). The electron-dense regions are called *bands*, and the more transparent intermediate regions are the *interbands*. A detailed analysis of many structural features of collagen, which we will only summarize here, will be found in Ref. 11. Collagen seems to be made up of molecular fibrils, or protofibrils, of about 12 A diameter. The interbands represent ordered regions of the fibrils, and the bands indicate less ordered regions. When a collagen fiber is placed under tension it stretches, and the x-ray diffraction pattern shows characteristic changes. The low-angle pattern (or large spacings) shows increased spacings that are proportional to the elongation of the fiber, but the high-angle pattern remains unchanged until the fiber lengthens about 3%, beyond which the spacings increase slowly with elongation. Cowan, North, and Randall conclude that the increase in low-angle spacing comes from the straightening of the individual fibrils within a fiber. All the fiber stretch does not arise from orientation, because the original disorientation, as shown by the angular width of the diffraction pattern, is too small. Some of the extension must come from the elongation of poorly ordered regions. The high-angle spacing corresponds to the detailed structure of protofibrils. As can be seen in Fig. 5–21(a), many of the meridional reflections are missing in the large-angle pattern, and a helical type of structure is indicated. The first meridional arc corresponds to a spacing of 2.95 A. The third layer line represents a spacing of 10 A. Thus there are about $3\frac{1}{3}$ repeat units per turn, or an integral number of units per three turns, or 30 A. The repeat units are obviously the amino acids which make up collagen.

The x-ray patterns of collagen are not detailed enough to locate the atoms in the protofibrils of collagen. Rich and Crick, and Ramachandran and Kartha, stimulated by the work of Pauling, Corey, and Branson on the structure of keratin, have proposed a model of collagen that seems to fit the observed x-ray pattern. It consists of three helical polypeptide chains (with three residues per turn) that slowly wind around each other in a direction opposite to the helical turns, so as to make a coil that will have more than three residues per 10 A, as required by x-ray diffraction data. This particular type of structure is possible for substances like polyglycine, polyproline, and collagen, in which the amino acid sequence —gly—pro—hypro— occurs often.

5–9 The structure of globular proteins. Globular proteins, unlike fibrous ones, form crystals whose x-ray diffraction patterns show great detail. Although the diffraction pattern of no protein crystal has been completely analyzed, the general features of globular protein structures emerge from the analyses. The most thorough and painstaking x-ray diffraction study of a globular protein molecule has been carried out by Perutz and his collaborators, Boyes-Watson, Bragg, Davidson, Howells, and Kendrew, on horse methemoglobin. The magnitude of the undertaking may be gauged by a quotation from an early paper* of Perutz's. "The diffraction pattern of wet hemoglobin crystals extends to a spacing of 2.5 A, but indexing was not carried beyond 2.8 A spacing, since only isolated weak reflexions occurred beyond this range. Even so, the limiting sphere contained 62,700 reciprocal lattice points [reflection planes] which symmetry reduces to 7,480 reflexions relevant for analysis. The photographing, indexing, measuring, correcting and correlating of some 7,000 reflexions was a task whose length and tediousness it will be better not to describe. . . . The intensities had to be recorded on three sets of 45 oscillation photographs taken respectively about the 100, 001, and 102 zone axes. The range of oscillation was 3°, with 1° overlap between successive photographs."

The details of the complete analysis of globular protein cannot be given here, but some of the techniques and shortcuts that can be used to obtain knowledge of the structure of hemoglobin will be mentioned. The changes in the dimensions of the hemoglobin crystal on drying may be seen from Table 5–1. The change in the dimension perpendicular to the ab-plane, as shown in Fig. 5–22, is much larger than those in the other two directions. Thus there is an indication of liquid layers parallel to the ab-plane. If the crystals are put into a potassium sulfate solution, the massive potassium ion diffuses into these liquid layers, and we find from the resulting change in the intensity distribution of the diffraction pattern that there is only *one* liquid layer in the unit cell. The change in cell dimension on drying arises from the slip of one molecule past another, not

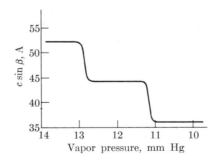

FIG. 5–22. The unit cell height perpendicular to the ab-plane for a wet crystal of horse methemoglobin in equilibrium with water vapor at different relative humidities.

* *Proc. Roy. Soc.* **A195,** 474 (1949).

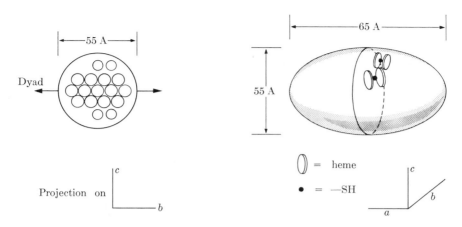

FIG. 5–23. A schematic picture of hemoglobin. The line labeled *dyad* is a symmetry axis. The location of the four heme groups is only one of four possible ones, but their orientation is correct. [After Bragg, Howells, and Perutz, *Acta Cryst.* **5**, 135 (1952), and Ingram, Gibson, and Perutz, *Nature* **178**, 906 (1956).]

from a rearrangement inside the individual molecules. The diffraction pattern at large angles is associated with the interatomic spacings of the molecules. The analysis of the intensities of the large-angle diffraction pattern shows two important regularities. If we take planes parallel to the ab-plane, it is found that there are regions of high electron density running down these planes in the form of rods parallel to the a-axis. It is reasonable to identify these high-density rods as polypeptide chains. These rodlike regions are separated from one another by 10 A. Within each rod there is a repeat distance of 5.1 A. Note that these two spacings correspond to those found in the x-ray patterns of α-keratin. This is a very useful correlation, since it implies that there exist common rules which guide such different structures as fibrous and globular proteins. A schematic picture of hemoglobin is shown in Fig. 5–23. The positions of the S—H groups are found by substitution of Hg for H. This type of substitution leaves the unit cell unchanged, and hence does not affect the positions of the intensity maxima but does change the intensity distribution. It is known as an *isomorphous transformation*. The intensity change may be used to calculate the change in the structure factor, which then yields a knowledge of the positions of the Hg atoms and, more important, some information about the phases of the structure factors.

It is easy to summarize the results of the x-ray investigation of hemoglobin. Obtaining them is another matter. The magnitude of the task may be judged from the fact that the initial analysis of hemoglobin showed only four layers of rods, whereas Fig. 5–23 shows five layers. Earlier views

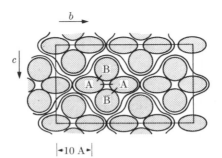

FIG. 5–24. An end-on view of a possible model of an insulin crystal. Each molecule, of four chains, is made up of two A and two B chains. The shaded groups are $a/2$ below the unshaded ones. [After Low, Ref. 5.]

pictured hemoglobin as a cylinder 57 A in diameter and 34 A high. The present view gives the molecule an ellipsoidal shape with an axial ratio of 1.18, which agrees with data obtained by sedimentation and diffusion methods. The shape of a molecule is very difficult to find by x-ray diffraction, because the molecules in a crystal are so close together that it is hard to say where one molecule begins and another ends.

Obviously there are many unresolved questions about the structure of hemoglobin. The *five* layers of polypeptide chains do not fit the known *four* subgroups or the *six* end groups. The five layers are, of course, simply projections on the yz-plane, and they could represent four layers that are warped to give five projected layers. Since x-ray data show that not all of hemoglobin is organized into parallel chains, the detailed determination of the structure is complicated. Lastly, the structures of the polypeptide chains in hemoglobin are not known.

Three other crystalline proteins have received intensive study: insulin, ribonuclease, and myoglobin. In end-on projection, the first two proteins show evidence of arrays of parallel, or near parallel, rods. A tentative model of insulin is shown in Fig. 5–24. Here, too, the structure of the polypeptide chains is not known even though the order of the amino acids is.

The three-dimensional *secondary and tertiary* structure of myoglobin has been determined by x-ray diffraction. Myoglobin has 152 amino acid residues and a molecular weight of 17,000. It has only one heme group. The phases of the various reflections were determined by substitution of a number of different heavy metal atoms to give isomorphous transformations, and the density distribution was calculated to a resolution of 2 A. Such resolution, which required the use of 10,000 reflections, is sufficient to show general positions of the chains. A model of myoglobin to

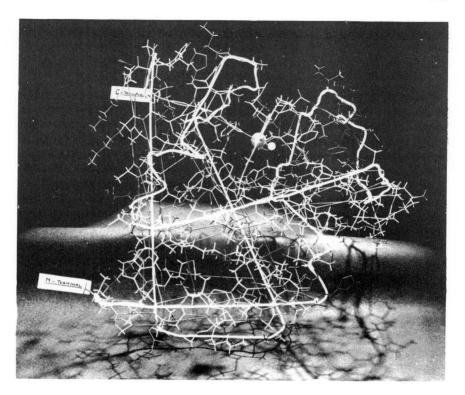

FIG. 5–25. A photograph of a three-dimensional model of the myoglobin molecule. At this resolution, 2 A, most of the individual amino acids may be identified. The polypeptide chain follows the tortuous path shown by the solid white line. The heme group, with its central iron atom, may be seen in the upper right-hand side of this model. [Courtesy of John Kendrew.]

this resolution is shown in Fig. 5–25. The most obvious feature is the lack of symmetry in the polypeptide chains. The chains, which are about 10 A apart, are only more or less parallel to one another and are folded to form an approximately flat disk.

5–10 The structure of polypeptide chains. In the method of structural synthesis that we have described, the spacings and intensities observed in the x-ray pattern of a crystal are used to derive the positions of the atoms making up the crystal. For simple crystals this is a comparatively easy task. For complex crystals it is almost impossible, and indeed has not been carried through to completion except in the case of myoglobin, although much valuable information about the molecular architecture of molecules has been obtained. Another line of attack is to determine first the exact structure of the constituent amino acids making up a protein molecule and then to fit these amino acids together to make the entire molecule. This method, pioneered by Pauling, Corey, and Branson, has been very fruitful. It has opened up a new method of attack (model-building with known constraints) on biological structures. The general principles used by Pauling, Corey, and Branson for α- and β-keratin and synthetic polypeptides have been applied to collagen and, as we shall see in Section 5–13, also to nucleic acid polymers.

X-ray analysis of amino acid crystals not only gives all the interatomic spacings, but also allows us to say that the peptide linkage is a *planar* configuration. The reasoning behind this latter point, which has an important bearing on determining protein structure, is quite simple. The observed distance between the carbon and nitrogen is 1.32 A. A single-bond spacing would be 1.48 and a double-bond spacing would be 1.28 A. The observed spacing corresponds to about 50% double-bond character, and is due to resonance (see Chapter 6) between the forms.

The extra stability conferred on the peptide bond by this resonance is of the order of 1 ev. We shall see that double-bond groups have a potential minimum when the group is planar. A 10° distortion would correspond to an energy increase of 0.9 kcal/mole, and a 20° distortion to 3.5 kcal/mole, or 0.15 ev. The most stable configuration, then, is certainly planar or very close to planar. Using this fact and all the other observed distances obtained for amino acids, we obtain the structure of an extended polypeptide chain, as shown in Fig. 5–26. This extended configuration is not necessarily the most stable one, because we know from infrared data, for example, that there is a large number of hydrogen bonds in a molecule of this type. One would suspect that the larger the number of hydrogen bonds, the more stable the configuration. The problem of ascertaining the form of a polypeptide chain is really one of minimizing the energy, subject to the known bond angles and separations shown in Fig. 5–26. Pauling, Corey, and Branson assumed that the possible structures would have a high degree of symmetry (that is, they would look like helices, for example) but found no reason to suppose that there must be an integral number of amino acids per turn of such a helix. If there are a nonintegral number of residues per turn, the symmetry of the helix is somewhat complicated. To go from one residue to another involves not only a rotation but also a

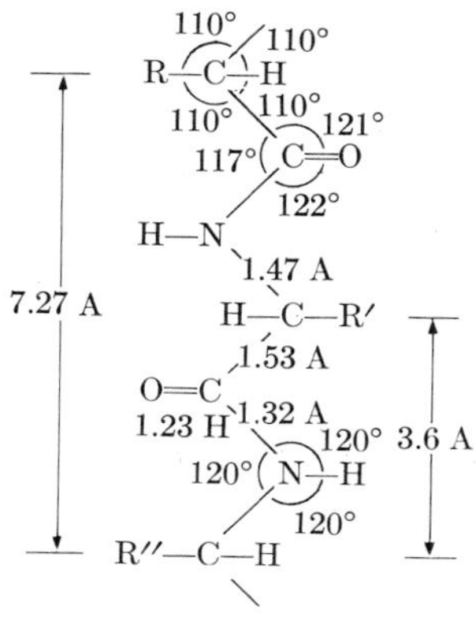

FIG. 5–26. The dimensions of an extended polypeptide chain. Note that the sequence CCNC is planar.

translation along the helix axis. Pauling and co-workers took care to satisfy the condition that a large number of strong hydrogen bonds are needed to minimize the energy. Hydrogen bonds (see Chapter 6) represent an electrostatic force between hydrogen and electro-negative groups such as oxygen. This type of interaction could take place between the $-N-H$ and $-C=O$ groups of proteins to give $-N-H \ldots O=C-$ if the NH and CO groups were in the correct positions. The interaction energy associated with a hydrogen bond will be strongest when, for example, the NHO group lies on a straight line. The distance between the nitrogen and oxygen atoms is normally found to be about 2.75 ± 0.05 A. Again, too wide a divergence from this value is not expected. The hydrogen bond energies are greater than $\frac{1}{4}$ ev when the angle between the NH and NO directions is less than 30°.

Of the many possible structures, three, namely two types of pleated sheets and one helix, called the α-helix, satisfy these minimum energy considerations.

5–11 The pleated sheets and β-keratin. Polypeptide chains are made up of planar groups C—CONH—C linked together about a tetrahedral carbon atom. One possible way of orienting these planar groups is shown in Fig. 5–27. As a result of the pleating, the repeat distance along the y-axis is 6.7 A/$2 = 3.3$ A in β-keratin but is 3.6 A for a fully extended polypeptide chain. The other β-keratin spacings, as shown in Fig. 5–27, represent sidewise distances between the chains (4.7 A) and the large spacing of 10 A which results from the extension of the amino acid side chains above and below the xy-plane. Every $-NH$ and $-CO$ group participates in a hydrogen bond. The hydrogen bonds in this model are

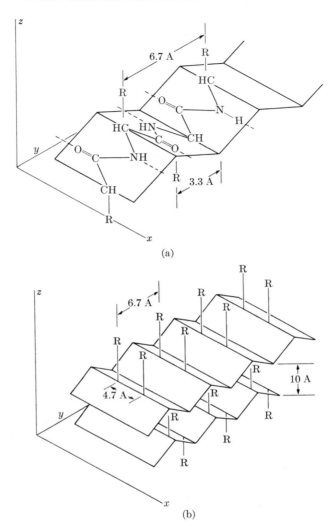

FIG. 5–27. (a) An extended polypeptide chain, which is the basis of the pleated sheet model of β-keratin. H bonds are shown as dashed lines. (b) An array of polypeptide chains to give pleated sheets.

interchain bonds and, in agreement with the absorption of polarized infrared light, they are oriented perpendicular to the fiber axis. The model shown in Fig. 5–27 is not complete, in that the relative directions in which the polypeptides run is not specified. The chains may be either parallel or antiparallel sequences of amino acids. Each possibility gives rise to a pleated sheet of the type shown in the figure and each fits the β-keratin structure.

5–12 The α-helix and α-keratin. The system of planar groupings that make up polypeptide chains may be rotated about the α-carbon atoms. If the rotation from plane to plane is constant, a helix results   (The pleated sheets are special cases of helices.) The α-helix is easily seen if the planar groups are represented by playing cards glued edge-to-edge to give the rotational dimensions shown in Table 5–2. Figure 5–28 shows some of the α-helix. Each C=O and N—H group participates in a hydrogen bond in which the NH direction is within 12° of the chain axis. These hydrogen bonds are *intrachain* bonds.

The number of residues per turn is not integral, but 3.7. Slight variations in hydrogen bond distances could change the dimensions of the helix slightly. Thus one might expect to find in actual practice 48 residues in 13 turns, 11 residues in 3 turns, 15 residues in 4 turns, or 18 residues in 5 turns. Although some of these deviations from the simple α-helix may appear large, they are certainly not impossible in any particular molecule, since there will be effects arising from the R groups and from the interactions between adjacent helices.

There is one obvious feature of the α-helix that does not appear on any other model for protein structure. There is a repeat distance of 1.5 A along the axis corresponding to the axial displacement between adjacent amino acids. This repeat was looked for after the proposal of the α-helix model, and was found to exist in hair, porcupine quill, muscle fibers, and hemoglobin. (Such a small spacing would appear at so large an angle that it had not been photographed in earlier pictures of hemoglobin.) The discovery of this spacing in fibrous proteins and hemoglobin was a great triumph for this molecular model and indicated that the α-helix was an important, though not unique, structural part of these proteins. Not all globular proteins are made up in part of α-helices. Ribonuclease does *not* show the 1.5 A spacing.

For two reasons, the α-helix cannot represent the final picture, even for α-keratin. First, the density of the structure, 1.15 gm/cm^2, though

TABLE 5–2

THE DIMENSIONS OF THE α-HELIX

Rotation between residues	97.2°
Residues per turn	3.69 A
Translation per residue	1.47 A
N—H direction from axis	12°
Helix radius	1.81 A
N—H—O angle	10°
Pitch	5.44 A

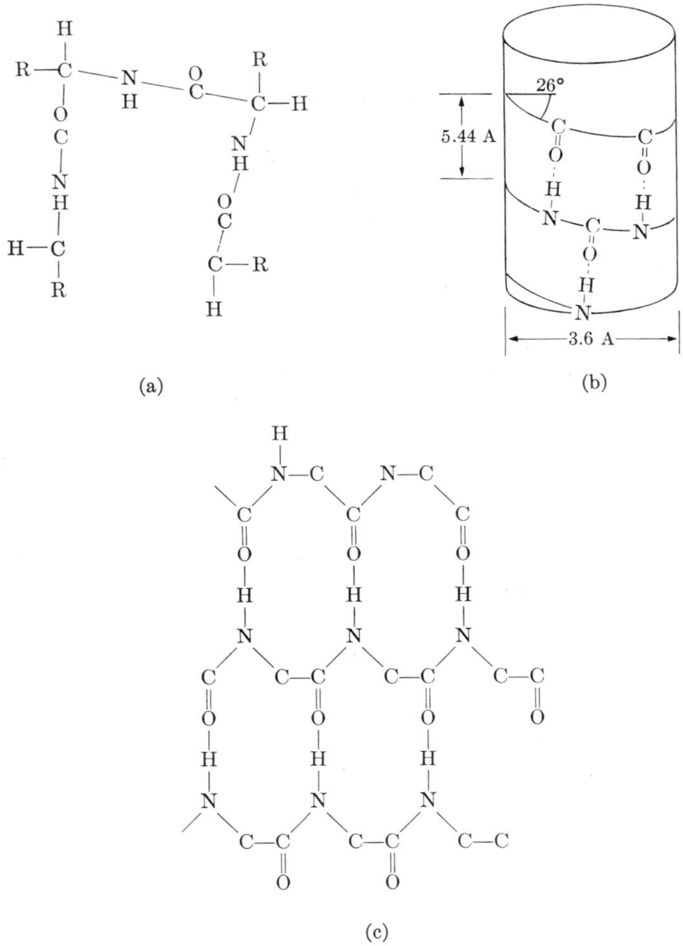

(a)

(b)

(c)

FIG. 5–28. The α-helix. (a) Top view of three residues, showing the planar groups. (b) The cylinder to which the planar groups are tangent. (c) The amino acid plan that is obtained when the cylinder is cut along one side and unrolled.

similar to that of synthetic polypeptides, is too small compared with the 1.3 gm/cm³ of α-keratin. Secondly, the α-helix does not give rise to the axial repeat of 5.2 A shown by α-keratin. Both objections were eliminated by Pauling and Corey in the following manner. They assumed that there could be small systematic changes in the hydrogen bond distance because of the amino acid order, for example. If these systematic changes took place at every seventh amino acid residue (not quite two turns of the

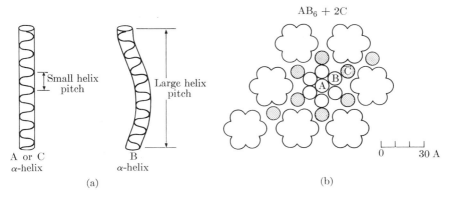

FIG. 5–29. (a) The α-helix units of the cables making up α-keratin. (b) A cross section of an α-keratin fiber, showing the helices which comprise it.

α-helix), the axis of the α-helix would itself traverse a helix of large pitch (200–400 A) of diameter 10 A. Six of these helical α-helices may be wound around one straight helix to give a seven-stranded cable. The elements of this cable and the manner of its packing are shown in Fig. 5–29. Such a structure has a density of 1.3 gm/cm^3 and at the same time accounts for the 5.2 A meridional spacing as follows. If *every seventh* hydrogen bond is different, there should be a repeat distance along the axis equal to 7 × 1.47 A = 10.36 A. This repeat distance is not observed because it is weak and masked by the diffuse reflection arising from the interhelix distance. The second-order reflection has a high intensity and occurs at an angle equivalent to a spacing of 10.36 A/2 = 5.2 A. Thus the 5.2 A spacing does not exist in α-keratin. The meridional reflection corresponding to this distance represents a spacing that arises from the super helix.

The analysis of the structure of proteins by x-ray techniques is advancing rapidly, and the information derived from these studies will be of crucial importance in describing the detailed role of proteins in molecular biophysics.

5–13 The structure of nucleic acid polymers. The most important compounds in molecular biophysics are the nucleic acid polymers, DNA and RNA. The genetic nature of DNA was mentioned in Chapter 2, and the part played by both RNA and DNA in protein synthesis will be speculatively described in Chapter 15. A firm knowledge of the structure of these polymers (given very generally in Chapter 2) is of crucial importance. Impressive advances in this knowledge have come about within the past few years, but since there are many more data available on DNA than on RNA, the following discussion will be concerned with DNA.

The gross dimensions of DNA may be found by flow-birefringence, light-scattering, or viscosity measurements. These techniques indicate that DNA is a long, thin, relatively rigid structure whose molecular weight is $\sim 6 \times 10^6$, although the individual genetic units are much smaller than this. Its dry density of 1.6 gm/cm^3 indicates that the purines and pyrimidines are closely packed. DNA is very hygroscopic, and its density at a relative humidity of 75% is 1.47 gm/cm^3.

Chemical evidence indicates that the PO_4 groups are very reactive, but that the $-NH_2$ or $-CO$ groups are not readily titratable. It was thought at one time that the four common bases in DNA, namely, thymine, adenine, cytosine, and guanine, occurred with equal frequency. The recent analyses of Wyatt and Chargaff indicate that this is not so, but that the ratio of thymine to adenine is unity, and the ratio of cytosine or its derivatives to guanine is also about unity, as is indicated in Table 5–3.

The absorption of polarized infrared light indicates that the $-NH_2$ and $-C{=}O$ groups of the bases are oriented perpendicular to the molecular axis. The $P{=}O$ groups, on the other hand, are inclined at an angle of $\sim 55°$ to the axis. Ultraviolet absorption measurements show that the bases themselves are oriented with their planes perpendicular to the molecular axis, and the x-ray diagrams of Astbury indicated that the planes of the bases were separated by a distance of 3.4 A.

TABLE 5–3

PURINE AND PYRIMIDINE COMPOSITION OF
SOME DNA'S IN MOLAR RATIOS (TOTAL = 4.00)*

	Adenine	Thymine	Guanine	Cytosine	5-methyl cytosine
Calf thymus	1.13	1.11	0.86	0.85	0.05
Bull sperm	1.15	1.09	0.89	0.83	0.05
Ram sperm	1.15	1.09	0.88	0.84	0.04
Rat bone marrow	1.15	1.14	0.86	0.82	0.04
Herring sperm	1.11	1.10	0.89	0.83	0.08
Wheat germ	1.06	1.08	0.94	0.69	0.23
E. coli	0.92	1.10	0.96	1.03	0.00
Gypsy moth	0.84	0.80	1.22	1.13	0.00
Silkworm polyhedral virus	1.17	1.12	0.90	0.81	0.00
T2r phage†	1.29	1.31	0.73	0.00	0.00 (0.66)‡

* From G. R. Wyatt in *Chemistry and Physiology of the Nucleus*, ed. by V. T. Bowen. Academic Press, N. Y., 1952.

† From *Cold Spring Harbor Symp. Quart. Biol.* **18,** 133 (1953).

‡ 5-hydroxy methyl cytosine.

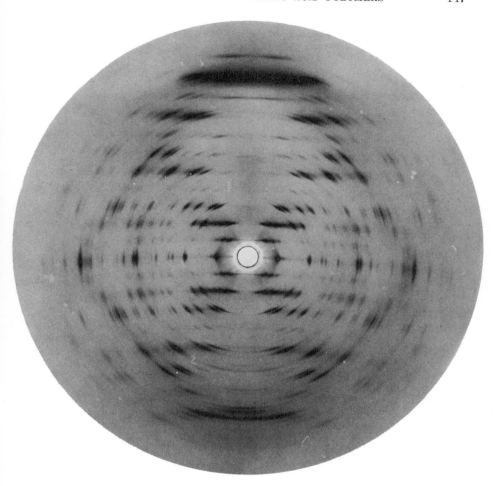

FIG. 5–30. An x-ray diffraction photograph of a fiber of the lithium salt of DNA at 66% relative humidity. The top of the photograph is different from the bottom because the fiber was tilted. [By kind permission of M. H. F. Wilkins.]

The rapid advances in knowledge of the structure of DNA came from (1) the excellent x-ray photographs of oriented thymus DNA fibers by Franklin and Gosling,* (2) the identification by Wilkins, Stokes, and Wilson* of a similar pattern in sperm heads, bacteriophage, and the transforming principle of pneumococcus, and (3) the recognition by Watson and Crick of the specific base pairing in DNA.* An x-ray pattern of a fiber of the lithium salt of DNA fibers is shown in Fig. 5–30. This beautiful

---

* *Nature,* **171,** 737 (1953).

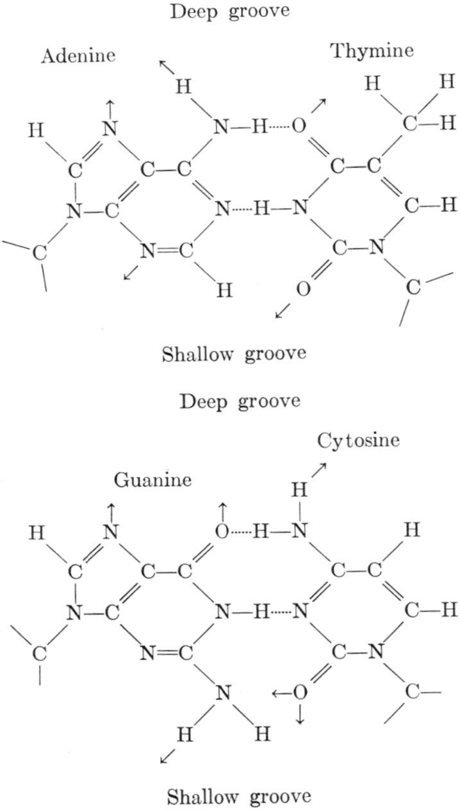

Fig. 5–31. The specific pairing by means of hydrogen bonds (dotted lines) of thymine-adenine and cytosine-guanine. The arrows represent other hydrogen bonding sites which are exposed in the shallow and deep grooves of the double spiral (see Fig. 5–32).

photograph shows clearly, as the reader should recognize by now, that DNA has a helical structure. The layer-line spacing corresponds to 34 A, but the first meridional arc shows up on the 10th layer line, i.e., at 3.4 A. The helical DNA has a pitch of 34 A with 10 repeat units per turn. The detailed measurement of the intensities of the diffraction maxima and the necessity of the fiber having a high density indicate that the fundamental structure is not one helix but two right-handed helices of radius ∼8.5 A, spaced about one-half the pitch apart.

The helices which make up DNA are obviously the polynucleotides. But what forces hold the two helices together? The answer comes from the work of Watson and Crick on the possible configurations of the base pairs in a double helix whose interatomic dimensions were known from the

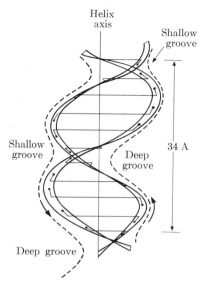

FIG. 5–32. A schematic diagram of DNA. The two spirals represent the phosphate-sugar backbone, the rods represent the bases, and the dots represent the P atoms. The dashed line traces the outline of the molecule.

work of Furberg. They pointed out that the pairs of purines and pyrimidines which occur in equal amounts in DNA, namely, thymine-adenine and cytosine-guanine, have complementary structures which easily form hydrogen bonds. Figure 5–31 shows this pairing. Watson and Crick found that the bases would be in the proper positions for strong hydrogen bonds if the two helical chains had sequences of atoms in opposite directions. The helical chains are the phosphate-sugar backbones. The bases extend toward the center of the helix and hydrogen bond across the axis of the double helix. Thus the DNA spirals are held together by *interchain* bonding, whereas protein helices keep their configuration by means of *intrachain* hydrogen bonds. Figure 5–32 shows a schematic diagram of such a double spiral. Because the helices are traversed in *opposite* directions and because phosphorus atoms do not lie in the plane of the bases, the mass distribution in the double helix is not uniform. As is seen in Fig. 5–32, there are two "grooves" of different depths running spirally around the molecule. The shallow and deep grooves seem important in the structures of nuclear proteins because these grooves contain hydrogen bonding sites, as indicated in Fig. 5–31.

The double spiral for the structure of DNA has very practical and interesting properties concerned with information storage and the duplication of genetic material. These fascinating aspects of structural analysis will be taken up in Chapters 13 and 15.

5-14 The structure of nucleoproteins. Nucleic acids usually are combined with proteins to form a complex. Obviously, the specific interactions between nucleic acids and proteins are the important factors in living processes. A direct way of investigating these interactions is by the structural analysis of particular nucleoproteins. The nucleoprotein, nucleoprotamine, derived from the sperm heads of many species, forms fibers, and good x-ray diffraction patterns have been obtained from them. In the basic protein, protamine, two-thirds of the amino acids are arginine,

$$
\begin{array}{c}
\overset{|}{HN} \\
\overset{|}{HC}\!-\!CH_2\!-\!CH_2\!-\!CH_2\!-\!\overset{H_2^+}{N}\!-\!\overset{}{C}\!-\!NH_3^+ \\
\overset{|}{C}\!=\!O \qquad\qquad \overset{\|}{\underset{H_2^+}{N}} \\
\end{array}
$$

and sequence analysis shows that a very common grouping is $-\text{arg}-\text{arg}-$

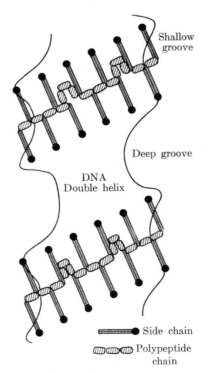

FIG. 5-33. A schematic drawing showing how protamine may be wrapped around DNA. [After Wilkins in Ref. 14.]

arg—arg—RR′—. R and R′ are nonbasic groups. The large positive charge on arginine produces a big force between it and the negatively charged phosphate groups of DNA. A structure that fits both the x-ray and the chemical data is shown in Fig. 5–33. The nonbasic residues occur in pairs and form folds in the polypeptide chain so that every basic side chain is electrostatically linked to DNA.

To learn the details of the binding of more complicated proteins to nucleic acids, both DNA and RNA, will necessitate knowing the structures of nucleic acids and proteins. The task ahead is difficult; the reward for success is fabulous.

5–15 The analysis of virus structures. We have alluded above to the difficulty of determining the structures of RNA and of nucleoproteins. There do exist systems which are ideal for these purposes. They are the crystallizable viruses. Plant viruses, for example, are complexes of RNA and protein, and they are readily purified in large quantities. The regular and complex diffraction patterns obtained from virus crystals indicate the uniformity and symmetry of these viruses. The analysis of virus structure may lead to our understanding the structure of nucleoproteins and RNA before the completion of the analyses of nucleoprotein and RNA extracted from cells.

Tobacco mosaic virus is a long, thin structure averaging 150 A in diameter and 3000 A in length. It contains 6% RNA and 94% protein. The infectious agent of the virus is the nucleic acid, which, unlike the protein part of the virus, can cause the production of complete virus particles. If the RNA is mildly extracted it can recombine with the protein to form intact virus. Obviously, the workings of this RNA-protein system are important in finding out about specific nucleic acid-protein forces and the manner in which RNA induces a host cell to manufacture whole virus.

Figure 5–34 shows a particularly pretty x-ray diffraction pattern of an oriented gel of TMV. The typical features of the helical diffraction pattern are apparent. Every third layer line shows a meridional reflection indicating a pitch of 69 A, which is equal to the spacing of these lines. Further quantitative measurements plus chemical evidence on the protein end groups indicate that the protein is made up of 2130 subunits in a helical array of 49 units in three turns (69 A). The molecular weight of the subunits is 18,000. The phosphorus atoms of the RNA part of the virus have been located by comparing the x-ray pattern of the virus with that of the virus protein. Figure 5–35 shows a schematic picture of part of a TMV particle. The mean radius as found from electron microscopy and interparticle distances in dry samples is less than the maximum value found by x-ray scattering from TMV particles. This is the reason for the helical groove on the outside of the particle.

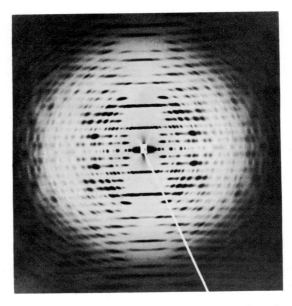

FIG. 5–34. An x-ray diffraction pattern of a 20% solution of oriented TMV taken with CuK$_\alpha$ radiation. [Courtesy of K. C. Holmes and D. L. D. Caspar.]

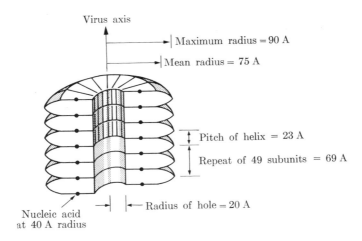

FIG. 5–35. A schematic section of a short length of a TMV particle, showing the helical arrangement of protein subunits, the location of the RNA, a central hole, and the external grooving. [From Franklin, Klug, and Holmes, p. 39 of Ref. 15.]

Not all the structures of molecular biophysics are helical. The structure of tomato bushy stunt virus, which is a crystalline plant virus, is spherical. The x-ray diffraction photographs taken by Caspar* of crystals of this virus show that the virus must have a large amount of symmetry. The spherical virus must be made up of a number of subunits. The number of subunits is a multiple of 12 and probably is a multiple of 60. Chemical data indicate that the actual number may be 300.

5–16 Conclusion. Molecular biophysics is concerned with the explanation of biological phenomena in terms of the reactions of both the simple and complex molecules that make up living systems. The use of x-ray diffraction is one of the most powerful techniques for determining the details of molecular structure. Therefore it is one of the most useful tools of the biophysicist. Its future seems bright and unbounded.

PROBLEMS

1. Derive the approximate relation relating the minimum x-ray wavelength, λ_{min}, to the potential difference across the tube [λ_{min} in A $\cong 12345/V$ in volts].

2. The following data represent the absorption coefficient divided by the density, μ/ρ, for nickel and cobalt at different wavelengths.

λ, A	μ/ρ for Ni, cm^2/gm	μ/ρ for Co, cm^2/gm
1.389	286	267
1.432	325	———
1.484	40.5	400
1.537	48	———
1.604	———	51.6

(a) What thickness of nickel will reduce the copper K_α line intensity by 50%? What is the percent transmission of the K_β line of copper for this thickness?

(b) What thickness of cobalt will reduce the copper K_β line intensity by 50%? What is the percent transmission of the K_α line of copper for this thickness?

3. The spacing between a *row of atoms* perpendicular to the wave-normal is b. Calculate the angular deflection of the first layer line if b equals (a) 100 A, (b) 34 A, (c) 5.0 A, where λ = 1.00 A in each case.

4. The spacing between a set of *parallel planes* is d. Calculate the angular deflection of the incident wave corresponding to the first diffraction maximum for d equal to (a) 100 A, (b) 34 A, (c) 5.0 A, where λ = 1.00 A in each case.

* D. L. D. Caspar, *Nature*, **177**, 475 (1956).

5. For λ = 1.54 A, find the Bragg angle for interplanar spacings of 3.4 A and 10 A.

6. If the thickness of the crystal in Problem 5 is 100 A, what is the angular width of the diffraction maximum?

7. Use the data for dry insulin crystals in Table 5–1 to compute the molecular weight of insulin.

8. Draw the planes (140), (250), and (321).

9. Assume that you are given a crystal of size 10a by 10b by 10c. What is the average number of atoms per plane for planes (100), (110), (010), (120), (130), and (230)? What is the average number of atoms per plane per unit cell?

10. Compute graphically the relative structure factors in directions [100], [010], and [001] of the unit cell shown in Fig. 5–36.

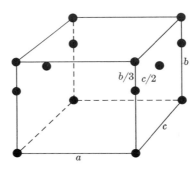

FIGURE 5–36

11. Do Problem 10 for directions [200], [020], [002], [300], [030], and [003].

REFERENCES

1. K. LONSDALE, *Crystals and X-rays*. Van Nostrand, N. Y., 1949.

2. K. M. RUDALL, "Fundamental Structures in Biological Systems," *Prog. Biophys.* **1**, 39 (1950).

3. A. ENGSTROM, "Use of Soft X-rays in the Assay of Biological Materials," *Prog. Biophys.* **1**, 164 (1950).

4. R. D. PRESTON, "Biophysical Aspects of Polysaccharide Structure in Plants," *Prog. Biophys.* **2**, 17 (1951).

5. B. Low, "The Structure and Configuration of Amino Acids, Peptides and Proteins," in *The Proteins: Chemistry, Biological Activity, and Methods*, Vol. I, Part A, ed. by H. Neurath and K. Bailey. Academic Press, N. Y., 1953.

6. J. C. KENDREW and K. BAILEY, "Structure Proteins," in *The Proteins: Chemistry, Biological Activity, and Methods*, Vol. II, Part B, ed. by H. Neurath and K. Bailey. Academic Press, N. Y., 1954.

7. J. C. KENDREW, "The Crystalline Proteins: Recent X-ray Studies and Structural Hypotheses," *Prog. Biophys.* **4,** 244 (1954).

8. H. D. SPRINGALL, *The Structural Chemistry of Proteins.* Academic Press, N. Y., 1954.

9. F. H. C. CRICK and J. D. WATSON, "The Complementary Structure of Deoxyribonucleic Acid," *Proc. Roy. Soc.* **A223,** 80 (1954).

10. P. SCHMIDT, P. KAESBERG, and W. W. BEEMAN, "Small-angle X-ray Scattering from Turnip Yellow Mosaic Virus," *Biochim. et Biophys. Acta* **14,** 1 (1954).

11. *Fibrous Proteins and Their Biological Significance,* Symposia of the Society for Experimental Biology, No. 9. Academic Press, N. Y., 1955.

12. A. RICH and F. H. C. CRICK, "The Structure of Collagen," *Nature* **176,** 915 (1955).

13. F. H. C. CRICK and J. D. WATSON, "Structure of Small Viruses," *Nature* **177,** 473 (1956).

14. *The Structure of Nucleic Acids and Their Role in Protein Synthesis,* Biochemical Society Symposia, No. 14, ed. by E. M. Crook. Cambridge University Press, 1957.

15. *The Nature of Viruses,* ed. by J. and A. Churchill. Ciba Foundation Symposia, 1957.

16. L. PAULING, R. B. COREY, and H. R. BRANSON, "The Structure of Proteins: Two Hydrogen-Bonded Helical Configurations of the Polypeptide Chain," *Proc. Nat. Acad. Sci.* **37,** 205 (1951).

17. L. PAULING and R. B. COREY, "The Pleated Sheet, a New Layer Configuration of Polypeptide Chains," *Proc. Nat. Acad. Sci.* **37,** 251 (1951).

CHAPTER 6

INTRAMOLECULAR AND INTERMOLECULAR FORCES

The structure of the molecules making up all systems is determined by the type of forces that hold the atoms and molecules together. The structure of a large aggregate of molecules, such as a living system, is determined not only by its intramolecular forces, but also by the forces governing the behavior of the molecules relative to one another. Since the number of interactions in a large system is too great to analyze easily, in discussing a living system we will be concerned, on the one hand, with forces between adjacent molecules as samples of particular interactions and, on the other hand, with the general nature of interactions between large numbers of molecules. The interactions among large numbers of molecules may be treated by statistical mechanics or by information-theory methods. Before we can attempt to apply our knowledge of atomic and molecular interactions to living systems and their components, we must have our facts straight as to the physics of inter- and intramolecular forces. There is no reason to assume at present that we cannot use the known forces to explain the many and diverse behaviors of living systems. Until the contrary is proven, we must go on and attempt to use our knowledge to explain these phenomena.

6–1 Strong and weak forces. It is convenient to divide the forces we shall speak of into two classes, the strong and the weak. The yardstick by which we measure whether a force is strong or weak is thermal agitation. If a force is strong, the two groups held together by it will be stable against the random thermal bombardment of the surrounding medium. Two groups held together by a weak force will not have this stability, but it may be possible, as we now believe, for many of these weak forces to join in concert and so make the equivalent of a strong force. The backbone or primary structure of a large molecule, such as a protein, is held together by strong forces. The relative configuration or secondary structure of this backbone, whether it be an extended chain or a helix, is determined by weak forces. When a protein is denatured by heat, the weak bonds give way first. Thus the secondary and tertiary structure of the protein is lost, and the characteristic position of the polypeptide chain reverts to a purely random one, although the chain itself stays intact.

It is, of course, impossible to measure directly the force between two small objects such as atoms or even molecules, but in many cases we can measure the energy of interaction between the two. Two atoms which

TABLE 6–1

CONVERSION OF ENERGY UNITS

Unit	joule/particle	ev/particle	kcal/mole
1 joule/particle =	———	6.2×10^{18}	———
1 ev/particle =	1.60×10^{-19}	———	23
1 kcal/mole =	———	0.044	———

attract each other will lose potential energy, and by various chemical and physical means it is possible to measure this energy loss. Hence the primary observable quantity is the *interaction energy* and not the force, although if we know how the energy varies with distance between the particles, we can find the force. If the interaction energy, V, is thought of as a function of the coordinates x, y, z, the force components in these directions are

$$F_x = -\frac{\partial V}{\partial x}, \qquad F_y = -\frac{\partial V}{\partial y}, \qquad F_z = -\frac{\partial V}{\partial z}, \qquad (6\text{–}1)$$

or in vector notation,

$$\mathbf{F} = -\nabla V. \qquad (6\text{–}1')$$

Thus the term "strong force" is really a misnomer; "strong interaction" is a better one.

The energy associated with the random thermal motion of individual particles is kT, the product of Boltzmann's constant, 1.38×10^{-23} joule/°K, and the absolute temperature. The average thermal energy of a mole of particles is RT, where R is the gas constant per mole, 1.98 cal/mole. At room temperature, thermal energy is given by

$$kT = 1.38 \times 10^{-23} \text{ joule/°K} \times 3 \times 10^{2}\text{°K} = 4.14 \times 10^{-21} \text{ joule/particle}$$
$$= 2.59 \times 10^{-2} \text{ ev/particle} = \tfrac{1}{40} \text{ ev/particle}$$
$$= 0.60 \text{ kcal/mole}.$$

These are alternative ways of expressing this energy. Table 6–1 is a conversion table of these units. Being physically minded, we should like to emphasize the interactions between individual particles, and so by and large we shall use ev/particle as our unit. To avoid implying that the reactions in living systems are necessarily reactions among great numbers of molecules, we shall not emphasize energies per mole.

6–2 The uncertainty principle and the Pauli principle. To understand the strong interaction that can take place between atoms, it is necessary to know something about atomic structure and atomic energy levels. Obviously it would take us too far afield to go into this phase of our subject in detail. The Bohr theory of atomic structure is sufficient to describe the simpler features of the hydrogen atom, but the representation it uses of electron orbits is incorrect. Particles cannot be localized in this way. The proper way of describing a hydrogen atom is to specify the electron density in this atom as a function of position. We are implying, of course, that the electron in a hydrogen atom has no unique position, and all that we can consider is the probability of finding the electron in a given volume of space. One way of making this diffuseness of the electron a little more precise is by the use of the *uncertainty principle*, which says in a simple form that the uncertainty in position, Δx, times the uncertainty in momentum, $\Delta(mv_x)$, in a particle is always greater than or equal to Planck's constant divided by 2π. Symbolically,

$$\Delta x \cdot \Delta(mv_x) \geq \frac{h}{2\pi} = \frac{6.63 \times 10^{-34} \text{ joule·sec}}{6.28} = 1.05 \times 10^{-34} \text{ joule·sec.}$$

If we attempt to confine an electron to a small region of space, Δx, the uncertainty in its momentum, and therefore the minimum possible average momentum, may get very large. As a result, the electron's kinetic energy is large, and unless there is a big decrease in potential energy, the *total* energy will also become large. The uncertainty principle is intimately associated with the *wavelike* properties of particles. The simplest example of the uncertainty principle applied to an atomic system is the calculation of the *minimum* energy of the hydrogen atom. If the electron, with charge e and mass m is a distance r from the nucleus, the total energy of the atom may be written in mks units as

Total energy = potential energy + kinetic energy

$$= \frac{-e^2}{4\pi\epsilon_0 r} + \frac{1}{2} mv^2 = -\frac{e^2}{4\pi\epsilon_0 r} + \frac{(mv)^2}{2m}, \qquad (6\text{--}2)$$

where

$$\frac{1}{(4\pi\epsilon_0)} = 9 \times 10^9.$$

The minimum total energy will be obtained when *both* r and (mv) have their smallest values. But clearly the lower limit to them is their uncertainty. We could not, for example, find an average momentum less than the uncertainty in the momentum. Thus $r_{\min} \cdot (mv)_{\min} = h/2\pi$, and if this is substituted into Eq. (6–2), then

$$\text{Minimum total energy} = \frac{-e^2}{4\pi\epsilon_0 r_{\min}} + \frac{h^2}{8\pi^2 mr_{\min}^2}.$$

The appropriate value of r_{min} to use is found by setting the derivative of the above expression with respect to r equal to zero and solving for r_{min}. When this is done, we find

$$r_{min} = \epsilon_0 \frac{h^2}{\pi m e^2} = 0.5 \times 10^{-10} \text{ m,}$$

and thus

$$\text{Minimum total energy} = -\frac{me^4}{8\epsilon_0^2 h^2}$$

$$= -2.16 \times 10^{-18} \text{ joule} = -13.5 \text{ ev.}$$

This value is the same as that found experimentally, and the agreement illustrates the role of the uncertainty principle in setting the minimum energy of atomic systems. The fact that the uncertainty in the electron's position is about the same as its average distance from the nucleus is the reason we must think of atoms as smeared-out charge distributions. The actual charge distribution may be determined by finding the solutions of the *Schrödinger wave equation* for the atomic system under investigation. The solutions of the wave equation are known as *wave functions*, because of their close connections with the wavelike properties of particles. The spatial dependence of the wave functions is related to the energy state of the atomic system (that is, whether the atom is in the ground state or an excited state), and the probability of finding an electron in a volume of space defined by the coordinates x, y, z and $x + dx, y + dy, z + dz$ is given by the square of the wave function, ψ, times the size of the volume element $\psi^2(x, y, z)\,dx\,dy\,dz$.

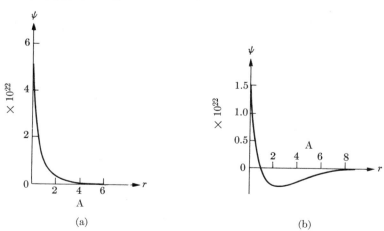

FIG. 6–1. The wave functions of the hydrogen atom for (a) the ground state, and (b) the first excited state with zero angular momentum.

Figure 6–1 shows how ψ varies with r for two of the states of hydrogen. For states representing atoms with nonzero angular momentum, the wave function is more complicated, and it is not spherically symmetrical. While our discussion has been about hydrogen, the simplest of atoms, similar conclusions hold for all atoms. But we need one more general principle because so far our minimum energy condition would mean that all the electrons, in polyelectronic atoms, would be at the same average distance from the nucleus. We know this is *not* so. The atomic diameters do not increase more or less uniformly with atomic number.

The extra principle we want is the *Pauli exclusion principle*. A practically applicable version of the principle says that only *two* electrons can occupy the same energy state, and these two electrons must have spins, or angular momentum about their axes, in *opposite* directions. If, for example, we define a direction in space by a magnetic field direction, the electron in a hydrogen atom may only have a component of spin momentum in this direction of either $s = \frac{1}{2}(h/2\pi)$ or $-\frac{1}{2}(h/2\pi)$. These are shown in Fig. 6–2(a). For a helium atom, with two electrons, the spins of the electrons in the ground state are in opposite directions and the total spin of the atom is zero, as shown in Fig. 6–2(b). (This type of state is known as a *singlet* state because the total spin can have only the single value zero in a given direction.) If the two electron spins in the helium atom were parallel, as in Fig. 6–2(c), the electrons would not be in the same energy state and the energy of the atom would not be minimum. In this case the total spin of the atom would be 1 $h/2\pi$. (This is known as a *triplet* state because the total spin may have as possible components $h/2\pi$, $-h/2\pi$, or 0 in a given direction.) For the next atom in the periodic table, lithium,

A fixed spatial direction, z, such as a magnetic field

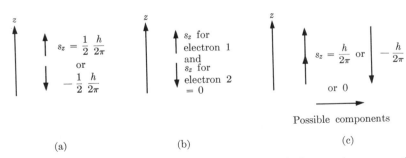

(a)   (b)   (c)

FIG. 6–2. The possible orientations of electron spin relative to a known spatial direction. (a) The two possibilities for a single electron. (b) Two electrons with antiparallel spins. (c) Two electrons with parallel spins give a resultant $h/2\pi$ which has the three possible components shown.

only two electrons may be in the lowest energy level, and the third is in the next level. So the Pauli principle, plus the condition of minimum energy, is sufficient to explain the ordering and properties of the elements in the periodic table. Quite often we shall describe the electrons as being in some particular position in space. The reader should not be misled by this loose terminology. He should remember that an electron cannot be localized exactly. It is smeared out over an atom, and its probability distribution determines its energy and bonding properties.

I. Strong Interactions

6–3 The covalent bond. The simplest example of a strong interatomic force is that shown by the interaction of two hydrogen atoms in forming a hydrogen molecule. As two hydrogen atoms approach each other, the spins of the two electrons may be either parallel or antiparallel. Moreover, because one electron cannot be distinguished from another, it is not correct to say that electron number 1 is always associated with nucleus A and electron 2 is associated with the other nucleus. *Both* electrons are *associated* with *both* nuclei. The Pauli principle would permit the two electrons to be in the lowest energy state if they had opposite spins. The wave function for the two-electron system with antiparallel spins is shown in Fig. 6–3(a). Because the electrons are now associated with two nuclei, they have a larger region of space which they may occupy and enjoy. The positional uncertainty is *greater* than if the two atoms were separated, and by virtue of the *uncertainty principle*, the average momentum and therefore kinetic energy may be lower than for the separated atoms. As the two atoms approach each other from a great distance, the kinetic energy decreases because of this sharing or *exchange* of electrons. If the nuclei get too close together, the kinetic-energy term rises because the system is confined to a small volume again. Thus this part of the total-energy term has a *minimum value* at some particular value of internuclear separation. We have oversimplified the problem because we have omitted

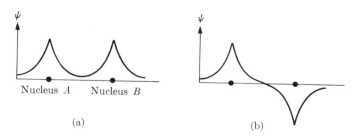

Fig. 6–3. The wave function for two hydrogen atoms when (a) the electron spins are antiparallel, and (b) parallel.

the contribution of the electrostatic potential energy to the total energy. The inclusion of this term will not change our general conclusion about the existence of an energy minimum at some particular internuclear separation. The exchange interaction and its quantitative evaluation for H_2 was first carried out by Heitler and London. The interaction arises from a sharing of an electron pair. It is known as a *covalent bond*.

If two hydrogen atoms, each in its ground electronic state, come together with parallel spins, none of these conclusions hold. Both electrons cannot get into the same energy state without violating the Pauli principle. Another way of looking at this situation is in terms of the wave function shown in Fig. 6–3(b). The wave function is *zero* between the two nuclei (because the electrons are not in the same state), and the small positional uncertainty gives a big momentum uncertainty. As the two atoms approach with parallel spins, the energy *increases* and they repel each other.

The pictorial way of presenting these results is by a graph of energy *versus* internuclear separation. Figure 6–4 shows such curves for parallel- and antiparallel-spin orientations. The parallel-spin, or triplet, state has no energy minimum and represents a repulsion between the nuclei. The nuclei, in the stable state, may be thought of oscillating back and forth between two internuclear separations, and because, for an oscillator, the total energy is equal to the maximum potential energy, the curves in Fig. 6–4 are often called *potential-energy curves*. The energy necessary to separate the nuclei from the most stable position, or lowest energy level, to infinity is the *dissociation energy* of the bond, or simply the bond energy.

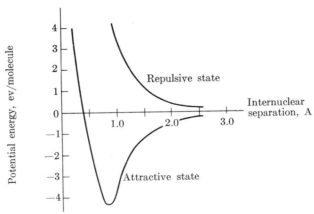

Fig. 6–4. Interaction energy curves for two hydrogen atoms as a function of internuclear separation. When the electron spins are antiparallel, a stable molecule is formed. The parallel-spin case represents a repulsion between the atoms. Zero energy corresponds to infinite separation.

TABLE 6–2

DISSOCIATION ENERGIES OF TYPICAL BONDS

Bond	Dissociation energy, ev
H—H	4.40
—C—C—	2.55
—C—H	3.80
—C—N	2.13
—C—N (peptide)	3.03
C=C	4.35
C=O	6.30
—C≡C—	5.35

More complex atoms, such as carbon, oxygen, and nitrogen, can also interact with one another by this same mechanism. In these cases there may be more than one pair of interacting electrons. In general, we shall represent each pair of interacting electrons by a line drawn between the two nuclei in question. The dissociation energies for these covalent bonds may be quite large. They too can be expressed in terms of the energy which would have to be put into the molecule in order to pull the nuclei apart. Typical values for these dissociation energies are shown in Table 6–2.

6–4 The ionic bond. The ionic bond represents an extreme case of the covalent bond. The electrons are shared in a very asymmetrical fashion, so that the majority of the force may be regarded as purely electrostatic, as in the case of sodium chloride. A decrease in this electrostatic force, as when the molecules are placed in a medium of high dielectric constant such as water, can cause dissociation. The electrostatic interaction energy

V between two charges q_1 and q_2 a distance r apart in a medium of permittivity ϵ is the Coulomb interaction

$$V = \frac{q_1 q_2}{4\pi\epsilon r^2}.$$

6–5 Resonance. When several configurations of a system of nuclei and electrons are equally, or almost equally, probable, then because of the uncertainty in electron position, we cannot describe the system of atoms by just one possible configuration. Instead, we must describe it as a sort of weighted sum of all the possible configurations. Because all these various configurations are highly probable, the region of space associated with the electrons is increased, and following the argument we used in the case of the hydrogen molecule, the energy is decreased. The best example of this effect, of course, is the benzene molecule, which has to be regarded not as one of the two principal forms A and B shown in Fig. 6–5(a) but as an intercombination of the two. The benzene structure has a much higher stability than either of the forms A and B. The extra stability is said to arise from *resonance*, but the reader should recognize that the electronic configuration of benzene does not oscillate between the two forms; it is a combination of both. It is our simplified picture of covalent bonds which requires us to draw diagrams such as those in Fig. 6–5. The evidence for the existence of resonance is not only the extra stability it confers on a bond, but also the values of bond distances derived from x-ray diffraction studies. The ordinary carbon-to-carbon bond has a separation of about 1.54 A. The $C=C$ bond is 1.34 A, and the benzene spacing is 1.39 A.

The existence of resonance in the peptide bond is indicated by the interatomic distances $C-N$, 1.48 A; $C=N$, 1.28 A; $C-N$ (peptide), 1.32 A. In this case the additional stabilization energy due to resonance is about 1 ev, or 23 kcal/mole.

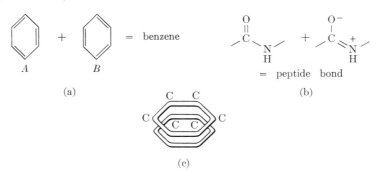

FIG. 6–5. Examples of so-called resonant forms whose mixture represents the electronic configuration of the molecule (a) benzene, (b) the peptide bond, (c) the nonlocalized density distribution of the mobile electrons in benzene.

We have described the formation of molecules from the point of view of the attraction of individual atoms for one another. In explaining and calculating this attraction, we used the wave functions, or *orbitals* of atoms, and the changes in these functions with internuclear distance. In many cases of interest, such as the resonance situations described above, the changes in atomic orbitals are so large that the resulting molecular wave function, or molecular orbital, bears very little relation to the original atomic orbital. In such situations it is obviously of more use to fix the nuclei of the molecule at the experimentally observed positions and calculate the electron distribution for this nuclear configuration. This type of calculation is the molecular orbital approach. For benzene it leads to the result that there are six mobile electrons, that is, six electrons associated with the ring as a whole rather than with individual nuclei. These electrons are located in rings above and below the plane of the molecule, as indicated in Fig. 6–5(c).

II. Weak Interactions

6–6 Dipole-dipole interaction. The weak interactions between molecules and atoms are very much the same as the molecular forces which give rise to the deviations from the ideal gas law. Since they can be described experimentally in terms of the van der Waals equation of state, they are often called van der Waals forces. The simplest of these to understand is the interaction between two electric dipoles, which we call a dipole-dipole force. A dipole is simply two separated charges. The dipole moment, p, of a dipole is equal to the product of one of the charges q times the distance l between them:

$$p = ql.$$

Typical dipole moments are shown in Table 6–3.

Table 6–3

Dipole Moments of Some Molecules

Molecule	p, coul·m $\times 10^{30}$
CO_2	0.00
HCl	3.4
H_2O	6.0
NH_3	5.0
Glycine	50
Egg albumin	830

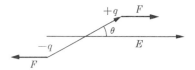

FIG. 6–6. A dipole in an electric field has a torque exerted on it by the field. Torque $= Fl \sin \theta = Eql \sin \theta = pE \sin \theta$.

If a dipole is placed in an electric field, E, as indicated in Fig. 6–6, there will be a torque on it tending to align it parallel to the field. To rotate it from a position parallel to the field to an angle θ with E requires work. We can calculate this work and hence, via the Boltzmann distribution, the number of dipoles that make angles θ with the field in the following way. The work, dW, required to rotate the dipole from θ to $\theta + d\theta$, by external means, is the product of the torque and $d\theta$, or

$$dW = + pE \sin \theta \, d\theta.$$

If we take as our zero of potential energy $\theta = 0$, we have for the potential energy of an angle θ,

$$V_\theta = \int_0^\theta dW = pE \int_0^\theta \sin \theta \, d\theta = pE(1 - \cos \theta). \qquad (6\text{–}3)$$

Because of thermal agitation, the dipoles will be distributed about the lowest energy configuration, according to the Boltzmann distribution

$$\frac{n_\theta}{n_0} = e^{-V_\theta/kT},$$

where n_θ and n_0 are the number of dipoles making angles θ and 0 with the field direction and kT is the average thermal energy. For the energy given by Eq. (6–3),

$$\frac{n_\theta}{n_0} = e^{-pE/kT} e^{pE \cos \theta/kT}. \qquad (6\text{–}4)$$

Because the first exponential term is constant, the angular distribution goes as $e^{pE \cos \theta/kT}$, and the number of dipoles between θ and $\theta + d\theta$ decreases as θ goes from 0 to π. For small molecules, and for electric fields that can be maintained in the laboratory, the ratio n_θ/n_0 never varies much from 1 because kT is large compared with pE. For example, if E were 3×10^7 volts/m and $p = 3.3 \times 10^{-30}$ coul·meter, $pE = 10^{-22}$ joule. At room temperature, $kT = 4.1 \times 10^{-21}$ joule, $pE/kT = 0.024$, and $e^{pE/kT} = 1.02$.

We may now solve the problem we are interested in, namely, the interaction, attraction or repulsion, between *two* dipoles, p_1 and p_2. Dipole p_1

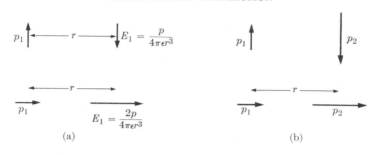

Fig. 6–7. (a) The electric fields a distance r from a dipole p_1. (b) The lowest energy orientation of p_2 in the field of p_1.

produces an electric field E_1 which exerts a torque on p_2. Dipole p_2 will rotate so it is in the lowest energy position, and the energy of the two dipoles will now be less than if they were infinitely far apart. They therefore attract each other. To simplify our calculations we shall make some crude approximations. As shown in Fig. 6–7(a), the electric field E_1 originating from a dipole p_1 depends on the orientation of p_1 relative to the line joining the two dipoles we are interested in. We shall take as the average electric field of dipole p_1

$$E_1 = \frac{p_1}{4\pi\epsilon r^3},$$

where ϵ is the permittivity of the medium. Moreover, since the interaction energy V goes as $-p_2E_1\cos\theta$, we shall take $V = -p_2E_1$. Thus dipoles p_1 and p_2 interact and

$$V = -p_2E_1 = -\frac{p_1p_2}{4\pi\epsilon r^3}.$$

If $p_1 = p_2 = 10^{-29}$ coul·meter and r is 5 A, the interaction energy is about 0.02 ev for free space. This interaction is close to average thermal energy, 0.025 ev, and the similarity of the numbers indicates that we have neglected one very important consideration in computing this interaction, namely the *random orientation* of the two dipoles, an orientation they would tend to assume, if they were free to rotate, by virtue of thermal agitation. Owing to these random positions, each dipole will tend to occupy any spatial position, and if this is true there will be on the average as much attraction as repulsion, and thus no net interaction except for the fact that the attractive case has a *smaller energy* than the repulsive configuration by an amount easily shown to be $2p_1p_2/4\pi\epsilon r^3$. Thus the antiparallel configuration is favored because of the electric field $p_1/4\pi\epsilon r^3$. The second dipole will have a preferential alignment along this field whose magnitude may be calculated from the distribution given in Eq. (6–4). The preferential alignment is usefully expressed in terms of the *average* dipole moment $\bar{p}_2$ of p_2 in the direction of E_1. If the interaction is *small* compared with thermal energy, that is, $p_2E_1 \ll kT$, it is easy to show that

$$\bar{p}_2 = \frac{1}{3}\frac{E_1p_2^2}{kT}. \tag{6-5}$$

Thus the interaction energy between two dipoles subject to relatively large thermal agitation is given by

$$V = -\bar{p}_2E_1 = -\frac{1}{3}\frac{E_1^2p_2^2}{kT} = -\frac{1}{3}\frac{p_1^2}{(4\pi\epsilon)^2}\frac{p_2^2}{kT}\frac{1}{r^6}. \tag{6-6}$$

This is the proper expression for the interaction between two weak dipoles, or between two strong dipoles at large distances.

There are two important points to note about Eq. (6-6). The first is that the interaction falls off rapidly with increasing r. The effective range of the dipole-dipole force is less than a few A owing to the dependence on the sixth power of the separation. The second is that the interaction depends on the inverse square of the permittivity. If the dipoles are in water and relatively far apart, $\epsilon/\epsilon_0 = 80$. If the dipoles are close together,

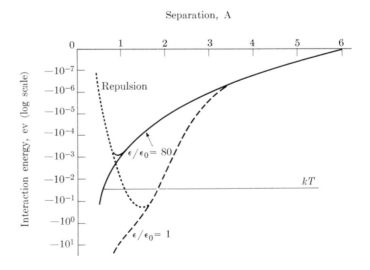

Fig. 6-8. The interaction energy as given by Eq. (6-6) between two permanent dipoles as a function of the distance between them, where $p_1 = p_2 = 3.3 \times 10^{-30}$ coul·meter, $T = 300°K$, and $\epsilon/\epsilon_0 = 80$. The dashed curve indicates, schematically, the result of the decrease in the effective dielectric constant at small distances. At distances less than about 2 A, the repulsion between electron clouds becomes important and the interaction energy rises.

there may be no room for water between them, and the dielectric constant of the space between them will approach unity. This consideration also means that these forces are of *short range*. The rapid change of the interaction energy with distance is shown in Fig. 6-8. The minimum in the curve of interaction energy *versus* separation arises because at very small distances the electron clouds begin to intermingle and the dipoles repel each other.

6-7 Permanent-dipole, induced-dipole interaction. The interactions between molecules are not only the result of dipole-dipole forces. A molecule with a permanent-dipole moment, such as H_2O, can exert a force on an ordinarily nonpolar molecule, such as CO_2, because of the dipole moment *induced* in the nonpolar molecule. The permanent dipole, p_1, produces an electric field, $E_1 = p_1/4\pi\epsilon r^3$, in the neighborhood of the nonpolar molecule, and the induced-dipole moment is given by

$$p_2 = \alpha E_1. \tag{6-7}$$

The proportionality constant, α, is known as the *polarizability* of the molecule. The two molecules interact, and, as before

$$V = -p_2 E_1 = -\alpha E_1^2 = -\frac{\alpha p_1^2}{(4\pi\epsilon)^2 r^6}. \tag{6-8}$$

We may get a rough estimate of the constant α by the following argument. If two *permanent* dipoles interact, the *average* dipole moment of one of them in the field of the other is given by Eq. (6-5). The constant of proportionality for this case is $\frac{1}{3}p_2^2/kT$. The "polarizability" for a permanent dipole is approximately the square of the dipole moment divided by its average energy. Now we may think of a nonpolar molecule as made up of a *fluctuating charge distribution* whose average may be given by functions such as shown in Fig. 6-1. At any instant the molecule may have a dipole moment (ea_2) where e is the charge on the electron and a is the atomic or molecular size. The fluctuation of this instantaneous dipole, which gives an average of zero in the absence of an electric field, takes place about an average energy which is the *binding energy* of the electron, not kT. The binding energy is approximately equal to the ionization potential of the atom. If we call it V_B, we have for the polarizability, by analogy with Eq. (6-5),

$$\alpha \cong \frac{(ea_2)^2}{V_B}, \tag{6-9}$$

and the interaction between a permanent dipole and the induced dipole, given by Eq. (6-8), becomes

$$V = -\frac{p_1^2}{(4\pi\epsilon)^2 r^6} \frac{(ea_2)^2}{V_B}. \tag{6-10}$$

This interaction also depends on $1/\epsilon^2 r^6$, and so it too is of short range. The binding energies of the valence electrons of most atoms are around 10 ev, whereas average thermal energies are 1/40 ev. Thus temperature plays a negligible role in this type of force. The permanent-dipole, induced-dipole interaction can also, of course, represent a part of the interaction between two permanent dipoles.

6–8 Transient-dipole, induced-dipole interaction.

The dipole forces we have discussed are not sufficient to explain even very simple physical phenomena. Nonpolar molecules, such as hydrogen or the rare-gas atoms, which are symmetrical, attract each other yet have no dipole moments. The interaction between H_2 molecules due to the quadrupole moments of H_2 is smaller than that observed by a factor of 100. Rare-gas atoms do not have multipoles. Moreover, the permanent-dipole forces are not additive. Two dipoles that attract each other will not both attract a third dipole. A force which explains the observed effects is that between a *transient dipole* and an *induced dipole*. This particular type of van der Waals force originates from two nonpolar atoms, which, as in the induced-dipole case, we think of as electronic charge distributions that *fluctuate* with time. The fluctuations take place about an average, roughly speaking, of the ionization potential. At a particular instant, one of the nonpolar atoms may have a large transient dipole. This dipole produces an electric field which can induce an average dipole moment in the second atom. The two dipoles now have a net attraction for one another, given by an expression of the type in Eq. (6–10) except that the permanent moment p_1 must be replaced by the fluctuating dipole moment of atom, or molecule, number 1, (ea_1). At the fluctuation frequencies involved, $\sim 10^{15}$ times/sec (about the same as visible and ultraviolet-light frequencies), the molecules of the surrounding medium do not have time to rotate and the dielectric constant, ϵ/ϵ_0, must be replaced by the square of the *index of refraction, n*. Since in addition to atom number 2 having an induced moment arising from the field of atom 1, the converse is also true, the expression for this interaction will be of the form

$$V \cong - \frac{(ea_1)^2 (ea_2)^2}{(4\pi\epsilon_0)^2 n^4 r^6 (V_{B_1} + V_{B_2})} ; \qquad (6\text{–}11)$$

and using Eq. (6–9),

$$V \cong \frac{\alpha_1 \alpha_2 V_{B_1} V_{B_2}}{(4\pi\epsilon_0)^2 n^4 r^6 (V_{B_1} + V_{B_2})} . \qquad (6\text{–}11')$$

As with the other two dipole forces, this interaction goes as $1/r^6$. For small molecules with small permanent-dipole moments, the transient-dipole, induced-dipole force is the largest. For molecules of all sizes in solution, it is the predominant term because n^4 is much less than ϵ^2/ϵ_0^2.

TABLE 6–4

THE COEFFICIENTS OF $-1/r^6$ IN EQ. (6–12) FOR
VARIOUS MOLECULES*

$\epsilon/\epsilon_0 = 1$. Units are electrostatic units (cgs) except
for the "binding energies," which are in ev. $T = 293°$K.

Molecule	p, $\times 10^{+18}$	α, $\times 10^{+24}$	"Binding energy," ev	$\frac{2}{3}p^4/kT$, $\times 10^{+60}$	$2p^2\alpha$, $\times 10^{+60}$	$\frac{3}{4}\alpha^2 V_B$, $\times 10^{+60}$
CO	0.12	1.99	14.3	0.0034	0.057	67.5
HI	0.38	5.4	12	0.35	1.68	382
HBr	0.78	3.58	13.3	6.2	4.05	176
HCl	1.03	2.63	13.7	18.6	5.4	105
NH_3	1.5	2.21	16	84	10	93
H_2O	1.84	1.48	18	190	10	47

* From Ref. 7.

For water, $\epsilon^2/\epsilon_0^2 = 6400$ and $n^4 = 3.2$, and this term alone gives the transient dipole term an advantage of 2000 times. Because the fluctuation frequencies in the transient dipole force are the equivalent of light frequencies, we can evaluate the constants in Eq. (6–11') from the *dispersion* of light, that is, from the change in refractive index with frequency. This type of force is also called *dispersion force*. It was first proposed by London, and sometimes his name is applied to it.

The importance of the dispersion force is shown by the data of Table 6–4, which represent the magnitudes of the various dipole interactions between similar molecules in the gas phase. In this case the value for the dielectric constant, or refractive index, has been taken as one. Even for molecules with a large permanent moment, the dispersion interaction is large. The total interaction energy is computed from an expression that is the sum of Eqs. (6–6), (6–10), and (6–11) except for the use of more precise numerical factors than we have used. The general expression is

$$V = -\frac{1}{r^6}$$

$$\left[\frac{1}{(4\pi\epsilon)^2}\left(\frac{2}{3}\frac{p_1^2 p_2^2}{kT} + p_1^2\alpha_2 + p_2^2\alpha_1\right) + \frac{1}{(4\pi\epsilon_0)^2 n^4}\frac{3}{2}\alpha_1\alpha_2\frac{V_{B_1}V_{B_2}}{V_{B_1} + V_{B_2}}\right].$$

$$(6–12)$$

It may seem as if the coefficients in Table 6–4 are small numbers. Remember, however, that the magnitude of the interaction energy is obtained by dividing them by r^6. If $r = 1$ A, then

$$\frac{10^{-60}}{r^6} \text{ erg·cm}^6 = 10^{-12} \text{ erg} = 0.6 \text{ ev.}$$

This energy would be tremendous compared with kT.

6–9 Dispersion forces between large molecules. The transient-dipole, induced-dipole interaction between two atoms or diatomic molecules is, as indicated in Table 6–4, given by an expression of the type

$$V = -\frac{B}{r^6}, \quad \text{where } B \cong 10^{-58} \text{ erg·cm}^6 = 10^{-77} \text{ joule·m}^6. \quad (6\text{--}12')$$

If two *large* molecules are close to each other, each atom in the first attracts each atom in the second, and likewise each atom in the second molecule attracts each atom in the first. The forces are, to a good approximation, *additive*. If N is the number of atoms per cm^3, the interaction will depend on N^2 and, of course, on the shape of the two molecules. Thus if we wish to find the interaction energy between two spheres, each of radius a, we must add up the interactions between all *pairs* of atoms. (Some simple cases are treated in the problems.) The procedure is somewhat similar to the gravitational case, but for the van der Waals force a sphere does not act as if its entire mass were concentrated at its center. The reason is that its interaction energy depends upon the inverse sixth power of the distance between atoms rather than on the inverse square of the distance. For the spheres shown in Fig. 6–9, the interaction energy is given by the expression

$$V = -\frac{\pi N^2 B}{6} \left(\frac{2}{s^2 - 4} + \frac{2}{s^2} + \frac{\ln s^2 - 4}{s^2} \right), \quad (6\text{--}13)$$

where B is the interaction constant for two atoms. If the distance H between the spheres is considerably less than the radius of the sphere, the

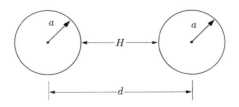

Fig. 6–9. The dimensions and definition of parameters for the attracting spheres whose interaction energy is given by Eq. (6–13). $s = d/a = (H + 2a)/a$.

interaction energy is given approximately by the expression

$$V \cong - \frac{\pi N^2 B}{12} \frac{a}{H}. \tag{6–13'}$$

Thus for close distances, the interaction between two spheres falls off, not as the sixth power of the distance, but as the *first power* of the distance. The decay remains less than $1/H^2$ for distances up to $H/a = 0.4$. The reason for this slow dependence on distance for spheres is easy to see. As the spheres move farther apart, the force of attraction between atoms decreases as r^7. At the same time, however, the component of these forces in the horizontal direction increases, and since the resultant force is the sum of all the horizontal components of force between atoms, the resultant force does not decrease as rapidly as the force between individual atoms.

It might seem that the interaction energy between the spheres would approach infinity as the spheres become larger and larger. This is not true. As the dimensions become large, the time it takes for an electric field to be propagated becomes an appreciable fraction of the fluctuation times of the electronic clouds. In a large object all the induced dipoles will not be in phase, and the forces will no longer be additive. A rough estimate of this limiting size can be made as follows. The fluctuation frequency of the electronic clouds is around 10^{15} per sec. In a time 10^{-15} sec, light would travel about 3×10^{-7} m, or 3000 A. This distance would correspond

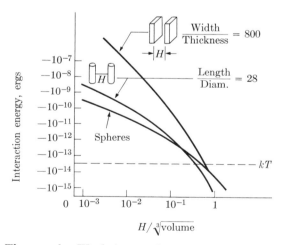

FIG. 6–10. The van der Waals interaction energy as a function of the ratio $H/\sqrt[3]{\text{volume}}$, the separation distance to the cube root of the molecular volume. Both scales are logarithmic, and all molecules are assumed to have the same volume but the indicated shapes. $\pi N^2 B$ is taken as 3×10^{-12} erg. [From M. Vold, *J. Colloid Science* **9**, 451 (1954).]

crudely to a complete fluctuation cycle. If all the forces are to be additive, the distances involved must be somewhat less than this, of the order of 1000 A, or 0.1 μ. This is one of the few cases in biology in which the velocity of light appears with some importance. Because of the finite velocity of light, objects that are too large may not have a large van der Waals attraction. As long as we confine ourselves, however, to distances less than 1000 A, we see that for large particles the van der Waals attraction may extend for an appreciable distance. For small particles this is not the case.

The computation of the attractive interaction between large molecules is complicated by the geometrical difficulty in the summation of the pairs of forces. M. Vold* has derived the important result that the attractive interaction is of the order of thermal energy if the separation between the particles is approximately equal to the cube root of the molecular volume. She has shown that this result is not too dependent on particle *shape* although, as is obvious, two flat plates will attract each other more strongly than two spheres. For example, in Eq. (6–13′) if $H = 2a$, $V = -\pi N^2 B/24$. If we take $N = 10^{23}$ atoms/cm^3, $\pi N^2 B = 3 \times 10^{-12}$ erg and V would equal about 1.2×10^{-13} erg, or 0.08 ev. Figure 6–10 shows how the interaction energy varies with distance for three different shapes.

6–10 The hydrogen-bond interaction. The next-to-last type of force which we shall describe, and probably the most important short-range molecular interaction in biology, is the *hydrogen bond*. The explanation of its existence is simple. A covalently bonded group formed from hydrogen and oxygen ($-$OH) or from hydrogen and nitrogen ($>$NH) has a large dipole moment. There is a net plus charge in the neighborhood of the hydrogen nucleus because the electron distribution has been shifted toward the heavier nucleus. Because hydrogen has only one electron, other negative groups (or the negative ends of other dipoles) in other molecules, or the same molecule, may get close to the proton before the electronic clouds interpenetrate and repel. Close interactions between charges go as $1/r^2$, and the dielectric constant is one. This electrostatic interaction, called a hydrogen bond, may give rise to interaction energies as large as 10 kcal/mole, or $\frac{1}{2}$ ev/particle. The hydrogen bonding between groups such as $-$OH and $>$C$=$O is usually indicated by $-$O$-$H . . . O$=$C$<$. It is hydrogen bonding that accounts for the difference in properties between water and other liquids.

Hydrogen bonding in biological molecules is important because proteins, nucleic acids, and polysaccharides contain many groups which may par-

---

* M. Vold, *J. Colloid Science*, **9**, 451 (1954).

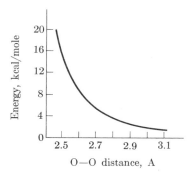

FIG. 6–11.   Interaction energy as a function of distance between oxygen nuclei for bonds of the type —O—H . . . O$\lessdot$.   [From E. R. Lippincott and R. Schroeder, *J. Chem. Phys.* **23**, 1099 (1955).]

ticipate in hydrogen bonding and which may be in a specific, regular order in the primary structure of such molecules. Thus if the molecular energy in these molecules is to be minimized, the number of hydrogen bonds must be maximized without increasing the energy of, or distorting, other types of bonds. Obviously hydrogen bonding is one of the major determinants of secondary and tertiary structures. We saw in Chapter 5 how hydrogen bonding determined structures such as the pleated sheet and α-helix of proteins and how it was the crucial element in determining the pairing of the purine and pyrimidine bases in the double helix of DNA. Life would be very different without hydrogen bonds.

Hydrogen bonding produces changes in the energy levels of molecular groups which may be detected by spectroscopic means. This will be taken up in some detail in Chapter 7. Figure 6–11 indicates how the energy of hydrogen bonds of the type —O—H . . . O$\lessdot$ varies with the distance between the two oxygen nuclei.

6–11 Charge-fluctuation interaction. Large molecules in solution have many ionized groups, such as —COO^- and —NH_3^+. At any instant when only a *fraction* of these groups are fully ionized (although each group, over a time average, may be partially ionized), the protons move in a more or less random way from one group to another and the dipole moment of the entire molecule fluctuates. Just as in the dispersion force, this fluctuation induces dipoles in the neighboring molecules and leads to an attractive interaction.* Since the fluctuation frequencies are about 10^7 per sec, this field must be divided by the square of the dielectric constant. The interaction, like all the other weak ones, is of short range.

---

* J. G. Kirkwood and J. B. Shumaker, *Proc. Nat. Acad. Sci.* **38**, 855 (1952).

III. Molecules in Solution

6–12 Debye-Hückel theory. Two large molecules in solution will attract each other because of the van der Waals force. But this attraction is not the whole story, for in the solution, which is the medium for living things, there are forces between the molecules due to charges on their surfaces. To reckon with these forces is really very difficult. The best we can do is to give the student an idea of how the problem has been tackled. It has not been solved in the general case.

Suppose a large molecule, such as a protein or nucleic acid, is in solution. If the solution is polar, as is the case with water, many of the groups of the molecule, such as the COOH groups, may become ionized because the force of attraction in ionic bonds is decreased by the large dielectric constant of the medium. The ionized situation represents a lower energy configuration than the non-ionized. Such a charged molecule will attract to itself from the solution ions of opposite sign. These so-called *gegenions* will cluster about the charged molecule and give rise to a double layer of charge: the charge on the molecule and opposite charge in the neighboring solution. Two charged molecules of this sort will not have as large a force of repulsion in solution as if they were in air, because the gegenions reduce the electric field surrounding each molecule. We have represented this situation in Fig. 6–12, where the electrical potential as a function of distance is shown for (a) a uniformly charged sphere in a medium with no free ions, and (b) in a medium with free $+$ and $-$ charges.

If the sphere has a radius a, the potential in the nonconducting medium falls off outside the sphere as $q/4\pi\epsilon r$, where q is the charge on the sphere.

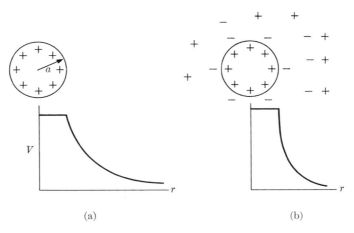

(a)   (b)

Fig. 6–12. The potential a distance r from a uniformly charged sphere (a) in a medium with no free ions, and (b) in a medium with free charges.

In the conducting medium, the ions of opposite sign tend to cluster about the charged sphere. If there were no thermal agitation, the charges in solution would neutralize the sphere and the field outside would be zero. In any actual case, the ions in solution are being bombarded by the surrounding medium, so that at every point in the medium there is actually a fluctuation of charge; the higher the temperature, the larger the fluctuation. We can certainly say, however, that close to a positively charged sphere there is an excess of negative charge in the solution and that at great distances there is an excess of positive charge. If we knew what the electric potential V was in every point in a solution, then of course we could find the force on any charge placed in that solution, because the force on a unit charge is given by Eq. (6–1). Our problem, therefore, becomes: given a solution with large molecules and ions in it, what is the potential as a function of position? This problem leads us to a consideration of the Debye–Hückel theory.

Suppose we have a solution made up of many different types of ions, such as Na^+, Cl^-, OH^-, SO_4^{--}, etc. Let us call the charge on the ith type of ion q_i and call the number per unit volume of ions of this type n_i'. If the potential (i.e., the potential energy per unit charge) at a particular point x, y, z in space is V, the number of ions n_i' of type i at this point is given by the usual Boltzmann distribution

$$\frac{n_i'}{n_i} = e^{-q_i V/kT} \qquad \text{or} \qquad n_i' = n_i e^{-q_i V/kT}, \qquad (6\text{–}14)$$

where n_i is the *average* number of ions of type i per unit volume. (Alternatively, n_i is the number per unit volume at the position where $V = 0$.) The charge density, ρ, is obviously given by the expression

$$\rho = \sum_i q_i n_i'. \qquad (6\text{–}15)$$

It is important to recognize at the outset that the number of charges per unit volume n_i', the charge density ρ, and the potential V are all functions of position, however, on the average, not of time.

$$n_i' = n_i'(x, y, z); \qquad \rho = \rho(x, y, z); \qquad V = V(x, y, z).$$

We now need a relation between charge density and potential. This is Poisson's equation, which comes from the continuity of electric flux. It is:

$$\frac{\partial^2 V}{\partial x^2} + \frac{\partial^2 V}{\partial y^2} + \frac{\partial^2 V}{\partial z^2} \equiv \nabla^2 V = -\frac{\rho}{\epsilon}, \qquad (6\text{–}16)$$

where ϵ, as before, is the average permittivity of the medium. The charge density may be eliminated from Eq. (6–16) by means of Eq. (6–15), and

n' may be eliminated by using Eq. (6–14). So we finally obtain

$$\nabla^2 V = -\frac{1}{\epsilon} \sum_i q_i n_i e^{-q_i V/kT}. \tag{6–17}$$

We have thus ended up with an equation that contains the electric potential V, the charge on each ion, the average number of each ion per unit volume, and the coordinates. If this equation could be solved for V as a function of the coordinates, we should then know the potential at all points in the solution. Knowing the potential, we could find the charge density and the number of ions at various points in the solution.

To solve Eq. (6–17) we have to set up boundary conditions, that is, specify the value of the potential at fixed positions in space, just as we had to specify the values of the concentration at given times in solving the diffusion equation. The boundary conditions we would impose would depend on the problem we wished to solve. We might take a single charged sphere at a known potential with zero potential at infinity. If we wanted to find the force between two spheres, we would take as boundary conditions the values of the potential at the two surfaces, and zero at infinity, etc.

The form of Eq. (6–17) does not admit of a simple solution in any of these situations, and it has to be solved by numerical means in general. To get an idea, however, of what the solution looks like, it is useful, though of course *not necessary*, to make an approximation. If we assume that the potential energy $q_i V$ of a charge q_i at all points in the medium is small compared with kT, and if we assume that the total charge is zero (i.e., that the solution is neutral), we may set:

$$\sum_i q_i n_i = 0 \qquad \text{and} \qquad e^{-q_i V/kT} = 1 - \frac{q_i V}{kT}.$$

Thus Eq. (6–17) becomes

$$\nabla^2 V + \frac{1}{\epsilon} \sum_i q_i n_i \left(1 - \frac{q_i V}{kT}\right) = 0$$

or

$$\nabla^2 V - \left(\frac{1}{\epsilon kT} \sum_i n_i q_i^2\right) V = 0.$$

If we define κ so that

$$\kappa^2 \equiv \frac{1}{\epsilon kT} \sum_i n_i q_i^2, \tag{6–18}$$

we have

$$\nabla^2 V - \kappa^2 V = 0. \tag{6–19}$$

This approximate equation is easy to solve for some simple cases. If the boundary condition were an infinite plane coincident with the yz-plane with potential V_0, the potential would decrease according to

$$V = V_0 e^{-\kappa x};$$

whereas if there were no free charges, V would decrease *linearly*. If we had a charged sphere of radius a and potential V_0, the potential in the surrounding medium would be

$$V = V_0 \frac{a}{r} e^{-\kappa(r-a)}.$$

This is the equation of the curve shown in Fig. 6–12(b).

Roughly speaking, $1/\kappa$ is the distance in which the potential falls to $e^{-1} = 0.37$ of its initial value. Table 6–5 gives some values of κ. Equations (6–18) and (6–19) indicate that the important parameter in determining the potential distribution in a solution is $\sum_i n_i q_i^2$. Therefore, if the properties of solutions of different compositions are to be compared, this sum should be kept constant. It is an important enough sum to warrant a definition. The *ionic strength* of a solution is defined as $\frac{1}{2}\sum_i n_i q_i^2$. A $1\,M$ solution of NaCl has an ionic strength of one, but a $1\,M$ solution of $MgSO_4$ would have an ionic strength of four.

The resultant force of attraction between two charged, similar molecules in solution is the sum of the van der Waals attraction and the electrostatic repulsion between them. The van der Waals attraction goes to infinity as the distance between the molecules approaches zero, as indicated by Eq. (6–12). At very small distances, the attraction is counterbalanced by a repulsion due to the intermingling of the electronic clouds of the two molecules. We will not be concerned with this very short-range repulsion at present. The electrostatic repulsion, on the other hand, does not go to infinity as the molecules approach each other, because the potential at the surface of a molecule is finite. Thus for small separations there will always be a resultant attractive force and a minimum in the interaction energy *versus* distance curve. We have seen how to calculate the van der Waals attraction for two spheres. The calculation of the repulsive electrostatic

TABLE 6–5

VALUES OF κ FOR SEVERAL CONCENTRATIONS

Concentration, mole/liter	Monovalent salt, m^{-1}	Divalent salt, m^{-1}
10^{-5}	10^7	2×10^7
10^{-3}	10^8	2×10^8
10^{-1}	10^9	2×10^9

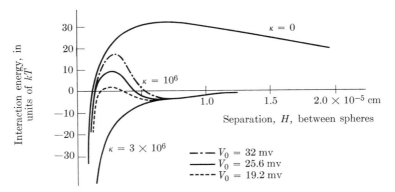

Fig. 6–13. The interaction between two similar charged spheres of radius 10^{-5} cm as a function of the smallest separation between them, showing the salt concentrations and the surface potentials of the spheres. A potential of 32 mv corresponds to a total surface charge of about 20 protons. [From Ref. 4.]

force in solution involves solving Eq. (6–17) for this boundary condition. It is quite complicated, but it has been worked out. The sum of these two interactions are presented in Fig. 6–13 for several salt concentrations and potentials of the spheres. It is seen that for high salt concentration (large κ) there is always a net attraction, while for low salt concentrations the repulsive force predominates at large distances. Proteins precipitate out of solution at high salt concentration. Since the salt concentration at which this occurs depends on the size, shape, and charges on the molecule, precipitation by this method is a way of purifying proteins. At intermediate salt concentrations, the curves of interaction energy *versus* distance all show minima at very large separations. This is because the repulsive force falls off more rapidly than the attractive force. It is the existence of such minima which account, for example, for the ordered array of tobacco mosaic virus particles in concentrated solution. Slight changes in salt concentration will change the value of the maximum interaction energy, and since the chance of two particles coming together depends upon their crossing over these potential hills, the probability of any reaction between similar molecules depends strongly on the salt concentration. It should be emphasized that because of the difficulties in solving some of the equations involved in the theory, only very simple cases have been worked out up to now. These are the cases of two infinite parallel planes and two identical spheres.

The existence of the attractive van der Waals force between flat plates has been verified by direct measurements of the force* as a function of the distance between the plates.

---

* A. P. Prosier and J. A. Kitchener, *Nature* **178**, 1339 (1956).

6–13 Antigens and antibodies as examples of short-range forces in solution. The forces between large molecules in solution may have a rather long range, but the forces between small molecules in solution, or between a large molecule and a small molecule, will all be of short range; that is, they will depend on an attractive potential which goes as $1/r^6$. The hydrogen bond is also a very short-range interaction. There are many examples in biology of the specificity of interaction between two molecules. Enzymes will act only upon very particular substrates. If the substrate does not have the correct configuration, the enzyme will not be able to catalyze its decomposition. The examination of enzyme-substrate interactions will be given in Chapter 8. For the present we shall deal with another type of specific reaction, the antigen-antibody reaction.

If a foreign substance such as a protein is injected into an animal, the animal goes to work and makes molecules of its own, called *antibodies*, which are structurally related to the foreign protein or *antigen*. If the foreign protein happens to be a virus, for example, the antibodies that the animal makes can combine with the virus and render it noninfective. Antibody formation is obviously of great practical importance to the survival of a species. The mechanism by which specific antibodies are produced by an animal is not known. The reactions between antigens and antibodies can be made to yield a lot of useful information because the reactions between the two types of molecules are reasonably specific, and it is possible to use antigens whose structure is known.

Antigens may be small molecules (molecular weights as small as 15,000), but antibodies are usually much larger. For example, the antibody molecules are found in the gamma globulin fraction of blood serum, and in the case of rabbit serum have molecular weights of around 150,000.

If the serum from a rabbit injected with antigen is mixed in a test tube with the antigen itself, a precipitate is formed. The precipitate contains both the antigen and the antibodies produced by the rabbit in response to the foreign protein. The amount of precipitate depends on the concentration of both antigen and antibody in the test tube. Figure 6–14 shows the amount of precipitate formed for different amounts of added antigen (egg albumin) and a fixed amount of antibody. For small amounts of antigen there is very little precipitate; as the antigen is increased, the amount of precipitate increases, goes through a maximum, and then decreases. We can account for this result by assuming that both antigen and antibody can combine with each other in two or more sites. Thus the antibody molecules can act as a bridge between antigen molecules until such a large structure is built up that the whole thing goes out of solution. When very large amounts of antigen are added to the solution, however, the antibodies will attach to this excess antigen and will no longer be able to form bridges between neighboring antigen molecules. A schematic

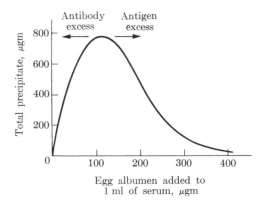

FIG. 6-14. The mass of precipitate formed by mixing different amounts of egg albumin (the antigen) with a fixed amount of antibody (anti-egg albumin). The regions below and above the maximum are known as the regions of *antibody excess* and *antigen excess*, respectively.

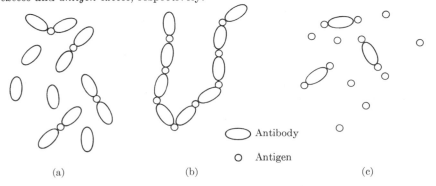

FIG. 6-15. The union of antigens and antibodies in the regions of (a) antibody excess, (b) equality, and (c) antigen excess. For simplicity each molecule is shown as having only two combining sites.

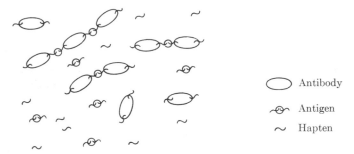

FIG. 6-16. A schematic picture showing how a hapten may inhibit the formation of a precipitate of hapten protein and antibody.

picture of the antigen-antibody complexes for the three regions of the pre-cipitation-reaction curve are shown in Fig. 6–15 for the assumed case of each molecule having two combining sites, that is, each is divalent. In actual practice antibodies may be multivalent.

It is possible to make good antigens by coupling very specific chemical groups to proteins such as egg albumin. The specific groups, known as *haptens*, do not by themselves stimulate an animal to make specific anti-bodies unless the hapten is coupled to a larger carrier molecule. Anti-bodies made in response to the injection of a hapten-protein are not homogeneous. Some of the antibodies react, as shown by the precipitin reaction, with the protein alone, others with the hapten-protein. This mixture of antibodies may be purified by treating it with the protein alone so as to precipitate the antiprotein antibodies and leave the antihapten-protein antibodies in solution. If a hapten such as paraazobenzene arsonate (PABA) is coupled

$$-N{=}N-\langle\underline{\hspace{1.5cm}}\rangle-AsO_3H^-$$

to a protein for use as an antigen, the resulting purified antibodies will precipitate the PABA-protein by the mechanism shown in Fig. 6–15. If, however, some azobenzene arsonate which is *not* coupled to a protein is added to the antigen-antibody solution, then the antigen (the hapten-protein) and the hapten will *compete* for the combining sites on the anti-body. Those antibody molecules which combine with the hapten will no longer be available for the precipitation reaction. Thus the amount of precipitate decreases as the amount of hapten added increases. Figure 6–16 shows how the competition works in a qualitative manner. Such a com-petition phenomenon provides us with a very powerful tool for measuring the specificity of combination of antigen and antibody. All that must be done is to have an animal make antibody that reacts specifically to a known substance, say PABA, by injecting the animal with hapten-protein and removing the protein-specific part of the antibodies as indicated above. A solution of antibody (specific to PABA) is mixed with PABA-protein and with *different* haptens such as orthoazobenzene arsonate and meta-azobenzene arsonate. We can measure the decrease in the amount of precipitate formed as a function of the *competing hapten* concentration. From the decrease we can get a quantitative measure of the specificity of the antibody to the antigen that induced its formation. Figure 6–17 shows a set of such inhibition data for different haptens. It is clear that the largest inhibition is produced by structures similar to the inducing hapten, PABA.

The competition technique is a powerful method of attack because, by using slight variations in the structure of the competitors, we can measure

TABLE 6–6

THE RELATIVE FREE ENERGY OF COMBINATION IN CAL/MOLE OF
VARIOUS COMPETING HAPTENS WITH ANTIBODIES TO
ORTHO- AND PARAAZOBENZENE ARSONATE

| Competing hapten | Antibodies to | |
	OABA	PABA
⬡—AsO_3H^-	0	0
HO—⬡—N=N—⬡ (—HO_3As)	−1360	+109
HO—⬡—N=N—⬡ (AsO_3H^-)	+500	−720
HO—⬡—N=N—⬡—AsO_3H^-	+2820	−1410*
⬡ (NO_2)(AsO_3H^-)	−970	+280
O_2N—⬡ AsO_3H^-	+1520	−950
⬡ (CH_3)(AsO_3H^-)	−690	+860
H_3C—⬡ AsO_3H^-	+980	−350
⬡—CH_2—AsO_3H^-	∼+4500	>5000
$CH_3AsO_3H^-$		>5000

* Absolute value = −7700 cal/mole.

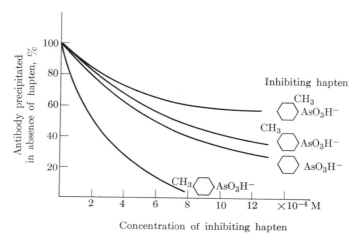

FIG. 6–17. A set of curves showing the inhibiting effect of different haptens on the formation of a precipitate of PABA-protein and the antibody induced by it. [From Ref. 6.]

the fine structure of the interactions between antibodies and antigens. A good measure of the specificity of an interaction is the free energy of combination, ΔF, of antibody and hapten. The more negative the ΔF, the stronger the interaction. Table 6–6 shows a selection of such data from an extensive series of investigations on the competing reactions of the type illustrated in Fig. 6–17 for two different types of antibodies. The relative values of ΔF given in the table may be found from curves of the type shown in Fig. 6–17, but the *absolute* value requires the much more difficult determination of the equilibrium constant K. The absolute value of ΔF is then found from

$$\Delta F = -RT \ln K.$$

As can be seen in Table 6–6, the antigens differ only in the relative positions of the arsonate group, and the antibodies to these antigens show big differences in behavior. The antibody to the orthoantigen reacts more readily to ortho than to para compounds, for example. Moreover, the antibodies only react strongly with haptens in which the arsonate group is attached directly to the benzene ring, rather than through an intermediate group. Clearly it is not just the positions of the arsonate ion that determines the interaction between hapten and antibody; the *entire configuration* of the hapten plays an important role in the interaction.

We can explain these results if we assume that in the process of antibody formation part of the antibody molecule is folded around the antigen. Let us think of the antibody as having cavities into which parts of the

Antibody to orthoazobenzene
arsonate

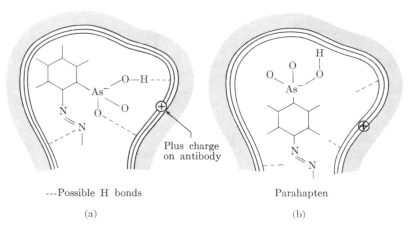

---Possible H bonds   Parahapten

(a)   (b)

Fig. 6–18. A schematic picture showing (a) the complementary nature of antibody and antigen, and (b) the decreased interaction between an antibody and a competing hapten. [From Ref. 6.]

antigen will fit. Then we can say that the interaction between a hapten and an antibody molecule will be determined by the relative sizes of cavity and hapten. Obviously if the hapten is too large, it cannot get into the cavity. Therefore the van der Waals attraction, which depends upon the inverse sixth power of the distance, and the electrostatic forces, and hydrogen-bonding interactions will be very small. By the same token, if the hapten is much smaller than the cavity of the antibody, the van der Waals interaction will be small. It is clearly possible to explain the specificity of antigen-antibody reactions by the *very short range* of the forces between small molecules, and to use this information to map out the configuration of the antibody combining sites as indicated in Fig. 6–18. The close fit diagrammed in the figure for the antigen-antibody reaction has led to a description of it as a lock and key arrangement. The close fit minimizes the interaction energy, and it is the short range of the interaction which gives them their specificities. The interaction between antigen and antibody thus becomes less and less specific as the distance between the two increases. It is doubtful if an antibody to orthoazobenzene arsonate could tell the difference between the ortho- and parahaptens at a distance of 10 A. These specific interactions are very nearsighted. Similar remarks will apply, as we shall see in Chapter 8, to the specificities of enzyme-catalyzed reactions. Their short range must be remembered in attempting to analyze the relations between, and the operations of, the structural elements of cells.

References

1. L. Pauling, *The Nature of the Chemical Bond.* Cornell University Press, Ithaca, N. Y., 1948.

2. M. Born, *Atomic Physics*, Chapter 8, 6th ed. Hafner Publishing Co., N. Y., 1957.

3. F. Rice and E. Teller, *The Structure of Matter.* Wiley, N. Y., 1949.

4. E. Verwey and J. Overbeek, *Theory of the Stability of Lyophobic Colloids.* Elsevier Press, Houston, Texas, 1948.

5. F. Booth, "Recent Work in the Application of the Theory of the Ionic Double Layer to Colloidal Systems," *Prog. Biophys.* **3**, 131 (1953).

6. D. Pressman, "Antibodies as Specific Chemical Reagents," *Adv. Biol. Med. Phys.* **3**, 99 (1953).

7. F. London, "The General Theory of Molecular Forces," *Trans. Faraday Soc.*, **33**, 8 (1937).

8. J. Lederberg, "Genes and Antibodies," *Science* **129,** 1946 (1959).

Problems

1. Assume that egg albumin is spherical and has an average charge of one electronic charge. Compute the electric potential (a) at its surface, (b) 1 A from the surface, and (c) 5 A from its surface, if the molecule is (i) in air, (ii) in water with no dissolved salt, (iii) in water containing 0.01 M NaCl.

2. Assume that a TMV particle of length 3000 A has a charge of $+e$ at one end and $-e$ at the other. What is the ratio of the number of particles at right angles to an electric field to the number parallel to the field if $E = 3 \times 10^4$ volts/m?

3. Show that the van der Waals interaction between an atom and an infinite plane distribution is of the form

$$V = -\frac{\pi N B}{2d^4},$$

where B = interaction constant between two atoms, N = number of atoms per m^2 of the plane a distance d from the single atom.

4. Show from Problem 3 that the interaction between a small molecule with n atoms and the plane is

$$V = -\frac{\pi N B}{2d^4} \cdot n,$$

and that the interaction energy per m^2 between two planes is

$$\frac{V}{m^2} = -\frac{\pi N^2 B}{2d^4}.$$

5. Show that as the distance of closest approach between two spheres gets small compared with their radii, the approximation given by Eq. (6–13′) holds.

6. Calculate the numerical values of the attractive interaction energy per unit area for two infinite planes separated by distances of 1 A, 10 A, and 100 A. Take the value of B given in the text, and assume that the surface density is 1 atom/A^2.

7. What is the repulsive electrostatic interaction energy per unit area between two planes each with a charge of one electronic charge per 100 atoms. Compare with the results of Problem 6.

8. Suppose the planes of Problem 6 have the charge distribution shown in Fig. 6–19(a). Calculate the interaction energy between the two for an area of 4 A^2 for values of $d = 1, 10, 100$ A.

9. Repeat Problem 8 for the charges shown in Fig. 6–19(b).

10. Repeat Problem 8 for the charges shown in Fig. 6–19(c).

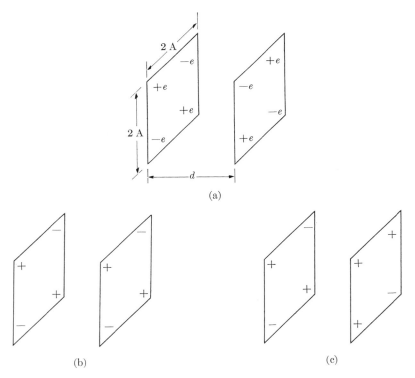

FIGURE 6–19

CHAPTER 7

ABSORPTION SPECTROSCOPY AND
MOLECULAR STRUCTURE

7-1 Introduction. The investigation of the structure and organization of molecules involves probing the molecules with all the means at the command of physics and chemistry. One standard method of physical attack is to send energy into the system under investigation and observe the results. For large and complicated systems, as many forms of energy should be used as are available. While each form of energy may give only a small amount of information, the total information received from all forms may be very useful. Some of the physical forms of energy that can be used are the following: (1) thermal energy; (2) electromagnetic radiation (infrared, visible, ultraviolet, and x-rays); (3) charged particles, such as protons and alpha particles; (4) uncharged particles (neutrons); (5) electric fields; and (6) magnetic fields. In this chapter we shall concentrate only on some of the specific results and interpretations of the interaction of electromagnetic waves with molecules and on how these interactions are influenced by external agents such as magnetic fields. Thus, for example, we are not going to be interested in the thermal effects of radiation. Actually the problem of the interaction of radiation with matter is a very complicated one, and we shall discuss it in only simple terms.

Electromagnetic radiation is quantized. The energy appears in discrete packets, and the energy of each packet, or photon, is equal to $h\nu$, where h is Planck's constant (6.63×10^{-34} joule·sec) and ν is the frequency of the radiation, which of course equals the velocity of light divided by the wavelength.

Since measurements of the wavelengths of sharp spectral lines have in the past been more accurate than those of the velocity of light, it is customary to give relative photon energies by the reciprocal of the wavelength, called the wave number $\bar{\nu}$, instead of in terms of frequency. The wave number times the velocity of light is the frequency.

$$\bar{\nu} = \frac{1}{\lambda} \quad \text{and} \quad \nu = \frac{c}{\lambda} = c\bar{\nu}. \tag{7-1}$$

And we have for the energy per quantum,

$$E = h\nu = \frac{hc}{\lambda} = hc\bar{\nu}.$$

Infrared radiation of wavelength 30,000 A has a wave number of 3.3×10^5 m^{-1}. The energy of such an infrared quantum is

$$E = \frac{6.6 \times 10^{-34} \text{ joule·sec} \times 3 \times 10^8 \text{ m/sec}}{3 \times 10^{-6} \text{ m}} = 6.6 \times 10^{-20} \text{ joule.}$$

Since one electron volt is 1.6×10^{-19} joule, the energy of this infrared photon is 0.4 ev. In a similar fashion we may compute the energy of a typical ultraviolet photon of wavelength 2500 A ($\nu = 4 \times 10^6$ m^{-1}) as 5.5 ev. A 1-ev photon corresponds to 8.067×10^5 m^{-1}.

7–2 Atomic energy levels. Not only the electromagnetic radiation is quantized; the atoms and molecules which absorb light are also quantized in that they may have only certain discrete energies. For example, the hydrogen atom can have only energies given by the relation

$$E_n = - \frac{me^4}{8\epsilon_0^2 h^2} \frac{1}{n^2}. \tag{7-2}$$

In this equation m and e are the electronic mass and charge, h is Planck's constant, and n is an integer. Each value of $n(1, 2, 3, \ldots)$ corresponds to a possible energy of the atom E_n. The energies E_n are less than zero because the zero energy level has been chosen for the electron infinitely far from the nucleus, i.e., for $n \to \infty$. Positive energy values are not quantized. They represent ionized atoms. The integer n is known as a quantum number. It represents, from a classical viewpoint, the orbit in which the electron travels. In view of the uncertainty principle, it really is not correct to describe electrons as traveling in a given orbit since we cannot effectively localize the position of an electron. Our discussion of atoms and molecules will not be concerned with the absolute positions of the various atomic and molecular components, but only with the precise energies the systems can have. To give some picture of these energy levels, we will describe the nuclei and electrons as having particular positions, but the reader must understand that the picture we are looking at is really a fuzzy one.

The hydrogen atom consists of a nucleus with one plus charge and an electron somewhere outside it. The electron is attracted to the nucleus by a coulomb force, that is, a force dependent on the product of the charges and inversely on the square of the distance between them. As the electron comes closer to the nucleus, its potential energy decreases. If, as is conventional in dealing with atomic systems, we call zero energy the energy when the electron is at rest at infinity, then as the electron approaches the nucleus its potential energy, given by $E_p = -e^2/4\pi\epsilon_0 r$, becomes more and more negative. The potential-energy curve for this system

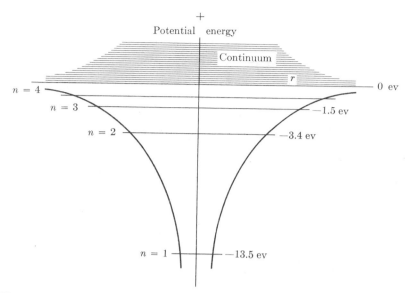

Fig. 7–1. Potential-energy curve for the hydrogen atom. The horizontal lines represent lines of possible *total* energy. The continuum for positive values of E means there are no quantized energy levels.

is shown in Fig. 7–1. It is immediately clear that as the electron gets very close to the nucleus, its potential energy becomes very small. If this were the whole story, we could say that the closer the electron came to the nucleus, the lower the potential energy and the more stable the configuration. A glance at the uncertainty principle, however, shows us that this is by no means the whole story. The reason is that if the electron gets so close to the nucleus that we may describe its potential energy as very small, then the uncertainty in its position will be very small and the uncertainty in its velocity will have to be large. Obviously the minimum value of the velocity of an electron is the uncertainty in its velocity. So we say that as the electron gets closer to the nucleus and its potential energy decreases, the electron velocity, and therefore the kinetic energy, increases. Thus the most stable configuration is not necessarily one in which the electron coincides with the nucleus.

Actually, by making the above argument quantitative, and the lowest energy of the hydrogen atom may be computed, as was done in Chapter 6. The results of this calculation comply with the Bohr theory of the hydrogen atom or with the more valid quantum-mechanical approach. The energy levels of the hydrogen atom are shown in Fig. 7–1. The depth of the lowest energy level is 13.5 ev. Ordinarily the hydrogen atoms are in the ground state, that is, at the lowest energy levels. When an assembly of hydrogen

TABLE 7-1

IONIZATION POTENTIALS*

Element or compound	IP_1, ev	IP_2, ev
H	13.5	
C	11.3	24.4
N	14.5	29.6
O	13.6	35.1
Na	5.14	47.3
P	11.0	19.7
S	10.4	23.4
CO	14.0	
NO	9.5†	
H_2	15.4	
N_2	15.58	
O_2	12.2	
CH	11.1	
CH_4	13‡	
C_2H_5OH	10.5‡	
Phenol	8.5‡	
Methyl amine	9.0‡	

* After G. Herzberg, *Atomic Spectra*, Dover Publications, 1944, and *Spectra of Diatomic Molecules*, Van Nostrand, 1950.

† H. D. Hagstrum and J. J. Tate, *Phys. Rev.* **59**, 354 (1941).

‡ K. Watanabe, *J. Chem. Phys.* **26**, 542 (1957).

atoms is illuminated by light of all wavelengths, only certain wavelengths will be absorbed, and the absorbed wavelengths correspond to a definite transition between the ground state of the hydrogen atom and some higher excited state. Thus, in general, the expression for the absorbed frequencies is $h\nu = E_n - E_1$. This simple equation is the key to the utility of using radiation to investigate atomic and molecular structure. Obviously the frequencies of radiation absorbed and emitted by a given atom or molecule are determined by the energy levels of the system. A superficial examination shows that different atoms and molecules have different spectra. Large molecules have characteristic spectra, and different large molecules have different spectra, but it requires considerable ingenuity to show this.

The ionization potential of hydrogen is 13.5 ev, a figure which is typical, as shown in Table 7-1, of almost all the light elements except for the alkali atoms. Photons of energy 13.5 ev correspond to a wavelength of about 900 A. Wavelengths < 1900 A are not readily transmitted through air, and therefore the range of wavelengths commonly employed is not sufficient to ionize atoms. When light is absorbed by an atom, the atom is raised to an excited state. It will lose its energy, perhaps by reradiating it, in a time of the order of 10^{-8} sec or less.

The energy levels of hydrogenlike atoms are really double instead of single, as given by Eq. (7-2). The doublet character arises from the two possible orientations (parallel or antiparallel) of the electron spin relative to the orbital angular momentum of the electron. The direction of electron spin is important, as we saw in Chapter 6, in covalent bonding. The fine structure of absorption spectra which enters into the consideration of electron spin is unimportant in the spectra of large molecules except for one case, namely paramagnetic resonance. When an electron is placed in a magnetic field it will have two different energies corresponding to the parallel and antiparallel orientations of its magnetic moment. If the electron is an *unpaired electron*, energy may be absorbed in the transition from one direction to another. The position of the absorption bands for this type of transition depends on the applied magnetic field. For a magnetic field of 10^4 gauss, the wavelength corresponding to the change in orientation of the spin is 1 cm. The details of these paramagnetic resonance spectra and the slight changes produced by nuclear magnetic moments will be taken up in Section 7-20.

7-3 Molecular energy levels. To describe the energy levels of molecules is more complicated than for atoms because of the additional types of motion that may take place. To a good approximation we may divide the energies of molecules into three parts: a part due to the *electronic configuration*; a part due to the *vibration* of the nuclei about some equilibrium position; and a third component representing *rotation* of the molecule as a whole. The energies of these three parts are: of the order of ev for electronic, of the order of tenths of ev for vibrational, and of the order of hundreths of ev for rotational.

As a simple introduction to the energy levels of molecules, let us consider the case of a diatomic molecule. We may represent this molecule by two mass points separated by a distance r. Such a molecule, with moment of inertia I about its center of mass and with angular velocity ω, rotates about its center of mass with a kinetic energy given by

$$E_k = \tfrac{1}{2}(I\omega^2) = \frac{(I\omega)^2}{2I} = \frac{(\text{angular momentum})^2}{2I}. \tag{7-3}$$

In quantum mechanics the angular momentum is confined to the values

$$\text{Angular momentum} = \frac{h}{2\pi}\sqrt{J(J+1)}, \tag{7-4}$$

where J is an integer that may take on the values 0, 1, ... In this case J

is known as a rotational quantum number. Since a simple rotator has no potential energy, its total energy is equal to its kinetic energy, and from Eqs. (7–3) and (7–4),

$$\text{Rotational energy} = E_r = \frac{h^2}{8\pi^2 I} J(J + 1). \tag{7–5}$$

Actually what we have written down is the energy of rotation about two axes perpendicular to the line joining the nuclei. We have not included the energy of rotation about the internuclear axis. The moment of inertia about this axis is due only to the electron cloud. Because the electron cloud has such a small mass relative to the nuclei, the moment of inertia about the internuclear axis is small, and from Eq. (7–5) we see that the corresponding energy is very large. Energy associated with rotation about this axis depends on the electron distribution, and therefore it is classed as electronic energy, not as rotational energy. Moreover, this energy is so large, of the order of ev, that this particular rotation, or degree of freedom, does not participate in the equipartition of energy. Thus in computing specific heats of diatomic gases, for example, only two rotational degrees of freedom need be considered.

When a simple rotator is illuminated by light, it may absorb energy from the incident light wave. There are definite limitations, however, to the possible energies that may be absorbed by the rotator. These limitations are usually expressed by a selection rule. In the case of the simple rotator, the selection rule is that $\Delta J = \pm 1$. That is, only those photons will be absorbed or emitted which change the energy of the rotator by values corresponding to a change in the rotational quantum number of

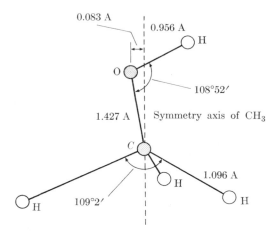

Fig. 7–2. The dimensions of methyl alcohol derived from spectroscopic data. [From P. Venketaswarlu and W. Gordy, *J. Chem. Phys.* **23**, 1200 (1955).]

±1. The rotational energies in general are very small compared with ordinary thermal energies. For example, in the case of the iodine molecule, the 75th rotational energy level must be reached before the energy is equal to thermal energies.

The importance of the rotational spectrum in the analysis of molecular structure stems from the dependence of the spectrum on the molecular *form*. Since rotational energy levels are independent of the interaction between atoms, they reflect the gross molecular morphology, which for these measurements means the moment of inertia of the molecule. The rotational analysis of a three-dimensional structure is obviously much more laborious than for a diatomic molecule, but in cases where the work has been carried out, the three principle moments of inertia of a molecule have been found. The microwave region corresponding to wavelengths greater than 1 mm is most useful for this work because of the high value of the moment of inertia in even the simplest polyatomic molecules. An example of the use of spectroscopic data to obtain molecular dimensions is shown in Fig. 7–2, where the interatomic distances and angles for methyl alcohol are given.

7–4 Vibrational energy levels. The nuclei of a diatomic molecule may oscillate, as well as rotate, about the center of mass. A simple harmonic oscillation, one in which the restoring forces are proportional to the displacement, is the easiest to work with. Moreover, by Fourier's theorem, a more complex type of motion may be resolved into the sum (possibly infinite) of a number of simple harmonic oscillations, so that an analysis of a simple harmonic oscillator (SHO) is really the most general type.

Consider the diatomic molecule made up of atoms of masses m_1 and m_2 shown in Fig. 7–3. If ξ_1 and ξ_2 are the distances from the nuclei to the center of mass, the center of mass is defined by $m_1\xi_1 = m_2\xi_2$. A restoring force proportional to the displacement is given by

$$F = -k(r - r_0), \qquad (7-6)$$

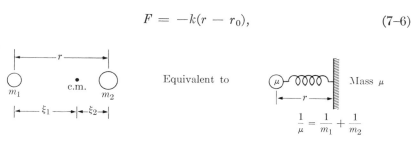

FIG. 7–3. A schematic diatomic molecule, showing the position of the nuclei. The motion of m_1 and m_2 about the center of mass as the origin of coordinates is equivalent to the oscillation of a single mass (the reduced mass) against an immovable wall.

where r is the internuclear separation, r_0 is the equilibrium internuclear separation (the value of r for which $F = 0$), and k is a proportionality constant with units of newtons/m. The system of *two* oscillating masses shown in Fig. 7–3 is equivalent to *one* oscillating mass point whose displacement is $x = (r - r_0)$ and whose mass μ (known as the reduced mass) is given by

$$\frac{1}{\mu} = \frac{1}{m_1} + \frac{1}{m_2}. \tag{7-7}$$

This relation exists because the displacements of the two nuclei are in opposite directions and are inversely proportional to the atomic masses if the center of mass of the molecule is fixed. (Motion of the center of mass represents translational energy, which does not enter our discussion.) The classical frequency of oscillation of the SHO is given by

$$f = \frac{1}{2\pi} \sqrt{k/\mu}, \tag{7-8}$$

and a classical oscillating dipole will absorb and emit radiation of this frequency.

The quantum-mechanical approach to this problem of the SHO proceeds via the potential function, V, which represents the interaction energy between the two atoms. Integration of Eq. (7–6) yields

$$V = \tfrac{1}{2}k(r - r_0)^2. \tag{7-9}$$

This parabolic potential function is shown graphically in Fig. 7–4. The

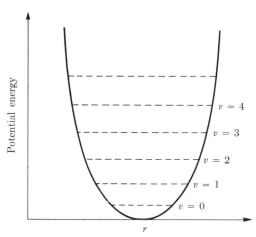

FIG. 7–4. Potential energy *versus* distance (solid curve) and the possible energy levels (dashed) for a simple harmonic oscillator.

nuclei are confined to this potential well, and as a result the possible total energy is quantized. These possible energies are given by

$$\text{Vibrational energy} = E_v = h\nu_0(v + \tfrac{1}{2}), \qquad (7\text{–}10)$$

where v is an integral quantum number, $v = 0, 1, \ldots, h$ is Planck's constant, and ν_0 is the classical frequency of oscillation given by Eq. (7–8). The dashed horizontal lines in Fig. 7–4 represent lines of constant total energy, and we may picture the oscillator as vibrating back and forth along these lines; at the extremes of its path, all the energy is potential, and in the center all is kinetic. The total energy of an oscillator is equal to the maximum potential energy. The amplitudes of vibration are of the order of 0.1 A. This viewpoint is satisfactory in classical terms, but it has shortcomings when examined quantum-mechanically. The fact that the oscillator cannot have zero energy is related to the uncertainty principle and is not explicable in classical terms.

There is a selection rule that governs the possible changes of the vibrational quantum number v in the absorption or emission of radiation by an SHO. It is

$$\Delta v = \pm 1.$$

Therefore the possible absorbed or emitted frequencies are given by

$$\nu = \frac{1}{h} \Delta E = \frac{1}{h} [h\nu_0(v + \tfrac{3}{2}) - h\nu_0(v + \tfrac{1}{2})] = \nu_0.$$

The frequency ν_0 is identical with the classical frequency of the oscillator.

A diatomic molecule cannot be a simple harmonic oscillator. If it were, the dissociation energy, the value of $(V - h\nu_0/2)$ as $r \to \infty$, would be infinite. The potential-energy curve for a real molecule is of the form shown in Fig. 7–5. The confining potential-energy hole is not so narrow as for the SHO, and hence the energy levels are lower than those for an SHO, as is indicated in the figure. The amount of lowering increases as the energy goes higher. For energies above the dissociation limit, the system is not confined and there is a continuum of possible energies. The vibrational quantum numbers v number the levels, but the energies are no longer given by the simple expression of Eq. (7–10).

The selection rule for an SHO does not hold for an anharmonic oscillator. Each of the Fourier components of the oscillator has its own selection rule, which means that as far as v is concerned

$$\Delta v = \pm 1, \pm 2, \pm 3, \ldots.$$

The larger values of Δv, while possible, are very improbable, so that it is almost impossible to dissociate a molecule by the absorption of light with

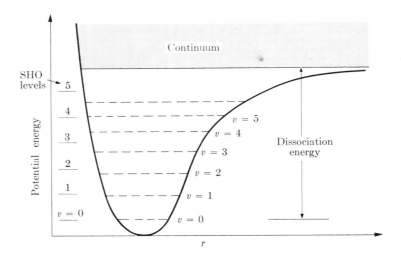

Fig. 7–5. Potential-energy curve for a real molecule. The dashed horizontal lines represent lines of constant total energy.

a transition from $v = 0$ to the continuum above the dissociation limit. Most of the molecules are found in the $v = 0$ level because they are distributed among the vibrational energy levels according to the Boltzmann distribution. If the anharmonicity is small, the lower portion of the potential-energy curve of Fig. 7–5 will be close to parabolic and the lower energy levels will be equally spaced. Because transitions with $\Delta v = 1, 2, \ldots,$ are permitted, the spectrum will consist of frequencies $\nu_0, 2\nu_0, \ldots.$ The spectral line of frequency $2\nu_0$, which is the first overtone, is much weaker than the fundamental of frequency ν_0. The higher overtones are not exact integral multiples of ν_0, but the ratio of the frequencies is close enough to integers so that the overtones are easy to identify, as we shall see below.

The necessary condition when a rotator or oscillator absorbs energy from an incident light beam is that the light contain photons whose energies correspond to the transitions permitted by the selection rules. This is not a sufficient condition, however, because obviously the rotator or oscillator must be able to interact with the light waves. The most important type of interaction is that between the oscillating electric field **E** of the light and the dipole moment **p** of the molecule. If the molecule has no dipole moment, as is the case for H_2 and N_2 for example, there will be no strong infrared absorption spectrum. An oscillator will absorb energy only if the electric field has a component *parallel* to the dipole moment, but a rotator will absorb energy only if the field has a component *perpendicular* to the molecule.

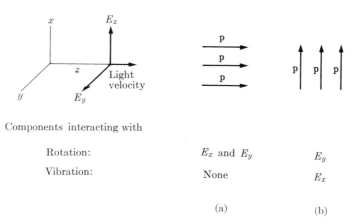

Components interacting with		
Rotation:	E_x and E_y	E_y
Vibration:	None	E_x

(a)   (b)

Fig. 7–6. A schematic indication of the components of an incident light wave that may interact with oriented dipoles. The light is incident in the z-direction and has components E_x and E_y. (a) Dipoles oriented parallel to the light velocity. (b) Dipoles perpendicular to the light velocity.

An oscillator such as HCl will not absorb energy if the incident electric field has no component parallel to the dipole. This situation is not met in the case of gases because the gas molecules are randomly oriented. If the incident photons are polarized and the absorbing dipoles are oriented, there may be directions of incidence for which there is no photon-oscillator or photon-rotator interaction and hence no transition. The use of polarized radiation, therefore, can give information, as we shall shortly see, not only about energy levels but also about the orientation of the absorbing dipoles. Figure 7–6 shows how the components E_x and E_y of an incident light wave may interact (if the frequency of the wave is correct) with the rotation and vibration of a molecule with dipole moment **p**.

7–5 Vibrations of polyatomic molecules. Molecules with more than two atoms may execute very complex vibrations. While the complexity is real, it is in a sense superficial since the complex motion can be resolved into the sum of many simple harmonic motions. (We shall assume that anharmonicity is negligible.) These simple harmonic oscillations, or *normal vibrations*, may be troublesome to find, but a great simplicity is obtained by their use.

If a molecule contains N atoms, $3N$ coordinates are needed to specify the coordinates of all the atoms. The molecule is said to have $3N$ degrees of freedom. Three of these degrees of freedom are translational and three are associated with rotation. The remaining number, $3N - 6$, is the number of *vibrational* degrees of freedom or the number of normal vibrations whose sum gives the actual vibration. For example, the entire complex two-dimensional periodic motion of a mass point, as in Lissajous figures, may be resolved into the sum of two simple harmonic vibrations of, in general, unequal frequency, amplitude, and phase at time zero. For each of the normal vibrations, all particles of the molecule have the same frequency and phase, but the particles have different amplitudes so that the center of mass of the molecule is fixed. The frequencies of the various normal vibrations are, of course, different. The possible energy of each of the normal vibrations is given by an expression similar to Eq. (7–10), and in the absorption of radiation the only possible change in the quantum number v_i of the ith normal coordinate is $\Delta v_i = 0$ or ± 1. In absorption or emission, at least one of the Δv_i must be nonzero. The total vibrational energy of a polyatomic molecule is the sum of its component energies, or

$$E_v = \sum_{i=1}^{3N-6} h\nu_i(v_i + \tfrac{1}{2}),$$

where ν_i is the frequency of the ith normal oscillation.

A linear molecule has only two rotational degrees of freedom, as for a diatomic molecule. Thus a linear molecule has $3N-5$ vibrational degrees of freedom. Figure 7–7 shows, as an example, the normal vibrations of the linear molecule CO_2. The nuclei oscillate about the positions shown. The motions represented by ν_{2a} and ν_{2b} have the same frequencies and are said to be degenerate. The degeneracy would disappear in the presence of an electric field. Not all the normal frequencies will appear in infrared absorption. The frequency ν_1 is absent because it has no changing dipole moment, but ν_2 and ν_3 are present. The frequency ν_1 may be found from transitions in which v_1 and v_2 or v_3 change (so-called "combination bands")

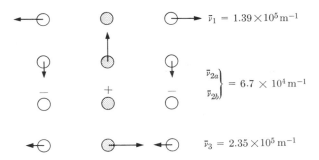

$\bar{\nu}_1 = 1.39 \times 10^5\,\mathrm{m}^{-1}$

$\left.\begin{array}{c}\bar{\nu}_{2a}\\[1mm]\bar{\nu}_{2b}\end{array}\right\} = 6.7 \times 10^4\,\mathrm{m}^{-1}$

$\bar{\nu}_3 = 2.35 \times 10^5\,\mathrm{m}^{-1}$

FIG. 7–7. The normal vibrations of CO_2. The center of mass remains fixed in each vibration, and the length of the arrows indicates the relative displacement of the nuclei. The plus and minus signs indicate "in" and "out" of the paper.

or from Raman spectroscopy, which is described briefly in Section 7–7. From a classical point of view it is easy to understand why the frequency ν_2 is much less than ν_1 or ν_3. For a small displacement of the nuclei at right angles to the internuclear axis there is a much smaller increase in internuclear distance. The restoring force per unit displacement, k, is small, and the frequency, given by Eq. (7–8), is not large. This result is characteristic of these frequencies, called "bending" frequencies as distinguished from the "stretching" frequencies represented by ν_1 and ν_3. The analysis of the absorption spectra of simple organic molecules gives the very important result that units which contain a double bond, such as

$$\begin{array}{ccc} \text{C} & & \text{C} \\ \diagdown & & \diagup \\ & \text{C}{=}\text{C} & \\ \diagup & & \diagdown \\ \text{C} & & \text{C} \end{array} \quad ,$$

are *planar structures*.

A protein of molecular weight 10,000 has about 1000 atoms, and the number of normal coordinates necessary to specify its vibrational motion is 3000. It is not possible to analyze a protein in these terms because all the details of protein structure are not known, and even if they were, the experimentally observed spectrum would not show fine enough detail to permit the analysis. Even the simplest amino acid, glycine, with 24 normal vibrations, has not been analyzed completely in the terms we have been discussing. For practical use, it is necessary to adopt the experimental and semitheoretical approach of looking for frequencies that are characteristic of particular *bonds* rather than of the molecule as a whole.

7–6 Characteristic bond frequencies. As an approximation we may look on the motion of a polyatomic molecule as made up of many diatomic oscillators rather than as being the superposition of the normal vibrations. Such an approach will be fruitful if the frequencies of the diatomic oscillators are the same from one molecule to the next. These characteristic bond frequencies will occur if the groups in question are sufficiently isolated from the rest of the molecule and have natural frequencies not too near that of other bonds. If the latter condition is not fulfilled, the interaction between the oscillators will shift the absorbed frequency. If the former is not obeyed, the characteristic frequency may disappear entirely. The only reason characteristic frequencies show up at all is that the force holding two atoms together may be roughly independent of other atoms bonded to these two.

The above criteria are best satisfied by the end groups of molecules. Where one of the atoms is hydrogen, neighboring groups have little influence on it. Because of its small mass, the hydrogen atom may be

TABLE 7–2

SOME CHARACTERISTIC BOND FREQUENCIES IN
CM^{-1} OF GASES AND LIQUIDS*

Group	Stretching vibration, $cm^{-1} \pm 100\ cm^{-1}$	Group	Bending vibration, $cm^{-1} \pm 100\ cm^{-1}$
≡C—H	3300	≡C—H	700
=C—H	3020		
—C—H	2960	=C (H, H)	1100
—O—H	3680 (3400)†		
—S—H	2570	C—C≡C	300
—N—H	3500 (3300)†	—N—H	1600
—C=O	1700		
—C=N—	1650		
—C≡C—	2050		
C=C	1650		
—C—C—	900		
P=O	1250–1300‡		

* Except where noted, all values are from G. Herzberg, *Infrared and Raman Spectra*, D. Van Nostrand, 1945.

† Liquid, hydrogen bonded. From Ref. 3. All other values are for non-hydrogen bonded groups.

‡ From R. C. Gore, *Faraday Soc. Disc.* (1950).

regarded as vibrating against a massive wall. The reduced mass of the oscillator, as shown by Eq. (7-7), is independent of the mass of the wall. The determination of characteristic bond frequencies involves the measurement and correlation of the spectra of many known compounds. Checks on the assignments can be made by isotopic substitution. For example, the substitution of deuterium for hydrogen in bonds of the form $\equiv C-H$ would decrease the hydrogen frequency by a factor of $1/\sqrt{2}$, as is indicated by Eq. (7-8). The characteristic frequencies derived from investigations on gases (in which the molecules do not interact and hydrogen bonds are not formed) and liquids (in which there is hydrogen bonding) are given in Table 7-2. Obviously the use of these and other characteristic frequencies is very helpful in determining the composition and structure of unknown molecules. Equally as obvious is the fact that infrared absorption data will not tell the whole story about molecular architecture.

As an example of the empirical correlation among absorption bands, we may take the infrared spectra of the pyrimidine uracil and some of its derivatives, as shown in Table 7-3.

7-7 Raman spectra and the dipolar nature of amino acids. We have seen that measurement of the frequencies of light absorbed by a given molecular species permits the absorbing groups to be identified. In many cases the absorbed wavelengths may be found directly; in others they may be found from the *Raman effect*. Light incident on an assembly of molecules is scattered out of the incident beam. Most of the scattered radiation has the same frequency as the incident radiation. (The ratio of scattered to incident light depends on the gross molecular properties, discussed in Chapter 4, rather than on the details of molecular structure.) Some of the scattered quanta have lower frequencies than the incident ones because the molecules have absorbed some of the energy. If the incident frequency is ν_i and the scattered frequency is ν_s, the energy absorbed by the molecule is given by

$$\Delta E = h\nu_i - h\nu_s = h\,\Delta\nu.$$

The measurement of $\Delta\nu$ gives the energy levels of the scattering molecules or, in the terms of Table 7-2, $\Delta\nu/c$ gives the corresponding wave number and hence identifies the scattering groups.

The dipolar nature of amino acids in solution has been shown by Raman spectroscopy.* The Raman spectra of acetic acid CH_3COOH show a strong line of 1730 cm^{-1}, which corresponds to the $>C=O$ vibration. The spectrum of sodium acetate, on the other hand, does not show this frequency because the salt is completely dissociated and its structure, repre-

---

* See J. T. Edsall, Chapter 2 in *Proteins, Amino Acids, and Peptides*, by E. J. Cohn and J. T. Edsall. Reinhold, N.Y., 1943.

TABLE 7-3

THE ASSIGNMENTS OF THE ABSORPTION BANDS OF URACIL AND ITS DERIVATIVES*

Acetamide† $CH_3\overset{O}{\overset{\|}{C}}NH_2$	Phenol† OH	Uracil	5-Chlorouracil	Thymine	Assignment
—	7000	—	—	—	OH (1st overtone 2 × 3400)
6700	—	6670	6670	6620	NH (1st overtone 2 × 3300)
—	5980	6060	6060	5950	CH in ring (1st overtone 2 × 3020)
5710	—	—	—	5710	CH aliphatic (1st overtone 2 × 2960)
5000	—	5020	5020	5000	C=O (2nd overtone 3 × 1700)
—	4670	4700	4700	4670	Combination of 3020 and 1700

* From J. R. Lacher, D. E. Campion, and J. D. Park, *Science* 110, 300 (1949). The peaks of the absorption bands are given in *wave numbers* in order to simplify identification.

† Presented as checks on the assignments.

sented by the resonant forms

$$CH_3C\overset{O^-}{\underset{}{\diagdown}}O \quad \text{and} \quad CH_3C\overset{O^-}{\underset{}{\diagup}}O,$$

does not really have a C=O group, but something part way between C—O and C=O. The spectra of the amino acids at neutral pH do not show the existence of $>$C=O, which indicates that the —COOH group is ionized. In a similar way, the ionization of the —NH$_2$ is indicated; thus the structure of amino acids in neutral solutions must be represented by

$$+H_3N\overset{H}{\underset{R}{-C-}}COO^-.$$

7–8 The vibrational spectra of proteins. Raman spectroscopy is useful for work on substances in solution, but the technique is laborious and large amounts of material are needed. Direct absorption measurements, on the

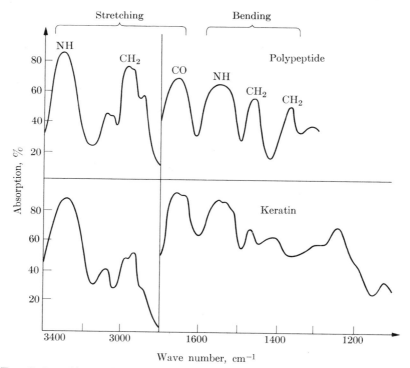

FIG. 7–8.   Absorption spectra of polyphenylalanine-leucine and keratin, showing identification of the individual bands. [From S. E. Darmon and G. B. B. M. Sutherland, *J. Am. Chem. Soc.* **69**, 2074 (1947).]

other hand, require very small amounts of material (less than 10^{-3} gm), but because of the high infrared absorption of water it is very difficult to obtain the spectra of biological material in aqueous solutions. The samples may be in the form of fibers or thin films. Figure 7–8 shows the absorption spectra of a protein and a synthetic polypeptide. As is to be expected, most of the characteristic groups involve hydrogen atoms. One of the marked features of these spectra are the N—H stretching frequencies at 3300 and 3100 cm^{-1}, which are lower than the gas-phase values of 3500 cm^{-1} and indicate the presence of hydrogen bonds. These infrared absorption data represent the strongest experimental evidence we have for the presence of hydrogen bonds in proteins and polypeptides. The fact that there is very little absorption in the spectral region corresponding to —NH groups that are not hydrogen bonded indicates that the great majority of the —NH groups participate in hydrogen bonds. Since the motion and bonding of hydrogen atoms show up so readily in infrared absorption (remember, they are unobservable in x-ray diffraction), it is important to consider in more detail how the interactions of hydrogen atoms with neighboring groups affect their motion.

7–9 The energy levels of hydrogen-bonded structures. Suppose we investigate the energy levels of an —O—H group which, because of the net plus charge on the hydrogen, is attracted to an electronegative atom such as N, O, or Cl. The attraction between the hydrogen and the electronegative atom increases the width of the potential-energy curve that represents the —O—H vibration. Classically speaking, the stiffness constant of the oscillator has been reduced. As shown in Fig. 7–9, the greater extent of space available to the hydrogen atom results, because of the uncertainty principle, in the depression of the energy levels. The energy

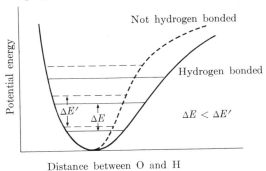

FIG. 7–9. Schematic potential-energy curve and energy levels for —OH in the absence and presence of hydrogen bonding. For simplicity, the zeros of the two curves have been made the same.

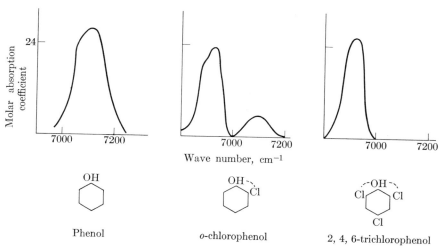

Fig. 7–10. Absorption spectra for the $\Delta v = 2$ transition (1st overtone) of the —OH stretching frequency in phenol, o-chlorophenol, and 2,4,6-trichlorophenol. The dashed lines indicates possible hydrogen bonds. The molar absorption coefficient is proportional to the number of absorbing molecules. [From L. Pauling, *The Nature of the Chemical Bond*. Cornell University Press, Ithaca, N. Y., 1948.]

change in the transition between adjacent energy levels is obviously less for the hydrogen-bonded configuration, and this is why the absorption maxima of hydrogen-bonded groups are shifted toward lower frequencies. Actually the situation may be more complicated than we have sketched above because of the splitting of the energy levels.

The shift in absorption frequency in hydrogen-bond formation is clearly seen in the absorption spectra of phenol, o-chlorophenol, and 2,4,6-trichlorophenol shown in Fig. 7–10. For phenol, the 1st overtone is at 7100 cm^{-1}, which is near the value $2 \times 3600 \text{ cm}^{-1}$ given in Table 7–2. In o-chlorophenol, the new large peak at 6900 cm^{-1} $(2 \times 3450 \text{ cm}^{-1})$ represents the absorption of an —OH group that is hydrogen bonded to the chlorine atom. Because the —OH group has more or less free rotation about the C—O bond, there is a good chance for the hydrogen to be on the opposite side of the molecule from the chlorine. In this case the energy levels correspond to the normal —OH group, and its characteristic frequency is observed. In 2,4,6-trichlorophenol, the hydrogen atom always participates in a hydrogen bond and only the lower frequency is observed.

The hydrogen-bond interaction in o-chlorophenol is weak, as shown in Fig. 7–10 by the double peak in its spectrum. If the hydrogen bond

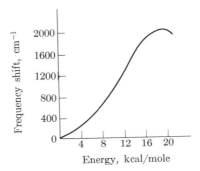

Fig. 7–11. The relation between the shift in absorption frequency and hydrogen-bond energy for −O−H . . . O bonds. The data were obtained from many different compounds. [From E. R. Lippincott and R. Schroeder, *J. Chem. Phys.* **23**, 1099 (1955).]

represented an interaction as large as $\frac{1}{4}$ ev (5.8 kcal/mole), the ratio of the number of molecules in which there was no hydrogen bonding to those in which there was hydrogen bonding would be given by an expression of the form of a Boltzmann distribution, assuming that the statistical weights of the two configurations are approximately the same:

$$\frac{n_{\text{unbond}}}{n_{\text{bond}}} \cong e^{-\Delta E/kT} = e^{-(1/4)/(1/40)} = e^{-10} \approx 10^{-4}.$$

In such a case the two absorption bands would not be observed. Just a frequency shift would be apparent, as in the case of proteins. The magnitude of the hydrogen-bond energy determines not only the relative height of the absorption maximum but also the size of the frequency shift. Figure 7–11 shows the relation between hydrogen-bond energy and frequency shift for bonds of the type −O−H . . . O. If we assume that these data apply approximately to o-chlorophenol, we see that the frequency shift of $200 \text{ cm}^{-1}/2 = 100 \text{ cm}^{-1}$ corresponds to 900 cal/mole, which is not much larger than the 600 cal/mole of thermal agitation.

7–10 Absorption coefficient and cross section. It is apparent from Figs. 7–8 and 7–10 that for liquid and solid systems the observed spectra are not sharp, as they are in the gas phase. The reason is that the high local fields surrounding the component oscillators may produce a splitting of the energy levels into many fine components. The observed spectrum then consists of unresolved transitions between *many* lower levels and the excited states. Since the absorption lines are broad, it is useful to characterize them not only by frequency but also by the magnitude of the absorption or by an absorption coefficient.

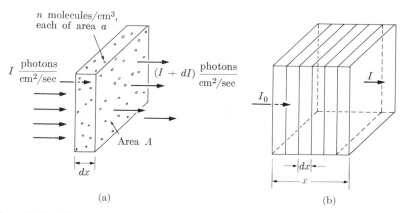

Fig. 7–12. The parameters involved in the absorption of light by (a) a thin slab of thickness dx, and (b) a finite thickness x that may be thought of as made up of infinitesimal slabs dx.

We may derive the relation between the light absorbed and the molecular parameters by a method we shall use again when we take up the effects of radiation on biological systems. At the moment we are concerned only with the effects of the absorbing system on the radiation.

Suppose, as indicated in Fig. 7–12, that incident on an absorbing medium of thickness dx and area A we have an intensity of I photons/unit area/sec, each of wavelength λ. Some of the incident photons are absorbed, and only $I + dI$ photons/unit area/sec are transmitted. Of course, the number of photons emerging is less than the number incident, so the increase in intensity dI is a negative number. The number of absorbed photons/unit area/sec is $-dI$. The absorbed energy is either degraded to heat or appears as re-emitted photons in *all* directions. In these terms the observed experimental absorption probability is $-dI/I$. Let us suppose that the absorbing medium is made up of n molecules per unit volume, distributed and oriented at random, each of average cross sectional area a. We may think of a as the area of the extent of the electron cloud making up the molecule. The relative area presented to the incident photons by all the molecules is the product of the area of each and the total number of molecules $nA\,dx$ divided by the area A, or $(a \cdot nA\,dx)/A = n \cdot a \cdot dx$. This quantity represents the chance that a photon will pass through a molecule. However, in passing through a molecule a photon will not always be effective in causing a transition. (If it does cause a transition from one level to another, it will be absorbed and disappear.) The photon may not have the energy corresponding to an allowed jump, and even if it does it may not be near enough to the particular group, e.g., $-N-H$, for its field to affect the group. Because of electric fields due to neighboring groups, a given type of vibrator (N—H again) may have slightly different energies in different parts of the molecule, in which case not all the —N—H groups can absorb the same frequency, and the photon-vibrator interaction may be small owing to a low value for the transition probability. We may lump these considerations together and simply say that p is the probability that a photon passing through the molecule will be absorbed. The theoretical absorption probability is then given by

$$p(n \cdot a \cdot dx) = n \cdot pa \cdot dx.$$

If we call $p \cdot a$ the absorption cross section s and equate the theoretical and experimental absorption probabilities, we have

$$\frac{-dI}{I} = ns\, dx. \tag{7–11}$$

Equation (7–11), or its integrated form, given below, is used to measure the value of the absorption cross section s.

If the absorbing sample has a thickness x and if light of intensity I_0 is incident on it, as in Fig. 7–12(b), it is necessary to integrate Eq. (7–11).

$$\int_{I_0}^{I} \frac{dI}{I} = -\int_{0}^{x} ns\, dx,$$

$$\ln \frac{I}{I_0} = -nsx \qquad \text{or} \qquad \frac{I}{I_0} = e^{-nsx}. \tag{7–12}$$

This relation, which indicates that the transmitted light intensity falls off exponentially with the concentration and path length through the sample, is known as the Beer-Lambert law. The exponential form arises from the random nature of the absorption process.

In the derivation of Eq. (7–12) or its differential form, Eq. (7–11), three assumptions have been made. They are that: (a) the absorbing units are independent of one another; (b) the absorbing units occupy random positions and are randomly oriented; and (c) the incident light is monochromatic. It is easy to see why these assumptions are necessary if the simple equations above are to hold. Suppose that an absorption line has the shape given by the graph of s versus λ in Fig. 7–13(a). If this absorption line is investigated by monochromatic light, Eq. (7–12) will be obeyed, as indicated by the dashed line of Fig. 7–13(b). But if the incident light has a big range of wavelengths, the relation between $\ln I/I_0$ and nx will be more like that shown by the solid curve of Fig. 7–13(b). Obviously some of the light will not be absorbed no matter how thick the sample is. If the light is monochromatic, and assumptions (a) and (b) are fulfilled, Eq. (7–12) holds, and at a particular wavelength, $\ln I/I_0$ should be

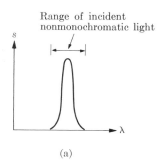

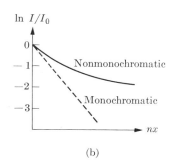

(a)   (b)

FIG. 7–13. The relation between $\ln I/I_0$ and nx for monochromatic and non-monochromatic light. (a) A schematic absorption line. (b) $\ln I/I_0$ for the two types of incident radiation.

proportional to nx (which represents the number of molecules per unit area) or to the surface density of the absorbing material. The slope of the solid line in Fig. 7–13(b) is $-s$. A graph of s versus λ is an absorption spectrum.

There are many other ways of writing the relations among the variables given in Eq. (7–12). One of the most popular forms is

$$\log \frac{I}{I_0} = -\epsilon c l \quad \text{or} \quad \frac{I}{I_0} = 10^{-\epsilon c l}, \tag{7–13}$$

where l is the sample thickness in cm, c is the concentration in moles/liter, and ϵ is defined as the molecular absorption coefficient. It is a simple matter to show that if s is measured in cm^2,

$$s = 3.8 \times 10^{-21} \epsilon. \tag{7–14}$$

In many absorption measurements either the concentration (which cannot be determined without a knowledge of the mass of the absorber and its molecular weight) or the thickness of the sample may not be known. In this case we represent the absorption spectrum by a graph of $\log I_0/I$ versus λ because $\log I_0/I$ is proportional to s. The quantity $\log I_0/I$ is known as the *optical density* or *transmittance* of the sample. It depends not only on the molecular properties but also on the sample thickness. For convenience, some of the parameters of absorption spectra are given in Table 7–4.

The necessity of the assumption of randomness may be quickly shown by the observation that if all the absorbers were in the lower half of the absorption cell, no more than 50% of the light could be absorbed; likewise, if all the absorbers were aligned with their dipole moments parallel to one another, then only 50% of incident unpolarized light would be absorbed.

TABLE 7–4

SOME TERMS USED IN ABSORPTION SPECTROSCOPY

Term	Expression	Units
Optical density	$D = \log_{10} I_0/I$	——
Molecular extinction coefficient	$\epsilon = (1/cx) \log_{10} I_0/I$	c: moles/liter x: cm
Molecular absorption cross section	$s = (1/nx) \ln I_0/I$	n: number/cm^3 x: cm

We will take up the latter situation more completely in Section 7–12, after a consideration of some of the experimental details of absorption measurements. Needless to say, if the absorption cross section is concentration-dependent, the general form of Eq. (7–12) will not hold but the exponential dependence of the transmitted intensity or path length will hold.

7–11 Experimental techniques for absorption measurements. The intimate and intricate details and exhaustive description of the various types of apparatus that may be used for absorption measurements cannot be gone into here. We shall be content with describing the general features of one of the more popular, and in many ways typical, spectrophotometers, a Beckman spectrophotometer. All other instruments are, in principle, similar. The general requirements are a source of monochromatic light of variable wavelength, a detection system to determine I/I_0, and an absorbing sample. Monochromatic light may best be obtained by use of a continuous light source, which emits all wavelengths, and some form of spectrograph like that shown in Fig. 7–14(a). Light from the source is focused on the entrance slit of the spectrograph by the mirrors m_1 and m_2. The light diverges from the slit, which is in the focal plane of the concave mirror M, and falls, as a parallel beam, on the quartz prism whose rear surface is coated with an aluminum reflecting coating. The light therefore passes through the equivalent of a 60° prism. The dispersed light would return along the path of the incident light, but because of a slight tilt of the mirror M it is brought to focus *below* the entrance slit in the plane of the exit slit. A spectrum is produced in the plane of the exit slit, and the exit slit itself defines a narrow wavelength interval of light. The light passes through the sample and falls on a light detector, say a photocell. The wavelength of the emergent light is controlled by rotation of the prism. Since all the other optics are reflecting surfaces, the instrument is achromatic and does not have to be refocused when the wavelength is changed.

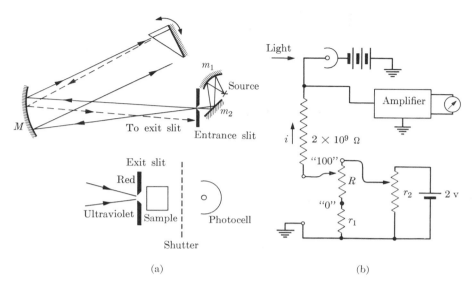

(a)   (b)

FIG. 7–14. (a) Schematic diagram showing the light paths in a Beckman spectrophotometer. (b) Schematic detection system.

If the absorbing material is dissolved or dispersed in another medium, such as water, we must determine the ratio of the light transmitted by the solution, I, to that transmitted by the solvent, I_0. An easy way to do this is to amplify the photoelectric current produced by the photocell and take the ratio of the currents, i/i_0, produced by light transmitted by solution and solvent. It is more accurate, however, to use the amplifier as a null instrument, as in Fig. 7–14(b). The electrons ejected by the incident light pass through the high resistance of 2×10^9 ohms and produce a potential difference across the resistance which is $\Delta V = i \times 2 \times 10^9$. The amplifier detects this potential difference and its output is used to give a meter deflection. The rest of the circuit is a potentiometer that applies a potential difference of variable magnitude and opposite sign to ΔV. When the bucking voltage from the potentiometer has a magnitude equal to ΔV, the amplifier indicates zero output and the value of the bucking voltage is proportioned to the light intensity because the photoelectric current $i\alpha I$. If one wishes to be sophisticated, the potentiometer slide wire, R, may be calibrated to read directly in percent transmission by the following procedure. When the shutter is closed, the sliding contact should be set at "0" and r_1 adjusted so as to buck out any dark current from the photocell. Now the shutter should be opened, and with the solvent cell in position and the sliding contact at "100," r_2 and/or the intensity of the light (by changing the slit width) should be adjusted so that the photocell output is again bucked out. We have now calibrated the slide wire so that "0" corresponds to no light and "100" corresponds to I_0. If an absorbing sample is placed in the light beam, the contact on the slide wire R will have to be set at an intermediate position for a null reading; and if the slide wire has been divided into 100 equal parts, the value of I/I_0 may be read directly.

Other types of absorption spectrophotometers may have dispersing elements that are diffraction gratings instead of prisms and may have detecting systems using thermopiles, photoconductive cells, or photo-multiplier tubes. The light sources for use in work in the infrared and visible regions of the spectrum are usually incandescent solids, and in the ultraviolet region they are hydrogen discharge tubes. Some absorbing systems, such as the one described in conjunction with the reflecting microscope of Chapter 12, use photographic recording.

7–12 Absorption by oriented dipoles. We have seen that the location of an absorption maxima and its intensity is sufficient, in many cases, to determine the chemical composition of the absorber and the number of absorbing molecules. Thus the location of the absorption bands in proteins which arise from the $-$NH group indicates that the hydrogen atom is participating in a hydrogen bond. If these $-$NH groups were aligned parallel to the axis of a long-chain molecule, and if the molecules themselves were oriented, the absorption of light whose electric vector was parallel to the molecular axis would be different from that of light whose electric vector was perpendicular to the absorbing molecules. The Beer-Lambert law, Eq. (7–12), would not hold for incident unpolarized light even though it holds for the two components, $I_{||}$ and $I_{\perp}$. Suppose *all* the absorbing dipoles are aligned parallel to one another and are in a plane perpendicular to the velocity of the incident light, as indicated in Fig. 7–15(a). If the

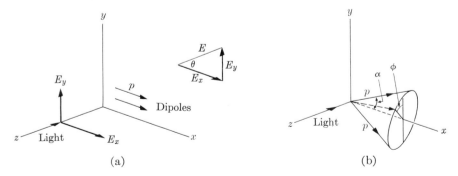

(a)   (b)

FIG. 7–15. Light with electric field components E_x and E_y incident on possible distributions of oriented dipoles. (a) All the dipoles parallel to the x-axis. (b) The dipoles making angles α with the x-axis but random angles ϕ.

incident light is *polarized* so that its incident electric vector makes an angle θ with the x-axis, the component amplitudes are given by

$$E_{x0} = E_0 \cos \theta, \qquad E_{y0} = E_0 \sin \theta,$$

and because the intensity, which is what is detected by devices such as photocells, is proportional to the square of the amplitude,

$$I_{x0} = I_0 \cos^2 \theta, \qquad I_{y0} = I_0 \sin^2 \theta,$$

with

$$I_{x0} + I_{y0} = I_0.$$

If the incident radiation were unpolarized, the two components would be equal in magnitude, that is, $I_{x0} = I_{y0}$. For both components, the exponential absorption law holds, and if we call $s_{||}$ the absorption cross section for light with electric vector parallel to the symmetry axis (the x-axis) and call $s_\perp$ the cross section for light whose electric vector is perpendicular to the symmetry axis, we have for the two components

$$\frac{-dI_x}{I_x} = ns_{||}\, dz \qquad \text{and} \qquad \frac{-dI_y}{I_y} = ns_\perp\, dz.$$

For the perfectly aligned distribution of Fig. 7–15(a), the value of $s_\perp$ would be zero, so that the integrals of the above equations yield

$$I_x = I_{x0} e^{-ns_{||}z} \qquad \text{and} \qquad I_y = I_{y0}.$$

The total transmitted intensity is given by

$$I = I_x + I_y = I_{x0} e^{-ns_{||}z} + I_{y0},$$

which clearly does not obey the Beer-Lambert Law.

A more reasonable distribution than the one we have been discussing would be that shown in Fig. 7–15(b), where the absorbing dipoles are pictured as distributed so as to make a fixed angle α with the x-axis but have a random azimuthal angle ϕ. Such a distribution could represent the orientation of the N—H . . . O= groups in an alpha-helix in which the helix axis is along the x-axis. Let $(\widehat{pE_x})$ and $(\widehat{pE_y})$ represent the respective angles between the dipoles and the x- and y-components of the electric field and let s_0 represent the cross section for absorption for p parallel to E. Then Eq. (7–11) takes the form

$$\frac{dI_x}{I_x} = -ns_0 \overline{\cos^2 (\widehat{pE_x})}\, dz = -ns_{||}\, dz,$$

$$\frac{dI_y}{I_y} = -ns_0 \overline{\cos^2 (\widehat{pE_y})}\, dz = -ns_\perp\, dz,$$

where the symbols have the same meaning as before and the bar over the $\cos^2$ indicates that the average value is to be used. The trigonometric averaging yields

$$\overline{\cos^2 (\widehat{pE_x})} = \cos^2 \alpha,$$

$$\overline{\cos^2 (\widehat{pE_y})} = \tfrac{1}{2} \sin^2 \alpha,$$

whence

$$I_x = I_{x0} e^{-ns_{||}z} \qquad (s_{||} = s_0 \cos^2 \alpha),$$

$$I_y = I_{y0} e^{-ns_\perp z} \qquad \left(s_\perp = \frac{s_0}{2} \sin^2 \alpha\right).$$

$$(7\text{--}15)$$

Clearly, a useful way to express the degree of orientation of an absorber is in terms of the ratio $s_{||}/s_\perp$, called the *dichroic ratio*. The dichroic ratio is independent of the absorber thickness. In practice it may be found from the ratio of the optical density for light vibrating parallel to the symmetry axis to that for light vibrating perpendicular to the symmetry axis. It is a function of the distribution of dipoles. For perfect alignment, which is a special case of the conical distribution, the dichroic ratio is infinite, as is evident from a qualitative description, and for the conical distribution it is given by $2/\tan^2 \alpha$. The dichroic ratio is shown as a function of the cone half-angle in Fig. 7–16. Other assumed distributions, such as one in which the dipoles are distributed with a gaussian distribution about the x-axis, will yield different results. If the cone half-angle is 55°, the dichroic ratio is one, and both electric field components will have the same absorption coefficients. The alpha-helix described in Chapter 5 has

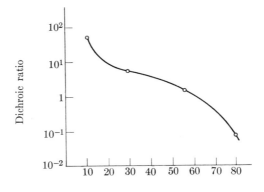

Cone half-angle, degrees

Fig. 7–16. The dichroic ratio for the conical distribution of Fig. 7–15(b) as a function of the cone half-angle.

the $-N-H \ldots O=$ groups making angles of 12° with the helix axis. This angle corresponds to a dichroic ratio of 44.

Two cautions concerning the interpretation of polarized absorption data are appropriate here. First, the observed dichroic ratio depends on the orientation of the absorbing groups within the molecule and on the orientation of the molecules relative to one another; therefore the calculated dichroic ratio for a set of parallel molecules is never observed in practice because all the molecules are not parallel. Second, the absorbing dipoles are not necessarily parallel to molecular dipoles because a large polyatomic molecule is only approximately the sum of diatomic groupings.

7–13 Dichroic ratios of proteins and nucleic acids. The measurement of dichroic ratios of biological systems to determine their structures requires polarized light and oriented structures. Polarized infrared light may be produced by reflection from or transmission through films of selenium, 4μ thick, set at the polarizing angle to the incident light. Some of simplest structures to orient are polymers of amino acids. These polymers are dissolved in a volatile solvent, and the solution is placed on a metal plate. When the solvent evaporates, the resulting thin polymer film may be either stretched or rolled to produce a degree of orientation among the polymer chains, and the polymers may be investigated by x-ray diffraction techniques and polarized light absorption. The absorption spectra of a stretched film of poly-γ-benzyl glutamate,

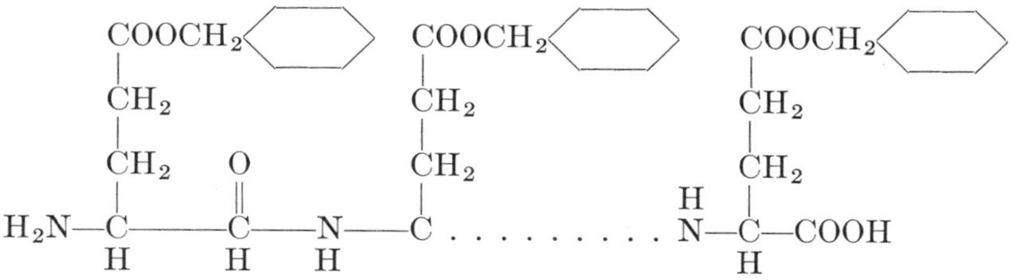

are shown in Fig. 7–17 for light parallel to and perpendicular to the molecular axis. X-ray diffraction pictures indicate that the structure is similar in general form to that of α-keratin and actually fits the α-helix type of structure described in Chapter 5. The absorption spectra shown in the figure were of great help in figuring out this structure. For this folded type of polypeptide chain, the stretching vibrations of $-N-H$ and $>C=O$ absorb more for light parallel to the molecular axis, which indicates that these molecular groupings are parallel to the molecular axis. The dichroic ratio at 3300 cm^{-1} is 14, which is close to the theoretical 44 of the α-helix. This large dichroic ratio rules out structures whose $N-H$ groups make angles of more than 20° with the molecular axis. The bending vibra-

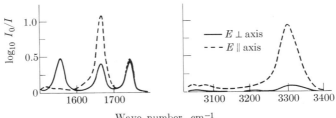

Wave number, cm^{-1}

FIG. 7–17. Absorption spectra of poly- α -benzyl glutamate for light with the electric vector parallel (dashed curve) and perpendicular (solid curve) to the molecular axis. X-ray diffraction data indicate that the molecule is of the α-keratin type. [From E. J. Ambrose and A. Elliott, *Proc. Roy. Soc.* **A 205,** 47 (1951).]

tions of N—H have, as is to be expected, a dichroic ratio less than one because the bending motion will preferentially be excited by light vibrating perpendicular to the N—H bond.

The spectrum of a fiber of denatured insulin in the region of the C=O stretching and N—H bending frequencies is shown in Fig. 7–18(a). The polarization properties of such fibers, which are of the β-keratin or extended polypeptide type, are the opposite of those for the folded polypeptide in Fig. 7–17. This is the evidence that the C=O and N—H groups are arranged perpendicular to the molecular axis and that the hydrogen bonds in these extended structures are *inter*chain bonds.

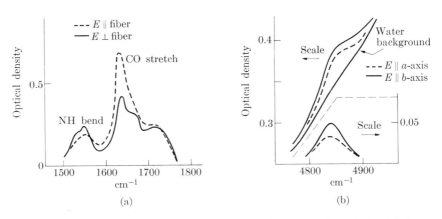

(a)   (b)

FIG. 7–18. Part of the absorption spectra of proteins in polarized infrared light. (a) A fiber of denatured insulin. [From E. J. Ambrose and A. Elliott, *Proc. Roy. Soc.*, **A 208,** 75 (1951).] (b) A hemoglobin crystal in water. In the lower part of the figure the background absorption due to water has been subtracted out. [From A. Elliott and E. J. Ambrose, *Faraday Soc. Disc.* (1950).]

TABLE 7–5

POLARIZATION PROPERTIES OF PROTEIN
ABSORPTION BANDS*

Absorption band	Dichroism and frequency, cm^{-1}	
	Folded chain	Extended chain
N—H bend	σ1545	π1525
C=O stretch	π1660	σ1640
N—H stretch	π3300	σ3300
N—H combination	σ4830	π4825

* π = greater absorption with electric vector parallel to the axis. σ = greater absorption with electric vector perpendicular to the axis.

A summary of polarized absorption data obtained with known structures is given in Table 7–5.

Most of the spectra we have given are of thin films or fibers in the absence of water because the very high infrared absorption of water obscures the spectra we are interested in. However, there exists one absorption region of proteins that can be seen through the background absorption of water. This is the absorption band at 4825 cm^{-1}, which corresponds to a combination of N—H bending and N—H stretching frequencies and shows, as indicated in Table 7–5, the polarization properties of the N—H bending frequency. This absorption band may be used to investigate the orientation of N—H groups in crystals of proteins. Figure 7–18(b) shows the absorption of a hemoglobin crystal at this frequency. Since the absorption is greater for the electric vector parallel to the b-axis of the crystal, we conclude that the hydrogen bonds are oriented perpendicularly to this axis. Because hemoglobin has folded rather than extended chains, the hydrogen bonds are parallel to the chain axis, and the data of Fig. 7–18(b) show that the polypeptide chains have a preferential orientation perpendicular to the b-axis, in agreement with the x-ray interpretation in Chapter 5.

Polarized infrared techniques have also been applied to the analysis of nucleic acid structure. Figure 7–19 shows an absorption spectrum of a thin film of DNA. The position of the N—H and O—H frequencies indicates that these groups participate in hydrogen bonds. The dichroism of the N—H, O—H, and C=O groups indicates that the hydrogen bonds are preferentially oriented *perpendicular* to the molecular axis, and so they probably represent intermolecular regions of attraction. The P—O—C groups also have a component perpendicular to the molecular axis, but

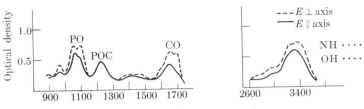

Wave number, cm^{-1}

FIG. 7–19. Absorption spectrum of a thin film of DNA with the electric vector of the incident light parallel (solid curve) and perpendicular (dashed curve) to the molecular axis. The assignments of bond frequencies are given. [From M. J. Fraser and R. D. B. Fraser, *Nature* **167**, 761 (1951).]

the absence of any dichroism in the P=O absorption band at 1250 cm^{-1} implies that they are oriented, as indicated in Fig. 7–16, at angles of 55° to the molecular axis. The structural model of DNA discussed in Chapter 5 is in agreement with these findings.

7–14 Electronic energy levels. There are many possible electron configurations, even in simple atoms such as hydrogen. This is not surprising, since each distribution usually corresponds to a particular electronic energy level of the atom. If we were to visualize the building of molecules from atoms, we could describe the molecular energy levels associated with the electron configuration as dependent on the internuclear separation, as in the curves shown in Fig. 6–4. As two atoms, each in its ground state, are brought together, the original single energy level splits into two molecular energy levels. One level represents the configuration with parallel spins and the other represents antiparallel spins. If N atoms were brought together to form a molecule, the original single energy level would split into N components representing different spin combinations. Obviously the electronic structure of polyatomic molecules becomes very complicated. The complications are even worse than we have indicated because the excited states of molecules may arise not only from combinations of atoms in their ground states but also from atoms which are initially in excited electronic states of their own. All this means that the number of excited electronic states of molecules is much larger than the number of atomic states from which they are derived.

We would do best to consider the simplest molecule, H$_2$. In a diatomic molecule, the binding energy and the shape of the potential-energy curve depend on the electron distribution; hence each electronic state may be represented by its own potential-energy curve. If we think of splitting the energy of a molecule into the sum of electronic and vibrational energies (a permissible procedure, because the electrons move so much faster than

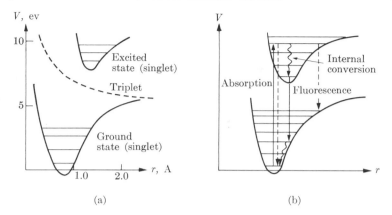

FIG. 7–20. (a) Some of the potential-energy curves for H_2. The solid curves and their associated vibrational energy levels are singlet states. The dashed curve is the lowest triplet state. (b) Some of the possible transitions in the absorption and re-emission of radiation by a diatomic molecule.

the nuclei that the vibrational motion represents a slow pulsation of the electronic cloud), each potential-energy curve will have its full complement of vibrational energy levels. Some of the potential-energy curves and their vibrational energy levels for the hydrogen molecule are shown in Fig. 7–20(a). As we saw in Fig. 6–4, the ground state is represented by zero total spin. Since zero spin can only have one component, zero, in a given direction, this state is known as a *singlet* state. The state just above the ground state has two parallel electron spins. The resultant spin of one may have components $1, 0$, or -1 in a given direction, so this state is called a *triplet* state. Just one of the excited singlet states which arise when an atom in the first excited state and a normal atom are brought together are also shown in the figure. Obviously the density of these states is high. There are also many stable triplet states above the low-lying repulsive one. The potential-energy curves for diatomic molecules must be replaced by potential-energy surfaces of $3N - 6$ dimensions when we consider a molecule of N atoms. Obviously such complex situations require much more analysis than we have time for.

When dipole radiation is absorbed by a diatomic molecule, it is very improbable that the total spin of the system will change. Thus if the ground state is a singlet state, the absorption of light will raise the molecule to an excited singlet state. In a transition from one electronic state to another, the electronic wave functions (electron distribution) change, and there is no selection rule which governs the changes in vibrational quantum number. The probability of a given change in vibrational level in an electronic transition is given by the *Franck-Condon principle*. In classical terms, this principle is described as follows. A change in the electron configuration of the molecule associated with the emission and absorption of a photon takes much less time than the time for a vibration. (The time for a vibration is $\sim 10^{-13}$ sec compared with the electron rearrangement time of $\sim 10^{-15}$ sec.) Hence the nuclear positions and velocities are unchanged during the electron rearrangement. This means that on a potential-energy diagram the transitions are indicated as taking place straight up and down. Since the molecules are most likely to be found at the extremes of the potential curves with zero velocity, the most probable transitions are straight up and down between the endpoints. The quantum-mechanical argument would deal with the overlapping of the wave functions and would yield the same result as the classical description for high vibrational quantum numbers. However, for the $v = 0$ level the most probable position of the oscillator is at the center of the level rather than at the extremes, and the most probable transition from the $v = 0$ level will be from its center. At room temperature most molecules reside in the $v = 0$ level, and almost all the absorption transitions start from this point.

According to the Franck-Condon principle, the absorption of light by a molecule would be indicated by the upward arrow in Fig. 7–20(b), where the molecule is pictured as being raised to an excited state that has potential minimum. If the molecule does not make collisions and so lose energy, it will fall back to the ground state along one of the paths indicated by dashed arrows in the figure and re-emit light. As may be seen, this fluorescent light has, in general, less energy than the absorbed light. The half-life of such excited states is 10^{-8} sec, a time not to be confused with the rearrangement time of the electronic motion. If the molecules which absorb radiation are in close contact with their neighbors, they may make many collisions before they reradiate their absorbed energy. If the vibration frequency is 10^{13}/sec, there will be 10^5 vibrations or collisions with neighbors in 10^{-8} sec. This means that a molecule initially in the $v = 3$ level of the excited electronic state (as shown in Fig. 7–20b) and therefore having a higher vibrational energy than its surroundings will lose this excess vibrational energy before light is reradiated. This loss of excess vibrational energy, or heat, is known as *internal conversion*. It leaves the electronically excited molecule in its lowest vibrational energy from which fluorescence takes place, as shown by the solid downward arrow. The cycle of energy transfers in solutions or solids is: absorption of a photon, raising the molecule to a high vibrational energy level of an excited electronic state; loss of excess vibrational energy to the surroundings; re-emission of a photon, with the molecule going to a high vibrational energy level of the ground state; and, finally, loss of vibrational energy to the surroundings by the "hot" molecule in the ground state.

7–15 Electronic spectra of polyatomic molecules. The big strides in the spectroscopy of diatomic molecules and in determining their structure were made because it was possible to obtain their emission spectra by exciting them, for example, in a gas discharge tube. Unfortunately this procedure cannot be followed for polyatomic molecules because this crude excitation process destroys the molecules. We are forced to use absorption and fluorescence spectroscopy. The changes in the electronic energies of molecules give rise to spectra in the near infrared, visible, and ultraviolet spectral regions. Spectra in the near infrared and visible arise from electronic changes in such molecules and groups as carotenes and

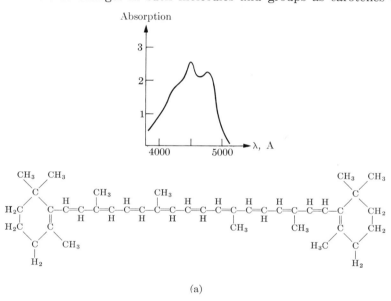

(a)

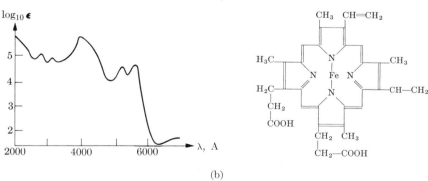

(b)

Fig. 7–21. (a) The structure and spectrum of β-carotene. (b) The visible spectrum of hemoglobin and the structure of its prosthetic group, protoheme.

porphyrins. Figure 9–17 shows the absorption spectra of phycoerythrin and chlorophyll. The spectra and structures of carotene and hemoglobin are shown in Fig. 7–21. The absorbing groups are large resonant structures, so the bonding electrons are shared, at least in part, by the entire structure. Their absorption spectra can be predicted with fair confidence.

Let us work out, as an almost trivial example, the energy levels of a group of electrons confined to a one-dimensional box of length L. This problem is close to that of β-carotene, where L is the chain length and N is the number of atoms in the chain because there is just about one free electron per atom. The wavelength of an electron is given by the de Broglie expression

$$\lambda = \frac{h}{p}, \tag{7-16}$$

where h is Planck's constant and p is the electron's momentum. If the electrons are *free*, there is no potential energy, and

$$\text{Total energy} = \text{kinetic energy} = \frac{p^2}{2m}, \tag{7-17}$$

where m is the electron's mass. If an electron is confined to a box of length L, its wave must vanish at the extremes, which means that the wave must have *nodes* at the ends of the box. Hence

$$L = \frac{n\lambda}{2}, \qquad n = 1, 2, \ldots. \tag{7-18}$$

We may solve Eqs. (7–16) and (7–18) for the momentum p in terms of L and substitute into Eq. (7–17), so that we get for the possible energies

$$E = \frac{n^2 h^2}{8mL^2}. \tag{7-19}$$

If the quantum number n changes from n to $n + 1$, the energy change is given by

$$\Delta E = \frac{h^2}{8mL^2}[(n + 1)^2 - n^2] = \frac{h^2}{8mL^2}(2n + 1). \tag{7-20}$$

Since the N electrons (assumed to be an even number) in the box obey the Pauli principle, they fill the lowest $N/2$ energy levels; therefore the *smallest* possible value of n in Eq. (7–20) is $N/2$, and we have for

$$\text{Minimum } \Delta E = \frac{h^2}{8mL^2}(N + 1). \tag{7-21}$$

The simple derivation leading to Eq. (7–21) illustrates an important point. The length of a resonating chain is proportional to the number of

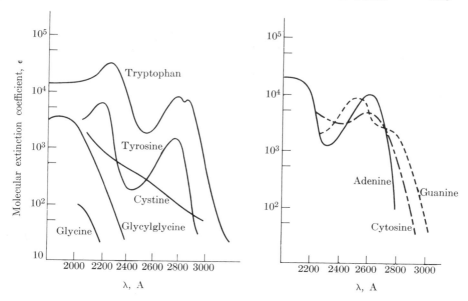

Fig. 7–22.   Absorption spectra of some amino acids and nucleic acids at neutral pH or in the dry state.

atoms in the chain, which in turn is roughly proportional to the number of free electrons in the chain. Therefore the minimum energy transition is approximately inversely proportional to L. The smaller resonating structures have energy levels which are far apart, and their absorption maxima are at short wavelengths. Thus, for example, the heme group of hemoglobin has its principal maxima above 4000 A; the smaller resonating amino acids, tyrosine and tryptophan, have absorption maxima at 2800 and 2200 A; the peptide bond, which shows only partial resonance character, has a maximum at 1900 A, and at still shorter wavelengths the electronic transitions of single bonds become important. Figure 7–22 shows the absorption spectra of some amino acids and nucleic acids.

Since water and other solvents become opaque below 1800 A, spectra at lower wavelengths must be obtained on dry samples. Because most commercial instruments, such as that described in Fig. 7–14, go no lower in wavelength than 2000 A, almost all the spectroscopic data on biological compounds is confined to higher wavelengths.

7–16 Ultraviolet absorption by proteins and nucleic acids. Almost all compounds have characteristic absorption spectra in the ultraviolet region, but we shall confine our attention to just two: proteins and nucleic acids. From the data shown in Fig. 7–22, we would expect that the absorp-

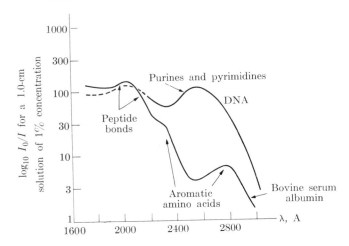

FIG. 7–23. Ultraviolet absorption spectra of a typical protein and nucleic acid at pH 7. The various maxima are identified with particular components of the molecules.

tion spectra of proteins would show maxima at 2800 and 1900 A and that nucleic acids polymers would have maxima at 2600 A. This is indeed the case, as is indicated in Fig. 7–23. The optical densities shown in the figure were calculated from data obtained on thinner and more dilute solutions on the assumption that the Beer-Lambert law, Eq. (7–13), holds. At the longer ultraviolet wavelengths, nucleic acids will have about 20 times the optical density of an equal mass concentration of protein. The explanation is that most of the amino acids are nonaromatic and contribute practically nothing to the protein absorption spectrum at wavelengths greater than 2100 A. The high and characteristic absorption by nucleic acids makes it relatively simple to detect them by ultraviolet spectroscopy and to localize them in cells by ultraviolet microscopes, as described in Chapter 12. Nucleoproteins will show spectra which are weighted averages of protein and nucleic acid absorption. For example, tobacco mosaic virus with 6% RNA and the rest protein shows equal absorption at 2600 and 2800 A.

The absorption spectrum of a large molecule, such as a protein or a nucleic acid polymer, is for the longer ultraviolet wavelengths due to electronic transitions in a relatively few types of groupings or subunits. These absorbing groups, which are the purines, pyrimidines, and aromatic amino acids, are approximately independent of one another. They are separated by large enough distances so that their electronic wave functions are separate and do not influence one another. We would therefore expect that the absorption cross section, s, of a large molecule would be approxi-

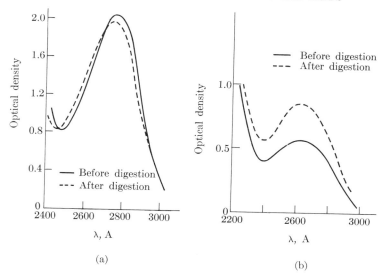

FIG. 7–24. (a) Absorption spectrum of serum globulin and its constituent amino acids. (From Ref. 4.) (b) Absorption spectrum of DNA and the sum of its constituents.

mately the sum of the cross sections, s_i, of its components.

$$s \cong \sum_i s_i. \qquad (7\text{–}22)$$

Figure 7–24 shows a comparison of the absorption spectrum of a protein with that of its constituent amino acids and of DNA with the equivalent sum of nucleotides. We see that Eq. (7–22) holds very closely for proteins and thus that absorption spectra may be used to determine the relative amounts of tyrosine and tryptophan in proteins. In this technique the protein absorption spectrum is measured at acid and alkaline pH, and because in alkalai the phenol group of tyrosine ionizes and its spectrum changes, the two spectra give an unambiguous determination. The slight shift toward higher wavelengths shown in Fig. 7–24(a) arises because in the native protein the —OH group of tyrosine participates in a hydrogen bond, which slightly lowers the electronic energy levels of

$$\text{\Large \hexagon}\text{—OH.}$$

The spectral change shown in Fig. 7–24(a) is more pronounced for a protein such as ribonuclease which contains tyrosine but no tryptophan, and it may be used to estimate how intact the tertiary structure is.

Figure 7–24(b) shows that depolymerized DNA has about a 30% higher absorption than the highly polymerized variety. We conclude that in a double helical structure the bases are *not* independent of one another because they are relatively close together and are all hydrogen bonded. The failure of Eq. (7–22) for DNA gives us a simple measure of the interactions between the bases, and it is used in the assay for the enzyme DNA-ase. Changes similar to those shown in Fig. 7–24(b) take place, under appropriate conditions, between polyadenylic acid and polyurydilic acid; thus the interaction between the two polymers may be followed spectroscopically.*

7–17 The fine structure in spectra. Most of the spectra we have shown have very little structure to them. Even if strictly monochromatic light had been used to obtain the absorption curves, they would not show the presence of many sharp absorption bands or lines. The absence of these definite characteristics in the absorption curves is due to the random and varying local fields of the molecules surrounding the absorbing ones. It might be expected that if the temperature of the absorbing medium were lowered so as to decrease this random perturbation and at the same time bring all the absorbing molecules into the ground vibrational state, the absorption spectrum might begin to show some fine structure. Some absorption spectra have been obtained at liquid air and liquid hydrogen temperatures. Of the compounds that show high absorption in the ultraviolet region of the spectrum, the pyrimidines in particular exhibit a very sharp absorption spectrum at these low temperatures. Figure 7–25 shows one of these absorption spectra. The absorption bands are roughly equally spaced in wave number, as is to be expected if they represent transitions from the zero level of the ground electronic state to the successive vibrational energy levels of the excited state.

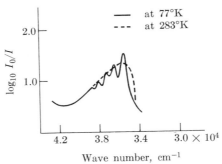

Fig. 7–25. Absorption spectrum of a thin film of thymine at room temperature and at liquid nitrogen temperature. [From R. E. Sinsheimer, J. F. Scott, and J. R. Loofbourow, *J. Biol. Chem.* **187**, 313 (1950).]

---

* G. Felsenfeld and A. Rich, *Biochim. et Biophys. Acta* **26**, 457 (1957).

7–18 Polarized ultraviolet light. The absorption of polarized infrared radiation can tell us something about the orientation of specific groups in nucleic acid and protein molecules. The absorption of visible and ultraviolet light does not depend upon the specific groupings, but is a result of the structure of ringlike resonating compounds. For example, the heme group consists of a large planar molecule whose capacity for resonance is great. Crudely speaking, we may think of this group as made up of an electron gas circulating about the ring. We would expect that these electrons would absorb radiation only if the incident electric vector is in the plane of the ring. Such a conclusion, of course, is not necessarily correct, because the observed absorption band may also be due to changes in vibration that take place perpendicular to the ring plane. Such vibrations would be equivalent to a puckering of the ring. We have, however, an experimental test of these two possibilities. If the latter one is correct, then there should be one direction of high absorption and two directions perpendicular to this of low absorption. If electric vectors in the plane of the ring are strongly absorbed, then there should be two directions of strong absorption and one of weak absorption. Data obtained in the visible region of the spectrum indicate that it is the vibrations in the plane of the ring which are strongly absorbed. The absorption spectrum of a crystal of hemoglobin is shown in Fig. 7–26(a) for two different orientations. This spectrum has been taken for only two directions, but other data in the region of 4000 A indicate that the b-axis is equivalent to the c-axis. Thus the heme groups have a preferential orientation parallel to the bc-plane. Their precise orientation, shown in Chapter 5, is obtained

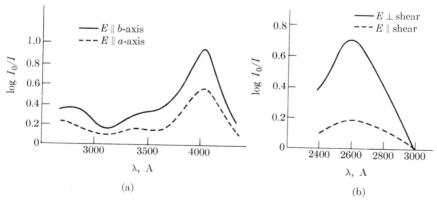

FIG. 7–26.   Absorption spectra in visible and ultraviolet polarized light. (a) A crystal of horse met-hemoglobin of mass $\sim 10^{-9}$ gm. [From Perutz, Jope, and Barer, *Faraday Soc. Disc.* (1950).] (b) Thymus nucleic acid (film at 90% humidity). [From W. E. Seeds and M. H. F. Wilkens, as reported by W. E. Seeds in Ref. 5.]

by paramagnetic resonance methods described in Section 7–19. The data at 2800 A indicate that the aromatic amino acids are also oriented with their planes parallel to the b-axis.

When a DNA gel is subjected to a shearing force, the long thin molecules will be aligned parallel to the shear direction. The fact that the electric vector perpendicular to the shear direction is more strongly absorbed, as shown in Fig. 7–26(b), indicates that the purines and pyrimidines are arranged with their planes nearly perpendicular to the chain axis. This is of course the case for the model shown in Fig. 5–31. At lower relative humidities, the dichroism decreases because the base planes make smaller angles with the chain axis.

The first use of polarized ultraviolet light to investigate the structure of a virus gave results similar to those for hemoglobin.* Tobacco mosaic virus particles were oriented by making them flow through a fine capillary. The absorption spectrum was obtained with the electric vector both parallel and perpendicular to the direction of flow. The results obtained indicated that in the region of 2800 A the absorption coefficients for E parallel were greater than for E perpendicular to the direction of flow, indicating that the planes of the aromatic amino acids are parallel to the particle axis.

7–19 Electron spin resonance. Molecules with *unpaired* electrons have, as we remarked at the beginning of the chapter, absorption spectra in the neighborhood of 1 cm. These spectra arise from electron spin resonance (ESR), i.e., the flip-flop of the electron spin in an external magnetic field when an electromagnetic wave of the proper frequency falls on the molecule. The ESR technique may be used to determine not only the number of unpaired electrons in a sample but also the *internal magnetic fields* which affect the energy levels. Some of the biological systems that have been analyzed by ESR methods are illuminated chloroplasts, heme proteins, oxidation-reduction reactions, and x-ray irradiated proteins.

For free electrons. The spin of an electron will be either antiparallel or parallel to the direction of an applied magnetic field H, and therefore the magnetic moment of the electron, μ_e, which is in the opposite direction from the spin of the rotating negative charge, will be only parallel or antiparallel to H. The two possible orientations of the magnetic moment represent different energies, and electromagnetic energy of frequency ν may be absorbed so that $\Delta E = h\nu$. The interaction energy between a magnetic dipole μ_e and a field H is given by the same expression as for an electric

---

* A. Butenandt, H. Friedrick-Freska, S. Hartwig, and G. Scheibe, *Z. Physiol. Chem.* **274,** 276 (1942). These authors had the incorrect sign for the dichroism. (See Ref. 5.)

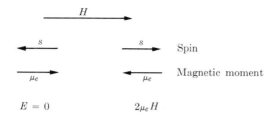

FIG. 7–27. The possible orientation of the spin and magnetic moment of an electron in a magnetic field H.

dipole in an electric field. It is

$$E = \mu_e H(1 - \cos\theta),$$

where θ is the angle between μ_e and H. Figure 7–27 shows the possible orientations, and because $\theta = 0$ or π, it is immediately apparent that

$$\Delta E = 2\mu_e H. \tag{7–23}$$

An incident electromagnetic wave may interact, by way of its oscillating magnetic field, with the electrons if its frequency is such that the energy of the photon equals ΔE or

$$h\nu = 2\mu_e H \qquad \text{(free electrons)}. \tag{7–23'}$$

For nonfree electrons. In actual practice the electrons in a liquid or solid are *not* free electrons. Their energies depend not only on the applied external field but also on their interactions with all the other nearby electrons. These interactions arise from the internal magnetic fields produced by the electrons making up the molecules under investigation. Therefore the splitting of the energy levels in an external field H is not given exactly by Eq. (7–23), but by an equation of similar form which is usually written as

$$\Delta E = g\mu_0 H. \tag{7–24}$$

The quantity μ_0, known as the Bohr magneton, is the magnetic moment of *classical* rotating charge e whose angular momentum mvr equals $h/2\pi$. In cgs electrostatic units it equals $eh/4\pi mc = 9.3 \times 10^{-21}$ erg/gauss. In mks units, the value of μ_0 is 9.3×10^{-24} joule per weber/m². (The electron which has a spin of $\frac{1}{2}h/2\pi$ nevertheless has a magnetic moment close to μ_0.) The constant g, which was introduced to explain the observations on the splitting of spectral lines in a magnetic field, is known as the Lande g-factor. It is known that $\mu_e/\mu_0 = 1.001$, so for *free* electrons Eqs. (7–23) and (7–24) give $g = 2.002$.

The general expression for the absorbed frequency is

$$\nu = \frac{g\mu_0}{h} H. \tag{7-24'}$$

The determination of ν at a given value of H, or of H for a preset value of ν, allows one to find the value of g for the transition and thus how close the system is to one of free electrons and how the molecular structure affects the energy levels. Equation (7-24') indicates that for $H = 10^4$ gauss,

$$\nu = \frac{2 \times 9 \times 10^{-21} \text{ erg/gauss}}{6.6 \times 10^{-27} \text{ erg·sec}} \times 10^4 \text{ gauss} = 2.8 \times 10^{10} \frac{\text{cycles}}{\text{sec}}.$$

Techniques. The physical setup and the experimental techniques used in ESR are very different from those used in optical spectroscopy, even though the fundamental ideas are the same. The sample is placed in a known magnetic field, and the power transmitted through a resonant cavity containing the sample is measured electronically. A schematic diagram of a simple, but insensitive, type of apparatus appears in Fig. 7–28. In practice it is difficult to vary the frequency ν of the incident wave so as to satisfy Eq. (7-24'). Instead, a fixed frequency ν is used and the magnetic field is varied to satisfy Eq. (7-24') and thus determine g. All absorption lines have a finite width and, because $\Delta\nu \alpha \Delta H$, these spectra are usually plotted as absorption *versus* the applied field H rather than as absorption as a function of frequency. Alternatively, we could plot absorption *versus* g-value. The sensitivity of ESR is so high that it can detect 10^{13} unpaired electrons/cm^3, or about 10^{-8} mole/1, if the width of the absorption line is 1 gauss. Wider absorption lines need more electrons if they are to be detected.

Results. Electron spin resonances have been observed in free radical reactions and in oxidation-reduction systems such as the oxidation of hy-

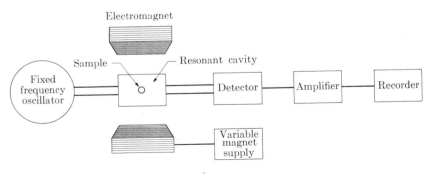

FIG. 7–28. Schematic diagram of the apparatus used to determine ESR spectra.

droquinones to quinone by way of the free radical semiquinoine. The resonance is, of course, typical of the free radical.

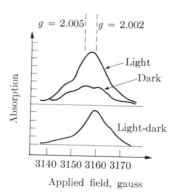

Free radical

Oxidation-reduction systems play a big part in biochemistry, and therefore it is noteworthy that ESR has been observed* in the reactions catalyzed by alcohol dehydrogenase, cytochrome C, cytochrome reductase, and cytochrome oxidase.

Dried or wet chloroplasts show ESR when illuminated by light,* indicating that the light-dependent steps in photosynthesis involve a semiconductor mechanism, triplet states, or free radicals. Figure 7–29 shows the ESR absorption curve of dried chloroplasts. The width of these absorption curves is about 20 gauss. The g-value of 2.002 at the maximum of the absorption curve for the illuminated system is the same as for free electrons. This fact supports the theory of a semiconductor mechanism for the chlorophyll-lipoprotein complex. The indication of fine structure

FIG. 7–29. ESR absorption curves for chloroplasts in the dark and in the light. The g-values corresponding to several values of H are indicated. $\nu = 9.000 \times 10^9 \, \text{sec}^{-1}$. [After B. Commoner, et al., Science **126**, 57 (1957).]

---

* B. Commoner, et al., Science **126**, 57 (1957).

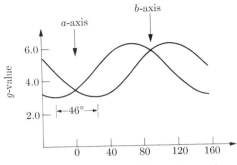

FIG. 7–30. The g-values of a single crystal of myoglobin for different orientations in the ab-plane relative to the applied magnetic field. [From J. E. Bennett, et al., *Phys. Biol. and Med.* **1**, 309 (1957).]

in the dark chloroplasts means that at least some of the electrons, instead of being free, are perturbed by the local molecular structure.

The heme groups of proteins show ESR spectra which depend on the orientation of the incident magnetic field. The g-value should vary with angle for reasons similar to those for the variation of optical absorption coefficient with angle. Also, measurements on single crystals of heme-containing proteins should locate precisely the orientation of the heme groups, because the g-value is a minimum in the direction perpendicular to the plane of the heme group. Figure 7–30 shows how the g-values for myoglobin vary with angle. Myoglobin is a muscle protein whose molecular weight is one-fourth that of hemoglobin. It contains only one heme group, but the unit cell contains two molecules of myoglobin. Since the heme groups of the two molecules are not parallel to one another, there are *two* absorption lines, or g-values, at each crystal orientation, as indicated in Fig. 7–30. The minima in g-values occur at angles of 23° to the a-axis; thus the projection of the heme normal (which is the minimum g-direction) makes an angle of 23° with the a-axis. In a similar manner, the angles between the heme normal and the other crystallographic axes are found. The orientations of the heme groups of myoglobin and hemoglobin mentioned in Chapter 5 were obtained in this way.

There is no doubt that electron spin resonance techniques will make big contributions to molecular biophysics.

7–20 Nuclear magnetic resonance. We have seen that the state of binding of electrons in molecules and solids may be examined by looking at the splitting of the energy levels in an applied magnetic field if the electrons we are considering have a resultant spin. The level splitting depends on the magnetic moment of the electrons, which in turn depends on the details of how they are bound. Nuclei also may have angular momenta or spins, and therefore they may have magnetic moments. A proton, which has a spin of $\frac{1}{2}$, has a magnetic moment that is much smaller than that of the electron because of its smaller angular velocity. Nuclear magnetic moments are usually given in terms of the nuclear spin I, a nuclear g-value g_n, and a nuclear Bohr magneton $\mu_n = eh/4\pi Mc$, where M is the proton mass.

$$\text{Nuclear magnetic moment} = g_n I \mu_n.$$

In an external magnetic field, the various possible orientations of nuclear spin will give rise to slightly different energies. If there is an oscillating component to the field, energy may be absorbed or emitted as the nuclear spin changes direction. This is known as nuclear magnetic resonance (NMR). The energy of the photons absorbed in such transitions is much smaller than in ESR because the nuclear magnetic moments are about

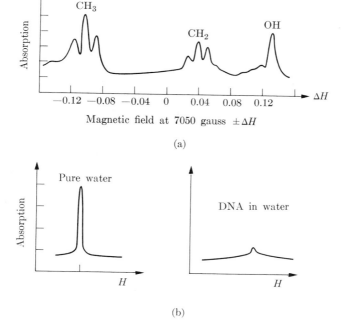

FIG. 7–31. Some nuclear magnetic resonance spectra. (a) High resolution spectrum of CH_3CH_2OH at 30×10^6 cycles/sec. (b) Spectrum of water and 1.6% DNA in water at 30×10^6 cycles/sec. Note the decrease in the proton absorption of the DNA in water as compared with that of pure water. [After B. Jacobson, W. A. Anderson, and J. T. Arnold, *Nature* **173,** 772 (1954).]

2000 times smaller than the electron magnetic moments. The value of μ_n is 5.05×10^{-24} erg/gauss, and for the proton $I = \frac{1}{2}$ and $g_n = 2.79$.

The difference in proton energy between the parallel and antiparallel configurations is given by an expression similar to Eq. (7–23) or (7–24),

$$\Delta E = 2g_n I \mu_n H.$$

And since $I = \frac{1}{2}$,

$$E = g_n \mu_n H. \tag{7–25}$$

Because μ_n is small, the resonant frequencies in NMR are much lower than in ESR. At a magnetic field of 10^4 gauss, ν is near 10^7 cycles/sec in NMR as compared with the value of 3×10^{10} cycles/sec for ESR. The experimental techniques in NMR are similar to those used in ESR. Each type of nucleus has a characteristic magnetic moment. The nuclear magnetic resonance spectrum of a sample will show absorption lines which are characteristic of the nuclear composition of the sample. Moreover, and here is another way in which the technique is useful, the individual nuclear absorption lines show *fine structure*. The fine structure arises because the magnetic field that determines the transition frequency is the sum of the external field and the field produced by the bonding electrons. Since different electron configurations give rise to different fields, the fine structure is characteristic of the state of chemical combination of the nucleus. Figure 7–31 shows two NMR spectra. The spectrum of ethyl alcohol at high resolution shows three types of absorption lines due to the proton magnetic moment. The spectrum of DNA in water shows a fine line due to free water and a broad absorption line arising from all the other protons. As in other types of spectra, the local perturbations in large molecules wash out the fine structure.

The energy differences between the spin orientations of nuclei are so small that large samples, of the order of 10^{20} nuclei, must be used. This fact necessitates a magnetic field that is homonogeneous over a bigger volume than in ESR.

PROBLEMS

1. The internuclear separation of H_2 is 0.8 A. For I_2 it is 2.7 A. For each molecule, calculate the value of the rotational quantum number J for which the rotational energy equals average thermal energy.

2. Assume that H_2 and I_2 interact with radiation. Calculate the frequencies and wavelengths absorbed in the transition $J = 0$ to $J = 1$. What wavelength would be observed if the value of J changed from the value found in Problem 1 to one higher?

3. Assume that a long, thin, cylindrical protein of length 100 A and diameter 5 A is free to rotate. (Note that in the liquid phase proteins *cannot* be considered as free rotators.) Calculate (a) the frequency corresponding to the $J = 0$ to $J = 1$ transition, (b) the value of J for which the rotational energy equals thermal energy, and (c) the frequency absorbed if the value of J in (b) increased by one.

4. For H_2 the wave number corresponding to the first vibrational transition is 4400 cm^{-1}. For I_2 it is 215 cm^{-1}. (a) Calculate the force constant k for each molecule. (b) What is the ratio of the number of molecules in vibrational level 1 to the number in level 0 at room temperature for H_2 and I_2?

5. Show that $s = 3.83 \times 10^{-21}\epsilon$.

6. Compute the wavelength of the first transition in a conjugated system approximating the electrons in a box model in which there is one electron per carbon atom and the distance between carbons is 1.39 A if there are (a) 20 carbon atoms, (b) 10 carbon atoms.

7. Assume that there is one free electron confined to move in the

grouping of the peptide bond. What is the wavelength of the first absorption maximum?

8. Assume a set of absorbing dipoles oriented on the surface of a cone of half-angle α about the x-axis. The concentration is such that $ns_0 = 1$. (a) If light is polarized along the x-axis and is incident in the z-direction, plot $\ln I_0/I$ versus z for $\alpha = 0$ and $\alpha = 30°$. (b) If unpolarized light is incident on the above dipoles, plot $\ln I_0/I$ versus z for $\alpha = 0$ and $\alpha = 30°$.

9. The molecular extinction coefficient of tryptophan at 2800 A is 5.5×10^3. (a) Calculate the concentration which would give 10% transmission for a path length of 1.0 cm. (b) What concentration would give 1% transmission for a 0.20-cm path length? (c) What concentration would give 30% transmission for a 0.20-cm path length?

10. What are the surface densities, in mgm/cm^2, for Problems 9(a), (b), and (c)?

11. What is the absorption cross section of tryptophan at 2800 A? How does this compare with the size of the molecule?

12. Compute the absorption probability p of bovine serum albumin at 1800 A. Take its molecular weight as 70,000 and consider the molecule to be spherical.

13. Assume that TMV is 6% RNA and 94% protein. Take the data given in Fig. 7–23 as representative of these compounds and compute the relative absorption spectrum of TMV.

14. How much light is transmitted through a bacteria of type *E. coli* at 3000, 2600, and 2300 A? Assume, for simplicity, that the cell has a constant thickness of 1μ. Use the data of Fig. 7–23 and the concentrations given in Chapter 2.

15. Given a group of 10^{13} electrons/cm^3 of g-value 2.00 in a magnetic field of 10^4 gauss. Calculate the ratio of the number of electrons with spins parallel

to and antiparallel to the field. What is the excess number/cm^3 with spins antiparallel to the field?

16. Given 1 cm^3 of water in a magnetic field of 10^4 gauss. Calculate the excess of protons with magnetic moments parallel to the magnetic field.

REFERENCES

1. G. R. HARRISON, R. C. LORD, and J. R. LOOFBOUROW, *Practical Spectroscopy*. Prentice-Hall, N. Y., 1948.

2. "Spectroscopy and Molecular Structure and Optical Methods of Investigating Cell Structure," *Faraday Soc. Disc.* (1950).

3. G. B. B. M. SUTHERLAND, "Infrared Analysis of the Structure of Amino Acids, Polypeptides, and Proteins," *Adv. Protein Chem.* **7,** 291 (1952).

4. G. H. BEAVEN and E. R. HOLIDAY, "Ultraviolet Absorption Spectra of Proteins and Amino Acids," *Adv. Protein Chem.* **7,** 320 (1952).

5. W. E. SEEDS, "Polarized Ultraviolet Microspectrography and Molecular Structure," *Prog. Biophys.* **3,** 27 (1953).

6. R. D. B. FRASER, "The Infrared Spectra of Biologically Important Molecules," *Prog. Biophys.* **3,** 47 (1953).

7. H. G. DAVIES and P. M. B. WALKER, "Microspectrometry of Living and Fixed Cells," *Prog. Biophys.* **3,** 195 (1953).

8. E. R. BLOUT, "Ultraviolet Microscopy and Ultraviolet Microspectroscopy," *Adv. Biol. Med. Phys.* **3,** 286 (1953).

9. H. D. SPRINGALL, *The Structural Chemistry of Proteins.* Academic Press, N. Y., 1954.

10. R. L. SINSHEIMER, "Ultraviolet Absorption Spectra," in *Radiation Biology,* Vol. II, p. 165, ed. by A. Hollaender. McGraw-Hill, N. Y., 1955.

11. J. R. PLATT, "Electronic Structure and Excitation of Polyenes and Porphyrins," in *Radiation Biology,* Vol. III, p. 71, ed. by A. Hollaender. McGraw-Hill, N. Y., 1956.

12. C. F. HISKEY, "Absorption Spectroscopy," in *Physical Techniques in Biological Research,* Vol. I, p. 74, ed. by G. Oster and A. W. Pollister. Academic Press, N. Y., 1955.

13. J. F. SCOTT, "Ultraviolet Absorption Spectrophotometry," in *Physical Techniques in Biological Research,* Vol. I, p. 131, ed. by G. Oster and A. W. Pollister. Academic Press, N. Y., 1955.

14. C. CLARK, "Infrared Spectrophotometry," in *Physical Techniques in Biological Research,* Vol. I, p. 206, ed. by G. Oster and A. W. Pollister. Academic Press, N. Y., 1955.

15. P. B. SOGO and B. M. TOLBERT, "Nuclear and Electron Paramagnetic Resonance and Its Application to Biology," *Adv. Biol. Med. Phys.* **5,** 1 (1957).

16. R. D. B. FRASER, "Interpretation of Infrared Dichroism in Axially Oriented Polymers," *J. Chem. Phys.* **28,** 113 (1958).

CHAPTER 8

ENZYMES

8–1 Introduction. Living cells are highly organized systems of reacting elements and chemical reactions. Their reactions do not appear to be a random series of processes such as would take place in a beaker. Each reaction must take place at the proper time and probably in the proper place in the cell. The way in which a cell grows is not uniform. For example, at various stages of the growth cycle some substance, such as nucleic acid, may accumulate much more rapidly than others but will not necessarily appear uniformly distributed throughout the entire cell. To a large extent the oxidative metabolism of many cells seems to be located in small granules or similar structures known as *mitochondria*. If the cell is the highly organized structure that we believe it to be, the chemical reactions within it must take place in an orderly fashion and rapidly enough so that thermal degradation does not destroy the growth process. The majority of the chemical reactions in living systems seem to occur through the intermediate action of substances called *enzymes*. Enzymes are biological catalysts. We believe that they have physical properties analogous to chemical catalysts. They seem to occur throughout cells, although various types of enzymes, such as the oxidative enzymes, may be localized in particular regions. It seems from the biochemical literature as if an enzyme exists for every conceivable purpose. We are not able, nor is it necessary, to consider all these enzymes. We shall discuss only what we think are a representative few, and attempt to generalize from some particular cases. The problem of how enzymes work is indeed a crucial one, because, as we have mentioned, all the important energy interchanges and structural rearrangements in the cell seem to take place through the intermediate action of these biological catalysts. It is just because enzymes have particular catalytic activities that the relations between enzyme structure and function are open to experimental attack. Enzymes are proteins, and many of them have been crystallized and purified by other means so that their physical and chemical properties are well defined. Ultimately, by the methods we have outlined in previous chapters, the primary, secondary, and tertiary structures will be known and their relationship with enzymatic activity will be ascertained.

8–2 The temperature dependence of enzyme kinetics. If we accept the identity of enzymes as catalysts, then we are forced to say (1) that enzymes may change the speed of a reaction but are unaltered by the pro-

239

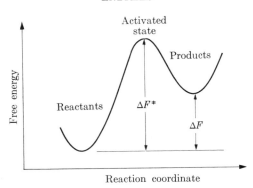

FIG. 8–1. Schematic diagram showing the over-all changes in free energy in the transition from reactants to products. ΔF is shown as positive.

cess, and (2) that enzymes cannot change the equilibrium concentration of reactants and products. The increase in reaction rate due to enzymes can be detected with very small amounts of the catalyst, i.e., with concentrations of the order of a microgram/milliliter or less. Suppose, to make things a little more definite, we think for a moment about the decomposition of urea according to the reaction

$$(NH_2)_2CO + H_2O \rightleftharpoons 2NH_3 + CO_2.$$

For the reaction to occur, a water molecule must approach the urea molecule with enough kinetic energy to overcome any repulsive force between the two, that is, to surmount a potential-energy hill. In more general terms, the water molecule must go over a *free-energy* barrier in approaching a urea molecule, as we discussed in some detail in Chapter 3. The molecules can then react, the urea can decompose, and the products diffuse away. The forward rate of the reaction depends on the probability of the molecules passing over the barrier in the right-hand direction in Fig. 8–1 (which is similar to Fig. 3–6), and the reverse reaction depends on the probability of its passing to the left over the barrier. As we showed in Eq. (3–11), the equilibrium constant K, which is the ratio of the product concentration to the reactant concentration, is given by

$$K = e^{-\Delta F/RT}, \tag{8–1}$$

where R is the gas constant per mole, T is the absolute temperature, and ΔF, as indicated in Fig. 8–1, is the free-energy difference per mole between products and reactants. In other words, the *rate* at which equilibrium is reached depends on the *height* of the barrier, while the final equilibrium depends only on the difference between the minima on either side of the barrier. What the enzyme does is to go to work on the barrier. It either lowers the barrier height or supplies an alternative reaction path which is of lower energy than the top of the hill. In any event, a catalyst speeds up the reaction rates in *both directions*.

The enzyme urease should catalyze the formation of urea from ammonia and carbon dioxide as well as catalyzing the decomposition of urea. But the free energy of ammonia and CO_2 is some 11,000 cal/mole less than that of urea; and because at room temperature RT equals 600 cal/mole, the equilibrium constant would be

$$K = e^{-(-11,000/600)} = e^{18.5} = 10^8.$$

The urea concentration would be approximately 10^{-8} that of ammonia, and it would be impossible to detect the small amount of urea formed. There are many cases, though, in which the reverse reaction may be detected. Chymotrypsin, for example, splits benzoyl-L-tyrosyl glycinamide into benzoyl-L-tyrosine and glycinamide. The reverse reaction cannot be detected due to the large value of the equilibrium constant. But the synthesis of benzoyl-L-tyrosine glycinanilide from benzoyl-L-tyrosine and glycinanilide is easily detected, since the resulting anilide is not soluble. Equilibrium is not reached and the reaction keeps on going to the left. In a somewhat similar fashion, nonspecific insoluble proteins may be formed by the action of trypsin on a solution of specific protein which has been hydrolysed by pepsin.

If the reaction *rates* of enzyme-catalyzed reactions are known at different temperatures, it may be possible to infer some of the details of the enzymatic process from the derived values of $\Delta H^{\pm}$ and $\Delta S^{\pm}$, the heat of activation and the entropy of activation, respectively, for the over-all reaction rate. Many measurements have been made on the temperature dependence of these rates, but because $\Delta F^{\pm} = \Delta H^{\pm} - T\,\Delta S^{\pm}$ and because the rate constant, as shown in Chapter 3, is of the form

$$k_1 = \frac{kT}{h}\,e^{-\Delta F^{\pm}/RT}, \tag{8-2}$$

the temperature dependence of k_1 is related to $\Delta H^{\pm}$, not to $\Delta S^{\pm}$. The temperature dependence is often expressed in terms of the ratio of the reaction rates at temperatures 10°C apart, k_{t+10}/k_t. This quantity, known as Q_{10}, is related to $\Delta H^{\pm}$ by

$$Q_{10} \cong e^{+\Delta H^{\pm}/18,600}.$$

As shown in Table 8-1, the values of $\Delta H^{\pm}$ are generally less than 16,000 cal/mole for enzyme-catalyzed reactions. The theoretical difficulty in analyzing these data fruitfully is that they apply to the over-all reaction,

TABLE 8-1

TEMPERATURE DEPENDENCE OF THE RATE OF SOME
ENZYMATICALLY CATALYZED REACTIONS

Catalyst or enzyme	Substrate	Q_{10}	$\Delta H^{\ne}$, cal/mole
Trypsin	Sturine	1.8	11,000
Emulsin	Salacin	1.15	2600
Luciferase	Luciferin	2.3	15,000
Invertase	Sucrose	1.5	7400
H^+	Sucrose	4.0	26,000
Pepsin	Casein	2.4	16,000
HCL	Casein	3.0	20,600
Amylase	Starch	1.9	12,000

whereas in actual practice the enzyme-catalyzed reaction takes place in several steps. One of these steps, depending on the reaction being studied, may be the one that limits the reaction rate, but a detailed knowledge of the steps is necessary before we know which one it is. Thus the data of Table 8-1 are not too valuable in themselves except insofar as they say that the heat of activation is lowered by enzymes. This is counteracted to some extent by a decrease in entropy of activation. But the velocity of an enzyme-catalyzed reaction still may be many orders of magnitude larger than the velocity of the same reaction occurring at the same pH in solution. Enzyme reactions, of course, can be first, second, or zero order. While we shall not be concerned with writing down all the differential equations of these reactions, there is one aspect of enzyme-catalyzed reactions that is important in understanding how enzymes work. This is the variation in the velocity of the reaction with the concentration of the enzyme and with the nature and concentration of the reactants. Here lies one of the keys to the interrelations between enzyme structure and function.

8-3 The enzyme-substrate complex. The principal reactant in an enzyme-catalyzed reaction is usually called the *substrate*. For example, in the reaction catalyzed by the enzyme invertase,

$$\text{sucrose} + H_2O \rightarrow \text{fructose} + \text{glucose},$$

sucrose is the substrate. In this reaction, if the sucrose concentration is 0.05 M, there are 1000 molecules of water per one molecule of sugar, and as the reaction proceeds the water concentration does *not* change. This reaction follows first-order kinetics; its rate is proportional to the sucrose concentration.

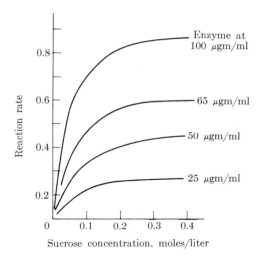

Fig. 8–2. The rate, in moles/liter/min, at which sucrose is split in the presence of different amounts of the enzyme invertase at different sucrose concentrations.

At still higher substrate concentrations the first-order reaction changes into a zero-order reaction; that is, the reaction rate is *independent* of the sucrose concentration. Figure 8–2 shows how the velocity of this reaction varies with substrate and enzyme concentration. A satisfactory theory to account for the variation in reaction rate with substrate concentration was proposed by Michaelis and Menten in 1913. They assumed that the splitting of sucrose, catalyzed by invertase, to take an example, proceeded in two steps: first, the reversible formation of an intermediate complex between the enzyme and the substrate; second, the irreversible decomposition of this *enzyme-substrate complex* into the enzyme and the reaction products. In equation form, these steps would be represented by

$$E + S \underset{k_2}{\overset{k_1}{\rightleftharpoons}} ES, \qquad ES \overset{k_0}{\rightarrow} \text{products} + E,$$

where the k's represent the specific velocity constants and E, S, and ES stand for enzyme, substrate, and enzyme-substrate complex. This scheme is a stepwise reaction, and it may be analyzed in the following way. Let C_E be the total enzyme concentration in moles/liter and let C_S and C_{ES} be the concentrations of substrate and enzyme-substrate complex. Usually C_S is much greater than C_E. Therefore the formation of the enzyme-substrate complex reduces the concentration of *free enzyme* to $C_E - C_{ES}$ but leaves the substrate concentration unchanged. After the enzymatic reaction has been going for a short time (usually $\sim$ seconds), the rate of appearance of products, $dP/dt = k_0 C_{ES}$, is constant in time. This means, in view of the stepwise nature of the reaction, that $dC_{ES}/dt = 0$. The rate of formation of the enzyme-substrate complex must equal the rate of destruction, or

$$k_1(C_E - C_{ES})C_S = (k_2 + k_0)C_{ES}. \tag{8-3}$$

It is customary to define a new constant, K_m, called the *Michaelis constant*, in terms of the reaction velocity constants as

$$K_m \equiv \frac{k_2 + k_0}{k_1}. \tag{8-4}$$

And from Eq. (8–3),

$$K_m = \frac{(C_E - C_{ES})}{C_{ES}} C_S,$$

from which we get

$$C_{ES} = \frac{C_E C_S}{K_m + C_S}. \tag{8-5}$$

The rate of production of products is thus given by

$$\frac{dP}{dt} = k_0 C_{ES} = k_0 \frac{C_E C_S}{K_m + C_S}. \tag{8-6}$$

At very high substrate concentration, $C_S \gg K_m$, all the enzyme is bound in the enzyme-substrate complex, and Eq. (8–6) becomes

$$\left(\frac{dP}{dt}\right)_{max} = k_0 C_E. \tag{8-7}$$

At very low substrate concentration, $C_S \ll K_m$,

$$\frac{dP}{dt} = \frac{k_0 C_E C_S}{K_m} = \frac{k_1 k_0 C_E C_S}{k_2 + k_0}. \tag{8-8}$$

The explanation for the relation between the reaction rate and the substrate concentration is as follows. At high substrate concentrations, the reaction rate is limited by the rate of decomposition of the enzyme-substrate complex, for at these concentrations there is no free enzyme, only enzyme-substrate complex. At low substrate concentrations, the rate is limited by the rate at which enzyme and substrate come together to form a complex. At high substrate concentration, the reaction velocity, as shown by Eq. (8–7), is independent of the substrate concentration. The reaction is zero order, and the total amount of substrate decomposed in a given time is proportional to the enzyme concentration. This fact forms the basis of most assays for enzyme activity. The reaction velocity given by Eq. (8–6) is half its maximum value when $C_S = K_m$. Therefore this measurement is an easy way to find K_m. For the urease-urea system it is 2×10^{-2} moles/liter.

Many refinements have been made to the original theory of Michaelis and Menten, such as taking into account the presence of competitive and noncompetitive inhibitors. However, the basic concepts of the theory stand.

8–4 Observation of the enzyme-substrate complex. It is a triumph for the original theory of Michaelis and Menten that the enzyme-substrate complex has been observed for one general type of enzyme, namely the catalases and peroxidases. These enzymes are combinations of proteins and heme prosthetic groups of the type shown in Fig. 7–21. They are therefore spectroscopically similar to hemoglobin and the respiratory enzymes, for which an action spectrum is given in Fig. 9–14. Catalase catalyzes the decomposition of hydrogen peroxide into water and molecular oxygen, and the reaction may be followed *spectroscopically* because the combination of enzyme and substrate has an absorption spectrum different from that of free catalase. Figure 8–3 shows some of these spectra in the visible spectral region. From these spectra it is possible not only to ascertain that an enzyme-substrate complex exists but also, by following the changes in the spectrum with time, to trace the course of the various stages of the reaction. This reaction,

$$2H_2O_2 \rightarrow 2H_2O + O_2,$$

is not, of course, as simple kinetically as the decomposition of sucrose,

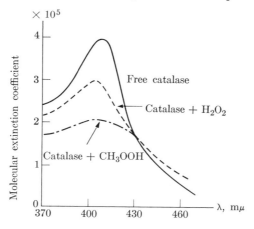

FIG. 8–3.   Absorption spectra of catalase, catalase-hydrogen-peroxide, and catalase-methyl-hydrogen-peroxide. [From B. Chance and D. Herbert, *Biochem. J.* **4,** 402 (1950).]

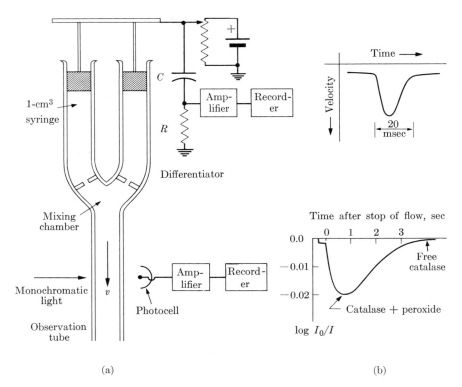

FIG. 8–4. (a) Schematic diagram of the apparatus to measure rapid reactions by spectroscopic means. (b) The recorder traces for the stopped-flow technique.

because in this case two hydrogen peroxide molecules must combine. Since the catalytic reaction is very rapid (it may be entirely over in a time of the order of minutes or less), it is necessary to adopt rather elegant and special experimental techniques to investigate the reaction rates involved.

The type of apparatus used by Chance* in following the course of these rapid reactions is shown schematically in Fig. 8–4(a). When the double syringe plunger is depressed, the reactants are rapidly mixed in the mixing chamber and travel down the observation tube with a velocity of the order of 10 meters per second. There are two ways of using a setup of this sort to observe the changes of a reaction with time. One is the *stopped-flow* method. The plungers are depressed only *momentarily* and then the changes in the reaction observed spectroscopically after the flow has stopped. In this case the device is simply one that starts the reaction at

_____

* *The Enzymes*, Vol. II, p. 428, ed. by J. B. Sumner and K. Myrbäck. Academic Press, N. Y., 1951.

a very precise time. On the other hand, if the reaction is very rapid, that is, something of the order of less than 30 milliseconds, it may be followed by depressing the plungers *continuously* and observing the light transmission at different points along the observation tube, each point corresponding to a particular time after mixing. Very small time intervals may be measured in this way, as the following simple analysis shows. The velocity of the solution in the observation tube is the ratio of the volume passing a point per second, dV/dt, to the cross sectional area, A, of the tube. The time Δt for the solution to go a distance s down the tube is

$$\Delta t = \frac{s}{v} = \frac{sA}{dV/dt}.$$

If we substitute reasonable numbers into this equation, we arrive at a minimum of 0.5×10^{-3} sec to observe the changes in the reaction with time.

It is obvious that the proper choice of wavelength or wavelengths will allow one to measure the relative concentration of catalase or of the catalase-peroxide complex. The minimum enzyme concentration is of the order of 5×10^{-7} moles of heme iron per liter. In the case of catalase, which has four heme groups per molecule, this would correspond to something of the order of 10^{-7} moles. The changes in percent transmission that take place during the reaction are relatively small. For example, see the values for the production and destruction of the catalase-methyl-hydrogen-peroxide complex in Fig. 8–4(b). Recording these small changes requires well-stabilized equipment. The velocity of flow of the reactants is easily measured by use of the differentiator circuit shown in Fig. 8–4(a). As the plunger is depressed, the potential difference across the capacitor C changes. A change in potential difference means a change in charge on the capacitor plates, and the rate of change of potential which is proportional to the plunger velocity therefore produces a current, which in turn produces a potential difference across the resistor R. This iR drop may be amplified and recorded, and then calibrated in terms of the flow *velocity*.

We cannot go into all the experimental and analytical details involved in the analysis of the data obtained in the catalase-peroxide reactions, but some general trends are easily seen and are quite fruitful in a discussion of enzyme action. The steps in the catalytic destruction of hydrogen peroxide by means of the enzyme catalase may be represented by the equations

$$E + S \underset{k_2}{\overset{k_1}{\rightleftharpoons}} ES, \qquad ES + S \overset{k_3}{\rightarrow} E + \text{products},$$

where, as before, S and E are substrate and enzyme respectively. The reaction constant k_1 for the formation of the enzyme-substrate complex

TABLE 8–2

REACTION RATE CONSTANTS FOR THE FORMATION OF
VARIOUS CATALASE–PEROXIDE COMPLEXES

Substrate	k_1, mole^{-1}/sec^{-1}
H_2O_2	5×10^6
CH_3OOH	8×10^5
CH_3CH_2OOH	2×10^4

depends on the substrate, as shown in Table 8–2. The differences between the three substrates shown are much too large to be accounted for by diffusion and must be attributed to differences in the free energy of activation for the formation of enzyme-substrate complex.

The enzyme-substrate complex can decompose spontaneously into enzyme and substrate with rate constant k_2. This reaction follows a simple exponential decay, as all first-order reactions do, and the specific rate constant for this process is 0.02 sec^{-1}. The reverse reaction is many orders of magnitude slower than the forward reaction. We may calculate the difference in free energy between the reactants and the enzyme-substrate complex by setting the equilibrium constant K equal to $e^{-\Delta F/RT}$. The equilibrium constant is the ratio of the specific velocity constants k_1/k_2 and is, for H_2O_2, $5 \times 10^6/0.02 = 2.5 \times 10^8$, from which we get $\Delta F = -11,000$ cal/mole. The fact that ΔF is such a negative number is simply another way of saying that the enzyme-substrate complex is *more stable* than the separated components. So far in our discussion of the catalase-hydrogen-peroxide system we have come only as far as the enzyme-substrate complex. For this system the enzyme-substrate complex does not dissociate and form the enzyme and reactants. Another hydrogen peroxide molecule must come up to the complex and react with it to produce water and oxygen; therefore the second step in the catalytic decomposition of hydrogen peroxide is a bimolecular reaction between hydrogen peroxide and the enzyme-hydrogen-peroxide complex. It is because of these many steps that the analysis is difficult. This reaction is clearly not the same as the classical one discussed by Michaelis and Menten. It is possible, however, to derive a value for the second step of the reaction. For H_2O_2 substrate it is $k_3 = 1.8 \times 10^7$ mole^{-1}/sec^{-1}. The reaction of a second H_2O_2 molecule with the enzyme-substrate complex is the most rapid step in the over-all reaction. This is to be expected from studies of synthetic catalytic models of catalase, which we shall discuss in Section 8–6.

Each of the rate constants may be used to compute the free energy of activation for the reaction from the expressions given in Eq. (8–2). These values, plus the free-energy difference between products and reactants, are sufficient to give the results shown in Fig. 8–5. The progressive decrease in free energy throughout the reaction is apparent. More insight into the meaning of these values could be obtained if there were data at several temperatures so that the values of the heat and entropy of the reactions could be found for the several configurations.

One other result concerning this system is important, and that is the mechanism of the second step in the reaction. Does the second hydrogen peroxide molecule react with the enzyme-substrate complex at or near the site at which the first hydrogen peroxide molecule is bound? Or does it react with one of the other three heme groups of catalase? The majority of the evidence is in favor of the former possibility. It is interesting that studies of the direct action of radiation on catalase also point to this conclusion.

A fruitful way of examining the binding of enzyme and substrate is to use an isotopically tagged substrate and measure the ratio of substrate bound to enzyme to free substrate. The ratio gives the equilibrium constant, and hence ΔF, directly. Such an experiment has been done for the enzyme chymotrypsin and the synthetic substrate acetyl 3,5-dibromo-L-tyrosine.

$$\text{H}_3\text{C}-\overset{\displaystyle \|}{\underset{\displaystyle O}{C}}-\text{N}-\overset{}{\text{CH}}-\text{CO}^{18}\text{OH}$$

This substrate is bound to the enzyme but it is not split by it. It acts as a true substrate in that studies with isotopic O^{18} in the position indicated have shown that this oxygen is exchanged with the oxygen of water. The enzyme is a catalyst for the exchange. If the bromine atoms are radioactive, i.e., Br^{82}, it is possible to determine, at different temperatures, the distribution of radioactive bromine bound to the enzyme and remaining in solution. This is feasible procedure in this case because the complex does not split up into products, but only involves a shifting of oxygen atoms. The difference in free energy between the reactants and the complex may be determined at different temperatures, and thus ΔS and ΔH may be obtained directly from $\Delta F = \Delta H - T\,\Delta S$. Values obtained in this fashion are shown in Fig. 8–6. The binding of enzyme and substrate,

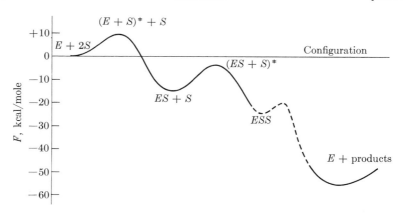

FIG. 8–5. The free energy for the system of catalase and $2H_2O_2$ for the various steps in the enzymatically catalyzed reaction. The value of F for $E + 2S$ is taken as zero. The superscript $\neq$ refers to an activated state.

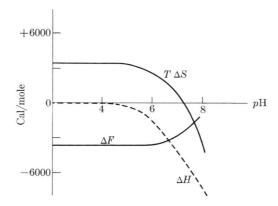

FIG. 8–6. The thermodynamic constants for the complex of chymotrypsin and acetyl 3,5-dibromo-L-tyrosine at different pH's. [From D. G. Doherty and F. Vaslow, *J. Am. Chem. Soc.* **74,** 931 (1952).]

as indicated by the small negative value of ΔF, is not strong. At low values of pH, it arises from the redistribution of energy levels associated with the *positive* value ΔS of the entropy term. The pH at which chymotrypsin is most efficient with substrates of this sort is 7.8. At this pH, ΔF is less negative, which implies weaker binding, and both ΔH and ΔS are *negative*. This entropy decrease would correspond to a decrease in the available degrees of freedom of the enzyme-substrate complex compared with the separated molecules.

8-5 Heat inactivation and the structure of enzymes. There are two general methods by which we can study the way enzymes operate. Either we can learn everything possible about the reactions of a particular enzyme and class of substrate and then generalize from this instance or we can study the features common to enzymes as a whole. At this stage of our knowledge it seems more fruitful to look at the general situation for clues to the mechanisms of enzyme action and then go on to the cases of some particular enzyme-substrate complexes. There are two things that stand out about enzymes: first, they are proteins, and second, in most cases they have a very high degree of specificity toward their substrates. Enzyme specificity will be discussed in Section 8-7.

The action of an enzyme is intimately connected with the structural integrity of a large part of the protein molecule. Studies of the action of both uncharged and charged radiation (Chapters 9 and 10) indicate that the $-S-S-$ bond of cystine is easily affected by radiation. As a result, the tertiary structure of the molecule is changed and it loses its enzymatic activity. On the other hand, there is clear experimental evidence which we shall give in Section 8-6, that only part of a molecule is necessary for its enzymatic activity.

Because enzymes act as very specific catalysts it is possible to determine accurately when a change in their physical or chemical constitution has occurred. Heating proteins in solution usually leads to a loss in solubility, called *denaturation*. Heating enzymes causes a loss in their enzymatic activity which may follow or precede the loss in solubility. It is possible to determine the specific reaction rate for the loss in enzymatic activity, and thus, as shown in Section 3-6, to determine the changes in free energy, entropy, and heat of activation for the inactivation process. As can be seen from Table 8-3, inactivation of enzymes in solution usually results in a large increase in the entropy of activation; inactivation of dry enzymes, on the other hand, results in a negligible entropy of activation. This behavior is the same as that shown for viruses in Chapter 3. It should be remembered that what is determined in experiments of this sort is the character of the *activated state*, not of the final state of the denatured protein.

Stearn* has given the following interpretation of the fact that the larger the value of $\Delta H^{\ddagger}$, the larger the value of $\Delta S^{\ddagger}$ for enzymes inactivated in solution. Assume that inactivation corresponds to the breaking of one $-S-S-$ bond and a number, n, of hydrogen bonds. This is a reasonable assumption because if a disulfide bond is broken due to thermal bombardment in solution but the hydrogen bonds are intact, there is a good chance that the disulfide bond will reform and so leave the molecule unchanged.

---

* E. A. Stearn, *Adv. Enzymol.* **9**, 25 (1949).

TABLE 8–3

THERMAL CONSTANTS FOR THE HEAT
INACTIVATION OF ENZYMES*

Enzyme	$\Delta H^{\ddagger}$, cal/mole	$\Delta S^{\ddagger}$, cal/mole°K
In H$_2$O†		
Insulin	35,600	23.8
Trypsin	40,200	44.7
Catalase	50,500	81
Pepsin	55,600	113
Invertase	110,400	263
Catalase in heavy water‡	125,000	300
Peroxidase (milk)	185,300	466
In dry state¶		
Urease	20,800	−22
Catalase	21,500	−16
Trypsin	21,600	−24
Invertase	30,000	0
Chymotrypsin	30,000	0

* E. A. Stearn, *Adv. Enzymol.*, **9**, 25 (1949).
† Values are *p*H and ionic-strength dependent.
‡ W. R. Guild and R. P. van Tubergen, *Science*, **125**, 939 (1957).
¶ E. Pollard, *Am. Scientist*, **39**, 99 (1951).

If a number of bonds break at about the same time, the chance that the tertiary structure will remain intact is negligible. If the breaking of one —S—S— bond corresponds to activated state parameters of $\Delta H^{\ddagger}_{-S-S-} = 20,000$ cal/mole and $\Delta S^{\ddagger}_{-S-S-} = 0$, and if the breakage of one hydrogen bond is associated with $\Delta H^{\ddagger}_{H} = 4000$ cal/mole and $\Delta S^{\ddagger}_{H} = 12$ cal/mole°K, the number of broken hydrogen bonds is given by

$$n = \frac{\Delta H^{\ddagger} - 20,000}{4000},$$

and the entropy of activation is then

$$\Delta S^{\ddagger} = 12n = 12\frac{\Delta H^{\ddagger} - 20,000}{4000}.$$

This expression fits the data of Table 8–3 well. Note that it implies that no hydrogen bonds must reach the activated state for dry inactivation, and that the number of bonds broken in the inactivation of catalase in D$_2$O is different from the number broken in H$_2$O. While this analysis may be correct, it should be noted that the range of observable values of $\Delta F^{\ddagger}$ is

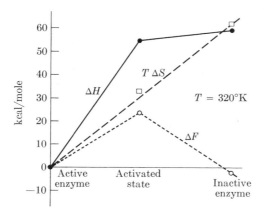

Fɪɢ. 8–7. Values of ΔH and $T\,\Delta S$ for the heat inactivation of soybean tryp-sin-inhibitor for the activated and final states. [From M. Kunitz, *J. Gen. Physiol.* **32**, 241 (1948).]

limited. If $\Delta F^{\ddagger}$ is below 20,000 cal/mole, the reaction will occur with such speed that the compound will have no stability at all. If $\Delta F^{\ddagger}$ is much above 30,000, the compound will be remarkably stable. Proteins are neither perfectly stable nor perfectly unstable at ordinary temperatures. Therefore the value of $\Delta F^{\ddagger}$ for inactivation must lie within a rather narrow range. Since $\Delta F^{\ddagger}$ is fixed, and $\Delta F^{\ddagger} = \Delta H^{\ddagger} - T\,\Delta S^{\ddagger}$, obviously there exists a relation between $\Delta H^{\ddagger}$ and $\Delta S^{\ddagger}$. This relation may have the physical significance outlined above, or it may be a purely numerological peculiarity.

There is a type of inactivation for which we have information on the final as well as on the activated state. Soybean trypsin-inhibitor, for example, under mild denaturing conditions, can exist in an inactive form. At low temperatures it is possible for this inactive form to revert to the normal active protein. In this case, then, we can measure not only the reaction rate in one direction, but also the equilibrium between the two forms, and thus obtain information about the thermodynamic constants for the steps in this reaction. These constants are shown schematically in Fig. 8–7, where it can be seen that there is a progressive increase in entropy as the enzyme goes from active form to the inactive one. It is reasonable to interpret this increase as a progressive unfolding of the molecule.

8–6 The relation between enzyme structure and function. The function of an enzyme is associated with a large number of linked amino acids but not necessarily with the entire molecule. In many cases some parts of proteins are useless appendages, in other cases they are necessary, and in

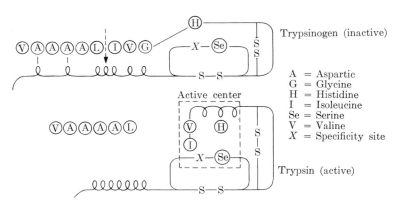

FIG. 8–8. Schematic diagram representing the conversion of trypsinogen to trypsin by trypsin. [From H. Neurath and G. H. Dixon, *Fed. Proc.* **16,** 791 (1957).]

still others inhibitory. For example, the enzymes trypsin and chymotrypsin are derived from the enzymatically inactive precursors trypsinogen and chymotrypsinogen. When the inactive precursors are treated with the proper proteolytic enzyme, such as trypsin, they are converted to the active form. In this conversion a polypeptide is split off from the precursor protein. Figure 8–8 is a schematic representation of the structural changes that take place in the conversion of trypsinogen to trypsin under the action of trypsin itself. If the enzyme action is associated with the proper and close positioning of the serine and histidine residues, the scheme of Fig. 8–8 indicates that in trypsinogen this positioning is not possible because the electrostatic interactions between the aspartic acid residues and the rest of the molecule are big enough to pull the histine away. When the hexapeptide is split off, the previously stretched section can revert to the helical configuration, now the one of lowest energy, and the molecule is enzymatically active. The *active center* represents the region of the protein to which the substrate binds. The enzymatic activity is associated with, as we have emphasized, the three-dimensional configuration of the active center. The preservation of the local three-dimensional configuration, however, may depend on other parts of the molecule. If, for example, one of the —S—S— bonds in Fig. 8–8 is broken by ultraviolet light, the configuration of the active center will change and the molecule will lose its catalytic activity even though no energy was absorbed in the active center itself.

Another good example of the relations between molecular structure and function is ribonuclease (RN-ase). The amino acid order is reasonably well known, and the enzymatic activity can be determined after various amino acids have been split off the molecule and the molecule has been

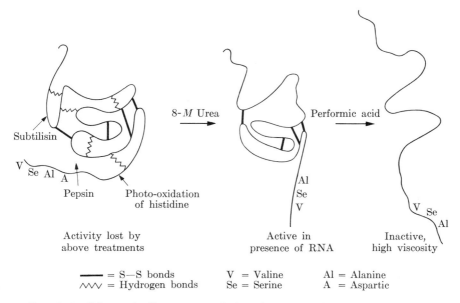

FIG. 8–9. Schematic diagram correlating changes in the structure of RN-ase with changes in its enzymatic activity. [From C. B. Anfinsen and R. R. Redfield, *Adv. Protein Chem.* **11,** 1 (1956).]

subjected to other environments, such as 8-*M* urea. Figure 8–9 schematically shows some of these changes in structure and in enzymatic activity. When valine, serine, and alanine are split off the C-terminal end by carboxypeptidase, no activity is lost; but when the next residue, aspartic acid, is split from the molecule, the activity disappears. The photo-oxidation of histidine causes activity loss, as does splitting the chain with subtilisin at the 20th residue from the N-terminal end. Richards* has found that the enzymatic activity is *regained* if the N-terminal peptide and the remaining protein are recombined without the reformation of the broken peptide bond. The catalytic activity is clearly associated with a large part of the molecule. Treatment of the enzyme with 8-*M* urea breaks hydrogen bonds but leaves the disulfide linkages intact. The increase in viscosity shows that the molecule is somewhat unfolded, as indicated in Fig. 8–9, but it still has enzymatic activity when in 8-*M* urea. The explanation is probably *not* that the molecule is active in the partially unfolded configuration but that the presence of the substrate, RNA, causes it to refold.† If more drastic treatment, such as splitting the

---

* F. M. Richards, *PNAS* **44,** 162 (1958).
† C. B. Anfinsen, Jr., *Fed. Proc.* **16,** 783 (1957).

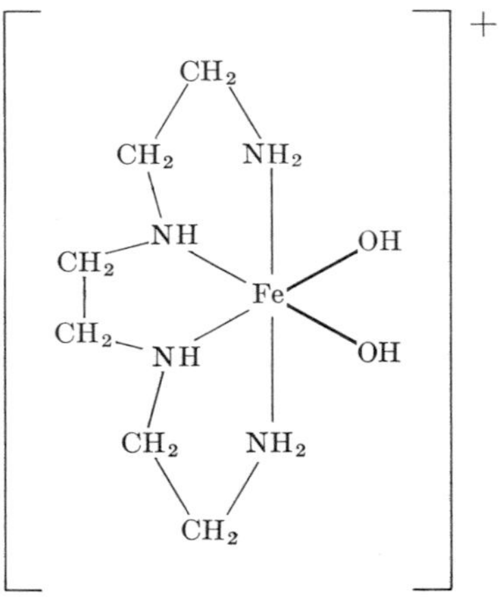

FIG. 8–10. The structure of triethylenetetramine-Fe (III) chelate, which acts as a synthetic catalase. The two bonds indicated by the darker lines can react with H_2O_2.

$-S-S-$ bonds with performic acid, is used, the molecule is further unfolded and has no enzymatic activity.

The best evidence that only part of a molecule may be necessary for enzymatic activity is supplied by the proteolytic enzyme papain. When papain is treated with another enzyme which removes amino acids from the N-terminal end, it is found that two-thirds of the 180 amino acid residues may be removed and papain still has its enzymatic activity.[*]

Still another approach to the structure-function relation is by the synthesis of nonprotein catalytic units that have properties similar to those of enzymes. Wang[†] has synthesized catalysts which are only 10^3 less efficient than catalase (they are 10^3 *more* efficient than hemoglobin). These catalysts are *not* heme-type groups, which are very inefficient, but are polyamineferric chelates. The structure of the most efficient of these, triethylenetetramine-Fe (III) chelate, is shown in Fig. 8–10. In alkaline solution the catalytic scheme is as shown in Fig. 8–11. (Of the six ferric iron bonds, only the two that react appear in the figure.) The enzyme substrate complex is

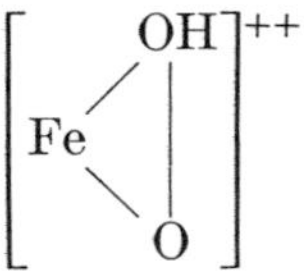

---

[*] R. L. Hill and E. M. Smith, *Biochim. et Biophys. Acta* **19,** 376 (1956).

[†] J. H. Wang, *J. Am. Chem. Soc.* **77,** 4715 (1955).

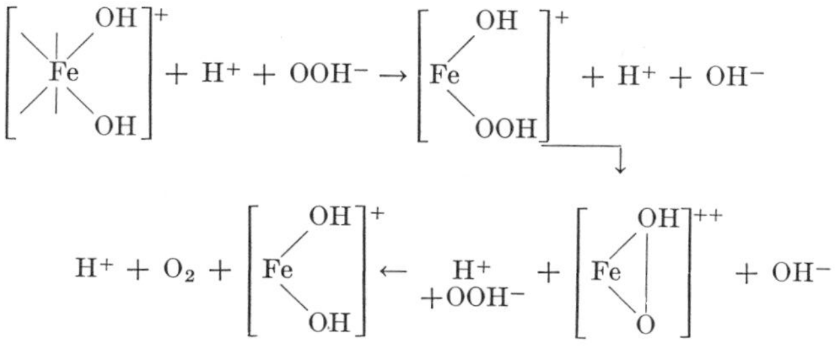

$$\left[\begin{array}{c} OH \\ \backslash | \diagup \\ Fe \\ \diagup | \backslash \\ OH \end{array}\right]^{+} + H^{+} + OOH^{-} \rightarrow \left[\begin{array}{c} OH \\ \diagup \\ Fe \\ \backslash \\ OOH \end{array}\right]^{+} + H^{+} + OH^{-}$$

$$H^{+} + O_2 + \left[\begin{array}{c} OH \\ \diagup \\ Fe \\ \backslash \\ OH \end{array}\right]^{+} \leftarrow \begin{array}{c} H^{+} \\ +OOH^{-} \end{array} + \left[\begin{array}{c} OH \\ \diagup \\ Fe \\ \backslash | \\ O \end{array}\right]^{++} + OH^{-}$$

or

$$2H_2O_2 \rightarrow 2H_2O + O_2$$

FIG. 8–11. The reaction scheme for the catalytic decomposition of H_2O_2 by a synthetic catalyst. [From R. C. Jarnagin and J. H. Wang, *J. Am. Chem. Soc.* **80**, 786 (1958).]

The $-O-O-$ bond is in a strained state, as indicated by the fact that its internuclear separation is about 1.3 A, whereas the value of 1.5 A is found in H_2O_2. When a second $[OOH]^-$ approaches the *ES* complex, the H atom quickly reacts with it, leaving O_2 behind. If these results are extrapolated to catalase, we conclude that the two peroxide molecules react at one heme group and that the liberated O_2 comes from a single H_2O_2.

8–7 Enzyme specificity.　There are untold examples of enzyme specificity. We shall cite just a few. Urease acts on urea but not on thiourea or on methylurea. The heme enzymes have specificities of their own which seem to depend more on an intimate chemical binding than on anything else. Trypsin catalyzes the splitting of peptide bonds *only* of the arginyl- and lysyl-type; this information is not only of value in determining how trypsin acts, but it also means that trypsin may be used as a *reagent* to break peptide chains at known places and so simplify determinations of amino acid sequence.

Chymotrypsin will attack a peptide or similar bonds only if the substituents on the peptide chain are in their proper places. It will catalyze the breaking of the indicated bond in compounds of the form

$$RCO-NH-CH(R')CO\diagup\!\!\!\!\diagdown R'',$$

where the most important side groups are, among others,

$$RCO = \text{benzoyl, glycol, acetyl, alanine;}$$
$$R' = \text{tryosine, phenyl, tryptophane;}$$
$$R'' = \text{amide or ethyl ester.}$$

While the hydrolyzed bond can be either an amide or an ester group, the surrounding substances determine whether the reaction will occur. This sort of specificity, which requires the existence of three particular groups or types of groups on the substrate, can be accounted for by assuming that the substrate comes toward the enzyme and, in forming the complex, makes a three-point landing on the enzyme surface. This three-point contact is a very specific one. All the interacting groups must be in their proper places. The *three-point landing* idea is a graphic way of saying that the specificity resides in the *three-dimensional* structure.

In many systems it may well be that three points are not necessary. Two may be enough, or even one. However, the idea of the three-point contact seems attractive, and while we shall not be dogmatic about it, the analysis that follows will assume that this is indeed the case.

The interaction between the enzyme acetylcholinesterase, which plays a key role in nerve action, and the substrate acetylcholine

$$(CH_3)_3N^+C_2H_4OCOCH_3$$

is best described by the diagram of Fig. 8–12. The information in the figure was derived from studies (similar to the hapten studies discussed in Chapter 6) on the inhibition of the enzymatic action by inhibitors of known structural configurations. The three-dimensional aspect of the binding, which is not illustrated in Fig. 8–12, is a result of the fact that the methyl groups attached to the nitrogen atom also contribute to the interaction. This interaction, the electrostatic one at the anionic site, and the covalent bond at the esteratic site are the three points of contact. A proposed detailed mechanism to describe the enzymatic process is indicated below.

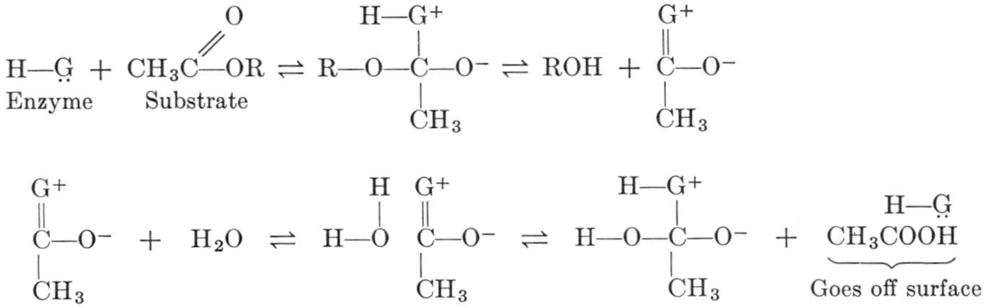

$$CH_3COOR + H_2O \rightarrow CH_3COOH + ROH$$

where $R = (CH_3)_3N^+CH_2CH_2-$

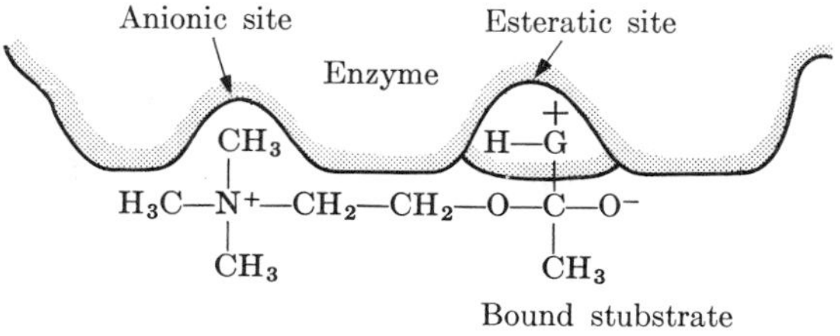

Anionic site   Esteratic site

Enzyme

$$H_3C-N^+-CH_2-CH_2-O-\overset{\underset{|}{CH_3}}{\underset{|}{C}}-O^-$$

Bound stubstrate

Fig. 8-12. A hypothetical diagram showing the interaction between acetyl-cholinesterase and the substrate acetylcholine. The interaction at the anionic enzyme site is primarily electrostatic, and at the esteratic site a covalent bond is formed. [From I. B. Wilson in *A Symposium on the Mechanism of Enzyme Action*, ed. by W. D. McElroy and B. Glass. Johns Hopkins Press, 1954.]

The mechanism is a three-step one in which the steps are acylation of the enzyme, the elimination of a part of the molecule, and then the deacylation of the enzyme.

The three-point concept is substantiated by work done on the pathway of the synthesis of citric acid from CO_2 by liver homogenates. Citric acid

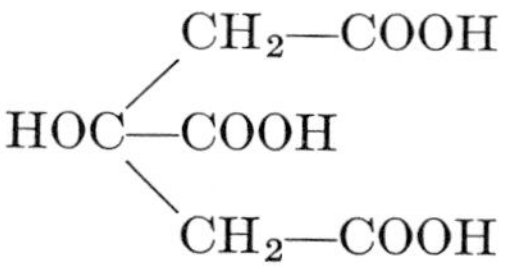

$$\begin{array}{l} CH_2-COOH \\ HOC-COOH \\ CH_2-COOH \end{array}$$

seems to be a symmetrical molecule, but if the citric acid made by the liver homogenate is degraded by enzymes present in liver to α-ketoglutaric acid, it is found that the degradation of citric acid is *not* symmetrical.* The reactions are followed by tracing the radioactive carbon, C^{14}, introduced as $C^{14}O_2$ in the following scheme.

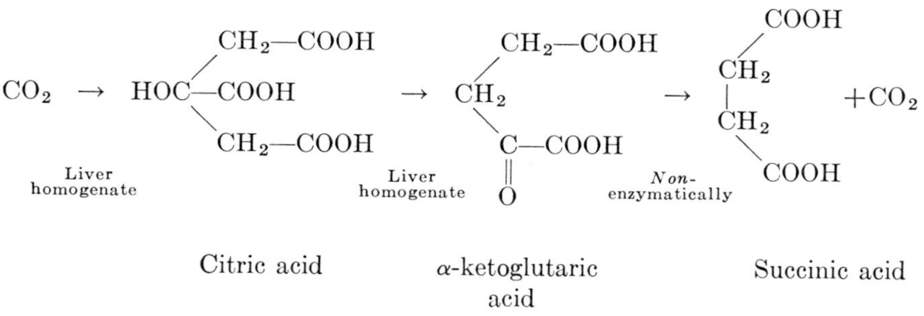

$CO_2 \rightarrow$ HOC—COOH $\rightarrow$ CH₂ $\rightarrow$ +CO_2

Liver homogenate   Liver homogenate   Non-enzymatically

Citric acid α-ketoglutaric acid   Succinic acid

* V. R. Potter and C. Heidelberger, *Nature* **164**, 180 (1949).

It is found that the last step in the reaction is (if we designate C^{14} by C^*)

$$\begin{array}{c} CH_2-COOH \\ \diagup \\ CH_2 \\ \diagdown \\ C-C^*OOH \\ \diagdown\!\!\diagdown \\ O \end{array} \quad \rightarrow \quad \begin{array}{c} CH_2-COOH \\ | \\ CH_2-COOH \end{array} \quad + \quad C^*O_2$$

That is, all the radioactivity appears in CO_2, which means it *all* came from the *last* carbon atom in α-ketoglutaric acid. This is understandable because α-ketoglutaric acid is unsymmetrical. However, it is derived from citric acid, which is *symmetrical*, and we would expect offhand that even if citric acid were labeled in only one carbon atom it would not yield asymmetrically labeled α-ketoglutaric acid. The reaction scheme seems to be

$$C^*O_2 \xrightarrow[\text{Enzymes}]{} \begin{array}{c} CH_2-COOH \\ | \\ HOCOOH \\ | \\ C^*H_2-COOH \end{array} \xrightarrow[\text{Enzymes}]{} \begin{array}{c} CH_2-COOH \\ | \\ CH_2 \\ \diagdown \\ C-C^*OOH \\ \diagdown\!\!\diagdown \\ O \end{array} \rightarrow \begin{array}{c} CH_2-COOH \\ | \\ CH_2-COOH \end{array} + C^*O_2$$

Either this series of degradation reactions of citric acid involves black magic or citric acid was labeled asymmetrically to begin with. It is hard to see how a symmetrical molecule such as citric acid can be labeled asymmetrically. The explanation is straightforward if we adopt the three-point idea. Suppose that the first step in degrading citric acid is its com-

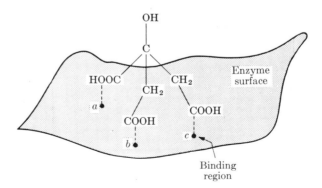

Fig. 8–13. The hypothetical binding of citric acid to an enzyme surface. If points b and c are *not* equivalent, the enzyme-substrate complex is asymmetrical. [After A. G. Ogston, *Nature* **162**, 963 (1948).]

bination with an enzyme surface at three points, as shown in Fig. 8–13. Since citric acid does not have three-fold symmetry, and since all binding points on the enzyme surface are certainly not the same, it is obvious that the reaction rate in the neighborhood of one of the COOH groups may be much larger than for the other. Thus we see that three points of binding are sufficient to explain the production of all radioactive CO_2 from what seems to be a symmetrical molecule but is in reality an asymmetrical enzyme-substrate complex. The explanation for the asymmetry in the complete cycle is now clear. Obviously if the degradation of citric acid is asymmetrical, the enzymatic manufacture of citric acid can also be asymmetrical. From the point of view of an enzyme surface, the CO_2 put into citric acid goes in only one of the two dissimilar groups. The groups only appear to be similar when the molecule is in solution.

The reason for all the emphasis on three-point binding is that three points determine a plane, and two or one do not. A molecule firmly bound at three points is much easier to warp than if bound at two. Let us keep this notion in mind for a moment while we delve a little more into the mysteries of specificity.

Do we need specific forces to bind substrate to enzyme? What is the range of the forces and what is the magnitude of the binding energy? The answer to the first question is that we know of no very specific forces other than covalent bonds. The answer to the second is that all the forces are short range. As we indicated in Chapter 6, they go as a high inverse power of the distance between the attracting groups. The interaction energy is proportional to $1/r^6$.

It is obvious that the attractive force, or the interaction energy, between enzyme and substrate must be within rather narrow limits. If it is too low, an enzyme-substrate complex will never be formed. If it is too high, there is the danger that the reaction products will stick to the enzyme and inhibit further enzymatic reactions. Since the charge distribution on a protein molecule depends on the pH of the solution, enzyme activity is very dependent on the pH.

The specification that substrate and protein bind at three points helps in two ways. First, there is a better chance of twisting the substrate out of shape; second, the substrate can be bound firmly before reacting and weakly afterward. Thus if, for example, the binding per contact corresponds to a weak hydrogen bond, which has an interaction free energy of 2000 cal/mole, the chance of finding (at room temperature) a *single* contact point or region *not* bound is $e^{-2000/600} = e^{-3.3} = 3.6 \times 10^{-2}$. But with three bonds cooperating in forming an enzyme-substrate complex, the chance of finding *all three* unbound is $e^{-6000/600} = e^{-10} = 4.6 \times 10^{-5}$. The three contact points mean that enzyme and substrate are close together most of the time. The chance of finding one bound group is 0.96, and the chance of all three groups being bound is $(0.96)^3 =$ 0.89. Because all these forces are *short-range* forces, they have high specificity, as in the case of the antigen-antibody reactions taken up in Chapter 6. Only specific enzyme and substrate combinations will represent maximum values of $1/r^6$ for the three contact points or for the entire *three-dimensional* interaction region. So much for enzyme specificity. There does not seem to be anything magical about it, and as pointed out in Chapter 3, it really does not require much information content. The close relation between structure and physical properties is shown by the comparison of normal adult hemoglobin with sickel-cell hemoglobin. The difference between the two types is only that a glutamic acid residue in each half of a normal molecule is replaced by a valine in the mutant type. This small alteration changes the charges on the molecules, and when they lose oxygen they aggregate so that the red cells take on a characteristic sickel shape.

8–8 Speculations about the mechanism of enzyme action. We are in a position to construct a semispeculative picture of how enzymes act. An enzyme must reduce the free-energy barrier over which the substrate must pass to yield the end products. It does so either by reducing the energy of activation as illustrated for catalaselike catalysts in Fig. 8–11, or alternatively by supplying what we might call configurational energy in the form of entropy. Either of these possibilities will reduce the free energy of activation $\Delta F^{\ddagger}$. It is not possible at present to decide which of these ways is more important, nor is there any reason to suppose that all enzymes are the same in this respect. In any event, both ways lead to the same sort of requirements for enzyme structure. Suppose for the moment we think only of reducing the energy of activation, that is, the energy required to disrupt a particular bond in the substrate, and assume, for simplicity of diagramming the process, that the entropy term is zero. For definiteness let us take the urease-urea system and suppose that urea makes a three-point landing on the enzyme surface as shown in Fig. 8–14(a). Before the enzyme and substrate interact, urea is a planar structure; after the interaction, it is *not* planar.

As the substrate approaches the enzyme it is attracted to it and the potential energy of the system decreases, as shown by the solid curve of Fig. 8–14(b). If the substrate had not changed its form, the loss in energy of the complex would have been greater, as shown by the dashed potential-energy curve in the figure. The reason for the difference is that some of the energy decrease is taken up by the substrate in the form of increased potential energy of its own bonds, as shown in Fig. 8–14(c). The energy increase of the substrate, $\Delta E'$, must be less than the difference in energy, ΔE, between the enzyme planar-substrate complex and the enzyme non-planar-substrate complex because some of the energy change will go into

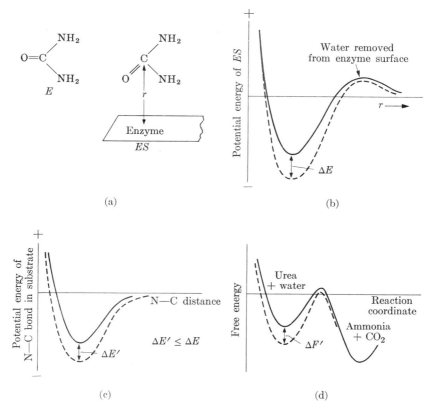

Fɪɢ. 8–14. A schematic urease-urea reaction. (a) The configuration of urea before and after it has interacted with the enzyme surface to form the enzyme-substrate complex. (b) Potential-energy curves for the enzyme-substrate interaction for the substrate becoming nonplanar (solid curve) and remaining planar (dashed curve). (c) Potential-energy curve for the N—C bond in urea for the substrate becoming nonplanar (solid curve) and remaining planar (dashed curve). (d) Free-energy diagram for the reaction of urea and water for urea in the nonplanar (solid curve) and planar (dashed curve) form.

potential energy of the enzyme and into heat. As indicated in Fig. 8–14(d), the free energy of activation for the reaction of water with the substrate is decreased by the warping of the substrate. Since reaction rates depend exponentially on the height of the free-energy barrier, even small changes in $\Delta F^{\neq}$ are important. Once the substrate has been split, the individual components of the substrate are held to the molecule by the forces that existed before; but now the interaction between the substrate and the protein has decreased because we no longer have three groups acting in *concert*, but three groups acting *individually*, and again under random thermal bombardments the products can dissociate themselves from the enzyme surface. If the attractive forces are too large, the products will not be freed from the enzyme surface and the enzyme will be poisoned or inhibited. As a matter of fact, the products of enzymatic catalysis quite often do act as inhibitors.

8–9 Speculations about the minimum size of an enzyme. The description in Section 8–8, in which the substrate is strained, places a very strict requirement on the structure of the enzyme because it implies that as a result of the interaction of substrate and enzyme, the substrate becomes warped and the enzyme remains fixed. Protein molecules must therefore represent very well-knit frameworks. If they are to last, they must be held in rather rigid patterns. On this basis we can immediately set simple limits to the minimum size of an enzyme. If we take as our model of a protein the Pauling picture of an alpha-helix, with 3.7 residues per turn, and take 120 as the average molecular weight of a residue, we have for one turn a molecular weight of around 500. One could guess, without any difficulty, that for a given helical chain to be stable against excessive local deformation by the substrate, it would have to have something of the order of five turns. The top and bottom turns of this chain would represent the stabilizing zones of the chain which would hold it in place while the substrate could be attached elsewhere near the center of the chain. Obviously an enzyme whose active site or substrate binding region was near the ends of the turns would be very vulnerable to thermal destruction while combined with the substrate. It would also seem reasonable to suppose that we would need more than one chain in an enzyme, because three points of attachment to one chain would again imply rather rapid destruction for this chain. Certainly a much more stable structure would result if we had three chains held in place by hydrogen bonds and sulfur bridges. These three helices would then have a total of about 15 turns. At a molecular weight of 500 per turn, this would give a total molecular weight of around 7000. This number represents purely an order-of-magnitude calculation, and indicates the general minimum size of an enzyme which is to function as a catalyst for the degradation of an ordinarily stable substrate. The stability of helical chains of this type is indicated by the fact that denatured proteins are more easily digested than globular forms. Pepsin will digest denatured pepsin, for example.

If we adopt the alternative view that the decrease in the free-energy barrier is due not to a decrease in the energy term but to an increase in the entropy of the system because of an opening up of some of the enzyme bonds, we are again led to the same general conclusion concerning the nature of the protein. If it is too small, then the opening of a few bonds will start a zipper action and the whole molecule will unfold. Again, a molecular weight of around 7000 is necessary for a stable enzyme. It is pertinent to remark that if this picture has any semblance of truth it could be possible to observe the interaction of enzyme and substrate in the infrared part of the spectrum. If the substrate is bound strongly, its infrared spectrum should change. If it is the protein which gives, then one might be able to find the changes in the hydrogen bonds in the protein. The latter would be more difficult to observe. There is perhaps one other reason why a large molecule is a better catalyst than a small. A large molecule with its many bonds is much more likely to have a part of it at an energy quite a bit above the average, and moreover, a water molecule with extra energy would have a better chance of transferring this energy to a large molecule than to a small one. Since a protein is a very well-knit and organized structure, it may be very easy for this extra bit of thermal energy to transfer to the substrate, where it can go into dissociation.

PROBLEMS

1. Calculate the ratio of products to reactants at 27°C if $\Delta F = 600$ cal/mole, 3000 cal/mole, and 15,000 cal/mole.

2. Verify from the known velocity constants the values shown in Fig. 8–5.

3. Calculate the Michaelis constant for invertase from the data in Fig. 8–2.

4. Assume that there is one invertase molecule per yeast cell and that the sucrose concentration is 0.5 M. What is the rate of splitting of sucrose in molecules per second? Use the data of Fig. 8–2, take the cell as a sphere of 3μ diameter, and use 120,000 as the molecular weight of invertase.

5. Calculate the equilibrium distribution at pH 5 and pH 7.5 of acetyl 3,5-dibromo-L-tyrosine and chymotrypsin between bound and unbound forms from the data of Fig. 8–6.

6. Assume that there is three-point binding between enzyme and substrate, with each point having a $\Delta F = -1200$ cal/mole. If all the binding energy goes into lowering $\Delta F^{\ddagger}$ (for the decomposition $ES \rightarrow$ products), what is the ratio of the reaction rate in the presence of the enzyme to that in the absence if the latter has $\Delta F^{\ddagger} = 25,000$ cal/mole?

7. Show that in the neighborhood of room temperature $Q_{10} \approx e^{+\Delta H^{\ddagger}/18,600}$.

REFERENCES

1. J. H. NORTHROP, M. KUNITZ, and R. M. HERRIOTT, *Crystalline Enzymes*, 2nd ed. Columbia University Press, N. Y., 1948.

2. J. B. SUMNER and G. F. SOMERS, *Chemistry and Methods of Enzymes*. Academic Press, N. Y., 1947.

3. J. B. SUMNER and K. MYRBÄCK, Eds., *The Enzymes.* Academic Press, N. Y., 1951.

4. E. BALDWIN, *Dynamic Aspects of Biochemistry.* Cambridge University Press, 1952.

5. W. D. McELROY and B. GLASS, Eds., *The Mechanism of Enzyme Action.* Johns Hopkins University Press, Baltimore, Md., 1954.

6. S. P. COLOWICK and N. O. KAPLAN, *Methods in Enzymology.* Academic Press, N. Y., 1955.

7. M. JOLY, "Recent Studies on the Reversible Denaturation of Proteins," *Prog. Biophys.* **5,** 168 (1955).

8. E. RACKER, "Enzymes as Reagents," in *Currents in Biochemical Research,* ed. by D. Green. Interscience Publishers, N. Y., 1956.

9. R. A. ALBERTY, "Enzyme Kinetics," in *Currents in Biochemical Research,* ed. by D. Green. Interscience Publishers, N. Y., 1956.

10. C. B. ANFINSEN and R. R. REDFIELD, "Protein Structure in Relation to Function and Biosynthesis, *Adv. Protein Chem.* **11,** 1 (1956).

11. O. H. GAEBLER, Ed., *Enzymes: Units of Biological Structure and Function.* Henry Ford Hospital Symposium #4, Academic Press, N. Y., 1956.

CHAPTER 9

ACTION SPECTRA AND QUANTUM YIELDS

9–1 Introduction. The interaction of light and molecular systems may be studied by investigation of (1) the effect on the light, and (2) the effect on the molecules. Studies of absorption spectra, i.e., the effect of molecules on incident quanta, can lead to a knowledge of molecular energy levels and of molecular composition and structure. Investigation of the effects of light on molecules will ultimately yield knowledge about the mechanism of energy transfer in large molecules, the atomic rearrangements within large molecules which take place after energy absorption, and the role such molecules and their parts play in the process of metabolism. In this chapter we will be concerned with the effects of light on molecules, viruses, and cells.

If a molecular system is to be affected by light, the light quanta must not only be absorbed, but must have enough energy to bring about a molecular rearrangement. Typical dissociation energies are 2–5 ev (Table 6–2), while ionization potentials are of the order of 10 ev (Table 7–1). The energy of light is quantized in packets of magnitude $h\nu$, where h is Planck's constant (6.63×10^{-34} joule·sec) and ν is the frequency of the light. The energies $h\nu$ associated with quanta of different wavelengths are given in Table 9–1. It is clear that infrared light, even though absorbed, will change only weak molecular configurations. Most of the work on the effects of light on living things and their components has been limited to wavelengths above 2000 A. Therefore the effects we shall describe are the results of dissociations and rearrangements of molecular groupings.

TABLE 9–1

ENERGIES OF QUANTA OF
DIFFERENT WAVELENGTHS

Wavelength, A	Energy, ev
10,000 (infrared)	1.24
7000 (visible)	1.77
4000 (visible)	3.1
2000 (ultraviolet)	6.2
1000	12.4

Light is a useful tool to use in molecular biophysics because (1) the energy released in a molecule when a photon is absorbed is known, and (2) the probability that a photon will be absorbed is a known function of the wavelength. The latter is, as a matter of fact, the absorption spectrum. For example, 2800 A photons will lose their energy mostly in the aromatic amino acids, and the observed effects may be different from those obtained with 4000 A radiation, which liberates energy in the heme groups. Obviously the correlation between the effects of light and known absorption spectra permits the identification of the compounds associated with the observed effects.

Even though an absorbed photon has enough energy to dissociate a group, dissociation need not occur, because the absorbed energy may be dissipated in other ways such as by fluorescence and vibration. The fact that some molecules return to their original configurations after the event of light absorption whereas others are changed in ways too subtle to be observed by our crude techniques shows that we actually know very little about the details of the processes by which light produces its effects.

The earliest appreciation of the effects of light on living things was shown in 1779 by Ingen-Housz, who correlated the oxygen evolution in photosynthesis with light incident on the green parts of plants. Experimental work on the inhibition of bacterial growth by light started in Pasteur's time. While the early work was mostly qualitative, it established the fact that light of wavelength 3000 A could kill bacteria and that light of shorter wavelength could do the same thing more effectively. Since the original work, a wealth of material has appeared on the irradiation of small molecules, proteins, viruses, and microorganisms. Some of the properties that have been investigated include: photosynthesis, death, mutation, division delay, growth rate, serological activity, enzymatic inactivation, solubility, viscosity, absorption spectrum, and odor.

Fruitful work on the effects of light on molecular systems requires, in addition to observing the irradiated material, controlling four variables associated with the irradiation procedure: (1) the wavelength of the light, (2) the average incident intensity, (3) the time of irradiation, and (4) the environmental conditions. The environmental conditions include temperature, pH, and the treatment of the irradiated systems before and after irradiation. For example, bacteria which will not form colonies after ultraviolet irradiation will do so if they are exposed to strong visible light or to higher than normal temperatures.

The energy carried by photons in the wavelength range of interest is much greater than the average thermal energy of vibration, 1/40 ev. This means that in most irradiated systems a change in temperature is a negligible perturbation on the processes initiated by the absorption of a quantum. The Q_{10} for most photochemical processes is 1.0. As with most generalizations, the exceptions are of great interest. The temperature during irradiation is important in three general cases. The first is one in which an incident photon may not have enough energy to initiate a process. A slight increase in temperature may add sufficient vibrational energy to the system so the reaction is energetically more probable. Such was the heroic experiment performed by de Vries* in which he increased his sensitivity to red light by raising his temperature, with a hot bath, to 102°F. The second case is when there is a possibility that a temperature change will alter the pathways by which the absorbed energy is degraded and so change the probability that dissociation occurs. Proteins irradiated at liquid air temperature, 90°K, are much less sensitive to ultraviolet light because a lot of the energy is trapped in relatively stable states which decay, not by dissociation, but by phosphorescence. The third case in which temperature control is important is where the absorption of light is followed by dark reactions, as in photosynthesis. If the dark reactions represent the rate-limiting step, a small temperature change may produce a large change in the light effect by its indirect action on the dark reaction. These remarks about temperature are not restricted to this specific environmental variable.   Experiments involving light must be carefully controlled, as must all experiments.

Since studies on the interaction of light and the constituents of living systems may be very informative, it is worth while to take care in the physical part of this type of experiment. Thus, it is just as important to use monochromatic light for irradiation studies as to use monochromatic light to determine absorption spectra. The physical apparatus necessary for irradiation work consists of three parts: a light source (Section 9–2), a means of isolating narrow spectral regions from this source (Section 9–3), and an intensity measuring device (Section 9–4).

9–2 Light sources and materials. For the visible region of the spectrum there are many available light sources, both continuous ones, such as incandescent filaments or the craters of carbon arcs, and discontinuous sources, such as mercury and sodium arcs. In the ultraviolet region, sources are limited by the fact that ordinary glass is not transparent below about 3000 A. Quartz may be used down to 1850 A. Irradiation may be performed at lower wavelengths by the use of lithium fluoride or calcite as windows for the apparatus. It must be remembered, however, that the oxygen in the air starts absorbing strongly below 2000 A, and water also becomes relatively opaque at these wavelengths. Figure 9–1 shows the absorption spectra of several substances over a range of wavelengths. Light sources, then, for the ultraviolet region, must be enclosed in quartz jackets

---

* Hl. de Vries, *Experentia* **4,** 357 (1948).

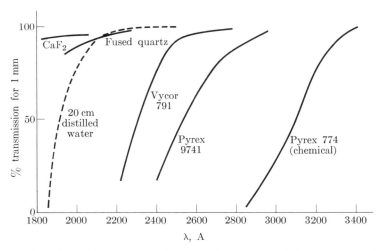

FIG. 9–1. Absorption spectra of some substances used in the irradiation of biological systems. (After Ref. 10.)

or in no jacket at all. Continuous sources in the ultraviolet consist of gas discharges, such as hydrogen, xenon, or high-pressure mercury arcs. A low-pressure mercury arc is a discrete wavelength source.

The germicidal lamp consists of a discharge through mercury vapor at a pressure of 6×10^{-3} mm of Hg, at which pressure the overwhelming majority of the emitted light comes from one particular energy transition.

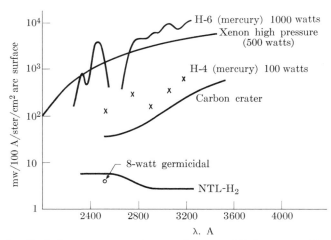

FIG. 9–2. Emission spectrum of several types of light sources in the ultraviolet region of the spectrum. The NTL—H_2 lamp is the type used in a Beckman spectrophotometer. The total energy output depends on the total arc area.

This transition gives rise to the so-called resonance radiation of mercury, the 2537 A line. Arcs of this type may emit as much as 90% of their total radiation and 20% of the input power at this one wavelength. The remainder of the energy appears primarily in the visible region of the spectrum. These arcs are similar to fluorescent lamps without the phosphor and with envelopes which will transmit the 2537 line, but nothing much shorter than that. Such a light source is essentially a monochromatic source as far as ultraviolet studies are concerned, and hence a very large amount of quantitative work has been done with this one wavelength. The low-pressure mercury arcs deliver more useful radiation than the data shown in Fig. 9–2 might imply because the area of these lamps is large. Roughly speaking, the energy output per unit area of arc surface is a constant for this type of lamp. High-power lamps are simply larger than low-power ones.

9–3 Monochromators. It is not possible to obtain monochromatic sources such as sodium and low-pressure mercury arcs for all parts of the spectrum. We must use sources that emit many wavelengths and, by one means or another, eliminate the unwanted ones. Glass absorption filters can be used to isolate the bright lines of the mercury spectrum in the visible region. These filters will transmit about 10% of the incident radiation. They pass a rather wide band of wavelengths, and so are acceptable only for discontinuous light sources. Narrow band-pass filters that may be used in conjunction with continuous radiation sources can be made by evaporating thin layers of a dielectric and sandwiching it between semireflective coatings. Such an arrangement, known as an interference filter, is a resonant cavity for light. It will transmit the resonant frequency or one of its harmonics. All other frequencies are not transmitted because of the destructive interference between the many reflected wavefronts. Interference filters must be used with parallel light if the small band-pass, or half-width, of the order of 100 A is to be obtained. The peak transmission of such filters may be as high as 30%. Figure 9–3 shows the construction and characteristics of such filters. In the ultraviolet region of the spectrum there are no such convenient filters available. Various solutions can be used, however, to isolate relatively large regions of the spectrum. They are by no means monochromatic filters, and in many cases are unstable in the presence of ultraviolet light. A comprehensive review of these and other types of filters may be found in an article by Mohler and Loofbourow.*

Each wavelength needs a separate filter, and since high spectral purity, especially in the ultraviolet region, is difficult or impossible to obtain by

---

* N. M. Mohler and J. R. Loofbourow, *Am. J. Physics* **20**, 499, 579 (1952).

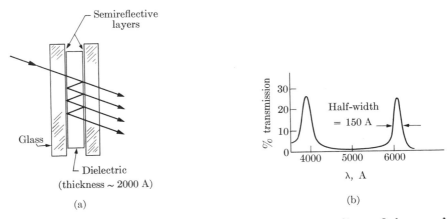

(a)

(b)

FIG. 9–3. (a) The construction of an interference-type filter. Only one of the incident parallel rays is shown. (b) The transmission curve of an interference filter. The two maxima are not a factor of two apart in wavelength because the index of refraction of the dielectric changes with wavelength.

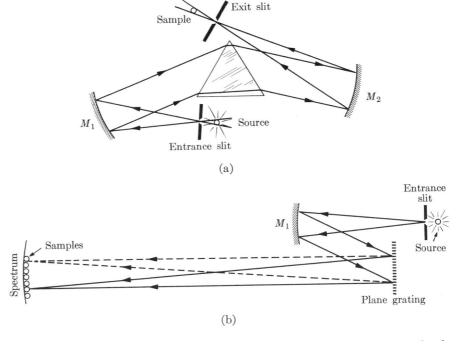

(a)

(b)

FIG. 9–4. Typical monochromators. (a) A prism monochromator, focal lengths of ∼1 m. (b) A grating monochromator with a grating-to-spectrum distance of ∼50 ft.

use of filters, monochromators are more conveniently used to isolate various spectral regions. Schematic diagrams of two types of mono-chromators are shown in Fig. 9–4. Light from the source of radiation passes through the entrance slit and is rendered parallel by the first mirror, M_1. In the prism monochromator the light is dispersed into its components in passing through the prism, and the second mirror forms an image of the entrance slit in the plane of the exit slit. The sample to be irradiated is placed behind the exit slit and is irradiated by the mono-chromatic light which emerges. The wavelength emerging from the exit slit may be changed by rotating the prism, and the wavelength range is determined by the dispersion of the instrument and the width of the entrance and exit slits. In the grating monochromator Fig. 9–4(b) the plane diffraction grating is illuminated by slightly convergent light, and as a result, the focused diffraction pattern extends over a big region of space. Samples at different wavelengths may be irradiated at the same time in such a device, but the intensity (not the total energy) will be less than in the type shown in Fig. 9–4(a). In one large installation[†] the distance between grating and spectrum is 50 ft. These monochromators look very much like ordinary spectrographs. The optical tolerances on a monochromator, however, are not nearly so strict as on a spectrograph. For example, we may be satisfied with a monochromator which will isolate a spectral band whose width is 50 A. In this case we can certainly tolerate an uncertainty of ±10 A, a situation which would be unthinkable in the case of ordinary optical instruments.

There is comparatively little flexibility in the design of a mono-chromator. For the ultraviolet region, for example, we can use only quartz and water as prism materials. Once we have chosen the prism material and the focal length of the mirrors, we have set the dispersion of the instrument, that is, the linear separation between two spectral regions at the exit slit. For example, a 60° water prism with mirrors whose focal length is 100 cm gives a dispersion of 25 A per millimeter. To iso-late a range of 50 A requires the use of slit widths of about 2 mm. There is a limit to how large the slit can be made, because if the monochromator is to be used efficiently, the light source must be large enough to fill the entrance slit with light. The light source must be at least as large as the entrance slit. Most light sources are less than 2 mm in width. Thus if we want to increase the total amount of power transmitted by a mono-chromator, it is necessary to increase the surface area of the mirrors and dispersing element. The increase in dimensions in a direction perpen-dicular to the light path means an increase in the solid angle of the instrument and the optics collect more light from the entrance slit. The

---

† G. S. Monk and C. F. Ehret, *Radiation Research* **5,** 88 (1956).

focal lengths of the mirrors, however, have little bearing on the problem. This may seem contradictory, because if the mirror focal lengths are decreased, the amount of light collected by them increases. However, at the same time it becomes necessary to decrease the size of the slit if the resolution of the instrument is to remain constant. These two factors, the increase in light gathered from the slit and the decrease in light transmitted by the smaller slit, just about cancel out each other. Simpler convenient instruments can be made with one concave mirror as the focusing element and with a plane mirror under a free water surface as the dispersing element. Inexpensive monochromators of this sort have one major defect. The intensity of stray light may amount to several percent in the wavelength region desired. Ordinarily this causes no harm, except when the stray light is much more effective biologically than the major component which passes through the exit slit.

9–4 Intensity measurements. Intensity has the dimensions of energy/area/time. Convenient units are ergs/cm^2/sec, watts/cm^2, and photons/cm^2/sec. The determination of the absolute intensity of a light beam is difficult. A detector such as a thermopile, which has a calibration independent of the wavelength of the light, is desirable. As shown in Fig. 9–5, a thermopile consists of small blackened receivers to which are attached several thermocouple junctions. When incident light falls on the thermopile, its energy is absorbed by one set of blackened receivers, whose temperature then rises. The temperature rises until the rate of energy input from the light beam is counterbalanced by the rate of heat loss due to conduction and radiation. If the thermopile has a very small heat capacity, it may reach a temperature equilibrium in times of the order of 0.1 to 10 sec. The small temperature difference between the

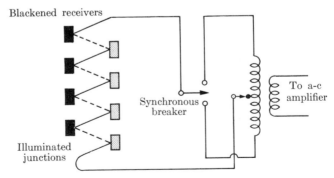

Fig. 9–5. A compensated thermopile connected to the input of a breaker amplifier. The unilluminated junctions are shielded from the incident light and compensate for changes in room temperature.

junctions, which may amount to 0.001°C, produces a thermal emf in the thermocouples. The thermal emf may be detected either by a sensitive galvanometer or by an amplifier and insensitive meter. A thermopile is a device of low impedance ($\sim$10 ohms) and of constant voltage. To amplify the d-c voltages, which are of the order of microvolts, demands special types of amplifiers. In one type the small d-c input signal is fed into a motor-driven switch which breaks the circuit and reverses the polarity eight times per second. The pulsating emf from the breaker is an alternating emf which can be amplified by a tuned a-c amplifier. The output may be rectified and read on a d-c meter. The sensitivity of thermopiles is about 1 μv/μw/cm^2. The minimum measurable intensity is determined by random thermal noise in the thermopile and in the associated detection equipment. It is of the order of 0.01 μw/cm^2.

The big advantage of a thermopile over other detection devices is that it responds equally to all wavelengths. It can be calibrated by placing it in the light beam emitted by a standard lamp. Because thermopiles are independent of wavelength, they respond to heat radiation, breezes, and people walking across the room. They are laborious to use. Photocells, on the other hand, are simple to use.

Photons falling on a metallic surface of a photocell eject electrons which give rise to a current that may be measured. The photoelectric currents are large enough to measure with a galvanometer or amplifier. A photocell is a device of high impedance and of constant current. As shown in Fig. 9–6(a), the output currents of about 0.1 μa may be passed through a resistance of 1 megohm, which changes the grid voltage of the amplifier tube. The change in plate current is proportional to the light intensity. A photomultiplier tube may be used instead of a photocell and amplifier. The photomultiplier, shown in Fig. 9–6(b), achieves its amplification by secondary electron emission. The photoelectrons ejected by light are accelerated to first electrode. They strike it with energy of around 100 ev, and eject about twice as many electrons. (The exact value depends on the accelerating voltage and the nature of the surface.) This multiplication process continues for about 10 electrodes and results in an over-all amplification of up to 10^6. Obviously such a device may be used directly with a microammeter. Its amplification depends on the magnitude of the applied voltage, and so it must be used with a stable high-voltage power supply. If a photomultiplier is used at high amplification, the normal thermionic emission at room temperature may give rise to large output currents. They may be eliminated by cooling the photomultiplier tube to a low temperature. Under these conditions its sensitivity is great enough, and the thermal noise small enough, so that it may be used as a photon counter. A photocell or photomultiplier responds to the total number of photons per second striking the sensitive

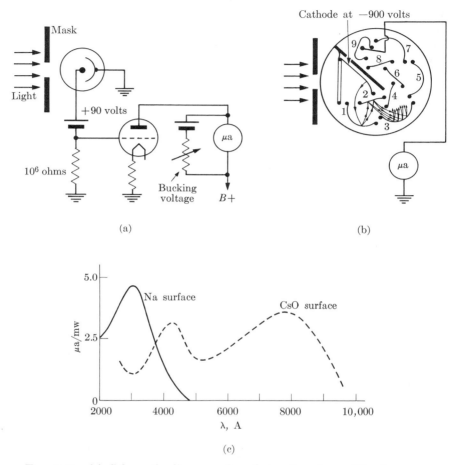

FIG. 9–6. (a) Schematic diagram of a photocell and amplifier to measure
light intensity. The bucking voltage on the meter is used to make it read zero
when no light falls on the photocell. (b) Schematic diagram of a photomultiplier
to measure intensity. The external connections to the intermediate electrodes
have been omitted. (c) Typical sensitivity curves of photocells.

surface. In this sense it does not measure intensity, since the photocell
does not discriminate between the light impinging on a small part of its
surface or on a large part. It is best, therefore, to use a photocell with
a limiting diaphragm in front of it. As shown in Fig. 9–6(c), photocells
do not respond equally to all wavelengths. Therefore they must be
calibrated at each wavelength against a thermopile or its equivalent.
Because of the big change in photocell sensitivity with wavelength, it
is important to know the spectral purity of the light that a photocell is

going to measure. For example, suppose a sodium photocell were being used to measure intensities in the region of 5000 A. If 1% of the light emerging from the monochromator were in the range of 3000 A, then the photocell would give a very distorted view of the intensities at the longer wavelength. Insofar as possible, a photocell should be chosen whose maximum sensitivity lies in the wavelength region being used. Despite all these necessary precautions that must be taken when photocells are used to measure incident intensities, they are by far the most convenient of the various detection devices.

There are many chemical reactions that may be used to detect the total light energy absorbed by a reacting solution. For example, uranyl oxalate is decomposed with a known efficiency by ultraviolet light. Such reactions are ultimately calibrated in terms of a thermopile, and they are more cumbersome to use than photocells. They measure the total incident energy, not the incident intensity as other detectors do.

9–5 Definition of action spectra. Table 9–2 shows orders of magnitude for the amount of light needed to affect various systems. As a general rule, the inactivation or activation of a specific function requires less energy than some generalized destruction such as the hemolysis of erythrocytes. It is also true that the smaller the structure irradiated, the fewer the number of absorbed photons needed to effect the transformation. Thus enzymes need many fewer photons to inactivate them than do

TABLE 9–2

TYPICAL NUMBERS OF ABSORBED PHOTONS OR INCIDENT
ENERGIES NECESSARY FOR CERTAIN PROCESSES

Process	Mass of unit, kgm	Incident energy per unit area, joule/m^2	Absorbed photons
Vision	—	10^{-13}	2
Photosynthesis	—	—	~10 per O_2 evolved
Photosynthesis, formation of 1 gm of carbohydrate	—	—	10^{23}
Sunburn at 3000 A	—	3×10^2	—
Hemolysis of rabbit red cells	—	—	10^{10}
Inactivation of bacteria	10^{-15}	10	10^6
Inactivation of viruses	10^{-19}	10	10^4
Inactivation of enzymes	10^{-22}	10^4	10^2
Dissociation of CO-myoglobin	3×10^{-23}	—	1

bacteria. In terms of the number of incident photons, however, the picture is just the opposite. Most of the photons incident on an enzyme molecule, for example, will not be absorbed. We saw in Chapter 7, Problem 12, that the probability of an incident photon being absorbed by a protein molecule is about 0.001. This means that to inactivate enzymes we need something of the order of 10^5 photons per molecular cross section. The absorption cross section for various systems is proportional to the molecular weight. Thus many of the photons incident upon a bacterium are absorbed, but the majority incident on an enzyme molecule are not. As may be seen from Table 9–2, the number of absorbed photons needed to inactivate a structure increases much less rapidly than the mass. This simply means that much lower incident intensities are needed to inactivate bacteria than enzymes, even though the efficiency per absorbed photon is much greater for the latter. Roughly speaking, we need several thousand joules per m^2 to inactivate enzymes, while only ∼10 joules per m^2 are needed to inactivate viruses and bacteria. The biological system being investigated will thus determine the type of radiation source that should be used.

The energy absorbed from a light beam by a reacting system may appear in one of three ways: (1) the absorbed energy may be degraded as heat or reappear as fluorescent photons; (2) it can supply the energy necessary for a complicated series of reactions, as in photosynthesis; and (3) it can disrupt the molecular organization in a random fashion, as in the inactivation of cells or enzymes by ultraviolet light. A graph of the response produced by incident light *versus* the wavelength is known as an *action spectrum*. It is worth while to spend a little time investigating the theoretical foundation of action spectra.

9–6 Action spectra theory. Suppose the irradiation of a biological system produces an effect which we designate as E. The effect might be the inactivation of virus particles or the photorestoration of bacteria, for example. The time rate of change of the effect may depend on (1) the incident intensity, (2) the wavelength, (3) the time during which the light has been incident on the sample, and (4) the properties of the irradiated system, such as the number of unaffected units and the ambient temperature. Since light is quantized, the intensity must be used in units of photons/area/time. If we let I = intensity, t = time, λ = wavelength, ξ = the rest of the properties of the system, and E = effect, we have

$$\frac{dE}{dt} = f(I, \lambda, t, \xi), \qquad (9\text{–}1)$$

where f may be an involved and unknown function of the variables.

We wish to compare the relative efficiency of two different wavelengths, λ_1 and λ_2. Equation (9–1) holds for both wavelengths.

$$\frac{dE_1}{dt} = f(I_1, \lambda_1, t_1, \xi_1), \qquad \frac{dE_2}{dt} = f(I_2, \lambda_2, t_2, \xi_2). \qquad (9\text{–}2)$$

The tacit assumption that the two wavelengths produce similar effects is indicated by using the same function, f, for the two. If the functional relation between dE/dt and the variables depends on the wavelength, it means that different processes produce the effect and the following analysis is *not* valid.

The relative efficiency of one wavelength, λ_1, to a second, λ_2, is obtained in the following way. Adjust the properties of the irradiated system so that $\xi_1 = \xi_2$, and choose times $t_1 = t_2$. In general, $dE_1/dt \neq dE_2/dt$. If the intensities I_1 and I_2 are varied so that $dE_1/dt = dE_2/dt$, the relative efficiency may be defined as

$$\frac{\text{Relative efficiency of } \lambda_1}{\text{Relative efficiency of } \lambda_2} = \left(\frac{I_2}{I_1}\right), \qquad (9\text{–}3)$$

where

$$\frac{dE}{dt} = \text{constant}, \qquad t = \text{constant}, \qquad \xi = \text{constant}.$$

If the relative efficiency indicated in Eq. (9–3) is to have meaning, the same ratio must be found at different times t. Equation (9–3) indicates that a high relative efficiency is associated with an effect produced by a low intensity. If all the relative efficiencies are expressed in terms of a particular wavelength, λ_0, the relative efficiency *versus* wavelength curve is the *action spectrum* for the effect E. We shall show that the action spectrum is parallel to the absorption spectrum of the absorbing molecule provided several simple conditions are obeyed. Figure 9–7 shows an

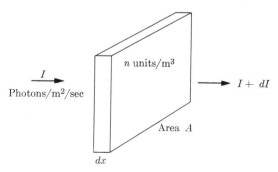

Fig. 9–7. Parameters of a medium irradiated by light for which Eq. (9–5) is derived.

irradiated sample of thickness dz and area A containing n units/m^3. The irradiated units may be molecules, viruses, bacteria, etc. The incident intensity is I and some of the light, $-dI$, is absorbed. We showed in Chapter 7 that

$$-dI = Isn\,dz, \tag{9-4}$$

where s was defined as the absorption cross section. In what follows we assume that the light absorbed by the sample is small enough so we may consider that all molecules see the same incident intensity. The total number of absorbed quanta per second is found by multiplying Eq. (9-4) by the area, yielding

$$\frac{\text{Absorbed photons}}{\text{Second}} = I \cdot s \cdot nA\,dz = sIN, \tag{9-5}$$

where N, which is the product of n (the units per cubic meter) and $A\,dz$ (the element of volume), is the *total* number of units irradiated. We mentioned previously that each absorbed quantum will not necessarily affect the absorbing unit because the absorbed energy may be dissipated along harmless pathways. Suppose a fraction, ϕ, of the *absorbed* photons are effective. We may write

$$\frac{\text{Affected molecules}}{\text{Second}} = \phi sIN. \tag{9-6}$$

The quantity ϕ is known as the *quantum yield* or *quantum efficiency*. It is the probability that an absorbed photon will be effective.

$$\phi = \frac{\text{number of molecules affected}}{\text{number of quanta absorbed}}. \tag{9-7}$$

It is reasonable to suppose that the rate of change of an effect E is a function of the number of units affected per second. Equation (9-1) therefore takes the form

$$\frac{dE}{dt} = g(\phi sIN). \tag{9-8}$$

In this expression the function g includes the environmental factors. The wavelength dependence appears in s and ϕ, and N represents the number of units at the time t. If two wavelengths, represented by subscripts 1 and 2, are to produce similar effects dE_1/dt and dE_2/dt, we must have

$$\phi_1 s_1 I_1 N_1 = \phi_2 s_2 I_2 N_2.$$

The expression for the relative efficiency, Eq. (9-3), now takes the form

$$\frac{\text{Relative efficiency of } \lambda_1}{\text{Relative efficiency of } \lambda_2} = \frac{I_2}{I_1} = \left(\frac{\phi_1 s_1}{\phi_2 s_2}\right), \tag{9-9}$$

where

$$\frac{dE}{dt} = \text{constant}, \qquad N = \text{constant}.$$

This equation is the key to all action spectroscopy because it says that from a knowledge of the relative efficiency as a function of wavelength (the action spectrum) and a knowledge of how ϕ varies with wavelength (with some important exceptions, it does not), we may determine the wavelength dependence of s, the absorption cross section. If the quantum yield is constant, the absorption spectrum is parallel to the action spectrum. Action spectroscopy may therefore be used to determine some of the crucial compounds involved in processes affected by light.

9–7 Inactivation of proteins and nucleic acids. In many cases it is possible to determine the change in the affected units themselves rather than some secondary effect dependent on this number. Such a situation might be the inactivation of the catalytic activity of enzymes. The increase in the number of units per second, $+dN/dt$, is the negative of the number affected per second given by Eq. (9–6).

$$+ \frac{dN}{dt} = -\phi s I N \qquad \text{or} \qquad \frac{dN}{N} = -\phi s I \, dt. \qquad (9\text{–}10)$$

Integration yields

$$\ln N = -\phi s I t + C.$$

The constant of integration is determined by the initial condition that at $t = 0$, $N = N_0$, the initial number of active molecules.

$$\ln \frac{N}{N_0} = -\phi s I t$$

or

$$\frac{N}{N_0} = e^{-(\phi s)(I t)}. \qquad (9\text{–}11)$$

If we call ϕs the cross section for inactivation σ, and call It the incident dose of radiation D in photons/m^2, then

$$\frac{N}{N_0} = e^{-\sigma D}, \qquad (9\text{–}12)$$

where $\sigma = \phi s$. The inactivation cross section is the relative probability that an incident photon will inactivate a molecule, just as the absorption cross section is the relative probability that an incident photon will be absorbed. It has the dimensions of area/photon.

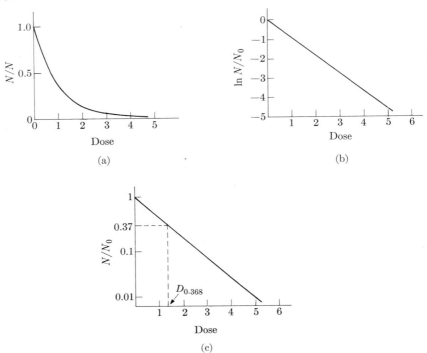

Fig. 9–8. Three different ways of plotting data represented by Eq. (9–12). (a) N/N_0 *versus* the dose. (b) $\ln N/N_0$ *versus* the dose. The slope of the straight line is $-\sigma$. (c) N/N_0 on a $\log_{10}$ scale *versus* the dose. σ equals the reciprocal of the dose for $N/N_0 = 0.368$.

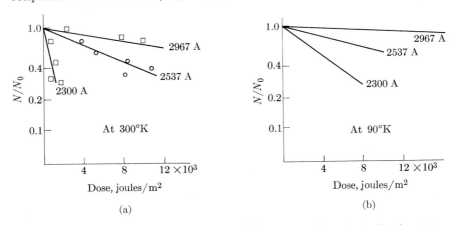

Fig. 9–9. The inactivation of activity of the enzyme trypsin in the dry state by different wavelengths of ultraviolet light. (a) The enzyme at 300°K during irradiation. (b) The enzyme at 90°K during irradiation.

Equations (9–11) and (9–12) represent a very simple case, one in which the relative number of surviving units depends on the product of the intensity and time. The same irradiation result may be achieved by using a high intensity for a short time or a low intensity for a long time. The so-called "reciprocity law" holds. This law has been shown to hold for enzyme inactivation for an intensity range of a factor 10^5. The law does not hold in rapidly metabolizing or changing systems or in systems where slow dark reactions follow the absorption of a photon before an effect may be observed.

Equation (9–12) is of the type observed in random processes in which a single event (a photon absorption) is sufficient to alter the structure. We shall have more to say from this point of view later. Equations of this form are familiar to us from the study of thermal inactivation. Figure 9–8 shows various ways of plotting inactivation data. As can be seen in the figure, if $\ln N/N_0$ is plotted against D, or if N/N_0 on a logarithmic scale is plotted against D, the resulting curve is a straight line. The advantage of these methods of representation is that an average straight line is the easiest curve to draw through experimental points. In Fig. 9–8(b) the slope is $-\sigma$. The inactivation cross section is also easily found from Fig. 9–8(c). We see from Eq. (9–12) that when $\sigma D = 1$, $N/N_0 = 1/e = 0.368$, or 37%. Therefore σ is the reciprocal of the $1/e$ dose.

Figure 9–9 shows some data for the inactivation of dry trypsin by ultraviolet light. It is seen that the enzyme is inactivated less rapidly when irradiated at 90°K than at room temperature. Its inactivation cross section is smaller at liquid air temperature.

The inactivation cross section and the quantum yield for inactivation may be calculated in the following way. We see from Fig. 9–9 that at 2537 A the $1/e$ dose is 12.0×10^3 joules/m^2. Thus the cross section is given by

$$\sigma = \frac{1}{D_{0.368}} = 0.83 \times 10^{-4} \frac{m^2}{joule}.$$

The proper units to use are m^2/photon. At 2537 A, the number of joules/photon is

$$\frac{6.63 \times 10^{-34} \text{ joule·sec} \times 3 \times 10^8 \text{ m/sec}}{2.537 \times 10^{-7} \text{ m}} = 7.8 \times 10^{-19} \frac{joule}{photon}.$$

So we obtain for σ

$$0.83 \times 10^{-4} \frac{m^2}{joule} \times 7.8 \times 10^{-19} \frac{joule}{photon} = 6.5 \times 10^{-23} \frac{m^2}{photon}.$$

To find the quantum yield we must also know the absorption cross section. Measurements on trypsin in solution show that at 2537 A a 1.0 mg/ml solution has an optical density of 0.47. If we take the molecular weight as 34,000 (a better recent value is 23,000), the use of Eqs. (7–13) and (7–14) gives for the absorption cross section

$$s = 0.6 \times 10^{-16} \frac{cm^2}{photon} = 0.6 \times 10^{-20} \frac{m^2}{photon}.$$

Thus from Eq. (9–12),

$$\varphi = \frac{\sigma}{s} = \frac{6.5 \times 10^{-23}}{0.6 \times 10^{-20}} = 0.011 \frac{molecules\ inactivated}{photon\ absorbed}.$$

The action spectra, graphs of σ *versus* wavelength, of trypsin at room and liquid air temperature are compared with the absorption spectrum of trypsin in Fig. 9–10. Since action and absorption spectra are not parallel, the inactivation of this enzyme is a case in which the quantum yield for inactivation, $\phi = \sigma/s$, depends on the wavelength. The reason the quantum yield varies with wavelength is that the different amino acids making up a protein not only have different absorption spectra but also have different sensitivities for protein inactivation. Cystine, which is important in maintaining the tertiary molecular configuration because it can link one polypeptide chain to another, seems to be the most sensitive

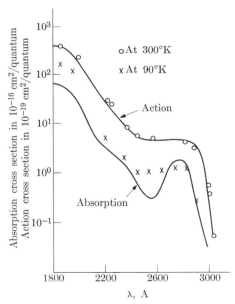

FIG. 9–10. Comparison of the absorption spectrum of trypsin and the inactivation spectra obtained at two different temperatures. The two spectra are not similar to each other.

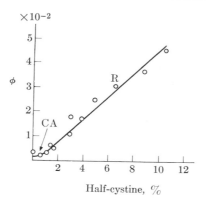

FIG. 9–11. An empirical relation between the quantum yield at 2537 A and the relative amount of half-cystine in the enzyme. Each point represents a *different* protein. For example, R represents RN-ase and CA represents catalase.

amino acid. It may be shown that the action spectra of Fig. 9–10 can be represented by the sum of a cystine component with a high quantum yield (0.05) and the aromatic amino acids with low quantum yields (0.005). The shape of the protein action spectrum shown in Fig. 9–10 is typical of enzymes which contain a relatively large amount of cystine. Enzymes with little cystine have action spectra which parallel their absorption spectra. As one might expect from the above discussion, the quantum yield for enzyme inactivation at 2537 A, where cystine has its *relatively* largest absorption coefficient (see Fig. 7–22), depends on the amount of cystine in the molecule. Figure 9–11 shows the quantum yield for many different enzymes as a function of the ratio of the number of cystines to the total number of amino acids. The functional dependence is clear-cut.

The generalizations that may be drawn from the above and other data about protein inactivation by ultraviolet light follow:

(1) The quantum yield for enzyme inactivation is of the order of from 10^{-2} to 10^{-3}.

(2) The quantum yield at 90°K is three times smaller than at 300°K.

(3) The quantum yield is proportional to the relative amount of cystine per molecule and is approximately inversely proportional to the molecular weight.

(4) From 1800 to 3000 A, when the absorption cross section changes by 10^4, the quantum yield changes by less than 10. To a first approximation, the action spectra for all proteins are parallel to the absorption spectra.

(5) Proteins with a lot of cystine have action spectra which are *not* exactly parallel to their absorption spectra. The quantum yield for such proteins has a maximum at 2500 A.

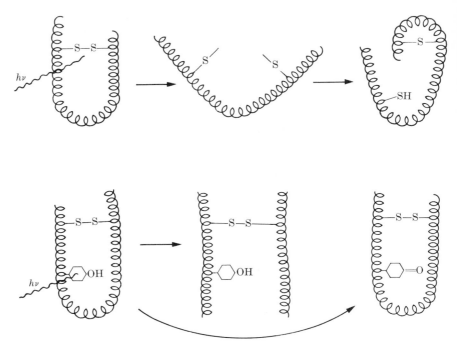

FIG. 9–12. Schematic inactivation mechanisms of proteins by ultraviolet light.

(6) At very low wavelengths, less than 1215 A, where the light ionizes the molecule, the quantum yield rises to unity.

Unlike the photo-oxidation of particular amino acids in the presence of dyes such as methylene blue, the inactivation of proteins by ultraviolet light arises more from a change in the structural integrity of the molecule than from changes in any particular amino acid. The splitting of the —S—S— bond of cystine may lead to an unfolded, inactive molecule. Some schematic inactivation mechanisms are shown in Fig. 9–12. The upper part of the figure shows the most probable mode of inactivation, the breakage of an S—S bond. The lower part shows two less probable ways, the breakage of a peptide bond and the photo-oxidation of tyrosine. The latter process would be effective only if tyrosine were part of the active site of the molecule or if its photo-oxidation led to a change in the tertiary structure.

McLaren* has pointed out that generalization (3) above implies that all small proteins contain a lot of cystine. Experimentally this is found to be approximately true, and the finding of such a relation illustrates the

---

* A. D. McLaren, *Biochim. et Biophys. Acta* **18**, 601 (1955).

unexpected rewards in one field of study which arise from pure research in other fields.

We have much less detailed information about the composition and structure of nucleic acids. Consequently much less is known about the details of the effects of radiation on nucleic acid polymers. Nucleic acid polymers may be single-stranded structures, as in RNA, or have the double helix represented by many DNA samples. One can study both the physical changes and the biological changes produced in these polymers by light. The most obvious physical change produced is the decrease in viscosity after irradiation. We would expect such a result from a break in a single-stranded RNA or from several nearby breaks in a double-stranded DNA. In the double-stranded DNA molecule, a break in one of the chains has a good chance of rejoining because of the hydrogen bonds holding the structure together. We would expect that if the two chains of DNA are to have nearby breaks and so give rise to a lower viscosity, big doses of radiation would be needed. This is found. The quantum yield for viscosity decrease in about 10^{-6}. If DNA is irradiated while dry, the opposite of a viscosity decrease may occur. Irradiated DNA may form an insoluble gel. A broken chain may recombine with a neighboring molecule, instead of itself, and a three-dimensional network of DNA fibrils may be formed. The efficiency of producing such gels depends on the incident wavelength, and the action spectrum is parallel to the absorption spectrum. Gel production takes place just as well at 90°K. The incident doses of light needed to affect DNA are much smaller than those used for protein inactivation. At 2652 A, an incident dose of 5 joules/m² can gel all but 37% of a DNA sample. The chief reason for the high DNA sensitivity is that the absorption cross section for nucleic acid is 20 times larger than that of an equal mass of protein. Therefore more incident photons are absorbed. The quantum yield for gelling DNA is not much higher than the values for inactivating enzymes. It is in the range of 10^{-2} to 10^{-3}.

Our knowledge of the effects of light on biologically active nucleic acid is limited to two cases. The first is exemplified by the transforming principle of *pneumococcus*. Double-stranded DNA extracted from a strain that is resistant to streptomycin can transform a second strain, which is sensitive to the drug, to streptomycin-resistant. The inactivation of the streptomycin-resistant DNA shows an inactivation curve that may be resolved into the sum of two exponential inactivations. The $1/e$ dose of the more sensitive component is about 1.5×10^2 joules/m² at 2537 A. At 77°K, the sensitivity is about two times less. The determination of the quantum yield for inactivation of this genetic marker requires a knowledge of the size of the active piece of DNA. The size of the unit is estimated, from the kinetics of the loss in transforming ability with

DN-ase treatment, as 1.6×10^3 nucleotides. From these data a quantum yield of $\sim 10^{-3}$ is obtained.* Different genetic markers may have somewhat different quantum yields.

The extracted infectious RNA from TMV has been irradiated at 2537 A. The quantum yield for inactivation was found† to be 3×10^{-4}.

A summary of the effects of ultraviolet light on nucleic acid polymers follows. (1) The action and absorption spectra are parallel to each other for the gelling of DNA. (2) The inactivation cross sections are 10 to 100 times larger than for proteins. (3) The quantum yield depends on the property observed. Values range from 10^{-2} to 10^{-6}.

9–8 Light action on respiratory pigments. Action spectroscopy first came into its own in the hands of Warburg, who used it to determine the absorption spectrum of the CO-compound of the oxygen-transporting enzyme, cytochrome oxidase. In this way he was able to clinch the identification of the enzyme as a heme-protein. The principles and procedures he used to reach this conclusion follow.

Carbon monoxide inhibits the respiration of yeast. The illumination of inhibited yeast cells results in increased respiration. The increase in respiration depends not only on the intensity of the incident light but also on the wavelength. The kinetics of the process may be described in the following simplified fashion. Assume that carbon monoxide competes with oxygen for the porphyrin groups of the proteins making up the respiratory system.

$$FeCO + O_2 \leftrightarrows FeO_2 + CO.$$

The equilibrium, and thus the respiration rate, can be shifted to the right by absorbed light. If the gas pressures are high and kept constant during any reactions that take place, then

$$\text{in the dark:} \quad \frac{d(FeO_2)}{dt} = k_d(FeCO) - k(FeO_2),$$

where the k's are specific velocity constants. The first term on the right represents the forward reaction and the second the back reaction. At equilibrium in the dark, the concentration ratio is given by

$$\text{in the dark:} \quad \frac{FeO_2}{FeCO} = \frac{k_d}{k}.$$

The effect of incident light is to increase the forward reaction constant

---

* L. S. Lerman and L. J. Tolmach, *Biochim. et Biophys. Acta* **33,** 371 (1959).

† A. D. McLaren and W. N. Takahashi, *Radiation Research* **6,** 532 (1957).

to $(k_d + k_l)$, and at equilibrium in the light we have

$$\text{in the light:} \quad \frac{\text{FeO}_2}{\text{FeCO}} = \frac{k_d + k_l}{k}.$$

If we take the respiration *rate*, R, as proportional to FeO_2 and use that fact that $R_{\max}$, obtained in the absence of CO gas, is proportional to the total iron concentration, which is $\text{FeO}_2 + \text{FeCO}$, we obtain

$$\frac{R}{R_{\max}} = \frac{k_d + k_l}{k + k_d + k_l}.$$

The constant k_l is the number of dissociations of FeCO per second under the action of incident light. It is given by Eq. (9–6) as $\phi s I$, where s is the absorption cross section of the FeCO compound, ϕ is the quantum yield, and I is the intensity

$$\frac{R}{R_{\max}} = \frac{k_d + \phi s I}{k + k_d + \phi s I}.$$

This expression is a particular form of the more general Eq. (9–8). It shows clearly that in the presence of CO the relative respiration rate depends on the light intensity. Figure 9–13 shows typical data on the oxygen uptake of yeast in the presence of CO and light. The slopes of the curves represent the respiration rates. It is possible to determine k, k_d, and ϕs by observing the respiration rate at different intensities. In this way the action spectrum, ϕs *versus* λ shown in Fig. 9–14, for the reduction of CO inhibition of yeast is obtained. If we assume that the quantum yield is constant and equal to one, as is the case for the simpler molecular systems described below, the action spectrum of Fig. 9–14 is

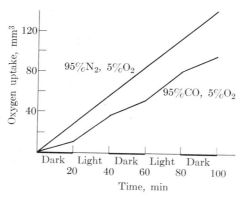

Fig. 9–13. The uptake of oxygen by yeast in the presence of CO, and the effect of light on the respiration rate. (From Ref. 1.)

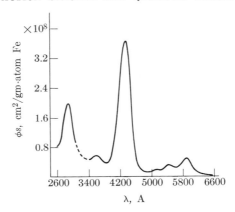

FIG. 9–14. Action spectrum for the reduction of the CO inhibition of yeast respiration. (After Ref. 1.)

the absorption spectrum of the pigment which is inhibited by carbon monoxide. This spectrum is very similar to those of iron-containing proteins [see Fig. 7–21(b) and note the different type of scale used] and led to the identification of cytochrome oxidase as a porphyrin-containing protein.

Similar data may be obtained from simpler systems, such as the combination of various iron compounds, including hemoglobin, with carbon monoxide. In these cases we not only can measure the amount of carbon monoxide split off from the molecule (that is, determine ϕs), but we also know the absolute values of the absorption cross sections of the molecules and we may determine the quantum yield ϕ.

The most interesting case is the splitting of CO-myoglobin by light. Myoglobin is a red-pigmented muscle protein of molecular weight 17,000, whose structure we described in Chapter 5. It has one heme group. The dissociation by light may be determined from the difference in absorption spectra between the CO- and O_2-myoglobin. The results obtained by Bücher and Kaspers are shown in Table 9–3. The quantum yield is independent of wavelength. The importance of this result is that at the lowest wavelength used, 2800 A, almost half the absorbed light is absorbed by the aromatic amino acids, but at all other wavelengths the photons are absorbed in the heme group. This is direct evidence for the transfer of sufficient energy from the protein to the prosthetic group so that CO is knocked off. Similar results have been obtained for heme groups coupled to polypeptide chains containing phenylalanine as the absorbing group.* A schematic picture of the process is shown in Fig. 9–15. The high transfer efficiency for energy absorbed at 2800 A may very likely

---

* W. Broser and W. Lautsch, Z. *Naturforsch.* **11b,** 453 (1956).

TABLE 9–3

THE QUANTUM YIELD FOR THE
DISSOCIATION OF CO-MYOGLOBIN*

Wavelength, A	Quantum yield, ±3%
5460	0.91
3660	0.99
3340	1.09
3130	0.97
2800	1.01

* T. Bücher and J. Kaspers, *Biochim. et Biophys. Acta* **1,** 21 (1947).

be due to "sensitized fluorescence," since protein and heme have large absorption (and hence similar energy levels) in the same region.

The conclusions we reach from the work of Warburg and his collaborators on iron-containing proteins is that for the dissociation of CO, the quantum yield is just about constant, and the action spectrum parallels the absorption spectrum. These conclusions do not necessarily hold for other systems. The visual pigment rhodopsin, which consists of a protein and a conjugated chain prosthetic group, can be bleached by the action of light, but the bleaching action follows the absorption spectrum only in the visible region. Light absorbed in the protein component has little if any bleaching effect. However, it cannot be concluded that the protein component is not an essential part of the visual mechanism.

9–9 Photosynthesis. The best-known effect of light, other than sunburn, is photosynthesis, i.e., the reduction of CO_2 to yield carbohydrate and molecular oxygen. The photosynthetic process is a complicated biochemical chain of events, of which only one step is the supplying of energy by absorbed light. The general type of reaction that takes place in the

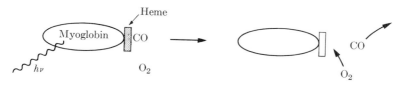

FIG. 9–15. A diagram to illustrate that light absorbed in the protein dissociates CO from the heme group.

chloroplasts of green plants is

$$CO_2 + 2H_2O \xrightarrow{h\nu} (CH_2O) + O_2 + H_2O.$$

(CH_2O) represents a general carbohydrate product. The two molecules of water on the left side of the equation are there to indicate that the evolved oxygen gas comes primarily from water and *not* from CO_2. The rate at which CO_2 is removed from the surrounding medium, or the rate at which oxygen is evolved, depends on the light intensity or rate of absorption of light. We obtain a lower limit to the number of photons necessary for the ultimate reduction of a molecule of CO_2 from a knowledge of the heat of combustion of the reverse reaction. This value is 112,000 cal/mole or 4.9 ev/molecule. Photosynthesis takes place readily in light of wavelength 7000 A, for which the energy per photon is 1.77 ev. Thus at least $4.9/1.77 = 2.8$ photons are needed. Since photons may not be split in this convenient way, at least three photons are necessary to reduce one molecule of CO_2. The determination of the maximum quantum yield for photosynthesis is difficult because of the many complications, such as method of cultivation and the determination of gases absorbed and evolved, which enter into the experiment. These factors are important because photosynthesis consists of a set of dark reactions (on which we shall not dwell) as well as the light reaction. The actual value of the quantum yield has been the subject of many heated controversies, with Warburg and his collaborators obtaining values of $\frac{1}{4}$ and most other people obtaining $\frac{1}{8}$. In either case, the photosynthetic process is an efficient one.

Photosynthesis is a process associated with plants which contain chlorophyll. Other pigments may be associated with photosynthesis, but they

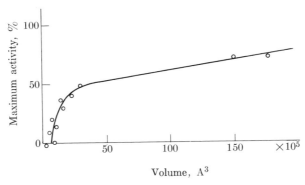

Fig. 9–16. The rate of O_2 production in the Hill reaction for grana which have been fragmented to the size indicated. (From Ref. 12.)

never work in the absence of chlorophyll. Chlorophyll is organized in the *grana* of the chloroplasts, and for efficient photosynthesis the grana must be above a certain size. If the grana are fragmented by ultrasonics, their ability to evolve oxygen in the Hill reaction, which is the liberation of O_2 in the reduction of ferric salts according to

$$4Fe^{+++} + 2H_2O \overset{h\nu}{\rightleftharpoons} 4Fe^{++} + O_2 + 4H^+,$$

is decreased. The Hill-reaction activity is related to the average granum size, as shown in Fig. 9–16. The minimum diameter that is efficient in the Hill reaction is about 100 A. Such a particle contains 100 chlorophyll molecules. These results indicate that the *organization* of chlorophyll molecules with protein and lipid in the grana is the important feature in the light reaction of photosynthesis. The detailed mechanism by which the light energy is used is not clear.

For most green plants the dependence of photosynthetic rate on wavelength is close to the absorption spectrum of chlorophyll. There are many algae, however, for which this is not true. The action spectrum is totally unlike that of chlorophyll. Figure 9–17 shows a photosynthetic action spectrum for a red alga. It may be regarded as consisting of two parts, an inefficient part due to chlorophyll and a very efficient part due to the dye phocoerythrin, which gives the algae their color. Phycoerythrin is apparently not involved in photosynthesis. The energy absorbed by it is transferred to the chlorophyll. The chlorophyll, with its extra energy, now takes part in photosynthesis. In these cases the action spectrum for photosynthesis looks more like the absorption spectrum for the entire plant rather than for a single component. We are not justified in concluding from the action spectrum that phycoerythrin is an essential mole-

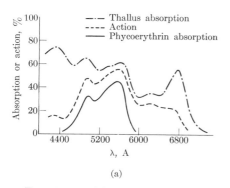

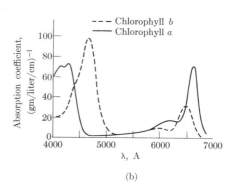

(a)   (b)

FIG. 9–17. (a) The photosynthetic action spectra in red algae, and the absorption spectrum of the dye phycoerythrin and of the cells themselves. [After F. T. Haxo and L. R. Blinks, *J. Gen. Physiol.* **33,** 389 (1950).] (b) The absorption spectra of chlorophyll in methanol.

cule in the photosynthesis operation. This may seem to be a trivial point, but it is one which must be borne in mind whenever the identification of specific molecules by an action spectrum is attempted. The action spectrum may simply indicate the absorption spectrum of the system as a whole, and perhaps only one molecule of this system has a critical function. This molecule can be altered either by absorbing energy directly or by receiving it indirectly, as in the case of the chlorophyll-phycoerythrin system.

The transfer of energy from one molecule to another in the case of photosynthesis by red algae has features similar to the dissociation of CO-myoglobin by light absorbed in the protein component. The energy transfers in these cases could take place by one of several mechanisms such as the collision between an excited and unexcited molecule, the conduction of electrons in conduction bands of the structure, the emission and reabsorption of radiation, or by a process known as *sensitized fluorescence*. It is this last process which is thought to be the most important for the photosynthesis case.

9–10 Sensitized fluorescence. Sensitized fluorescence is a process whereby two molecules may exchange energies if they have overlapping energy levels. Since it takes place over distances less than the wavelength of light, the process may not be considered to be the emission and reabsorption of radiation. Actually two neighboring molecules with similar energy levels are not independent of each other, and we are not really entitled to say that a photon energy is localized in one or the other. Nevertheless, as a first approximation, we may assume that the energy is absorbed by one molecule and reappears in another. The efficiency of this energy-transfer mechanism depends on the distance between the molecules and the similarity between their energy levels. The similarity is judged by the overlap of the fluorescent emission spectrum of one and the absorption spectrum of the other. The molecule which receives energy via the sensitized fluorescence route may not return it because it might lose some energy by internal conversion [Fig. 7–20(b)] and not retain enough to raise the original energy-rich molecule to its excited state.

Calculations have been made for the sensitized fluorescence energy transfer in photosynthesis in the blue-green algae Chlorella.* In these algae the pigments which absorb light are chlorophyll and the dye phycocyanin. The fraction of light absorbed by the two components varies with wavelength. At 6000 A, 20% of the light is absorbed by chlorophyll and 80% by phycocyanin. If we let ϕ_{ch} and ϕ_{ph} represent the photosynthetic quantum yield for light absorbed in chlorophyll and

---

* W. Arnold and J. R. Oppenheimer, *J. Gen. Physiol.* **33**, 423 (1950).

phycocyanin respectively, the observed quantum yield of 0.078 at 6000 A may be written as

$$0.078 = 0.20\phi_{ch} + 0.80\phi_{ph},$$

and from data obtained at 6760 A, where most of the absorption is due to chlorophyll,

$$0.085 = 0.94\phi_{ch} + 0.06\phi_{ph}.$$

If we solve these equations for the two yields, we get

$$\phi_{ch} = 0.086, \qquad \phi_{ph} = 0.076.$$

The light absorbed by phycocyanin is almost as efficient as that absorbed by chlorophyll.

A molecule, such as phycocyanin, which absorbs light will ordinarily lose its energy in the form of heat and fluorescence, If, in addition, it transfers energy by sensitized fluorescence, the normal fluorescence, which shows up as emitted light, will be decreased. In solution, phycocyanin emits 20% of its absorbed energy as fluorescent radiation and the remaining 80% appears as heat. Inside cells, only between 1 and 2% appears as fluorescence, with an assumed 4 to 8% as heat. This means that *in vivo* between 95 to 90% of the energy absorbed in phycocyanin is transferred to chlorophyll by sensitized fluorescence. This high efficiency is sufficient to account for the large value of ϕ_{ph}. Calculations based on a knowledge of the energy levels and concentrations of the two pigments show that the theoretical efficiency of sensitized fluorescence is more than ample to explain the observed results.

9–11 Viruses and microorganisms. Some action spectra for the inactivation of the virus T1 bacteriophage are shown in Fig. 9–18. The action spectrum in solution is very similar to the absorption spectrum of the virus, which indicates that the quantum yield is independent of wavelength. The virus contains 30% DNA and 70% protein. At 2650 A the absorption cross section is 1.5×10^{-12} cm^2. One may calculate that the quantum yield is 6×10^{-4}. The inactivation cross sections obtained at liquid air temperature are less than those at room temperature at wavelengths of 2800 and 2300 A. At these wavelengths the absorption coefficients of protein have relatively large values compared with nucleic acid, and since proteins are less sensitive at 90°K, it is perhaps understandable that the inactivation cross sections are low.

Not all action spectra have to be as complete as the ones we have described. In many cases important conclusions may be reached by a very simple determination of the relation of incident light energy to cellular function. For example, certain yeast cells do not ordinarily utilize

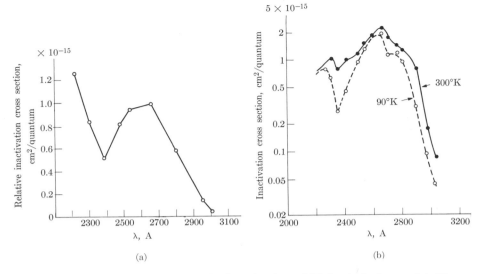

FIG. 9–18. Action spectra for the inactivation of T1 bacteriophage. (a) The virus in solution. [After M. R. Zelle and A. Hollaender, *J. Bacteriol.* **68,** 210 (1954).] (b) The virus dry at two different temperatures. [After D. J. Fluke, *Radiation Research* **4,** 193 (1956).]

galactose. If these cells are placed in a medium containing galactose, they adapt after a short while so as to metabolize this sugar. This process of adaptation can be inhibited by ultraviolet light. A yeast suspension with 2×10^8 cells per milliliter was placed in a quartz dish and irradiated from below with monochromatic ultraviolet light. The minimum amount of energy necessary to prevent the adaptation of the cells to galactose is shown in Table 9–4. Probably all the light incident on the suspension was absorbed. Clearly, radiation of wavelength around 2600 A is more effective in preventing this adaptation than others. Thus the sensitivity curve resembles the absorption spectrum of nucleic acids and not the absorption spectrum of proteins, whose maximum lies around 2800 A. The adaptation of yeast cells from metabolizing one sugar to another obviously is a very complicated procedure. The data in Table 9–4 show that the adaptation is intimately connected with nucleic acids. This is striking evidence for the close functional relationship between nucleic acids and protein synthesis.

9–12 Cooperative events in light action; the Poisson distribution. In our earlier theoretical treatment we mentioned that the reciprocity law held in many cases. The time rate of change of the effect is proportional to the intensity, or the effect itself depends on the product of the intensity and time. There is no reason why the law of reciprocity must hold

TABLE 9–4

MINIMUM ENERGY NEEDED TO PREVENT GALACTOZYMASE
FORMATION IN YEAST FOR AT LEAST FOUR HOURS*

Wavelength, A	Dose, ergs/mm^2
2345	3400
2537	1700
2654	1700
2804	3400
3025	14,000
3130	750,000

* From P. A. Swenson, *Proc. Natl. Acad. Sci.* **36**, 699 (1959).

in *all* cases. For example, when we are irradiating a growing culture of bacteria with a very low intensity, the rate of inactivation will be so low compared with the multiplication rate that there could possibly be no effect of ultraviolet light in this case. At the other extreme, when we are irradiating with very high intensities, it may be possible for two photons to be absorbed in the same molecule within a very small fraction of time; and two excitations at a given moment have a much higher probability of producing a molecular rearrangement than two excitations at different times. These two examples are not meant to imply that in all other cases reciprocity does hold. It is important in all radiation work, more especially with light than with charged-particle irradiation, to establish the fact that reciprocity holds. When reciprocity does not hold, then the resulting analysis of the data may be very complicated, since it is difficult experimentally to have the same incident intensities at many different wavelengths.

A situation in which the cooperative effects of radiation are important, one in which reciprocity *may* hold, is where more than one event is needed to produce an observable effect. If it is necessary to inactivate *both* genes of a homozygous pair before impairing a specific biochemical pathway, a different dose dependence will be found than if only one had to be inactivated. Let us suppose for the moment that we have a much more complicated situation than the ones we have discussed, and instead of needing just one event, or "hit," to produce the molecular rearrangement that we can detect, we need p hits. There are two possibilities that we have to consider: first, that the p hits take place in a single molecule or target, or second, that one hit is needed on each of p targets. The second possibility, the multitarget one, is more reasonable on physical grounds. The following analysis assumes that the law of reciprocity holds.

Suppose that as the result of irradiation we have produced a large number of hits per target. Let this average number be represented by x. Some of the targets will have more hits than x; some of them will have fewer. The distribution of hits may be represented by the Poisson equation,

$$P(p) = \frac{x^p e^{-x}}{p!}, \tag{9-13}$$

where $P(p)$ is the chance that if the average number of hits is x, we will observe p hits. It is easy to write down the explicit expression for this probability for the case of no hits, one hit, two hits, etc., and to show that the sum of these probabilities from zero to infinity is just one.

$$P(0) = e^{-x}, \qquad P(1) = xe^{-x}, \qquad P(2) = \frac{x^2}{2} e^{-x}.$$

The probability of no hits, $P(0)$, which equals e^{-x}, represents the number of irradiated entities which have received *no* hits. For processes such as enzyme inactivation, the relative activity is given by Eq. (9–12) as

$$\frac{N}{N_0} = e^{-\sigma D}.$$

This ratio is the probability of an enzyme receiving *no* inactivating hits, $P(0)$. Thus we have shown that the average number of hits per target, x, is equal to σD.

$$\text{Average number of hits per unit} = \sigma D. \tag{9-14}$$

This is a very useful result since, as we shall see, σD may be found easily, and thus for all radiation doses we can evaluate the average number of hits per target.

Suppose that to inactivate an organism with ultraviolet light we have to knock out two special sites of activity, two genes for example. We need one hit on each of two targets. Assume for simplification that all the targets are the same, i.e., they all have the same cross section σ. The chance that one of these targets is *not* hit is $e^{-\sigma D}$, and the chance that one is hit is simply $1 - e^{-\sigma D}$. To inactivate the organism we have to hit two of these targets, and the chance of hitting two of them is the product of the chances of hitting one, or $(1 - e^{-\sigma D})^2$. The chance of surviving, or the survival ratio, is one minus the chance of hitting the two targets, or

$$\frac{N}{N_0} = 1 - (1 - e^{-\sigma D})^2.$$

If we need one hit on each of p targets, then the expression becomes:

$$\frac{N}{N_0} = 1 - (1 - e^{-\sigma D})^p.$$

If for the multiple-target case we plot $\ln N/N_0$ against D, it is easy to see intuitively that the resulting curve will not be a straight line but will have zero slope at $D = 0$, and for large doses it will tend toward a straight line whose slope is minus σ. At very low doses, none of the organisms has received $p - 1$ hits, and therefore one more hit does not inactivate. At high doses, all the survivors have had their $p - 1$ hits, and so for this population a one-hit process holds.

The procedure for analyzing multiple-hit survival curves is simple enough, though laborious. We can determine the inactivation cross section by finding the slope of the logarithmic survival curve *versus* dose at high doses. By extrapolating this straight-line portion back to zero dose it is possible, from the intercept at zero dose, to find the multiplicity of the process. (See Problem 4.)

An example of the failure of the law of reciprocity and the use of the multiple-target type of analysis is shown in Fig. 9–19, where data are given on the inactivation of the *B. subtilis* spores by ultraviolet light of wavelength 2537 A. For dry irradiation, reciprocity holds over an intensity range of 12, and the resulting survival curve can best be fitted to a two-event curve. For the wet irradiation, reciprocity *does not* hold. The survival curves of the wet irradiation have multiplicities which vary with the intensity used. Any straightforward physical interpretation of these multiplicities is open to question.

Since reciprocity holds for the dry spores, it was possible for Morowitz to obtain the action spectrum for inactivation and also for mutation. The mutations were from biochemical deficient mutants back to the wild type. Such an ultraviolet-induced back mutation gives rise to a colony

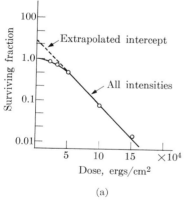

(a)

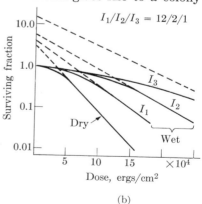

(b)

Fig. 9–19. Inactivation curves for spores of *B. subtilis* irradiated by 2537 A light. (a) Spores irradiated dry. (b) Spores irradiated wet at intensities in the ratios $I_1/I_2/I_3 = 12/2/1$. [After H. J. Morowitz, *Arch. Biochem. Biophys.* **47,** 325 (1953), and unpublished data.]

which can grow on minimal medium. The action spectra for inactivation and mutation are parallel to the absorption spectrum over a range of absorption cross section of 10^3. This means a constant quantum yield. The tentative conclusion is that two hits in any part of the bacterial spore inactivate it. We may also note that the mutation spectrum is similar to the inactivation spectrum. This implies that we can look upon inactivation as a lethal mutation.

We must always bear in mind that most of the photons absorbed produce no observable effect. In the case of *B. subtilis* something of the order of a million photons must be absorbed before the two right ones which do the trick are found. Whether these two photons must be absorbed in particular critical regions of the cell, or whether they are just two photons whose energy is dissipated in a particularly efficacious fashion, we cannot say. We do not even know the answer to this question in the case of small things such as enzymes.

One more example of a multiple-event type is the change in properties of influenza virus by the action of ultraviolet light. Among these properties are the infectivity and the ability of the virus to agglutinate red cells. Infectivity decreases exponentially with dose, and the infectivity action spectrum shows a maximum around 2600 A. Since influenza virus contains a large amount of protein, in this case the quantum yield for inactivation is not constant but shows a maximum in the neighborhood of the high absorption of the nucleic acids at 2600 A, again evidence for the important role of these substances in determining the course of biological synthesis. The hemagglutination data are presented in Fig. 9–20. The ordinate represents the dilution which will just give a precipitate, a high dilution corresponding to a high concentration of the agglutinating part of the virus. The curves shown are all of the multiple-target type. They indicate a maximum sensitivity in the neighborhood of 2800 A, and the doses needed are of the order of 10^4 times larger than those needed for the comparable reduction of infectivity. The hemagglutination properties of the virus could be said to be associated with several critical regions on the virus surface, and they are dependent on the existence of intact protein, not nucleic acid.

A very informative type of experiment* with ultraviolet light on the T-series of phages has made a point of the fact that the average number of hits per system is just the product of the inactivation cross section and the dose. The analysis which follows is no doubt an oversimplification, but its beauty recommends it. The starting point in this investigation was the observation of Delbruck and Baily that the active titer of an irradiated solution of phage depended on the concentration of phage

---

* S. E. Luria, *Proc. Nat. Acad. Sci.* **33**, 253 (1947).

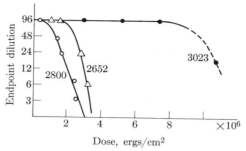

FIG. 9–20. The inactivation of the hemagglutinin of influenza virus by ultraviolet light of different wavelengths. The number of targets corresponding to the curves drawn through the experimental points are: 2800 A, 5; 2652 A, 40; and 3023 A, 100. [After I. Tamm and D. J. Fluke, *J. Bacteriol.* **59,** 449 (1950).]

when first placed in combination with the sensitive host. When 0.1 milliliter of virus is added to 1 milliliter of an *E. coli* suspension and the host-virus combination is diluted in broth 10^4 times before plating, a higher number of plaques is found than if the virus was first diluted 10^4 times in broth and then added to a bacterial suspension. This type of reactivation is known as multiplicity reactivation. The entire analysis of the problem would take us too far afield. Clearly, however, one possibility is that each phage has many individual units. When a phage is adsorbed to a bacterium and its DNA enters the cell, *all* these units must be present for the production of new phage. There is a chance that two inactive phage will contain between them the necessary subunits to make more phage. Schematically, four different inactivated viruses might be as shown in Fig. 9–21. Each phage itself can produce no more, but the following combinations, for example, can: (I, II) and (I, III, IV). The

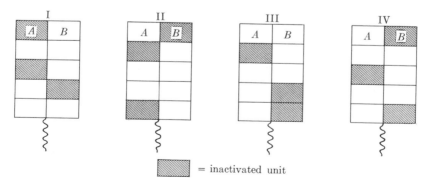

= inactivated unit

FIG. 9–21. Schematic diagram to illustrate hypothetical virus units which may be inactivated by ultraviolet light.

existence of this sort of recombination shows up when high concentrations of phage (mostly inactive) are mixed with sensitive host cells.

From experiments at very low phage/coli ratios, where never more than one virus adsorbs to a bacterium, we find that the survival ratio is $e^{-\sigma D}$. But the observed cross section σ represents the sum of all the units, since no reactivation is possible here. If there are n subunits, the surviving fraction of subunits will be $e^{-\sigma D/n}$. (It is important to recognize that we know the average number of hits per phage, σD; and if we knew the number of units, then we would know the average number of hits per unit, $\sigma D/n$.)

Suppose we increase the ratio of phage to bacteria so that, on the average, k particles are adsorbed per bacterium. Then if we think of unit A for the moment, we must find the chance that there will not be a hit on each of the units A. This is just

$$\text{Surviving fraction of unit } A = 1 - (1 - e^{-\sigma D/n})^k.$$

Since there are n types of units,

$$\text{Surviving fraction} = [1 - (1 - e^{\sigma D/n})^k]^n.$$

Experimentally we can vary σD and k independently and find both σ and n. Fitting the observed data to this expression yields the data of Table 9–5.

The analysis and interpretation we have given for multiplicity reactivation is somewhat oversimplified because all bacteria do not have the average number, k, of virus particles adsorbed to them. The actual number must be found from a Poisson distribution which takes into account the length distribution of the bacteria, because a long bacterium will have a better chance of being found by a diffusing virus than a short one will.

TABLE 9–5

PARAMETERS OBTAINED IN THE MULTIPLICITY REACTIVATION EXPERIMENTS ON BACTERIOPHAGES

Phage	Size, A		n	Relative σ
	Head	Tail		
T1	500	1200×100	8	1/10
T2	600×800	1000×200	40	1
T4	600×800	1000×200	30	1/4
T5	900	1700×150	15	1
T6	600×800	1000×200	50	1
T7	450	150×100	8	1/10

9–13 Photoreversal. The discussion of the effects of light on organisms, viruses, and enzymes would be incomplete without a consideration of the possibility that the inactivation can be reversed. It was found by Kelner that ultraviolet-inactivated microorganisms could be "reactivated" by exposure to high-intensity visible and near-ultraviolet light. At present this photoreversal cannot be done with viruses or enzymes, but a virus which has been inactivated can be reactivated after adsorption to its host. The photoreversal of viruses is obviously connected with the metabolism of the host, and is not connected with a primary molecular rearrangement of the virus induced by visible light. This view is substantiated by the fact that the action spectra for the photoreversal of *E. coli* and the virus T2 bacteriophage (after adsorption to *E. coli*) are the same, as is indicated in Fig. 9–22.

Photorestoration involves a series of complex steps, one of which is the absorption of photon. The others represent dark reactions whose speed may be studied with intermittent high-intensity light. The action spectrum is not definitive enough to permit the identification of the absorbing pigment. Photoreversal seems to be a process associated with the repair, or side-stepping, of nuclear rather than cytoplasmic damage. For example, the immobilization of *Paramecia* by ultraviolet light (the

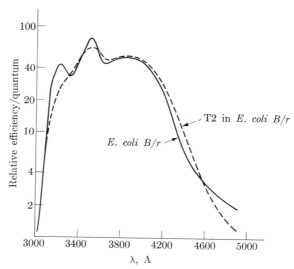

Fig. 9–22. The photoreversal spectra of *E. coli B/r* and T2 phage after adsorption to the bacteria. The inactivating wavelength was 2537 A. Doses of 1.8×10^5 ergs/cm^2 and 2.7×10^4 ergs/cm^2 gave 0.1% survival of bacteria and virus respectively. Photoreversal doses at 3500 A of 3.5×10^6 ergs/cm^2 and 1.3×10^6 ergs/cm^2 raised the survival level to 1%. [After J. Jagger and R. Latarjet, *Ann. Inst. Pasteur* **91,** 858 (1956).]

action spectrum is similar to that of a cystine-containing protein) cannot be photoreversed, but division delay (with an action spectrum similar to nucleic acid) can be reversed. Likewise, damage to the cytoplasmic RNA of wasp eggs cannot be reversed, but nuclear damage can be.

PROBLEMS

1. (a) Find, from the T1 wet action spectrum, the $1/e$ dose in ergs/cm^2 at 2800 A. (b) What incident dose, in ergs/cm^2 at 2800 A, would give 1% survival?

2. The following data were obtained for the inactivation of dry T1 phage at 2537 A. (a) Plot N/N_0 versus D. (b) Plot ln N/N_0 versus D and find the inactivation cross section. (c) Plot N/N_0 versus D on semilog paper and find the cross section.

Dose, joules/m^2	% Survival
0	100
2.0	72
3.0	59
4.0	43
7.5	20
10.2	12.0
12.0	7.1
14.0	5.0
15.5	3.0
18.5	1.9
22.0	0.78

3. The inactivation of influenza at 2650 A is single hit, and 3×10^4 ergs/cm^2 give 0.2% survival. The inactivation of hemagglutination is ~40 hit, and the 50% survival dose is 3×10^6 ergs/cm^2. If hemagglutination is lowered to 50%, calculate: (a) the probability of infectivity receiving zero hits, (b) the probability of infectivity receiving 1, 2, or 3 hits.

4. Show that the expression for the survival of a one hit on p-unit entity yields the following results: (a) As $D \to \infty$, ln (N/N_0) versus D has a slope of $-\sigma$. (b) If the high dose data are extrapolated to $D = 0$, $N/N_0 = p$.

5. Plot (as ln N/N_0 versus D or as N/N_0 on a log scale versus D) a single-hit, two-hit and 10-hit curves. Take σ as 10^{-16} cm^2, and use D in photons/10^{-16} cm^2.

6. If, at 2800 A, a dose of 10^3 joules/m^2 is given to (a) a dilute trypsin solution, and (b) a thin film of dry DNA, (so that the average intensity is the same in both cases), calculate, using the data given in Chapters 7 and 9, the unaffected fraction of each.

7. Repeat Problem 6 for 2200 A.

8. The following data were obtained in an experiment on the enzyme aldolase, whose molecular weight is 150,000, irradiated with 2537 A radiation. *Absorption data:* for c $= 1$ mg/ml, $\log_{10}(I_0/I) = 0.80$ for a 1-cm path. *Inactivation data,* obtained in a dilute solution:

Dose, $\times 10^3$ joules/m^2	Relative activity
0.00	100
1.0	60
2.0	40
3.0	20
5.0	7.0
10.0	0.90

Find the absorption and action across sections and the quantum yield at 2537 A.

REFERENCES

1. O. WARBURG, *Heavy Metal Prosthetic Groups and Enzyme Action.* Oxford University Press, 1949.

2. A. D. McLAREN, "Photochemistry of Proteins, Enzymes, and Viruses," *Adv. Enzymol.*, **9**, 75 (1949).

3. J. R. LOOFBOUROW, "Effects of Ultraviolet Radiation on Cells," *Growth Symp.*, **12**, 75 (1948).

4. H. F. BLUM, in *Biophysical Research Methods*, ed. by F. M. Uber. Interscience Pub. Co., N. Y., 1950.

5. A. C. GIESE, "Protozoa in Photobiological Research," *Physiological Zoo.*, **24**, 1 (1953).

6. E. C. POLLARD, *The Physics of Viruses.* Academic Press, N. Y., 1955.

7. M. ERRERA, "Mechanisms of Biological Action of Ultraviolet and Visible Radiations," *Prog. Biophys.*, **3**, 88 (1953).

8. A. HOLLAENDER, Ed., *Radiation Biology*, Vols. II, III. McGraw-Hill Pub. Co., N. Y., 1955, 1956.

9. R. SETLOW, "Action Spectroscopy," *Adv. Biol. Med. Phys.* **5**, 37 (1957).

10. L. R. KOLLER, *Ultraviolet Radiation.* Wiley, N. Y., 1952.

11. M. CALVIN, in *Currents in Biochemical Research, 1956*, ed. by David Green. Interscience Pub. Co., N. Y., 1956.

12. J. B. THOMAS, "Structure and Function of the Chloroplast," *Prog. Biophys.* **5**, 109 (1955).

13. C. P. WITTINGHAM, "Chloroplast Structure and Energy Conversion in Photosynthesis," *Prog. Biophys.* **7**, 319 (1957).

14. J. JAGGER, "Photoreactivation," *Bacteriol. Rev.* **22**, 99 (1958).

CHAPTER 10

THE ACTION OF IONIZING RADIATION ON CELLULAR CONSTITUENTS

10–1 Introduction. Ever since the discovery of x-rays and radioactivity, the ability of these radiations to penetrate living systems has excited great and sustained interest. One reason is that the effects produced by ionizing radiation on living systems are out of all proportion to the energy communicated to the system. For example, the rise in temperature occasioned by a lethal dose of radiation is so small as to be almost unmeasurable. Thus quite apart from its use in the diagnosis of damage and disease, ionizing radiation has a special interest of its own. The steadily increasing use of ionizing radiation in medicine and in industry, combined with the military espousal of nuclear weapons, have brought into sharp public focus questions that are also important to the molecular biologist. One example is that at Congressional hearings on the topic of the effect of radiation on living beings one of the central points of debate was the question of whether there is any threshold for the effect of ionizing radiation. It will become apparent as this chapter develops that full understanding of the action and behavior of the macromolecules that determine hereditary properties and of the nature of protein and carbohydrate synthesis may be necessary before correct answers can be given to some of the problems of public debate. It is for this reason that the combined study of molecular biology and ionizing radiation has become of great importance.

In addition to this rather intense and somewhat fearfully motivated region of research, is a second area of interest; namely, the use of the properties of ionizing radiation and of selected effects on the cell to tell us something about the *cell* rather than about radiation. Since this area has been of major concern to the authors for some years, we include a short chapter following this one on that special topic.

Ionizing radiation produces intense localized energy releases in its path. It is part of the inherent character of quantum mechanics and atomic structure that energy transfers between radiation and matter are discrete, and that many regions of no transfer at all, which therefore have no "knowledge" of the fact that radiation exposure has taken place, must exist. Thus we need to inquire into what happens to a cell, or a system of cells, when the great majority of the material of the cell has sustained no energy release but certain quite small regions have sustained considerable effect. To make this inquiry, the line of least resistance is first to describe what is known about the physical character of ionizing radiation, then see what we know about the consequences on macromolecules or systems of macromolecules, and finally attempt a synthesis of what the effect on the cell should be, a synthesis which should be capable of experimental verification. It will soon be apparent to the reader that we are on moderately firm ground in the physical description, rather shaky ground in molecular effects, and somewhat at sea in the final stages.

10–2 The nature of ionizing radiation. The two most commonly discussed forms of ionizing radiation, x-rays and neutrons, do not themselves ionize. This results in a little confusion, which a moment's patience soon resolves. Ionization is nearly exclusively produced by fast charged particles, and it is because x-rays and neutrons, in traversing matter, can form such fast charged particles that they are termed "ionizing." The major part of their action, which we will take up first, is in reality a secondary action. The way in which x-rays and neutrons produce fast charged particles will accordingly be described in Section 10–4.

We can look at the effect of a flying charged particle on matter in two ways. Perhaps the way which appeals most directly to our intuition is that of a *collision*. The first theory based on this concept, using the nuclear atom, was given by Bohr in 1915. We conceive that a fast electron, for instance, makes a collision with either an electron in an atom or the nucleus of the atom, and we attempt to describe what will happen. We soon find that there are two kinds of collision; namely, elastic, with conservation of kinetic energy, and inelastic, where some kinetic energy is temporarily removed as energy of excitation or ionization. This collision process, for the slightly esoteric case of fast particles traversing atomic hydrogen, was completely worked out in a monumental paper by Bethe in 1930. The methods of the theory were such that the *form* of the expressions deduced can also be applied to substances other than atomic hydrogen, although one parameter cannot be fixed by theory.

A second, and equivalent, method is to regard the flying particle as carrying automatically an electric field. The effect of this can be thought of crudely either as tending to push electrons out of nearby atoms if the flying particle is itself an electron or, in the case of a proton or deuteron, which is positive, as trying to pull them out as it goes by. This crude picture is quite helpful, but it can readily be elaborated a little more with considerable gain. Figure 10–1 gives a schematic summary of various features of radiation action. In part (a) the line is the path of a flying charged particle as it goes through a region where atoms are dense. In its path are two ionizations, represented by arrows, and one excitation, represented by the dotted circle. Part (b) shows the effect on one atom in particular and the path of the particle as it goes by. Part (c) plots the

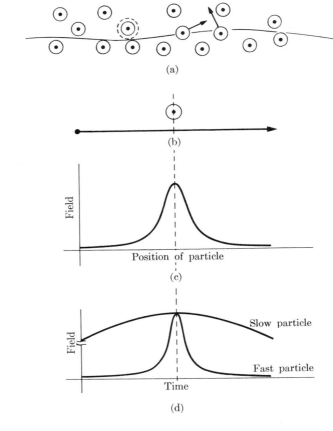

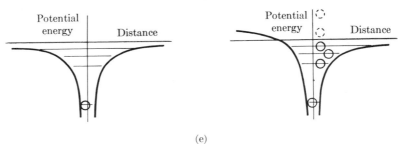

FIG. 10–1. (a) A particle traversing a number of atoms, with some consequent ionizations and excitations. (b) One atom and the particle going past it. (c) The electric field at the atom due to the fast charged particle in terms of the position of the particle, and (d) the same field in terms of *time*. (e) The potential-energy diagram of an electron in an atom before any additional field is imposed and also while the fast particle is adding its influence.

electric field produced at the atom as a function of the position of the particle. In (d) the field is plotted as a function of the time elapsed after the particle started to go by. For a slow particle the field is present for a long time; for a fast particle it rises and falls quickly. In (e) we show the effect of the external field on the potential-energy diagram with the atom in the ground state, along with a distorted diagram in which there is a probability that excited states can be occupied, including states which are not bound, i.e., ionized. These are indicated by the dotted circles.

We can now see the following very simple consequences of this type of added field. First, every atom near the fast particle is temporarily perturbed. Second, the duration of the perturbation is longer for a slower particle. Third, it is greater for a multiply charged particle, such as an alpha particle. Fourth, the field of a faster particle has more high-frequency components than that of a slower particle. Fifth, the mass of the fast charged particle is not important at all.

These consequences lead to some theoretical predictions which can be given first qualitatively and then quantitatively. The perturbation of atoms means that a probability of transition to some new, excited state exists. This is only a probability, and an atom which falls in the class of "failures" and not of "successful transitions" is *entirely unaltered*. Other atoms may be ionized or excited, with a probability depending on the duration and intensity of the perturbation. Thus a slow particle produces more transitions, as does a multiply charged particle. The higher-frequency components mean that transitions involving greater energy differences are possible for fast particles; and finally, the mass of the flying particle will not enter.

One or two decorative points can be mentioned. A particle moving close to the speed of light has a field which is laterally compressed, so that its effect is both more sudden and more intense. Transition probabilities must take this into account. Also, an electron in motion and an electron in an atom are identical particles and can exchange. This ability to exchange also modifies the transition probabilities.

The theory using this viewpoint was worked on by Fermi, Gaunt, and most completely by Bloch in 1933. The results are the same as those found by Bethe. Effects slightly off the path of the flying particle can be more readily estimated by the Bloch method; the energy of ejected electrons can be more readily estimated by the Bethe method. Both are fundamentally quite equivalent. The value best given by the theory is the rate of energy loss per unit length of path. If E is the energy of the flying particle moving with velocity v along the x-direction, then for heavy particles

$$-\frac{dE}{dx} = \frac{4\pi e^4 z^2 N}{mv^2} \; (B), \qquad (10\text{–}1)$$

where
$$B = Z\left[\ln\frac{2mv^2}{I_0} - \ln(1 - \beta^2) - \beta^2\right].$$

In this formula,

e is the electronic charge in esu,

z is the charge multiplicity of the fast particle,

N is the number of atoms per cm^3 of the material traversed,

m is the mass of the electron in grams,

β is v/c, where c is the velocity of light,

I_0 is the average ionization or excitation potential of the atom and has to be found by experiment,

Z is the number of electrons per atom.

The qualitative considerations we have described can be seen quantitatively when we survey Eq. (10–1). The interaction between charge and field can be seen clearly in the term e^4z^2, or perhaps more clearly in $(ze \cdot e)^2$, which is the square of the product of the charge on the flying particle and that of the electron in the atom. The velocity of the fast particle enters mostly as $1/v^2$ in the first term, with a small, more slowly varying feature $\ln 2mv^2$ in the second. The only mass concerned is the electronic mass, which is essentially the mass of the atomic particle that has to be excited. The mass of the flying particle is *not concerned*. The loss of energy is dependent on N, the number of atoms per unit volume in the path, and Z, the number of electrons per atom. The shrinking of the electric field laterally is expressed in the terms involving β, the ratio of the velocity of the fast particle to that of light.

The one term in Eq. (10–1) not covered by theory is I_0, the "average ionization potential." In principle, this is calculable from the statistics of the atomic electrons, that is, from their wave functions. In practice, it is too hard to do; conversely, the determination of I_0 by experiment is relatively easy. Therefore I_0, which varies very slightly with v for each

TABLE 10–1

Element	I_0, ev
H	16.0
C	64.0
N	81.0
O	99.0
P	165.0

element, is found by measuring dE/dx for known velocity particles in material of known composition. Fortunately the velocity of particles can be found independently by one or two methods, so that I_0 can be readily measured. Some values are given in Table 10–1.

We can see a very important aspect of Eq. (10–1) by considering the distribution in energy of the ionizations produced. Are there many small excitations and few energetic electron ejections, or is it the other way around? The answer to this was given by Bohr in 1915, and the relation controlling the distribution is

$$dn = \frac{2\pi e^4 z^2 NZ}{mv^2}\left(\frac{1}{W_1} - \frac{1}{W_2}\right) dx, \tag{10–2}$$

where dN is the number of releases of energy exceeding W_1 but less than W_2. The differential form is

$$d\left(\frac{dn}{dx}\right) = \frac{2\pi e^4 z^2 NZ}{mv^2} \cdot \frac{dW}{W^2}. \tag{10–3}$$

Note that the rate of energy loss is the value $W\, d(dn/dx)$ for any incremental energy loss, and therefore the total energy loss is

$$\int_{W_{\min}}^{W_{\max}} \frac{2\pi e^4 z^2 NZ}{mv^2} \frac{dW}{W},$$

where $W_{\max}$ and $W_{\min}$ are the maximum and minimum energy releases possible. This is a very simple idea, but it becomes less simple when actual values for $W_{\min}$ are investigated. $W_{\max}$ poses no problem, for it is the largest possible energy transfer in a direct collision and is determined by the conservation of momentum to be $(4m/M)E$, where M is the mass of the flying particle and E is its energy. For the simple, nonrelativistic case, $E = \frac{1}{2}Mv^2$; thus we see that $W_{\max}$ is $2mv^2$. The value of $W_{\min}$, however, is determined by the nature of atomic transitions. If it is set as I_m, an arbitrarily chosen value for the minimum energy transfer, then the resulting expression for the energy loss dE/dx becomes

$$-\frac{2\pi e^4 z^2 NZ}{mv^2}\int_{I_m}^{2mv^2} \frac{dW}{W}$$

and yields the value

$$\frac{dE}{dx} = -\frac{2\pi e^4 z^2 NZ}{mv^2}\ln\left(\frac{2mv^2}{I_m}\right).$$

This is obviously very much like the expression given in Eq. (10–1). The value of I_m, the smallest possible energy transfer, is clearly not the same as I_0, the average excitation energy per electron. If we suppose that I_0 is the geometric mean between the maximum energy transfer $2mv^2$ and the least value I_m, we have

$$(I_0)^2 = I_m \cdot 2mv^2$$

or

$$I_m = \frac{(I_0)^2}{2mv^2}.$$

We then obtain

$$\frac{dE}{dx} = -\frac{2\pi e^4 z^2 NZ}{mv^2} \ln \left(\frac{2mv^2}{I_0}\right)^2 = -\frac{4\pi e^4 z^2 NZ}{mv^2} \ln \frac{2mv^2}{I_0},$$

which is precisely the formula (10–1), given before for the nonrelativistic case.

These expressions are basic to an understanding of the effect of radiation on the enzymes, nucleic acids, and hormones of cells. To fix ideas, suppose we consider a solid protein, whose molecular composition is $C_4H_8NO_2$. Its density can be taken to be 1.3, and we can readily find the number N of various atoms per unit volume. To estimate the energy loss we use the *Bragg additive law*, which states essentially that chemical combination can be ignored and that each type of atom separately produces its own rate of energy loss. Thus if we use N_C, Z_C, and I_C for carbon atoms, N_H, Z_H, and I_H for hydrogen, and so on, we can set, for singly charged particles ($z = 1$),

$$\frac{dE}{dx} = -\frac{4\pi e^4}{mv^2}$$

$$\times \left(N_C Z_C \ln \frac{2mv^2}{I_C} + N_H Z_H \ln \frac{2mv^2}{I_H} + N_N Z_N \ln \frac{2mv^2}{I_N} + N_O Z_O \ln \frac{2mv^2}{I_O} \right).$$

Calculations made in this way are tedious but straightforward; some sample results are given in Table 10–2.

A glance at the table shows at once that the passage of a fast charged particle through a protein molecule is likely to make a difference to the molecule. In the case of a 4-Mev alpha particle and a protein molecule of thickness 30 A, 390 ev of energy are lost in the molecule, on the average. Since a normal chemical bond has an energy of 3 ev, the energy release is sufficient to break, at least temporarily, 100 bonds. This will almost certainly alter the protein molecule. Putting this fact together with the considerations of Chapter 3, where the importance of a very few molecules in a cell was stressed, we can see that the disruptive effect of ionizing radiation *at single, nearly unique locations* may be very great. It will be seen that this theme is capable of great elaboration.

TABLE 10–2

Energy	Kind of particle	Energy loss per 100 A protein, ev
10 Mev	Alpha particle	662
	Deuteron	93
	Proton	57
	Electron	2.9
4 Mev	Alpha particle	1300
	Deuteron	194
	Proton	117
	Electron	2.6
1 Mev	Alpha particle	2520
	Deuteron	540
	Proton	320
	Electron	2.5

While the figures in Table 10–2 are very informative, it is necessary to have some idea of the way in which the energy is actually released. Very early experiments by C. T. R. Wilson, using the cloud chamber, showed that the energy releases are discrete and large, as we have learned to expect from atomic theory. C. T. R. Wilson went beyond this. By deliberately waiting until after a fast particle had traversed his cloud chamber before he caused the expansion, he permitted the ions to diffuse and so separate, and obtained pictures of the individual ions at each energy release. He found that they were in *clusters*, with a variable number in the cluster, but averaging three ion pairs per cluster. His results, combined with more recent work by Beekman, have been analyzed by Hutchinson (Ref. 9) to give the figures of Table 10–3, where the relative frequency of various numbers of ion pairs is given. The general trend for lower energy

TABLE 10–3

Number of ion pairs in a cluster	Percent of such occurrences
1	50
2	25
3	10
4	5
5 and more	10

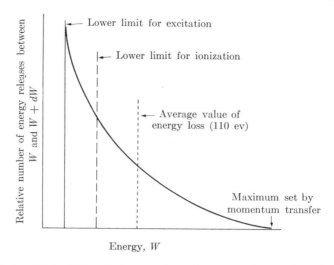

FIG. 10–2. Plot of the relative number of energy releases of a given energy range in terms of the energy of each.

releases to predominate is clearly present, as expected from Eq. (10–2). A value for the average energy release at a *primary ionization,* or ionization directly due to the main fast particle, can be derived from a number of cloud-chamber studies. The figure we adopt for this is 110 ev per primary ionization.

In Fig. 10–2 we show a graph of the relative number of energy releases between energy limits W and $W + dW$. The maximum energy release is set by momentum transfer as $2mv^2$ for a heavy particle and mv^2 for an electron. The lower limit for both ionization and excitation is set by atomic transition properties.

If now we represent the energy releases for a fast charged particle pictorially, they appear as in Fig. 10–3. The regions marked a are primary ionizations. The large release, $a(\delta)$, indicates that a secondary electron

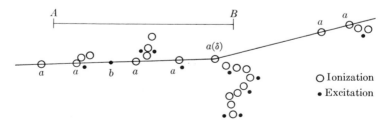

FIG. 10–3. Representation of the energy releases along the track of a heavy fast particle.

of rather high energy has been produced. This is called a *delta ray*, or sometimes a *spur* (see also Section 10–10). A primary excitation is indicated at *b*. The intervals between events are randomly distributed in length.

The scale of the spacing between events depends on the charge carried by the particle and on its velocity. Thus if the particle were a 4-Mev alpha particle, the distance *AB* would correspond to 31 A, or about the thickness of a protein molecule.

It can be seen that this distribution of energy releases somewhat changes the statement about "sufficient to break 100 bonds" given above. The energy releases are *localized and large*, and the results they produce strongly reflect this fact.

Another value of great use is the average energy loss per ionization (whether primary or produced by a released secondary electron). This can be measured by collecting all the ions produced in a volume of gas in which a known energy has been lost. The value, for air, is 32.5 ev per ionization.

10–3 The measure of radiation: the roentgen. When irradiation is by x-rays or gamma rays, it is customary to measure dosage in *roentgens*, a unit which dominates radiology and radiobiology but is somewhat difficult to measure because of its definition. A roentgen is the amount of radiation which causes one electrostatic unit of separated charge due to ionization in 1 cm^3 of air, better defined as 0.001293 gm of air. The radiation and air must be such that no *transition effects* are present; therefore, the 1 cm^3 of air must be imagined as surrounded by quite thick air.

When high-energy photons traverse a boundary between two media, the rate of absorption changes and therefore the amount of local ionization changes. The manner of the change depends on the range and energy of the secondary particles and also on the initial photon energy. Fortunately, it is possible to estimate corrections for this kind of change, which is what we mean by a transition effect, otherwise the absolute measurement of ionizing radiation would be very difficult.

Approximate equivalents for roentgens exist. Thus, 93 ergs absorbed per gram of tissue is called one roentgen equivalent physical, or 1 *rep*. Also, 100 ergs absorbed is called 1 *rad*. Other useful equivalents are 6.13×10^{11} primary ionizations per cm^3 in protein and 7.54×10^{11} primary ionizations per rep in nucleic acid.

10–4 Ionization by x-rays, gamma rays, or neutrons. For x-rays and gamma rays two predominant effects take place: photoelectric absorption and Compton recoil. The former causes complete removal of the photon of x- or gamma radiation and replaces it by a fast electron; the latter is a process of partial energy transfer. Both these processes, and indeed the transfer of energy by neutrons, are effectively random. For any random energy-transfer process, a relation such as that derived in Section 9–7 for light absorption also holds; namely,

$$\frac{i}{i_0} = e^{-NSx}, \tag{10–4}$$

where i/i_0 is the ratio of the intensity of radiation on the far side (i) of a slab of thickness x to that on the near side (i_0); N is the number of absorbing units (atoms, electrons, nuclei); and S is a *cross section* which expresses the probability of the absorption.

In the case of photoelectric absorption, the photon of energy $h\nu$ (the familiar Planck's constant times the frequency) is absorbed, causing an excitation energy in the atom of value W and releasing an electron (mass m) with a velocity v according to the relation

$$h\nu = \tfrac{1}{2}mv^2 + W.$$

The cross section for the process, in cm^2, is S_{ph}, where

$$S_{ph} = (2.04 \times 10^{-30}) \frac{Z^3}{E^3} (1 + 0.008Z).$$

Here Z is the atomic number of the atom and E is the photon energy in Mev. The effect is thus much more probable for low-energy photons and for elements of high atomic number. The effect is of interest because electrons of uniform energy are produced.

The process of Compton recoil differs in that the electron is effectively free and recoils without requiring the absorption of the photon. Accordingly, *two* energy sources remain after Compton recoil: the degraded photon (which has lost most of its energy) and a fast electron. The degraded photon is usually rapidly absorbed by the photoelectric effect. The appearance in the two cases is therefore as shown in Fig. 10–4, which is an attempt to give an impression of the ionization due to 100,000-volt and 1-Mev gamma radiations. Part (a) shows the appearance of ionization in a region of density slightly above that of water after the arrival of $\tfrac{1}{3}$ millirad of 100-kev x-rays. It is filled, in a random way, with photoelectron tracks, each of which is of the appearance shown at the top. There are some Compton recoils, but they are a definite minority and difficult to show. Part (b) shows a much larger region, drawn to a scale 100 times smaller than (a), in which 10^{-7} rad, at 1 Mev, has arrived. The energy transfer is predominantly by Compton recoil at first, followed by photoelectric absorption of the degraded electromagnetic radiation. Thus there is a mixture of rather long tracks and a nearly equal number of quite short

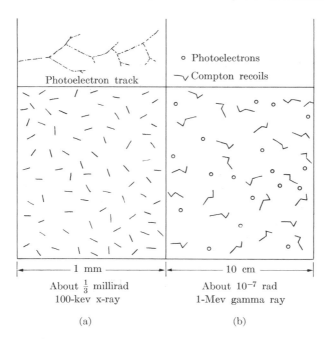

○ Photoelectrons

∿ Compton recoils

Photoelectron track

|◄——————— 1 mm ———————►|◄——————— 10 cm ———————►|

About $\frac{1}{3}$ millirad   About 10^{-7} rad
100-kev x-ray   1-Mev gamma ray

(a)   (b)

Fig. 10–4. The appearance of ionization in the case of (a) photoelectric absorption and (b) Compton recoil.

tracks that are similar to the photoelectric tracks in (a). The density of ionization along the Compton electron track (b) is considerably less than along the photoelectron track (a), a fact which is concealed by the change of scale.

The Compton recoil cross section varies rather slowly with the energy of the radiant photon, and is directly proportional to the number of electrons per atom. For radiation of energy in biological material in excess of 0.3 Mev, it is the major method of absorption.

For very high-energy gamma radiation a third method of absorption, rather analogous to the production of photoelectrons, exists. This is *pair formation.* An energy in excess of 1 Mev is needed. In biological material Z is usually low and the effect of pair formation is small.

Neutrons are exclusively absorbed by producing some effect on nuclei. Since nuclei are small, neutrons are not readily absorbed. In many experiments distinction is made between *slow neutrons* and *fast neutrons.* Pushing this distinction to its extreme (which is not very easy to do in biological irradiation), we say that a slow neutron is one which has the same class of velocity as if it were a gas molecule mingled in with the material, while a fast neutron has an energy in excess of 500 kev.

In biological systems a slow neutron reacts in two major ways. The first is with nitrogen, according to the nuclear reaction

$$_7N^{14} + n \rightarrow {}_6C^{14} + {}_1H^1 + 0.6 \text{ Mev}.$$

The second, discovered by D. E. Lea, is

$$n + {}_1H^1 \rightarrow {}_1D^2 + 2 \text{ Mev}.$$

The first reaction predominates, and most of the energy is delivered, by momentum transfer, to the hydrogen produced. Over 90% of the effect of slow neutrons is thus in terms of 600-kev protons. The remainder appears as 2-Mev photons produced in the second reaction. Slow neutrons are thus rather specific in that they ultimately cause ionization by a rather slow, heavy particle, with a rate of energy loss corresponding to five primary ionizations per 100 A.

Fast neutrons are not so homogeneous in their action. They predominantly collide with hydrogen nuclei, transferring part of their energy by momentum transfer to give quite fast protons. They can also lose energy by inelastic scattering, giving rise to high-energy photons, and ultimately produce nuclear reactions. Therefore any oversimplification of the action of fast neutrons is suspect. So that the reader may put them in a broad category, we can say that the major effect of fast neutrons is due to fast recoil protons.

Cross sections for the two slow-neutron reactions are 1.76×10^{-24} cm^2 for the $N^{14}(np)C^{14}$ reaction and 3.13×10^{-25} cm^2 for the $H^1(n\gamma)$ D^2 reaction, both at a velocity of 2.2×10^5 cm/sec for the capture by hydrogen. The cross section in each case depends on $1/v$, where v is the neutron velocity.

The fast-neutron recoil cross section with hydrogen is 1.5×10^{-23} cm^2 for neutrons of about 200 kev and 5×10^{-24} cm^2 for neutrons of 1-Mev energy.

10–5 Dosimetry. After the foregoing very brief account of the nature of the action of fast particles, electromagnetic radiation, and neutrons, the reader may well wonder how it is possible to make any quantitative estimate of the amount and character of any ionizing radiation. The answer is that the technique is indeed complex. The art of such measurement, called *dosimetry*, is well developed but requires considerable skill. Long treatises on the subject exist, yet each year sees more useful material added to the catalog of technique. Fortunately, approximate dosimetry is easy to apply in many cases, otherwise the subject of quantitative radiobiology would advance very slowly.

The standard method of operation is to find some suitable effect of radiation which is easy to measure, and which responds linearly, or in a simple manner, to the dose, and then to rely on a measurement of that effect plus a separately done calibration. Examples of such effects are:

(1) Elapsed time in a standard position for the case of a radioactive source such as radium or cobalt.

(2) The current and time at a known voltage on an x-ray machine, the irradiation being done at a fixed distance from the target of the machine.

(3) The ionization produced in a standard type of ionization chamber located at the point of irradiation and exposed for a known time.

(4) The actual current for a known time in the case of primary charged particles such as fast electrons or deuterons.

(5) The amount of ferrous iron oxidized to ferric iron in a standard solution.

(6) The amount of virus, or enzyme, inactivated by a given exposure.

(7) The amount of current flow permitted in a crystal of cadmium sulfide exposed to the radiation.

(8) The number of counts of a Geiger counter placed in a definite location with respect to the irradiation source.

(9) The number of neutron-induced recoil tracks in a photographic emulsion.

(10) The current in an ionization chamber filled with $B^{10}F_3$ and exposed to a beam of slow neutrons.

The above is by no means an exhaustive list, but it gives the reader some idea of the various means available. One of the commonest methods used, in view of the fact that 250-kv x-ray machines are also rather commonplace, is the Victoreen thimble ionization chamber and electrometer. This very convenient instrument consists of an ionization chamber, comprising an insulated rod ending in an air space, bounded by a carefully chosen and shaped plastic, one surface of which is conducting. The insulated rod is charged by some means (sometimes by a rather frustrating frictional charger), and then carried over to the irradiation zone where it is irradiated for a known time. The ionization current causes the rod to discharge to a value dependent on the amount of ionization, and by reading the voltage on an electrometer, the operator can measure the amount of radiation received. Usually the electrometer is calibrated directly in roentgens. A subsequent calibration of the meter against a standard source of radiation enables the whole measurement to be made to about 2% or so. For most biological purposes this is adequate.

The reduction of the physically, or chemically, made measurement to numbers suitable for quantitative estimates of biological action is a second step that has to be taken. It is by no means easy to complete in a rigorous way but, again, can be handled approximately with fair ease.

The process can be seen most simply for the case of bombardment by fast electrons. The dose can be measured physically, simply by measuring the electron-beam current, the time, and the area of exposure. We then know the total number of electrons traversing one square centimeter. If the velocity of the electrons is known, and if the atomic composition and density of the material irradiated is known, then application of the energy-loss formula, Eq. (10–1), together with the Bragg additive law, enables the energy loss per centimeter to be calculated. Since the area is one square centimeter, we now know the energy loss per unit volume. This is the best starting point for any quantitative analysis of biological action. For example, if we need to know the number of primary ionizations, or clusters of ionization, we can use the value of 110 ev per primary ionization, and dividing the energy loss per cubic centimeter (in electron volts) by 110, we get the number of primary ionizations per unit volume, a value we designate later by I.

For gamma rays, x-rays, and neutrons, the process is more complicated, and may become so complicated that accurate radiation studies may be impossibly hard. It is first necessary to estimate the amount of photon energy absorbed, or neutron energy absorbed, and then estimate how it is distributed. By this last we mean how many photoelectrons and of what energy, and how many Compton recoils and of what energy; or, for neutrons, how many hydrogen recoils and their energy, how many gamma rays produced and their fate, and so on. For gamma rays an estimate has been made that one roentgen releases 93 ergs per gram of "tissue," tissue being material of average biological atomic content and density unity. Even after the above estimates have been made there still remain some uncertainties. For example, low-voltage x-rays produce their energy loss in rapidly ionizing slow electrons. Thus it would not be safe to assume that the energy loss is uniformly distributed unless the grouping of energy along these tracks is duly considered. In a very important study (Ref. 1), D. E. Lea has treated and tabulated a variety of cases of energy loss and ionization distribution. The reader who wishes to go further in this subject is referred to his book and to the other reference material given at the end of the chapter.

After the somewhat disquieting note of the previous paragraph, we should point out that selection of the type of radiation is now much more easy and inexpensive than it was 20 years ago. Thus irradiation by fast electrons, or by heavy fast charged particles is quite possible, and many of the complexities mentioned above do not exist in these cases. Also, sources of Co^{60} are now widely available, and the 1.1-Mev gamma rays they emit cause effects which are predominantly due to fast electrons and so can be analyzed relatively confidently. Reasonably accurate and convenient irradiation and subsequent analysis is therefore quite practical, and certainly as easy and inexpensive as ultracentrifugation or electronmicroscopy.

10–6 Action of ionizing radiation on molecular systems. The first effect of ionizing radiation is predominantly to *ionize*. Some excitation also occurs, but it is probably less frequent than ionization and is responsible for only a small fraction of the energy lost by the flying particle. This is immediately apparent on looking at a cyclotron beam in air (using suitable mirrors). A beam of 10-Mev deuterons of intensity 10 microamps is dissipating 100 watts in around 1 meter. Its light intensity is far below that of a 100-watt glow discharge. Therefore, to a first and good approximation, we can follow up the ionization to see what its ultimate molecular effects will be.

In a small molecule, such as an amino acid or an alcohol, the effect of ionization is to cause a rupture, which is probably nearly random in character. If the yield of fragmented substances is measured, the number of a particular class of fragment produced per 100 ev of energy absorbed (the G-value of radiation chemistry) can be measured. This usually runs to about unity, with variations from 0.1 to 4 or so. Although in some experimental systems chain reactions are possible and high G-values result, cells and biological molecules do not seem to be systems where chain reactions are possible. The initially produced fragments are generally reactive. In experimental systems of great homogeneity, they may react with one another. In biology they are more likely to react with other molecules in the cell.

An important small molecule is water. A great deal of study has been given to the action of ionizing radiation on water. The discovery that irradiated water could produce chemical action was made by H. Fricke in 1927. He suggested that water became "activated," a description that is still probably the most adequate. Nowadays effects on water are described in terms of free radicals, which are secondary products of the first act of ionization, possibly according to the following scheme:

$$H_2O \xrightarrow{\ \sim\!\sim\!\sim\ } H_2O^+ + e^- \qquad \text{(the first ionization process)}.$$

There then result the further reactions

$$H_2O^+ \rightarrow OH + H^+,$$

$$e^- + H_2O \rightarrow OH^- + H.$$

The ions present promptly cause orientation of the polar molecules of water and become *solvated*, in which condition they are normal ions of H^+ and OH^- in such small concentration as to be of no real concern. The H and OH radicals are more important. They will ultimately recombine with a half-life of 2×10^{-6} sec (in ordinary water), or they can react with one another to form H_2 or H_2O_2. In addition, if oxygen is present in solution, the formation of HO_2, of half-life about $\frac{1}{10}$ sec, is possible.

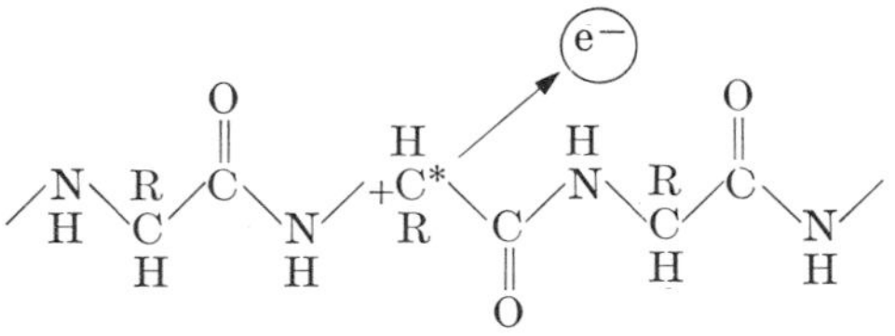

FIG. 10–5. Representation of an ionization at a point in a polypeptide chain.

Numerical values regarding the concentrations of these chemical agents are hard to give. The concentration of free H and OH radicals around a primary ionization in pure water is in the vicinity of $10^{-5}\ M$. The concentration of H_2O_2 produced by 1-Mev electrons was measured by Ebert and Boag to be around $1.5 \times 10^{-9}\ M$.

All the products of radiation action on small molecules stand a chance of diffusing, and since most cells are quite small physical systems, this diffusion may play a very important part.

We now turn to large molecules, known to be of major importance in living systems. Here a somewhat different situation is found. In a large molecule, of molecular weight in excess of 100,000, there are of the order of 10,000 chemical bonds. Therefore its structure is more analogous to that of a small crystal than to the structure of a single, simple molecule. The consequence is that an ionization inside such a large structure need not necessarily cause rupture, with an attendant separation into two. Studies to be described in the next section, however, indicate that when energy releases exceeding about 100 ev take place in such a molecule, it loses its biological function. Let us see how this can happen.

Consider a polypeptide chain, as shown in Fig. 10–5, and note that the whole chain is covalently bonded. This covalent bond is due to the exchange of an electron between two adjacent atoms. Suppose that a carbon atom, as indicated by the asterisk in the figure, becomes ionized and loses an electron. This is the electron which binds it to its neighbor. In a small molecule this event would cause disruption. In a large molecule the integrity of the whole structure can be expected to hold the atom in place, at least for a fraction of a second. The carbon atom is accordingly positively charged, as indicated in the figure. Because of this charge there is a strong tendency for an electron from a neighboring atom to move over to settle around the carbon atom. If this happens, there will result a migration of the positive charge to, say, the nitrogen. However, it has not ceased its restless existence, and can move on to still the next carbon, or can return, or can go into a side-chain. All these processes take place with the speed of one electronic traversal of an atom, a time of the order of 10^{-15} sec. This type of "random walk" will result in the positive charge having moved to every location available in the chain within

10^{-12} sec. If, because of weakness in one or more of the bonds, the chain can take up an alternative configuration, the opportunity to do so will arrive as the result of the migrating positive charge. We would not expect there to be only one way of producing an incorrectly bonded molecule, and there is abundant evidence that several ways have been found in experiment. The important point is that there is an excellent opportunity for migration of this particular class of excitation energy along covalently bonded chains, while energy transfer to regions outside the confines of the molecule (or if you prefer, small crystal) is not nearly so favored.

The suggestion that small molecular regions might trap energy in the way just described was made by Dessauer in 1923. His description of the process is not in quite the terms used above; instead, he used the phrase "point heat." Nevertheless, there is no doubt that he intended to convey the same idea of a favored migration inside a large molecule, and his publication* must be regarded as a major advance at a very early stage.

In our account we have not mentioned the released electron. This will very soon be brought to rest, and may, of course, also ionize in its own right. Once it is caught by an atom it will perform something like the same bond-breaking role as the positive atom, and migration will again occur. In a very short time, of the order of 10^{-12} sec, the two charges will recombine, with a considerable local excitation. This energy will then transfer from one form of excitation to another until it becomes the vibrational energy associated with heat. In this form of excitation energy it is quite able to go from one molecule to another, and so the time of "holdup" within the large molecule is over.

For the moment we can leave the question of the way in which the molecule can lose its precise integrity and consider some experimental results which bear on the whole process.

10–7 Experimental results of bombarding large biological molecules.
When samples of virus, bacteria, or enzymes are exposed to the action of x-rays, gamma rays, deuterons, etc., one very commonly observed experimental result is that the logarithm of the "survival ratio" is proportional to the "dose." To make this somewhat heavily radiological statement have a precise meaning we can describe a simple experiment.

Suppose we take a simple enzyme, invertase. A solution of this is made, a small amount pipetted onto a series of cover slips, and allowed to dry. Two are chosen for controls, while the remainder are placed in the line of a beam of ionizing radiation. A deuteron beam from a cyclotron is excellent. The various samples are then given varying exposures, measured

---

* H. Dessauer, *Zeit. für Phys.* **20**, 288 (1923).

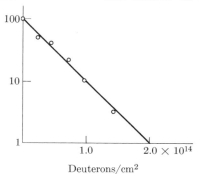

Deuterons/cm^2

FIG. 10–6. The inactivation of the enzymatic ability of an invertase preparation under deuteron bombardment, as observed by Dr. W. F. Powell.

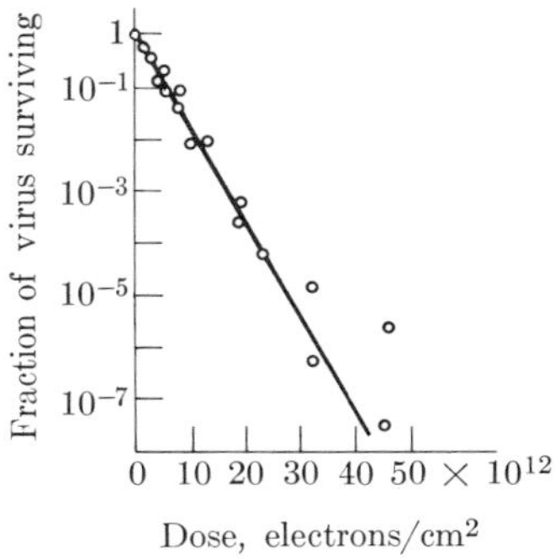

Dose, electrons/cm^2

FIG. 10–7. The inactivation of T1 bacteriophage by 2-Mev electrons, as observed by Dr. D. J. Fluke. The logarithmic inactivation relation is obeyed over a very wide range.

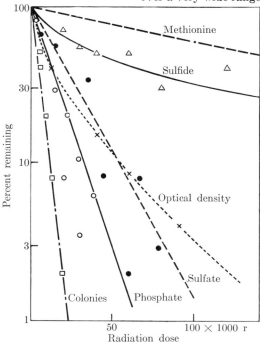

FIG. 10–8. The effect of x-rays on several properties of a bacterium, *E. coli*. [Data due to Jane Kennedy and Dr. E. S. Kempner.] The various properties are: colony formation, which is the most sensitive to the radiation; growth, as measured by optical density, giving a curved line; uptake of phosphate and sulfate, having rather high sensitivity and a logarithmic response; uptake of sulfide, much less sensitive and not logarithmic; and the uptake of methionine, which is markedly less sensitive than the other properties.

in terms of numbers of deuterons per cm^2 of the aperture of the beam. When x-rays are used, the number of roentgens on each sample is varied. The enzyme activity is then measured, and the ratio of the activity after bombardment to that of the controls is found. This is the *survival ratio*. It is found that the ratio (n/n_0), if plotted on a logarithmic scale, gives a straight-line relationship with the dose, measured appropriately as described. The results of such a bombardment of invertase are shown in Fig. 10–6. The manner of plotting in the figure shows that the amount remaining is related to the dose by the equation

$$\ln \frac{n}{n_0} = - \text{ (constant) (dose).}$$

Several possible processes of inactivation can give this result. For example, heating a virus for various lengths of time at the same temperature gives rise to a similar relation, as described in Section 3–5. Such processes can conveniently be interpreted by supposing that some critical point, a special bond for example, is destroyed in a random manner. If the resulting activity depends linearly on the number of critical bonds left, then the above result can be expected.

To illustrate some of the characteristic effects of ionizing radiation we give three examples of the results of irradiating biological substances. The first, Fig. 10–7, shows the effect of fast electrons on a bacteriophage, T1, of the *E. coli* system, indicating that over a range of more than a million the above relation holds.

The second example, Fig. 10–8, shows a variety of effects of ionizing radiation on *E. coli* bacteria. In the figure we see first the effect of x-rays on the ability of the irradiated culture to form colonies when plated on nutrient agar. The bacteria are very sensitive, and lose the ability very easily. The second method of observing bacterial growth, by observing the turbidity of the culture, shows that the bacteria which do not readily form colonies nevertheless have considerable ability to grow. Microscopic examination shows that in place of division, long filaments are formed. Moreover, the loss of this function does not seem to obey the simple logarithmic relationship we have described. This may well be because the measurement does not express the effect, or it may have biological significance. When biochemical metabolic processes are studied, the ability to incorporate radioactive phosphate is found to be very sensitive to radiation, while the ability to incorporate sulfate is less so, but still sensitive. If the radioactive sulfur is provided as sulfide, the sensitivity is definitely less than was found for sulfate. At a still greater extreme, Fig. 10–8 includes the initial part of a line showing the loss of ability to incorporate one labeled amino acid, methionine. Evidently quite heavy irradiation is needed to remove some kind of uptake of an amino acid. It is thus obvious that a bacterium does not act toward ionizing radiation as a single molecule, but has quite different reactions, depending on the circumstances of study. This must never be forgotten in reasoning about radiation action.

A third example of the result of irradiating biological substances would be provided by bombarding small *colonies* of bacteria. The effect of radiation on the subsequent growth of these colonies is such that they develop as though no irradiation had occurred, until rather suddenly the number of colonies starts to diminish. The reason is that until *all* the members of a small colony are inactivated, the regrowth of the colony is not stopped. Thus there is a delay of the apparent effect of radiation until only single viable cells exist in each colony, after which the *coup de grace* is given in the usual way.

It is in place now to consider some kind of theoretical analysis of these types of response curves.

10–8 Target theory. The idea of a critical point that we mentioned in the previous section is usually applied as a *target theory*, devised by Dessauer, Crowther, Condon, and Terrill and enlarged on by many others, notably Lea, and more recently Zirkle and Tobias. According to this theory, a "target," or sensitive region, of volume V finds itself in a bombarded region in which I inactivating events are randomly distributed per unit volume. Although the major concepts of this line of reasoning have been given in Section 9–12, we repeat the reasoning here so as to express the findings in terms suitable for ionizing radiation. The simplest form of the theory examines the "total escape" probability and suggests that survival only occurs if ionization has not occurred in the target molecule.

The average number of "hits" made by these ionizing events is then the product of the sensitive volume times the inactivating events per unit volume, or VI. If we now consider the probability of a certain number, n, of hits being acquired by the volume V, the Poisson formula is seen to be applicable. If $P(n)$ is the required probability, then we have

$$P(n) = \frac{e^{-IV}(IV)^n}{n!}.$$

(10–5)

If $n = 0$, the sensitive volume has not encountered any ionization and so will have certainly survived. For this to happen (bearing in mind that $0! = 1$), $p(0) = e^{-VI}$ so that the probability of escape, which is measured experimentally by the survival ratio, is

$$N/N_0 = e^{-IV}$$

or

$$\ln N/N_0 = -IV,$$

(10–6)

which is of the form already observed experimentally and shown in Fig. 10–5. It remains only to re-express the "dose" in terms equivalent to inactivating events per unit volume. Then the value of V can be found. Thus when the simple logarithmic type of inactivation is observed, Eq. (10–6) can be applied, and the quantities derived from its use may prove to have some significance.

In 1944, Lea, Smith, Holmes, and Markham applied Eq. (10–6) to the x-ray inactivation of ribonuclease and myosin. On the assumption that a single ionization inactivates, but that these are grouped in three's (as found by C. T. R. Wilson), they obtained figures for V in each case. Such a volume can conveniently be re-expressed as a "molecular weight," a more familiar term. The molecular weight is the mass of 6.03×10^{23} particles. If the density of the two proteins above is taken as 1.3, the molecular weight M is then

$$M = V \times 1.3 \times 6.03 \times 10^{23}.$$

The above workers found 30,000 and 230,000 respectively for the molecular weights of ribonuclease and myosin. These are in the right region for the true molecular weights. Follow-up work on this by a group at Yale (Pollard, Forro, Setlow, Powell, and Hutchinson) has led to the idea that the value of V for enzymes and antigens irradiated dry and *in vacuo* is actually closely related to either the whole molecule or some subunit or polymer of it. This will be discussed in Section 10–11; in the meantime, a little more elaboration of target theory can be given.

Let us use the line of reasoning developed above and in Section 9–12. If for survival to cease n hits rather than a single hit are necessary (a "multihit" case), then the probability of survival is given by

$$P(0) + P(1) + P(2) \ldots P(n - 1),$$

corresponding to the various possibilities up to n. This leads to a survival ratio of

$$\frac{N}{N_0} = e^{-IV}\left[1 + IV + \frac{(IV)^2}{2} + \frac{(IV)^3}{3!} + \cdots + \frac{(IV)^{n-1}}{(n-1)!}\right],$$

or more compactly,

$$\frac{N}{N_0} = e^{-IV} \sum_0^{n-1} \frac{(IV)^k}{k!}. \tag{10–7}$$

A mathematical expert would see with a glance at Eq. (10–7) that the series in the summation is a truncated version of e^{+IV} stopped at a finite number of terms. Since e^{-IV} is not stopped short, the inevitable result is that when IV becomes large the term in e^{-IV} predominates. The final slope fits the simple relation $N/N_0 = e^{-IV}$ and can be calculated. This is the case of a single, insensitive target.

Suppose, however, that we have a population of targets, m in number. If it is required that *all* must be hit to prevent a colony from growing (the case for yeast, or bacteria, or virus clumps, and of importance in radiation sterilization), then we can argue that the probability of being hit is unity (the probability of all things) less the probability of *survival*, which gives us

$$P \text{ (hit)} = 1 - e^{-IV} \sum_0^{n-1} \frac{(IV)^k}{k!}.$$

If there are p to be hit, the probability that p will be inactivated is then $[P \text{ (hit)}]^p$ or

$$\text{Probability of inactivating } p = \left[1 - e^{-IV} \sum_0^{n-1} \frac{(IV)^k}{k!} \right]^p.$$

Since we are interested in survival, which is often easiest to measure (not always, since mutations are not "survivals"), the probability that one or more will survive is the probability of all events (unity) less the probability of inactivating p. This is

$$\frac{N}{N_0} = 1 - \left[1 - e^{-IV} \sum_0^{n-1} \frac{(IV)^k}{k!} \right]^p. \tag{10-8}$$

This expression can be used in the study of populations. For a single hit case, it reduces to

$$\frac{N}{N_0} = 1 - (1 - e^{-IV})^p. \tag{10-9}$$

All these relations have their counterpart in action by ultraviolet light, and the reader will see, by referring to Section 9–12, that we have effectively already derived Eq. (10–9).

10–9 Variable linear energy transfer. Before returning to the subject of the action of ionizing radiation on large molecules, let us take up one additional phase of bombardment, namely the use of variable ionization density along the path of the ionizing particle. This is often referred to as variable linear energy transfer, sometimes shortened to "LET." Bombardment in this way adds a very powerful and useful second dimension to radiation studies. The method of analysis of such molecular studies which appeals to the authors as the most direct is the following.

We consider that a heavy ionizing particle cuts a dense swath of ionization, and as a first approximation the swath is considered as infinitely dense. The tracks are, however, still randomly distributed in *area*. So, to match the previous treatment of random bombardment, we endow the sensitive region with an *area*, S, called by analogy with other cases in atomic and nuclear physics a *cross section*. Now, if the dose is measured in an appropriate relation to area (no longer to volume) as the average number of particles per unit area, say D, then SD is the average number of traversals made by inactivating particles. As before, the probability $P(n)$ of n traversals is

$$P(n) = \frac{e^{-SD}(SD)^n}{n!}.$$

If *one* passage suffices, the probability $P(0)$ of no passage is accordingly $P(0) = e^{-SD}$, and therefore the survival ratio is given by

$$\frac{N}{N_0} = e^{-SD} \qquad \text{or} \qquad \ln \frac{N}{N_0} = -SD.$$

In this way a value for the cross section can be found. It must be pointed out that both V, the inactivation volume, and S, the cross-sectional area,

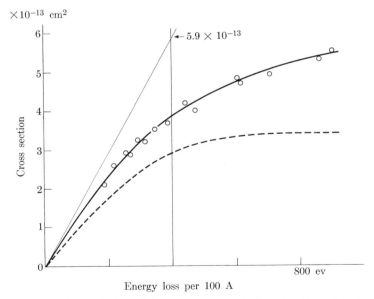

$\times 10^{-13}$ cm^2

$\leftarrow 5.9 \times 10^{-13}$

Cross section

800 ev

Energy loss per 100 A

FIG. 10–9. The variation of the cross section for inactivation of an invertase preparation as the energy of the bombarding beam of deuterons is lessened, thus increasing the rate of energy loss to the invertase.

are constructs of a theory. It remains for active comparison with known molecular sizes to establish that they have any physical significance.

If we suppose that the particle is very densely ionizing and that no energy transfer from outside can get into a molecule, then S should be the cross section of the molecule itself. It is possible, by varying the energy of the particle, to show that the inactivation cross section, in some cases, rises and flattens as the linear energy transfer increases. An example of this is invertase, which follows the type of relation shown in Fig. 10–9, where it can be seen that the cross section increases but appears to be tending toward a maximum. This maximum is related to the geometrical cross section of the sensitive unit of the molecule, and expresses the fact that energy beyond that needed to inactivate will do no further damage. The maximum is not definite because energy is lost away from the track of the particle, largely due to long-range secondary electrons (delta rays) whose contribution to the inactivation somewhat obscures the true maximum. The dashed line shows a correction for the effect of these secondary electrons which is simple, but approximate, and is described in Section 10–10.

A theoretical relation for the solid curve of Fig. 10–9 can be deduced by assuming that S is determined by the probability that, in a molecule of thickness x, a particle may traverse the molecule but still may not produce an ionization. Suppose that the average number of primary ionizations in a thickness x is px, where p is the average number of primary ionizations per unit length, a way of setting a number to correspond to the LET. Then the probability $P(y)$ of y such ionizations is

$$P(y) = \frac{e^{-px}(px)^y}{y!}.$$

As before, we can say that the molecule is not damaged only in the case where no ionization occurs. For this we have

$$P(0) = e^{-px}.$$

Thus the probability that *at least one* primary ionization occurs is the probability of all events (unity) less the probability of no ionization, or $1 - e^{-px}$. The efficiency of a particle which has been assumed to a first approximation as ionizing in an infinitely dense swath is then $1 - e^{-px}$, and we may put

$$S = S_0(1 - e^{-px}), \qquad (10\text{–}10)$$

where S_0 is the "true" cross section for infinitely dense ionizing swaths and S is the measured cross section. Note that a complete curve for S versus p enables us to calculate x. This is the valuable added dimension.

10–10 Effect of secondary electrons, or delta rays. If it were true that for heavy particles such as deuterons, protons, or alpha particles we had ionization confined accurately to the particle track, then bombardment by such particles would be a most powerful method of studying biological systems because they would be line probes of varying effectiveness, as outlined in the last paragraph. Unfortunately such ionization is only a bare majority, if that, of the total ionization produced by the particle. A considerable fraction of the energy is lost as rather long-range secondary electrons, known as *delta rays*, or *spurs*. Since there is no reason why a set of randomly arranged molecules should not encounter such ionization, clearly it can be ignored only in a very first approximation. Methods for allowing for the effect of this kind of ionization are given by Lea (Ref. 1). There is some uncertainty regarding the ranges of slow electrons, and more recent direct measurements of electron ranges (Table 10–4), made by M. Davis,* tend to diminish somewhat the corrections Lea gives.

TABLE 10–4

RANGES OF SLOW ELECTRONS IN PROTEIN

Electron energy, ev	Range, A
300	50
600	90
900	230
1200	400
1500	620
2000	1130

We can use Eqs. (10–1) and (10–3) to derive a correction to a first approximation, as follows. Table 10–4 gives some figures for the *ranges of*, or distances traversed by, electrons of various energies in enzymes. Consulting the table, we first decide what energy track will lie outside the target. Thus if the target is a virus of radius 200 A, an energy of 1000 ev would be necessary to produce ionization outside the virus if the particle track were down the center of the virus. For a molecule of an enzyme, a much smaller energy would suffice. Let us call this limiting energy E. Using the notation of Eq. (10–3) we can now calculate the amount of energy lost in secondary electrons whose energy ranges between E and the

* *Phys. Rev.* **94,** 243 (1954).

maximum permitted by the conservation of energy and momentum, namely $2mv^2$. Then, dividing by the average energy per primary ionization, we can find the number of primary ionizations per centimeter of track which are produced in these relatively long-range secondaries.

Since these secondaries are spread out, and they themselves scatter, the ionization produced in this way can be thought of as random in volume and used to give an estimate of the amount of inactivation in a target of volume V, just as before. This can then be added to the in-activation due to the swath of dense ionization to give a correction to the cross section.

Applying Eq. (10–3), we find for E_d, the energy loss per centimeter-path per fast particle, in secondaries, the value

$$
E_d = \int_E^{2mv^2} W d\left(\frac{dN}{dx}\right) = \frac{2\pi e^4 z^2 NZ}{mv^2} \int_E^{2mv^2} \frac{dW}{W}
$$

$$
= \frac{2\pi e^4 z^2 NZ}{mv^2} \ln \frac{2mv^2}{E} \text{ per cm-path.} \qquad (10\text{–}11)
$$

If E_p is the energy loss per primary ionization (110 ev), then each deuteron contributes a number E_d/E_p of primary ionizations per centimeter, or if there are D deuterons per cm^2, a value of $D \cdot E_d/E_p$ of primary ionizations per unit volume, which is the equivalent of a value for I in Eq. (10–6). We have, then, if n/n_0 is the survival ratio,

$$
\ln \frac{n}{n_0} = -SD - VI = SD - VD \frac{E_d}{E_p}
$$

$$
= -D\left(S + V \frac{E_d}{E_p}\right).
$$

Thus if we have an estimate of V, the volume of the target, we can estimate what fraction of the observed inactivation is due to the lines of dense ionization and what fraction is due to the secondaries.

The merit of the above reasoning lies not so much in its ability to correct as in the fact that Eq. (10–11) shows the factors at work. A doubly charged particle will have a correction term four times as large as a singly charged particle of the same velocity. As the particle slows down, the correction becomes greater, but not quite inversely with energy because the term in the logarithm tends to diminish the effect somewhat. The larger the target, the greater the correction in absolute terms. But because the limiting energy E is greater for a large target, the correction may well be relatively not so important if S is large. The dashed line on Fig. 10–9 shows the application of the correction for a volume of 1.5×10^{-19} cm^3 and a value of E of 400 ev.

10–11 Features of the radiation sensitivity of large molecules. If we are to take the approach of molecular biophysics, it is very important to understand the precise nature of the effect of ionizing radiation on the large biological molecules. Studies such as those described in Section 10–7 have been carried out on a considerable variety of enzymes, antigens, nucleic acids, and viruses, and some pattern of explanation is beginning to develop. In the same spirit as in Chapter 9, we can first describe some of the results that seem to us to be established, and then attempt to fit them to the pattern of explanation.

(1) A release of between one and four ionizations inactivates a volume which is very close to that of one molecular unit.

(2) Lowering the temperature will diminish the inactivation volume by about a factor of two. Raising it will increase the volume by as much as a factor of three, with the increase taking place most sharply just below the temperature at which thermal inactivation becomes appreciable.

(3) The physical state of the molecule, with regard to adsorption of ions or other molecules onto it, may diminish, or even increase, its sensitivity.

(4) Bombardment in the presence of oxygen, even though the enzyme may be dry, may have an increased effectiveness.

(5) A bombardment which does not inactivate can still leave a modified molecule, partially damaged, in its wake.

(6) The best evidence indicates that there is no observable radiation damage until the molecule encounters the process of solution.

In Section 10–6 we pointed out that the locale of a positive charge produced by ionization could wander, particularly if the molecule is covalently bonded. Some very important studies by Gordy, Ard, and Shields employing microwave spectroscopy have shown that irradiated proteins develop paramagnetic resonances, due to unpaired electrons, which are characteristic of one or two of the amino acids and of special linkages. For example, the presence of the $—CH_2—S^+—S—CH_2—$ linkage can be seen in either irradiated cystine or irradiated protein. Gordy points out that such a linkage is actually a stronger bonding as far as physical forces are concerned. It may well be very reactive chemically, however, especially with water or oxygen. The pattern of explanation that develops is then as follows. The macromolecule, which is ionized randomly in its structure, is so bonded that the effect of the ionization can wander until it reaches one of a few bondings that are chemically vulnerable, probably mainly to water. The chemical action, which takes place at what might be called the radiological lesion, then produces an alteration in the molecule which may or may not express itself in biological change. The evidence would seem to be that in most cases the chemical action does produce a biological effect.

The process we have described is very likely to be close to the truth for protein. For nucleic acid we are not able to be so assertive. Probably the effect of radiation is either to break the chain, again as the result of a chemical action with water, or else to produce a cross linking with more neighboring nucleic acid. As it stands now, the evidence is that both kinds of nucleic acid must be fully intact in rather large units in order to function biologically, and so again the effect of radiation is drastic, though approximately confined to that particular molecular unit.

We are almost completely lacking in knowledge of radiation action on polysaccharides. Work needs to be done in that field.

10–12 Molecular effects by agents that diffuse. What we have understood by radiation action so far is best exemplified by effects in the dry state. However, some of the products of radiation action on water, plus many products of action on small molecules and combinations of them, can diffuse within the cell. The part they play in the biological action of radiation is still, unfortunately, largely unknown. Nevertheless some indications of how they act can be obtained, which we shall present in this section.

Inactivation of enzymes in solution. The inactivation of enzymes in solution by x-rays was observed quite early by Hussey and Thompson and by Northrop. That the inactivation was due to migrating agents was first realized by Dale in 1940. A variety of enzymes have since been studied, notably by Dale, Barron, Ross, and Hutchinson and by Augenstine. The inactivation proceeds according to the familiar logarithmic relation, but the "inactivation volume" is not related in any way to the molecular size, being far too great. One significant way to analyze this type of experiment is in terms of the amount of enzyme inactivated for

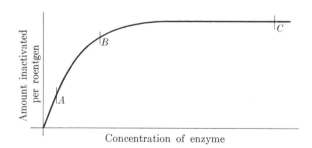

Fig. 10–10. The amount of enzyme inactivated per roentgen in dilute solution plotted against the enzyme concentration. At *A* the molecules of enzyme are so spaced that the regions of high radical concentration near the ionizations may not include an enzyme molecule. At *B* an enzyme molecule is likely to be found; at *C* there is a great preponderance of enzyme and every radical is used.

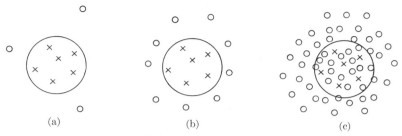

$\times$ = Active agents, probably radicals
$\bigcirc$ = Molecules of enzyme

FIG. 10–11. A pictorial representation of the effect of increasing the concentration of enzymes in the face of active agents which have a tendency to recombine or to be removed and consequently have a short half-life. Only in case (c) are the active agents used with full efficiency.

a given dose as a function of the concentration of the enzyme. A curve of the form shown in Fig. 10–10 is obtained. The absolute yield increases in a $1 - e^{-x}$ manner until a plateau is attained. The reason for this increase can be seen in Fig. 10–11, where the large circles denote the spheres within which active agents (probably free radicals) exist before they are removed as a result of either recombination or combination with some substance which is not enzyme.

From studies of the inactivation of monolayers of catalase and bovine serum albumin, where the geometry for diffusion calculations is simple, Smith* has estimated that in moderately pure water the active agents have a half-life of 2×10^{-6} sec. Such a value explains the kind of curve found for the yield in Fig. 10–10. Very probably the true recombination half-life of radicals produced in very pure water is longer. Using intense pulsed sources of electrons, Hutchinson† estimated a half-life of 1.6×10^{-5} sec. Almost certainly the half-life of a radical in a cell is determined by the close proximity of many kinds of reactive molecules and is in the neighborhood of 10^{-9} sec.

The yield along the plateau of the curve in Fig. 10–10 can be measured, and the number of enzyme molecules inactivated per 33 ev of radiation energy can be calculated. In Table 10–5, due to Hutchinson, we give such values.

Nucleic acid in solution. Many studies of the effect of ionizing radiation on the physical properties, such as viscosity, of nucleic acid have been reported. Recently the discovery that the pneumoccus transforming principle is a pure DNA has made it possible to study the action of radia-

---

* *Arch. Biochem. and Biophys.* **50,** 322 (1954).
† *Radiation Research* **9,** 13 (1958).

TABLE 10–5

TYPICAL IONIC YIELDS FOR ENZYMES IN DILUTE SOLUTION

Enzyme	Yield, molecules/33 ev	Ref.
Invertase	0.05	a
Catalase	0.03	b
Cytochrome C	0.10	c
Ribonuclease	0.48	d
Alcohol dehydrogenase	0.93	b
Coenzyme A	0.90	d

(a) F. DeFilippes, unpublished data.
(b) E. S. G. Barron, *Ann. N.Y. Acad. Sci.* **59**, 578 (1955).
(c) H. Rajewsky, G. Gerber, and H. Pauly, *Adv. in Radiobiology.* Oliver and Boyd, London, 1957, p. 25.
(d) F. Hutchinson and D. A. Ross, *Radiation Research* **10**, 477 (1959).

tion on it in solution. The first results of this kind of study were obtained by Ephrussi-Taylor and Latarjet, with preparations bombarded in the presence of yeast extract. They concluded that the transforming principle is very sensitive to the "indirect effect" but gave no numerical figure for the G-value, or yield per 100 ev. Later studies made by Guild and DeFilippes showed that as the preparations were more and more carefully purified the G-value increased until it reached the very high value of 0.6 for the inactivation of a molecule assumed to have a molecular weight of 10^6. Nucleic acid is thus a vulnerable molecule, regardless of whether the ionization occurs in the molecule itself or energy is brought to it by diffusion from elsewhere in the solution.

10–13 Protective action against diffusing agents. It is easy to see that inactivation by diffusing agents can be interfered with. If the conditions of the experiment are such that the action being measured is due to a particular diffusing agent, then quite simple means of "protection" can be used. Thus a reaction due to hydrogen peroxide can be greatly diminished by catalase. Reactions due to oxidizing radicals can be diminished by cysteine, thiourea, or glutathione. Any biologically inert material exerts a protective action so long as it will chemically react with the diffusing agents. The protective action of broth on virus preparations was discovered in 1941 by Luria and Exner and Friedewald and Anderson. Dale discovered protective action on enzymes. Not nearly enough accurate measurements are available to describe protective action. As far

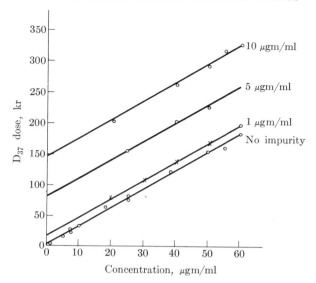

Fig. 10–12. The inactivation of methylene blue in distilled water to which varying amounts of thiourea have been added. The protective effect of the thiourea can be seen. Taken from Ross and Hutchinson.

as the biological action of radiation is concerned, it is probably not unreasonable to consider that the area exposed by an organic molecule is a rough measure of its protective action. The basis for a theoretical treatment and of a valuable numerical tabulation was begun by Lea, and data by Dale afford a valuable start in this direction.

It should, in principle, be possible to make measurements which would characterize protective action numerically. Work by Ross and Hutchinson, and by Hutchinson, is aimed in this direction, and a somewhat complementary approach has been taken by Augenstine. The effect of irradiating methylene blue in distilled water with varying amounts of thiourea present is shown in Fig. 10–12. It can be seen that the addition of 10 micrograms per milliliter of thiourea roughly triples the amount of radiation necessary to produce a given effect.

Quantitative studies can be made to yield a figure for the probability that a diffusing radical which has made a collision with a molecule of solute will react with it so as to be removed from the solution. Hutchinson estimates that for methylene blue, coenzyme A, thiourea, sulfanilamide, invertase, and alcohol dehydrogenase, the probability is nearly equal and approximately 0.5. Radicals are clearly reactive. Augenstine has turned this reactivity into a means of estimating how much of an enzyme molecule is essential for its function. If we take a representative figure for the yield of an enzyme inactivated per 100 ev as 0.4 molecule, and further take the figure of 6 radical pairs per 100 ev released in water, the number of radicals required to inactivate a trypsin molecule is 15. This would indicate that about one fifteenth only of the trypsin molecule is essential for its enzymatic function.

It is quite important to realize that the rather vaguely specified "diffusing agents" about which we have spoken may be quite varied in character. If a protein or a nucleic acid can actually experience contact with 20 or so active radicals without losing its specific activity, it by no means follows that small fragments are not detached without being observed. These fragments may be highly active. Protection against such agents may require quite specific action. A great deal more work is needed before the nature of the family of biologically active products of radiation is understood. Until then, it will not be easy to make predictions regarding radiobiological action.

It is not only action due to diffusing agents which is susceptible to protection. Experiments on the dry irradiation of enzymes and antigens show that the physical combination of two molecules (as, for example, enzyme and substrate or enzyme and inhibitor) can modify their radiation sensitivity. This may play a very important part in altering the sensitivity of a cell at various times.

10–14 The oxygen effect. One of the remarkable, and to some extent surprising, agents which modify radiation action is oxygen when present in the medium surrounding the region where the energy releases take place. The effect was discovered by Thoday and Read for the production of chromosome breaks in *Vicia faba* and confirmed by Giles and Riley for breaks in *Tradescantia*. To state the nature of the phenomenon more clearly, what is observed is a drop in sensitivity of a factor between two and three when oxygen is prevented from being in the medium. The effect has been found in many simpler systems, for example in the inactivation of dry trypsin by Alexander, and it is hard to observe in some rather remarkable cases, notably the action of x-rays on enzymes in dilute solutions. The drop in sensitivity is much less when irradiation by sources of high ion density are used. To make a statement as to the reason for the oxygen effect would be to invite much criticism. We can only remark that the process we have invoked for the inactivation of protein molecules, namely the production of a radiological lesion by the primary ionization, followed by a chemical action, could easily be imagined as influenced by the chemical agents in the medium. An effect similar to that of oxygen has been found for nitric oxide by Howard-Flanders and Jockey. Ebert, Hornsey, and Howard have found that the oxygen effect can be reduced by the inert gases, notably xenon, in a proportion related to their lipid solubility, a fact which suggests that biological membranes may be involved with the oxygen effect. Whatever the reason involved, there is no doubt that the presence of oxygen and its modifying action must be carefully considered in any radiation experiment.

10–15 A theoretical analysis of radiation effects on a cell. Without claiming that the following analysis provides an explanation for the action of ionizing radiation on the cell, we intend to show numerically the inactivating effect of 1000 roentgens on a bacterial cell. The observed action can be compared with these values, and, in addition, the analysis shows what other types of radiation action need to be looked for.

Suppose we consider a bacterial cell of the composition given below. This is 70% water, and has 2.1×10^4 molecules of DNA, 4.2×10^4 of RNA, 4.7×10^6 of protein, 2.5×10^7 lipid, and 1.6×10^7 phospholipid. It has a volume of 2.25×10^{-12} cm^3.

Bearing in mind that one roentgen is equivalent to 6.1×10^{11} primary ions per cubic centimeter, we can rather quickly estimate the damage due to nondiffusing energy releases. Assuming a molecular weight of 10^6 for both kinds of nucleic acid, 100,000 for each protein molecule, and 1000 for each kind of lipid, the volumes of the molecules are 1.1×10^{-18}, 1.28×10^{-19}, and 1.7×10^{-21} cm^3, respectively. We made the point in Section 10–2 that the energy release of 110 ev at an average primary ionization will inactivate any nucleic acid or protein molecule. It seems likely that the much smaller lipid molecule would also lose any specific function it had. So we can say that the probability of inactivation of any one of these molecules is the probability that by chance a primary ionization will occur in the volume of the molecule. For 1000 r this is $6.1 \times 10^{14} \times 1.1 \times 10^{-18}$ for nucleic acid, or 6.7×10^{-4}; for protein it is 7.8×10^{-5}; for lipids, 1.04×10^{-6}.

Comparing these with the numbers of molecules present we see that there will be $2.1 \times 10^4 \times 6.7 \times 10^{-4}$ or 14 molecules of DNA inactivated. There will be 28 of RNA, 3.7×10^2 of protein, 26 of lipid, and 17 of phospholipid.

These figures are remarkably small. Accordingly, a first impression is that unless some other action is present, radiation does very little to the cell.

We can now consider the effect of diffusible agents. It is here that the theoretical analysis becomes very weak, for we do not know what the diffusible agents are, or how many are formed, or how effective they are. In default of this knowledge we can make an approximation by saying that the diffusible agents are the same as in water and that they inactivate quantitatively as if they were in water. Then the only difficult problem is the relative division of the inactivating agents among the cellular molecules. Again, as a first approximation we can divide them according to molecular surface. Taking each nucleic acid molecule as having a length of 2300 A and a diameter of 23 A, the surface area per molecule is 1.67×10^{-11} cm^2. Assuming proteins and lipids to be spherical, the surface areas are 1.22×10^{-12} cm^2 and 5.6×10^{-14} cm^2. The three total areas are then

Nucleic acid, DNA	3.5×10^{-7} cm^2
Nucleic acid, RNA	7.0×10^{-7} cm^2
Protein	5.7×10^{-6} cm^2
Lipid	2.3×10^{-6} cm^2
Small molecules	2.4×10^{-6} cm^2

In a volume of $0.7 \times 2.25 \times 10^{-12}$ cm^3 of water, 10^3 r will release $5.8 \times 10^{14} \times 0.7 \times 2.25 \times 10^{-12}$ or 910 units of 100 ev. Note that this is itself not a large number compared with the number of molecular units in the cell. These will divide, according to our hypothesis, as below.

Nucleic acid, DNA	28
Nucleic acid, RNA	56
Protein	460
Lipids	182
Small molecules	190

We recall that measurements showed that one 100-ev unit inactivated 1.7 molecule of nucleic acid as transforming principle. Using this, the only available figure for the radiation sensitivity of nucleic acid, we calculate that 28×1.7 or 48 molecules of DNA and 96 of RNA are inactivated in this way.

Turning to protein, we see that each unit of 100 ev inactivates on the average 0.5 molecule. Thus 230 protein molecules will be damaged. In default of knowledge about lipids we can assume that 1 unit of 100 ev inactivates one molecule. Putting all these together, we see that the total damage in a cell, based on the best measurements now available, should be as in Table 10–6.

Once again, looking at Table 10–6, it would seem as though the effect of 1000 r on the bacterium should be negligible. However, if it is indeed true that, as McIlwain pointed out, the formation of many essential molecules such as vitamins is due to single enzyme molecules, then we can see that the 600 protein molecules could contain the sole representative of a class of enzyme. Under such circumstances the cell will gradually run out of its supply of, say, some vitamin, and unless this is provided

TABLE 10–6

MOLECULES DAMAGED IN A BACTERIAL CELL BY 1000 ROENTGENS

Type of molecule	Number present	Number damaged due to ionization within the molecule	Number damaged due to agents formed in water	Total
DNA	2.1×10^4	14	48	62
RNA	4.2×10^4	28	96	124
Protein	4.7×10^6	370	230	600
Lipids	4.1×10^7	43	182	225

from outside it will cease to grow and so may ultimately die. Thus the only immediate effect on the cell is a latent one, a block in a production line which shows up when the essential unit becomes short in supply.

What we have said about protein becomes of great significance when we consider that it is likely that protein synthesis depends on nucleic acid. If we remember that a bacterial cell, with a division time of 30 minutes, synthesizes nearly five million protein molecules in that time, we see that each molecule of nucleic acid is indeed busy. If we suppose that the RNA is responsible for the protein synthesis (and the reader with decided views on this will please remember that our interest really lies in *rates* at this stage, not in processes), then each RNA molecule is concerned in the synthesis of 114 protein molecules before division. The fact that 96 have been damaged means that roughly 10,000 protein molecules will not enter the next division at the right time. This is more than 10 times the pure radiation damage.

By the same token, if we recall that nucleic acid itself has to be synthesized, then we can suppose that a part of the DNA is responsible for this, and therefore the damage to 62 DNA molecules may entail a latent damage to of the order of 124 more RNA molecules.

Thus it is possible to see that the biosynthetic processes offer a way by which the really very small effects of radiation can be magnified to give quite serious consequences. These effects are nearly all *delayed*. Indeed, the most striking feature of the biological action of radiation is its delayed character.

In Section 10–6 we asserted that chain reactions are unlikely in living cells. By "chain reaction" we mean a reaction of a chemical type in which the products of one reaction cause a second, and so on. For this to occur the whole medium must be quite homogeneous, otherwise the reaction products encounter nonreactive material. Unless such chain reactions can be demonstrated either in polypeptide bonds, or the base-sugar bonds of nucleic acid, or in the carbon-carbon chains of lipids, there are no regions in the cell with the desired homogeneity. Therefore we feel that chemical, as distinct from biological, chain reactions are not likely.

It is interesting to compare the above discussion with the results of experiment. It is found that 1000 r reduces the number of colony-forming *E. coli* cells from 100% to 80%. Thus only about one cell out of five or so receives sufficient damage to become inviable. If we analyze the events solely in terms of nucleic acid molecules, this can be taken to mean that damaging 189 × 5 or about 1000 nucleic acid molecules will give a unity chance of survival.

By far the most valuable lesson to be learned from studying the biological action of radiation is the clear demonstration it affords of the importance of a limited number of molecules. The analysis we have just given shows that no more than a few hundreds of molecules, *disrupted without total destruction*, can cause measurable action, and indeed may even prevent cellular multiplication. We have made the point many times before and we emphasize it again here.

A discussion by Errera (Ref. 7) is of some interest in considering the above numerical analysis. From a review of 19 enzyme systems for which a study of the effect of radiation has been made, Errera concludes that the only immediate effect of ionizing radiation is on DNA metabolism.

There are some glaring deficiencies in our above analysis, which we will point out. First, we have taken no account of the organization of the molecular structure of the cell. Thus we know that the enzymes RNA-ase and DNA-ase exist in the cell, yet they do not produce their expected enzymatic action on their substrates. Presumably, in many cases either the enzyme or the substrate is so combined as to be inaccessible. Yet we have supposed free accessibility, particularly to diffusible agents. Certainly if the agents which synthesize protein are the RNA-protein granules, the intercombination of the two will produce a change in sensitivity of both. We have disregarded any such effect. The same is true of DNA. Moreover, we have supposed that diffusion is not limited. This, in a cell which is a 25% solution, may not be right. All these factors of uncertainty stand in the way of our understanding of radiation action. Nevertheless, if we resolutely pursue the attempt to make such a theoretical analysis by making measurements on cell-free systems of protein synthesis when they become available and by fixing all the necessary parameters of radiation action, such as distances diffused, molecular sensitivities, and so on, there is clear promise in the method. Limited as it is, the analysis we have given calls attention to the factors at work. They may not be *all* the factors, but even to see the relative effectiveness of some is of value. It is in that spirit that we have written the last few paragraphs.

10–16 The action of ionizing radiation on chromosomes. The discussion in Section 10–15 applies to a bacterial cell, where the apparatus of chromosomes and of mitosis is not so apparent as in many cells. We should therefore include a brief account of the effect of ionizing radiation on chromosomes, a subject which has received a great deal of attention. Unfortunately, no *brief* account is possible. The subject is complex and vast. However, we can mention one or two features of radiation action on chromosomes which are worth a moment's thought. The point should, of course, be made that any damage as serious as a chromosome break almost inevitably results in some kind of damage to the cell.

The physical structure of a chromosome is not known. Possibly it is the task of radiation studies to elucidate it. It seems very likely that chromosomes are multiple threads of nucleoprotein, located in a selected and highly specific environment which makes it possible for the accretion and duplication of the essential chromosome structure itself. Because their physical structure is unknown, it is very hard to interpret the action of ionizing radiation on chromosomes. We can make one or two comments on the essential nature of chromosomes to guide thought on the subject.

The chromosome thread must retain at least the vast majority of its integrity from division to division. If we accept the figure given by Sax,[*] that a chromosome has a diameter of 1000 A, we can consider two aspects of a chromosome "break" quite apart from any radiation studies. The first concerns the layer of water molecules which would form on the two new surfaces of a broken chromosome. In Section 3–4 we pointed out that a free energy change ΔF is given by $-NkT \ln Z$, where Z is the partition function, the "sum over states" $\sum e^{-E_r/kT}$. Now, any water molecules fastened to the surface are not free to rotate. This means that a change of free energy corresponding to the rotational degrees of freedom of two layers of water molecules must have taken place. The value of Z for rotation, calculated from simple quantum mechanics,[†] is $(8\pi^2 IkT)/h^2$. The value of I, the moment of inertia of a rotating molecule, is 10^{-40} gm cm^2 for water, and the resulting value of Z per molecule is of the order of 75. The free energy per molecule is then $-kT \ln 75$, or $-4.3kT$. When each molecule is bound, the free energy per molecule becomes essentially zero instead of a negative figure. The free energy has therefore increased as a result of the break of the chromosome. Since the increase is very large, because the two new surfaces can certainly bind 10^5 water molecules, the free energy change is of the order of 10^4 ev.

---

[*] K. Sax, *Genetics* **23**, 496 (1938).

[†] See, for example, Johnson, Eyring, and Pollisar, *The Kinetics of Molecular Biology*, John Wiley, New York, 1957, Chap. IV.

This may be high, for there is some energy of binding, and water molecules are probably not freely rotating in the cell. We can assume 10^3 ev. We recall that $TS = U - F$, and we know that entropy changes must be either zero or increase; therefore an amount of energy equal to 10^3 ev must be made available. In other words, it takes not less than 10^3 ev of efficiently applied energy to break a chromosome. Alternatively, the chromosome already has sectional units with water molecules in between. This alternative must be remembered later. It is also possible that the basic structure of the chromosome is much smaller.

We can see another side to the nature of chromosomes by considering that in a cycle of division there has to be a very low probability that the chain of genes will break and so go awry. We can suggest that 99% must remain intact. Let us suppose that there are 1000 regions where breaking can occur; then if f is the chance that one will break, the chance of remaining intact is $1 - f$, and we have therefore, for 1000 potential breaks:

$$(1 - f)^{1000} = 0.99,$$

$$f = 10^{-5}.$$

If we re-express this in terms of the Boltzmann factor,

$$f = e^{-E/kT},$$

we find $E = 11.5kT$, or about 0.3 ev. Perhaps a more valid way is to introduce a time element as well and require that the reaction velocity for breaking a chromosome be that given by the spontaneous rate, which Kotval and Gray* found to be 0.003%, accumulated over about a year. This gives a rate of roughly 10^{-12} per second. Using the theory of absolute reaction rates, we have, remembering there are 1000 regions to break,

$$10^{-15} = \frac{kT}{h} \exp - \left(\frac{\Delta F^{\ddagger}}{kT}\right),$$

(where we express F in ergs for comparison with kT). The resulting value of $\Delta F^{\ddagger}/kT$ is 63, or $\Delta F^{\ddagger} = $ approximately 2.1 ev. This compares favorably with the value of $\Delta E^{\ddagger}$, the energy constant in the Arrhenius equation deduced from the temperature variation of mutations, for which $\Delta E^{\ddagger}$ is 1.3 ev.

Thus with this kind of reasoning the energy of activation to be overcome before a break occurs is around 2.1 ev. This is very much less than the energy required for the formation of two fresh surfaces covered by

---

* J. P. Kotval and L. H. Gray, *Journal of Genetics*, **48**, 135 (1947).

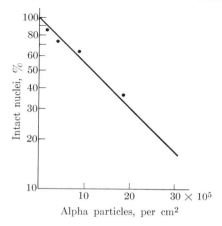

FIG. 10–13. A presentation of the findings of Kotval and Gray on the number of chromosome breaks produced by alpha particles in *Tradescantia* microspores.

water. It forces us to consider the idea that chromosomes are aggregates of separate units, fully hydrated (including the surface), and bound together by physical forces which owe their strength more to the relatively large surfaces of binding than to specific chemical bonding.

Let us return to radiation. Perhaps the most significant experiment on chromosome breakage is that done on microspores of *Tradescantia* by Kotval and Gray, who subjected *Tradescantia* anthers to irradiation by radon gas in solution, thus bombarding them with alpha particles of high ion density. The number of various classes of chromosome break could be counted after various exposures. The dose in energy liberated per unit volume could be calculated from the time of exposure and the radon concentration, and the anthers were placed in water for 24 hours after exposure before fixation for cytological examination. The cells at metaphase were observed, and counts of normal cells, chromatid breaks, isochromatid breaks, interchanges of various kinds, and intrachanges were made.

One simple analysis of Kotval and Gray's data is shown in Fig. 10–13, where the percent of normal cells is plotted against the dose in alpha particles per square centimeter, clearly showing the familiar semilogarithmic relation. Using the analysis given in Section 10–9, we find that the cross section for chromosome breaking by alpha particles is 6.0×10^{-7} cm^2. Since the area of the nucleus of a *Tradescantia* microspore is 11.3×10^{-7}, the sensitive area which must be traversed by an alpha particle is less than half that of the nucleus. We can calculate the relation of this to the chromosomes as follows. The total length of chromosome in the nucleus is 972μ, to be thought of as randomly arranged lines of sensitive material. A linear target which is randomly oriented with respect to a bombarding particle presents less than its true area to the particle. By a simple geo-metrical calculation, the effective area is seen to be $\pi/4$ times the true area. Allowing for this, the true cross section is accordingly $4/\pi$ times the observed cross section, or 7.6×10^{-7} cm^2. Thus if t is the thickness of the chromosome,

$$9.72 \times 10^{-2}t = 7.6 \times 10^{-7},$$

$$t = 7.8 \times 10^{-6} \text{ cm, or 780 A.}$$

The value given by Sax is 1000 A. Therefore the effective target appears to be less than that of a chromosome.

This simple analysis shows that an intimate relationship must exist between the chromosome thread and the ionizing particle which causes a break. The value given above is actually too low, because among the normal cells we have listed many cells that have undergone breaks but have also had the breaks heal. This factor of repair is very hard to esti-mate. Kotval and Gray, from a very careful analysis of their own and other data, use a figure of 0.35 for the probability that a break is actually seen. This increases the cross section in the ratio 1:0.35, and makes the estimated chromosome width 2200 A, or about double the value given by Sax. Accepting this, we see that a break is produced every time an alpha particle traverses a chromosome, or approaches within 600 A of either side of it.

No other data available at the present is as satisfactory for simple analysis. A study of chromosome breaks produced by neutrons was made by Thoday and by Giles, with definite results. However, neutrons do not afford a single, simple type of irradiation like alpha particles. Neverthe-less, it is quite clear that with neutrons which produce recoil protons of about 3-Mev energy, the cross section calculated from data like that of Fig. 10–13 is far less, being about 3×10^{-8} cm^2 in place of 6.0×10^{-8} cm^2. Since the ionization density of an alpha particle is about 12 times that of such a proton, the two values indicate a very roughly linear increase of cross section with ionization density, a feature observed in the inactivation of some bacteriophages and of yeast.

Chromosome breakage is complicated by the feature of restitution. Chromosomes tend to break and restitute in the normal process, and it is the fact that this occurs at meiosis, which is responsible for genetic crossing over. Therefore any observed cytological damage may be far less than the original damage. That this is so is shown by dose fractionation, where x-rays are applied in bursts with intervals in between. Such experi-ments show that chromosome breaks can remain open for of the order of five minutes before rejoining, and Sax has shown that the number of breaks observed can be increased by quite gentle centrifugation.

Where the observed cytological damage requires two breaks and a union between them, it is found that sparsely ionizing radiation, such as gamma radiation, produces effects proportional to the square of the dose, implying a two-hit process. Densely ionizing radiation, which presumably produces related breaks with some certainty, causes effects proportional to the dose.

The early work of Sax led him to give a qualitative account of the nature of the action of ionizing radiation on chromosomes. A quantitative account on the same topic was attempted by Lea. Lea concluded that 20 ionizations in a small chromosomal volume of the order of one cubic micron can cause a break and that of these, a high fraction rejoin, either to revert or to form a new combination. Not everyone accepts his analysis, and we are in no position to give an opinion other than to say that any carefully worked out numerical analysis is of value because it becomes susceptible to numerical test. Quantitative data to disprove Lea's hypothesis do not seem to have been accumulated yet.

The figure of 20 ionizations is not nearly large enough to provide the energy for a clean break with the formation of two fresh-water-covered surfaces. We are therefore led, from radiation studies, to the idea that a chromosome must be an aggregate of nucleoprotein units held together by some sort of van der Waals attraction and hence also susceptible to the repulsion of ionic atmosphere forces and so to the concentration of metallic ions. In some way radiation induces a change in one of these units which modifies the attraction at the boundary and causes a break. The process is still unknown. In any event, the sensitive region of 500 A around each thread, plus the thread itself, is so large that the overwhelming preponderance of the action of ionizing radiation on living systems must be action on the chromosomes. We refer the reader to the large amount of literature on this subject for further wisdom in this field.

10–17 The effects of ionizing radiation on human beings.

This is a subject which has increased in importance since the biological effect of ionizing radiation was discovered early in the century. Acceptable estimates of human tolerance to radiation have been steadily revised downward, and at the present time there is a considerable public concern occasioned by the testing of nuclear arms, the arrival of nuclear power plants, and the increased medical use of x-rays. The reader can find several reasonably authoritative summaries of the action of ionizing radiation on human beings. We do not intend to deflect the reader from perusing such summaries—in fact, the reverse is our wish—but we would like to give a short account of the theoretical side of one or two features of radiation action.

TABLE 10–7

IONIZING RADIATION AND HUMANITY*

Background radiation	
Cosmic ray	
At sea level	30 mr/yr
At 5000 ft	70 mr/yr
Natural radioactivity	
In the open	50 mr/yr
In buildings	80 mr/yr
Representative total	120 mr/yr
Average dose due to medical x-rays (gonads)	100 mr/yr
Estimated dose in U. S. from fallout at rate preceding 1956	3 mr/yr
Estimated dose to double the spontaneous rate of mutation in man	5–150 r
Maximum permissible doses	
Whole population	1.4×10^6 r per 10^6 population up to age 30
Occupational	
Accumulated	5 (age — 18) r
Weekly	3 r over 13 weeks
Emergency	25 r, once only in a lifetime
Life shortening due to 1 r	5–15 days
Dose due to one set of dental x-rays	
To face	300 mr
To gonads	5 mr (male), 1 mr (female)
Dose due to one chest x-ray (large film)	50 mr
To gonads	0.4 mr
Dose due to pelvimetry in pregnancy	
Mother	1300 mr
Child	2700 mr
Mean lethal dose (whole body)	500 r
Dose for sickness symptoms	150 r
Dose for radiation burn	300–1000 r local to skin
Local dose in cancer treatment	3000 r
Dose due to radioactive wrist watch	At skin 600 mr/yr
Dose due to foot x-ray machines	
Feet	Up to 25 r!
Gonads	75 mr (male), 15 mr (female)

* Reference 11.

We first give a self-explanatory chart (Table 10–7) that summarizes the most salient figures.

We would like to comment on two important and somewhat controversial topics: the existence of a threshold for radiation effects (by which is meant that no effect is produced until a certain amount of ionizing radiation has been received) and the long delayed effects of radiation.

Certainly many effects exist for which there is a threshold. Reddening of the skin is one of them. What is more important is the question as to whether an effect which is linear with the dose above 10 r is also linear with the dose at 0.01 r. It seems likely to us that it is, for the following reasons. First, each energy release has exactly the same large value regardless of the dose rate. Second, the molecular units of the cell, which seem to determine its action, are rarely more than 0.1 micron in size; the primary events associated with a 10 r dose are separated by about six times this distance. Thus it would seem that the separation in the region of known linearity is already greater than the size of the units involved. We would expect that increasing the separation would reduce the frequency of a reaction to radiation, but only proportionally to the amount of the increase. It seems to us, therefore, that the burden of proof that an effect which is linear at moderate doses is nonlinear at low doses rests on the individual who makes that assertion. It may be true, but it would be surprising.

One of the sad features of radiation action is the delayed appearance of serious disease like leukemia or bone cancer. We feel that such an occurrence could be predicted for the following reasons. If we consider that one roentgen will render one percent of a group of cells unable to divide correctly, then one percent of the cells may need to be replaced by the normal process of growth. The question now arises as to whether the normal process of growth produces exact replicas of the disabled cells. It would seem likely that it does not, because the very process of differentiation requires that some change occur in cells all derived from one ancestor. Pushing the cell replacement rate up would seem to be rather like increasing the rate of aging, and thus hastening the origin of diseases which are normally incident late in life. It seems quite safe to predict that if we continue to lengthen the life span at anywhere near the rate we have achieved in the past 50 years, the concern over radiation damage in 50 more years will be much greater than it is now.

PROBLEMS

1. Calculate the velocity of: (a) a 2-Mev deuteron, (b) a 1-Mev electron, (c) a 160-Mev O^{16} nucleus, (d) a 100-ev electron.

2. Calculate the rate of energy loss of 10-Mev deuterons in water.

3. Calculate the amount of energy released in primary ionizations exceeding 400 ev for (a) a 10-Mev deuteron, (b) a 20-Mev alpha particle, (c) an 80-Mev O^{16} nucleus.

4. Given that the absorption cross section per electron for 1.1-Mev gamma rays is 2.6×10^{-26} cm^2, calculate the energy loss per cm^3 in carbon of density unity and hydrogen of the same density. Assume 10^{10} gamma ray photons per cm^2.

5. A sample is subject to irradiation by 10^{10} photons of energy 1 Mev and the same number of photons of energy 50 kev. If the area of the sample is 1 cm^2 and the material has absorption coefficients of 0.1 and 1 for the two kinds of radiation, compare the rates of energy loss at depths of 1 cm and 10 cm.

6. Estimate the 37% dose for the inactivation of an enzyme of 100,000 molecular weight, using Co^{60} gamma radiation.

7. A mixture of 10 micrograms of transforming principle, assumed to be pure DNA of molecular weight 10^6, and 100 micrograms of RNA-ase, assumed to be a spherical protein of molecular weight 15,000, is irradiated in pure distilled water with 100 r. Estimate the amount of each substance which is inactivated.

8. Assuming that 100 r of radiation will render 63% of mammalian cells in tissue culture unable to divide normally, comment on the fact that the mean lethal dose to a whole animal is about 500 r, and that death takes some days to occur.

REFERENCES

1. D. E. LEA, *Actions of Radiations on Living Cells.* Cambridge University Press, 1956. A valuable classic which is essential reading for all interested in radiation and living systems.

2. N. W. TIMOFEEFF-RESSOVSKY and K. G. ZIMMER, *Das Treffer Prinzip in der Biologie.* Hirzel, Leipzig, 1947. This is a most useful book which treats the subject in a manner different from that of Lea, including in particular a more complete account of the multiple-hit processes.

3. *Symposium on Radiobiology,* ed. by J. J. Nickson. John Wiley & Sons, N. Y., 1952.

4. Z. M. BACQ and P. ALEXANDER, *Fundamentals of Radiobiology.* Academic Press, N. Y., 1955.

5. L. H. GRAY, in *Actions Chimiques et biologiques de radiations,* ed. by Haissinsky. Masson, Paris, 1955.

6. E. C. POLLARD, W. R. GUILD, F. HUTCHINSON, and R. B. SETLOW, "The Direct Action of Ionizing Radiation in Enzymes and Antigens." *Prog. Biophys. and Biophys. Chem.* **5,** 72 (1955).

7. M. ERRERA and A. HERVE, *Mechanismes de l'action biologique des radiations*. Masson, Paris (1951).

8. W. M. DALE, L. H. GRAY, and W. J. MEREDITH, *Phil. Trans. Roy. Soc.* **A 242,** 33 (1949).

9. F. HUTCHINSON, *American Naturalist* **94,** 59 (1960).

10. *Biological Effects of Atomic Radiation.* Report of National Academy, National Research Council, 1956.

11. *U. S. Congressional Hearings on Nature of Radiation Fallout and Its Effects on Man (1956).* Report of the United Nations Scientific Committee on the Effects of Atomic Radiation, New York, 1958.

12. H. L. ANDREWS, *Radiation Biophysics*, Prentice-Hall, Englewood Cliffs, N. J., 1961.

13. *Conference on Molecular and Radiation Biology.* Ed. R. A. Deering, Publication 823, National Academy–National Research Council, 1961.

CHAPTER 11

THE USE OF IONIZING RADIATION TO STUDY CELL STRUCTURE

11-1 Introduction. Ionizing radiation can penetrate the cell wall or the surface layer of a virus without necessarily producing any effect. Once the radiation is inside the cell, it produces localized energy releases of very great size. As described in the last chapter, these releases can have effects on cells which are greater than would be expected in view of the rather small total energy transfer. The explanation we put forward in Chapter 10 is deeply involved with the fundamental ideas of molecular biology, namely that there are small molecular structures which control the processes of the cell, and that when energy is released in one of these structures, drastic consequences could result.

The study of radiation action on living systems can be approached in two ways. One is to seek to understand the effect of radiation and to use it for some human value, such as the treatment of cancer or the survival of a population after a nuclear war. The other way, which we intend to use in this chapter, is the reverse of the first; it involves using the knowledge provided by nuclear physics and x-rays to make deductions about the molecular biology of the cell. The two approaches are really quite different, though they interact to some extent. Thus the research worker whose aim is to improve the treatment of cancer will never wander very far from the study of radiation effects on normal and malignant cells. On the other hand, the research worker seeking to use radiation to understand the cell will look for systems in which he is most confident of his knowledge of the physical action of radiation, and so may find himself studying bacterial spores, viruses, and the enzyme systems of bacteria. The first approach appeals very strongly to human emotion, while the second can only claim the intellectual appeal of understanding some part of a cell a little better. For this reason most research in this field has been directed at understanding the action of radiation, and very little has been aimed at studying the cell. Nevertheless, accurate conclusions regarding cell structure can be made, and have been made, by using ionizing radiation in statistical studies of damage to cells. Since we believe such studies to be a promising branch of molecular biophysics, we give a short account of the present state of the science.

11-2 The principle of the method. Almost nowhere is the essential difference between the approach of biochemistry and biophysics more

352

apparent than in the use of ionizing radiation as a means of studying the cell. Consider for a moment a parallel method of study which is biochemical in character: the use of chloramphenicol to inhibit protein synthesis. How this chemical agent acts is not known, how it enters the cell is not known, and what, if any, differential actions it produces in the cell are not known. Nevertheless, the biochemist has established that it acts to prevent protein synthesis in some cells, and a cell properly treated with chloramphenicol has a one-sided behavior which can be most informative about the processes involving nucleic acid. The beauty of the use of chloramphenicol is its effect on one aspect of the cell. Used as a disturbing agent, it has a great appeal to the biochemist for he can consider metabolic pathways, precursors, and so on, in an altered but interesting system. He cannot find out anything about physical size or structure except in a rather roundabout way, but such a limitation is one he lives with all the time and therefore does not notice.

Ionizing radiation, on the other hand, does not act in any selective chemical way. There are probably at least 10 different and important ways in which ionization acts on biological molecules. To suppose after irradiating a cell that one particular process has been blocked, with no other effects, is open to much more question than in the case of cell treatment with chloramphenicol. Nevertheless it is true that whatever effects radiation may produce, they are separately and statistically distributed, independently of any special chemical species. If such localized effects produce a cellular response, then one quite legitimate line of inquiry is related to the probability that such statistical distribution could have interacted with the particular molecular part of the cell which is concerned with the response. One simple aspect of such probability is influenced by relative size. Thus, if ionizing radiation is any use to us in cell study, it is likely to be in the direction of telling us something about the size, shape, and distribution of the parts of the cell which do the work of the cell. Here is where the cellular biophysicist believes he plays his part.

The principle of the method of using ionizing radiation can be seen most easily from Fig. 11-1. A cellular unit (which could be a system which synthesizes a particular protein or could be an enzyme or a system which controls the formation of a protein synthesizing system) is represented as a circle in a region of the cell which is 1000 A square and 100 A deep. If x-ray irradiation in the amount of 10,000 r is delivered to the cell, then one primary ionization will be produced on the average in the region of the figure. The effects this ionization can produce in the cytoplasm can migrate through a distance of about 30 A. In part (a) of the figure the migration is illustrated by a little dotted circle around the ionization. It is clear that the cellular unit has a 98% chance of escaping any effect whatever. In the succeeding three parts of the figure we have

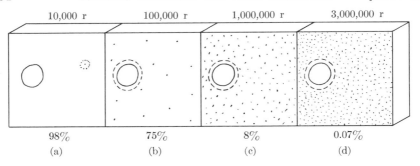

FIG. 11–1. Representation of how the probability of escaping an ionization decreases as the dose increases. The probability of survival depends also on the size of the sensitive volume, and some estimate of this volume can be made from the statistical analysis of radiation effects.

used a common trick in collision theory by adding the 30 A to the target molecule, leaving the ionizations as points. It can readily be seen that as the dose increases, the probability of escape decreases. The dose range in which the probability of escape is about 50–50, (actually 37%, or e^{-1}) gives us quite a fair idea of the size of the system which can be subject to damage.

So the plan of action is as follows. We find some cellular property which is influenced by ionizing radiation, for example, the ability to synthesize a particular protein. We study the survival of this property as a function of the dose delivered, and from our knowledge of the way in which ionizations are distributed by such a dose, we infer the size of object which must be responsible for the property. Later we intend to discuss ways in which the shape as well as the volume of the particular region can be found. In the meantime we can look more closely at what is involved in our inference about size.

One very desirable possession is the accurate knowledge of what ionizing radiation does to the cellular molecules. Unfortunately, as of 1960 we have only an imperfect grasp of such knowledge. We do know, however, that both protein and nucleic acid are very sensitive to ionizing radiation, both in the dry state and in solution. Quite a large range of experiments, as described in the last chapter, show that a primary ionization which arrives in either of these molecules will stop their biological operation. Experiments show that nucleic acid is equally sensitive to the effects produced in water by ionization if, in their migration, the effects encounter the molecule of nucleic acid. Protein in solution is not quite so capable of generalization, some protein molecules being more sensitive than others.

We could proceed on this basis, without any rationale for the action we have just described. Fortunately, the situation is not quite that bad. It seems likely that in nucleic acid we are generally dealing with a long, thin molecule which is readily susceptible to being broken upon ionization or upon reaction with a free radical. If the coil of nucleic acid is such that adjacent strands are close together, then there can also be some cross linking, which again is unfortunate for the functioning of the molecule. In the case of protein, the covalently bonded chain permits the migration of the positive region left after ionization until it occupies a statistically most probable region in the molecule. This region also seems to be vulnerable to reaction with water, to produce a damaged molecule. Therefore, with some reservations, we can start out with the premise, first assumed by Lea, that one primary ionization inactivates one molecule and see whether our results need a great deal of correction. It will be seen that by and large they do not.

To be certain that the migration of free radicals does not blur the deductions we make about size, it is desirable to irradiate in the dry state, where no free diffusion can take place. For viruses and spores this is quite possible, and it can also be done for some cellular properties (for example, enzymes). However, such a limitation is rather severe, though no more than encountered by the electron microscope, and one would like to be able to make some deductions from material irradiated under conditions where the cells are living. As a working hypothesis we propose to adopt the suggestion made by Hutchinson, based on studies on enzyme inactivation in wet and dry cells, that migration of radicals can add as much as 30 A to the effective radius of the target molecule. In a good many cases a lower figure is to be expected. In some studies by Pollard and Nancy

TABLE 11–1

INACTIVATION OF β-GALACTOSIDASE

In dry state			In C minimal medium		
Dose, $\times 10^6$ r	% Survival	Volume deduced, $\times 10^{-19}$ cm³	Dose, $\times 10^6$ r	% Survival	Volume deduced, $\times 10^{-19}$ cm³
2.8	39	5.5	0.8	81	6.5
8.4	10	4.5	1.6	55	7.5
11.5	3.7	4.7	2.1	35	10.0
14.2	2.1	4.5	3.2	21	9.8
17.4	1.1	4.3	8.6	8	5.9
Average volume	4.7×10^{-19} A³			7.9×10^{-19} A³	
Radius if spherical	48 A			57 A	

Barrett the inactivation of β-galactosidase in the dry state and in cells in minimal medium yielded the figures of Table 11–1. It can be seen that in this case the increase in target radius due to migrating elements after irradiation is less than 30 A. Very probably the enzyme is part of some membrane and so is covered for part of its surface, thus being less susceptible to damage from the outside.

We should point out that every method we can employ to study cell structure, except our imagination, is in some degree destructive. Even the light microscope, when pushed to a resolution where cell organelles begin to show structure, has to employ ultraviolet light which destroys the functioning of the cell while the observations are being made. The electron microscope can only work with entirely dead and drastically fixed preparations. Although it has given remarkable knowledge of some cellular processes, the technique of using parts of cells obtained from ultrasonically broken or pressure-burst or enzymatically weakened and broken cells is still faced with the fact that the organization of the cell has been damaged. Thus we have to take the information we gain from these various destructive methods and assemble a theoretical picture of the working of the cell. The penetrating property of ionizing radiation, and the feature of local energy releases, make it a very attractive agent for studying cell structure. It too is destructive of the cell function, but in quite a different way from breaking the cell open and centrifuging or other similar techniques. This very difference renders it interesting.

11–3 Early radiation studies of structure. A very early instance of the use of ionizing radiation for structure studies was the discovery by Zirkle in 1932 that the sensitivity of fern spores to alpha particles depended on the direction of irradiation. This discovery was nicely correlated with the assumption of a nucleus that is acentric and therefore more accessible to alpha particles on one side and not accessible on the other. In 1925, at just about the time when the rediscovered Mendelian genetics had reached definite maturity and the mapping of linkage groups was progressing with confidence, Muller discovered that x-rays had the power to produce chromosome breaks. This provided the agent needed to make it possible to identify the linkage groups, which are constructs of genetic law, with the physically observable chromosomes.

Gowen and Gay, in 1933, and Lea, in 1940, attempted to use ionizing radiation to estimate the size and number of genes. The survival ratio of *Drosophila* that have been irradiated by x-rays can readily be measured. In addition, it is possible to measure the number of a particular mutant form produced per unit of dose. If we assume that lack of survival is due to the production of one of many lethal mutations and that the production of a specific mutation is due to localized action in one place, it is possible to argue somewhat as follows. A dose of 4000 r will permit a 37% survival rate in *Drosophila*. Since 1 r is equivalent to 6.1×10^{11} primary ionizations per cubic centimeter, the relation $\ln n/n_0 = -VI$ tells us that the value of V corresponding to these results is 4.1×10^{-16} cm³ (which is equivalent to a molecular weight of 3.2×10^8). On the other hand, since one specific mutation was observed for 500 flies which survived this dose, the probability that a particular mutation will be produced by this irradiation is 1/1000 (allowing for the flies which have not survived). If we use dn to represent the number of mutants in n flies, and if a mutation is supposed to occur when an ionization falls in a region of volume V, then if dI is the number of ionizations per unit volume, then $V\,dI$ is the average number of "hits" which occur. Thus we deduce

$$dn/n = v\,dI,$$

and we can derive $v = 4.1 \times 10^{-19}$ cm³, corresponding to a molecular weight of 320,000. Thus these early experimenters estimated that the number of genes must be roughly in the ratio of V/v or 1000. A present-day estimate of the number of genes is 3000. An estimate of the molecular weight of a gene poses sharply the question of what is meant by a "gene." Nevertheless, bearing in mind the early date of the estimate, we see that it is not at all out of line with modern ideas.

Lest the reader conclude that such reasoning is above all criticism, we need to remind him that it is only hypothesis that a primary ionization released inside a molecular unit will cause a heritable change in that unit, and indeed an hypothesis which is rather hard to justify. Even so, the possible agents related to ionization are closely limited in volume, so that whatever the cause of mutation the fact that the original source of energy was ionizing radiation demands that the effect be localized. Thus we *are* justified in saying that genes have a volume comparable to a molecule of 300,000 molecular weight and that there must be something like 1000 of them. We are *not* justified in being dogmatic about the exact figures until the mechanism of mutation by ionizing radiation is understood.

Another very interesting application was made by Preer to the problem of the *kappa* factor in *Paramecia*. *Kappa* is an extranuclear agent which, when present together with the appropriate genes, can cause *Paramecia* to produce a toxic substance lethal to other organisms. Preer found that the activity of the factor *kappa* was reduced to 37% of its potency by 3500 r of x-radiation and concluded that the responsible agent must therefore be a relatively large particle. Subsequent microscopic observation showed that this is true. Gray has deduced that the radiation-sensitive volume must have a diameter of 1.15 microns, which is less than that of the observed particle. It is quite clear that careful radiation studies on *kappa* would tell us a great deal about its internal structure.

A further very important line of radiation work concerns the size of viruses. The critical stage of the development of this work was reached in several different places during World War II, and therefore rather similar but quite independent studies went forward in the scientific isolation of that time. Thus work by Gowen, Luria, and Exner in the United States, by Hollweck and Lacassagne in France, and by Lea and Salaman in England actually formed the basis for a means of determining the size and to some extent of the structure of viruses. Only recently has a proper appraisal of the various separate efforts been made. An early review (Ref. 10) of the subject, including the description of a very simple method of irradiating viruses in solution with dissolved radon, was given by Bonet-Maury. He showed the clear agreement between virus-sensitive cross sections and accepted virus dimensions, giving figures for some viruses not measured earlier. In the next section we discuss virus size and structure more fully, including information on more recent results.

11–4 Radiation studies of the structure of viruses. The remarkable advances made in the past 20 years have shown that viruses have many characteristics other than that of being "infectious agents." Let us consider a well-known animal virus, Newcastle Disease virus (NDV), which produces a very serious influenza in chickens and which was dreaded by poultry farmers until an effective vaccine was discovered. We can study the following properties of NDV:

(1) Its ability to multiply on the chorioallantoic membrane of the chick embryo, or on sheets of chick cells in tissue culture, where plaques are very nicely visible.

(2) Its ability to agglutinate red blood cells.

(3) Its ability to lyse red blood cells.

(4) Its ability to combine with specific antibody.

(5) Its ability to elicit antibody formation in an animal.

This is by no means a complete list of the known properties of the virus, but it affords a good start.

The first of these properties, which we will call the property of "infecting" for short, can be very effectively reduced by ionizing radiation. The inactivation of this property by x-rays or by Co^{60} gamma rays follows the familiar logarithmic relationship with dose. By the methods outlined in Chapter 10, the inactivation volume is found to be 1.27×10^{-16} cm^3, which, if we treat the region as spherical (tried as a first approximation), gives a radius of 310 A. This is considerably below the electron micrographic radius, which is 550 A, and gives some indication that the virus has a differential internal sensitivity of some kind. The RNA content of the virus is about 3% of the whole, and there is clearly some correlation between the reduced size of the radiation-sensitive region and the RNA,

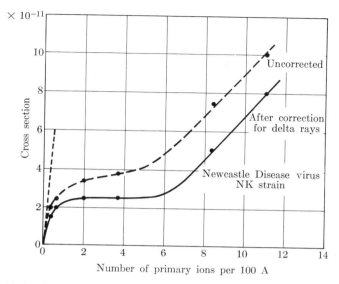

FIG. 11–2. Variation of the survival cross section for Newcastle Disease virus, as observed by Wilson. The cross section is plotted against ionization density. Two regions of sensitivity corresponding to structural features of the virus can be seen.

which, if it were located at the center, would have a radius of 170 A. This correlation between nucleic acid content and radiation sensitivity, first pointed out by Epstein, is a useful first approximation though there are exceptions to its validity.

To pursue this differential sensitivity still further, two methods of approach have been used. The first is to employ particles of different ionization density as bombarding agents and to use the densely ionizing particles to give some estimate of the cross section of the sensitive region. The first experiments of this kind were by Woese and one of the authors, but somewhat more complete measurements taken by Wilson are shown in Fig. 11–2. It can be seen that the sensitivity, which is analyzed for these densely ionizing particles according to the relation

$$\ln \frac{n}{n_0} = -SD,$$

where S is the cross section and D is the dose in particles per square centimeter, varies in a rather complex way. There seem to be two levels of sensitivity, one at a cross section of 3.5×10^{-11} cm^2 and one reaching a high value of 10×10^{-11} cm^2. In addition, the inactivation by sparsely ionizing radiation can be represented on this kind of graph if we use the fact that the two relations $\ln n/n_0 = -VI$ and $\ln n/n_0 = -SD$ are really parametric representations of inactivation. Then we can say that for one particle with an energy loss of 110 ev per 100 A per square centimeter, D is unity and I is 1 cm divided by 100 A, or 10^6. Thus the inactivation volume tells us the initial slope of the graph of cross section *versus* energy loss, and we draw the graph by plotting $V \times 10^6$ at the point where the energy loss is 110 ev per 100 A. When this is done, the complex character of the curve is even more clear, and the question is what can we learn from it.

One very simple and trivial explanation for the increase in cross section at high ionization densities may lie in the fact that only part of the energy release lies along the track. A considerable fraction may lie along the tracks of secondary electrons and so be far removed from the track of the ionizing particle. One way to correct for this was given in Chapter 10. A method more suitable for large sensitive volumes was suggested by Lea, but when this is applied there is still a marked plateau at 2.5×10^{-11} cm^2, with a rise at higher rates of energy loss. The suggestion can therefore be made that the virus has a very insensitive outer coat and a much more sensitive inner region, one which is quite possibly a tightly structured nucleoprotein unit.

A very interesting way of studying directly the sensitivity of a virus as a function of the depth inside its structure is the technique of low-voltage electron bombardment. This method, originally used by Hutchinson and Davis, will be described more fully in Section 11–6. When it is possible to obtain very potent preparations of virus which can be spread in monolayers and dried without too great a loss of their ability to infect, the irradiation can be done with electrons of energy so low they will only penetrate into the top surface layers of the virus. By increasing the energy, we can increase the penetration until the sensitive region, if there is one, is reached, whereupon there is a dramatic increase in the effective cross section of the electrons. The results of such an experiment made by Wilson are shown in Fig. 11–3. It can be seen that the low-voltage electrons have very little effect, but that after a penetration of 250 A there is a considerable increase in the effectiveness of the electrons. The range-energy relation for electrons in protein has been measured by M. Davis. On the basis of her figures, the thicknesses of penetration have been deduced. They are given in Fig. 11–3. Thus the evidence of ionizing-radiation studies points to there being a centrally located sensitive region of radius 280 A, surrounded by a less sensitive region of thickness 230 A, making a total radius of 510 A.

We can now turn to some other properties of the virus. Its ability to agglutinate red blood cells is of great interest. It proves to be very difficult to remove this property by radiation, far more so than to reduce the virus' ability to infect. Studies by Woese indicated that the agglutinating

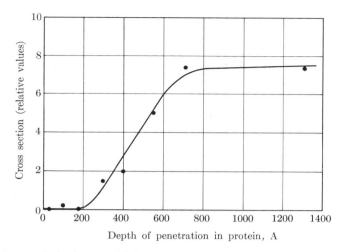

Fig. 11–3. Relative sensitivity of Newcastle Disease virus to electrons of different energies, and hence of their ability to penetrate. An inner sensitive region is seen to be surrounded by an insensitive coat. Data due to Wilson.

property resided in a unit of an effective molecular weight of 500,000. At the same time he made these studies, he also measured the sensitivity of the virus' ability to combine with antibody, thus neutralizing its ability to agglutinate. He found this last sensitivity to be exactly half that of the agglutinating ability, which suggested strongly that the agglutinating property is involved with a pair of subunits of the virus, placed approximately opposite to each other and so able to hold two red cells together. How many of such units there are is not easy to say from these measurements.

It is of interest that Buzzell, Brandon, and Lauffer found that the sensitive region of influenza virus is about one-eighth of the whole virus, and that the hemagglutinin has a sensitive radius of 95 A and a multiplicity of inactivation of three. The indication is again that roughly paired factors must be present to cause red blood cells to agglutinate.

One further property of Newcastle Disease has been studied, namely its ability to lyse chicken red blood cells. Wilson found that when radiation sufficient to remove all signs of the virus' ability to lyse such cells was applied, the inactivation followed a multihit type of curve, corresponding to about 15 hits. The final slope of the curve, which can be used to measure the inactivation volume, corresponded to a molecular weight equivalent of 350,000. On bombarding with densely ionizing particles, Wilson found the cross section to be greater than expected for the volume observed. He concluded that the hemolysin property is concerned with a set of platelike molecules, around 15 in number, spread over the surface of the virus par-

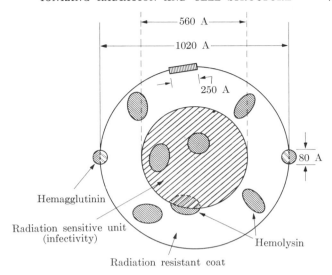

Fig. 11–4. Schematic representation of Newcastle Disease virus based on radiation studies. A central sensitive region is surrounded by a coat, on which there are units for lysing red cells and for agglutinating red cells.

ticle. The composite picture of NDV derived in this way is shown in Fig. 11–4. The reader already realizes the inferential nature of such a picture. For instance, there is nothing in the radiation work to contradict the idea that all the hemolysins are concentrated on one side of the virus. Thus they are spread out in the figure for esthetic reasons only, and may not necessarily be right. That there are many of them, and that they are about as drawn, is probable.

Electron micrographic studies of this virus have been made by Morgan, Rose, and Moore. They show a rather larger particle than suggested by radiation work but are most interesting in that the appearance in thin section shows that there seem to be two rings. Possibly we should identify the inner region with the infectious property and the outer ring with the material carrying the abilities to agglutinate and to lyse red blood cells.

Bacterial viruses lend themselves to radiation studies. T1 bacteriophage, operating on *E. coli*, is very easy to study since it is quite stable when dry. Also, quite a range of properties are available for study. The following have been studied, largely in the authors' laboratory:

(1) Its ability to infect bacteria and make plaques on sheets of growing bacteria.

(2) Its ability to combine with antibody.

(3) Its ability to attach to the bacterium.

(4) Its ability to kill the host.

(5) Its ability to donate genetic markers to another strain of virus which is also infecting the bacterium.

(6) Its ability to make specific protein.

All these properties have definitely different radiation sensitivities. The ability of the phage to infect and ability to kill the host react in similar ways to different types of irradiation in that they show a relatively small inactivation volume when bombarded by fast electrons and a rather uniformly increasing cross section when densely ionizing particles are used. The host-killing property is one-third as sensitive as the infectivity property. About the best analysis of the data can be given by supposing that the sensitive part, for both properties, resides in a long, thin unit—one of less than 50 A in diameter and of around 3000 A in length for infectivity and 1000 A in length for bacterial killing.

The ability of T1 phage to combine with antibody is totally different. Really very large bombardment is necessary to have any effect at all, and the conclusion reached is that the ability to combine with antibody must be somehow involved with a surface of many small units. The ability to attach is also relatively insensitive to irradiation, though not to the degree of combination with antibody. Since it is doctrine in studies of bacteriophage that such viruses attach by their tails, the attachment unit corresponds to a part of the end of the tail.

The ability of this bacterial virus to donate genetic markers is a very sensitive property. J. Till[*] found that it corresponds to 60% of the ability to infect, indicating that there is a genetic string of sensitive material in a single unit. When this is broken or cross linked, the passing of genetic information to a second virus particle is prevented. The sixth property, that of infecting and making virus (not bacterial) protein, is also very sensitive, being about 40% of the total sensitivity for plaque formation, as found by G. Whitmore.[†]

The fact that T1 can be readily dried and gives a very sensitive assay was taken advantage of by M. Davis[‡] to study the infectivity as affected by low-voltage electrons. She found very little effect until a voltage of 990 was reached, corresponding to a penetration of 125 A. Thus for T1 there is also an insensitive outer coat, as found for T2 by Hershey and as indicated for NDV in the experiments described above. The thickness of the tail, as seen in electron micrographs, is 150 A. There can thus be no infectious material in the tail, for the electrons can travel more than halfway across it without producing any effect.

------

[*] J. Till and E. Pollard, *Radiation Research* **8**, 344 (1958).

[†] G. Whitmore and E. Pollard, *Radiation Research* **8**, 392 (1958).

[‡] M. Davis, *Arch. Bioch. Biophys.* **49**, 417 (1954).

TABLE 11-2

DEDUCTION REGARDING VIRUSES FROM RADIATION INACTIVATION

Virus	Property	Sensitive region				Equivalent mol. wt.	Ref.*
		Volume	Length	Thickness	Radius		
Influenza	Infectivity	3.8×10^7 A^3	420 A	420 A	—	3×10^7	1
	Interference	2×10^6 A^3	250 A	40 A	—	1.6×10^6	2
	Hemagglutination	3.4×10^5 A^3	140 A	21 A	—	190,000	1
NDV	Infectivity	5.8×10^5 A^3	—	—	280 A	8×10^7	3
	Hemagglutination	—	—	50 A	—	44×10^5	5
	Hemolysin	—	—	20 A	120 A	7.0×10^5	4
	Serological combining power†	—	—	—	—	2.2×10^5	5
Polio	Infectivity	—	—	—	140 A	—	9
TMV	Infectivity	3.1×10^7 A^3	3070 A	100 A	—	—	6
	Antibody combining power	—	—	—	8 A	—	8
Southern beam mosaic	Infectivity	3.4×10^6 A^3	—	—	11 A	6,000	7
	Antibody combining power	—	—	—	18 A	15,000	8
Vaccinia	Infectivity	—	—	—	240 A	—	14
	Hemagglutination	—	—	—	45 A	—	14
T1 phage	Infectivity	1.9×10^6 A^3	Long	Thin	—	—	10
	Attachment	—	177 A	504 A	—	326,000	12
	Bacterial killing	0.6×10^6	Long	Thin	—	—	11
	Latent-period extension	1.9×10^6 A^3	—	—	—	—	10
	Serological combining power	—	86 A	22 A	—	25,000	13

† Half hemagglutinin.   * See opposite page.

REFERENCES FOR TABLE 11–2

1. J. JAGGER, and E. POLLARD, *Rad. Res.* **4**, 1–19 (1950).
2. W. F. POWELL, and E. POLLARD, *Virology* **2**, 321 (1956).
3. D. W. WILSON and E. POLLARD, *Rad. Res.* **8**, 131 (1958).
4. D. W. WILSON, *Rad. Res.* **8**, 142 (1958).
5. C. WOESE and E. POLLARD, *Arch. Bioch. Biop.* **50**, 354 (1954).
6. E. POLLARD and A. E. DIMOND, *Phytopathology* **46**, 214 (1956).
7. E. POLLARD, *Physics of Viruses.* Academic Press, N. Y., 1952, p. 84.
8. E. POLLARD, *Physics of Viruses.* Academic Press, N. Y., 1952 p. 137.
9. M. BENYESH, *et al.*, *Virology* **5**, 257 (1958).
10. E. POLLARD, *Advances in Virus Research* **2**, 129 (1954).
11. D. I. FLUKE and E. POLLARD, *Ann. N.Y. Acad. Sci.* **59**, 489 (1955).
12. E. POLLARD and JANE SETLOW, *Rad. Res.* **4**, 87 (1956).
13. E. POLLARD and JANE SETLOW, *Arch. Bioch. Biop.* **50**, 376 (1954).
14. J. F. McCREA, *Ann. N.Y. Acad. Sci.* **83**, 692 (1960).

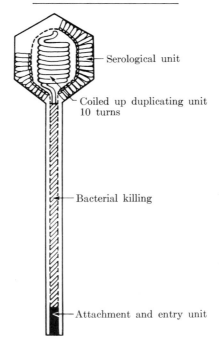

Serological unit

Coiled up duplicating unit
10 turns

Bacterial killing

Attachment and entry unit

FIG. 11–5. Schematic representation of T1 phage based on radiation studies.

We are led to a picture of T1 shown in Fig. 11–5. The general shape of the virus is taken from electron micrographs, notably those of Fluke and of Williams and Fraser. The DNA has been divided into two parts, one concerned with bacterial killing and virus protein synthesis, the other concerned with the genetic part and also presumably with the replicative function proper. The ability to combine with antibody, which was measured by Jane Setlow and Pollard in terms of the ability of irradiated virus to block antiserum, must be concerned with many small units all over the virus, and has been so represented.

We conclude this section with Table 11–2, which summarizes much of the evidence about viruses found from radiation work. Although the table shows the extent of information available about viruses, we must stress that many of the results shown there are predictive in the sense that they await confirmation (or refutation) by other methods of study. Radiation methods are not lagging behind other methods of study.

11–5 Differential radiation studies on bacteria. While the simplicity of the structure of viruses gives them a strong appeal to the biophysicist, one is reluctantly forced to the conclusion that the interest in the virus only really begins as it interacts with the host, and that then the host itself begins to be of the utmost importance. Therefore, although living cells are very much more complicated than viruses, it becomes necessary to attempt to understand them in detail, even in order to see how a virus works. Recent work on bacteria and on mammalian cells in tissue culture, using ionizing radiation, has been most informative. We give in this and the next section a short account of the kind of experiment which has been performed and some of the conclusions tentatively drawn.

The effect of ionizing radiation on two simple aspects of bacteria has been extensively studied: the ability to divide and form colonies visible on plates of agar, and the ability to grow and so scatter light. The former is very sensitive. But the situation is not a simple matter of inactivating one single large target. The sensitivity depends sharply on the nature of the medium on which the bacteria grow. This is to be expected. After all, the process of division requires the whole capability of the cell, and many vulnerable regions must exist. Some of the vulnerability may well lie in the fact that damaged regions are producing analogs which are harmful when they accumulate. So it is not wise to draw too many conclusions from data on the formation of colonies until further studies have been made.

If we turn to the measurement of cell mass, usually achieved by means of a measurement of optical density in a simple spectrophotometer, the effect of radiation is markedly less sensitive. Cell suspensions in which the ability to form colonies has dropped by a factor of a thousand will continue to grow. The growth is largely in the form of long filaments, and occasionally a normal cell will form at the end of one of these and proceed to form a normal colony. It is quite clear that the process of synthesis and growth is not nearly as vulnerable as that of division.

These studies are at one extreme of the totality of cellular processes. If we ask what is the sensitivity of the ability of the cell to incorporate a

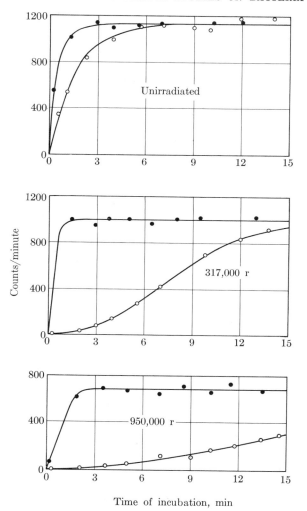

FIG. 11–6. The effect of gamma radiation on the uptake of radioactive proline by *E. coli* into two fractions, as observed by Kempner.

particular amino acid, or glucose, or one of the nucleic acid bases, the answer is that relatively huge doses of radiation have to be given to produce any effect. In Fig. 11–6 we reproduce a graph, plotted by Kempner, of the uptake of radioactive proline by *E. coli*, as affected by radiation from a Co^{60} source. The upper lines are for incorporation into the whole bacterium; the lower lines indicate that part which is insoluble in cold trichloroacetic acid (TCA). It can be seen that even after almost a million roentgens have been delivered there is a measurable uptake of radioactive

TABLE 11–3

Compound	Volume, $\times 10^{-18}$	Length	Radius, A
Glucose	5.9	Spherical	80
Uracil	15.1	Spherical	155
Methionine	10.0	Spherical	130
Proline	8.6	1.8μ	12.2
Arginine	5.3	1.5μ	10.5
Histidine	4.8	1.0μ	12.2
Leucine	5.6	1.5μ	10.9
Isoleucine	6.9	0.94μ	15.5

proline into a fraction which is insoluble in cold TCA, and so is presumably incorporated within a large molecule of some kind. The cellular units responsible for the uptake of proline therefore seem to be relatively small. Kempner has made a comparative study of the effect of gamma rays, deuterons, and alpha particles on the uptake of several amino acids, glucose, and uracil. As was described in the last chapter, one can infer a sensitive volume from the gamma-ray studies, and can get some idea of the area and thickness of the volume by employing densely ionizing radiation. The studies show that for glucose, uracil, and methionine the target area is about that to be expected from the volume of a spherical target, while for all amino acids other than methionine the area is much greater and the thickness far smaller than would be expected. In Table 11–3 we give the values of the sensitive volume and estimated thicknesses and lengths for the substances studied. It is tempting to identify the long, thin units with long RNA-protein molecules, unfolded, and to identify the spherical units with ribonucleoprotein particles which are folded into a compact shape. Both are probably forms of ribosomes.

The technique of measuring radioactive tracer uptake, described more fully in Chapter 13, can be applied to this kind of study of the effect of ionizing radiation on the functioning of cells in a wide variety of ways. The simplest is to study the uptake of an elementary metabolite such as phosphate or sulfate. The results of doing so for *E. coli* were shown in Fig. 10–8. Two features of such work are of interest. The first is that if labeled metabolite is given to irradiated cells, there is little or no change in their initial behavior. Then, as observed by Billen, there is a rather sharp change at a time which is shorter as the radiation increases; and a linear, as opposed to exponential, uptake is seen. The slope of the linear part is less as the dose increases. It is these slopes which have been compared in Fig. 10–8. The "breakaway" occurs very slightly later for sulfate than for phosphate, but the linear increase is essentially parallel. The other feature of interest is the rather high sensitivity, which, while not as high as for colony formation, is much higher than for the incorporation of a single amino acid. It seems likely that some organized system is disrupted by the radiation. Whether this is a complex set of enzymes needed to reduce and activate the metabolite or whether the nucleus of the cell has a membrane which can be broken by radiation or what, indeed, is the organization involved is hard to say at present.

Preceding and paralleling these studies are some very interesting observations, made by Billen, Stapleton, and Hollaender,* on the ability of *E. coli* to conduct respiration after irradiation. The effect of radiation on respiration is very small, indicating that this function is carried out by a relatively small and very multiple part of the cell.

All the experiments so far described concern growth, division, the uptake of radioactivity, or respiration. If we study the formation of an adaptive enzyme, we are observing the total synthesis of a useful protein. Such studies were first made by Billen and Lichtstein† on the enzyme formic hydrogenlyase in *E. coli* and indicated 37% survival dose of about 30,000 r. Very elegant measurements of such effect of radiation on the enzyme lysin decarboxylase in *B. cadaveris* have been made by Pauly, Rajewsky, and Bucker. Some of their data are shown in Fig. 11–7. It can be seen that considerable doses of radiation are needed to reduce the amount of enzyme formed to 37%, a figure of 70,000 r being a reasonable estimate. Such a figure, while expected to be far greater than that necessary to prevent division, is still smaller than found by Kempner for the incorporation of amino acids. A similar study made by Pollard and Vogler on the effect of gamma radiation on the formation of β-galactosidase showed that the time elapsed after giving the radiation was very important. This enzyme can be studied either in bacteria which have been grown on lactose and so have developed the ability to make the enzyme, or in bacteria previously grown on glucose and which must undergo the process of induction before they can make the enzyme. In the first case, the effect of radiation on the immediate synthetic process is not great, and quite probably doses of about the same size as needed for the destruction of the ability to incorporate amino acids are needed for immediate effects. However, if the amount of enzyme formed is measured at later times, it is found that a considerable effect of radiation has taken place. In the case of cells which must first adapt to the new carbon source, the initial

---

* *J. Bacteriol.* **65**, 131 (1953).
† *J. Bacteriol.* **63**, 533 (1952).

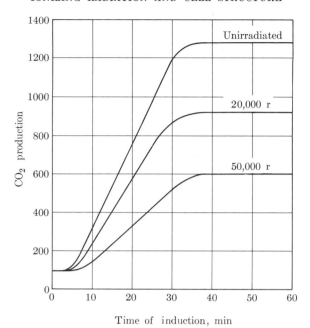

FIG. 11–7. The effect of x-rays on the induction of lysin decarboxylase, as observed by Pauly, Rajewsky, and Bucker.

formation of the new enzyme is not greatly sensitive, but the formation after three hours or so is drastically reduced by 45,000 r.

This development of radiation action after the lapse of time presents a challenge for interpretation. If we take the currently accepted idea that the genetic information in the bacterial cell is contained in the DNA and that this is somehow transferred to RNA, which operates to make the enzymes used by the cell for the processes of metabolism and synthesis, we can examine the time sequence after radiation. We have made the point that the effect of the high energy release of ionization is destructive of some molecular system, which happens to encounter the ionization, and that elsewhere the structures are intact. If we study the effect of radiation on an already present enzyme, measured in terms of its activity on an individual substrate, then we find that very large doses indeed are needed, of the order of 3×10^6 r. Thus we can feel confident that doses as low as 50,000 r probably do not concern individual enzyme action, and we note that such individual enzyme action would not be expected to be delayed. We then look one stage further back in the process and observe that damage to the mechanism which synthesizes protein from smaller metabolites would produce a delay in action on the over-all enzymatic action of the cell. The *new* enzyme supply would be deficient, and the

TABLE 11–4

TIME AND DOSE RELATIONSHIPS FOR DNA IN CONTROL
AND IRRADIATED CELLS OF *E. coli*

Time, min Dose	0	30	60	90	120
13,000 r	1	0.96	0.84	0.85	0.83
21,000 r	1	1	0.87	0.73	0.59
26,000 r	1	0.90	0.84	0.80	0.61
39,000 r	1	0.90	0.60	0.62	0.49
52,000 r	1	0.90	0.80	0.78	0.58
78,000 r	1	0.92	0.77	0.46	0.42

deficiency would show after a time determined by the rate of synthesis of protein. Recent evidence indicates that in bacteria this rate of synthesis is such that a new protein molecule can be formed in less than a minute. The effects of longer delay are thus out of line with this particular time-table. The diminution in the incorporation of amino acids is observed to occur in a time less than ten minutes, and so it is justifiable to conclude that the radiation action upon this phase of the cellular activity is very likely on the synthetic mechanism for protein. It is gratifying to find that the sensitive volumes reported in Table 11–3 are in good agreement with the suggestions of others as to the site of protein synthesis.

The delays of minutes to hours we have mentioned must be due to damage to some other mechanism, and if we trace the sequence further back we find that the process of transfer of information from DNA to RNA offers one possibility, and yet another is offered by the synthesis of DNA itself. Both these occur far enough back in the cycle to operate with considerable delay. As reported in Table 11–4, the formation of DNA is diminished by relatively small doses of radiation, and an attractive theory of radiation action of this delayed type can be developed in terms of the reduction in the synthesis of DNA by the cell. The work of Kornberg* and his associates, however, seems to indicate that the synthesis of DNA is by a relatively simple polymerase, and it is thus surprising that so great a sensitivity should be associated with an enzymatic process. It is tempting to relate the sensitivity with the destruction of the organized form of the DNA, which might cause synthesis of faulty DNA by the polymerase system, and in turn affect the transfer of in-

---

* Lehman, Bessman, Simms, and Kornberg, *J. Biol. Chem.*, **233**, 163 (1958).

TABLE 11-5

SENSITIVITY OF VARIOUS FEATURES OF THE BACTERIAL ACTION OF *E. coli* TO IONIZING RADIATION

Property	Sensitive volume	Probable shape	Probable responsible organelle
Colony formation	8.5×10^{-16} cm^3	One dimension, thin	Nuclear membrane or part of DNA
Capacity to permit T1 phage to grow	1.73×10^{-17} cm^3	One dimension, thin	Part of DNA
Capacity to permit T2 phage to grow	1.2×10^{-18} cm^3	One dimension, thin	Part of DNA
Release of prophage	4×10^{-16} cm^3	One dimension, thin	Nuclear membrane or part of DNA
Uptake of P^{32} after initial stage is over	1.4×10^{-16} cm^3	Not known	
Uptake of SO$_4$ after initial stage is over	9.5×10^{-17} cm^3	One dimension, thin	
Effect on uptake of amino acids measured shortly after radiation; same for glucose	5×10^{-18} cm^3	Long and thin	"Unrolled" ribosomes
Respiration after two division times	6×10^{-18}	Spherical	RNA-protein particle
	7.2×10^{-18}	Not known	Series of enzymes?
Formation of adaptive enzyme after time lapse	9.5×10^{-17}	Not known	Part of DNA?
Enzyme activity of β-galactosidase	4.3×10^{-19} cm^3	Nearly spherical	Enzyme molecule itself

For comparison: Total cell volume $= 1.5 \times 10^{-12}$ cm^3.   Volume of DNA $= 5 \times 10^{-15}$ cm^3.
Volume of nucleus $= 1.1 \times 10^{-13}$ cm^3.   Volume of one ribosome $= 4 \times 10^{-18}$ cm^3.

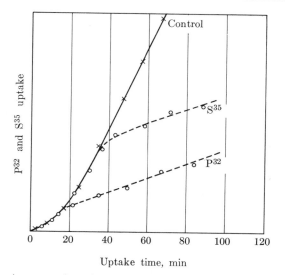

FIG. 11–8. A comparison between the uptake of radioactive P^{32} and S^{35} in control and irradiated cells. There is little change for a while, followed by a period of linear, and not exponential, uptake.

formation from DNA to RNA. Important evidence on the effect of radiation on the sequential processes of the cell is provided by the work of V. R. Potter and his group,* using the synchronized cells of regenerating rat liver.

To illustrate the nature of these delayed effects, we show in Fig. 11–8 the time course of uptake of P^{32} as phosphate and S^{35} as sulfate, for control, and cells irradiated by 36,000 r. In Table 11–4, due to Pollard and Vogler, we show the ratio of irradiated DNA to control DNA for various times and various doses.

The results of radiation studies on a number of bacterial features are summarized in Table 11–5. The first part of the table lists the observed sensitive volumes for various properties, together with some comparison volumes. The second part shows some of the time-dependent features. At the present time it is not possible to give a clear interpretation of the experimental results; the most simple "target" for the sensitive action, such as division, would seem to be some element connected with the nuclear structure. Radiation studies suggest that there is an accurately structured form to the nucleus, even in a bacterial cell, and that disruption of this form can hinder division, or even cause the release of a prophage from the bacterial chromosome. At the same time it is clear that

---

* F. J. Bollum, J. W. Anderegg, A. B. McElya, and V. R. Potter, *Cancer Research* **20**, 138–143 (1960).

there is a striking difference between the sensitivity of DNA within the cell, as expressed in terms of biological action, and the great sensitivity of such material as transforming principle, irradiated outside cells. The explanation of this discrepancy is one of the challenges of radiation studies. In smaller bacteria, the sensitive volume more closely approximates the volume of the DNA. It is of interest that the sensitive volume for the ability to develop a bacterial virus is not the same. In the case of T2, very little of the cell is seemingly necessary, while for T1 much more is needed. This is clearly related to the abnormal properties of the nucleic acid of T2, which evidently carries with it the power to conduct much more of its own assembly process, while T1 requires a large part of the cellular synthetic mechanism.

The delayed effects point to the fact that action on the more fundamental of the reproductive processes of the cell takes time to become expressed. It is possible that a quantitative analysis of the effect of various doses on the time course of several cellular processes might be very informative as to the nature of the reproductive processes themselves.

11–6 Bombardment of bacteria by particles limited in penetration. The technique described in Section 11–4 for studying the thickness of protein coat on a virus can be very effectively applied to studying the

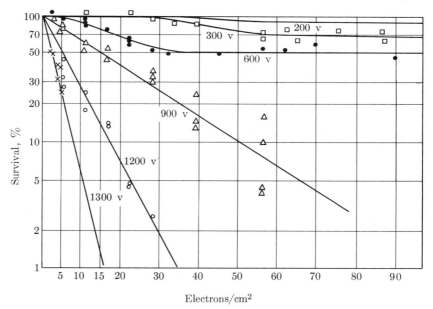

Fig. 11–9. The effect of low-voltage electrons on the viability of *B. subtilis* spores, as observed by Davis and Hutchinson.

location of various features in bacterial cells. The combined problem of how the specimen can retain viability and withstand a high vacuum while in a monolayer on a metal plate seems readily solved only by using bacterial spores. Work on spores of *B. subtilis* by Davis and Hutchinson is shown in Fig. 11–9. The figure shows the results of varying the dose at various voltages and seeing how many spores will still germinate and form colonies, as compared with the controls which have not been irradiated. It is quite easy to see that the normal semilogarithmic inactivation curve does not result for electrons of energy less than 900 volts. Instead, a small fraction is inactivated, after which the use of further bombardment is without effect. This argues for a thin skin surrounding the spore, of negligible sensitivity to ionizing radiation, which must be penetrated in order to permit damage to be produced. The fact that a part of the spores show sensitivity indicates either that there is a multiple population or that some feature of part of the cells is different. What seems to be the case is that on one side of the cells there is a thin region in the insensitive coat and below this there is a rather resistant, but not inert, region. Since the spores are randomly arranged, some have the thin part on the lower side and so are protected from the slow electrons. These accordingly always survive. When they were removed from the surface, resuspended, and bombarded, they were found to behave just the same as the original spores, which indicated that no selection of a population could be made.

The conclusions about the structure of the *B. subtilis* spore are summarized in Fig. 11–10. The spore membrane has a thickness of 230 A (except in one special region, where it is thinner) and has a secondary structure underneath. There is apparently no well-defined region in which something equivalent to a chromatin thread or nucleus exists. This does not mean that the spore has neither of these. It simply means that the

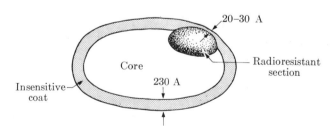

Fig. 11–10. A proposed structure deduced from the radiation studies for *B. subtilis* spores shown in Fig. 11–9. An insensitive membrane exists, which has a local thin part backed by a more sensitive region that is still less than normal sensitivity. The region inside is seemingly uniform in sensitivity, and highly so. Thus there seems to be no evidence for a local concentration of the function necessary for growth and division.

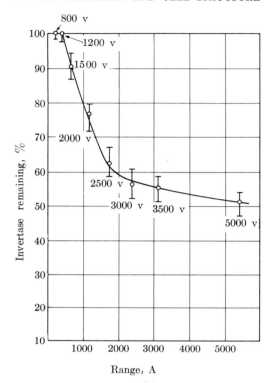

FIG. 11–11. Preiss' observations on the effect of electron bombardment at various energies, and hence on depths of penetration, on the amount of invertase remaining in yeast. The zero effect of low-voltage electrons indicates a protective insensitive layer, while the sharp drop indicates that the majority of the invertase is immediately below the protective layer. Preiss deduces that the depth of the invertase zone does not exceed 500 A below the protective layer.

spore is vulnerable not only in any genetic region which might be expected to be in such a thread, but also elsewhere. This is perhaps a characteristic of the state of a spore, which before entering that condition has conserved only the vitally important functions.

That all spores do not have such a pattern was shown by the comparable work of Knauss on *B. megaterium* spores. The sensitivity steadily increased with the voltage, and no simple analysis into a layered structure could be made. The spore wall seemed to be between 1500 and 2000 A in thickness.

While the requirement of viability is hard to achieve, many cells retain their enzymatic ability after drying in a monolayer. By using large areas of cells, involving a rather large vacuum chamber, Preiss was able to study the localization of invertase in yeast cells. Figure 11–11 shows the summarized results of his studies. He has been able to deduce that there is a resistant protective coat, of about 500 A in depth, and that the invertase is contained within an additional layer, close to the surface, of depth 500 A. The enzyme catalase was found to be distributed deeply in the cell with its outer bound 2000 A from the surface. Such studies should be capable of extension to a variety of enzymes in a variety of cells.

11–7 Orientation studies. Whenever a biological preparation can be prepared with a definite alignment and bombarded with densely ionizing particles, the possibility of examining the orientation of the internal structure exists. An example of the bombardment of an oriented preparation is shown in Fig. 11–12, where data taken by Whitmore on TMV are shown. It is quite certain in the case of this long and thin virus particle that the sensitive region must conform to the over-all shape of the particle itself. This is clearly shown in the finding that the cross section of the virus to alpha-particle bombardment is less when the virus is pointed toward the beam than when it is perpendicular to the beam. In the case of phages with long tails, the property of the tail, when it is determined, would also show such orientation effects. Preliminary results indicate that the property of "infectivity" (that is, of multiplication in the host) is not susceptible to differentiable effects in oriented preparations. On the other hand, studies have not yet been made on mutual interference and bacterial killing, which might well be found to show such behavior.

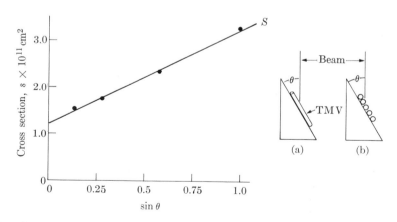

Fig. 11–12. The effect of changing the orientation of pencil-shaped tobacco mosaic virus with respect to the beam. In case (a) the virus can be tilted at different angles, and the cross section is found to vary with the sine of the angle between the virus and the beam. In case (b) no change is found. This experiment shows clearly that the sensitive target is real and not a parameter of statistics.

11–8 Conclusion. The reader may wonder whether the results of studies as described in this chapter repay the effort which goes into them. Certainly in comparison with the wealth of pictorial information given by the electron microscope, the inferential sketches given here are meager. However, it must be remembered that this method is very much in its infancy, and that electron microscopy has attained a breadth of application which goes far beyond the relatively limited efforts in ionizing radiation work. And it must be further remembered that the two methods are very much complementary. The electron microscope cannot reveal what the structural element does, but can only tell us that something appears to be there, whereas the ionizing radiation technique is completely concerned with the function of the section of the organism. Thus quite vital auxiliary information can come from the radiation studies. In addition, the sizes which can be measured by ionizing radiation are rather smaller than can conveniently be measured microscopically. Therefore the promise of the radiation method is considerable, and it should form a useful branch of biophysics.

PROBLEMS

1. The following figures are derived from work by Pollard and Setlow for the inactivation of the ability of T2 to interfere with T1, and by Powell and Pollard for the inactivation of the interfering ability of influenza virus. Calculate the molecular weight of the unit responsible for interference in each case.

T2/T1 interference		Influenza interference	
% left	Electrons/cm^2*	% left	Electrons/cm^2*
60	5×10^{13}	60	5×10^{13}
23	1.1×10^{14}	23	10^{14}
10	1.9×10^{14}	11	1.5×10^{14}

    * Electrons of this energy lose their energy at 2.74 ev per 100 A.

2. Assuming the nucleus of *E. coli* to lie 1300 A from the surface, calculate the energy of low-voltage electrons needed to inactivate with high efficiency. What effect of random bacterial orientation would you expect?

3. Calculate the 37% dose for a single hit process on:

    (a) a chromosome of diameter 1000 A and length 10 microns,

    (b) polio virus, radius 150 A,

    (c) a molecule of hemoglobin,

    (d) a molecule of thiamin.

REFERENCES

1. E. C. POLLARD, "Ionizing Radiation Methods for Determining Biological Structure," *Proceedings of New York Academy of Sciences* **59**, 469 (1955).

2. E. C. POLLARD, "Ionizing Radiation and Viruses," *Adv. Virus Research* II, 109 (1954).

3. E. C. POLLARD, "Use of Ionizing Radiation to Study Virus Structure," *IRE Transactions on Medical Electronics* **PGME–6**, 56 (1956).

4. E. C. POLLARD, "Ionizing Radiation and Cell Structure," *Rev. Mod. Phys.* **31**, 273 (1959).

5. M. DAVIS, "Irradiation of Bacterial Spores with Low-Voltage Electrons," *Arch. Biochem. and Biophys.* **48**, 469 (1956).

6. H. P. KNAUSS, "Penetration of Slow Electrons Through Spore Walls of *Bacillus megaterium*," *Science* **124**, 182 (1956).

7. J. JAGGER and E. C. POLLARD, "Inactivation with Fast Charged Particles of Infectivity and Hemagglutination in Influenza A Virus," *Rad. Res.* **4**, 1 (1956).

8. D. WILSON and E. C. POLLARD, "Radiation Studies on the Infectious Property of Newcastle Disease Virus," *Rad. Res.* **8**, 131 (1958).

9. J. W. PREISS, "The Localization of Invertase in the Yeast Cell with Low-Voltage Electrons," *Arch. Bioch. Biophys.* **75**, 186 (1958).

10. P. BONET-MAURY, "L'Ultra-Microscopie Statistique des Virus," *Revue Canadienne de Biologie* **5**, 489 (1946).

CHAPTER 12

MICROSCOPES

12–1 Introduction. The aim of molecular biophysics is to explain the operation of living things in terms of the known properties of molecules such as nucleic acids, amino acids, sugars, and ions. We have seen that one of the important properties of these substances, as far as life is concerned, is the way in which they are organized in the polymers of DNA, proteins, and polysaccharides. But the specification of this small-molecule organization is not sufficient to account for the processes we are interested in. There exists a higher level of organization which we must know about if we are to complete our description of cellular workings. This higher level of organization is concerned with the arrangement of large molecules to form structures whose dimensions are 100 A and bigger. This level of organization cannot easily be investigated by experimental methods such as sedimentation and diffusion or x-ray diffraction. (An exception is small-angle x-ray diffraction, which may be used to determine the large repeat distances in large repetitive structures such as muscle and collagen.) We are forced to fall back on well-known microscopic techniques which magnify small objects to the point where the organization is visible to the eye. We shall take up briefly both light microscopes and electron microscopes. In both cases we shall be concerned with three important aspects of microscope utilization, namely magnification, resolution, and contrast. Although we shall consider them separately, the three quantities are not independent of one another. Insofar as possible, the light and electron microscopes will be analyzed together since the fundamental concepts are common to both.

12–2 Magnification. The normal eye is just able to resolve two objects which subtend an angle of one minute of arc (3×10^{-4} radian) at the eye. Objects that are closer than this angular separation will not be seen as separate, and a single complex object which subtends a smaller angle will appear to be structureless. The resolution of the eye is set by diffraction from the eye pupil, lens aberrations, and the angular separation of the cones (one-half minute of arc).

If the objects are 25 cm away (the distance of closest approach which is comfortable), they must be at least 0.07 mm apart if they are to be resolved. If we wish to see objects whose dimensions are smaller, the image of the object must be made to subtend an angle greater than one minute of arc on the retina. This is achieved with a simple magnifying glass

380

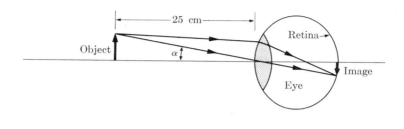

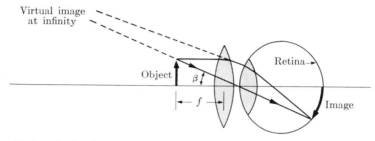

FIG. 12–1. A simple magnifying glass. Since the object is close to the eye, the angle it subtends (β) is larger than the angle when the lens is absent (α).

(Fig. 12–1) by placing the object at the focal point of the lens. The light falling on the eye then acts as if it comes from infinity, a comfortable distance to look at. The ratio of the angle subtended on the retina by the image to the angle subtended by the object when it is 25 cm away is clearly $25/f$ if all the angles concerned are small. It is impossible with this simple system to achieve high magnification and relatively high light intensity and at the same time eliminate the aberrations such as spherical aberration, astigmatism, coma, and chromatic aberration associated with single-element lenses. Some of Leeuwenhoek's simple lenses had magnifications of 250×, but because of aberrations they had much less than the theoretical resolution (see Section 12–3).

Higher magnification with much less aberration and distortion may be achieved with a combination of lenses, as in the compound microscope. Schematic diagrams of compound light microscopes and compound electron microscopes are shown in Fig. 12–2. Both microscopes have (a) *condensing systems* to illuminate the object, (b) *objective lenses* which project an enlarged image of the object on the first-image plane, and (c) *projection lenses* to project an enlarged image, I_2, of I_1 on the second-image plane. In the light microscope the projection lens may be the combination of eyepiece and eye, as shown, or a camera lens.

In actual practice the simple lenses shown in Fig. 12–2 for the light microscope are replaced by combinations of lenses, such as shown in

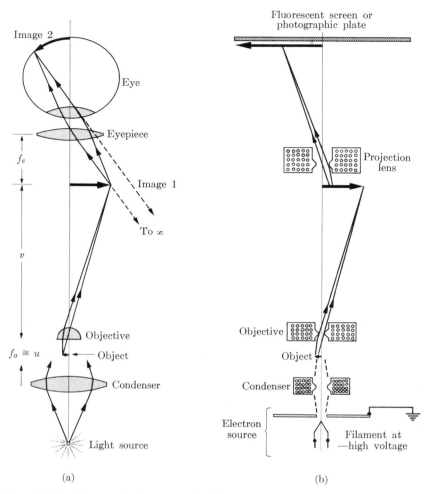

FIG. 12–2. Schematic diagrams of (a) a compound light microscope, and (b) a compound electron microscope. Not to scale.

Fig. 12–3, which enable the lens designer to obtain a large aperture (useful for high resolution) and still minimize the lens aberrations. The magnification of a compound microscope is the product of the magnifications of objective lenses and projection lenses. For the microscopes shown in Fig. 12–2 the magnifications would be:

$$\frac{I_1}{0} \cdot \frac{25}{f_e} = \frac{v}{u} \cdot \frac{25}{f} = \frac{v}{f_0} \cdot \frac{25}{f_e}$$

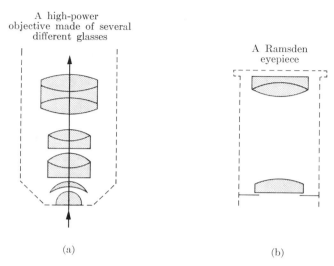

A high-power
objective made of several
different glasses

A Ramsden
eyepiece

(a)   (b)

FIG. 12–3. (a) A high-power objective made of several different glasses. (b) A Ramsden eyepiece.

for the light microscope and

$$\frac{I_1}{0} \cdot \frac{I_2}{I_1} = \frac{I_2}{0}$$

for the electron microscope. In the electron microscope the magnification is shared equally between the two lenses, but in the light microscope most of the magnification is achieved by the objective lens. The maximum useful magnifications of the two types are limited, as shown in Section 12–3, by diffraction to the values 200,000× and 2000×.

The big differences between electron and light microscopes are the methods of focusing and the practical fact that the sample in the electron microscope must be in a vacuum. Light is bent by use of materials of different indices of refraction, and therefore a light microscope is focused by changing the distance between objective and object. An electron beam is bent by magnetic lenses whose magnetic field strength, and therefore focal length, may be changed *continuously* by altering the electric current through the magnet windings. The principle of a magnetic lens, but not the complexity of designing a good one, is illustrated in Fig. 12–4, where the path followed by an electron in a magnetic field is indicated. Because the force exerted on a moving charge by a magnetic field is always perpendicular to its velocity, the paths followed by the electrons are helical and the images are rotated with respect to the object. Magnetic lenses are only converging, and it is therefore not possible to

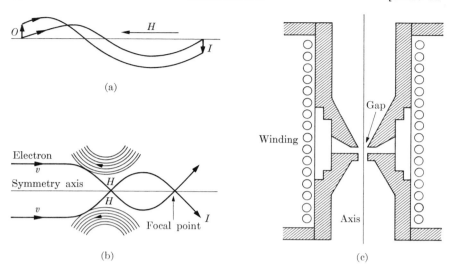

Fig. 12–4. The principle of a magnetic lens. (a) A uniform magnetic field has a magnification of one. Electrons moving parallel to H are *not* deflected. (b) A nonuniform magnetic field has a magnification of greater than one. Electrons moving parallel to the symmetry axis are focused. (c) A cross section of a high-power magnetic lens.

correct their aberrations by using diverging lenses, as in the optical case. This limits the entrance angle to an electron microscope to 5×10^{-3} radians, compared with about 1.7 radians for the light microscope. If the nonuniform magnetic field is concentrated in a small region of space, the lens will have a short focal length. Figure 12–4(c) shows a cross section of such a lens. The magnetic field produced by the magnetic windings is confined to the region between the pole pieces, which are kept in position by the brass spacer between them.

12–3 Resolution. It should be clearly recognized that a microscope has a maximum useful magnification. There is no sense in magnifying an object if physical limitations make it impossible to resolve details of the object. The physical limitation which acts in the case of a microscope is that of diffraction. Neither light nor an electron travels in a straight line when passing through an aperture. The smaller the opening, the larger the diffraction image that is obtained. When the diffraction images from two nearby sources overlap considerably, it is not possible to distinguish the sources; they seem to act as one. The size of the diffraction pattern depends on the ratio of the wavelength to aperture dimensions. It is in this ratio that the big difference between light and electrons exists. The range of optical wavelengths used is from 2000 to 7000 A. Electron wave-

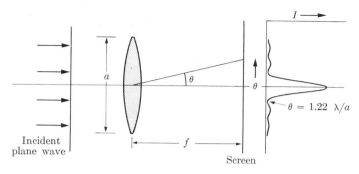

Fig. 12–5. The diffraction pattern of an incident plane wave in the focal plane of a lens of diameter a.

lengths, on the other hand, are less than 0.1 A for the electron energies used today. The waves associated with electrons are interpreted as probability waves. If the wavelength of an electron is 0.01 A, then we certainly cannot localize an electron any better than this. Thus the considerations of diffraction and resolving power that apply to optical instruments also apply to electron microscopes or to other particle microscopes. The wavelength of an electron is given by the de Broglie relation, $\lambda = h/mv$, where h is Planck's constant and mv is its momentum. An electron with an energy of 50 kev has a momentum of 1.3×10^{-17} gm·cm/sec,* and thus the wavelength is equal to 0.05 A.

A slightly detailed analysis of the diffraction pattern applicable to light and electrons follows. When light from a distant point source passes through a circular lens, a point image will not appear, but the resulting diffraction pattern in the focal plane of the lens will consist of a series of concentric circles. The relative intensities of these circles as a function of the angular deviation from the axis of the lens is shown in the Fig. 12–5. The angular separation between the central maximum and the first minimum is, if the angles are small, equal to $1.22 \lambda/a$, where λ is the wavelength of the light or particle and a is the lens diameter. This diffraction pattern arises from interference among the various parts of the wavefront traveling through the aperture. If we have two light sources, each source will give rise to its own diffraction pattern, and the intensity in the focal plane of the lens will be the sum of the two intensity patterns. The resolution of a lens is expressed in terms of its ability to separate two light sources which are close to each other. The criterion proposed by Rayleigh is that two sources shall be considered as resolved if the maximum of the diffraction pattern of one coincides with the first minimum of the other.

* The relativistic expression must be used for these quantities; this is one of the few cases we know of in which relativity theory applies to biophysics.

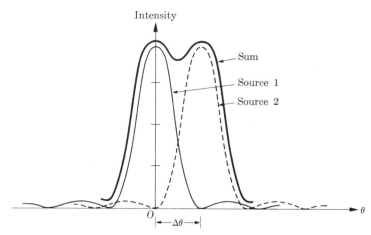

FIG. 12–6. The diffraction pattern produced by two sources separated by an angle. $\Delta\theta = 1.22\,\lambda/a$.

The intensity pattern produced by two sources separated by this angular separation of $\Delta\theta = 1.22\,\lambda/a$ is shown in Fig. 12–6. In practice it is possible to resolve two sources which may be separated by a slightly smaller angle, $\Delta\theta = \lambda/a$.

The Rayleigh criterion for resolution indicates clearly why high resolution is achieved with short wavelengths (electrons, for example) and large aperture. The effect of decreasing the aperture of a lens on its resolving power is indicated in the photographs of Fig. 12–7.

It is more difficult to use the Rayleigh criterion to determine the minimum separation which can be resolved with a microscope because a microscope does not use plane waves from the object to form an image in the focal plane of the objective lens. Light from the object diverges toward the objective and is focused a distance v from the lens, as shown in Fig. 12–8. Since the distance v is very large compared with $f \cong u$, we may think, to a first approximation, of the light emerging from the lens and converging to infinity instead of to v. If we now imagine that the light paths are *reversed*, we have the situation shown in Figs. 12–5 and 12–6 of light from infinity focused in the focal plane of a lens of aperture a, and we can apply the Rayleigh criterion to the minimum resolvable angular separation. Because the object is very close to the objective lens (that is, u may be less than 1 mm), the angle θ is very large. The angle ϕ, on the other hand, is much smaller, since the distance v is about 160 mm. To an excellent approximation, $\sin\phi = \tan\phi$, and the lens aperture is related to v and ϕ by

$$a = 2v \sin \phi. \tag{12–1}$$

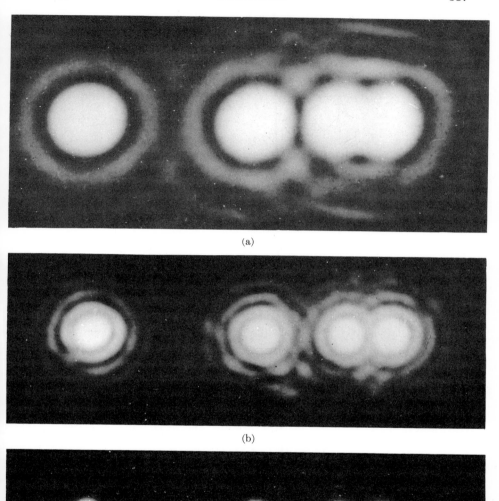

(a)

(b)

(c)

FIG. 12–7. The diffraction patterns of four point sources with a circular aperture in front of the lens. In (a) the aperture is so small that the two right-hand sources satisfy the Rayleigh criterion. In (b) and (c) the aperture is larger. [From F. W. Sears and M. W. Zemansky, *College Physics,* Third Edition, Addison-Wesley, 1960.]

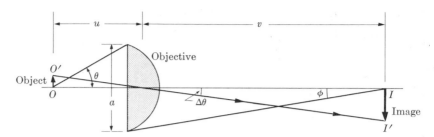

FIG. 12–8. The distances and angles involved in the derivation of the formula for the resolution of a microscope. Angle θ is large, angle ϕ is small, and $\Delta\theta$ is *very* small.

If the image points I and I' are to be resolved, we find from the reversibility argument above that they must be separated by an angle $\Delta\theta$, where

$$\Delta\theta = 1.22 \frac{\lambda}{a}. \tag{12-2}$$

As indicated in Fig. 12–8, this minimum angle is also the angle subtended by the object OO' at the objective. To obtain the minimum object-size that may be resolved, we proceed in the following way.

Because $\Delta\theta$ is a very small angle,

$$\Delta\theta = \frac{OO'}{u} = \frac{II'}{v} = 1.22 \frac{\lambda}{a}. \tag{12-3}$$

If the object is in a medium of refractive index n and the image is in a medium of index 1, then a general formula, due to Helmholtz, states

$$n \cdot (OO') \sin \theta = (II') \sin \phi. \tag{12-4}$$

On combining Eqs. (12–1), (12–3), and (12–4), we obtain for the minimum resolvable separation

$$OO' = u \, \Delta\theta = v \frac{(OO')}{(II')} \cdot \frac{1.22\lambda}{a} = v \frac{\sin \phi}{n \sin \theta} \cdot \frac{1.22\lambda}{2v \sin \phi} = \frac{1.22\lambda}{2n \sin \theta}$$

or

$$OO' = \text{minimum resolvable separation} = 0.61 \frac{\lambda}{n \sin \theta}. \tag{12-5}$$

The quantity $n \sin \theta$ is known as the numerical aperture of the system:

$$n \sin \theta = \text{NA}. \tag{12-6}$$

The minimum separation then is simply 0.61 times the wavelength divided by the numerical aperture. As we mentioned previously, in actual practice one can do slightly better than the Rayleigh criterion, and in general we can use the simpler expression, namely that the minimum separation is the wavelength divided by twice the numerical aperture, or

$$h = \text{minimum resolvable separation} = 0.5 \frac{\lambda}{\text{NA}}. \tag{12–7}$$

Unfortunately, a microscope that can resolve small objects is said to have a high resolution.

It is apparent from Eq. (12–7) that high resolution may be obtained in a microscope by using small wavelengths and high numerical apertures. The maximum value of the angle θ, subtended by the objective lens at the objective, is 90°, and if the object is in air or a vacuum (for which $n = 1$) the resolution distance is $\lambda/2$. For green light, of wavelength 5000 A, the resolution distance, h, is 2500 A, or 0.25 μ, which is about one-fourth the dimensions of a bacterium of *E. coli*. An ultraviolet microscope, working at 2500 A, would have $h = 0.12\,\mu$ for a numerical aperture of one. A more important reason than higher resolution for using ultraviolet microscopes is the fact that ultraviolet light is strongly absorbed by such substances as nucleic acids and protein, and therefore the specimen may be seen with good *contrast*. The subject of contrast, i.e., the difference in intensity between adjacent parts of the image, is a very important one and will be taken up in Sections 12–4 through 12–11. Suffice to say now that if the contrast is poor in an image, the resolution distance may be much larger than that given by Eq. (12–7).

An electron microscope obtains its high resolving power by using waves (electrons) whose wavelength is much shorter than that of visible light. Theoretically, for a numerical aperture of one, electrons of wavelength 0.05 A (corresponding to an energy of 50,000 ev) would yield a resolution distance of 0.02 A. Modern electron microscopes fall short of this ideal by a factor of 500; they have resolutions of only 10 A. Such a resolution is nothing to be ashamed of. It is at least 100 times better than the light microscope. The reason for the comparatively low resolution of electron microscopes is the large aberrations of the magnetic lenses. Large aperture lenses distort the image so much that the resolution distance actually increases with numerical aperture. Figure 12–9 shows how the resolution depends on the entrance angle of the microscope objective. The best resolution, 10 A, is obtained at 5×10^{-3} radians, or 15 minutes of arc. If an optical microscope had such a small numerical aperture, its resolution with optimum contrast would be 50 μ, which is not much better than the eye's 100 μ. The electron microscope obtains its high resolution because its very small wavelength outweighs the small numerical aperture.

The numerical aperture of an electron microscope is limited by lens aberrations, but for light microscopes the numerical aperture may be

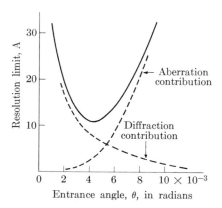

FIG. 12–9. The dependence of the resolution of an electron microscope on the entrance angle θ is shown by the solid curve. The contributions to this curve from diffraction and aberration are indicated.

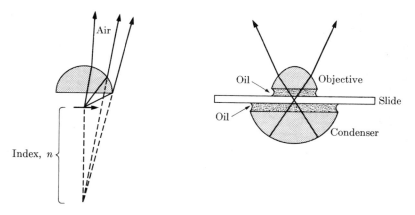

FIG. 12–10. The light paths when an oil-immersion objective is used.

greater than one. Such high values are obtained by immersing the object in a medium of refractive index, n, greater than one. Oil of cedar is a common immersion medium. It has $n = 1.4$. Under these conditions the minimum resolution distance with 5000 A light is 0.18 μ, whereas it is 0.25 μ without oil. Another, not so obvious, advantage of oil immersion is the lack of spherical aberration if, as shown in Fig. 12–10, the slide, object, oil, and objective lens have the same refractive index. This advantage permits the use of lenses whose resolution is governed by diffraction instead of aberration.

There are two other points of interest about the numerical aperture. The amount of light which passes through the microscope depends on the square of the numerical aperture, and the depth of field decreases as the numerical aperture increases. The depth of field, D, is the range of depth in the *object* which may be seen in good focus without readjusting the microscope. It is given by the approximate expression

$$D \cong \frac{2h}{\tan \theta} = \frac{\lambda \cos \theta}{\sin^2 \theta}, \qquad (12\text{–}8)$$

where h is the minimum resolvable distance given by Eq. (12–7) and θ is the entrance angle. For a light microscope with large θ (high aperture) the depth of field may approach the resolution distance. In that case the only way to see all parts of an object is to observe separately its many different planes. Because an electron microscope has such a small entrance angle, it has a very large depth of field. Since θ is small, we may set, in Eqs. (12–7) and (12–8), $\theta = \sin \theta = \tan \theta$ and obtain

$$\text{Electron microscope depth of focus} = \frac{\lambda}{\theta^2}.$$

If $\lambda = 5 \times 10^{-2}$ A and $\theta = 5 \times 10^{-3}$, then $D = 2 \times 10^3$ A, or a depth of field 200 times its resolution distance of 10 A.

The lower limit to the attainable resolution with a microscope really sets a limit also on the magnification which should be used. There is no sense in magnifying the minimum distance up to a point where it is much more than twice the minimum separation that the eye can observe. In the light microscope the minimum distance is near $0.2 \, \mu$. Since the eye can resolve 0.1 mm or 100 μ, a magnification of 500 is sufficient. A magnification of 1000 or 1500 would be easier to use because the eyes would not be subject to as much strain as when they are working at maximum capacity. An electron microscope with a 10 A resolution would need a magnification of 10^5 to bring this minimum resolvable distance up to the point where it can be seen by the naked eye. Not all the magnification must be done by the microscope itself. The image projected on a photographic plate by the projection lens may be further enlarged photographically by as much as 10 times.

12–4 Contrast. We have not yet discussed the most important consideration in our discussion of microscopes—contrast. To be seen, an object must be different from the surrounding medium. If it is not, all the resolving power in the world will be useless, and it is questionable if one is entitled to speak about an object which cannot be detected. The intensity difference between the image of an object and the image of the surrounding medium is called *contrast*. Many ingenious methods have been developed for increasing the contrast in microscope images. Some of these techniques are identified in the following sections, but not all of them are discussed at length.

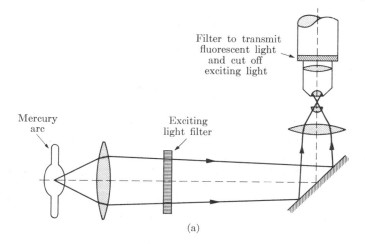

Filter to transmit
fluorescent light
and cut off
exciting light

Mercury
arc

Exciting
light filter

(a)

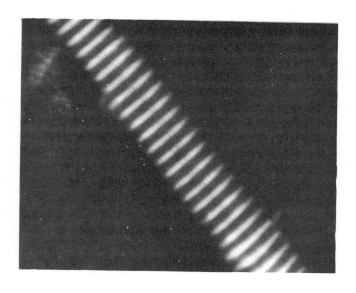

(b)

FIG. 12–11. (a) Schematic diagram of a fluorescence microscope. (b) A photograph illustrating the use of fluorescence microscopy. A chick myofibril was stretched, extracted with glycerol, and treated with fluorescein-labeled antibody to myosin. The labeled antimyosin is localized only in the A-bands of the sarcomeres. (Courtesy of Howard Holtzer.)

12–5 Staining. If the parts of an object absorb a substance, say a dye, differentially, the absorption of light will vary across the object and the light intensity in the image will vary from point to point. Since dyes may be chosen which are reasonably specific for particular chemical groupings, it is possible to visualize the location of cellular compounds. Most staining techniques involve killing the cell. Special "staining" techniques have been developed for electron microscopy. They will be taken up in Section 12–12.

12–6 Fluorescence. By use of stains the object is rendered opaque. The fluorescent technique makes the object luminous. The object, if it will fluoresce, is illuminated by strong ultraviolet light, usually 3650 A, and the object is seen by its fluorescent light. The exciting light must be filtered out, as shown in Fig. 12–11(a), if it affects the detection mechanism. Most cellular constituents such as proteins, nucleic acids, and various structural elements are at best only weakly fluorescent. Therefore the technique is best used with cellular dyes or to observe the location of non-fluorescent molecules to which have been coupled fluorescent groups. Figure 12–11(b) shows a photograph which indicates the concentration of fluorescent antibody.

12–7 Polarization. Objects which have asymmetrical regions or are made up of oriented molecular structures may be transparent to un-polarized light, but when they are illuminated by polarized light, intensity differences will appear between the random and oriented cellular parts. The principle of the method is to examine the object between crossed polarizers. If the object is isotropic, the field will appear dark. The anisotropic regions will appear as bright areas in the image plane. The ideas of the method were discussed briefly in connection with flow birefringence in Chapter 4.

The arrangement of the optical components is indicated in Fig. 12–12. The polarizer and analyzer are set so that the directions of the oscillating electric fields of the light waves transmitted by them are at right angles. Let the light intensity transmitted by the polarizer and incident on the sample be I_0. It is split up by the asymmetrical object into two equal components (because we have assumed the angles shown in Fig. 12–12):

$$I_{x0} = I_{y0} = \frac{I_0}{2}.$$

On entering the object, the electric fields of the two components are in phase. They are given by

$$E_x = E_{x0} \sin \omega t, \qquad E_y = E_{y0} \sin \omega t,$$

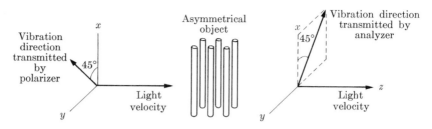

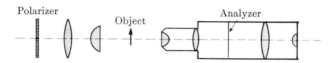

Fig. 12–12.   The orientation of the optical components in a polarizing micro-scope. For simplicity, the angle between the direction of vibration of the incident light and the axis of the oriented structures is taken to be 45°.

where ω is 2π times the light frequency. Since the intensity is proportional to the square of the electric fields, the amplitudes of the two components are

$$E_{x0} = E_{y0} = \frac{E_0}{\sqrt{2}}.$$

The ratio of the two *incident* components is constant at all times, which indicates that the light is plane polarized.

Because the sample is anisotropic, one of the components travels with a greater speed than the other. If the x-component has the lower index of refraction, it will have the higher velocity, and so the y-component will lag *behind* the x-component by some fraction, δ, of a period of oscillation. When they emerge from the sample, the two components may be represented by

$$E_x = E_{x0} \sin \omega t, \qquad E_y = E_{y0} \sin (\omega t - \delta).$$

These two components are now incident on the analyzer. To find the light transmitted through the analyzer, we must find the components of E_x and E_y parallel to the analyzer direction.

E_x contributes $\dfrac{E_x}{\sqrt{2}} \sin \omega t = \dfrac{E_0}{2} \sin \omega t,$

E_y contributes $-\dfrac{E_y}{\sqrt{2}} \sin (\omega t - \delta) = -\dfrac{E_0}{2} \sin (\omega t - \delta).$

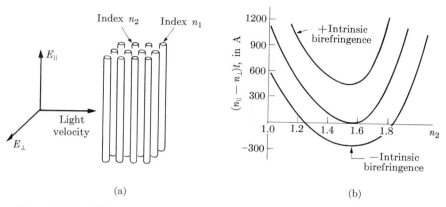

(a)   (b)

FIG. 12–13.   (a) A system of parallel rods which would give textural birefringence.   (b) Birefringence as a function of the index of refraction of the
medium, n_2.

The resultant electric field, E_A, transmitted by the analyzer and detected
by an observer is

$$E_A = \frac{E_0}{2}\left[\sin \omega t - \sin (\omega t - \delta)\right]$$

$$= E_0 \cos \left(\omega t - \frac{\delta}{2}\right)\sin \frac{\delta}{2}.$$

The amplitude transmitted by the analyzer is proportional to $\sin \delta/2$.
Obviously if the medium is isotropic, the two waves travel with the same
speed, $\delta = 0$, and the transmitted intensity is zero.   If one wave lags
behind the other by $\lambda/2$, or 180°, the transmitted intensity will be a
maximum.   In general, anisotropic cellular regions will appear bright when
viewed between crossed polarizer and analyzer.

The polarizing microscope can be used quantitatively so as to determine
the magnitude of the phase lag δ between the two components.   We shall
not go into the details of the techniques except to say that they involve
introducing a known phase lag, by use of quartz plates of suitable thickness,
to counteract the lag δ introduced by the unknown substance.

Substances having different light velocities for electric field vibrations
in different directions are said to be *birefringent*.   The birefringence may
be associated with anisotropic molecules, in which case it is called *intrinsic
birefringence*, or it may be associated with the asymmetrical orientation
of isotropic molecules, which is called *textural birefringence*.   The textural
birefringence depends only on molecular packing and not on molecular
structure.   It may be calculated from an assumed distribution, such as that
shown in Fig. 12–13(a).   If the medium has a refractive index n_2 and the

rods (DNA fibers, for example) have an index n_1, the medium (though not necessarily the molecule) is anisotropic and the electric vector $E_{||}$ will be transmitted through the sample with a lower velocity than $E_\perp$ even though both may be going in the same direction. Let $n_{||}$ and $n_\perp$ be the indices of refraction for light vibrating parallel and perpendicular to the symmetry direction. That is, $n_{||}$ is the ratio of the velocity of light in a vacuum to the velocity of component $E_{||}$. The phase difference δ between the two components is $(2\pi/\lambda)$ times the optical path difference, where λ is the wavelength in vacuum. The optical path difference is $(n_{||} - n_\perp)$ multiplied by the sample thickness t. So we have

$$\delta = \frac{2\pi}{\lambda}(n_{||} - n_\perp)t. \qquad (12\text{–}9)$$

The quantities δ, λ, and t are measurable, and thus the birefringence, $n_{||} - n_\perp$, is obtained.

If the index of refraction of the medium, n_2, is altered, the birefringence will change. When n_2 equals n_1, the textural birefringence will vanish, and any remaining birefringence arises from the anisotropy of the molecules themselves. Figure 12–13(b) shows schematically how the observed birefringence varies with n_2. Proteins show positive intrinsic birefringence, but nucleic acids have negative intrinsic birefringence because the orientation of the bases perpendicular to the molecular axis is equivalent to a set of parallel plates. Such a structure always has negative birefringence.

12–8 Ultraviolet microscopes. We have pointed out that the use of shorter wavelengths permits higher resolution to be obtained. The other reason for interest in ultraviolet microscopy is the high absorption coefficients of cellular components, such as nucleic acids and proteins, in this spectral region. Because of this absorption, specimens show contrast without special staining. It is very difficult to build a refracting microscope which will be in focus over a large range of ultraviolet wavelengths. The original instruments used by Caspersson in his pioneer work on ultraviolet microscopy had to be refocused for each wavelength used. Moreover, since such a microscope is not achromatic, it must be illuminated by monochromatic light.

The experimental setup used in ultraviolet microscopy of cells with a refracting microscope is shown in Fig. 12–14. Light from an ultraviolet source, such as a mercury arc, is passed through the monochromator. The resulting monochromatic light illuminates the quartz microscope. The intensity of the resulting enlarged image may be found by photoelectric or photographic means. The minimum size of object-area whose light transmission can be obtained is determined not only by the resolution of

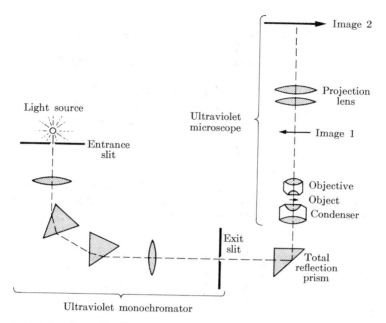

Fig. 12–14. Schematic diagram of an ultraviolet refracting microscope.

the microscope but also by the scattering of light by the object. The minimum size has a diameter in the neighborhood of 0.6 μ.

A solution to the limits imposed on the refracting ultraviolet microscope is to use a reflecting microscope. Since mirrors have the same focal points for all wavelengths, they can be focused in the visible region and will then be in focus in the ultraviolet and also in the infrared. It is difficult, however, to attain large numerical apertures with simple spherical reflectors. A spherical mirror of large aperture has a large amount of spherical aberration. It will not focus parallel rays to a point. It has been found possible to design aspherical surfaces for use in a reflecting microscope. A schematic diagram of this type of condenser-objective system is shown in Fig. 12–15. When oil immersion is used, objectives of this type can get up to a numerical aperture of about one. The advantage of a microscope of this sort becomes immediately apparent if we are interested in studying the absorption of cells or of particular cellular regions over a range of wavelengths. Since the image is in focus for all wavelengths, it is possible to project the image onto the slit of a spectrograph. The spectrograph disperses the light into its component wavelengths, and the result is a picture of the image at many different wavelengths. It is possible to take these spectrograms in a relatively short time, so that any ultraviolet damage to the structures being visualized will be

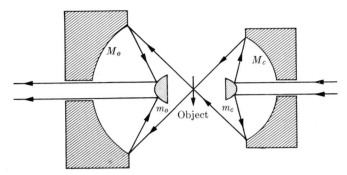

FIG. 12–15. The condenser and objective of a reflecting microscope. M_o and M_c are aspherical; m_o and m_c are spherical. Note the large working distance. This Burch system has a numerical aperture of 0.65.

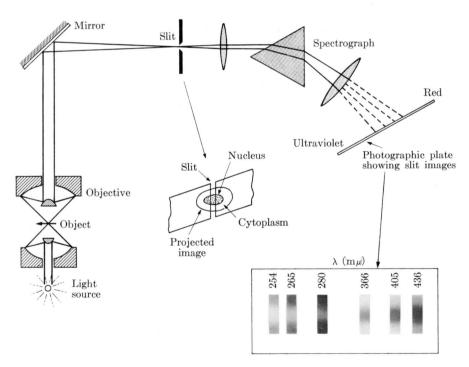

FIG. 12–16. An ultraviolet microscope projects an enlarged image on the slit. The spectrograph disperses the light to give the spectrum shown. Note the large nuclear absorption at 260 mμ and the large cytoplasmic absorption around 400 mμ. [After R. Barer, Ref. 3.]

kept at a minimum. A picture of some frog red blood cells taken with this apparatus is shown in Fig. 12–16. The absorption of the hemoglobin is clearly seen to be a maximum in the neighborhood of 400 mμ, while the nucleus shows its maximum absorption in the region of 260 mμ. Reflecting microscopes cannot only be used to determine cellular absorption spectra, but are indispensable in finding absorption spectra of small crystals or fibers. Some of the absorption curves shown in Chapter 7 were obtained by this technique.

12–9 Interference microscopes. Since most objects, as we have indicated above, show little contrast in visible light, special techniques are required if the image is to be seen. The basic difficulty is that most biological specimens are nonabsorbing in the visible region even though the object may have a refractive index different from its surroundings. This difference in refractive index means that the light forming the image is not in phase with that forming the background. But because it has the same amplitude, the ordinary detectors such as eyes, photocells, and photographic plates do not detect the differences between image and background. The image would be observable if the "phase" image were changed into an "amplitude" image. This transformation is effected by the interference microscope, which makes the phase image interfere with a known light beam so as to produce an interference pattern. We shall see below that the phase microscope is a special, and in some ways inferior, case of the interference microscope.

Suppose the object we wish to "see" is a bacterium of thickness 10^{-4} cm, having a refractive index of 1.34 whereas the surrounding medium's index is 1.33, as shown in Fig. 12–17. The difference in optical path between the two media is 10^{-4} cm $\times (1.34 - 1.33) = 10^{-6}$ cm. If green light of wavelength 5×10^{-5} cm is used, the phase difference between light passing through the object and background is $2\pi/\lambda$ (path difference) $= 0.126$ radians $= 7°$. One way of converting this small phase difference into an amplitude change is to use the "round-the-square" interference

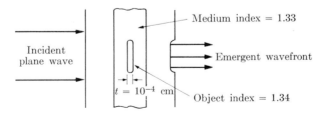

FIG. 12–17. A plane wave incident on a thin object emerges as a distorted plane wave.

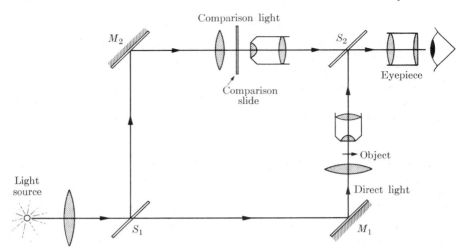

FIG. 12–18. A "round-the-square" interference microscope. The final image is produced by the sum of the direct and comparison beams.

microscope shown in Fig. 12–18. Light from a source is split by the half-silvered mirror S_1 into two parts. One part travels along the path $S_1 M_1$ (object) to the half-silvered mirror S_2, where it is reflected into the eyepiece. The other light beam travels along the path $S_1 M_2$ (comparison) to S_2, where it is transmitted into the eyepiece. The observed image, therefore, arises from the sum of two light beams as in more conventional interferometers. The advantage of the arrangement shown in Fig. 12–18 is that the comparison beam is under the control of the experimenter and thus both its intensity and phase may be altered at will. The difficulty in constructing such a microscope is not only that *two* microscope objectives must be precisely aligned, but also that the two objectives must be identical if the observed image is to have a one-to-one correspondence with the object.

The behavior of the interference microscope is best described in terms of a vector diagram in which the amplitude of the light emerging from a particular part of the object is represented by the magnitude of a vector

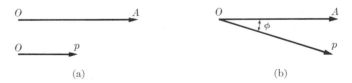

FIG. 12–19. The vector representation of light waves. **OA** represents the light incident on an object. **Op** represents the light transmitted. (a) An absorbing object. (b) A phase object.

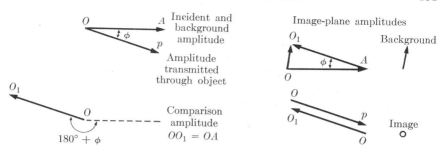

FIG. 12–20. The production of an amplitude image from the sum of the light from a phase object and a comparison beam which has been retarded by $180° + \phi$ relative to the incident light, **OA**.

and the phase is represented by the orientation of the vector. Figure 12–19 shows the relations between the vectors representing the incident and transmitted beams for an absorbing object (with the same refractive index as the surroundings) and a phase object (with the same absorption as the surroundings). The observed intensity is proportional to the square of the amplitudes. Therefore the intensity of the phase object, represented by the square of Op [Fig. 12–19(b)], is the same as that of the surroundings, represented by the square of OA. The object is differentiated from the background only by the fact that the light passing through it has been retarded by an angle ϕ. Suppose the comparison beam has been retarded relative to OA by an angle $180° + \phi$. The resultant image, which is the sum of the direct and comparison beams, will now *not* have the same amplitude as the background and will show amplitude contrast, as indicated in Fig. 12–20. In practice it is not necessary always to adjust the retardation of the compensation beam so that it cancels the transmitted beam. The general case is considered in Fig. 12–21. The solid circle represents the light transmitted through the object. It has a radius $OA = a$. The vector **OO$_1$** represent the magnitude and phase of the compensation light. The resultant amplitude of the image is given by the vector sum **OO$_1$** + **Op** = **OP**. It is easily seen that the locus of the point P is a circle of radius $a = |$**OA**$|$ with the center at O_1. This image circle is shown by the broken circles in Fig. 12–21. All possible non-absorbing objects are represented by points p, and the corresponding image points by P. This scheme changes objects of constant amplitude, $|$**Op**$|$, into images of different amplitudes, $|$**OP**$|$.

Thick objects may have regions in which ϕ is greater than 360°. In this case the space between the thin and thick places will, in the image, be occupied by interference fringes. These regions of alternate high and low intensity are produced by the change in $|$**OP**$|$ as ϕ goes through more than one revolution. A measurement of the retardation yields, more or less

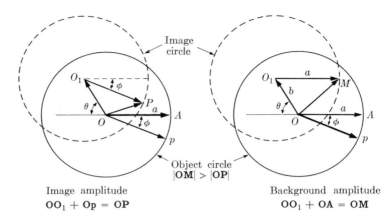

Image amplitude
$OO_1 + Op = OP$

Background amplitude
$OO_1 + OA = OM$

Fig. 12–21. Reference circles for the analysis of the interference microscope. The incident light is given by **OA**. The light through the object (retarded by ϕ) is given by **Op**. The interference light has a magnitude OO_1 (not necessarily equal to OA) and makes an angle θ with **OA**, and the resultant image vector is **OP**.

directly, the surface density of the object, i.e., its mass per unit area. The phase angle ϕ is given by the analog of Eq. (12–9),

$$\phi = \frac{2\pi}{\lambda} t \cdot \Delta n, \qquad (12\text{–}9')$$

where t is the object's thickness and Δn is the refractive-index difference between object and surrounding medium. We mentioned in Chapter 4 that the refractive index of a solution was proportional to the concentration, c, and that for protein solutions $\partial n/\partial c = 0.18$ per gm/cm^3. Therefore, calling the proportionality constant α,

$$\Delta n = \alpha c.$$

Substitution gives

$$\phi = \frac{2\pi}{\lambda} \alpha t c.$$

But tc is the concentration per unit area or surface density σ, so

$$\phi = \frac{2\pi}{\lambda} \alpha \cdot \sigma.$$

If we measure ϕ we can determine σ (without knowing the cell thickness), and a knowledge of the cell's area, A, gives the difference between the cell's mass and the mass of an equal volume of surrounding medium, $\Delta m = A\sigma$. This is equivalent to knowing the *dry* mass of the cell.

Interference microscopes can be made without two sets of objectives as shown in Fig. 12–18, but elaborate attachments are needed above and below the object so as to split the light beam into two parts, only one of which goes through the object.

12–10 Phase microscopes. Another way of visualizing transparent substances is with the phase microscope invented by Zernicke. The phase microscope is a special case of the interference microscope. In the phase microscope the image is produced by interference between the undiffracted and the diffracted light, whereas the interference microscopes described above produce images by interference between all the transmitted light and another *independent* light beam. As we shall see, phase microscopes have defects not shared by interference-type instruments, but their greater simplicity and ease of adjustment outweigh the disadvantages. The theory of operation of phase microscopy is a beautiful example of the complexities involved in image formation in microscopes. To obtain an inkling of how phase microscopy works, it is instructive to delve a little more thoroughly, but by no means completely, into the theory of image formation.

Suppose that we think of a very simple and somewhat artificial situation, one in which the object is a diffraction grating of spacing d made up of opaque and transparent regions, illuminated by parallel monochromatic light. As shown in Fig. 12–22, the lens forms an enlarged image of this

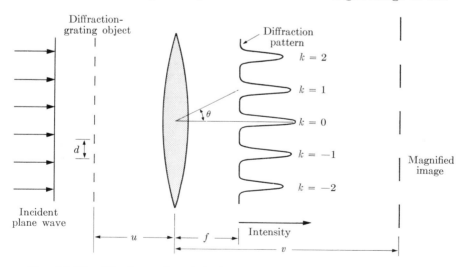

Fig. 12–22. The formation of the image of an amplitude grating by a simple lens.

so-called "amplitude" grating, and the position of the image can be found by the usual lens equation,

$$\frac{1}{u} + \frac{1}{v} = \frac{1}{f}.$$

Anyone familiar with the diffraction grating will recall that in addition to the image of the grating, which is not discussed in diffraction-grating theory, there is obtained, in the focal plane of the lens, a diffraction pattern. With incident monochromatic light, this diffraction pattern consists of a number of bright lines given by the equation

$$k\lambda = d \sin \theta. \tag{12–10}$$

The designations of these lines shown in Fig. 12–22 correspond to the path difference between consecutive openings in the grating. They result from constructive interference. If we represent the light from each opening by a vector, the diffraction maxima will occur when all these vectors are parallel to one another. The vector addition to give the maxima is shown in Fig. 12–23. When $k = 1$, the phase difference between vectors representing adjacent openings is 2π, etc. Note that the diffraction maxima have the *same* phase as the central maximum. The light falling at each of these diffraction maxima comes from all parts of the diffraction grating, which is the object. By the same token we can consider each of the diffraction maxima in the focal plane of the lens as *new* light sources. These new light sources produce a pattern in the plane of the image, a pattern which is simply a magnified one of the object. What we have shown by these rather simple considerations is that the image is produced by light which comes from *all* the diffraction maxima. This light covers the entire image plane, and it is only because the conditions for interference hold that we get an image formed. In general, then, the image of a given object, which of course in the case of a microscope is small, is produced by light from *all* parts of the object. If the object is very large, the diffraction pattern consists almost entirely of the zero-order or central image, and geometrical optics can describe the entire situation. But when the object is small, all parts of the object contribute to all parts of the image.

The diffraction pattern in the focal plane of the objective is related to the resolution limit of the microscope, because, as we have shown, the

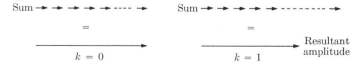

FIG. 12–23. Addition of vector amplitudes to give the diffraction maxima of an amplitude grating.

image is formed by the light coming from the diffraction maxima. If the maxima for $k > 1$ are at such large angles θ that they are not accepted by the microscope, the image is formed only by light from $k = 0(\pm 1)$, and it will have lost some of its detail. This situation is analogous to the representation of a complex wave by the sum of its Fourier components. As more of the Fourier components are omitted, the series representation becomes a poorer approximation to the complex wave. If the grating spacing d is so small that $\lambda/d > 1$, we see from Eq. (12–10) that none of the diffraction maxima pass through the optical system, and therefore the final image is formed only by the central maximum. But this is equivalent to forming an image from a single point source, and such an image will have no relation to the original object. Resolution will be nonexistent for such an array of small objects. The above resolution criterion, $\lambda/d \cong 1$, is similar to Eq. (12–7). The two expressions are different because we have considered the diffraction grating as illuminated by parallel rather than divergent light, and a diffraction grating represents a repetitive array of small objects rather than one small object.

Now let us return to the point of this analysis, namely the detection of phase images. Suppose that as our object we do not have a regular array of transmitting and absorbing components, such as an amplitude diffraction grating, but a regular succession of thick and thin regions or high and low refractive-index regions, as shown in Fig. 12–24. In those parts of the object with larger optical paths, n_2t_2, the light wave lags behind the waves transmitted through n_1t_1. We shall assume, for the moment, that $(n_2t_2 - n_1t_1)$ is small. The light transmitted through the grating will

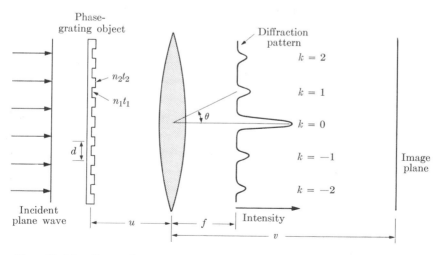

FIG. 12–24. Formation of the image of a phase grating by a simple lens.

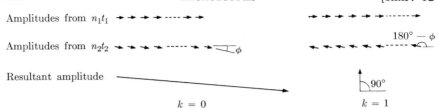

FIG. 12–25. Addition of amplitudes to form the diffraction maxima for $k = 0$ and $k = 1$ of a phase grating. The angle $\phi = 2\pi/\lambda$. It is assumed that $(n_2 t_2 - n_1 t_1)$ is small.

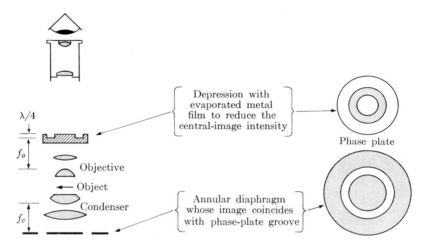

FIG. 12–26. Schematic diagram of a phase microscope.

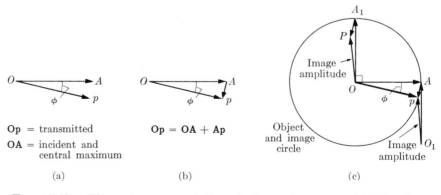

FIG. 12–27. The vector representation of phase microscope. (a) The phase lag of the transmitted light. (b) The resolution of transmitted light into undeviated plus diffracted light. (c) The result of advancing the phase of the undeviated light by 90°.

form a diffraction pattern in the focal plane of the lens in the way shown in Fig. 12–25. The central maximum is large, as in the amplitude grating, but the secondary maxima are small because when $k = 1$, $d \sin \theta = \lambda$ and the phase difference between regions $n_2 t_2$ and $n_1 t_1$ is $180° - \phi$, which means that the two regions *almost* cancel each other, as indicated in the figure. (This cancellation does not exist in the amplitude grating because the region $n_2 t_2$ is opaque.) The other difference between the diffraction patterns of the amplitude and phase gratings is in the relative phases, or time of arrival, of the diffraction maxima. Figure 12–23 indicates that in the case of the amplitude grating all the maxima are *in phase*. But in the phase-grating diffraction pattern, the central maximum differs from the other maxima by 90°, as in Fig. 12–25.

So much for the diffraction pattern of a phase grating. The important point to remember is that the image of the grating, which is formed by light from the diffraction pattern, will *not* be seen because it has no variations in amplitude. If, however, we are able to change the phase-diffraction pattern of Fig. 12–25 into the amplitude pattern of Fig. 12–23, the resulting image of the phase grating which is formed from the diffracted light will show *amplitude* variations. This is the beautiful experimental trick of phase microscopy—the conversion of a phase-diffraction pattern into that arising from an amplitude grating.

The way in which this trick is worked experimentally can be seen by referring to Fig. 12–26. On the lower side of the condenser is a diaphragm with a transmitting annular ring in the condenser focal plane. Parallel light emerges from the condenser, passes through the object, through the objective, and goes on to form the final image. On its way, however, it passes through the focal plane of the objective. In this plane there is an image of the annular diaphragm, the central image of the diffraction pattern produced by the object, and any secondary maxima which arise from diffraction of light by the object. In the back focal plane of the objective, the positions of the diffraction maxima depend on the object, but the central maximum, i.e., the image of the annular diaphragm, is always in the same place. Therefore, in the focal plane of the objective we can put a disk in which there is an annular groove one-quarter of a wavelength deep. The groove is placed so as to coincide with the direct image of the condenser diaphragm. The undeviated beam passes through this groove and is advanced one-quarter wavelength further than the diffracted light. The intensity of the central maximum may also be decreased (so as to make it more nearly equal to the diffracted intensity of Fig. 12–25) by evaporating a semitransparent metallic film onto the annular ring. There is no compelling reason why one-quarter wavelength has to be used. One could retard the direct beam by one-quarter wavelength or by small fractions of a wavelength. But in any event the ultimate purpose of all these

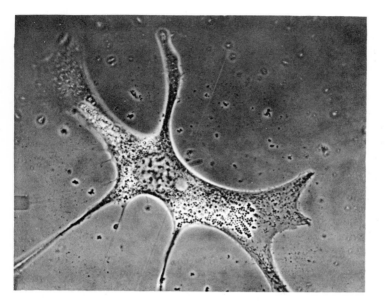

(b)

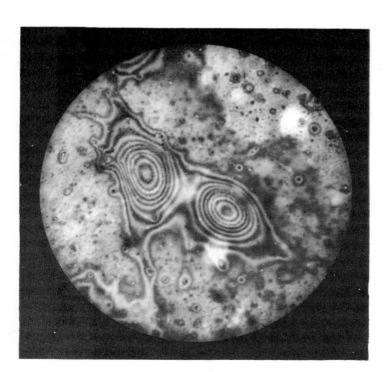

(a)

Fig. 12–28. A comparison of sarcoma cells in tissue culture, obtained with interference and phase microscopes. (a) A multiple-beam interference pattern, at 546 A, of two cells mounted in air. Magnification 1000×, reduced to 80%. (b) A phase-contrast image of a single cell in aqueous medium. Magnification 1000×, reduced to 40%. [Both courtesy of Robert Mellors.]

manipulations is to obtain a large amplitude contrast resulting from a contrasting index of refraction in the object.

Vector representation of phase microscopy. The analysis we have gone through above is particular in that a specific type of object, a diffraction grating, was chosen for discussion. A simple and elegant method of analysis is based on the vector representation we used in discussing interference microscopy. Let the incident light be represented by **OA** in Fig. 12–27. This vector will also represent the undeviated light, which forms the central image, in the back focal plane of the objective. The light passing through the object is retarded by ϕ and is indicated by **Op**. If we assume no absorption, $|\mathbf{OA}| = |\mathbf{Op}|$. As shown in Fig. 12–27(b), the transmitted light may be resolved into

$$\mathbf{Op} = \mathbf{OA} + \mathbf{Ap},$$

which means it is made up of the undeviated light plus a component, **Ap**, which represents the *diffracted* or *scattered* light from the object. Note that for small angles ϕ the diffracted light is approximately 90° out of phase with the undeviated beam. If, as in Fig. 12–26, the undeviated light is advanced by $\lambda/4$, or 90°, the image intensity will be [as shown in Fig. 12–27(c)]

$$\mathbf{OP} = \mathbf{OA_1} + \mathbf{AP} = \mathbf{O_1p} = \mathbf{O_1A} + \mathbf{Ap}.$$

The amplitude of the image intensity is given by the vector joining O_1 and the point p on the circle, which represents the image. For the case we have drawn in Fig. 12–27, the amplitude of the image intensity O_1p is less than the amplitude of background $|\mathbf{O_1A}|$. A phase change has been converted into an amplitude pattern, and the image is now visible.

Phase microscopy in which the undeviated light is advanced 90° in phase is known as *positive contrast*. Objects having slightly higher optical path lengths than their surroundings (that is, ϕ is negative, as in Fig. 12–27), will appear *dark* compared with the background. Other possible types of contrast in which **OA** is shifted by other than 90° and in which its magnitude may be changed (by putting an absorbing layer on the phase-plate depression) are also easily analyzed by the vector representation.

It should be obvious from this vector treatment that the phase microscope is just a special case of the interference microscope, but an inferior one. For example, it is not possible to separate completely the direct and scattered beams. Best separation, and therefore best contrast, is obtained for small objects or for the boundaries or discontinuities of objects. The images in a phase microscope are surrounded by halos which come from diffraction from the phase-plate annulus. Figure 12–28 shows a comparison of the images observed by phase microscopy with those observed in an interference microscope.

12–11 Electron microscopy. The electron microscope is superior to light microscopes as far as resolution is concerned, but it is still plagued with the problem we have been attempting to solve by various ingenious methods, the problem of contrast. If the high resolution of the electron microscope is to be used, the image must show contrast between parts of itself and the surrounding background.

The incident electron beam is not absorbed by the object. It is *scattered*, and many of the emerging electrons no longer pass through the microscope's optical system. Because the maximum numerical aperture is limited by spherical aberration to 5×10^{-3} radians, an electron only has to suffer a slight deflection before it fails to reach the photographic plate in the image plane. To ensure elimination of these scattered electrons, an opaque disk with a hole of about 50 μ in diameter may be placed in the back focal plane of the objective lens. The undeflected beam passes through the hole, which is infinitely greater than the size of hole which would cut off some of the diffraction pattern from the incident beam. Since the scattering power of an object depends on the density of electrons in the object, contrast depends on differences in density between one part of the object and another. Most biological objects have only small variations in density from one point to another and have the same density as the backing support on which they are placed. Therefore the contrast is negligible and must be increased by special means. Two methods for increasing contrast are shadowing and staining. Before describing them, we shall digress to describe the general method of mounting samples.

Electron-microscope samples must be mounted in a vacuum so as to avoid scattering of the electron beam by the air. If high resolution is desired, the samples and their supporting backings must be thin enough so that the incident electron beam loses a negligible amount of energy in traversing the sample. If the electrons do lose energy, they will not be focused in the image plane because of "chromatic" aberration in the magnetic lenses, and the image will be blurred and show poor resolution. The maximum sample and support thickness which will yield 20 A resolution (assuming adequate image contrast and microscope adjustment) is about 200 A for a 50-kv electron beam and about twice this for accelerating voltages of 100 kv. The advantage of the higher-energy machine is very useful. There is another reason, other than increased resolution, which favors thin samples. The theoretical depth of focus of an electron microscope is very high (about 1000 A). The image of a thick sample will show all the detail of the object as on the same level, and the three-dimensional positioning of the internal structures of the object is very difficult. The three-dimensional uncertainty may be eliminated by taking *stereoscopic pairs* of pictures. In this technique electron micrographs are taken of a sample which is inclined to the electron beam at two different angles. When these two pictures are looked at through a stereoscopic viewer, the three-dimensional structure stands out with brilliant clarity. It was in this way that Anderson* was able to show that tailed bacteriophages attach to the bacterial surface by their tails.

The specimens for electron microscopy are supported on thin (100–200 A) films of collodion or formvar, or even thinner (50 A) films of carbon. These thin films are prepared by letting a drop of collodion dissolved in amylacetate spread on a water surface until the desired thickness is obtained or, in the case of carbon, by letting it evaporate in a vacuum onto a clean surface from which it may be removed. These thin films are, in turn, supported mechanically on fine wire meshes having the order of 200 wires per inch.

A specimen, such as a virus preparation, may be put on the specimen holder in the form of a small liquid drop, which is then allowed to dry. The objection to this method of sample preparation is the possible distortion of the object as the liquid is removed and as the liquid surface passes through the object when the liquid evaporates. The surface-tension forces are large and may cause appreciable flattening of the object. One way out of this difficulty is to freeze-dry the samples. Another way is to use a liquid, such as CO_2, that may be removed by taking the

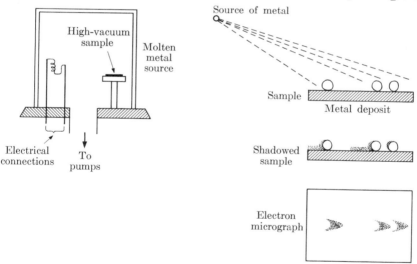

Fig. 12–29. The technique of evaporating a thin metal film onto a three-dimensional object to bring out its contours. The sizes of the objects are greatly exaggerated.

---

* T. F. Anderson, *Cold Spring Harbor Symp. on Quant. Biology*, XVIII, 197 (1953).

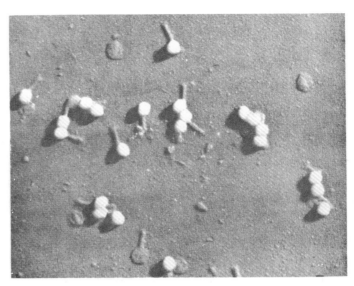

FIG. 12–30(a). A purified suspension of T6 bacteriophage. Note the presence of some protein coats or ghosts. Magnification 70,000×, reduced to 88%. [From R. W. G. Wyckoff, *The World of the Electron Microscope.* Yale University Press, New Haven, 1958.]

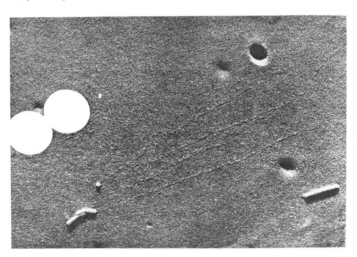

FIG. 12–30(b). Tobacco mosaic virus treated with hot detergent. The particles are nucleoprotein-rod segments of 150 A in width. The thin fibrous structures are thought to be single RNA chains which are visible because of adhering contaminating material. The large white spheres are latex spheres of known size. Magnification 65,000×, reduced to 70%. [From R. G. Hart, *Biochim. et Biophys. Acta,* **28,** 457 (1958).]

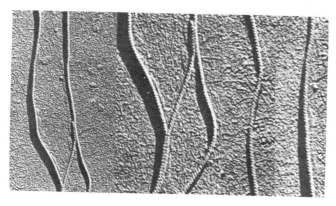

Fig. 12–30(c). Parts of some bacterial flagella showing their stringlike structure. Magnification 50,000×, reduced to 72%. [From L. W. Labaw and V. M. Mosley, *Biochim. et Biophys. Acta*, **15**, 325 (1954).]

sample to a pressure and temperature above the critical point and thus going into the gas phase without producing a boundary between the liquid and gas phases.

The contrast shown by objects deposited from solution onto specimen holders is small if the objects are thin. It is possible to increase the contrast of objects, and at the same time give a three-dimensional effect to the image, by depositing on the object a thin layer of heavy metal atoms such as palladium or uranium. In this process, developed by Williams and Wyckoff, the outline of the object is brought out beautifully but the internal structure may be obscured. A diagram of the evaporation apparatus is shown in Fig. 12–29. The evaporated metal covers the sample holder except in the regions behind the object, since in a high vacuum the metal atoms travel in straight lines. The electron beam incident on this evaporated metal object is scattered in all regions except where the metal was not deposited behind the objects. The electron micrograph is *dark* where no metal was deposited, and light elsewhere. The resulting picture looks as if the objects were casting shadows of a light source located where the evaporation source was placed. The length of the shadow gives the height of the object if the angle of shadowing is known. Figures 12–30(a), (b), and (c) show electron micrographs of preparations which have been shadowed to bring out their forms.

Since the best resolution is achieved with thin samples, a large amount of effort has gone into the development of microtomes which can cut thin sections reproducibly and with a minimum distortion to the sample. As a result, the cutting of thin sections is almost routine. The sample (tissue or bacteria, for example) is first fixed in osmium tetroxide at a *p*H of

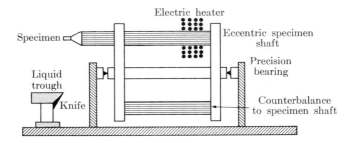

FIG. 12–31. Schematic diagram of an ultramicrotome. [After Sjöstrand, Ref. 9.]

about 7. The osmium tetroxide not only immobilizes the cellular components with a minimum of distortion, but also acts as a staining agent because it has a high electron density. Any cellular components which absorb the osmium are good electron scatterers, and show up well in electron micrographs. After fixation, the sample is usually impregnated with a plastic monomer, such as methacrylate. The plastic monomer is then polymerized by the addition of a catalyzer to yield a solid plastic

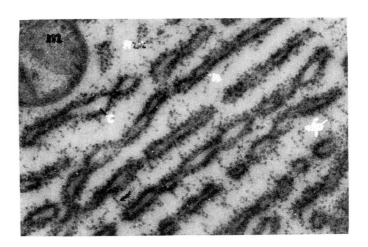

FIG. 12–32. An electron micrograph of a thin section of the basal region of a pancreatic exocrine cell of the rat. Part of a mitochondrion appears at m. The rest of the field is made up of the endoplasmic reticulum which appears as membrane-limited cavities. There are small particles, of $\sim$150 A in diameter, attached to the outer surface of the membranes and in the regions between them. The particles contain RNA and protein. Osmium tetroxide stain. Magnification 50,000×, reduced to 78%. [From G. E. Palade, in *Microsomal Particles and Protein Synthesis*, ed. by R. B. Roberts. Pergamon Press, New York, 1958.]

block which may be cut into thin sections. The small uniform advances of the microtome between sections may be obtained by the thermal expansion of a metal bar, whose rate of expansion may be 10^4 A per minute. If a section were cut every second, its average thickness would be 160 A. A schematic diagram of an ultramicrotome designed by Sjöstrand is shown in Fig. 12–31. The eccentrically mounted sample holder goes by the knife, which may be a piece of glass or a specially sharpened razor blade, once a second. The electric heating coil causes the bar to expand, and the sections which are cut float off onto the liquid surface behind the knife where they may be picked up on specimen holders. Figures 2–3 and 12–32 show two examples of thin-section electron micrographs obtained by the above procedure. Heavy metal compounds other than osmium may be used as electron stains. For example, phosphotungstic acid gives excellent contrast in collagen fibers, as shown in Fig. 5–21.

The field of electron microscopy is a rapidly moving one. For particular details about methods and techniques the reader should consult the articles by Anderson, Sjöstrand, and Gettner and Ornstein cited in the references.

Problems

1. (a) Plot the minimum resolvable distance as a function of entrance angle for the range $\theta = 10°$ to $75°$ and a wavelength of 5000 A. (b) Plot the maximum useful magnification *versus* θ. (c) Plot the depth of focus *versus* θ.

2. (a) What is the wavelength of an electron of energy 50 kv? 100 kv? (b) What is the theoretical resolution of such waves if the numerical aperture $n \sin \theta = \theta = 5 \times 10^{-3}$ radians?

3. Assume that the index of refraction of light of wavelength 5000 A vibrating parallel to the rods of Fig. 12–13(a) is 1.30 and that $n_\perp$ is 1.28. What sample thickness will give a phase difference of 90° between the two components?

4. If incident polarized light makes an angle of 45° with the rods of Fig. 12–12, and $(n_{||} - n_\perp) = 0.02$, plot the intensity transmitted by the analyzer (set at right angles to the polarizer) as a function of thickness for light of wavelength 5000 A.

5. Use the vector diagram of Fig. 12–2 for the interference microscope, and take $OO_1 = OA$ and $\theta = 90°$, to determine the amplitude of the image as a function of the phase retardation ϕ. Work the problem graphically, *not* analytically, and present the results as a graph of relative amplitude *versus* ϕ.

6. Plot the intensity *versus* ϕ for the situation given in Problem 5.

7. Use the vector diagram of Fig. 12–27 for the phase microscope, and take $O_1A = OA$ and $\theta = 90°$, to determine the relative image intensity as a function of the retardation.

8. Work Problem 7 with $\theta = -90°$, $O_1A = OA$.

9. Work Problem 7 with $\theta = 90°$, $O_1A = \frac{1}{2}OA$.

10. An absorbing object, whose index of refraction is the same as its surroundings, is examined in +90° phase contrast. Use a vector diagram to obtain the relative observed image intensity as a function of the percent transmission of the object. (Remember that intensity is proportional to the square of the amplitude.)

REFERENCES

1. T. F. ANDERSON, "Electron Microscopy of Microorganisms," in *Physical Techniques in Biological Research* III, ed. by G. Oster and A. W. Pollister. Academic Press, N. Y., 1956.

2. R. BARER, "Phase-contrast, Interference-contrast and Polarizing Microscopy," in *Analytical Cytology*, ed. by R. C. Mellors. McGraw-Hill, N. Y., 1955.

3. R. BARER, "Microscopy," in *Cytology and Cell Physiology*, ed. by G. Bourne. Oxford University Press, N. Y., 1951.

4. E. R. BLOUT, "Ultraviolet Microscopy and Ultraviolet Microspectrometry," *Adv. Biol. Med. Phys.* **3**, 285 (1953).

5. M. E. GETTNER and L. ORNSTEIN, "Microtomy," in *Physical Techniques in Biological Research* III, ed. by G. Oster and A. W. Pollister. Academic Press, N. Y., 1956.

6. G. OSTER, "Birefringence and Dichroism," in *Physical Techniques in Biological Research* I, ed. by G. Oster and A. W. Pollister. Academic Press, N. Y., 1955.

7. H. OSTERBERG, "Phase and Interference Microscopy," in *Physical Techniques in Biological Research* I, ed. by G. Oster and A. W. Pollister. Academic Press, N. Y., 1955.

8. O. W. RICHARDS, "Fluorescence Microscopy," in *Analytical Cytology*, ed. by R. C. Mellors. McGraw-Hill, N. Y., 1955.

9. F. S. SJÖSTRAND, "Electron Microscopy of Cells and Tissues," in *Physical Techniques in Biological Research* III, ed. by G. Oster and A. W. Pollister. Academic Press, N. Y., 1956.

10. C. E. HALL, *Introduction to Electron Microscopy*, McGraw-Hill, N. Y., 1953.

11. R. W. G. WYCKOFF, *Electron Microscopy*. Interscience Publishers, N. Y., 1949.

CHAPTER 13

ISOTOPIC TRACERS IN MOLECULAR BIOPHYSICS

13–1 Introduction. Among nature's building blocks are neutrons and protons. From these the nuclei of elements are formed, and around the nuclei the electrons settle into the charge clouds which determine the valence and chemical properties of each element. The charge clouds settle in patterns determined only by the number of protons. The mass and the stability of the atom reside predominantly in the nucleus and depend on both neutrons and protons.

The fact that only a part of the atomic nucleus is concerned with chemical properties makes it possible to vary the kind of atom in a molecule without varying the chemical properties. Such varied atoms are called *isotopes*. Work with isotopes is given the name *tracer* work, although, as will be seen, their ability to trace atoms is only a part of their usefulness in cellular studies. Preliminary to an account of the use of abnormal atomic species in biological studies, we shall begin with a short description of the nature of the atomic nucleus and of its potential behavior when it is not fully stable.

Neutrons and protons in an atomic nucleus form a very confined system. By a huge margin, the nucleus is the most dense part of space that exists. In any confined atomic system, the laws of atomic physics hold, and there is no reason to believe that they fail to do so in the nucleus. This being the case, the neutrons and protons occupy various levels of energy, and the requirements of the Pauli exclusion principle are also imposed on the number and character (whether neutron or proton) of the nuclear particles in each level. This simple and natural statement, clearly consistent to the student of atomic physics, has very important consequences. The density of the nucleus is so great, and the forces between particles are so large, that the enforced occupancy of a higher energy level by either a neutron or a proton entails a considerable change in energy. In many cases this change in energy means that a combination of different proportions of neutrons and protons has considerably less total energy in the nucleus. This means that a change from a neutron to a proton, or *vice versa*, will give an evolutionary advantage to the new nucleus. The mechanism of evolution, explained by Fermi, consists either of a change of the neutron into a proton, electron, and neutrino or the change of a proton into a neutron, positive electron (positron), and neutrino. The change involves an energy difference, positive for the neutron becoming a proton and negative if a proton alters. In all these processes,

417

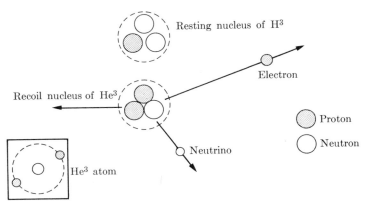

FIG. 13–1. Change of H^3 into He^3. The resting nucleus, after a time which is not determined for any one atom, suddenly converts a neutron to a proton, with the events as shown. The energy released is divided between the recoil nucleus, the electron, and the neutrino. Since the neutrino is almost undetectable, a part of the energy is apparently missing.

the neutrino is not detected, even though it may carry energy, momentum and angular momentum.

The net result of this ability of the nucleus to change character is a process as drawn in Fig. 13–1. In the upper part of the figure, the resting nucleus is shown, with a dashed line indicating the approximate extent of nuclear forces, which is about the best that can be done to delimit the nucleus. In the lower part, the actual moment of transition is shown. The real event is the change of the neutron to a proton, which takes place inside the nucleus. Accompanying this event, and more dramatic from the outside, is the ejection of an electron and neutrino, with the recoil of the much heavier nucleus. The energy release is divided among the three moving elements, very unequally, because the lighter particles take much the greater proportion. The energy taken by the neutrino is almost undetectable, because the neutrino has so slight an interaction with matter, and this results in a somewhat unusual uncertainty in the energy of the electron because it is sharing energy with a "silent" partner. The final part of the process, when the smoke has cleared away, is the completion of the initial process. The new charge caused by the new proton attracts an extra electron from the surrounding matter. This is almost certainly not the original electron which went out, but another electron dislodged from matter in some way. Since there are always as many electrons as there are positive particles (if some of the transient particles of cosmic rays are excepted), there is always an electron available. The total result is therefore a complete atom of helium, which takes its place in the chemistry of the surrounding matter. This last stage is shown (on a very different scale) in the left-hand insert in Fig. 13–1.

One or two features of this process need mention. The first is the obvious one that elements other than hydrogen can be radioactive and go through this change. In fact, every element can exist in a radioactive form. The second is the variable probability with which the radioactive decay can take place. It is always very low, particularly in terms of what might be called nuclear times, but the low figure is also quite variable from element to element. The probability of decay per unit time is called the *decay constant*, denoted by λ. The law of radioactive decay is expressed in the familiar form as

$$\frac{dN}{N} = -\lambda \, dt,$$

which can be expressed in the integral form as

$$\ln \frac{N}{N_0} = -\lambda t.$$

If t_h is the time at which N is $\frac{1}{2}N_0$, we have $t_h = (\ln 2/\lambda)$. The value of t_h, or the *half-life*, is expressed in more familiar time units and has caught the imagination as the way to describe the probability of decay. Half-lives vary from small fractions of seconds to billions of years. The half-life is therefore a most important property of a radioactive element.

A third feature of the process is the fact that it is quite possible that the daughter nucleus formed after the decay is actually not in the final energy condition. If it is not, it will shortly reach that condition by emitting electromagnetic radiation or *gamma radiation*. Accordingly, gamma radiation is sometimes an important feature of a radioactive process.

On the whole, nuclei seem to be more stable when there are more neutrons than protons, particularly if the nuclei are complex. The excess of neutrons need not always be the same, which means that quite often elements can have one, two, or even more neutrons than the number necessary to give stability. These nuclei are quite different in nuclear properties, but are, nevertheless, charge centers essentially indistinguishable from the charge center that is characteristic of the element. Since they have the same number of protons, they behave chemically in the same way. But because they have a different number of neutrons, they have different masses, and this difference can be used to distinguish them and indeed separate them. Thus stable isotopes, with unusual concentration of the various species, can, in conjunction with means for detecting mass, be used to label some part of a cellular process. The same is true, of course, of radioactive isotopes, except that the radioactivity is generally so obvious a phenomenon that mass detection is not necessary.

We summarize this introduction by saying that unusual nuclei permit the tracing of a particular chemical process by either detecting radioactivity or measuring the proportion of unusual mass isotopes in a sample.

13–2 Detection and measurement of isotopes. Probably no more intensive effort has gone into any form of instrumentation than that of detecting isotopes and radioactivity. It is almost impossible that the reader knows nothing about this; indeed it is likely that he has already used several forms of nuclear particle detection, and quite probably has some decided opinions about their use. In fact, so far has the art of detection progressed that it is with a sense of dismay that the authors contemplate the array of weapons available for the purpose. Nevertheless, in spite of the formidable contents of manufacturer's catalogs, and the list of model numbers therein, some very simple principles exist for isotopic detection. Since these concern biophysical observation, we propose to discuss them briefly here.

The problem of detecting radioactivity is dominated by the process of ionization and excitation as a fast charged particle passes through matter. Matter enters in two ways, either as an absorber or the detecting agent. If the amount of matter which intervenes before the detecting is accomplished is too high, the particle cannot be detected. This, then, becomes a big factor if the energy of the particle is small, as is the case for tritium or C^{14}. The detecting agent is conditioned by the form of detection selected. One of the simplest is the observation of a small ionization current produced in a gas by the ionization of the particle or group of particles if the source of activity is high enough. The observation is made possible by the large forces between small electrostatic charges, which cause a gold leaf to deflect or a quartz fiber to twist on its suspension. The ionization current is used to neutralize these charges, thus causing a diminished repulsion and a movement of the gold leaf or the fiber.

Such a method is very hard to adapt to the detection of single decays, in other words, to *counting*. It can be modified by replacing the gold leaf or quartz fiber with an electronic amplifier, but then there is the extra complication of fluctuations in the much larger currents under control in the vacuum tubes. In a physics laboratory, where the necessary shielding and stabilization of power sources can be used, this method of amplification has been employed. In biological laboratories, where elaboration is undesirable, two modifications of this method have evolved. The first is to replace the gas in which the ionization current flows by a clear solid which emits light when the fast particle passes through it. The second is to use the phenomenon of ionization by collision to amplify the current initially produced. The first device is known as a *scintillation counter*; the second takes two forms, the *proportional counter* and the *Geiger-Müller counter*.

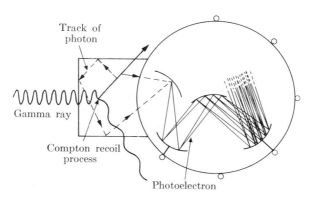

FIG. 13–2. Schematic drawing of the action of a scintillation counter. The gamma ray enters the sodium iodide phosphor, and its energy is converted by Compton recoil into an electron and a photon of longer wavelength. The electron ionizes and excites along its path until stopped. The light photons (shown dashed) spread out, and some reach the photocathode, there to start the photomultiplier avalanche.

The scintillation counter consists of a block of a material known as a *phosphor*, which both generates a relatively high fraction of light when the ionizing particle traverses it and does not itself absorb it. The phosphor is fastened to the surface of an electron multiplier tube in such a way that the light falls on the photocathode of the vacuum tube. The arrival of a fast particle then causes a tiny flash of light, which in turn gives rise to a burst of electrons in the photomultiplier tube—a burst so large that the detection process is essentially reduced to quite commonplace electronic trickery. The special design of the scintillation counter depends on its purpose. If it is intended to count energetic gamma radiation, then the block is made both large and dense so that the transfer of energy from the high-energy gamma-ray photon to a fast electron can take place with relatively high probability. A schematic drawing of a scintillation counter is shown in Fig. 13–2. The phosphor indicated is sodium iodide, which is dense and can be grown to large dimensions (upwards of a cubic inch). Cesium iodide is also now available. Such a phosphor is excellent for counting high-energy gamma radiation as from sodium or cobalt. Other forms can include a phosphor of a transparent plastic that can be made into a light trap which will turn corners. Such a phosphor can be used for counting inside an animal preparation and has even been inserted in the human brain. Liquid phosphors are also available and have many uses.

The second class of counters, the proportional and Geiger-Müller counters, use a region of very high electric field to accelerate electrons liberated by the flying particle to energies where they in turn will ionize. This

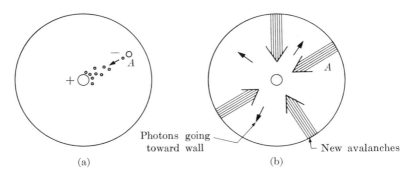

Photons going
toward wall

New avalanches

(a)   (b)

Fig. 13–3. Schematic representation of the action of (a) a proportional counter, and (b) a Geiger-Müller counter.

process, of *ionization by collision*, can cause the entering particle to develop many times the current originally produced. The action can be seen schematically in Fig. 13–3. The left-hand side shows the action of the proportional counter. The fast particle enters at A, where its track is shown end on. It ionizes, and the positive-negative ion pair promptly separates, with the electron going toward the positive wire and the positive ion moving slowly toward the outer case. The electron collides with gas molecules many times on its way toward the wire, and in such collisions it must never encounter a gas impurity which is electronegative (i.e., it likes to attach an electron to itself). If it successfully runs this course, it will reach the region near the wire where the fields are very high, and in between collisions it may acquire enough energy to ionize in turn. When this happens, there are now two electrons to ionize, and so on, until an avalanche of charge develops. This produces a local negative region that acts to diminish the electric field near the wire, which results in a cessation of the process. The electrons then rapidly enter the wire, changing its potential, and the positives move away, also changing the potential of the wire. In a time of about 10^{-5} second, everything is over and a new process can begin.

Because the potential change of the wire is small, some amplification is necessary. The amplification by ionization by collision in the gas (gas-amplification) has, however, brought the problem of detection out of limiting sensitivity into ordinary sensitivity, and the associated amplifier is not technically difficult. In the proportional counter the extent of the avalanche (and the consequent potential change) is statistically proportional to the original ionization. This is sometimes an advantage, sometimes a nuisance. In any event, a logical extension of this technique of gas amplification is to push the avalanche size up (by raising the interelectrode voltage) until it is so large that it generates sufficient photons to produce photoelectrons at the outer wall and start a discharge. This discharge effectively solves the detection problem, because the voltage on the wire can change by hundreds of volts if a discharge flows. On the other hand, it has to be put out. The Geiger-Müller counter, therefore, which employs this method, detects any ionization, triggers a discharge, and requires a quenching circuit, or special gas mixtures, including organic molecules, which are self-quenching.

Because a whole discharge does many things to a container of gas, a Geiger counter does not recover for a millisecond or so. This, in turn, means that a counting rate faster than 100 per second or so will be subject to error due to the fact that the counter may be in the recovery stage when called on to count. A proportional counter does not have such a long recovery time and can be used to count at very much more rapid rates.

Radioactive decay is completely random in character. Therefore, to establish statistical confidence in some experiment, a large number of decays have to be counted. A fluctuation as large as the square root of the number of counts is quite probable, and to make such a fluctuation of little importance it is often necessary to count a large number of particles. To do this may take time unless the counting is very rapid, and such rapid counting will not show on a mechanical register, which naturally has inertia. To overcome this, various *scaling circuits* exist, the delight of the electronic enthusiast. By now these are getting to be reliable and form a standard part of manufactured equipment.

Armed with the appropriate forms of counter, scaler, and registering equipment, we would find that the observation and numerical measurement of radioactivity is actually rather simpler than accurate weighing, and nearly as easy as pipetting.

Stable isotopes are a shade more difficult to use. Only the mass differentiates two isotopes, and somehow this mass difference must be used to observe and measure the various amounts of different isotopes. In the case of the very lightest isotopes, the ratio of masses is so large that relatively simple methods can be used. Thus it is possible to measure the amount of deuterium in a sample to one part in 500,000 by observing the rate of fall of a drop of water in fluorotoluene, which, having a density close to that of water, does not mix with it. The use of such differential density measurements can be extended by observing in a medium of known density gradient in an ultracentrifuge. Thus solutions of CsCl have been used to distinguish between DNA with and without N^{15} in its molecular structure.

In general, the differentiation and relative measurement of isotopes such as C^{13}, N^{15}, and O^{18} require the *mass spectrometer*. The mass spectrometer is an instrument in which a gaseous mixture of isotopes at low pressure is ionized. A sampling of the ions is then subjected to the action of electric and magnetic fields carefully designed to produce a focused beam of each ion, having a certain charge-to-mass ratio, on a slit. The current passing through the slit is then proportional to the amount of the particular ion, and with care, this is also proportional to the amount of the particular isotope one wishes to measure.

The separation of the beams of different ions requires long paths and narrow slits, so that very careful alignment is necessary, and under all circumstances the current measured is very small. The region in which ionization of the gaseous mixture is produced has to be at relatively high pressure while the rest of the system has to be at very low pressure; this requires a good deal of skill in pumping and arranging the position of slits. All these factors combine to make a mass spectrograph an expensive instrument with some problem of maintenance. Nevertheless, the mastery of all these factors is not beyond the ability of biological laboratories, particularly if sufficient research funds are available. The details of mass spectroscopy are not in place in this book. Reference material is given at the end of the chapter.

13–3 Experimental use of isotopic tracers. The already revolutionary subject of biochemistry has itself undergone a major revolution as a result of the use of isotopic tracers. A spot check of one issue of the *Journal of Biological Chemistry* in 1955 showed that 40% of the articles were in some way concerned with isotopic tracers. To a large extent, therefore, the literature of isotopic tracers is the whole literature of biochemistry. It is thus clear that we cannot possibly review here the entire field of tracer discovery.

Instead, what can be done is to consider some particular experiments that bear heavily on molecular biophysics. Out of many possible choices we select five: the observation of the permeability of the cell membrane by small labeled metabolites (Section 13–4); the study of aminoacid incorporation (Section 13–5); the study of the induction of enzyme formation (Section 13–6); the study of replicating deoxyribonucleic acid by incorporating radiophosphorus or tritium (Section 13–7); and lastly, observing the destruction of function as the radioactivity decays (Section 13–8). Since these five experiments do not cover anything like the whole range of available radioactive substances, we give in addition a short survey of the isotopes most useful in molecular biophysics (Section 13–9).

13–4 The permeability of the bacterial cell to small molecules. One of the most obvious and attractive subjects to study with radioactive tracers is cell permeability. Some of the very earliest studies (of erythrocyte permeability) were made with radioisotopes made with the authors' cyclotron. Many have been made since. For the purposes of this book we choose one set of studies made in a very sustained manner by the group at the Carnegie Institution of Washington, notably Roberts, Abelson, Cowie, Bolton, and Britten (Ref. 5). These studies have mainly been concerned with the two organisms *E. coli* and the yeast *Torulopsis utilis*.

The basic technique of the experiment is very simple. Cells are grown to a high concentration, cooled so that they no longer divide, washed, and placed in a nutrient medium, which contains, for example, sodium sulfate having some S^{35}. With only a short exposure to the radioactive medium, the cells are then spun down in a centrifuge at 14,000 g, which rapidly precipitates them into a pellet. The supernatant solution is decanted, and the pellet is washed with salt solution. The radioactivity in the pellet is found by taking a known fraction of it, spreading it on a disk of paper covered with a detergent, and counting it with a thin-window counter. The results showed that the amount of radioactivity in the cells per milliliter was 72% of the radioactivity of one milliliter of the medium. The total time of exposure was not in excess of eight minutes. For these cells, then, 72% of the total cell volume can be used to contain sulfur. In other experiments this figure approached 75%. Now, if the cells are dried, it is found that the amount of water lost amounts to 75% of the volume. So it appears that all the water involved in the cells, namely the water inside the cells, the water between the cells, and indeed the water bound into the structural elements of the cells, is freely available to include sulfur. By immersing the bacteria in labeled large protein molecules, the authors were able to estimate the volume of the water space trapped between cells, finding an upper limit of one-third of the whole space. So the freely accessible region includes a considerable volume which is inside the cells. These experiments thus suggest strongly that permeability into the cell is essentially complete, as far as this batch of bacteria is concerned, and also as far as the sulfate used is concerned.

Similar experiments were conducted for a wide variety of labeled substances, including phosphate ions, glucose-1-phosphate, fructose-1-phosphate, potassium, rubidium, cesium, and sodium ions, sulfur-labeled cystine, sulfur-labeled methionine, carbon-labeled glutamic acid, and sulfur-labeled glutathione, a compound of glutamic acid, cysteine, and glycine. Except in the case of glutathione, the ratio of the cell radioactivity to medium radioactivity was 75%. In the case of glutathione it was less, being about 63%. Later experiments have shown rather lower figures, perhaps one-half as great, for the ratio than those in the series described here. But even with these lower figures, the startling fact seems to emerge that at least for some bacterial cells, the membrane is not functional in selecting small molecules for the use of the cell, but rather is simply a physical container for the larger structural molecules of the cell. Thus one is driven to the idea that the synthetic and enzymatic mechanisms of the cell are open to access by all small molecules, and that only when some deliberate incorporation process has taken place is a molecule retained inside the cell. The range of cells for which this has been shown is very small, and it may prove to be far from a general principle. But even so, the fact that selective permeability is not readily shown is of great significance.

13–5 Amino acid incorporation; isotopic competition. The experiments described above were made with resting cells and aimed at a study of permeability. It is possible to carry out similar radioactive studies aimed deliberately at finding out the pathways of metabolic synthesis. A very large body of research has developed around this objective, and the results have already been of revolutionary significance. We propose to describe the general technique of study of amino acid incorporation in *E. coli* and to indicate some of the general results.

In experiments involving metabolism it is clearly necessary that the bacteria be fully growing. Therefore the experiments are done with rapidly dividing bacteria, in proper growth medium and at temperatures which support active growth. To the medium is added some radioactive component, which can be chosen for a purpose but which for the purposes of the description of technique is not important. The metabolic processes are then allowed to proceed, and at some time, again chosen for the purposes of the particular investigation, the bacteria are spun down, or filtered off, and subjected to analysis. One standard analysis is as follows.

(1) The cells are exposed to 5% trichloracetic acid at 5°C for 30 minutes, and then spun down. The supernatant is then one fraction, which contains small molecules, such as glucose and amino acids.

(2) The residue is subjected to 75% ethanol at 45°C for 30 minutes. This is again centrifuged, and the supernatant decanted. This supernatant contains peptides, some proteins, and lipids.

(3) The residual part is heated to 100°C with 5% trichloracetic acid (TCA) for 30 minutes and again centrifuged. The supernatant contains nucleic acids.

(4) The part which remains as a hot TCA precipitate is considered to be mainly protein.

This broad separation into four categories can, of itself, be most informative. It can be made much more powerful, however, by two-dimensional chromatography. The process of chromatographic separation depends on the fact that, in general, substances have differing solubilities in various solvents, and that if a mixture of, for example, amino acids is placed on a filter paper, which will accordingly adsorb them, a solvent will free them from the filter paper at different rates. This process can be made to separate out various fractions by letting the solvent rise on the filter paper by capillary action, so sweeping through the spot of mixed amino acids, and then carrying the separated components with it in its upward flow. The process of elution proceeds at different rates for different amino acids, with the net result that in many cases one acid is eluted completely while another has not yet started to be released from the paper. Each component is then carried up in turn and forms a band. Usually such bands contain several amino acids which are not separated completely. By turning the paper through 90° and choosing a different solvent for a repeat of the process, one can make the separation much more complete.

Such chromatographic analysis is a very important technique in most laboratories concerned with amino acids and small biologically important molecules generally. It lends itself admirably to work with tracer radio-activity, for the chromatograms can be placed in contact with a sheet of photographic paper and the positions of the radioactivity determined, or the spot can be cut out from the paper, after location by photographic methods, and counted with an end window Geiger counter. Such a technique is very powerful, and it is not surprising that it has already given us a penetrating insight into some of the processes of cellular synthesis.

The kind of experiment which can be done is, then, as follows. A particular substance is elected to be the source of radioactivity. This is then introduced into the medium, the cells are allowed to grow, and after a suitable increase (usually measured by the optical density of the culture) in the number of organisms, the cells are spun down and the separation procedure put into effect. Where the radioactivity goes is determined by observing the chromatograms, and this can be done with some accuracy.

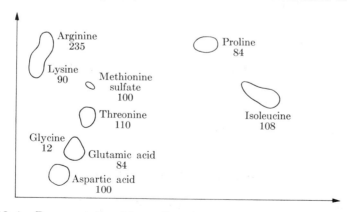

FIG. 13–4. Representation of a radioautograph taken by Roberts, Abelson, Cowie, Bolton, and Britten (Ref. 5) indicating what happens when *E. coli* are grown in the presence of $C^{14}O_2$ and glucose. The numbers indicate the relative activities of the various amino acids.

TABLE 13–1

PERCENT SUPPRESSION OF RADIOACTIVITY

Supplement	Argi-nine	Aspar-tic acid	Glu-tamic acid	Isoleu-cine	Lysine	Methi-onine	Pro-line	Threo-nine
Amino-butyric acid	0	0	0	90	0	0	0	0
Arginine	100	0	0	0	0	0	0	0
Aspartic acid	20	60	60	60	70	60	60	60
Casein digest	100	60	90	100	100	100	90	90
Citrulline	100	0	0	0	0	0	0	0
Glutamic acid	30	60	90	60	70	60	90	60
Homocysteine	0	0	0	0	0	80	0	0
Homoserine	0	0	0	90	0	90	0	90
Isoleucine	0	0	0	100	0	0	0	0
Lysine	0	0	0	0	100	0	0	0
Methionine	0	0	0	0	0	100	0	0
Ornithine	65	0	0	0	0	0	0	0
Proline	0	0	0	0	0	0	90	0
Threonine	0	0	0	100	0	0	0	90

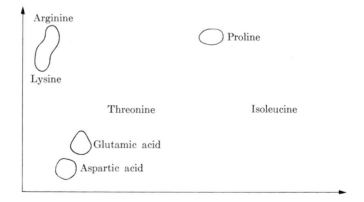

FIG. 13–5. Representation of a radioautograph taken by Roberts, Abelson, Cowie, Bolton, and Britten in which *E. coli* were grown in the presence of labeled CO_2 and glucose, with an excess of unlabeled threonine present in the medium. A comparison with Fig. 13–4 shows that both threonine and isoleucine are suppressed on the chromatogram, indicating that threonine is needed for the synthesis of isoleucine.

An excellent example of the technique is seen in the work of Roberts and the Carnegie Institution group on the way in which $C^{14}O_2$ is incorporated into cells of *E. coli* grown in the presence of glucose. A representation of a radioautograph of their work is shown in Fig. 13–4. The radioautograph is of a chromatogram of the products of hydrolysis of the protein fraction. The positions of the various amino acids are indicated on the figure. In actual practice the density of the spots shows roughly the activity of each.

A very powerful method of studying the actual synthetic process is the method of *isotopic competition*, utilized by the Carnegie Institution group. In this method an excess of one amino acid, unlabeled, is added to the medium. Since the cell wall is essentially permeable, the amino acid enters the cell where it can substitute for an amino acid which is being synthesized from glucose and CO_2. If the synthetic process of the cell is such that the operations of the cell do not require this amino acid in the free state, then no effect will be observed. This is not normally seen. On the other hand, if the particular amino acid is one needed in the formation of other amino acids, these will be formed from the excess of unlabeled acid and not from the process of synthesis of amino acids from glucose and CO_2. In Fig. 13–5 is shown the result of competition with unlabeled threonine in excess. The same process of fractionation used in the experiment shown in the previous figure was followed, and the resulting chromatogram is shown. It can be seen that the pattern is different in that both threonine and isoleucine are notably missing from the chromatogram. Threonine is expected to be missing, since it competes with itself, but isoleucine must be somehow formed from threonine at some point, as it is also completely missing.

Very penetrating studies can be made relatively rapidly by this method. In Table 13–1 are listed the various degrees of suppression in some amino acids by various supplements. From the table alone it is already apparent that there are certain synthetic pathways. The degree of understanding becomes even more profound, however, when other sources of radioactive carbon are used in the same class of experiment. For example, if sodium acetate is used, the addition of glutamic acid in excess reduces the radioactive carbon markedly in proline, arginine, lysine, aspartic acid, glutamic acid (as is expected), and threonine, but does not affect the amount taken into leucine.

A great many experiments can be performed rather quickly by use of this technique, and when put together they give evidence for the existence of a cycle of synthesis in *E. coli*, which is very much like the Krebs cycle, as indicated in Fig. 13–6. It can be seen that acetic acid, which enters the cycle after the direct synthesis of aspartic acid, is more concerned with the formation of glutamic acid than with aspartic acid. Experiments in which the various acids of the cycle were used as competitors showed the

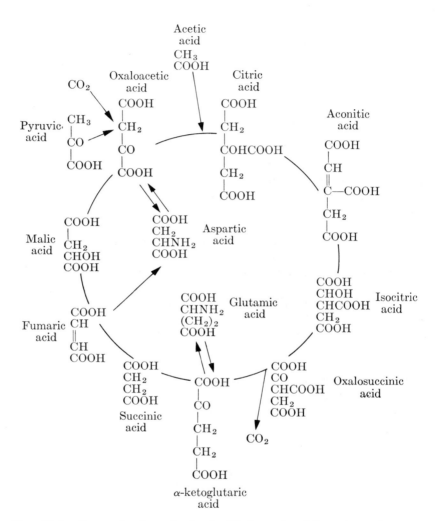

FIG. 13–6. One cycle of synthesis, the Krebs cycle. When the various compounds of the cycle are used as competitors, it is possible to show the general validity of the scheme in synthesis in *E. coli*. In addition, it is possible to make quantitative estimates of the amounts of each component formed in the cycle and so determine the effect of changes in the medium provided to the cells on the operation of the cycle.

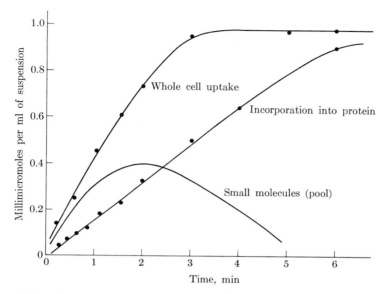

FIG. 13–7. The rate of incorporation of C^{14} proline into *E. coli* as measured by Britten. The total incorporation is nearly matched by the part on the protein fraction in three minutes, while the part in small molecules rises and falls again very quickly.

validity of the scheme; in fact, the experiments do even more in that they permit an estimate of the various rates of synthesis. These rate studies reveal one very important feature of bacterial metabolism, which is its flexibility. The addition of glutamic acid or aspartic acid, or its product amino acid, immediately changes the flow pattern. If cells are grown in the absence of air, and glucose is the major carbon source, very little glucose enters the cycle, and very little CO_2 is released. Change in the rates in the cycle can also result from adaptation in the whole organism. So that while the Krebs cycle is responsible for the formation of glutamic acid (and with it, proline and arginine) and aspartic acid (and with it, threonine, isoleucine, methionine, lysine, and pyrimidines), the operation of the synthetic mechanisms of the cell may not be wholly dependent on it. Experiments in other microorganisms indicate that the same kind of cycle occupies the same important role in metabolism.

Returning to the topic of *amino acid incorporation*, we can ask what happens to an amino acid once it is either made in the synthetic process or enters through the cell wall from the medium. Some answer to this is afforded by some experiments of Britten on rapid kinetic studies with highly labeled proline and with methionine. In Fig. 13–7 is shown the counting rate in two fractions as a function of time in minutes. It can be seen that the rate of incorporation into protein is very rapid, and that the part in small molecular form rises to a maximum and diminishes very quickly. The rapid incorporation of proline or methionine requires the presence of glucose in the medium. Thus, if the cell is actively metabolizing, the rate of incorporation of amino acids is very rapid. Even if the cell is close to 0°C, there is evidence that an amino acid which enters the cell can proceed to a specific site and be bound there, weakly, it is true, but still sufficiently well to prevent free diffusion out of the cell again. This binding on to some kind of receptor site is *specific*, and offers a challenge in explanation. Britten's studies show that while 75,000 proline molecules can be held in the cell in a pool for protein synthesis, only 25 molecules per cell exist in the water space, i.e., are completely free to diffuse.

In these rapid kinetic studies, no evidence for di- or tripeptides being present is found. The general impression gained is that the process of synthesis of amino acids into protein is by the attachment of the amino acids to some kind of synthesizing surface where they are held in place until over-all synthesis of the protein takes place. Some additional evidence indicates that an intermediate stage of combination with soluble RNA occurs. In addition to the general impression, there are specific experiments in which it can be shown that the absence of one amino acid completely inhibits the formation of any kind of protein. This general impression is substantiated by the work on induced enzyme synthesis, which will be described next. We emphasize to the reader that when we describe an impression we are emphatically not creating a dogma. The powerful techniques we have just described have been far from fully exploited, and the final story is by no means in.

13–6 The induction of adaptive enzymes. It has been known for many years that bacteria differ markedly in their ability to grow on different media. A bacterium like *thiobacillus thiooxidans* can grow on a medium of inorganic salts plus sulfur, and produces sulfuric acid as a product. At first glance it looks as though the bacterium should resemble a chemical plant, with special noncorrosive materials and a highly specialized production line. In fact, it synthesizes protein with the same amino acids as the majority of other proteins, and operates with the same use of nucleic acid as other bacteria, by and large. This must mean that it contains a rich variety of effectively operating enzymes in order to perform the chemical miracles needed for growth and division. On the other hand, bacteria which have been associated with some organ of an animal have a much richer nutrient medium in their past tradition, and so are not so well equipped with enzymes, since they can be expected to find many of the amino acids provided from the medium. By some skill, it is possible to devise a medium which lacks one item of fundamental necessity, and then the bacteria will not grow. When this happens, one reason for the lack of growth may be the lack of a particular enzyme which can synthesize some needed metabolite from the medium and so make up the deficiency. Studies of bacterial growth led Monod and Spiegelman to the discovery that a bacterial population which is static because of the lack of an enzyme can nevertheless suddenly develop normal growth, and examination of the culture reveals that the necessary enzyme has been formed in the new culture, which is accordingly *adapted*.

This very interesting phenomenon has been followed by much study in which isotopic experiments have played an important part. It has been found that the adaptation process is greatly accelerated by the presence in the medium of molecules of an *inducer*, which can be the substrate for the enzyme needed to make up the deficiency, or a molecule something like it. This substance acts to cause the formation of a protein molecule that can perform the necessary synthesis.

A great deal of work has been done on the induction of the enzyme β-galactosidase, which hydrolyzes lactose and so makes it available as a carbon source for *E. coli*. The addition of lactose to the medium which has previously been devoid of it causes a great increase in the amount of the enzyme. Now the ordinary expectation regarding such a process would be that the new enzyme represented some change in an already existing protein, or at any rate an already existing polypeptide precursor, and that the effect of the inducer is merely to add a small molecular configuration and turn out the completed enzyme. The use of tracers shows that this is not so. If the medium on which the cells are grown before induction is rich in S^{35}, the cells will develop well-labeled protein. Since β-galactosidase contains sulfur, it can also develop label. Now if at the moment of induction the cells are transferred to "cold" medium and induced with lactose, the newly formed enzyme can be separated out and examined for radioactivity. It is found to be "cold." This is a strong indication that the whole enzyme is made afresh after the inducing process has taken place. The same experiment can be done in reverse, since the previous history of the cells is that of being in "cold" medium, and then the process of induction takes place in "hot" medium. The resulting β-galactosidase is radioactive. These experiments underline the conclusions from purely metabolic studies mentioned above, namely, (a) that the formation of protein from precursors seems to indicate that the precursors are small molecules, and (b) that the protein seems to grow by a process of over-all assembly very rapidly.

This whole technique of labeling becomes very powerful as an adjunct to other methods of studying the cell. Recently it has become possible to disrupt cells and separate the microsomal particles or ribosomes by a centrifugal method. These ribosomes should have, by analogy with the microsomal particles of liver cells, a vital part in protein synthesis. Roberts has been able to use pulses of label as short as four seconds to see where the label goes among the various fractions of the ribosomes. The incorporation of labeled amino acid seems to occur first in the larger microsomal particles and to move into other fractions later. If the experiments continue to show the same pattern for other conditions, then it is clear that one important locale of protein synthesis in the bacterial cell is on these ribosomes. The physical structure of ribosomes is thus of great importance to study, and it is certain that as this book appears, exciting structural discoveries will be in course of being made.

13–7 Effect of incorporated phosphorus–32 on the viability of a bacterial virus. Radioactive phosphorus, sulfur, and carbon have played a very important part in the study of virus development and growth. In the case of plant viruses, where quantities are larger, N^{15} has also been employed.

One of the earliest and most important studies of bacterial virus development was the demonstration by Cohen in 1947 that virus phosphorus is almost wholly incorporated from phosphorus in the medium after infection, so that relatively little of the bacterial pre-existing phosphorus was used. This was followed by an important finding by Putnam and Kozloff, who showed that in the first generation of infection by radioactive virus, 35% of the phosphorus is found in the progeny. Watson and Maaløe extended this to the second generation and showed that 50% of the P^{32} of the second infection is found in the progeny.

Since P^{32} can be incorporated into virus with quite high efficiency simply by growing the virus on bacteria in "hot" medium, it is of some interest to see whether the P^{32} incorporated into the virus does any damage when it decays to S^{32}. This damage could occur in three possible ways. First, the act of change involves the emission of a beta ray which is an ionizing particle and could damage the virus by ionization in the ordinary way. Second, the change from the chemical form of phosphorus to sulfur could produce a structural defect in a large molecule. Third, the recoiling S^{32} nucleus could carry an atom clear out of the molecular structure and so cause damage.

The demonstration of decay inactivation (often called "radioactive suicide") was made by Hershey, Kamen, Kennedy, and Gest in 1951. They found that the *E. coli* bacteriophages T2 and T4, when grown on medium of high specific activity and stored for some weeks, lost their activity in a manner clearly related to the decay constant of P^{32}. If it is assumed that each decaying atom has a probability α of inactivation, that there are N^* of them per phage particle, and that there are S phage particles present which are viable, then we expect

$$-\frac{dS}{dt} = \alpha \frac{dN^*}{dt} S.$$

But the law of radioactive decay states that $(dN^*/dt) = \lambda N^*$ so that we obtain

$$-\frac{dS}{dt} = \alpha N^* \lambda S.$$

Now if we put N_0^* for the number of radioactive atoms per phage particle at $t = 0$, we have, by the law of radioactive decay,

$$N^* = N_0^* e^{-\lambda t}.$$

So we obtain

$$-\frac{dS}{dt} = \alpha N_0^* \lambda S e^{-\lambda t}.$$

Integrating, we obtain

$$\ln S = -\alpha N_0^* e^{-\lambda t} + \text{constant}.$$

And if $S = S_0$ when $t = 0$, we obtain

$$\ln S = -\alpha N_0^* e^{-\lambda t} + \ln S_0 + \alpha N_0^*$$

or

$$\ln \frac{S}{S_0} = \alpha N_0^* (1 - e^{-\lambda t}).$$

According to this relation, a plot of $\ln S/S_0$ versus $1 - e^{-\lambda t}$ should give a straight line. Such straight lines are very nicely obtained. The slope of the line determines the quantity αN_0^*. Now N_0^* can be estimated from the specific radioactivity of the growth medium and the total number of phosphorus atoms per virus particle, using Cohen's finding that the incorporated phosphorus is derived from the medium. With this estimate, the value of α can be found. It is remarkably high, 0.1 to a first approximation.

To consider the cause of inactivation, we can show that the effect of ionizing radiation is apparently less than this figure. A single beta ray, of average energy 0.7 Mev, is absorbed in approximately 3 mm of protein-like material. This corresponds to a loss of energy in traversing a virus particle of diameter 10^{-5} cm of $(10^{-5}/0.3) \times 7 \times 10^5 = 23$ ev. Radiation studies on these viruses show that an energy loss of 23 ev randomly distributed throughout the phage particle has a probability of only about $\frac{1}{30}$th of causing inactivation. So the great majority of the inactivation is presumably due to recoil, or to change of element, or to the fact that ionization has certainly occurred in the nucleic acid.

In some more recent experiments Stent and Fuerst have repeated the original work and extended it to T5, T1, T3, T7, and λ. Values for α are given in each case. In addition, the remarkable fact that the value of α *depends on the temperature of storage* was found.

This last fact, together with the feature that α rises to as high as 0.35, renders it unlikely that the figure of 0.1 for α means that only one of ten disintegrations is in a "vital" unit. Rather it would seem to suggest that some phosphorus locations are favorably situated to cause damage to the genetic chain of the virus and that others are not. Tessman has shown that in the very small phage $\phi X174$, the efficiency of "suicide" is unity. He links this with the fact that in this small phage the DNA is single stranded. Thus "radioactive suicide" appears to be a potent new method of study of virus development.

13–8 Radioautographic studies of biological duplication. The ability to introduce P^{32} at high specific activity into microorganisms, and the use of tritium-labeled thymidine and uridine, make it possible to study in remarkably fine detail the process of self-duplication by using radio-autographic methods of studying the distribution of radioactivity after the duplication has taken place. This kind of radioactive analysis has been employed, notably by Levinthal, Forro, and J. H. Taylor.

Levinthal's work on the bacterial virus T2 is in some ways the simplest to describe, and can be treated first. Highly radioactive T2 virus cultures are grown by using very radioactive medium for bacterial growth during the virus infection. These are then separated from all bacterial debris and are carefully cleaned. After this preliminary processing, they are used to infect bacteria which are growing in cold medium. The resulting "lysate," which contains many new virus particles synthesized during this fresh infection, is then mixed with some liquid nuclear emulsion. The mixture is then placed on a microscope slide, allowed to gel and dry. After a few days, the emulsion is developed and examined under the microscope to see how many tracks of beta rays are found associated to-gether. Since each virus particle which is radioactive is a center for many decay processes, there should be a considerable number of beta rays seen where each particle rests and very few anywhere else. This is found by Levinthal. Now the interesting question arises as to the way in which the number of tracks at each "star" is distributed. If the radioactivity of the original virus was distributed among all the other progeny, there would be expected to be large numbers of stars with very few beta tracks, and only occasionally would there be a large number of tracks per star. This is not the distribution found.

If the original labeled virus particles are studied, then it is found that the number of tracks per "star" is, say, 100. Now if we repeat the experiment (except that a cycle of growth in "cold" P^{32} is allowed to take place), the number of tracks per star drops to 20 on the same scale. Repeating for another cycle in cold P^{32}, however, does *not* give a further drop to 5; instead, what is found is again 20. The drop from 100 to 20 in the first cycle seems out of line, therefore. Levinthal found that if, instead of looking at intact virus particles, he first opened them up by a rapid change from high-concentration medium to distilled water, a process known as "osmotic shock," there were not 100 per star, but 40 per star. "Shocking" the first-generation "cold" virus *did not* reduce the number of tracks, nor did it for the second generation. Thus he is led to the idea that there is a "big piece" of DNA which is vital to the virus and that this has 40% of the label. This now divides *once* and thereafter resolutely holds its label for another vigorous cycle of growth.

The conclusion would appear to be that the duplicating part of the virus, which in the case of T2 is DNA, is orginally in two parts. One of these is a single unit comprising 40% of the original phosphorus, while the remainder is either capable of being divided many times or else is in small units at the start. The large single unit is capable of division *once*, and thereafter retains its integrity, accounting for the stars at 20% activity. Levinthal relates the ability to divide once with the double helical structure for DNA proposed by Watson and Crick, suggesting that each of the chains has separate integrity. Clearly, refined studies using this method can be most powerful in establishing the nature of molecular self-duplication.

A different but equally powerful approach has been taken by Forro. Using the organism *Micrococcus cryophilus*, cells were grown to high radioactivity content. One specific organism was then chosen under the microscope, and observed until it divided, when the progeny were separated and manipulated apart. This process of watching and manipulating was continued until there were effectively 256 cells all derived from the original "hot" parent and all grown on cold medium. The slide was then covered with emulsion, allowed to become exposed to beta rays, and developed at the end of several weeks. The distribution of grain count, rather than of tracks, was used in Forro's work, but the aim is the same, namely, to see whether there is a statistical bias away from the distribution expected if the P^{32} distributes itself uniformly among the progeny. The results clearly show two things. First, a considerable share of the P^{32} does indeed divide itself among the progeny; second, the division of P^{32} is not what would be expected if all the P^{32} were continually spread at random among the generations.

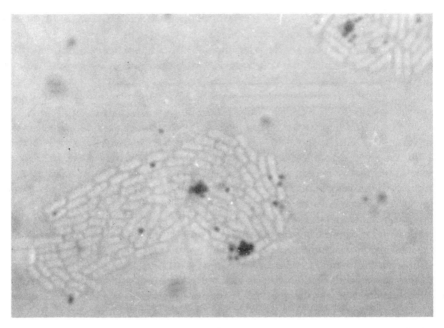

Fig. 13–8. A combined radioautograph and phase-contrast micrograph of a colony of *E. coli* grown on "cold" medium from cells which have been labeled heavily with tritiated thymidine. The localization of the tritium autograph in very few of the cells is apparent, suggesting that a small number of DNA units, which retain their integrity, exist. Data due to F. Forro.

The simplest explanation of these findings is that the part of the label incorporated as RNA can be considered as divided into many relatively small parts which can become spread among the progeny, while the part in DNA stays in relatively large units that preserve their integrity to a great extent upon division.

A remarkably powerful extension of this kind of work has become possible with the discovery that it is very easy to incorporate tritium into thymidine simply by catalyzed exchange, and that such tritium remains bound where the exchange takes place. This development has been used by J. H. Taylor, and also by Painter, Forro, and Hughes, in some very informative experiments. Since we are considering the division of bacteria, we can take Painter, Forro, and Hughes' work first. The great attraction of using tritium is the fact that in a radioautograph the very limited range of the low-energy beta ray operates to give a very confined heavy spot of developed film localized right at the point of decay. The use of thymidine guarantees that the label goes into DNA and not into RNA, because thymine is not found in RNA. So this labeled compound, together with the autographic process, is indeed powerful. Painter, Forro, and Hughes used the labeled thymidine in the medium of thymine-deficient *E. coli* and so grew heavily labeled bacteria. One of the simplest and most striking experiments can be instantly understood by a glance at Fig. 13–8, in which the microcolony resulting from growing such a "hot" bacterium on "cold" medium has been fixed and radioautographed. It can be seen that mainly only two bacteria have retained the label. Thus at a glance one can see that a DNA molecule has a permanent existence, and thus that the process of replication involves the synthesis of new material and not the division of the old many, many times. It is as though the hereditary code script remains intact and serves as an actual physical mold which can form the copies.

Another aspect of this work is shown in Fig. 13–9. In this experiment one heavily labeled cell is placed on the stage of the microscope in "cold" culture medium and watched. Upon division, the daughters are separated by micromanipulation and again watched until they, in turn, divide. The process is repeated for several generations, resulting in a very large number of cells. This array, whose genealogical table is fully known, is then fixed and autographed. The observations yield the final number of grain counts in the last generation, and the patience of the observer is rewarded by the fact that the genealogical table can now be read back to the original cell, as has been done in the figure. Forro has watched many such sets of divisions; we pick one of the simpler experiments. In Fig. 13–9 we see that for the first three divisions the DNA has retained the simple character of an even split. At the fourth division one of the fractions has subdivided again, however *not* evenly. Thus Forro's work shows (a) that an even split is likely, and (b) that the even split is *not* the invariable rule. Both these findings are in agreement with two quite different experiments, one due to Meselson and Stahl on bacteria and one due to Taylor on broad bean root tips.

Meselson and Stahl used the fact that DNA which is fully labeled with N^{15} has a definitely different density from N^{14} DNA. Using $N^{15}H_4Cl$ with 96.5% N^{15} as a source of nitrogen, they grew cells of *E. coli* until the DNA was fully labeled. The cells were then opened and the DNA carefully extracted and purified. This DNA was placed in concentrated CsCl solution and spun for many hours at 140,000 g. The CsCl, which is small and can rediffuse, does not separate, but forms a density gradient, and the DNA seeks its region of equal density. The ultraviolet absorption at this region in the cell is high, as DNA absorbs in the ultraviolet, and if the photographic trace is measured with a densitometer the appearance is as shown in Fig. 13–10(a). It can be seen to be a single peak. If, now, the experiment is repeated with cells that, after full labeling, have been grown on N^{14} medium, the single peak shows as double, with a second component

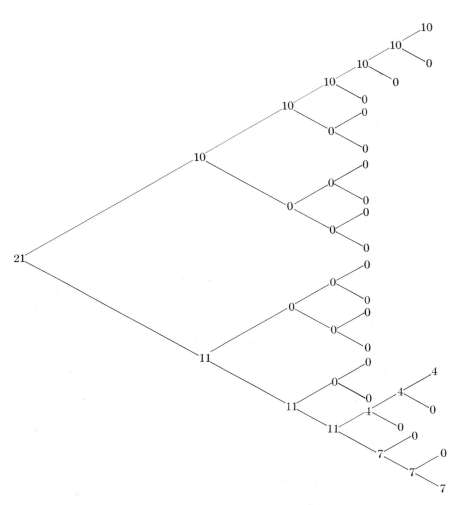

Fig. 13–9. Diagram of an array of micromanipulated cells grown from one parent, heavily labeled with tritium thymidine. The divisions are indicated, together with the grain count per cell. The predominantly all-or-nothing splits indicate the presence of conserved units of DNA, and the fact that fractional splits may also occur shows that a process of some sort of exchange is also possible. Data due to F. Forro.

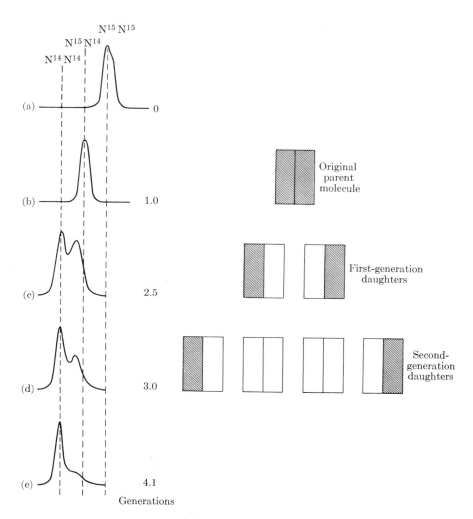

FIG. 13–10. Illustrating Meselson and Stahl's experiment on the change in fully N^{15} labeled bacterial DNA as the bacteria grow on N^{14} medium. The bacterial DNA is separated and purified and spun for many hours in a CsCl density gradient in an ultracentrifuge. The density trace of ultraviolet absorption is shown. As the generations progress, the fully labeled molecule modifies to a hybrid and then to a mixture of hybrids and unlabeled molecules, as shown in the diagram adjacent to the absorption patterns.

developing. At the first generation, the peak is single and corresponds neither to N^{14} DNA nor to N^{15} DNA, but is *exactly intermediate*. As the generations progress, a new peak of N^{14} DNA grows, but the mixed peak remains. The peaks at 0, 1, 2.5, 3.0 and 4.1 generations are shown in parts (a), (b), (c), (d), and (e) of Fig. 13–10. The conclusion is thus in exact agreement with Forro's quite distinctly different experiment: the DNA divides once, and then produces only hybrids or fully unlabeled cells. The diagram inserted on Fig. 13–10 illustrates the process.

We can conclude our sampling of tracer experiments with a short account of the very beautiful work of Taylor. Taylor used preparations of broad bean root tips, which are familiar material to the cytologist and in which the chromosomes can be made clearly visible simply by uniformly squeezing down and observing in the microscope. If this technique is combined with that of growing on tritium-labeled thymidine, then the tritium goes into the chromosomes and nowhere else, and thus can be observed by means of a radioautographic film spread over the preparation. If a single growth is observed, meaning that the label is taken up during the part of the cycle which corresponds to DNA synthesis, then upon division the chromosomes are seen to be equally, and essentially fully, labeled. Now a simple cytological technique can be used; it is to inhibit cell division with colchicine, which does not inhibit chromosome division, so that the chromosomes pile up within the cell. Then a treated cell with two sets of chromosomes has caused them to duplicate once, while a cell with four sets of chromosomes has duplicated twice. Thus it is possible, after colchicine treatment, to make radioautographs, and by observing the radioactivity in the cells with two sets and four sets, to come to some conclusion about the way the actual material of the chromosomes divides. By fully labeling, treating with colchicine, and growing further on "cold" medium, the autographs show the fate of the label. Taylor's results show that the future divisions of labeled chromosomes do *not* show a random distribution of radioactivity. The first division does indeed show an equal distribution, but the second shows many cases in which the new chromosome is not labeled at all, and the corresponding partner has all the label. Of equal interest is the fact that in those cases of second division where the label is shared, it is shared in *large blocks*, so that the two chromosomes each show label and nonlabel in a complementary pattern. This corresponds to the process of sister chromatid exchange, and indicates that the structure and replication of chromosomes must be capable of this kind of process. The findings are in agreement with Forro's later work on bacteria.

Such studies invite the construction of models. One such, due to Taylor, is shown in Fig. 13–11. Taylor has sought to avoid the unpleasant idea of an enormously long single molecule of DNA by using an ordered array of DNA stretching outward from a two-layered center strip. Such a model

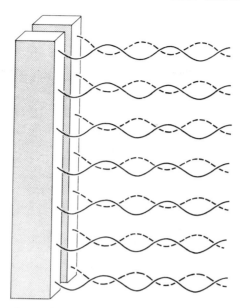

FIG. 13–11. A schematic model of a chromosome as suggested by Taylor, using evidence from radioautography to propose the model. The DNA threads are attached to protein units, which form part of a unit which can divide evenly.

has its difficulties, and almost certainly is oversimple. However, it is a starting point.

As we have already said, these examples of the use of isotopic tracer methods are only a very small fraction of the total possible to describe even today, and experiments arrive with every mail, so to speak. It should be clear that a biophysicist should be familiar with radioactivity and the methods of working with it, and that the greater his familiarity and the deeper his understanding, the more likely he is to devise some of the many new applications of radioactivity not yet used. Therefore we feel the topic has a place in this book. We conclude with a brief account of some of the more commonly used isotopes, with one or two remarks about each.

13–9 Remarks about commonly used isotopes. *Deuterium.* This is very cheap, readily available, and can be measured by density techniques very simply. It is possible to grow quite large organisms on heavy water, and a study of the results of such substitution should be very informative. Since the vibrational levels of a linked deuterium atom are quite different from those of a hydrogen atom, there should be some differences in the way in which a deuterium molecule reacts with a protein or RNA molecule. In fact, if the adiabatic process of passing from a condition in which a small molecule can move and rotate to one in which it is part of a large fixed system is important in biology, as we suggest in the last chapter of the book, studies with deuterated compounds should give much information about it. Thermal inactivation of enzymes operates with different constants in heavy water as compared with ordinary water.

Tritium. The striking characteristic of this is the very low-energy beta ray which it emits, having a maximum energy of 18 kilovolts. It can be readily detected by any means which has very little absorption, such as the photographic emulsion or a Geiger counter in which the tritium is introduced into the gas filling. At the present time, it is being extensively used in the form of tritiated thymidine as a means of labeling specifically DNA. It should be realized that such a compound could be a very serious hazard because it is specially geared to enter and so affect the genetic part of cells.

Carbon-13, nitrogen-15, and *oxygen-18.* These three stable isotopes, which are obviously keenly related to biological compounds, are reasonably available. The first two can be bought at up to 96% concentration, and so can be employed in studies involving very heavily labeled material. Meselson, Stahl, and Vinograd have made use of the technique of sedimentation in a density gradient to study the character of N^{15} labeled DNA after cell division, as described above, and the technique shows great promise. Rather long hours of sedimentation are called for, with consequent wear and tear on the rotor suspension, but the results justify the expense.

Carbon-14. This readily available isotope, with a long half-life of 5000 years, and a single beta ray of maximum energy 130 kilovolts, is probably the most important in biology. It has been synthesized into a number of biochemically important molecules, and many of these are available on the market. It requires some care in counting because the beta rays only travel about 15 cm in air, and any thickness in the sample, or the counter window, must accordingly be a source of worry. In spite of its long half-life, it is relatively safe if accidentally taken internally; the amount which can be tolerated is given as 250 microcuries. Special means for radiation monitoring have to be available in any laboratory which does extensive work with C^{14}, as is of course the case for tritium.

Sodium-24. This relatively short-lived, intensely active element (15 hr half-life, with a 1.4-Mev beta-ray energy and two gamma rays of energy 2.8 and 1.4 Mev) is readily available and can be used wherever a study of sodium is needed. Since sodium readily ionizes, it exchanges very rapidly. Thus the kind of study in which the pathway of a particular metabolite is followed is not normally possible with this element.

Sodium-22. This form has a much longer half-life (2.6 yr), and emits a positron of energy 0.54 Mev and a gamma ray of 1.3 Mev. It is much less available, for it has to be made by bombardment in an accelerator, using a reaction such as $Mg^{24}(d\alpha)Na^{22}$.

Phosphorus-32. Perhaps of equal importance with carbon is P^{32}, which is almost the perfect isotope to use. Its maximum beta-ray energy of 1.6 Mev makes it easy to detect; it has no gamma radiation, and so can be handled in relatively large quantities without danger. Its half-life of 15 days makes it possible to handle it in relatively long biochemical processes, and yet it will decay readily while in the process of being disposed of after use. It is made in two ways. The first is by irradiating phosphorus with neutrons, in which case very large activities, unfortunately also accompanied by large amounts of "cold" phosphorus, can be made. The second involves irradiating sulfur with neutrons of over 1-Mev energy. These are available in a reactor, but in fewer numbers than neutrons of low energy. The resulting P^{32} can be completely separated from the sulfur, and there results phosphorus of very high specific activity. This is the form in which it is most commonly used in molecular biology. The short half-life unfortunately makes it commercially difficult to make and store particular compounds, so that the catalogs do not contain radioactive phosphates of nucleic acid and bases. They can be made in the laboratory, however, and this is now being done.

Phosphorus-33. This most interesting isotope was discovered only recently. It has a half-life of 25 days, emits a single beta ray of 250-kv energy, and should be available in fair quantity when demand for it arises. It is made by a slow neutron reaction on S^{33}, and so can be obtained with high specific activity. It is always heavily contaminated with P^{32}, which is formed at the same time unless separated S^{33} is bombarded. Up to the present there has not been sufficient S^{33} produced to justify its use to make this isotope. With P^{33} and P^{32}, double labeling experiments should become possible.

Sulfur-35. With very much the same characteristics as C^{14}, except for the much shorter half-life of 80 days, S^{35} can be used as an important tracer in specialized protein studies. Nearly every protein contains one or more of the amino acids methionine, cysteine, and cystine, which contain sulfur. Since nucleic acid never contains sulfur, S^{35} clearly is concerned only with protein processes, even in the presence of much action on the part of nucleic acids. It is readily available, being produced by the reaction $Cl^{35}(np)S^{35}$, and is made in reactors.

Iron. This is available in two forms: Fe^{55}, with a half-life of 2.9 yr, decaying by K-electron capture; and Fe^{59}, with a half-life of 45 days, with two beta-ray energies of 0.46 and 0.26 Mev and gamma rays of energy 1.3 and 1.1 Mev. The former is rather hard to detect because it emits mainly the x-rays resulting from the electron space vacated at K-capture being refilled by electrons. Therefore thin windows are important, and the efficiency of detection is not high. However, the amounts available are considerable. Actually both isotopes have been used in many studies, primarily of blood and its formation. The two isotopes permit the ready use of double labeling, which has been more exploited for iron than for any other element.

13–10 Summary and conclusion. An attempt to sum up the subject of radioactive tracer work is not going to be too successful. In 1942, still not long ago, one of the authors presented an "outlook" in place of a summary. It is as though a chemist writing in 1830 had to summarize the use of weight-quantification, a technique which changed the whole emphasis in chemistry, put the atomic theory on a firm basis, introduced the idea of valence, and ultimately the periodic table of the elements. The impact of tracer research on biology and biochemistry is very nearly as great. Even now, when there has been time for a great industry to grow around isotopic research, the stage of discovery is still so early that no confident summarizing or lining up of conclusions is in order. What can be said is that the nature and succession of processes in the growth and development of the cell are rapidly being brought into a system. Whether we can say that we have an understanding of the system is doubtful, but the technique is so tremendously powerful and the drive and interest in it are so great that the future does indeed look bright.

PROBLEMS

1. A thin-window Geiger counter has an efficiency for S^{35} (including solid angle) of 75%. A culture of bacteria will grow to 10^9 cells per ml in S^{35} medium. How many microcuries per ml of S^{35} should be used to produce 1000 counts per minute in a filtered sample from 1 ml of culture?

2. Bacteriophage are grown on phosphate consisting of 1 millicurie P^{32} per 100 milligrams P^{31}. A cleaned-up sample, after washing, gave 10^9 plaques per ml. The counts from 1 ml, dried down, were 500 per minute, with an efficiency, including solid angle, of 20%. How many atoms of phosphorus are there per phage?

3. It is desired to follow the P^{32} activity of a culture through eight divisions. Assuming that the cells will utilize P^{32} until starved of phosphorus, how much P^{32} is necessary to label an initial culture of 10^7 cells, assuming that the limit of detectability is 100 atoms per cell?

4. In a two-week period a bacterium having a length of two microns and a radius of one micron which has been labeled with tritiated thymidine is observed to have undergone 40 decays. Assuming that each decay leaves energy in a sphere of radius 4000 A and has an average value of 8,000 ev, calculate the dose in roentgens. Assume 90 ergs per cm^3 per roentgen. Give your answer

according to two assumptions: (a) that the overlap factor between decay events is the ratio of the volume of the 4000 Å sphere to the volume of the bacterium, and (b) that there is 90% overlap, corresponding to all events being in a nucleus of the bacterium.

REFERENCES

1. C. L. Comar, *Radioisotopes in Biology and Agriculture*. McGraw-Hill, N. Y., 1955. A very well-planned book which covers all the field, including chromatographic and ion-exchange methods, as well as preparation, detection, and properties of isotopes.

2. M. Kamen, *Radioactive Tracers in Biology*. Academic Press, N. Y., 1951.

3. W. E. Siri, *Isotopic Tracers in Biochemistry and Physiology*. McGraw-Hill, 1946. Very valuable as a handbook of many radiation facts and processes.

4. J. Sacks, *Isotopic Tracers in Biochemistry and Physiology*. McGraw-Hill, N. Y., 1953.

5. Roberts, Abelson, Cowie, Bolton, and Britten, *Studies of Biosynthesis in Escherichia Coli*. Carnegie Inst. Wash. Publication 607, Washington, D. C., 1957.

6. F. W. Putnam, "Bacteriophages: Nature and Reproduction," *Advances in Protein Research* **VIII,** 177 (1953).

7. C. Levinthal and C. A. Thomas, Jr., "Molecular Autoradiography," *Biochim. et Biophys. Acta* **23,** 453 (1957).

8. F. Forro, Jr., "The Distribution of Radioactive Phosphorus Among the Progeny of a Single Labled Bacterium," *Exp. Cell Res.* **12,** 363 (1957).

9. R. B. Painter, F. Forro, Jr., and W. L. Hughes, "Distribution of Tritium Labeled Thymidine in *E. coli* During Cell Multiplication," *Nature* **181,** 328 (1958).

10. F. Forro and S. Wertheimer, "The Organization and Replication of Deoxyribonucleic Acid in Thymine Deficient Strains of *E. coli*," *Biochim. et Biophys. Acta* **40,** 9 (1960).

11. J. H. Taylor, "The Duplication of Chromosomes" *Scientific Am.*, June 1958, p. 36.

12. M. Meselson, F. W. Stahl, and J. Vinograd, *Proc. Natl. Acad. Sci.* **43,** 581 (1957).

13. M. Meselson and F. W. Stahl, "The Replication of DNA in *E. coli*," *Proced. Natl. Acad. Sci.* **44,** 671–682 (1958).

CHAPTER 14

MOLECULAR BIOPHYSICS AND MUSCLE, NERVE, AND EYE STUDIES

Four decades of research have left no doubt in the author's mind that there is only one life and living matter, however different its structures, colorful its functions, and varied its appearance. We are all but recent leaves on the same old tree of life; even if this life has adapted itself to new functions and conditions, it uses the same old principles over and over again. There is no real difference between the grass and he who mows it. The muscles which move the mower need the very same two substances for their motion as the grass needs for its growth, potassium and phosphate, the two substances we put on our lawn as fertilizer so as to have something to mow—a strikingly simple demonstration of the basic unity of living nature. So, in principle, it does not matter which material we choose for our study of life, be it grass or muscle, virus or brain. If we only dig deep enough we always arrive at the center, the basic principles on which life was built and due to which it still goes on.

A. Szent-Gyorgyi, 1951

14–1 Introduction. Throughout this book we have made little reference to physiology. The functioning of large organisms, by which the processes of muscular action, nerve signals, vision, excretion, respiration, and so on, are actually made to operate, has not concerned us much. Our interest has been in molecular and cellular structure, and really only in the previous chapter have we touched on the working processes of the cell, and even there only in an illustrative way. We make no apology for this, because the preceding material is all necessary to the understanding of molecular biophysics. If we have been unable to include all aspects of the study of living systems, we are not the first to meet our limitation.

Furthermore, the aims of the study of physiology are really different from our aims, though as time progresses the two seem to converge. It was a tremendous advance in physiology when it was established that nerves deliver impulses, detectable electrically, which were always equal in individual intensity but variable in number according to the degree of stimulus. Thus, from the many possible ways that a message could be transmitted along a nerve, a single specific means was isolated. It is not surprising that a very large body of experimental work has been devoted to the study of nerve impulses and many attempts made at their understanding.

Nevertheless, to a person interested in cellular processes, in growth, division, and differentiation, such a study can very easily seem to be an expensive diversion. In the study of nerve impulses one does not encounter molecular genetics, which arouses our keen interest in the replication of DNA, nor protein synthesis, where we have a strong interest in the relation of amino-acid order to genetic order, and in turn the relation to enzymatic behavior. The question of how a growing system lays down its new chemical products in the required molecular array is not one which, at first, is the concern of the electrophysiologist. For this reason, there has been a sharp division among physically minded biologists. Those who work with cells and viruses and macromolecules have had little in common with those who design amplifiers, recorders, thermocouples, and the whole elaborate array of instrumental study now used to determine in finer detail the nature of nerve and muscular action.

It is our view that this early phase is ending. Already the molecular structure of muscle can be described with some accuracy. And the energy-transfer mechanism of muscle, when established, may be of the utmost use in describing energy transfer in more ordinary cells and hence in clarifying the processes of synthesis and growth so vital to the cellular biophysicist.

Accordingly, even though our experience is heavily limited to macromolecules and simple cells, we are essaying in this chapter to describe muscle, nerve, and eye as they appear to us, expecting some of the approach to be naive, but confidently hoping that our remarks will help to speed up the attainment of a common goal by two different lines of attack.

I. Muscle Studies

14–2 Muscle fiber as a model. A variety of muscles exist. Most consideration is given to vertebrate skeletal muscle, which is attached to bone and is under the control of the nervous system. Involuntary muscle, as in the walls of the stomach, has many features in common with skeletal muscle, but as might be expected, is organized differently. Although we have called attention to the fact that differences between types of muscle exist, it is not in our province to describe them comparatively; rather, we need to consider the area of the general similarity of function of types of muscle. For this reason we will consider in most detail a skeletal muscle exemplified by the rabbit psoas muscle or the frog sartorius muscle.

A whole muscle is made of an aggregate of bundles of individual fibers. Surrounding the whole is a sheath called the *epimysium*, and each bundle is in turn surrounded by a sheath, the *perimysium*. Within each bundle is a set of fibers, which are multinucleate cells of a very elongated character, confined by a cell wall called the *sarcolemma*. In between the fibers blood capillaries can be found. Each fiber has nerve junctions, the *myoneural* junctions, which connect it to a nerve fiber and thus render it under control by the nervous system.

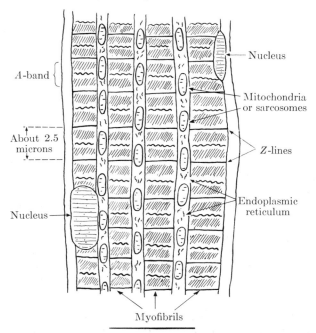

FIG. 14–1. A schematic representation of a single muscle fiber, showing only a fraction of the length. The neuromyal junction is not included. Such a structure can be inferred from the optical microscope. The distance from one Z-line to the next, called a *sarcomere*, is about 2.5 microns.

A major characteristic of muscle is its separability into fibers. A whole muscle can be dissected into bundles of fibers; these can in turn be dissected into single fibers, each surrounded by a sarcolemma; these contain *myofibrils*, which are aggregated molecular structures having a definitely related molecular pattern, first shown by Hall, F. O. Schmitt, and Jakus, which is clearly of great significance. As the study of muscle has progressed, the question has continually been asked as to whether each of these subunits carries its full fractional share of the whole function. Put more simply, is each subunit a model for the whole muscle action? The answer has been "yes," for at least each subunit comes near enough to being a model. Thus muscle is really a wonderful model for molecular biophysics because once the molecular processes are understood, one can rapidly scale up to see the whole process.

Since we are concerned with molecular structure and behavior, we do not need to consider the whole muscle. A starting point is a single fiber, which is illustrated schematically in Fig. 14–1. Such a structure can be inferred from observations with the light microscope. It can be seen to be a multinuclear structure, characterized by many longitudinal fibrils, the

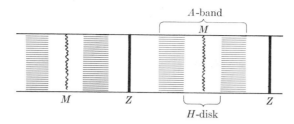

FIG. 14–2. Representation of part of a myofibril in finer detail to present some of the descriptive nomenclature now current.

myofibrils, aligned and accurately organized in the pattern shown. The dark lines across the center, the Z-lines, mark out a natural unit called the *sarcomere*, which has a length (notably variable in muscle) of approximately 2.5 microns. The region in between the myofibrils includes the *sarcoplasm*, which contains the mitochondria (or *sarcosomes*) and the endoplasmic reticulum as described for other cytoplasms.

Each myofibril can be described in more detail. In Fig. 14–2 we show a schematic diagram to represent the various features. It is possible, of course, to consider even finer detail. Before doing so, we shall describe some of the biochemistry of muscle.

14–3 Biochemical character of muscle. A glance at Fig. 14–1 will convince the reader that the biochemical make-up of muscle will differ from that of a less specialized cell. The greater part of the muscle fiber is made up of a set of specialized protein molecules which are in some way concerned with the process of muscular action. The water content does not differ much from that of the bacterial cell we dealt with in Chapter 2, nor does the protein differ much. But there is far less nucleic acid and very little ribonucleic acid. The specialized molecules constitute about two-thirds of the protein, while the remaining one-third is concerned with the enzymatic use of the substances brought in by the blood capillaries that surround the fiber in the whole muscle.

Since the process of muscular action is still not understood, it is reasonable to believe that one or more compounds of great importance to muscle action have not yet been described. Even so, several which obviously play extremely important parts are well known, and will now be set forth. The first is the complex of *actin* and *myosin*, two proteins found in the sarcomere. The second is adenosine triphosphate, ATP, which is thought to play a part in the energy-transfer processes that must go on when muscle action takes place. The third is a "factor," called the Marsh-Bendall factor, which acts as an inhibitor to the process of splitting ATP. Each of these is worth some description.

For many years it has been known that muscle contains a protein of high molecular weight, called *myosin*. In 1939 Engelhardt and Ljubimowa discovered that myosin is an enzyme which catalyzes the conversion of ATP to the diphosphate, ADP, with consequent release, or transfer, of configurational energy. More thorough studies by Banga and Szent-Gyorgyi showed that two proteins were involved in "myosin," namely *actin* and *myosin*, which form a combination known as actomyosin, a combination capable of changing shape in a manner very reminiscent of the behavior of muscle itself. Subsequent purification and separation procedures have brought out that the molecular weight of myosin is 450,000, with an axial ratio of about 50 and a total length of 1600 A. That of actin is 60,000, with an axial ratio of 12 and a length of 290 A.

A third protein, *tropomyosin*, which has a molecular weight in the neighborhood of 50,000, an axial ratio of 25, a length of 385 A, a strong tendency to polymerize, and great stability, has more recently been found. It is not yet clear what its function is, but this is not surprising since the whole operation of muscle, though tantalizingly clear in very broad aspects, is not at all understood in detail.

These proteins, which comprise 15 to 20% of the content of the myofibril, form part of a gel, the remainder being water and salts. The organization of the myofibrils will be described later. Surrounding the myofibril, and certainly to some extent penetrating into it, is the sarcoplasm, which contains 20 to 30% of the total muscle protein and occupies about 20% of the cell volume. It is thus rather *more* concentrated in protein than the average concentration of the myofibril. The sarcoplasm contains the mitochondria, or sarcosomes (the two terms are nearly interchangeable and seem to be becoming more so with time), which contain enzymes to oxidize metabolites (particularly glycogen) and to make ATP. In those muscles with very high oxidative ability, like flight muscles and cardiac muscles, the mitochondria are very large and significantly arranged in rows closely associated with the A-bands. Studies with C^{14} glycine show that the myofibrillar parts do not turn over glycine to any great extent, while the rate in the sarcoplasmic fraction is quite normal.

It is possible, by centrifugation, to separate the two components of the sarcoplasm, the particulate, containing the mitochondria, and the soluble fraction. Sacktor has shown that a large part of the enzymatic activity, such as the oxidation of the citric-acid cycle intermediates, is in the particulate fraction alone but that both fractions had to be combined to oxidize several other substrates, including glycogen. Since myofibrils played no part in these processes, the energy provision is definitely in the sarcoplasm.

The average diameter of a protein molecule in the sarcoplasm is 50 A. Some of the molecules penetrate into the myofibrils, since there is no membrane apparent between the two parts.

To conclude this brief section on the biochemistry of muscle, we can say that ATP, whose general structure was described in Chapter 3, is a triphosphate of adenine and ribose. The structural formula is

and it is characterized by a phosphate grouping which, upon hydrolysis, can yield a diphosphate and orthophosphoric acid, with the result that a more stable total configuration of the same atoms is produced. This increase in stability means that energy is released when the process takes place. If the event can occur while the ATP is attached to a protein molecule, and there exists a mechanism for energy transfer within the protein, this energy can be transmitted along the protein molecule until it produces some effect which converts the energy to some other form. It is reasonably certain that ATP is closely concerned with muscle action, and that the above mechanism is involved. Exactly what the process is, as has already been said, is not yet so certain.

Related to ATP action, and still somewhat obscure in nature, is a protein that certainly has some enzymatic properties, but which also has the power to inhibit the action of ATP in the myofibril. This protein, called the Marsh-Bendall factor, is one component of the sarcoplasm. It may well be a complex of two small proteins, for it would seem to have one component that is very sensitive to heat and one that is very stable. Elucidation of the nature of this factor would be of the utmost service.

It can thus be seen that in the muscle fiber we have present myosin, an enzyme which can catalyze the breakdown of ATP (and also of other nucleoside triphosphates), and a protein, or set of proteins, which can inhibit this catalysis. It should be possible to conceive a mechanism for contraction and relaxation of muscle in terms of these features of the fiber.

14–4 The molecular architecture of the muscle fiber. Biophysical methods for studying the molecular structure of muscle fiber are far from lacking. In fact, very few biological preparations offer the same opportunity for physical study; it might be said that if muscle action is not soon elucidated, then biophysics had better look to its laurels. Muscle fibers are birefringent; they can be pulled apart down to smaller and smaller size and studied in the electron microscope in various ways, notably by thin-section technique. The protein components can be studied by centrifugation and by electrophoresis, and definite reflections can be obtained by x-ray diffraction.

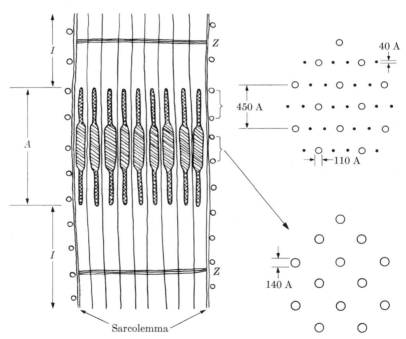

FIG. 14–3. The molecular structure of skeletal muscle, along the lines proposed by H. E. Huxley and J. Hanson. The sarcomere, the distance from Z to Z, is made up of interleaved molecules, one a fine set and the other much thicker. The cross-sectional dimensions of the molecular array are shown on the right, the upper for the outer part of the A-band, and the lower for the H-band. It is A. F. Huxley's view that the nerve impulse travels down the sarcolemma, along the Z-band. H. E. Huxley believes that this causes a sliding of the thin actin molecules in between the thicker myosin molecules.

This battery of attack has been able to force considerable inroads into the understanding of the structure of muscle. We have already described the molecular weights of actin and myosin, and indicated the rough shape of these molecules. Much more detail than we have given can readily be filled in. Perhaps the most sensational advance has come from section electron microscopy, which yields two pictures of the ultrastructure of muscle, as indicated in Figs. 14–3 and 14–4. The first is a representation of the structure of skeletal muscle, due to H. E. Huxley and J. Hanson, and the second is of insect flight muscle, due to Hodge.

Taking the skeletal muscle first, we can see that it has a very precise molecular architecture. The sarcolemma is about 200 A thick, with a loose covering of collagen fibers on the outside. It is attached to the Z-bands. According to A. F. Huxley and Taylor, the sarcolemma, which is normally polarized electrically, upon receipt of the message from the neuromyal junction, drastically changes polarization in a manner that travels along

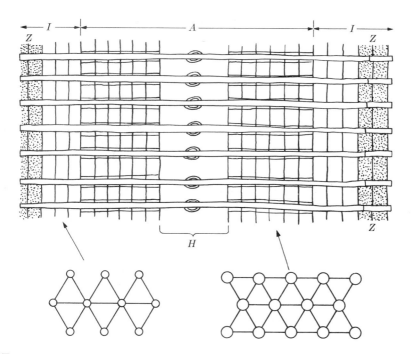

FIG. 14–4. The schematic structure of insect flight muscle as proposed by Hodge on the basis of light and electron microscopic observations. It differs from the proposals of Huxley and Hanson in the shorter I-bands, the cross links, and the lack of thickening in the H-band, plus the important feature of the absence of any interleaving. This flight muscle has a function which calls for very rapid development of tension with very little contraction.

the sarcolemma, proceeding into the myofibrils by way of the Z-bands, which communicate the message to the molecular structure. This accordingly sets into effect the contraction. The myofibril itself is a fourfold structure, with thin actin filaments attached to the Z-bands and interleaved with thicker myosin molecules as far as the start of the H-band, which is simpler in cross-sectional structure. The A-band is thus the extent of the myosin fibrils in each sarcomere, while the I-band is not so readily definable since it is partly concerned with the actin and partly with the myosin molecules. It will be seen later that the contraction and stretching properties of muscle are mostly in the I-band.

Turning to the pattern for insect flight muscle (Fig. 14–4), we see that it is remarkably similar in general outline, with some clear differences. The I-bands are shorter, and the interleaving is not obvious, but rather there is a definite bridged structure to both the A- and the I-bands. The very beautiful electron micrographs taken by Hodge show the bridges very clearly. In fact, they form a most impressive indication of molecular structure in a living system. The differences could quite possibly reflect the difference in function. The insect flight muscle has to develop good tension over a small working range several hundred times a second. It could be that the firm structure provided by the cross links is related to this need. In any event, it is not our province to consider which of a set of studied preparations is to be regarded as showing the general features of muscle, but rather to call attention to the possibilities of interpretation latent in the molecular models. With this in mind we can turn to the behavior of muscle, and see whether it can be related to the molecular biophysics of muscle.

14–5 Muscle behavior. Muscle preparations are among the easier separate biological systems to study. A muscle will retain its major properties in an oxygenated salt solution for weeks, and can readily be worked with for the duration of a day or two. As a result, it has been possible to study various kinds of length-tension relationships, as done by Fenn and Hill, and also, largely due to the persistence and skill of A. V. Hill, thermal relationships. These form our basic knowledge of muscle behavior.

When a whole muscle preparation, which includes the neuromyal junction, is studied, it is found that upon stimulus a wave of excitation, or perhaps more correctly, of depolarization, travels relatively slowly along the muscle. At 0°C the rate of travel of this stimulating wave is about 30 cm/sec, a rate so slow that different parts of the muscle are stimulated at different times, and a rate that makes some of the experimental methods needed rather complex, especially when very short times are involved. A single excitation can produce a single twitch, in which tension is developed, and which lasts for about 45 msec at 0°C in the frog and about 10 msec if the temperature is raised to 20°C. If the stimulus is repeated at shorter and shorter intervals, the muscle goes into a condition of tetanus, a steady contraction. Raising the temperature decreases the tension per twitch, but increases the tension in tetanus. Increase in hydrostatic pressure will increase the tension in a twitch. The maximum tension occurs when the muscle remains at its resting length and does not shorten at all. This maximum is about 5 kgm/cm^2 of muscle cross section. When the muscle shortens, a smaller tension P is exerted. The value of P depends on the time rate of shortening in a manner discovered by Hill, and described by the Hill equation, called by him the "characteristic equation,"

$$(P + a)(V + b) = P_0 b,$$

where P_0 is the maximum tension exerted, V is the velocity of shortening, and a and b are constants for any one kind of muscle preparation. The value of a/P_0 is roughly constant for a variety of muscles ranging from tortoise to man. Hill's equation is strictly only valid when V is measured at the resting length of the muscle, but a similar form can be used to describe tension-velocity relations at other lengths by replacing P_0 with the maximum tension at the muscular length being studied. The two constants a and b remain the same.

Production of heat is an important characteristic of muscular processes. It is very difficult to measure accurately, because the temperature rise is very small and several trivial heat effects are quite comparable in magnitude. For example, the movement of muscle brings a new area under any thermocouple system, and this may not be at the temperature of the part under study. Also, evaporation can change local temperatures very seriously. With much ingenuity, and many years of experience, A. V. Hill has succeeded in assembling a consistent picture of thermal processes in muscle. In outline, they are as follows. Three separate kinds of heat evolution exist: *resting heat*, associated with the metabolic process of the living muscle and not directly concerned with the heat changes during the action of the muscle as such; *initial heat*, which is associated with the process of development of tension, or of contraction, following the stimulus; and *recovery heat*, which is heat produced while the muscle is returning to its resting condition.

Resting heat is the heat evolved in the normal metabolic processes of the muscle cell. It is to some extent determined by the state of the muscle, being affected by the amount of stretch and by the ionic nature of the salt solution. A typical value for resting heat is 2×10^{-4} calorie per gram.

Initial heat occurs in two fractions, one dependent on the degree of contraction. The two are referred to as *maintenance heat* and *shortening heat*. When the heat developed is plotted versus time after stimulus, then for the case where the muscle does not change in length (isometric contraction) there is a fairly sharp rise followed by a more gradual rise. This is the maintenance heat. If the muscle is allowed to shorten, then more heat is developed, and this extra heat is the shortening heat. The rate of heat production is accurately a linear function of the distance shortened, and is independent of the load against which the shortening takes place, a rather surprising result. The maximum rise in temperature per twitch is 3×10^{-3}°C, which corresponds to 3×10^{-3} calorie per gram of muscle. If we express the rate of heat production in terms of energy, then the relation between the rate of heat production, E, and the velocity of shortening, V, can be written as $E = aV + ab$, where the value of a is now the same as that of the constant a in the Hill equation, and ab is the maintenance heat.

These two relationships can be used to derive two others. The *total* heat, the sum of heat and work, is deduced to be a diminishing linear function of the tension P as follows:

$$
\begin{aligned}
\text{Total heat rate} &= E + PV \\
&= aV + ab + P_0 b - Pb - aV \\
&= ab + P_0 b - Pb.
\end{aligned}
$$

By substituting for P from Hill's characteristic equation, a more complicated relation between total heat and V can be derived.

The last category of heat is the recovery heat. The short-term energy requirements of the muscle-contraction process are supplied by the hydrolysis of ATP and also of creatine phosphate, which have to be replaced. Heat is developed during this recovery process. It is most interesting that the process of relaxation, which needs to be distinguished from recovery, involves no heat change (apart from the work done in returning). Recovery heat is markedly (twentyfold) affected by the presence of oxygen, which increases it.

One figure of interest is the efficiency of muscle, defined as the work performed divided by the sum of work and heat. It is about 20%.

14–6 Molecular biophysics and muscle action. After the somewhat lengthy introduction of the previous section, it remains to be seen whether molecular biophysics can shed any light on muscle action. One might put this rather more directly by asking whether the dissection of muscle into fibers, and then into myofibrils, and then into actin-myosin threads has left us with a system which resembles muscle in any way. And if it has, does it prove revealing to make studies at this molecular level? The answer to both questions seems to be a rather hesitant "yes," unless one is a convinced molecular biologist, in which case the "yes" is resounding and very persuasive. Before beginning to consider the molecular biophysics of muscle, it is well to remember the rules of the game. Any attempt to make a molecular explanation of a biological system necessitates synthesizing that system in our minds, and then trying to see how it would behave. Therefore we are in trouble at the start unless the known building blocks are adequate, or nearly so. The short account of muscle has indicated that perhaps a relatively simple system may act as a model for muscular action. It is too much to hope that a simple model system will be 100% successful in explaining and correlating muscle processes in our minds by the molecular description. The least we can expect is that it will not lead us astray into experiments that waste our time.

Following the discovery by Engelhardt and Ljubimowa that myosin catalyzes the hydrolysis of ATP, Szent-Gyorgyi discovered that actomyosin threads contract very definitely on addition of ATP. This discovery was made during World War II, and suffered somewhat from the relative isolation of Axis science from Allied science. Nevertheless it stimulated the search for simple models in molecular terms, which progressed steadily in the hands of Szent-Gyorgyi and his school. At the present time, many varieties of muscle preparations exist, including glycerol extractions of rabbit psoas muscle and molecular actomyosin with ATP. A very thorough and careful review of the findings of these preparations has been given by H. H. Weber and Portzehl, who have themselves been major contributors to this field. Examining the behavior of various models and comparing them with the whole muscle preparations in terms of elastic state, tension and shortening, birefringence, speed of shortening, and efficiency, Weber and Portzehl conclude that the resemblance is very considerable. They call attention to differences. Among these is the continued presence of ATP in living muscle, ATP which is not split in the resting state, while the molecular preparations always split ATP if it is present in the right environment. Also, the speed of contraction is not great enough to compare with living muscle, and the maximum rate of splitting of ATP is far less. It would therefore seem that an attempt to describe some important features of muscular action by molecular biophysics is not out of place.

Among the results on the simplest molecular models, namely actin-myosin mixtures, we can mention the effect of ATP on viscosity, flow birefringence, and light scattering. Viscosity and flow birefringence were both found to drop sharply on addition of ATP by Dainty, Kleinzeller, Lawrence, Miall, Needham, Needham, and Shen. Johnson and Landolt observed a decrease in light scattering on addition of ATP. A very interesting application of the technique of studying the depolarization of fluorescent light has been made by Tsao. A fluorescent dye can be coupled to actin, and the relaxation time of the molecule can be studied by observing the rate of depolarization of fluorescent light. The relaxation time depends

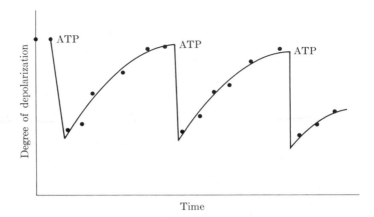

F_IG. 14–5. Depolarization of fluorescent light by actomyosin, as observed by Tsao. The drop in depolarization when ATP is added seems to indicate that a dimer is formed. In any event, the depolarization is always too great to correspond to a large molecular aggregate of the size expected from a combination of actin and myosin.

on the molecular volume, and on the ratio of the viscosity to temperature, with a shape factor introduced for nonspherical molecules. By plotting the reciprocal of the degree of polarization in fluorescent light *versus* the ratio of temperature to viscosity, a straight-line relationship is obtained, from which the relaxation time and the molecular volume can be found. The data can be obtained accurately, and relaxation times can be measured to an accuracy of a percent or so.

Thus the fluorescent depolarization technique is a powerful means of determining the ability of a molecule to rotate, and possibly also of determining the size of a unit which is rotating. In Fig. 14–5 we show Tsao's results on the polarization of actomyosin, when ATP is added. It can be seen that depolarization abruptly *diminishes* when ATP is added, meaning that less rotation is possible and thus presumably a larger molecule is formed. A similar conclusion has been reached by Morales, on the basis of light-scattering and ultracentrifugal studies. This can be taken to mean that the effect of ATP is to cause a monomer to become a dimer. Of even greater interest is the fact that the depolarization is always too big to correspond to the rotation of a whole actomyosin molecule of about a million molecular weight. Thus, apparently, the complex of actin and myosin is not a simple binding of two molecules to form one tight unit.

Many suggestions for molecular processes in muscle have been made. As we do not pose as muscle experts, it could hardly be possible for us to arrange these in the correct historical order, nor would it serve the purposes of this book to do so. In addition, none of the suggestions to date has attracted the universal acclaim that goes with undoubted success, so that we really do no harm by making some selection. The selection is one which appeals to us as molecular biophysicists, and we do not claim that it is the best.

The first we choose is that of Riseman and Kirkwood in 1948. They proposed that the actomyosin thread, in the relaxed condition, is in reality held in place by electrostatic forces that prevent it from giving way to the action of Brownian movement, which will tend to make multiple bends in a long molecule and so produce a shortening. In looking for a mechanism for the formation of electrostatic charges, they call attention to the presence of high percentages of hydroxamino acids, serine and threonine (which together make up 9% of the myosin amino acids), and suggest that these become phosphorylated by ATP, and that the H_2PO_4 becomes singly ionized at pH-7 to —HPO_4, giving a negative charge. These charges hold the actomyosin threads in an extended form. When the signal to contract is received, the ATP becomes enzymatically split, and the phosphorylation of the actomyosin thread is removed, with the result that the molecule becomes a random coil and contracts. There is thus a gain in configurational entropy in contraction.

Riseman and Kirkwood calculated the spacing between the phosphorylation sites as follows. If a random coil forms, with a charge alteration of n elementary units of charge e apiece, and if the linear molecule has a molecular weight M and the structure has a density ρ with a distance between net points of L, then with an effective dielectric constant of D_e, and N for Avogadro's number, the change in elastic modulus is ΔT, where

$$\Delta T = -\frac{8N\rho n^2 e^2}{3M\ D_e L}.$$

Inserting the values $\Delta T = 10^5$ dynes/cm^2, $\rho = 1$, $M = 10^6$, $L = 10^4$ A, and $D_e = 100$ (rather a large value), they deduced that n is 100, and so there are phosphorylation sites every 100 A. This is quite plausible for the distribution of the right kind of amino acids, but does not fit with the fact that the repeat unit for ATP molecules corresponds to only about one per 360,000 molecular weight units. Since the calculations were never intended to be interpreted with precision, it is foolish to condemn the theory on the basis of a number. For example, as Pollissar has pointed out, the use of a much smaller dielectric constant could remove most of the discrepancy.

A theory, similar in principle but differing in the details of the origin of the electric charges, has been given by Morales and Botts, who consider rather carefully a wide range of evidence. They propose that the relaxed state, as in the above theory, is due to the operation of electrostatic forces

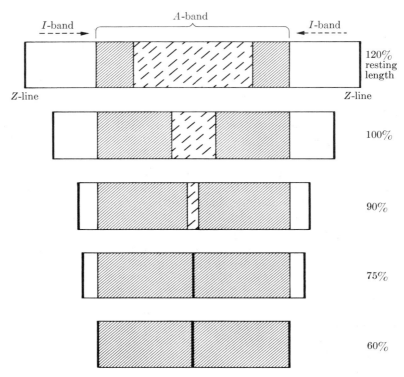

FIG. 14–6.   A schematic drawing, after H. E. Huxley, of the behavior of the *I*-bands and *A*-bands during stretch and contraction.   It appears that the *I*-bands slide within the *A*-bands.

that are due to the adsorption of bivalent cations.   The anion of ATP, as it becomes bound to myosin, neutralizes these charges and causes a contraction by removing the force that keeps the molecule straight.   As the enzymatic action of myosin takes over and changes the ATP to ADP, which is not bound, the straightening out operation begins again and the muscle relaxes.

A somewhat different mechanism has been advanced by H. E. Huxley and Hanson.   While the motivating thought behind the two proposals above has been the idea that contraction is due to the release of threads to become subject to random bombardment, the thought behind the proposal of Huxley and Hanson is based on the observation that during stretch and contraction, the *I*-band, to be thought of as thin actin molecules, does all the changing in length, while the *A*-band does not change at all.   Figure 14–6, due to H. E. Huxley, shows the process which is envisaged.   It can be seen that the property of extension and contraction lies in the changing character of the *I*-band. Section electron-microscopy of the outer part of the *A*-band in the normal condition shows the double array of fibers, as already indicated in Fig. 14–3. Huxley suggests that the thin filaments are actin and the thicker ones are myosin, and that the process of muscle action is concerned with a sliding of the one into the other.

The observations of section electron microscopy are so insistent in showing almost crystalline structure in muscle fibers, and these observations are so well supported by x-ray diffraction pictures, that the "interdigitating" hypothesis mentioned above, which exploits these findings, is worth a little more attention. The evidence for thick and thin filaments is good, and so also is the evidence that the thick filaments are myosin. There is also good evidence for cross bridges between the two, although the all-important detailed structure of thin cross bridges is not known. H. E. Huxley and Jean Hanson, and also A. F. Huxley, have suggested a way in which the cross bridges could be used to cause the "interdigitating" sliding (so called because at this moment any lecturer is practically forced to put the fingers of his two hands together and slide them to and fro). H. E. Huxley suggests that the cross links have their firm base in myosin, but can attach to sites on the thinner actin. The cross links are thought of as able to move back and forth until they become attached, but on attachment there is some kind of ratchet action which prevents them from moving in both directions. As they attach and pull the filament, a molecule of ATP loses a phosphate and so provides the energy necessary for the motion. About 100 of such actions per second would be necessary, and this fits the rate of catalysis of ATP to ADP and phosphate by myosin.

A. F. Huxley has expanded this idea into a rather definite theory, using a specific and intriguing model, with results which bear a clear relation to the relations due to Fenn and Hill. Since his model permits some numerical estimates in terms of molecular pattern, we present an outline of his reasoning. The model is shown in Fig. 14–7. The process of interdigitating motion is supposed to be due to the "catching" of two sites, *M* on the myosin and *A* on the actin. The "catching" is governed by a rate constant *f*, and the release by a second rate constant, *g*. This rate constant is associated with the energy release of combination with, for example, a high-energy phosphate bond, denoted by combination of *A* with "*XP*," some phosphate compound. The third reaction is the breaking up of this combination into its separate parts. The scheme is then

$$A + M \rightarrow AM \qquad \text{(rate constant } f\text{)},$$
$$AM + XP \rightarrow AXP + M \qquad \text{(rate constant } g\text{)},$$
$$AXP \rightarrow A + X + P.$$

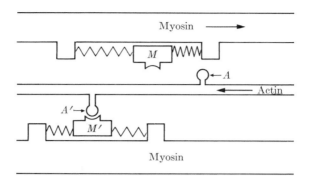

FIG. 14-7. Schematic drawing of the process of attachment site and Brownian movement, which causes the relative motion of thin actin and thick myosin in muscle. The attachment sites are at A, M, A', and M', while the springs simply denote schematically the process of to-and-fro random motion. The model explains the Hill equation and also the heat production in muscle.

In the absence of excitation of the muscle, the "catching" must not occur. Huxley suggests that, among other reasons, this could be because the third reaction cannot occur. Upon excitation, this reaction is freed. Now catching will occur in a manner mediated by relative distance and random thermal motion, represented pictorially by the springs in the model. To introduce the ratchet action, and also set some finite distance to the molecular action, g, the breaking constant, is supposed to be high to the left of the center point and also to rise slowly to the right. The rate constant f is zero to the left of center and rises linearly to a distance $+h$, after which it is zero. On the right, f exceeds g, up to the limit h.

If n is the number of combined sites, the rate of change of n with time is equal to the rate of fresh formation less the rate of breaking, or

$$\frac{dn}{dt} = (1 - n)f - ng.$$

Introducing the velocity, V, as $-dx/dt$, we have

$$-V\frac{dn}{dx} = f - (f + g)n.$$

This velocity, V, is the rate of molecular motion. If the sarcomere is of length s, and v is the rate of shortening in the whole muscle, $V = sv/2$. (Only half the velocity is in the actin.) Thus

$$-\frac{sv}{2}\frac{dn}{dx} = f - (f + g)n.$$

To calculate the energy released, we take the number of times *each M* site undergoes the process and multiply by the energy release per phosphate bond, e, and the number, m, of sites per unit volume of muscle. In a distance dx the number of potential sites is dx/l, where l is the total length between A sites available for reaction. The number per second is then

$$\frac{dx/dt}{l}.$$

The actual reactions are given by the product of this, times the number available to react, times the rate constant, times the increment of time, or

$$\frac{dx/dt}{l} \int f(1 - n)\, dt \quad \text{or} \quad \frac{1}{l} \int f(1 - n)\, dx.$$

The limits of the integral are set by the nature of f and can be considered to be from minus to plus infinity.

The tension can be found by introducing k as the Young's modulus of muscle. The work done at one single site is then $\int kx\, dx$, or for n sites combined is $\int nkx\, dx$. The limits are again set by the prescribed limits to the motion and can be set as infinite. The average force per combined sites is then the total work divided by the total length of travel, which is l, or $\int (nkx\, dx)/l$. For a cubic centimeter of muscle, the total tension is then this figure times the number of sites in one-half of the sarcomere, or for unit area, the number $ms/2$. So we find P to be

$$P = \frac{msk}{2} \int nx\, dx.$$

Introducing the appropriate values for g and f [namely $g = g_2$ for negative x and $g = g_1(x/h)$ for positive x, and $f = 0$ for negative x or x greater than h and $f = f_1(x/h)$ for x between zero and h], Huxley evaluates these equations, and by adjusting two quantities

$$\frac{kh^2}{2e} \frac{f_1 + g_1}{f_1} \quad \text{and} \quad \frac{f_1 + g_1}{g_2},$$

obtains remarkably good fit to the relations derived by Fenn and Hill. The fit is close, but not functionally right; thus Huxley shows slight curvature when the Hill relation is straight. However, as Table 14–1 shows, the agreement is quite as good as the experiments suggest.

Fitting these curves, together with other data, permits Huxley to calculate the actual values of h, the extent of the "catching" zone, and l, the distance between A sites. He obtains values of 156 A for h and 153 A for l. While l should exceed h, which is disturbing, the figures are inter-

TABLE 14–1

COMPARISON OF HUXLEY'S THEORY WITH
HILL'S CHARACTERISTIC EQUATION

Tension (fraction)	Speed of shortening, Hill (fraction)	Speed of shortening, Huxley (fraction)
0	1.0	1.0
0.2	0.44	0.41
0.4	0.23	0.21
0.76	0.066	0.066

esting and bear comparison with current research on the molecular architecture of myosin and actin.

This interdigitating model is very attractive and its proponents are very persuasive. It has trouble because muscle can shorten down to one-fourth of its length and can also exert tension when stretched beyond the observed overlap of the digits. Both these difficulties may well be explained away, but they remain at present.

At the outset of this chapter we have quoted the very expressive words of Szent-Gyorgyi, who has linked the study of muscle with that of life itself. It is worth a moment to assess what we have learned about life from muscle, and more particularly from the molecular biophysical studies of muscle. Perhaps the outstanding feature of muscle is the amount of attention that has been paid to it. Review articles with over 300 references are quite to be expected. What has emerged has been the fact that it is possible and useful to make studies on preparations which are more and more isolated from the whole living organism and that these can give repeatable data, full of meaning. A relatively simple structural plan for muscle has appeared, which is capable of dissection to the molecular level without losing all the properties of muscle. A biochemical analysis has started, and the terms in which it is now given are not hopelessly complex, even though probably incomplete. Above all, it has become clear that in looking at a functioning physiological unit, we are not wasting time at all if we inquire as to its molecular architecture and how this is related to what it does.

Here we run into one of the problems encountered by science in the unseen world of small things. No *one* experiment, no *one* masterly research will tell us the nature of muscle. In all molecular and atomic physics, there is no single definitive experiment. It is the aggregate synthesis of a wide variety of experiment that has yielded us our confident knowledge of things atomic and molecular. It will have to be so with muscle. This means we need to be very tolerant of speculation and hypothesis. We need to encourage theoretical biology, remembering that a good theory is still good even if it is not fully comprehensive. As physically trained individuals, the authors are acutely conscious of the seemingly hopeless tangle of successful and faulty theory which characterized the first thirty years of modern atomic research following the discovery of the electron. All this tangle is now neatly coiled and cataloged, perhaps somewhat banally in the eyes of a pioneer experimentalist. It is well to realize that somewhat the same process lies ahead in understanding muscle. So if some molecular explanations work for some aspects but not for others, it behooves us to look beyond for the grand synthesis of all. When this is done, and it may not be long, muscle will have contributed in a major way to the understanding of life.

II. Nerve Studies

While in studies of muscle we are considering the basic motor process of living beings, in nerve study we are involved with the operation of a system of functioning parts for the use of the whole. The study of nerve is thus far more than the study of a curious way of behavior of excitable tissue; it is also the starting point for any study of the behavior of a whole living being. So its importance in physiology cannot be underestimated. The study of nerve is also of interest in biophysics because the technical revolution of electronics has here had its impact in perhaps the greatest degree in biology. Electronic means of biophysical study of nerve abound, and an electrophysiological laboratory can look like home to a physicist. This very fact has rather disconcerting implications for molecular biophysics, because a readily measurable potential can unfortunately be caused by a variety of processes. Thus in spite of a wealth of measurement, the concluding analysis and explanation is even less satisfying than in the case of muscle.

14–7 Cell membranes. Electrical studies are easily and simply related to conducting and nonconducting processes. The relation is only easy and simple in principle, we hurry to add, but even allowing for the inevitable complications of undesired geometries, it is possible to make electrical measurements which give us an idea of the thickness of the nonconducting part of a cell. The same type of measurement has been applied to a nerve, and this can be discussed later. In the meantime we can profitably consider what can be learned about cell membranes from electrical measurements.

A very early consideration of the resistance and capacitance of suspensions of cells was made by Fricke in 1924. He generalized an expression given by Maxwell for the specific resistance of a suspension of spheres to the case of spheroids, and applied it to suspensions of red blood cells. In the course of this general line of work, he considered the capacitance of a suspension of spheroids which have a thin insulating membrane, and derived the expression

$$C = \alpha \left(1 - \frac{r_1}{r}\right) qC_0,$$

where α is dependent on the ratio of the axes of the spheroid, r is the resistance of the suspension, r_1 is the resistance of the medium, q is the major axis of the spheroid, and C_0 is the capacitance of one square centimeter of the membrane. By making measurements of capacitance as a function of concentration, Fricke was able to determine the value of C_0, showing that it is extremely high. Subsequent refinement of this method by Fricke, and by Cole, has shown that for a variety of cell membranes the capacitance per square centimeter is close to one microfarad.

To see where this leads us, consider a parallel plate condenser, for which the capacitance per unit area is C_0 and the dielectric constant is K. Then

$$C_0 = \frac{K}{4\pi d},$$

using electrostatic units, or

$$C_0 = \frac{8.8K}{d}$$

if C_0 is measured in microfarads and d is in angstroms. It can be seen that in order to calculate d, the thickness of the membrane, we need to know the dielectric constant of the membrane. Unfortunately it is not definitely known, because the nature of the membrane is not known either. But if we assume that the insulating material is the commonest biological insulating material, namely lipid, we can take a dielectric constant of 3, and promptly deduce that the membrane has a thickness of 26 A. This is far smaller than the thickness of any membrane seen in the microscope, and for a number of years seemed to be quite out of line with other knowledge about cells. The recent work on section electron microscopy has to a large extent removed the conflict, and it now seems to be reasonable that the actual barrier to conduction imposed by the cell is very thin, and certainly of the order of one or two molecular thicknesses. A reasonable suggestion is that the membrane is made of a double layer of lipoprotein molecules, of lipid thickness about 30 A with protein thickness making a total of about 100 A. Such a suggestion was made by Danielli.

K. S. Cole suggests that a typical resting cell, heavily qualifying the idea of a "typical" cell, has for its electrical character a membrane with a capacitance of 1 μf/cm^2 that has a leakage resistance of 1000 ohms·cm^2 and an inside to outside negative potential difference of 70 mv. As far as present measurements have gone, the inside is roughly homogeneous with a specific resistance of 100 ohms·cm.

Electrical characteristics of a single nerve fiber of the squid were made by Curtis and Cole, and show the same type of capacitance per square centimeter. It seems, therefore, that a nerve is no exception to the apparently general pattern of a thin lipoprotein layer as the essential membrane of the cell.

14–8 Electrical effects associated with membranes. While it is very tempting to draw a picture of a membrane as we have just described it, we have deliberately withheld the pictorial representation. The reason is that all we can legitimately draw is a repeat of the endoplasmic reticulum featured in Chapter 2, and one which may very well contain quite large openings that permit free passage of even large molecules. It seems more in order to see first what the effect of a double layer, even with quite big holes, could do in the way of developing electrical effects. And the first thing to do is to ask why we expect electrical effects at all, and if they are likely to be of any significance.

The most prolific sources of electrical effects we know are: electrical discharges, generators, and solutions of ions. All have mechanisms to cause the separation of charge that is ordinarily closely associated either in atom, conductor, or molecule. In the case of a discharge, there has to be a strong applied field, coupled with a relatively long, collision-free path, so that an electron can acquire sufficient energy to cause ionization. In the generator the relatively weak field caused by moving a wire in a magnetic field has a very large effect because of the large number of electrons in a conductor that are not bound to atoms. As long as all the processes of interest are confined to conductors, the generator is a potent piece of equipment.

Neither of these processes seems to be very apt for explaining any electrical effects in cells. The third is different. Many compounds exist in which the atomic configurations are such that an individual atom, or group of atoms, can hold an excess electron, or cheerfully lose one. Since matter is accurately electrically neutral, when enough of it is present, each excess negative electron has a matching positive charge, and very often these can form an aggregate, which is an ionically bonded molecule. Alkali metals and halogens are the standard examples. Sodium chloride is such a molecule. In the presence of polar solvents, pre-eminently water, a different aggregate can take place, in which the charged atom, or ion,

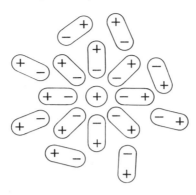

Fig. 14–8. Schematic diagram of an ion in solution. The positive atomic ion is surrounded by a polarized aggregate of polar water molecules. It is thus quite extensive.

can be a stable unit, surrounded by polarized water molecules, which have the appearance shown in token fashion in Fig. 14–8. Such an *ion* is clearly far more extensive than the atomic radius of the bare elemental ion itself, and, indeed, the very motion of such an ion is a question of great interest because it is by no means necessary that the same cloud of polarized molecules be found around it, so long as there *is* a cloud, of the right kind. This means that either the whole cloud can move, or a fresh set of polar water molecules can be found in a new place, and so the ion can move.

Because there is not the least doubt that such ions are present in living cells, and in their environment, we need to consider what electrical effects they can produce. Before doing this, we can see whether chemical reactions exist that can produce such a charge separation. A moment's thought shows that they do. Any element that can operate with more than one valence has this latent ability. While realizing this, we must still remember that to separate two atoms which are attracting each other because of being ionized, we have to provide about 3 ev of energy. Not many of the enzymatically catalyzed processes of biology have this much energy to spare. On the other hand, if we do not ask so drastic a charge separation, it is not nearly so hard to imagine processes that will redistribute charge. Thus, in the case of the transition from ferrous chloride to ferric chloride, a chlorine atom, which very readily attaches an electron and forms a negative ion, becomes attached to an iron atom. This will change the existing equilibrium among charges and so achieve the effect we are discussing.

Another process, really similar in character, involves influencing the ionization of amino or carboxyl groups. If a hydrogen ion is added to an amino group, it then carries a net positive charge, and if hydrogen is re-

TABLE 14–2

Element	Li$^+$	Na$^+$	K$^+$
Radius in crystal lattice, A	0.78	0.98	1.33
Radius in solution, A	3.66	2.81	1.88

moved from carboxyl, it becomes negative. The most studied process for changing these charges is change in the pH, which can alter the number and location of charges. In addition, it must be remembered that any process that alters the binding of the hydrogens in the protein also can influence the amount of local charge. Thus there exist means, not only for altering ionic concentrations, but also for changing the charge distribution on protein molecules in membranes. We can now see what to expect from these two potentialities.

In the first place, whenever a particular ionizable substance exists in a different concentration in two localities, there is a potential difference between them. If we treat a penetrable membrane as causing the concentration difference, and if u and v are the ionic mobilities of the $+$ and $-$ ions, with c_1 and c_2 the two concentrations, the potential difference is ΔV millivolts, where

$$\Delta V = 58 \frac{u - v}{u + v} \log_{10} \left(\frac{c_1}{c_2}\right).$$

Thus, if a concentration ratio of 10 exists, and some difference in mobility is present, a potential difference of the order of millivolts will be present. There is little doubt that many bioelectric potentials, which are just about in this range, are due to this cause.

In the second place, we can consider the nature of the ionic size. As we have described an ion in solution, it is a much larger unit than the same kind of ion in a crystal lattice would be. In fact, it is to be expected that the larger an ion in the crystal lattice, the smaller will be the size of the solvated ion. The reason is that the energy of attraction to the ion of opposite sign must be less if it is bigger and hence farther away, so that the energy of polarization of water molecules needed to hold the ion free in solution is less, and hence there is less water held by it. Thus for the three alkali metal ions, we have the radii shown in Table 14–2. It is clear that while there are many similarities chemically among the alkali metals, there are striking differences physically among the ions in solution.

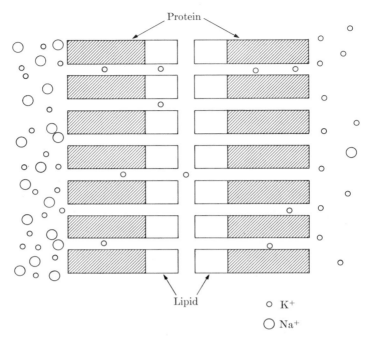

FIG. 14–9. Schematic representation of a lipoprotein cell membrane immersed in ions of two different solvation sizes, namely Na$^+$ and K$^+$. The narrow interstices will permit the smaller ions to pass, but not the larger. There is thus a difference of potential across the membrane.

Now we can consider a process such as is indicated in Fig. 14–9. Here we have exercised our imagination a little, in drawing a lipoprotein membrane in the manner suggested by Danielli, and put it in an environment of ions of various kinds. The sodium ions and potassium ions are drawn roughly to scale, and it can be seen that it is easy to think of potassium diffusing through relatively uniformly, while sodium has a strong concentration gradient across the cell. This concentration gradient will enable a potential difference, measurable in the millivolt range, to be developed.

We can now return to the second potentiality of a membrane, that of altering the surface charge distribution by altering the number of ionized carboxyl or amino groups. This can be achieved *internally* in a protein molecule by an alteration in bonding that changes the hydrogen ion concentration at which an ionization will take place, or it can be achieved *externally* by a change in pH or ionic strength. If such a change takes place, then we can see an effect as shown in Fig. 14–10, where a more enlarged view of one of the pores in the lipoprotein molecule is drawn. The ionized carboxyl and amino groups are shown simply as charges, and the

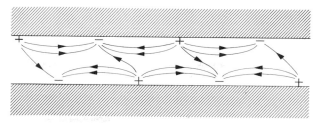

Fig. 14–10. Schematic drawing of a set of charges localized in a protein part of a membrane pore. It can be seen that in order to pass through, an ion has to move back and forth, gaining and losing speed. Such a process could have a strong differential effect on ionic transport through a pore, depending on the sign and size of the ion to be transported.

kind of fields present in the membrane can thus be imagined. It is quite clear that the whole process of ionic permeation *could* be controlled by molecular changes in protein molecules. The fact that the local fields accelerate and decelerate ions and also move them back and forth means that an ion having a polar molecule atmosphere around it which differs from that of another ion will be affected differently, and probably drastically differently.

Some of the problems of pores in cellular membranes have been studied by tracer techniques by Solomon and his group. By using Poiseuille's law for flow of a viscous liquid through a narrow pipe, and a simple diffusion equation, it is possible to derive a radius for the pore. The type of result found is shown in Table 14–3, which is taken from a paper by Solomon. The variation is great, and it is clear that biological pores have character and are interesting. Solomon gives the picturesque analogy of a bowl of spaghetti which is continually shaken, so creating and closing passages.

TABLE 14–3

Tissue	Equivalent pore radius, A
Squid peripheral nerve membrane	16
Human red cell	3.5
Frog ovarian egg	29
Frog body-cavity egg	2.2
Amoeba	2.0
Frog gastric mucosa (two sizes)	60 (7%) 2.5 (93%)

The last question we said we would consider in this section is the *significance* of electrical effects. We can promptly say that as indicator devices they are excellent. They permit the use of very powerful physical tools in their detection and measurement. Also, when some idea of the cellular process involved comes to mind, the electrical data can serve as one piece of evidence for or against the idea. On the other hand, a huge set of potential measurements are needed to deduce any charge distribution, and it is the charge distribution that is the molecular process of interest. It seems to the authors that this inherent difficulty has stood in the way of a clear molecular description of bioelectric phenomena in general and of nerve excitation in particular. With this, for us, unusually gloomy remark, we can proceed to give a very short account of a nerve and the method of transmission of nervous impulses.

14–9 Nature of a nerve and a nerve cell. A moment's thought shows that the kind of nerves we use for piano playing, hearing, seeing, and tasting can hardly be single pieces of cable. They are, in fact, complex multicellular units in which the cells themselves are complex, not only in the usual way, but as to their function. What we loosely call a nerve is a compound object made up of a set of detecting and stimulus-transferring units, all somewhat alike, and yet also all somewhat different. By means of this object, subtleties of sensation and control are possible, ranging from the ability of a conductor to detect undesired overtones from a single instrument in an orchestra, to the color sense of a skilled interior decorator. In studying nervous processes, biophysics begins to play a part in the understanding of the individual as a system, and it is not at all surprising that quite different motives actuate research in this field.

A nerve cell, or *neuron*, is a sort of nightmarelike inversion of the ordinary cell such as we have described formerly. Its nucleus, and its reproductive parts, which are usually so important, and indeed are most important in the neuron, are in the background. The cell has many outgrowths, called *dendrites*, which spread out in a semirandom way. It also has one major outgrowth, the *axon*, which has a specialized structure. These cells are used as a sensing and communication network in which the major operation, repeated many times, is the transmission of change along the axon and communication to another neuron. The manner in which this is done, and the astonishing diversity of function that can be accomplished by a relatively simple repetition of the same process, shows the architecture of a living being to be truly far more beautiful in concept and performance than any other architecture yet seen.

It would be fair to say that we know very little about the molecular structure of this nervous system in relation to what it does. We know something about the axon, and we know the way in which the axon reacts

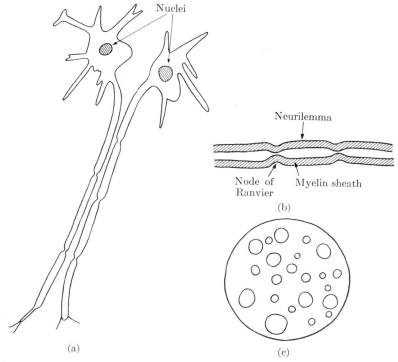

FIG. 14–11.   Schematic drawings illustrating features of nerve.   (a) A bundle of two neurons.   (b) The most basic features of a myelinated axon.   (c) A cross section of a more complex bundle than that shown in (a).

to a stimulus and what kind of a signal it transmits. How it does it, we do not know, though there are some good surmises. Since we are concerned with molecular biophysics, we have to admit that much research remains to be done before we can write this section. So we shall simply describe the major features of transmission by an axon and leave the rest to the research world. Before we do this we call attention to the schematic diagram of a multiple nerve shown in Fig. 14–11. The whole nerve is composed of many cells with axons, as indicated in part (c) of the figure. Two of these are shown in (a), and the general character of the section of an axon longitudinally is shown in (b).

The neuron is not to be thought of only as a highly specialized cell, one lacking the normal nucleus and cytoplasm of a more usual cell. Actually, the material down the core of the axon, the *axoplasm*, is steadily moving along and hence requiring continual renewal. To create the quite diverse contents of the axoplasm, including a fibrous protein, there has to be a very active cytoplasm with all the synthetic apparatus—mitochondria, ribonucleoprotein particles, and endoplasmic reticulum. The very action of the nerve definitely requires active metabolism, and one of the important lacks in our knowledge is how this active metabolism is coupled to the way in which the nerve functions.

The axon itself has a complex structure. In many nerves it has a set of sections of *myelin* sheath surrounding it, with short intervals between the sections, known as nodes of Ranvier. The structure of the myelin sheath is beginning to be described, and a very good summary of the knowledge has been given by F. O. Schmitt. The myelin sheath is spirally wrapped around the axon until it forms many layers, each of which are lipid protein structures, rather less than 200 A thick and containing a closely organized molecular pattern of lipids, for example, phosphatidyl serine, cholesterol, cerebroside, and sphingomyelin. This organized molecular system is certainly involved in nervous action, and active research is in progress to relate the two.

If a multiple neuron nerve is removed and kept in salt solution, it can be stimulated into action by applying a potential from a pair of electrodes placed at one end. An electrode placed anywhere farther down the nerve and connected to the right kind of amplifier will detect a pulse of voltage, due to the nerve action passing by. The shape of the detected wave depends on the electrode system, and too much should not be made of it unless this has been carefully designed and considered. We are resolutely going to avoid all discussion of electrophysiological electronics, since that field is one *par excellence* for the specialist, and we cannot produce our union card. From a compound nerve the response is complex, ranging over about a millisecond, with a very large component initially. When the much harder experiment of observing the effect on a single axon (made easier by the cooperation of the squid, which in turn renders it necessary to spend the summer at Woods Hole, which accounts for some of the interest in this field) is done, it is found that the action current is much simpler, that it travels at a velocity of six meters per second per micron diameter of the fiber, that there is a refractory period of about 0.6 msec, and that it is of the order of 50 millivolts. The process is *not* that of electrical conduction down the nerve, but resembles the burning of a fuse, a remark inserted to discourage any physicist who might be reading about the action of a nerve for the first time.

The actual electrical properties of the axon can be measured by carefully applied electrical techniques, a field in which K. S. Cole, Hodgkin, and Huxley are major leaders. The capacitance of the membrane runs in the vicinity of $1 \, \mu f/cm^2$, and a parallel resistance and potential source are usually represented as well, in order to give a parametric description of the impedance of the axon. In a very striking experiment, Cole and Curtis demonstrated that an impedance change is closely associated with the

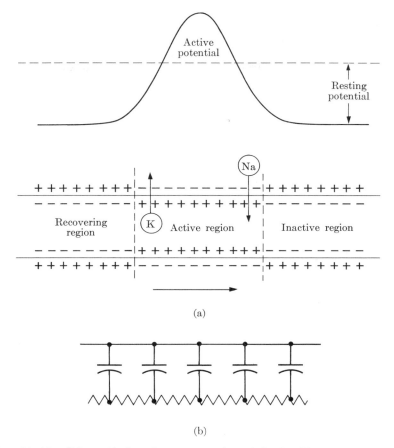

(a)

(b)

FIG. 14–12.   Schematic (very) representation of the fuselike process of nerve excitation. To start the process, a minimum stimulus has to be given. The nerve is then refractory for a short while and, if the stimulus is still operating, will "fire" again. A strong stimulus thus produces more of the potential spikes, but not any greater individual potential change.   Thus a nerve is well suited to transmit information in binary code.

action potential, and thus the idea that a change in ionic permeability can be associated with nerve action is supported.

The action of the nerve axon is thus to transmit a partly physical, partly chemical, partly electrical pulse in material which has been prepared for the event by its previous metabolism. The kind of effect can be represented schematically (only), as in Fig. 14–12. The axon is represented as having a center core of axoplasm, with a polarized sheath. When the appropriate stimulus is applied, and this needs to be great if applied for a short time but can be less if applied for a longer time, the nerve "fires," and the active region has a reversed polarization. Behind the active region is the recovering region where the membrane potential is being restored by the maintaining processes of metabolism. Such an "all-or-nothing" response thus nicely provides a means for transmitting a binary (on–off, black–white) code.

This reversal of a polarized surface pattern is clearly correlated with the sodium and potassium content of the axoplasm. In the unstimulated nerve there is a strong discrimination in favor of potassium ions and against sodium ions. The process, which is not understood, is referred to as the "sodium pump," although the "pump" does more than keep sodium out: it also favors the K^+ ion. The "pump" is clearly related to metabolic activity, whether by changing the charge in pores, or by associating ions with large molecules, or by some other means, is not known. The operation of this metabolically controlled process is drastically altered if the magnitude of the potential difference is changed by passing a current into the nerve center. The change takes place rather abruptly at a voltage which depends on the length of the excitation, being less the longer the excitation is kept up. The abrupt change is due to a regenerative de-polarization that produces a sharp rise from the normally negative potential to a positive potential, returning to its original state in a millisecond or two. This "spike" or "action potential" travels down the nerve at a speed depending on the kind of axon, being faster in those with myelin sheaths and nodes.

The process of propagation is connected with a completely different property of the nerve, the electrical cable property. An ordinary transmission line which operates on an alternation between a current due to an electric field and an electric field due to the magnetic field set up by the current can be designed to have a very low resistance. Such lines will transmit over very great distances with low attenuation. The nerve is a much humbler kind of cable. It has no real reliance on recreating the electric field by the changing magnetic field, but it does have, in the 1 $\mu f/cm^2$, a remarkable means of storing electrical energy in a small space. If we think of (as the very simplest circuit) a series of parallel capacitances connected at one side and attached to a long resistance on the other side, as shown in Fig. 14–12(b) then if one capacitance is charged, current will flow into the next and on to the remainder. Nothing acts to regenerate voltage, but nevertheless the charging of one capacitance will cause others, farther down, to charge. The voltage developed is attenuated rapidly, in fractions of a millimeter, but even so, it provides the necessary threshold voltage and current to cause the inactive region to "fire." The recovering region is also stimulated, but the metabolic processes take time and the condition for firing is not yet restored. So the spike travels down the nerve. In the case of the myelin sheath with breaks at the nodes, the units of the myelin sheath act as separated capacitances and the efficiency of transmission is higher, including a faster rate of transmission.

With our strictly amateur status, this is all we intend to say about nerve behavior. We would like to quote from someone with a more advanced status to conclude this section on the proper note. These remarks from A. V. Hill seem far more fitting than we can possibly write. They are taken from his article in the first Cold Spring Harbor Symposium.

I do not know how many motor and sensory medullated nerve fibers there are in a man, but let us guess. Assume that they weigh altogether 100 grams, that they have an average length of 50 cm and an average diameter of 14μ. This would give about a million of them. I expect this is an underestimate. Let us think of a man running in a quarter-mile race, exerting himself to his utmost. I think we admit an average of at least 10 impulses per second to each of the fibers; total, ten million waves per second. This hurricane of coordinated impulses is raging in our runner. Even at rest I suppose we may allow him one-twentieth of this, half a million per second. Each of these impulses could be picked up and recorded or made audible by modern electrical technique. Each wave has the same general characteristics. Each is a reasonable and intelligible thing. The properties of a gas depend on the average behavior of its molecules, but that is governed by statistical rules. The properties of a man depend upon the total behavior of his nerve impulses, but these—although so many—are coordinated and adjusted. Truly, as David said, we are fearfully and wonderfully made.

III. Studies of the Eye

14–10 The eye as a model. Anyone seriously wishing to contemplate the mechanical construction of the equivalent of a living organism would do well to think about the nature of the eye. It is not that the authors want to discourage attempts to stimulate and reproduce living systems; quite the contrary, for such attempts often give great insight. It is because of the overwhelming functional perfection of the eye as a sensory mechanism and as an optical system that we suggest that it is worthy of thought. As a sensory mechanism it can detect a single quantum. But it does even better; it registers the fact only when there are enough quanta present to be worth considering as part of a pattern. It can also handle intensities over a range of 10^9. As an optical system it has greater than 180° angular coverage, something which is impressive in itself, and also has the ability to change focus, at an instant's notice, over a range from a few inches to infinity. It has sensitivity for alertness, and a means for detailed observation of a narrow region, all built in and fully automatic. So, again, it is worth some thought.

To describe an eye in broad terms, it is a lens that focuses images onto a retina. The dimensions of the eye have been determined by use of a narrow beam of x-rays. The axial length of the eyeball in normal subjects is 22.9 mm. In myopes it is around 24.9 mm, and in hypermetropes it is 21.3 mm.

A very large number of topics related to the eye are open to the biophysicist. The geometrical optics of the eye is itself of great interest, and mature physical insight is required to understand it. The problem of *acuity*, the smallest resolvable angle, the relation of polarized light to vision, and the ultimate sensitivity of the eye are a few more topics to add to the list. Some selection has to be made. We propose to consider briefly the microhistology of the retina, or rather of elements of the retina, and then to consider the quantum nature of vision, which bears on molecular biophysics.

14–11 The retina. The appearance of a section through the retina is shown schematically in Fig. 14–13. This is intended to be used much as the map of a continent is first consulted to know something about the location of a particular state. In the next two figures two more stages of detail are shown. The rods and cones, which form so dramatic a part of the operation of the eye, are not themselves connected to the nervous system, but apparently are connected through two discontinuities joined by a small-scale nervous system. Thus histologically it would appear that no discrimination by a single rod or cone is possible, but that they have to be taken in groups.

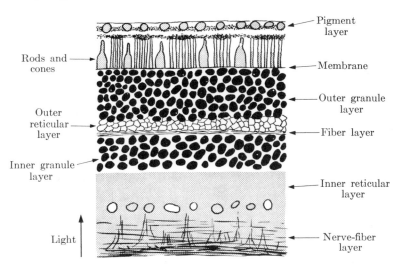

FIG. 14–13. Schematic drawing of a section through the retina to give an idea of the general organization. Perhaps the most surprising feature is the direction of the light.

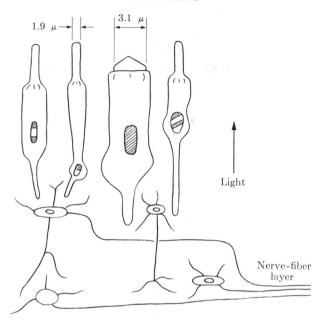

FIG. 14–14. A schematic drawing of the retina to show the relative positions of the rods and cones and of the network of nerves, cells, and fibers which form the retina.

Perhaps the most surprising feature in Fig. 14–13 is the direction of the light, which is a severe shock to most physicists first encountering the subject. It might almost be used as a warning sign to anyone who feels that living systems are just logical extensions of known physical instruments.

There are many more rods than cones. The most sensitive region of the eye is the *fovea*. Here the density of sensory units is greatest. At the center of the fovea there are roughly 10^5 cones per mm^2, dropping in number to 6×10^3 at 3 mm from the center. Close to the edge of the fovea, the rods (which are missing in the center) start to rise sharply in number to about 2×10^5 per mm^2, and drop gradually in number to 3×10^4 away from the fovea, again in round numbers. Thus, in the rather dense regions there will be found about one rod or cone per 10 square micron.

A second stage in the localization of the rods and cones is shown in Fig. 14–14. This serves to show the general character of the rods and cones, although as will be seen from Fig. 14–15, the very fine structure is much more detailed than might be expected at first.

One of the early triumphs of osmium-stained, methacrylate-embedded, section electron microscopy was in the revelation of the remarkable struc-

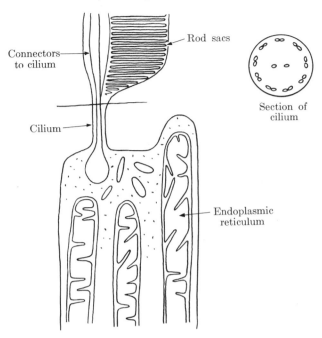

Fᴵɢ. 14–15.   Schematic diagram of part of the outer and part of the inner segment of a rod, modified from figures by Sjostrand and de Robertis. The rod consists of many flat platelets, enclosed in a membrane and connected to the cilium, which in turn connects to the inner segment containing long, thin mitochondria and the endoplasmic reticulum.

ture of the rods. A somewhat similar structure also holds for the cones. Figure 14–15, adapted from Sjostrand, who first determined the general characters (plus some added features found by de Robertis) shows the microstructure revealed by this means. It can be seen that each rod is double, with a receptor segment separated from the rest of the cell. The connection is made by a cilium, whose cross section shows it to have nine pairs of tubules, in close similarity to the cross section of the cilia in *Paramecium*. The receptor segment is a stack of platelets, enclosed by a membrane. The platelets are occasionally connected to the cilium, and are also connected to each other. Details on these disks are given in Fig. 14–16.

The inner segment is a more-or-less normal cell, with tightly packed, long, thin mitochondria and elements of the endoplasmic reticulum. The disks of the outer segment contain lipid and protein in the ratio of two to three. In Fig. 14–16, the type of molecular structure which is present is shown. Sjostrand feels that the repetition of disks increases the probability

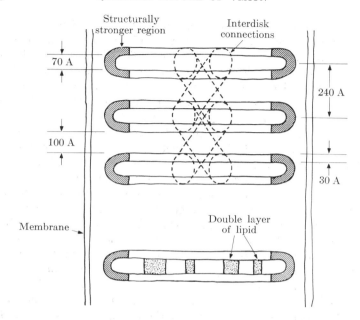

Fɪɢ. 14–16. Molecular structure of the rod disks as suggested by Sjostrand. Since the width is variable, no scale is included.

for the absorption of a photon in such a way as to excite the membrane of one of the elements and that the resulting excitation is communicated to the inner segment via the elements.

Sjostrand suggests that the place of lipid, shown in early polarization studies by Schmidt to be parallel to the axis of the rod, lies inside the disks, as a double layer. It is of great interest that Schmidt's polarization studies led him, in 1934, to suggest the presence of lamellae and to separate the organization of lipid and nonlipid materials. The diagrams in his paper are highly suggestive of the structures shown by the electron microscope.

It is interesting that one other efficient absorber and utilizer of light, the plant chloroplast, has structure rather similar to the retinal rods. A comparative study by Wolken has shown that the chloroplast in *Euglena*, while having wider and thicker photoreceptors than in the frog retinal rod, has about the same number of pigment molecules per photoreceptor, with a molecular weight of somewhat the same order.

14–12 Quantum nature of vision. It has been known for many years that the dark-adapted eye has a very high sensitivity. Use was made of this knowledge in the observation of single radioactive particles by the pioneers of atomic and nuclear physics. In a careful study of the process of the detection of scintillations from alpha particles, Chariton and Lea concluded that the eye can detect between 17 and 30 photons at maximal sensitivity when a scintillation is observed. This figure is probably rather low, but it shows at once that the eye must have a sensory part which can detect a very small number of quanta, probably as low as two or more.

A very careful and elaborate study of the sensitivity of the eye was made by Hecht, Shlaer, and Pirenne in 1941. They made use of the fact that the eye is most sensitive at about 20° away from direct viewing, and set up a shutter device which would deliver a single pulse of light of any desired wavelength when the observer called for it by pushing a button. The intensity could be varied by a second experimenter so that each pulse contained a known amount of light. In this way, by recording the number of times that a pulse was actually seen, the sensitivity of the eye could be measured. They found that the minimum detectable energy was between 2.1 and 5.7×10^{-10} ergs, measured at the cornea. This corresponds to between 58 and 148 photons of light at 5100 A wavelength. To estimate the actual amount absorbed by the rods, one must allow for the reflection at the cornea, which is 4%, the absorption in the light path of the eye, which is 50%, and the transmission through the retina, which is 80%. Making these allowances, we find that the figure becomes a range from 5 to 14 quanta.

A very interesting confirmation of this low figure, which also brings out rather nicely the quantum nature of vision, is found in terms of the frequency of observation of a pulse as the intensity is varied. If indeed as low a number as 5 quanta can be detected, then a pulse having on the average 5 quanta will show many fluctuant values. The Poisson formula, already well known to the reader, describes these, and use can be made of the fluctuations to see whether the actual detection by the observer matches the expected fluctuations.

To see how this is followed out in detail, suppose that the average number of photons in a pulse is a. Then the probability that actually n will be present is $P(n)$, where

$$P(n) = \frac{e^{-a}a^n}{n!}.$$

Now if we arbitrarily set n as having a certain value, the values of $P(n)$ can be determined for various values of a, the average number of photons, a number that can be determined by the second experimenter. For example, if the average number of quanta is 10, the probability that 5 will actually be all that are in the pulse is 1.8%. Thus under those conditions, an observer who required 6 photons for detection would not observe the flash. Actually the flash would not be observed for less than 5 photons either, so that a summation of the various probabilities has to be taken.

TABLE 14–4

Number of quanta at cornea	Frequency of seeing	Theory for $n = 6$
46.9	0.0	0.05
73.1	9.4	10.0
113.8	33.3	33.3
177.4	73.5	76.0
276.1	100.0	96.0
421.7	100.0	100.0

This poses no problem, since the Poisson function is tabulated over a wide range of values, and a little work soon develops a theoretical set of curves corresponding to the probability of seeing for various presupposed quantum sensitivities and average numbers of quanta. Hecht, Shlaer, and Pirenne drew up a series of such curves in which the logarithm of the average number of quanta at the cornea (i.e., before absorption and reflection are considered) is plotted against the theoretical probability of seeing. The results found by Hecht in one experiment were as listed in Table 14–4. It can be seen that the fit with theory is remarkably good. If the value of n is set as low as 5 or as high as 8, the fit is not so good. Thus this independent proof of the low number of quanta necessary is very satisfying. In the experiment, Shlaer recorded a sensitivity of 7 photons and Pirenne of 5.

These are not the only measurements of the limiting sensitivity of the retina. In particular, Bouman and Van der Welden have concluded that the sensitivity can be as low as two photons.

In view of the histology of the retina, wherein we have already seen that no one rod is directly connected to the optic nerve, but rather to a set of nerve networks, it seems to be reasonable to say that *one photon can excite one rod*.

14–13 The biochemistry of retinal detection. The process of retinal detection is concerned with photosensitive pigments. Among these is *rhodopsin*, present in rods. It is a protein molecule, with a diameter of about 40 A, and hence quite capable of being part of a mosaic which forms the platelike structures shown in Fig. 14–16. The protein has attached to it a small molecule, *retinene*, which is a carotenoid, the structural formula of which (in one form) is shown in Fig. 14–17. Under the action of light, retinene is split away from the protein, the residue of which is called an *opsin*. The retinene is then reduced to vitamin A by the combination of an alcohol

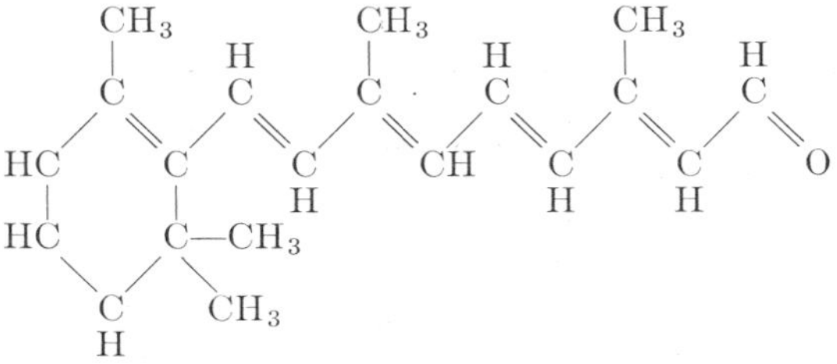

FIG. 14–17. One structure for retinene. Note the large number of conjugated double bonds.

dehydrogenase plus cozymase. The reverse process is not dependent on light and may approach completion in the dark, so as to restore the ability to respond to light.

We owe a great deal of the knowledge of the biochemistry of the retina to Wald. He makes the suggestion, among other possibilities, that the resting visual pigment is not an enzyme, that possibly the retinene is an inhibitor. The action of light, in his phrase, "uncorks" the enzyme by removing the inhibitor. The freed enzyme can now produce ample chemical change to give a response in the network of nerves near the rod or cone.

This mechanism enables us to see why the limiting sensitivity of vision, with regard to its registration by the mind, is more than one photon. If we are to suppose that one protein molecule which has become "uncorked" can set into being the whole process of nerve excitation so that a set of spikes travel along a nerve fiber, then we must consider what the possibility of random thermal excitation is. If we set the threshold for the uncorking process at 1.5 ev, and if we take the average energy corresponding to kT to be 1/30 ev, which is also reasonable, then the probability that a particular molecular configuration will be found to be 1.5 ev is $e^{-1.5/(1/30)}$, or e^{-45}. This is 10^{-19}. Now there are 10^8 rods, each having about 1000 layers, with each layer having about 1000 rhodopsin molecules, making 10^{14} sensitive units in all. Thus purely random processes can give excitation to rods somewhere in the eye about $10^{14} \times 10^{-19}$, or 10^{-5}, of the time. Since the eye certainly responds to a process which occurs in one thousandth of a second, and probably far less, the eye would be vulnerable to a set of meaningless stimulations every second or so, in a way which would give constant unnecessary alerts to the mind.

By using a detection system requiring two related excitations, the eye eliminates this background in exactly the same way as the nuclear physicist reduces the background from a scintillation counter by requiring a coincidence of two counts closely related in time before his circuit will register. Thus the eye is not only ultimately sensitive, but also has designed into itself means for making use of this ultimate sensitivity.

This very limited discussion of the eye is in reality intended only to start interest on the part of the reader. No physiological organ impresses the physicist with the perfection of design of a greatly evolved living being more than the eye. It is worthy of much deep study by all kinds of scientific methods.

IV. Conclusion

We conclude this chapter by returning to our remarks at the outset. In the topics of muscle, nerve, and eye, we have picked three which clearly involve physiological function. It has been our aim to show that molecular biophysics offers hope in the interpretation of such physiological systems. We have seen that in muscle studies the function of shortening can be related to molecular changes and that molecular means of energy transfer seem to offer means of explanation of muscle energetics. In the study of nerve we are not so far along, but again the thinness of the undoubtedly molecularly functioning membrane leads us to consider the nature of nerve in terms of molecular units. And, finally, the eye, with an almost crystalline structure to part of the rods, and an ultimate quantum sensitivity of one, also calls for explanation in terms of molecular biophysics. So the only thing we can wish is, not that we were better physiologists as such, but that we knew our business of molecular biophysics even better, for then we would stand a chance of explaining the function of these three organs.

Problems

1. Using Riseman and Kirkwood's equation, calculate the number of phosphorylation sites for a dielectric constant of 3 and a change in elastic modulus of 5×10^4 dynes/cm^2.

2. Calculate the capacitance per square centimeter of a lipo protein membrane in which the lipid has a thickness of 50 A and a dielectric constant of 3. Estimate the percent of lipid in cells having such a membrane for: (a) cell radius 1000 A, (b) cell radius 4000 A, length $2\,\mu$, (c) cell radius $10\,\mu$.

3. If the electrical potential due to auxin in a plant is caused by the concentration difference of a singly charged $+$ ion of mobility twice that of the $-$ ion, calculate the ratio of concentration needed to give a potential difference of 50 mv.

4. Draw a theoretical curve for the relation between logarithm of average number of photons incident on the retina and percent observation of flashes for a required number of photons for vision of 3.

5. If the threshold of release of effect in a rhodopsin molecule is 1 ev and there are 10^{14} total sensitive units, calculate the frequency of apparent flashes due to thermal action if (a) one molecule triggers the nervous system, and (b) two molecules must be excited within 10^{-3} sec of each other for a response to be recorded.

REFERENCES

1. H. E. HUXLEY, "Muscular Contraction," *Endeavour* **15,** 177 (1956).

2. S. V. PERRY, "Relation Between Chemical and Contractile Function and Stru cture of the Skeletal Muscle Cell," *Physiol. Rev.* **36,** 1 (1956).

3. A. SZENT-GYORGYI, *Chemistry of Muscular Contraction.* Academic Press, New York, 1951.

4. G. H. BOURNE, ed., *Structure and Function of Muscle.* Academic Press, New York, 1960.

5. M. MORALES and JEAN BOTTS, "A Model for the Elementary Process in Muscle Action," *Arch. Biochem. Biophys.* **37,** 283 (1952).

6. A. V. HILL, *Proc. Roy. Soc.* **B126,** 136 (1938).

7. A. V. HILL, et al., *Proc. Roy. Soc.* **B137,** 40–87 (1950).

8. A. J. HODGE, "Studies on the Structure of Muscle," *J. Biochem. Biophys. Cytol.* **1,** 361 (1955).

9. H. FRICKE, *Cold Spring Harbor Symposia* **1,** 117 (1933).

10. H. DAVSON and J. F. DANIELLI, *The Permeability of Natural Membranes.* Cambridge University Press, 1952.

11. J. A. V. BUTLER, *Electrical Phenomena at Interfaces.* Methuen, London, 1951. See, particularly, articles by W. F. Floyd, titled "Membrane Potentials and Electrical Properties of Living Cells" and "Electrical Properties of Nerve and Muscle."

12. H. DAVSON, *A Textbook of General Physiology.* Little, Brown and Co., Boston, 1959.

13. T. TEORELL, "Transport Processes and Electrical Phenomena in Ionic Membranes," *Prog. Biophys.* **3,** 305 (1953).

14. M. H. PIRENNE, "Quantum Physics of Vision," *Prog. Biophys.* **2,** 193 (1952).

15. E. STEINMANN and F. S. SJOSTRAND, "Ultra Structure of Chloroplasts," *Exp. Cell. Res.* **8,** 17 (1955).

16. F. DE ROBERTIS, "Electron Microscope Observation on the Submicroscopic Organization of the Retinal Rods," *J. Biochem. Biophys. Cytol.* **2,** 319 (1956).

17. K. S. COLE, "The Electric Structure and Function of Cells," *Proceedings of the First National Biophysics Conference.* Yale University Press, 1959, p. 332.

18. A. K. SOLOMON, "Equivalent Pore Discussions in Cellular Membranes," *Proceedings of the First National Biophysics Conference.* Yale University Press, 1959, p. 314.

19. Articles by F. O. SCHMITT, A. J. HODGE, M. F. MORALES, H. S. BENNETT, A. F. HUXLEY, B. KATZ, and C. M. CONNELLY, in "Biophysical Science: A Study Program," *Rev. Mod. Phys.* **31,** Nos. 1 and 2, 1959.

CHAPTER 15

THE PHYSICS OF CELLULAR PROCESSES

15–1 Introduction. In this chapter we intend to attempt some of the synthesis of our knowledge of the parts of cells and of the way in which they might behave according to the laws of physics. We hope to change our scale of being, and for a while live in the unseen submicroscopic world of the cell, trying to determine how this world will look to us. We can never see it precisely, and what we observe may be artifacts, because even the detail of an electron microscope is no better, perhaps not as good, as the detail in an Egyptian mummy preserved by "fixatives" for a few hundred generations. But we will try to construct, in terms of our best knowledge, how the cell might behave, using the laws of physics and chemistry as best we can apply them, and then see whether the behavior we predict bears any relation to the behavior of a living cell. What we are really doing is attempting an essay in theoretical biology. We need to remind ourselves that so doing is well worth while, because all our knowledge of atomic physics and chemistry, dating from the first use of weighing and volume measurements by Lavoisier and Avogadro, is theoretical. If we are ever to understand the cell, it will be by theory—theory checked and counterchecked against quantitative observation.

Unfortunately, theoretical biology can hardly be said to be an established science. Thus we cannot draw upon a whole library of authoritative texts. Instead, we have to try to start, in a tentative way, a process which others will challenge, correct, and finish.

Clearly one cellular process that must be considered is *growth*. A second is *replication*, a third is *division* and a fourth is *differentiation*. We can start with growth.

15–2 Growth. In keeping with the spirit of numerical description, we can consider some rates of growth. An *E. coli* bacterium divides under optimum conditions in 20 min, or roughly 1000 sec. In that time it synthesizes its own weight of 2.5×10^{-13} gm, doubles its length of 2×10^{-4} cm, and doubles its area of external surface of 10^{-7} cm^2. Since about 60% of the dry weight of the cell is protein, this means that 1.5×10^{-13} gm of protein is synthesized in the 1000 sec. If we take the molecular weight of protein to be 100,000, then the weight of one molecule is 1.6×10^{-19} gm and the number of protein molecules synthesized *per second* per cell is 1000, in round numbers. Since each molecule involves the correct ordering of something like 1000 amino acids, it is clear that a very remarkable synthetic method must exist. We shall return to the nature of this process in Section 15–3, but in the meantime we wish to keep our attention fixed on the process of growth.

Growth in the living cell is something very different from the growth of a crystal or the expansion of a bubble. Although the factors which enter into the process of crystal growth or the expansion of a bubble of gas probably enter into the whole process of the growth of the cell, they are subordinate to a number of factors that are highly characteristic of living material. To illustrate this point, let us consider the growth of the cell membrane. As far as we can tell, the membrane grows only in its own plane. Therefore new material has to be fed into the surface in some way, without permitting it to thicken at any point. The new material does not have the same macromolecular constitution of either the outside or inside of the cell; it is membrane material. Also, in the process of growing, the membrane retains a certain geometrical shape—not exactly, to be sure, but still a rod-shaped bacterium remains a rod during the growing time. A very challenging question is: how does such a membrane grow?

Without giving an answer, we can see, in terms of some further ideas that in turn need to be examined rigorously, how the membrane might grow. While we consider this question, it is well to recall the structure of the cell that we outlined in Chapter 2, particularly of the double lamellae which form a part of the endoplasmic reticulum. One feature of these double lamellae, of which we are still not certain, is that they are essentially closed double sheets. We might take the bold attitude that such closed double sheets are one of the biological units and that the double sheet is one element which has to be able to grow.

In Fig. 15–1 we show one of our inferential schematic diagrams for a simple unit of the reticulum and, in much enlarged form, an idea of how it might be made up on the molecular scale. The simple unit is made up of a small, double surface with a "granule" somehow attached to it. In the endoplasmic reticulum these granules appear very frequently, and we wish to stress that we have deliberately chosen to represent the simplest possible unit of the reticulum. What we know about it from electron microscopy is shown in part (a) of the figure. Speculation about it (which is quite legitimate in this chapter) is shown in part (b).

The center of synthesis is supposed to be the "granule," which is probably composed of RNA and protein. It is an integral part of, but not necessarily covalently bonded to, a single continuous sheet of protein. We endow the granule with the ability to attach amino acids in the correct order and location and to "zipper" them together to form protein molecules, as represented by dumbbells in the figure. As each protein molecule is finished, it naturally finds its place in the membrane and causes it to grow. The membrane of protein molecules is held only by forces of the

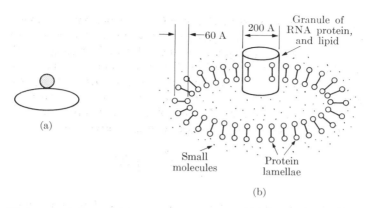

Fig. 15–1. An inferential representation of the smallest unit of the endoplasmic reticulum, shown in (a) as it would be seen in the electron microscope. On the molecular scale, it is imagined to look as shown in (b). The granule is shown as a cylindrical particle of ribonucleoprotein, with probably some lipid in it, and it is supposed to have the ability to make whole protein molecules (shown as dumbbell-shaped objects) out of the small amino acids which are inside and outside the lamellae. As each protein molecule is formed, it is fed into place in a kind of two-dimensional crystal, which is the continuous lamella. The whole process appears only in section, but is in reality concerned with the formation of a sheet, not a loop.

van der Waals type and so is not fixed and tight. As it gets larger it may become looser. And if there are more granules on the outside, due to a second synthetic process that makes them, the granules can find a temporary space and fit in so that the number of granules per surface increases. In this way, a single unit of the reticulum can grow until it is of considerable size.

This method proposed for the process of growth of a membrane is only one possible method. It is, however, one which appears plausible. It is worth while to examine the physical processes that will be involved in such a process of growth. In so doing, we shall find that the processes will have to be considered for almost *any* model for growth. Therefore the speculative aspect of our suggestions need not get in the way of due physical thinking.

Let us first consider the forces between the protein molecules that form the reticulum. Each molecule has neighbors to the north, east, south, and west and must be attracted to them all. Thus it would seem as though the forces would not be too specific. The molecules cannot be bound too tightly together, because if they were, the space between them would be too small to permit the diffusion of amino acids and of water, both of which are necessary to achieve the synthesis of protein. The kind of force available for this is the London dispersion force, which is one of the van der Waals forces, discussed in Chapter 6. A rather careful review of the nature of these forces has been given by Vervey and Overbeek. It is found that between any one pair of molecules of simple character, the force varies as the inverse sixth power of the separation. For large molecules this apparently feeble force is quite important, because so long as retarded electric potentials are not necessary, the force between each atomic pair is additive. Thus if v_1 and v_2 are the volumes of two particles containing q atoms per unit volume, the potential energy is given by

$$V = -\int\limits_{v_2}\int\limits_{v_1} \frac{q^2\lambda\, dv_1\, dv_2}{r^6},$$

where r is the distance between two increments of volume and λ is the London constant for "dispersion" forces.

The attraction between spheres and parallel plates was worked out by Hamaker and is fully described by Vervey and Overbeek. As we mentioned in Chapter 6, a very valuable set of calculations has more recently been made by M. Vold. She has considered the potential resulting from the above formula for various kinds of rods and plates. For the case of rods, of length l, width w, and thickness t, a comparison between the attractive energy for various alignments has been made. The resulting curves are shown in Fig. 15–2. It can be seen that the attractive energy is always greatest for the alignment that brings most of the interparticle distances as close to the average as possible. In terms of actual energies, the case where long rods are arranged parallel to one another gives an attractive energy which is about $3kT$ when the separation is such that the *surfaces* of the two molecules are separated by about one-tenth of their diameters. If we say that the protein molecules have diameters of about 40 A, then when they are arranged parallel to one another, the attractive energy will hold them loosely, but adequately, when the surfaces are 4 A apart. Such a separation might be enough to allow free passage of amino acids and water. In any event, there would be nothing like enough energy to hold the molecules end to end unless they were always in direct contact.

The first glance at the growth process, then, tells us that there do exist physical forces that could cause a stable membrane to form and grow in this way, provided that the miracle of protein synthesis happens. Before leaving the subject of interprotein forces, however, we need to point out some more consequences of invoking physical forces in this process.

In the first place, there is no reason for the molecules of protein to be separated at all. If we use simply the London-Hamaker type of force, then the attraction is greatest when the molecules are in contact. If they are in contact, it is very difficult to see how an amino acid like, say, tryptophan can get through to the inside of the membrane. Perhaps it

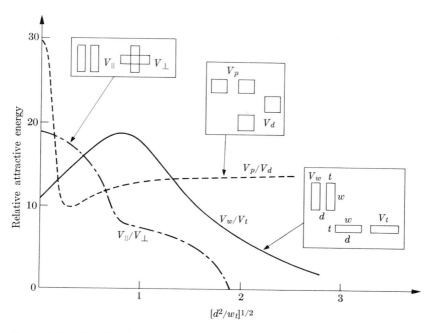

Fig. 15–2. M. Vold's calculations of the relative attractive energies for various orientations of rod-shaped particles. It can be seen that the parallel case, where extremes of distance are minimized, is always heavily favored.

doesn't. If so, we have said right away that all the protein synthesis is on the outside of the reticular double lamellae. This is surprising, and probably too bold a statement. So we have to look for the kind of force which will repel protein molecules and produce a potential minimum that is not zero. Such a force is at hand in the Debye–Hückel force produced by charge on the protein and the gegenions of an ionic atmosphere, again as described in Chapter 6. If such forces exist, and it is very difficult to see how they can fail to be present, then the interacting ionic atmospheres will cause a repulsion that will be superposed on the attraction due to dispersion forces. Therefore it is possible to conceive a separation between the protein molecules large enough to permit some passage of water and metabolites.

Having said this, we realize that we have also said that any change in the salt concentration of the cell will cause the lamellae to open and close their molecular sieves and produce a startling change in the concentration of various molecules in the inside of the endoplasmic reticulum lamellae. At this early a stage, such a mechanism does not seem to be undesirable, inasmuch as changes in salt concentrations are known to produce big

changes in the configurations of polyionic structures such as polynucleotides and ribosomes. If changes are due to the modification of the potential minimum between the protein molecules of a membrane, then they
should follow a definite pattern; thus doubly charged ions should have
four or more times as much effect as singly charged ions.

The surface strength of a cell membrane is also worth consideration.
It is possible, by using the figures for surface tension of cells, as found by
Harvey and others, to see what kind of binding would be expected between
protein molecules in a membrane such as we have described. With this
method the figure of about 5 ergs/cm^2 has been found. If each protein
molecule is considered to occupy a radius of 25 A, then there are 5×10^{12}
protein molecules per square centimeter, or each has an energy share of
1.25×10^{-12} erg. Since at 300°K the value of kT is 4.5×10^{-14}, the
energy of binding is in the order of $30kT$. We should point out that such
measurements were made on amoebae, whose membranes are thicker than
a single monolayer. There is still no real conflict between such figures and
the probable energy of binding as calculated by Vold.

The second feature of such a process of growth of a protein layer is, of
course, the ability of protein to be synthesized. Rather than considering
this in the simple context of growth, it seems wiser to consider the process
of protein synthesis as carefully as we can and then to see whether any
profound conflicts are present.

15–3 Protein synthesis. In this early essay on theoretical biology we
wish to disclaim any absolute knowledge about the process of protein
synthesis. We crave the reader's indulgence while we engage in some
hopeful thinking about it.

The advances resulting from the discovery of adaptive enzyme formation, or more correctly, induced enzyme formation, and from the use of
labeled amino acids in studies of their incorporation have had a profound
effect on the current ideas of protein synthesis. As described in Chapter
13, the work of Spiegelman and Monod has shown that an adaptive enzyme
is formed out of a wholly fresh supply of amino acids, and not by the modification of a protein already there. The work of Roberts, Cowie, Britten,
and Bolton has shown that there seem to be negligible concentrations of
peptide intermediates on the way to the formation of a whole protein.
During the last decade evidence has steadily accumulated to show that
one point of protein synthesis is in the ribosomes. The early evidence for
this important conclusion is reviewed by Loftfield; and two recent experimental studies by Dintzis, Borsook, and Vinograd* using rabbit

---

* H. M. Dintzis, H. Borsook, and J. Vinograd, in *Microsomal Particles and
Protein Synthesis.* Pergamon Press, New York, 1958.

reticulocytes and by McQuillen, Roberts, and Britten* using *E. coli* are particularly convincing. These ribonucleoprotein particles are thus presumably the template on which the protein is assembled from its separate amino acids. One suggestion for the way in which the template operates is afforded by the work of Zamecnik, Hoagland, and their group.† The scheme proposed is as follows.

Enzyme + AA + ATP ⇌ E(AMP-AA) + PP   (a)

SRNA-AA + E + AMP   (b)

AA in protein   (c)

In the above scheme, (a) is activation, (b) is attachment to RNA, and (c) is transfer to ribosomes. Each amino acid is first activated, by being enzymatically attached to ATP. In this condition it is then attached to RNA of relatively low molecular weight (about 25,000), called "soluble" RNA (usually shortened to SRNA) or also called "transfer" RNA. The attachment between SRNA and each amino acid is quite specific, and the appropriate binding region on the ribonucleoprotein template is determined by a specific base pairing between the template RNA and the SRNA-AA.‡ The amino acid is thus carried onto the template by a specifically matched vehicle, and is presumably bound to the other amino acids of the incomplete protein chain, while it is held in place by the SRNA. The SRNA acts as an "adaptor" between the template and the amino acid.

Not everyone accepts this proposal, but it suits our purpose to analyze it physically because it contains several steps in the synthetic process and so might be considered as describing a rather slow process. As we shall see, the speeds of molecular processes at close quarters are high enough to permit the process to occur.

15–4 Random collision and specific selection. We do not know how living systems operate. One widely held hypothesis is that they are rather specialized organic chemical systems, where the word "organic" is used in its modern sense, not in the sense used prior to Wohler's synthesis of urea. These chemical systems operate by the laws of physics and chemistry, and that they appear to be living is due to their special nature and not to any extra principles involved in how they operate. In Chapter 1

---

* K. McQuillen, R. B. Roberts, and R. J. Britten, *Proc. Nat. Acad. Sci.* **45,** 1437 (1959).

† M. B. Hoagland, in *The Nucleic Acids*, vol. III, ed. by E. Chargaff and J. N. Davidson. Academic Press, N. Y., 1960, p. 349.

‡ F. H. C. Crick, *Symp. Soc. for Exp. Biol.* **12,** 138 (1958).

we asked whether such a hypothesis would be upheld by our increasing knowledge of living systems. One place where we can examine living behavior in terms of physical mechanism is in the process of synthesis. The physical process available for specific synthesis is dual in character: the various molecules needed as parts of the larger molecule to be synthesized are supposed to be moving randomly, and so making many encounters with many kinds of molecule or indeed with the surface of organelles in the cell; at the same time, actual combination only occurs at an encounter which is *specifically right*. Thus, out of a huge surplus of encounters, the mechanisms of the cell select only those which are needed and reject those which are not.

This dual process of what may be called random encounter and specific selection must operate both swiftly and accurately in the process of protein synthesis. Therefore, if we can subject it to some kind of numerical analysis, we are in a position to see whether it might work. The Hoagland scheme, plus the idea of synthesis on ribosomes, is very suitable for such examination. Written schematically, it is

$$AA \rightarrow Act\ AA \rightarrow SRNA\text{-}AA \rightarrow template \rightarrow protein$$

$$\text{Enzymes}$$

We can examine the mechanism from the two points of view of (a) the amount of specific material around a ribosome and (b) the possible rates of synthesis.

15–5 Content of the volume around a ribosome. In *E. coli* there are, roughly, 10^4 ribosomes. The total volume available for these, if we exclude a volume for the nucleus, is 10^{-12} cm^3, in round numbers. Thus the volume associated with one ribosome is 10^{-16} cm^3. To study this volume we need the material listed in Table 15–1. Three points need comment, otherwise the table speaks for itself. The first is that the amino acids themselves, even in rather high concentration, do not make up much material. They are therefore not in the table. The second is that we have assumed 80 SRNA-AA molecules to be present. This number follows from the discussion on rates, given next, but it is also reasonable that an excess of the SRNA-AA would be necessary to supply, by random means, the various combinations of amino acids in the chain. We have chosen four times the minimum of 20. The last point is the guess that 20 completed protein molecules would remain near a ribosome before they found a destination somewhere in the growth pattern of the cell. Whether the reader likes these last two points or not, it is clear that the space around a ribosome is very crowded, *but not especially more than the average for the cell*. There is

TABLE 15–1

Material	Volume, cm^3	% of whole available
1 ribosome	4.2×10^{-18}	4.2
20 activating amino acid enzymes	2.4×10^{-18}	2.4
80 SRNA-AA	2.4×10^{-18}	2.4
20 other enzymes	2.4×10^{-18}	2.4
20 protein	2.4×10^{-18}	2.4
		13.8

therefore no visible absurdity about the process. Overzealous addition of three more "activating enzymes" per amino acid, or the discovery of three more steps requiring enzymatic action, would involve a shortage of space. As it is, there is room.

15–6 Random collisions and the rates of each step in synthesis. The analysis of the rates involved in a four-step consecutive process involving 20 separate amino acids is clearly complicated and difficult. In spite of this fact, there remains the reality of a synthesis of protein at a remarkably fast rate. In Section 15–2 we estimated that a bacterial cell synthesizes 1000 protein molecules per second. This is one protein molecule every 10 seconds per ribosome. We are conservative in requiring 100 amino acids to be linked per second per ribosome. So rapid is this whole process that it is worth while to consider one extreme of the whole range, namely when every process happens as fast as could reasonably be expected. Thinking in this way will help us decide whether the scheme proposed is possible, and it also helps us visualize some of the conditions under which the cell must be working.

We first consider the two enzymatic steps, the formation of activated amino acids and subsequently of SRNA-AA complex. While no reaction kinetics are available for either of these, we can obtain some insight from recent measurements by Strother and Ackerman[*] on the action of catalase on hydrogen peroxide. The particular aspect they studied was the molecular nature of the reaction, and they varied the very important parameter of the viscosity of the medium. In general, they found that the catalase-H_2O_2 reaction is not limited by diffusion for low viscosities, but that it can become so limited at higher values. They show that under such cir-

---

[*] G. K. Strother and E. Ackerman, *Biochim. et Biophys. Acta* **47,** 317 (1961).

cumstances the reaction between catalase and H_2O_2 is in broad agreement with the idea that a sufficiently accurate collision produces a reaction. The "target" is very small, a radius of 0.6 A, but the fact that a diffusion-limited reaction can be observed, with reasonable agreement with collision theory, suggests an approach to the problem we are considering. If we suppose that each enzymatic process requires an exact collision, and if we make a guess at the size of the target, taking care that we overestimate rather than underestimate so as to retain our philosophy of examining extremes, we can see whether useful conclusions can be drawn.

Before we begin, it is necessary to consider the type of collision theory to use. In the theory of colloidal reactions as worked out by Smoluchowski and Collins and Kimball,* the problem of collision and reaction is some-what complicated by the removal of reactants by the reaction itself. In the case of the cell, however, the amino acids used up will be replaced by metabolism, and so we have a close approximation to a steady state which is a rather simple case. Thus we can consider three-dimensional Brownian motion, which is closely related to the problem of random flights. The direct approach to the solution of this problem is to assign a critical volume within which a collision has to take place, to use the expression for the probability of such a collision, and to integrate the expression over all distances from which the collision can occur. When this is attempted, the importance of very small distances becomes apparent, and it is difficult to assign the smallest value without being rather arbitrary. A way out, as taken by Smoluchowski, is to note that the expression for the probability of a collision is formally the same as a solution of the diffusion equation in the three-dimensional form

$$\frac{\partial c}{\partial t} = D \left(\frac{\partial^2 c}{\partial x^2} + \frac{\partial^2 c}{\partial y^2} + \frac{\partial^2 c}{\partial z^2} \right),$$

where c is concentration and D the diffusion constant, with boundary conditions as imposed by the process considered. If each collision is sup-posed to occur at a radius R, and is supposed to remove the metabolite at collision, then the concentration of metabolite at radius R is zero. At infinity it can be set at a value c_0. Under these circumstances it is quite easy to show† that the rate of collision is given by ϕ, where

$$\phi = 4\pi DRc_0. \tag{15-1}$$

The particular solution of such an equation depends on the boundary

---

* F. C. Collins and G. E. Kimball, *J. Coll. Sci.* **4**, 425 (1949).

† See J. Th. G. Overbeek, in *Colloid Science*, ed. by Kruyt. Elsevier Publishing Co., Inc., New York, 1952.

conditions. This result applies to the collision of two equal molecules of radius R, with the sum of their diffusion constants being D. If a small molecule of radius R collides with a large molecule, such as a ribosome, then the ribosome is accessible only on one side, and this halves the rate. Also, the smaller radius, that of the colliding molecule, has to be used.

As a start, we can therefore use Eq. (15–1), slightly modified, to describe the collision process. The next problem is to describe the specificity. We can suppose that the colliding molecules interact with two kinds of forces. The first are the London forces, which are additive, and do not depend on whether the molecule is rotating as it approaches, and which also extend to distances of the order of R, the radius of the colliding molecule, as would be indicated by Vold's calculations referred to in Section 15–2.

The second kind are forces that depend on a pairing of some kind. This type of force includes covalent bonding, ionic bonding, and hydrogen bonding, which are the three kinds of force that would be expected to bind firmly a *specific molecule*, for a definite relationship must be present before binding can occur. Thus for the covalent bond, an atom of one surface must have an electron which can share an orbital with an atom of the colliding molecule. Such sharing will not take place until the orbitals overlap, which requires that the two atoms approach within about 1.5 A of each other. Similar considerations apply to the other two forces, and in their case also there has to be very close approach.

This suggests that we can give some expression to specificity by requiring that in the collision there is only a fraction of the surface of the colliding molecule which is "active," and that this fraction is relatively small. To get some idea of how small it has to be, we can refer to the analysis of specific reactions according to information theory given in Chapter 3. There it was suggested that seven to nine bits of information were involved in the requirements of specificity. Not all this information may be expressed simply in the fraction of active area at a collision, but if six bits are taken to be involved with that part, then there is a fraction $\frac{1}{64}$ of the total which is "active." This suggests, therefore, that the collision is abortive unless the aspect, at collision, is such that $\frac{1}{64}$ of the surface area of the colliding molecule makes contact with the right region on the surface of the enzyme or ribosome. With this idea, we can rewrite Eq. (15–1) to read

$$\phi = 2\pi \, DRgc_0, \tag{15–2}$$

where g is the factor expressing the specificity.

This equation can now be used with the known values of synthetic rates, using the molecular values of R, and if possible, known values of D, to calculate c_0. The concentrations so calculated then represent the concentrations necessary to provide the observed rates by the process of random collision and specific selection. If they are much higher than observed in the cell, it is in place to question either the process or the theory. Before attempting to use Eq. (15–2), we point out that it can be used in two ways: one ignoring molecular rotation, and the other taking it into account. The former is simpler, and once it is used, the latter can be readily included.

Equation (15–2) can be further simplified if the theoretical value for D is used. This is $D = kT/6\pi\eta R$, where η is the viscosity. Making this substitution,

$$\phi = \frac{kTgc_0}{3\eta}.$$
(15–3)

If the temperature is taken to be 37°C so that $T = 310°$K, then

$$\phi = 1.4 \times 10^{-14} \frac{gc_0}{\eta}.$$
(15–4)

If we are willing to take the value of $\frac{1}{64}$ for g, then the only problem we encounter is the value of the viscosity. For the bacterium $E. coli$, unpublished measurements by F. L. Gardner of the viscosity of the "juice" from bacteria opened under pressure gave values exceeding six poise. This very high figure is probably partly due to the presence of degraded DNA from the rupture of the bacterial nuclei, but a figure of one poise seems to be reasonable to assume. We can now see what concentrations are required by Eq. (15–4).

Assuming that the 20 enzymes activate five amino acids apiece per second per ribosome, which is at the required rate, we can substitute five for ϕ, and deduce $c_0 = 2.3 \times 10^{16}$ molecules per cubic centimeter. Since the volume of the cell can be taken to be 10^{-12} cm³, the number of one particular amino acid per cell must be 2.3×10^4, and the number of all amino acids must be 4.6×10^5. The total mass of amino acids in the protein of the cell is 1.5×10^{-13} gm. And if the average molecular weight of an amino acid is taken as 150, the number of such bound amino acids is 9×10^8, so that we are asking that less than 1% of the amino acids be free. This is certainly quite reasonable.

Now if we turn to the process of attaching SRNA-AA, the complex of soluble RNA and amino acid, on to the template, the same rate can be assumed, and so the same concentration is deduced. However, the molecular weight of SRNA is more than 100 times as great as the molecular weight of an average amino acid, so the amount of SRNA is now seen to be much too great. This suggests that either the theory is not describing what takes place or the supposed process is wrong. It will be seen that the introduction of the possibility of rotation, with a very temporary combination of a loose kind, removes much of the difficulty.

15–7 Temporary complex formation. In Chapter 8 the idea of the *enzyme-substrate complex* was introduced, and its use in describing enzyme kinetics was brought out. We have just mentioned the fact that the London forces are not specific and that they operate over a relatively long range. If we suppose that at a collision the colliding molecule is held very momentarily by the operation of the London forces, and that the molecule is also free to rotate while it is held, then the opportunity for the active part of the molecule to be presented to the specific surface on the enzyme or ribosome will be increased. To get some idea of how much speed is gained by this method, use can be made of the fact that attraction is appreciable, according to Vold, when the two molecules concerned approach within a surface-to-surface distance equal to their radius. We can now inquire into (a) how long it takes a molecule to diffuse a distance R, and (b) how much angle is covered by rotational Brownian movement in that time. It develops that a rather intriguing and simple relation results, which shows that the value of g taken above is definitely too small.*

The distance x diffused in a time t in one dimension is given by Eq. (4–6) as

$$\overline{x^2} = \frac{2kT}{6\pi\eta R}\, t,$$

for a spherical molecule of radius R. The corresponding equation for the angle θ traversed by rotational Brownian movement was worked out by Einstein and is very similar. It is:

$$\overline{\theta^2} = \frac{2kT}{8\pi\eta R^3}\, t.$$

If we use this equation to find the angle traversed while the molecule is diffusing a distance R, we find the result that $\overline{\theta^2} = \frac{3}{4}$, independently of both the value of the viscosity and of the radius R. Thus the colliding molecule describes nearly one radian of angle while under the influence of the attractive field. To present all aspects, it only needs to describe 2π radians, so that *even if there is no more complex formation than present in one approach*, a reasonable value for g would be $1/(2\pi)$. Any longer delay due to the attractive force would increase the fraction to still closer to unity. Thus the rotation of the molecule as it approaches speeds up the process by a factor of at least 10. This means that all the concentrations so far computed are unnecessarily high by a factor of 10, and so the concentration of SRNA required, at 4.6×10^4 per cell, requires a mass of roughly 2×10^{-15} gm, which is rather high, but not impossible.

---

* E. Pollard, *J. Theor. Biol.*, in press (1961).

Thus the simple idea that random motion, with the expected diffusion constants, together with the idea that only specifically right collisions take part in the synthetic process, is capable of explaining the high speeds of synthesis. It is, of course, clear that the simple feature of the collision process is by no means all that is involved. A very similar approach was applied to enzyme rates many years ago by Moelwyn-Hughes, with the conclusion that the rates were definitely slower than expected from collisions. The slower rate is easily understood in terms of an *activation energy*, and in some cases the measured activation energies explain the behavior of the reaction rates without invoking the need for collisions and diffusion processes. The presence of any kind of potential barrier to a reaction, or even of any reason for reducing the probability of reaction at a "correct" collision, will slow down the rates drastically and will also increase the concentrations needed to achieve fast synthesis. The figures above suggest that there can be very little activation energy for the process of attachment of SRNA-AA to the ribosome template.

Before we leave the subject of protein synthesis, it is worth while to look at the general question of diffusion in the cell and to see what the effect of electric fields would be upon the speeds of transport offered by diffusion.

15–8 The speed of diffusion in the cell. In a time t a molecule of diffusion constant D moves a root-mean-square distance x, where

$$x^2 = 2\ Dt.$$

This result, which is a slight modification of Eq. (4–6), applies to linear diffusion. For diffusion on a surface, we take a root-mean-square distance of $4\ Dt$, and for three dimensions, $6\ Dt$. Now for glycine in water, D is 9.6×10^{-6} cm^2/sec, so that the actual path traveled in one second in water is roughly 10^{-2} cm. Thus it will not be possible to maintain a concentration of a small molecule at one end of a cell, for it can easily diffuse to the other end in one hundredth of a second. At first glance, it seems as though diffusion can transport metabolites quite effectively. Certainly no concentration differences of small metabolites can last very long unless some force field exists which can maintain them. We discuss the effect of electrophoresis as such a force field in the next section.

In Section 15–6 we examined one special case of protein synthesis in the bacterial cell. We employed the idea of a specific collision between a molecule of radius R and some specific surface. The operation of diffusion, or rather three-dimensional Brownian movement, in a larger cell can be seen if the requirement is that a collision occur in a small definite element of volume situated a distance r from a required metabolite. This problem was worked out by Rayleigh,* who used ordinary mathematical methods, and is discussed by Chandrasekhar,† who used Markoff's n-dimensional analysis. The result, as we can use it, states that the probability of a collision within a volume $d\tau$ at a distance r from a starting point is given by $W(r)\,d\tau$, where

$$W(r) = \frac{1}{(4\pi\ Dt)^{3/2}}\, e^{-r^2/4Dt}, \tag{15-5}$$

D being the diffusion constant and t the time.

For a given r, this expression is small for both small t and large t. The explanation is that in the former case the exponential is very small, corresponding to requiring great good fortune in diffusing to cover the required distance. In the latter case, $1/(4\pi\ Dt)^{3/2}$ is small, while the exponential is nearly unity, corresponding to the fact that the "target" volume is now a small part of the whole volume comprised in diffusion for longer times. In Eq. (15–5), $W(r)$ is a maximum for $6Dt = r^2$. Now the value of r is determined by the distance which has to be diffused by some metabolite in order to reach the point where it is wanted. If Eq. (15–5) is examined for various assumed values of r, it becomes clear that the value of $W(r)$ increases as $1/r^3$, and hence a fast reaction depends on the presence of metabolites very close to the reacting site. If the reaction initially takes place in a space of uniform concentration, then reaction by molecules close to the "target" will remove them and set up a concentration gradient, which leads to the reaction process described by Smoluchowski and given in Eq. (15–1). However, in a large cell, one metabolite may be made in one place, and the reacting site may be quite distant in the cell. The efficiency of synthesis would then go sharply down, and the growth of the cell would become slow. Stated a little differently, the region making the metabolite has to fill the whole cell with its product in order to get one molecule into place in time.

It seems likely that in much larger cells than bacterial cells an additional mechanism for making efficient use of diffusion exists. This is the lamellar structure described in Section 2–2. These large and extended areas confine the region within which metabolites need to travel and reduce the distance required for random molecular motion. The fact that microsomal particles are very often seen to be attached to these layers suggests that the layers operate to stop metabolites and permit them to diffuse in two dimensions along their surfaces until they reach the synthetic particle. Two-dimensional random motion involves a probability relation similar

---

* Rayleigh, *Scientific Papers*, vol. 6. Cambridge University Press, 1920, pp. 604–626.

† S. Chandrasekhar, *Rev. Mod. Phys.* **15**, 2 (1943).

to Eq. (15–5), but the first term falls off as $1/r^2$. The maximum is thus further out, so that the cell can still handle relatively dilute metabolites with the required speed. The endoplasmic reticulum thus serves the important function of restricting the three-dimensional, semi-aimless Brownian motion into still aimless, but confined, motion in two dimensions.

Before leaving this consideration of diffusion we should once more mention the very important question of the *aspect* of the colliding molecule as it approaches an enzymatic surface or some other region where it will react. Treating the relation between traversal of angle by random motion and traversal of distance by the same process, we have the two equations,

$$\theta^2 = 2\Theta t$$

and

$$x^2 = 2Dt,$$

where Θ is the rotational diffusion constant, given for a spherical molecule of radius R by

$$\Theta = \frac{kT}{8\pi\eta R^3}.$$

In a time t the ratio of the square of the angle covered to the square of the distance traversed is Θ/D, and with the theoretical values for spherical molecules, the ratio of angle covered to distance traversed is $0.86/R$. Thus a molecule need only diffuse a distance of 10 times its radius in order to have presented every possible aspect. For a small molecule such a distance may well be within the range of some attractive force. For a large molecule the distance is more open to question, but, as was discussed earlier, the London forces may have the required extent.

The strong forces available to biological systems would appear, at a first glance, to be electrical. In the next section we examine the kind of effect the expected electrical forces would exert.

15–9 Electrical effects in diffusion. In our discussion up to the present we have effectively disregarded any specialized concentration, which would serve to permit a much larger target for collision, with a mechanism for "homing" onto the precise area or, alternatively, a mechanism that would select a higher concentration in a particular region. To produce a specialized concentration, some kind of influence field has to be present in the cell. The only obvious force field existing is electrical. Magnetic and gravitational effects would not be expected to be large in a single cell, although the latter obviously play a part in large organisms. The electrical character of many cell processes cannot be doubted. One that comes to mind is that of the attachment of phage to bacteria, which has an initial phase that is due to electrostatic forces.

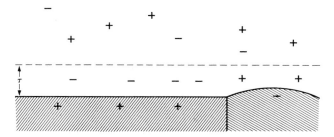

Fig. 15–3. A representation of the charged character of part of the surface of a protein molecule. It has supposedly acquired three positive charges in the left-hand region and one minus charge in the right. As a consequence, near it there will be an atmosphere of opposite, or gegen, ions, resulting in an ill-defined region where an average neutralizing layer, forming the double layer, can be supposed to be. Following Helmholtz, the thickness of this layer is supposed to be τ.

Two sides to the problem exist. First, how great are the electrical fields in a living organism? Second, what effects do these fields have on the motion of all classes of biological molecules?

Let us consider the size of the field first. One essential characteristic of amino acids and proteins, as we have stressed before, is their possession of $-NH_2$ and $-COOH$ groups that can very readily remove an H^+ from solution or lose an H^+ to it. Such groups then become positively or negatively charged, and very real and indeed large charges are produced on the molecule as a result. To indicate the latent electrical effects, we can suppose that each unit of 1000 molecular weight carries a net positive charge. Then a flat layer of protein can be thought of as having one net charge per 100 A^2, as a rough figure. The electric field near a plane surface is $(2\pi\sigma/K)$, where σ is the surface density of charge and K is the dielectric constant. The value of σ is $(4.8 \times 10^{-10})/10^{-14}$, or 4.8×10^4 esu/cm^2. The electric field then works out to be slightly over a million volts per centimeter, a truly impressive figure.

These huge fields do not actually exist in living organisms, although they represent a temporary possibility under some circumstances. The reason that they do not exist is that there are ionic atmospheres, due to the presence of ions of various valences, in the medium around these molecules. The study of such ionic atmospheres was begun by Helmholtz, who treated them as producing mixed *double layers*. Motion of particles in ionic atmospheres was treated by Smoluchowski, and the first approximate theory of ionic atmospheres, as was indicated in Chapter 6, is due to Debye and Hückel. Let us consider the nature of the charge near a protein molecule. It will appear somewhat as shown in Fig. 15–3. The protein molecule is supposed to have acquired three $-NH_3^+$ groups, giving positive charges, at the left and one $-COO^-$, giving a negative charge, at the right. The ions around the protein then form a not very exact grouping, as shown, and the net result is a rather loosely defined double layer, of thickness τ, which Helmholtz considered (as an aid to theory) to be a rigid, definite, double layer.

Now if an applied electric field X is directed to the left, the protein will tend to go to the left and the liquid ions to the right. This will produce a *shear*. It can be supposed that the shear will increase until it has the size corresponding to the shear that can be tolerated by the liquid when it is undergoing viscous flow. That is to say, a velocity gradient will be set up by the two motions. It will be related to the force per unit area caused by the charge and the electric field in the familiar way for viscous motion.

Thus if σ is the net surface charge per unit area and v_0 is the velocity developed by the protein molecule relative to the double layer, the velocity gradient is v_0/τ, and we see that the relation between force per unit area and viscous motion per unit area is

$$X\sigma = \eta \frac{v_0}{\tau},$$

or

$$v_0 = \frac{X}{\eta} \sigma\tau. \tag{15-6}$$

where η is the coefficient of viscosity,

The quantity $\sigma\tau$ was referred to by Helmholtz as the *moment* of the double layer. It is usual today to refer to a potential, ζ, which is that of the surface of shear, defined by the relation

$$\zeta = \frac{4\pi\sigma\tau}{K},$$

where K is the dielectric constant. In terms of the *zeta potential*, then,

$$v_0 = \frac{XK\zeta}{4\pi\eta}. \tag{15-7}$$

This replaces the product of a relatively unknown charge and a relatively unknown thickness by a product of a relatively unknown potential and a relatively unknown dielectric constant. The situation would be very unfortunate except that measurements of v_0 can be made very accurately and the product $K\zeta$ accordingly found. The ratio of v_0 to X is called the *mobility*.

If we now make some assumptions about the shape of the protein—for example, that it is spherical, of radius r, and that the shear occurs also at this radius—then

$$\zeta = \frac{Q}{Kr}.$$

If the Debye-Hückel treatment is used to determine the nature of the double layer, the surface of shear is extended outward by a factor $1 + \kappa r$, where κ is the Debye-Hückel quantity defined by

$$\kappa^2 = \frac{4\pi\epsilon^2}{KkT} \Sigma n_i z_i^2,$$

where ϵ is the elementary electric charge, n_i is the number of ions of type i per cubic centimeter, and z_i is the number of elementary charges on each ion. For a univalent electrolyte of concentration c moles per liter,

$$\kappa = \frac{c^{1/2}}{3 \times 10^{-8}},$$

approximately. Then we get, using Eq. (15-7),

$$v_0 = \frac{XQ}{4\pi\eta r(1 + \kappa r)}. \tag{15-8}$$

If the spherical protein is small enough, the viscous flow is in streamlines around the sphere and not laminated, so that the kind of treatment used

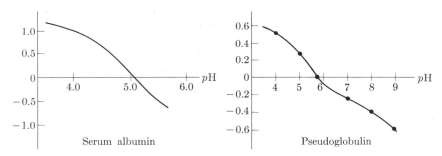

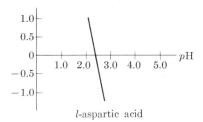

Fig. 15-4. The electrophoretic mobility of serum albumin, pseudoglobulin, and l-aspartic acid as influenced by pH. Changing pH alters the number of —NH$_3$ and —COO$^-$ groups.

to derive Stokes' law has to be used. For this case,

$$v_0 = \frac{XQ}{6\pi\eta r(1 + \kappa r)}.$$ (15–9)

Since our purposes will never require us to decide between these cases, we propose to use Eq. (15–9) for calculations.

Many measurements of electrophoretic mobility have been made. In Fig. 15–4 we show the values of mobility for serum albumin, pseudoglobulin, and l-aspartic acid. The value of the pH markedly affects the mobility and the net charge. This well-known effect is related to the formation of $-NH_3{}^+$ or $-COO^-$ groups. The actual values of the mobility do not seem high at first, but they are large enough to speed up the apparent transport of amino acids across a cell.

These measured values of electrophoretic mobility tell us what to expect of a charged molecule in a given field in a medium of given viscosity. They do not tell us what sort of fields to expect unless we apply some of the previous equations to calculate fields around protein molecules which fit with the charges on them. Thus if we take serum albumin to be a spherical molecule of radius 3.3×10^{-7} cm, assume a molarity of 10^{-2} for univalent ions, giving κ a value of 3×10^6, we find from Eq. (15–9) a value of Q of a little over five elementary charges. Now the potential near such a sphere is, according to Debye-Hückel theory,

$$V = \frac{Qe^{-\kappa(x-a)}}{(Kx)(1 + \kappa x)}.$$

If we set $x = 5 \times 10^{-7}$ cm, under the above conditions, with the assumption that the dielectric constant K is 80, we find $V = 4 \times 10^{-4}$ volt.

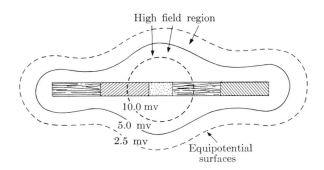

Fig. 15–5. Indication of how the region of high net charge near one of an array of protein molecules can produce a high electric field and so aid in the concentration of certain amino acids near that protein.

This is actually smaller than many measured values of the zeta potential. The value of the electric field is dV/dx and, again very approximately, is 300 volts per centimeter. Thus we have every reason to expect that very real fields will exist very near to molecules which can carry a net charge. A small amino acid, in conditions of favorable pH, would be expected to migrate at something like 3×10^{-2} cm/sec toward a definite point. So it would be unwise to write off electrical effects as not augmenting the random diffusion processes in cells.

We can, in fact, suppose that a set of enzyme molecules, as are supposed to exist in a mitochondrion, might have an electric field distribution somewhat as in Fig. 15-5. Each enzyme presumably has a rather different isoelectric point (meaning the pH at which it carries no net charge), and therefore the equipotential lines that surround it are probably curved in a manner as shown. This variable field will cause a variable mobility of specialized amino acids, which might in turn convert the local environment from one in which only random encounters can take place to one in which particular metabolites may be selected for particular places.

15-10 Specificity of transport. The only specificity introduced by diffusion is in terms of size, and it is not very great. The diffusion coefficient of RNA-ase is only 10 times less than that of acetic acid; therefore the specificity of diffusion among the amino acids would involve a factor of two at the most. We have just seen that electrophoretic effects could account for some specific transport. Possibly the cell makes some use of this process. It is interesting that if it does so, it should be possible to exert some influence on cell growth with an externally applied electric field. Some such effects have been reported, and it might be worth while to correlate them with change in pH, which should be much more dramatic because it affects the net charge on the protein. Of course, pH effects are observed, although even so the range of pH covered by the cheerfully growing organism seems to preclude the use of transport specificity by electrical means to any great extent.

In Table 15-2 we list the isoelectric points of a few amino acids. It can be seen that they vary over a range of nearly five pH units. A glance at the electrophoretic mobility of l-aspartic acid as given in Fig. 15-5 shows that the mobility changes rapidly with pH and hence that the selection for a particular amino acid by this means could occur. Such an effect would be superimposed on the pH variation of enzyme action, and so it would be difficult to detect directly.

To get some idea of how great an increase in concentration due to electrophoresis is possible, we can make a rough calculation as follows. If we say that a molecule has to travel 1000 A to reach the proper site, then by diffusion alone it will move to a point 1000 A distant in a time t

TABLE 15–2

ISOELECTRIC POINTS, pI, OF AMINO ACIDS

Amino acid	pI
Glycine	5.97
Alanine	6.00
Valine	5.96
Leucine	5.98
Isoleucine	6.02
Serine	5.68
Proline	6.30
Aspartic acid	2.77
Glutamic acid	3.22
Arginine	10.76
Histidine	7.59
Cysteine	5.07
Cystine	5.05

given by the relation $\delta^2 = 6\,Dt$ already familiar to us. On substitution of 1000 A or 10^{-5} cm for δ, we find (for a molecule of diffusion constant 10^{-5}) a value of t of 1.7×10^{-6} sec, in round numbers. Now we can suppose that the effective concentration of this molecule is such that there is one of it in a sphere of radius 10^{-5} cm. But if there is electrophoresis, there will be no need for the molecule to diffuse all this way. In fact, it is only necessary for the molecule to diffuse 1000 A, *less* the distance gone by electrophoresis, in this time of 1.7×10^{-6} sec.

If the electrophoretic mobility is m and the field strength is X volts/cm, the distance gone is $Xm \times 1.7 \times 10^{-6}$ cm. If X is taken to be 300 volts/cm and the mobility is 10^{-3} cm/sec/volt, the distance saved is 5×10^{-7} cm, again in round numbers. This means that the sphere has shrunk to 1000 minus 50 A, and so the concentration has risen in the ratio $(1000/950)^3$, or by 20%. Had the distance of diffusion been 10 times greater, the increase would have been a factor of eight. Thus electrophoresis does offer a little selectivity which, although not decisive and not wholly specific, could be of great importance in a large cell. Only if the fields near a template were greater than 3000 volts/cm could the concentration differential for short diffusion distances approach a factor of two. We find it hard to believe that electrophoretic effects are of any importance in a bacterial cell. In a larger cell they may play a part.

15–11 Fluctuations in the cell. In considering the mechanism by which one of the cellular processes, namely protein synthesis, can occur, it is wise to introduce an important method of judging a process. It was first pointed out by Schrödinger that the fidelity of duplication of an organism required that fluctuations be somehow ignored. He suggested that the molecular character of a gene could do this by utilizing the regularity of atomic order in an "aperiodic crystal" to convey the hereditary pattern to the next generation. Since this general idea is applicable beyond the hereditary apparatus, we have to examine each of the basic cellular processes to see whether they can continue to function in spite of fluctuations.

To make the point more clearly, let us consider some of the possible momentary abnormalities to which a cell can be exposed. First consider pH. At pH 7 the concentration of hydrogen ions is $10^{-7}\,M$; thus there are 6×10^{13} hydrogen ions per cubic centimeter in round numbers. In a bacterium of volume $2 \times 10^{-12}\,\text{cm}^3$ there are therefore only 120 hydrogen ions on the average. Hence we have no right to consider a fixed pH in a bacterium, because a fluctuation of numbers of ions up or down by a factor of two can occur easily. Thus the pH is fluctuating between 6.7 and 7.3 even when the average is 7. Near any one protein molecule it can vary even more, so that even if we had a specific transport process introduced by electrophoresis, there would many times be exceptional conditions that would concentrate the wrong amino acids.

Secondly, consider the small concentrations of limiting vitamins. Biotin, in a concentration of one molecule per cell, produces an observable effect. The cell can hardly guarantee that this molecule is in the right place by the process of diffusion. Until it is, the cell has to be able to continue development, utilizing the biotin-induced process at various times in its history. The same is true of small concentrations of various metallic ions.

The varying of charge on proteins will cause electro-osmotic pressures. With a protein of surface area $10^{-12}\,\text{cm}^2$, a change of charge of one elementary unit introduces a surface charge density of nearly $500\ \text{esu/cm}^2$. This will cause local pressure fluctuations of up to 100 atmospheres. Such pressures will, momentarily, disrupt some processes, and the cell has to be able to take this disruption in its stride.

Many other forms of fluctuation are possible to conceive. In a small system like a cell, where the number of molecules is often in the thousands or less, the fact of fluctuation always has to be considered. What is of deep interest is that the actual behavior of the cell has a considerable regularity in spite of being subject to these many fluctuations.

Some idea of the kind of regularity called for in protein synthesis can be obtained from the fact that a precise amino-acid order can be found for insulin and ribonuclease. In this last enzyme there is evidence that the alteration of more than one amino acid has a decisive effect on the action of the enzyme. We can thus make a generalization that protein synthesis has to be correct to one amino acid in 200. It should, of course, be remembered that a faulty enzyme will only affect the way in which the cell operates if it is actively making unwanted products, or is the only representative of its kind in the cell. It may be true that a measurable fraction of the protein in the cell is not exactly right. Thus our estimate of one in 200 is perhaps reasonable.

The only mechanism which can be seen at present for achieving this accuracy is indeed that of Schrödinger. The amino acids must be specifically accepted at the right place, and rejected firmly elsewhere. Then fluctuations will only change local *rates* and not local *results*. This is achieved in the Hoagland scheme by requiring that there be 20 SRNA molecular species exactly matched (a) to an amino acid and (b) to a specific part of the ribosome. The matching process will merit considerable study, for on the one hand it must not require so exact a collision that the rates of formation of SRNA-AA and of template-SRNA-AA are too slow, thus forcing a high concentration of both to secure the proper speed of synthesis. On the other hand, the matching process must not be too sloppy, or a chance fluctuation may carry a high concentration of the wrong substance into the synthetic zone and produce an improbable and unfortunate bonding of the wrong amino acid in the order. The reader can sense that quite precise molecular biological processes must be at work and that they will need equally precise thinking about molecular events before they are fully explained.

15–12 The duplication of DNA. The second fundamental process we considered early in this chapter is replication. Undoubtedly, the heart of this process is the duplication of the chromosomes. For the purpose of molecular biophysics we intend to simplify still further and consider the duplication of DNA. As with all topics in this chapter, it is most unwise for us to be dogmatic or take any very strong attitude. Many of the factors regarding the duplication of DNA have been discovered in only the last four years or so, and we are highly vulnerable to the fact that equally important discoveries will almost certainly be made soon after this book appears. Not so long ago the symbol for DNA replication was a "Y," with double-stranded DNA becoming two double strands at the split. Now it is thought to be a process involving synthesis at opposite ends, and the symbol must be quite different. So we are forced to consider what knowledge about DNA can be considered to be sure and to confine ourselves to a biophysical analysis of various features of the process of replication, without assuming too much detail.

We can be quite sure of the biochemical nature of DNA as described in Chapter 2. We can be sure that the pairing of complementary strands, with opposite sense as suggested by Watson and Crick, is one form which can be taken by DNA. We have an indication from the work of Marmur and Lane* and of Doty, Marmur, Eigner, and Schildkraut† that the strands of DNA may separate and recombine, even to the extent of combination between two kinds of bacteria. The ultraviolet action studies of Setlow and Setlow‡ suggest that phage DNA can become disorganized soon after infection. The work of Kornberg, Lehman, Bessman, and Simms has shown that an enzyme system working in the absence of living cells can cause the formation of new DNA from old "primer" DNA to the extent of more than 20 times the original material. The enzyme system has already been rather firmly characterized, and we propose to start from the idea that the Kornberg "polymerase," which, in Kornberg's words, "takes its direction from a template," is the mechanism by which DNA replicates. We propose to give a brief, biophysically oriented, description of the enzyme system, and then see what biophysical analysis can be made.

$$\begin{matrix} n \ dTPPP \\ n \ dGPPP \\ n \ dAPPP \\ n \ dCPPP \end{matrix} + \begin{matrix} DNA \\ primer \end{matrix} \rightarrow DNA - \begin{bmatrix} dTP \\ dGP \\ dAP \\ dCP \end{bmatrix} + n \ PP$$

FIGURE 15–6

The over-all reaction for the synthesis of DNA is shown in Fig. 15–6, where dTPPP, dGPPP, dAPPP, and dCPPP stand for deoxythymidine triphosphate, deoxyguanosine triphosphate, deoxyadenosine triphosphate, and deoxycytosine triphosphate. The letters PP mean pyrophosphate. The actual mechanism suggested by Kornberg is shown in Fig. 15–7. The importance to us is the fact that it occurs at the free sugar which is at one end of the DNA chain. Therefore the process occurs at only one end, and the Y-type of DNA replication cannot occur.

We can now examine the process in terms of (a) synthetic rates involving random diffusion and selection, (b) rates of uncoiling, (c) precision of assembly of new DNA, and (d) the transition from rotation to vibration.

15–13 Random diffusion and specific selection in DNA synthesis. The discussion we have applied to the process of protein synthesis can be applied also to the process of DNA synthesis, with the result that some rather restrictive statements can be made. The process envisaged is simple enough: a base on the primer somehow attaches to the enzyme and forms

* J. Marmur and D. Lane, *Proc. Nat. Acad. Sci.* **46,** 452 (1960).

† P. Doty, J. Marmur, J. Eigner, and C. Schildkraut, *Proc. Nat. Acad. Sci.* **46,** 461 (1960).

‡ J. K. Setlow and R. B. Setlow, *Proc. Nat. Acad. Sci.* **46,** 791 (1960).

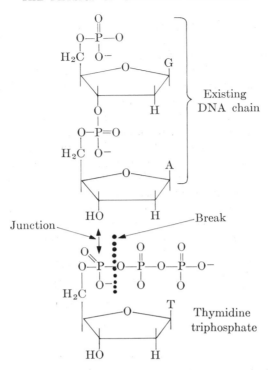

Fig. 15–7. Kornberg's postulated mechanism by which the DNA chain is lengthened. The first phosphate attaches to the free sugar and pyrophosphate is dropped off.

a "coenzyme." With this base in place the enzyme will only tolerate the complementary base. That is, if adenine is the coenzyme, only thymine will be able to join onto the end of the already formed DNA. The base on the primer must move on and off the enzyme with precision, and we can now examine first the over-all rates, and second, the chance of making an unwanted repetition in the chain due to the sluggish operation of the enzyme and primer.

Let us consider rates first. In *E. coli*, in synthetic medium, 8×10^{-15} gm of DNA is synthesized in 50 min, or 5×10^3 nucleotides are fastened into place per second. A comparable estimate can be made for T2 phage. The DNA synthetic process for T2 occupies a little less than half the latent period of 22 min, in round numbers 10 min or 600 sec. Luria[*] showed that the process is exponential and not linear. In the latent period it is possible to have a "burst" of 1000 phage particles produced, so in 600 sec the

---

[*] S. E. Luria, *Cold Spring Harbor Symposia Quant. Biol.*, **16**, 463 (1951).

DNA complement of 1000 particles is made. If x is the number of generations, $2^x = 1000$ or $x = 10$, again in round numbers. Thus one DNA complement is made in 60 sec, and if we accept Levinthal's idea (see Chapter 13) that there is a single piece of molecular weight 6×10^7, this means that one enzyme is capable of assembling $(6 \times 10^7)/300$ or 2×10^5 nucleotides in 60 sec, that is to say at a rate of 3×10^3 per second in approximate agreement with the *E. coli* figure.

We can now try to reconcile these rates with the idea of random collision and specific target. The target can be estimated from Fig. 15–7. The phosphorus and oxygen must approach very closely, and an estimate of the target area of 1 A^2 does not seem to be too severe a restriction. If we take this figure, and a molecular weight of 450 for a triphosphate, then the radius of such a molecule is approximately 4.7 A, and its area is 280 A^2. The expected value for g is therefore rather low unless a temporary complex with free rotation can form. Assuming no complex and $g = 1/300$, we find, for synthesis at *one* point, from Eq. (15–4),

$$3 \times 10^3 = 1.4 \times 10^{-14} g c_0 = \frac{1.4 \times 10^{-14}}{300} c_0$$

or

$$c_0 = \frac{9 \times 10^6}{1.4 \times 10^{-14}} = \frac{6.4 \times 10^{20}}{cm^3}.$$

This is roughly one molar. It is 6.4×10^8 per cell, or roughly 5×10^{-13} gm, far too many to be reasonable. With a g value of unity, corresponding to the formation of a complex, and with time for rotation to select the proper region, the concentration requires roughly 1/300 as much, or 1.6×10^{-15} gm, still surprisingly high. The conclusion reached is, then, that synthesis cannot occur at one point, but must occur at something in excess of 10 places. Quite independently it has been remarked* that the rate of DNA synthesis in *E. coli* requires something of the order of one percent of the cellular protein to act as enzyme. This would correspond to something like 10,000 separate units, unless the enzyme molecule is unusually large or the rates in the cell are greater than in cell-free systems. It seems most probable to us that our estimate of 100 enzyme molecules is not too high.

The problem of uncoiling DNA is of interest and has been discussed by Levinthal and Crane.† If we take the figure of 7×10^3 nucleotides per second for T2 and remember that one nucleotide pair is separated from the next by an angle of approximately 30°, then the rate of rotation required

---

* R. B. Roberts, K. McQuillen, and I. Z. Roberts, *Ann. Rev. Microbiol.* **13**, 1 (1959).

† C. Levinthal and H. R. Crane, *Proc. Nat. Acad. Sci.* **42**, 436 (1956).

in uncoiling is 580 revolutions per second. This may seem to be surprising in the supposedly gentle environment of a cell. The figure is not by any means absurdly high. In fact, as soon as one considers the intimate chemical details of any molecular process, they seem to be explosively violent, and indeed they are. An explosion is remarkable only in that we observe for a large mass what is actually required in any reaction. We need to be prepared to think of vigorous action in a multiplying cell, and evidently part of the action is rapid rotation. To make this point more definitely, we observe that the kinetic energy of rotation, given by $\frac{1}{2}I\omega^2$, where I is the moment of inertia and ω is the angular velocity, for a 6×10^7 molecular weight unit, of radius 10 A, is roughly 6×10^{-24} erg per molecule, while kT is 4×10^{-14} erg per molecule. The more cogent question, perhaps, is to inquire as to what slows down the DNA, preventing the more vigorous Brownian movement from interfering with DNA synthesis.

This leads to the next question we wish to discuss, which concerns the precision of assembly of the DNA. Before starting the discussion, we point out that if the deoxy-triphosphate of either 5-bromouracil or 5-iodouracil is presented to the DNA assembly system, it is accepted in place of thymidine triphosphate. 5-bromocytosine triphosphate will be accepted in place of cytosine triphosphate. These are only a few examples of rather close analogs which can be introduced. It will be noticed that the unusual triphosphate always substitutes for the base which is close to it structurally.

Thus while there is a little "sloppiness" about the assembly process, it does not extend to putting one of the four bases in the wrong place. The seriousness of such erroneous assembly if it should happen is beginning to be apparent. Gierer and Mundry* have shown that the change of a single base in the infectious RNA of tobacco mosaic virus causes a mutation, and similar evidence, discussed in Section 2–7, holds for DNA. We can therefore suppose that the observed spontaneous mutation rate in bacteria represents something like the number of errors made in the assembly line. Those rates were studied by Novick and Szilard† for mutation to resistance to T5 phage and for our purpose can be taken as 10^{-8} per bacterium per 50-minute generation time. Assume that this mutation refers to one of the bases in a cistron which we take to be 1000 nucleotides in length. If the alteration of any one base results in a mutation to T5 resistance, this means that each nucleotide has a chance of 10^{-11} of being incorrectly assembled. Now the rate of assembly of nucleotides is about 5×10^3 per second, and if we accept the idea that there are 100 enzyme systems or

---

* A. Gierer and K. W. Mundry, *Nature* **182**, 1457 (1959).

† A. Novick and L. Szilard, *Proc. Nat. Acad. Sci.*, **36**, 708 (1950).

loci engaged in nucleotide polymerization, each locus handles 50 nucleotides per second. Thus *if time is a determining factor*, the change from one "coenzyme" to the next must occur within $10^{-11}/50$, or 2×10^{-13} sec.

This remarkably short time eliminates two methods of action on purely physical grounds. If we suppose that the "primer" DNA actually moves along, to bring a new base into a specific location on the protein of the enzyme, and if we assume a molecular weight of not less than 6×10^6 for the primer, then the energy per "jump" can be calculated. If the distance between nucleotides, namely 3.4 A, is covered in 2×10^{-13} sec, the velocity is 1.7×10^5 cm/sec and the kinetic energy involved is 9×10^4 ev, hopelessly out of line. Even if the enzyme moves and not the primer, we cannot reduce the figure below 100 ev. Thus we see that if the process of specific synthesis involves a continuous bombardment by four nucleoside triphosphates, with a changing specific selection, the speed of change required to avoid selection of the wrong base is so fast that it cannot be achieved by a physical translation of either the primer or the enzyme.

We can also eliminate the idea that the DNA is uncoiling as it performs the task of being the primer. The uncoiling process requires 30° per base of rotation. To do this in 2×10^{-13} sec requires an angular velocity of 2.5×10^{12} radians per second and a rotational energy for the DNA molecule of 2.0×10^5 ev.

So accurate is the time requirement that we can momentarily consider the operation of the uncertainty principle. Using it in the form

$$\Delta E \cdot \Delta t \sim \frac{h}{2\pi},$$

where ΔE is the uncertainty in energy and Δt that in time, we see that ΔE cannot be less than 5×10^{-15} erg, about $\frac{1}{10}kT$. The attachment process must therefore have a "band width" which is relatively broad.

These considerations force the conclusion* that the physical operation of the Kornberg system must be either (a) in terms of a high multiplicity of enzyme systems or, (b) by the attachment of a whole length of primer to the enzyme, and the operation of successive regions on the complex, to give each new endpoint a new specificity. Or again, the enzymatic process might be inactive until the new coenzyme was ready. In other words, rapid accurate synthesis cannot take place on a moving production line unless energies of a most unlikely magnitude are available to move the line.

To continue the physical analysis, we can consider the quantum-mechanical problems involved in the process of attaching a nucleotide. Recently Szent-Gyorgyi has written most provocatively of the need for a

---

* E. Pollard, *J. Theor. Biol.*, in press (1961).

"submolecular biology." We can see the kind of problem which must be faced in the processes we have discussed. It has become apparent that the collision process for a specific acceptance of a molecule involves rather a small target, so small that the aspect at collision must be considered. We saw in Section 15–8 that the proper aspect of the colliding molecule could be provided if the molecule were undergoing rotational Brownian movement. Actually such motion, to which we ascribe the average energy kT, is quantized, and at the moment of collision has a specific value. After attachment, the random rotation of the molecule ceases and is replaced by a set of new forms of quantized energy in which vibration takes a part.

Whenever such a transition takes place, there are bound to be the equivalent of "selection rules." To mention an extreme, if the new position of an attached molecule required a change in an electron's direction of spin, the process would be most unlikely. There is really very little of such theory worked out, at least to our knowledge, and it may prove to be very difficult. We make three suggestions. The first is that an attachment should occur at a bond where free rotation can take place after attachment, for then there is less need for energy to be transferred instantly from one form to another. The second is that attachment is likely to occur in two stages, the first being in a form bound by weak forces, where the van der Waals or hydrogen bonds, together with the relatively large mass of the attaching molecule, can have vibrational levels closely spaced so that the change from the closely spaced rotation levels to vibration is not too drastic. In addition, since the first level for vibration is not at zero, but at

$$\frac{1}{2} \frac{h}{2\pi} \sqrt{\frac{k'}{m}},$$

where k' is the force constant for the vibration and m is the vibrating mass, this level should lie low enough to agree with the rotational energy. The third suggestion is that the large value of ΔE, or the large line width, which we deduced from the uncertainty principle, may be necessary to reduce the restriction placed on molecular transitions from rotation to vibration imposed by the selection rules we are discussing.

In view of the above factors, which are only sketched with the finest of preliminary lines, we agree with Szent-Gyorgyi that submolecular biology has an important future.

15–14 The formation of ribosomes. One serious gap in our knowledge of the cycle of the cell involving genetically fixed DNA, which forms genetically determined RNA that in turn forms enzymatically operating protein, is the knowledge of how the RNA is made by the DNA. Almost certainly by the time this book is read there will be much more information about the process of forming RNA from DNA or from RNA itself. At this time there is very little definite knowledge, particularly regarding the way in which DNA influences the formation of specific RNA. An enzyme which causes the synthesis of polyribotides has been found by Ochoa and his associates, and it has been very useful in producing synthetic material for physical study. Somehow there nevertheless seems to be a link missing. In spite of this lack of information, we can estimate the rate at which ribosomes are formed and can see whether separately formed protein and RNA can migrate over to each other and combine to form ribosomes at a reasonable rate.

Since there are 10^4 ribosomes per cell and the cell can divide in 1200 sec, a figure of 10 ribosomes made per second is not out of line. Suppose we assume that 10 RNA molecules are formed per second, say at the surface of the nucleus, and inquire as to the concentration of protein necessary to ensure combination at the rate of 10 per second. It is reasonable to suppose that 10 protein molecules combine with each RNA molecule, since the amount of protein equals that of RNA in many cases, and protein molecules are about one-tenth the size of nucleic acid molecules. Thus the rate of combination of protein molecules is 10 per second per RNA molecule. Using Eq. (15–4), with g unity and $\eta = 1$, we find

$$10 = 1.4 \times 10^{-14} c_0, \qquad c_0 = 7 \times 10^{14},$$

or 700 protein molecules per cell must be available to keep the rates high enough. This is quite reasonable. If, however, g has to be taken as a small fraction, indicating that many abortive collisions occur, then the cell must be prepared to let protein molecules accumulate to provide the needed concentration to cause the combination. The specificity of combination between RNA and protein to form ribosomes is obviously important to study. It is quite possibly not very specific at all.

15–15 "Long-range" forces. The reader will sense from much of the above that some directed character to the forces between molecules and their specific sites would be very desirable. Many biologists are emotionally convinced that "long-range" forces may one day be found. So far, physicists have not accepted the idea that such forces exist, and the reports, from time to time, of their existence have met with strong skepticism. In our foregoing analysis we have excluded them. It is possible we have been too severe. Normal electrostatic forces have ample range of action, but we discarded them because of the neutralization of the gegenions. It is possible that the local ionic atmospheres in the neighborhood of a synthesizing RNA molecule are specially cleared. If so, then electrical forces could act to aid the arrival of a wanted molecule and greatly reduce the stringency of the target volume required for a specific collision. It should not be hopeless to design experiments to see whether such is the case, especially as cell-free synthetic systems become more available in the laboratory.

The London-van der Waals force, while it is not "long range," nevertheless has the property of additivity, which results in a weak but extensive influence of one molecule on another. Actual measurements of van der Waals forces in biological environments would be of great value in deciding how large a role they play.

In this connection it is worth considering the purely hydrodynamic consequence of removing 200 amino acids per second from the medium in a location whose area is probably not much more than 100 A^2. The rate of flow is about 10 A per second, which is about one order of magnitude too small to make any difference. If for some reason the synthetic rate were faster (as would be the case if fewer ribosomes were working at any one time), then the fact that a directed fluid flow were taking place locally just where it is needed would undoubtedly act to speed up the necessary transport. How to measure local fluid motion in a bacterial cell is a problem for which a solution has not yet suggested itself to us.

15–16 The process of cell division. Early in the chapter we outlined cell division as one of the topics to discuss. It is, as yet, a subject on which very little firmly established knowledge, suitable for biophysical analysis, is available. We can, nevertheless, discuss it briefly. The process of differentiation, which is our last subdivision, we cannot discuss at all.

All the evidence seems to show that the process of cell division is separate in many ways from the processes just described. It is far and away the most vulnerable process as far as ionizing radiation is concerned. Moreover, the process of synthesis of the cell membrane and wall is not sensitive, since giant cells, or "snakes," can be made after radiation. We therefore suggest that the process of growth we described earlier causes the cytoplasmic membrane to grow steadily. This membrane, in turn, has some means to condition the formation of cell wall. At the moment when the last unit of DNA has passed through the "polymerase," there comes a very short interval in which the two chains are wholly separated. The new DNA chains have to find their new "polymerases," a process which may not take long (possibly only seconds) but which gives time for the two nuclei to separate. The momentary cessation of synthesis will cause many changes: local temperatures will alter, triphosphates will accumulate, any systematic motion may cease, or change form. The result is a change in the cell pattern. We can suppose that there is a momentary stage in which membrane synthesis outstrips the other growth. This will mean that the membrane must fold, and it can only fold inward because of the con-

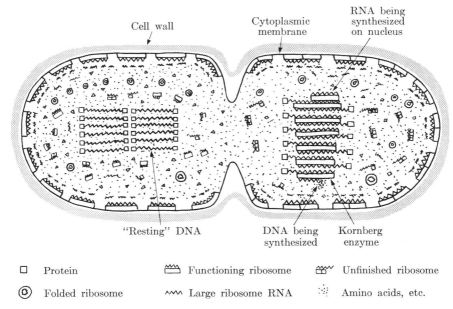

Fig. 15–8. Conceptualization of *E. coli* which involves some of the ideas about structures and processes. The left-hand member of the cell is about to divide. On the right is represented the appearance of the cell during normal growth. It has been speculated that there are two kinds of ribosome, one attached to the membrane and being functional, and the other, just formed, which is folded and appears spherical. The polymerases, for the synthesis of DNA and RNA, appear on the right, and we have drawn them rather large in accordance with the idea that synthesis moves along the enzyme surface and not by transport of the enzyme.

fining action of the cell wall. It does so, and the inward folding results in a joining to form two separate cytoplasmic membranes. The cell has now effectively segregated its primary mechanisms. The cell wall, which also continues to synthesize, grows closer to the separated cytoplasmic membranes, comes inward, and completes a dividing wall. The two cells then fall apart.

Since, in spite of some justified criticism, we like inferential pictures, we show, in Fig. 15–8, a picture of the cell that contains these ideas. We would like to emphasize for the reader (and any critic with a grain of tolerance) that such a picture is only meant to stimulate thought and to produce better pictures from those with more acumen. In this connection we quote Roberts, apropos of a different model proposed by the Carnegie group. "Such models have a considerable usefulness in that they organize a number of otherwise unrelated facts and they serve to suggest further experiments. At this stage a model should be considered successful if it presents a pleasing composition of the known facts and is suggestive even though it is by no means an accurate working diagram of a living cell."

15–17 Conclusion. The kind of theoretical biology we have described in this chapter is a mixture of the trivial and the profound. It is trivial in the sense that almost anyone who has the patience to accumulate numerical facts about a cell in terms of composition, size, rate of growth, etc., and who will mentally live in the world of that cell, can repeat, extend, and modify what we have said. To do so is a fascinating and rewarding exercise, and we greatly hope that we have encouraged others to try their hand at it. The profundity comes not from special physical skill or mathematical intuition; it comes from Nature herself. For it appears, dramatically and inescapably, that the beauty, regularity, and order of inanimate Nature is transcended only by the beauty, regularity, order, and developing form of living beings. One entry into the conceptual world where we first see this beauty and regularity, and the one peculiar to the physicist, is by imaginative numerical description. To do so opens a window for a moment, and the conceptual world shows itself across the page of figures, or sketch of a model, or even the rising line of smoke in the seminar room. And it is because this conceptual world will one day become the believed and accepted description of living cells and their behavior, and because of the surpassing beauty which such description will clearly contain, that the humble, almost menial, approach of the biophysicist carries such profound incentive.

"He that has eyes to see: let him see." If the eyes prove to be centrifuge diagrams, x-ray patterns, chromatogram charts, clicks of a Geiger counter, plaques on a sheet of agar, figures flashing across a slide rule, queer numerical integrals or fantasylike models, they are the eyes of the biophysicist. It is our deep hope that he may see.

Problems

1. Calculate the surface tension of a double layer of protein molecules wherein the average energy per molecule is $5kT$. The radius of each protein molecule is supposed to be 25 A, and the separation between their surfaces is 4 A.

2. The application of 200 atmospheres pressure is found to reduce the uptake of radioactive proline in *E. coli*. Assuming that the effect is due to a shrinkage in radius of the individual ribosome particles (radius 130 A) by 5 A, calculate the bulk modulus of elasticity of the particles.

3. Suggest the order of magnitude of applied electric field which would produce a 5% change in growth rate along the field.

4. Treating the rotation during replication of a DNA molecule as though it had a hydrodynamic radius of 15 A, a length of 10 microns, and were rotating in an outer cylinder of 100 A radius in a liquid of viscosity 0.01 poise, calculate the power needed to cause a rotation of 250 rps. At the peak of virus replication, 100 such processes are going on. Calculate the rise in temperature of a bacterial nuclear body of radius 1000 A and length 1 micron.

References

E. J. W. Verwey and J. Th. G. Overbeek, *The Theory of the Stability of Lyophobic Colloids.* Elsevier Publishing Co., Inc., New York, 1948.

H. R. Kruyt, ed., *Colloid Science*, vol. I. Elsevier Publishing Co., Inc., New York, 1952.

R. B. Loftfield, "The Biosynthesis of Protein," *Prog. Biophys. and Biophys. Chem.* **8**, 348 (1957).

Nucleoproteins. 11th Solvay Conference, Interscience Publishing Co., New York, 1960.

A. Kornberg, "Biosynthesis of Deoxyribonucleic Acid," *Science* **131**, 1503 (1960).

A. Szent-Gyorgyi, *Introduction to a Submolecular Biology.* Academic Press, New York, 1960.

Majorie J. Vold, "Van der Waals Attraction Between Anisometric Particles," *J. Coll. Sci.* **9**, 451 (1954).

ANSWERS TO SELECTED PROBLEMS

CHAPTER 2

1. 9×10^{-14} gm protein
   3×10^{-15} gm phospholipid

3. 10^{-7} cm^3

5. (a) 4×10^3 A
   (b) 4×10^5 A
   (c) 7×10^5 A

CHAPTER 3

1. (a) 0.60 ev
   (b) 1.85
   (c) -3.6×10^2 cal/mole

4. 28,200 cal/mole
   0.0 cal/mole/°K

6. (a) $\sim 3.5 \times 10^4$
   (b) 200

CHAPTER 4

1. (a) 31 A
   (b) 5.8×10^{-8} dyne per cm/sec
   (c) 3×10^{-12} sec

3. 5×10^{-3} sec

4. (a) 7×10^{-2}
   (b) 0.02
   (c) 0.46, ~ 0.0000

6. 127,000

9. (a) 10^8
   (b) 10^7 sec
   (c) 1.4 cm

11. (a) 10^{-41}
    (b) 0.37

12. (a) 4 hr
    (b) 400 hr

14. 1.86×10^{-13} sec

16. (a) 11,600 A
    (b) 9400 A

CHAPTER 5

2. (a) 0.0016 cm, 1.8%
   (b) 0.0003 cm, 40%

4. (a) 0.57°
   (b) 1.68°
   (c) 11.4°

6. 1.9°

CHAPTER 6

1. (a) .575, 0.0072, 0.0072 volts
   (b) .555, 0.0069, 0.0064 volts
   (c) .48, 0.0060, 0.0045 volts

2. 0.70

7. repulsive force $= 2.9 \times 10^9$ newtons/m^2

9. 24 ev
   2.6×10^{-3} ev, 2×10^{-6} ev

CHAPTER 7

1. 2
   75

3. (a) 10^6 sec^{-1}
   (b) 3500
   (c) 3.7×10^9 sec^{-1}

7. 700 A

9. (a) $36\,\mu\mathrm{gm/ml}$
   (b) $360\,\mu\mathrm{gm/ml}$
   (c) $94\,\mu\mathrm{gm/ml}$

11. $2.1 \times 10^{-19}\,\mathrm{cm}^2$
    $\sim 10^{-15}\,\mathrm{cm}^2$

14. 99%,   83%,   80%

15. 0.9955, $4.5 \times 10^{10}\,\mathrm{cm}^{-3}$

CHAPTER 8

1. 0.36,   0.006, 10^{-11}

3. $5 \times 10^{-2}\,\mathrm{moles/1}$

5. bound/unbound $= 250$,   25

6. 400

CHAPTER 9

1. (a) 10^4
   (b) 4.6×10^4

3. (a) 10^{-280}
   (b) 10^{-273}, 10^{-271}, 10^{-269}

8. $s = 4.6 \times 10^{-20}\,\mathrm{m}^2$, $\sigma = 4.3 \times 10^{-22}\,\mathrm{m}^2$, $\phi = 9.5 \times 10^{-3}$

CHAPTER 10

1. (a) $1.4 \times 10^9\,\mathrm{cm/sec}$
   (b) $2.8 \times 10^{10}\,\mathrm{cm/sec}$
   (c) $4.3 \times 10^9\,\mathrm{cm/sec}$
   (d) $5.8 \times 10^8\,\mathrm{cm/sec}$

3. per 100 A of protein
   (a) .023
   (b) .092
   (c) 1.5

5. 1 Mev photons: 9×10^{14} and $3.7 \times 10^{14}\,\mathrm{ev/cm}$
   50,000 kev photons: 1.8×10^{14} and $1.2 \times 10^{10}\,\mathrm{ev/cm}$

7. $9.8\,\mu\mathrm{gm}$, $4.4\,\mu\mathrm{gm}$

CHAPTER 11

1. 3.9×10^5
   4.4×10^5

3. (a) $210\,r$
   (b) $1.2 \times 10^5 r$
   (c) $1.9 \times 10^7 r$
   (d) $5 \times 10^9 r$

CHAPTER 12

2. (a) 0.053 A,   0.037 A
   (b) 5 A,   4 A

3. $6.2\,\mu$

CHAPTER 13

1. $0.3\,\mu\mathrm{c/ml}$

3. $3.6\,\mu\mathrm{c/ml}$

CHAPTER 14

1. 12 sites

3. $c_1/c_2 = 380$

5. $\sim 10^6\,\mathrm{sec}^{-1}$

CHAPTER 15

1. $2.1\,\mathrm{erg/cm}^2$

3. $3 \times 10^6\,\mathrm{volt/m}$

CONVERSION TABLE

QUANTITY		UNIT	EQUIVALENT	
Mass	m	gm	10^{-3}	kilogram, kgm
Force	F	dyne	10^{-5}	newton, n
Energy	E	erg	10^{-7}	joule, j
		ev	1.6019×10^{-19}	
		cal (15°C)	4.1861	
		kcal	4.1861×10^3	
Power	P	erg·sec^{-1}	10^{-7}	watt, w
		cal·sec^{-1}	4.1861	
Pressure	p	dyne·cm^{-2}	10^{-1}	n·m^{-2}
		atm (standard)	1.0133×10^5	
		cm-mercury	1.3332×10^3	
Density	ρ, D	gm·cm^{-3}	10^3	kgm·m^{-3}
Charge	q, Q	statcoul (esu)	$1/(3 \times 10^9)$	coulomb, coul
		abcoul (emu)	10	
Potential difference	V	statvolt (esu)	300	volt, v
		abvolt (emu)	10^{-8}	
Capacitance	C	statfarad (esu)	$1/(9 \times 10^{11})$	farad, f
		abfarad (emu)	10^9	
Permittivity	ϵ	esu	$1/(36\pi \times 10^9)$	f·m^{-1}
Electric field intensity	E	v·cm^{-1}	10^2	v·m^{-1}
		dyne-statcoul^{-1} (esu)	3×10^4	
Electric flux density or electric displacement	D	esu	$1/(12\pi \times 10^5)$	coul·m^{-2}
		emu	$10^5/4\pi$	
Current	i, I	statamp (esu)	$1/(3 \times 10^9)$	ampere, amp
		abamp (emu)	10	
Magnetic flux density or magnetic induction		gauss (emu)	10^{-4}	weber·m^{-2}
		esu	3×10^6	

INDEXES

AUTHOR INDEX